ACCOUNTING FOR MANAGEMENT

ACCOUNTING FOR MANAGEMENT

For B.Com., B.Com. (CA), BBA, BBM., M.Com., M.Com (CA), MBA, MCA, Courses of all Indian Universities and Commerce, Management Courses of Periyar University

By

Dr. V.R. PALANIVELU
M.Com., MBA, M.Phil., Ph.D.,
Reader
Periyar Institute of Management Studies (PRIMS)
Periyar University
Salem, Tamil Nadu

UNIVERSITY SCIENCE PRESS
(An Imprint of Laxmi Publications Pvt. Ltd.)
An ISO 9001:2015 Company
BENGALURU • CHENNAI • GUWAHATI • HYDERABAD
KOCHI • KOLKATA • LUCKNOW • RANCHI
NEW DELHI

ACCOUNTING FOR MANAGEMENT

Printed and bound in India
Typeset at : ABRO Enterprises, Delhi
First Edition : 2007, *Second Edition* : 2009, *Third Edition* : 2013, *Reprint* : 2016, 2017, 2020, *Edition* : 2025
ISBN : 978-93-81159-38-5

Branches

✆	Bengaluru	080-26 75 69 30
✆	Chennai	044-24 34 47 26
✆	Guwahati	0361-254 36 69
✆	Hyderabad	040-27 55 53 83
✆	Kochi	0484-405 13 03
✆	Kolkata	033-40 04 77 79
✆	Lucknow	0522-430 36 13
✆	Ranchi	0651-224 24 64

PUBLISHED IN INDIA BY

UNIVERSITY SCIENCE PRESS
(An Imprint of Laxmi Publications Pvt. Ltd.)
An ISO 9001:2015 Company
113, GOLDEN HOUSE, GURUDWARA ROAD, DARYAGANJ,
NEW DELHI - 110002, INDIA
Telephone : 91-11-4353 2500, 4353 2501
www.laxmipublications.com
info@laxmipublications.com

C—00502/024/09
Printed at : Ajit Printing Press, Delhi

ACKNOWLEDGEMENT

I would like to extend my gratitude to my parent Institution Periyar Institute of Management Studies (PRIMS) Periyar University Salem Providing great academic and infrastructural support.

I would like to express my whole hearted thanks to the Vice Chancellor of Periyar University Prof. Dr. K. Muthuchelian without whose approval and encouragement, I would not have been complete this revised work. I am grateful to Dr. S. Gunasekaran, Registrar, Periyar University and Dr. N. Rajendhiran Prof-Cum-Director PRIMS Periyar University Salem, for their support and motivation for this revised edition.

I would like to thank Prof. Dr. M. Karunanithi Chairman and Secretary, Vivekanandha Educational Institutions, Tiruchengode, Dr. P. Vikkraman Director (I/c) Anna University of Technology Coimbatore, my Research Supervisor Dr. A. Jayakumar, Periyar University, Salem, Dr. M. Ravichandran, Faculty, Department of Management Studies, Anna University of Technology, Trichy and Dr. G.Vadivalagan, Chairman, Faculty of Management Studies, Anna University of Technology, Trichy for their continuous Support and guidance for the completion of this revised edition.

I would like to thank my colleagues faculty members and countless students from various institutions for their encouragement and suitable suggestions for this revised edition.

The second revised edition would not been easy task without the emotional and psychological encouragement from my wife Sasikala and daughter, Kavina son Kowranth. Several thanks for their Support.

I would like to thank my parents G. Rangasamy, Pappayee and family members Ravindran, Balasundran, Senna Krishnan for their moral support for completion of this work. At the time of preparing this revised edition, I have been assisted by my Research Scholars Srividhya, Sankar Ganesh and Manavazhagan. Thanks for there continues work.

I record my gratitude to our publisher Laxmi Publications (P) Ltd., its Managing Director Saurabh Gupta and his team of Editors, Production personnels, Designers, Marketing specialists and sales representatives who ensured that this book got into the hands of students and faculty in record time.

—Author

PREFACE TO THE FIRST EDITION

Accounting is very much essential for successful operations of all business concerns. Accounting information provides valuable guidance to the management specifically for the decision-making activities. Anna University has introduced MBA and MCA courses. It has rightly incorporated one paper on Financial and Management Accounting in the first semester of this course. This book has been specifically designed for the students of MBA and MCA courses according to the revised syllabus. And it is also helpful to the beginners of accounting.

Everywhere, the principles of Accountancy are the same in all walks of life. But, there are differences of opinion as to the suitable methods of incorporating these principles. This book is also helpful for non-accounting students as it provides simplified methods for the preparation of accounts in a lucid manner which will enable them to acquire sufficient theoretical and practical knowledge.

The foremost aim of introducing this book is to facilitate understanding of the matter at one reading without any strain in grasping the theories and illustrations. The book consists of four parts *viz.*, financial accounting, cost accounting, management accounting and financial management.

For the benefit of the students, nearly 250 problems have been collected from various university question papers. All the problems are worked out in a very simple method. For example, in the fund flow analysis, the increase or decrease in working capital is found out only on net result and not from item-wise comparison. In this way, problems in all the chapters are worked out in a short cut and easy method. For the simplification of all the chapters, procedures and/or formulas have been incorporated at appropriate places.

Generally, MBA, MCA students feel accounting is a difficult subject, but the readers of this book will realize that it is not so. At the same time, I do not claim any originality, but I have taken much pain to present the subject in simple and systematic manner. It is the outcome of my teaching experience in this subject for several years.

This book is useful not only for the management and commerce students but also more helpful to the students of BE courses of various branches of Anna University.

I have made serious efforts to remove the printing mistakes of the book. Apart from my serious efforts, if the reader finds any error, he is requested to convey the same to me. I believe that both the students and teachers will find the book very useful. I will be very happy in receiving constructive criticism and appropriate suggestions for improving the quality of presentation and standard of the book in the next edition.

I feel it is a great opportunity to construct the new edition of "Accounting for Management" book for the commerce and non-commerce students of MBA, MCA courses.

—Author

PREFACE TO THE THIRD EDITION

I have great pleasure to place before the esteemed readers of the third revised and enlarged edition of our book "Accounting for Management" I am greatful to the readers for giving a warm and wholehearted response to the first edition of our book.

The whole text has been completely revised and incorporating number of new problems set by the recent professionals and university examinations as clearly worked out. And also incorporated the latest theory questions at the end of each chapter. This review question can be used for discussion in the class room by teachers. Thus the revised and enlarged edition of the book will meet exhaustively the requirements of students appearing for the post graduate examinations of different universities and also those conducted by different professional institutes.

I am sure that the above aspects will make this book is invaluable asset for the students community and they will find the text book as instructive and enjoyable. It also provides an easy way of understanding the activities involved in business, industry and commerce.

I am greatful to Professor Dr. Vidhya Ratana. M. Karunanithi, Chairman and Secretary of Vivekanandha Educational Institutions, for his continuous support and encouragement for revising this book. I would like to thank to S. Meganathan, Chief executive, M. Chokkalingam, Administrative officer of the Vivekanandha Educational Institutions for rendering their continuous support for revising this book.

I would like to thank Dr. A. Somu, Director, Vivekanandha Institute of Information and Management studies, Tiruchengodu, Professor Dr. A Manikavasagam, Controller of examinations, Alagappa University, Karaikudi, My research supervisor Professor Dr. A. Jayakumar, Controller of Examination, Periyar University, Salem, Prof. Dr. L. Manivannan, Erode Arts College, Erode, for their personal interest and making their invaluable suggestion for revising this book.

My wife Sasikala, Daughter Kavina, Son Kowranth have been tremendous source of encouragement during the Writing of this revised edition. Several thanks to this three members.

I am obliged to many students and teachers who sent their valuable suggestions which have been duly incorporated in the present revised edition.

I made all the efforts to remove the printing errors found in the earlier editions.

Any criticism or suggestions for further improvement of the book will be greatfully acknowledged and highly appreciated.

—Author

PERIYAR UNIVERSITY

Salem-636 011, Tamil Nadu, India.

Prof. K. MUTHUCHELIAN, Ph.D., D.Sc., FNABS., FIEF (Canada) **Date : 03 Nov 2010**

Vice Chancellor

FOREWORD

I am immensely impressed by this exemplary work, "Accounting for Management" authored by Dr. V.R. Palanivelu. I appreciate his painstaking efforts in bringing out the book as a thoroughly revised third edition. The book contains 28 chapters with large quantum of solved problems and a number of unsolved problems for the students exercise. A careful consideration has been paid while framing of its contents, and it is written in simple language. In his rich experience of teaching accountancy, he has constructed this book "It will be more useful in addition to the existing large number of accountancy" books. I strongly recommend this book and it is more suited to the students of commerce and management courses of all Indian Universities. A few copiesl of this book can be made available in libraries of all Engineering and Arts and Science Colleges and it will be more beneficial to the faculties and student communities at large.

I congratulate the author for completing this task and wish him success.

3/11/10

[K. Muthuchelian]

CONTENTS

ACCOUNTING FOR MANAGEMENT
THEORY, TECHNIQUES, PROBLEMS & SOLUTIONS

S. No.	CONTENTS OF THE BOOK	Sub. Code	Sub. Code
1.	Introduction about the Accounting	BA1606	MC1605
2.	Basic Records Maintained by a Business Concern	BA1606	MC1605
3.	Revenue Recognition and Measurement	BA1606	—
4.	Preparation of Final Accounts	BA1606	MC1605
5.	Fund Flow Statement	BA1606	MC1605
6.	Cash Flow Statement	BA1606	MC1605
7.	Ratio Analysis	BA1606	MC1605
8.	Fixed Assets and Depreciation	BA1606	—
9.	Cost Accounting: Cost Sheet Accounting for Manufacturing Cost	BA1606	MC1605
10.	Job Costing	BA1606	
11.	Process Costing	BA1606	
12.	Activity Based Costing	BA1606	—
13.	Inventory Pricing and Valuation	BA1606	
14.	Standard Costing	BA1606	MC1605
15.	Management Accounting	BA1606	MC1605
16.	Marginal Costing	BA1606	MC1605
17.	Relevant Cost for Decision Making	BA1606	—
18.	Budget and Budgetary Control	BA1606	MC1605
19.	Inflation Accounting	BA1606	—
20.	Human Resources Accounting	BA1606	—
21.	Responsibility Accounting	BA1606	—
22.	Financial Management	—	MC1605
23.	Dividend	—	MC1605
24.	Cost of Capital	—	MC1605
25.	Capital Structure	—	MC1605
26.	Working Capital	—	MC1605
27.	Capital Budgeting	—	MC 1605
28.	Computerised Accounting	—	—

S. No.	Subject code	Name of the paper	Course covered
1.	BA 1606	Accounting for management	MBA I Semester
2.	MC 1605	Accounting and financial management	MCA I Semester

SECTION I : FINANCIAL ACCOUNTING

1

Introduction to Accounting

NEED FOR ACCOUNTING

The ultimate aim of any business is to earn a profit. Profit earning is not an easy task. For earning a profit the businessman will purchase the goods in one place at certain price and sell it at another place at higher price than the purchase price or convert the raw material into finished products and sell them to various customers at a certain price which will give some percentage of margin on cost of production. But, this may not be true in all cases, because the goods produced or purchased may go out of fashion or competitors may enter the market. Due to this reason, sales will decline automatically. The business runs at a loss or at a very small margin. However, the businessman wants to know the profit or loss for the consolidated transaction at the end of the financial year. So, he needs more information for planning control, evaluation of performance and decision making. This information can be provided only when business transactions are recorded, classified and summarised properly. In order to achieve the above purpose, it would be necessary to record the business transaction according to well defined Accounting system.

MEANING OF ACCOUNTING

Accounting is the art of recording, classifying, summarizing, analysing, and reporting of business transactions and interpreting their effect on the affairs of the business concerns.

As Accounting is commonly referred to as the language of business, accounting information has to be suitably recorded, classified, summarised and presented.

DEFINITION OF ACCOUNTING

In 1941, The American Institute of Certified Public Accountants defined accounting as follows. "Accounting is the art of recording, classifying and summarising in a significant manner the terms of money transaction and events which are, in part at least, of a financial character and interpreting the results thereof."

FUNCTIONS OF ACCOUNTING

A well designed Accounting System helps :

(*i*) To keep the proper records of financial transaction which enables to prepare final accounts.

(*ii*) To meet the legal requirements such as sales tax and income tax disputes as and when necessary.

(*iii*) To protect the properties of the business concerns.

(*iv*) To provide data to interested parties like owners, creditors, debtors, investors, employees, government authorities and researchers.

ACCOUNTING CONCEPTS

Accountants adopt the following concepts in recording the business transactions :

(*i*) *Separate Entity Concept*. According to this concept, the firm is separated from the owner of the business whenever the firm is born. Then, it is necessary to record the business transactions separately to distinguish it from the owner's personal transactions.

(*ii*) *Going Concern Concept*. In this concept, it is assumed that transactions are recorded hoping that the business concern is to exist even in the future. A firm is said to be a going concern when there is neither the intention nor the necessity to wind up its operations.

(*iii*) *Money Measurement Concept*. Measurement of business event in terms of money helps in understanding the state of affairs of the business in a better way.

In accounting, all transactions are expressed and interpreted in terms of money. Accounting records only those transactions which are being expressed in monetary terms though quantitative records are also kept.

(*iv*) *Cost Concept*. According to this concept (*a*) an asset is ordinarily entered in the accounting records as the price paid to acquire it and (*b*) this cost is the basis for all subsequent accounting for the asset.

(*v*) *Dual Aspect Concept*. This is the basic concept of accounting. According to this concept every business transaction has two aspects. (*a*) Debit, (*b*) Credit. If a firm has acquired an asset, it must have resulted in one of the following :

(*a*) The owner of the firm has contributed money for the acquisition of the asset.

(*b*) For the consideration of asset acquired, some other asset has been given up.

The reverse is also true. For example, A starts business with capital of ₹ 20,000/-. There are two aspects of transaction. On the one hand, business has an asset of ₹ 20,000 while on the other hand, the business has to pay to the proprietor a sum of ₹ 20,000/- which is taken as proprietory capital.

Capital (equities) = Cash (Asset)
20,000 = 20,000

The term 'Assets' denotes the resources owned by a business while the term 'Equities' denotes the claims of various parties against the assets. Equities are of two types :

- Owner's equity (or capital) is the claim of the owners against the assets of the business.
- Outsider's equity (or liabilities) is the claim of outside parties such as creditors, debenture holders against the assets of the business. Since, either owners or outsiders claim all the assets of the business, the total assets will be equal to total liabilities. Thus,

Equities = Assets, Liabilities + Capital = Assets

The term "Accounting Equation" is also used to denote the relationship of equities to assets. The equation can be technically stated as, "for every debit there is an equivalent credit". Entire system of double entry book keeping is based on this concept.

(*vi*) *Accounting Period Concept.* A Business life is assumed to continue indefinitely. According to this concept, the life of the business is divided into appropriate intervals for studying results shown by the business and the financial position after each interval. Suppose it would not happen within the stipulated time means, necessary corrective steps cannot be initiated. In accounting such a segment or time interval is called "accounting period". It is usually of one year and at the end of this period, income statement and balance sheet are prepared.

(*vii*) *Realisation Concept.* Accounting is a historical record of transactions. According to this concept, revenue is recognised at the point when property in goods passes to the buyer and he becomes legally liable to pay.

(*viii*) *Periodic Matching of Costs and Revenue Concept.* According to this concept income made by the business during a period can be measured only when the revenue earned during a period is compared with the expenditure incurred for earning that revenue. It is based on the accounting period concept.

IMPORTANT TERMS USED IN ACCOUNTANCY

Following are the Important Terms used in Accountancy :

Book Keeping

Book keeping is the systematic recording, classifying and summarizing the business transactions in the book of accounts in accordance with the principles of accounting. In the words of Carter "Book keeping is the art of correctly recording in book of accounts all those transactions that result in the transfer of money or money's worth".

Account

It is a consolidated statement of various transactions occurred between a customer and the firm. It should be clearly expressed and it is a concise record of the transactions relating to a person or a firm or a property or a liability or an income or expenditure. The abbreviation for account is A/c.

Transaction

Day-to-day business activities are called transaction. It may involve transfer of money due to exchange of goods or services between two parties or two persons. Transaction may be cash transaction and/or credit transaction.

For Example :

(*a*) Purchase of machinery worth ₹ 50,000/-

(*b*) Cheque Received from Ramu ₹ 15,000/-

Capital

In order to start and run the business, the owner has to contribute some initial amount to the firm for the purpose of producing and selling the goods. The amount invested in order to earn an income is known as capital. Capital may be classified as fixed capital and working capital.

Capital is the Liability of the business to its proprietor, because as and when the owner claims, firm is liable to repay the money to its owner.

Liability

It refers to any amount which a business firm has to pay legally to outsiders. All dues to others including proprietor's capital are said to be liabilities.

Asset

Anything possessed by the firm which is of certain monetary value is called Asset. In other words, assets refer to tangible object and an intangible right of an enterprise, which carries probable future benefits. It may be classified as current assets and fixed assets.

Income

Income is a flow of benefit to the enterprise arising out of resources controlled by it. The definition of income consists of both revenue and gain. Revenue arises in the course of ordinary activities of an enterprise. In manufacturing or trading enterprises revenues arise mainly from the sale of goods.

Example : Sales, dividend received, interest received, etc.

Expenses

It means an amount spent on any item by the proprietor to acquire benefit out of it. The expenses are classified into Capital Expenditure and Revenue Expenditure.

Capital expenditure refers to any amount spent to increase the earning capacity of the business or acquisition of asset.

Revenue expenditure refers to the amount spent for the purpose of acquiring benefit for the particular year alone.

Example : Payment of salaries, rent, etc.

Purchase

Buying of goods by the trader for selling them to his customers is known as purchases. Purchases may be cash purchases and credit purchases.

For example : Ramu purchases goods of ₹ 85,000/-.

Purchase Returns

Purchase returns means a firm or buyer returns to the vendor the goods purchased due to defective parts or product.

Sales

Exchange of goods for money is called sales. Simply sales means goods sent out from the organisation to its customers. Sales can be cash sales and credit sales.

For Example : Sale of finished goods to Murali ₹ 60,000/-.

Sales Returns

When a customer returns some of the purchased goods (due to some reasons) to the firm it is called sales returns.

For Example : Murali returns goods worth ₹ 5,000/-.

Creditor

Creditor is a person who supplies finance or goods to others *i.e.,* he has to get money from others. Suppose more than one person are supplying finance or goods to others. It means the consolidated names of suppliers is called creditor. The creditors are shown as liability in the balance sheet.

Debtor

Debtor is a person who owes money to others because he has purchased the goods or has got finance from others. Simply debtor is one who has to pay money to others. The Debtors are shown on the Asset side of the Balance sheet.

Goods

The things which a trader sells or purchases are called goods.

Drawings

It refers to the withdrawals of money or money's worth (goods) by the proprietor from his business for his personal use.

Journal Entry

Journal Entry means particular transactions are to be split into two parts *i.e.,* debit and credit based upon the accounting rules.

Ledger

A ledger refers to a summary statement of all the transactions relating to a person, asset, expense or income which have taken place during a given period of time and show their net effect.

Invoice

While making a sale, the seller prepares a statement giving the particulars such as quantity, price per unit, the total amount payable, any deductions made and shows the net amount payable by the buyer. This type of statement is called an invoice.

BRANCHES OF ACCOUNTING

In order to satisfy the needs of different people interested in the accounting information, different branches of accounting have developed. Accounting can be broadly classified into three types.

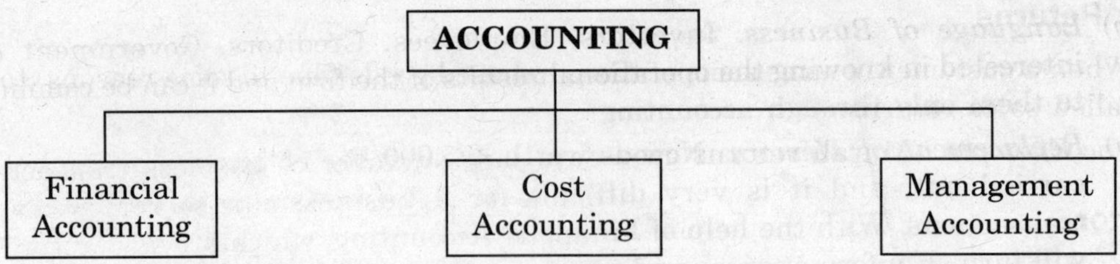

1. *Financial Accounting.* It is the original form of accounting. Financial Accounting records business transactions taking place during the accounting period with a view to prepare financial statements.

   American Institute of Certified Public Accountants has defined 'Financial Accounting' as "The art of recording, classifying and summarising in a significant manner and in terms of money transactions and events which are in part at least of financial character and interpreting the result thereof".

   Ultimate object of accounting is to measure the Profit or Loss of the concern and to ascertain the financial position of the business. Thus Profit and Loss Account is prepared for a particular period to determine the profitability of the concern and Balance sheet is prepared on a particular date to determine the financial position of the concern.

2. *Cost Accounting.* Cost Accounting is the process of ascertaining cost from the point at which expenditure is incurred or committed to the establishment of its ultimate relationship with the cost centres and cost units.

3. *Management Accounting.* The term Management Accounting refers to accounting for the management. Accounting which provides necessary information to the management for taking and implementing important decisions.

   Management accounting covers various areas such as cost accounting, budgetory control, inventory control, etc. This has been discussed in detail in the subsequent pages.

FUNCTIONS OF FINANCIAL ACCOUNTING

The main objectives of Financial Accounting are :

(*i*) *Recording Business Transaction.* The first and foremost objective of Financial Accounting is to record business transactions which are maintained systematically with the help of journal and ledger and also to prepare Final Account. With the help of these facilities it is easy to know the operating results and financial position of the organisation.

(*ii*) *Managerial Functions.* Decision making is an important process of the management. Financial Accounting provides necessary information to the managerial functions and decision making programmers. Without accounting proper decision making is not possible.

(*iii*) *Legal Requirement Function.* Business disputes are unavoidable. If there is any dispute properly maintained accounts are often treated as a good evidence in the court to settle a dispute. Auditing is compulsory in case of registered firms.

(iv) *Language of Business.* Investors, Employees, Creditors, Government etc., are interested in knowing the operational results of the firm and it can be communicated to them only through accounting.

(v) *Replacement of Memory.* Now-a-days large number of business transactions are carried out, and it is very difficult for a businessman to remember all the transactions. With the help of Financial Accounting, which provides records which will furnish information as and when needed and thus it replaces human memory.

(vi) *Comparative Study.* Financial Accounting provides necessary steps for comparative study of various aspects of the business such as Profit, Sales, Liabilities, Loans, Fixed assets etc. with that of previous year and helps the businessman to make changes if any.

(vii) *Sale of Business.* The circumstance arises when the businessman wants to sell his business means, he wants to determine the total value of his business with the help of systematic recording of financial data.

LIMITATIONS OF FINANCIAL ACCOUNTING

Financial Accounting suffers the following limitations :

(i) *Records of Monetary Transactions.* Accounting records are maintained only when transactions are expressed in monetary terms. At the same time, those transactions which cannot be measured in monetary terms are not to be recorded. It excludes qualitative elements like management reputation, employee morale, labour strike, etc.

(ii) *Recording Actual Cost.* Cost concept is found in financial accounting. If the effect of price level changes is not brought into the books, comparison of various years becomes difficult. Financial accounting records are based only on Actual Cost. This type of accounting techniques actually reduces the utilities and usefulness.

(iii) *Personal Bias of Accountant affects the Accounting Statements.* Normally, Accounting policies are framed by the Accountants. They differ on the use of accounting principles. And at the same time a number of conventions, concepts and postulates have been propounded in accountancy. Their use is greatly affected by the personal judgement of Accountants. Sometime different financial results are obtained from the same concern's financial statements. Because, these statements are prepared by two different accountants with varying personal judgement in using or applying particular conventions.

(iv) *Incomplete Information.* Financial Accounting discloses only the net result of the consolidated business transactions. It does not disclose profit or loss of each department's job, process, etc. The product-wise or job-wise cost of production cannot be found out.

(v) *Permits Alternative Treatments.* Financial Accounting permits alternative treatments within generally accepted accounting concepts. For example, closing stock may be valued by FIFO or LIFO or average method or market price method. Applications of different methods may give different results and at the same time results may not be comparable.

(vi) *Only Quantitative Information.* Financial Accounting will be taken into account only on those factors which are being quantitatively expressed. But, quantifiable information could not be considered. Because the management has to follow the government policies which relate to the Economic development of the country.

(vii) *Technological Revolution.* Due to the development of Science and Technology, all types of business information and data are needed for effective functioning of the organisation. But financial accounting provides only elementary information. So, this is not enough to meet out the current level of competition.

TEST QUESTIONS

1. Define Accounting. Explain the functions of Accounting.
2. What are the Basic Accounting Concept ? Explain their implications.
3. What do you meant by Basic Accounting Concept and Conventions ? Discuss in brief some of the important concepts and conventions of accounting.
4. Briefly discusses the Basic Accounting Concept and Fundamental Accounting assumptions. Is there a conflict between the two ?
5. Explain the major conventions followed in the preparation of Financial statements.
6. What is meant by Capital ?
7. What is mean by Transaction ?
8. Explain the meaning of Assets.
9. Who are Creditors ?
10. Who are Debtors ?
11. What are the Branches of Accounting.
12. What is meant by Financial Accounting.
13. What is Cost Accounting ?
14. Explain the meaning of Management Accounting.
15. Briefly explain the functions of Financial Accounting.
16. What are limitations of Financial Accounting ?

❑❑❑

2

Basic Records Maintained by a Business Concern

Small organisations have only limited transactions and they maintain very few basic accounting records such as journal book, ledger and a cash book. But in the case of large scale business organisation, they have a wider number of transaction. In this respect they maintain not only the journal book, ledger and cash book but also some other separate books which arc maintained for recording credit purchases, credit sales, bills transactions etc. These books are day book, sales day book, Returns inward and outward books, Bills receivable and bills payable books, petty cash book, etc.

SUBSIDIARY BOOKS

All the business transactions are first entered in the journal and then posted to the respective accounts in the ledger, to make sub divisions of journals into various books. Recording transactions of similar nature are called subsidiary books. These subsidiary books are also known as books of prime entry. The following are the important subsidiary books which are maintained by the large business organisation.

(*i*) Cash Book
(*ii*) Purchases day Book or purchases Book
(*iii*) Sales day Book
(*iv*) Purchase return Book
(*v*) Sales return Book
(*vi*) Bills receivable Book
(*vii*) Bills payable Book
(*viii*) Journal proper.

(*i*) *Cash Book.* It deals with the transaction relating to the receipts and payments of cash.

(*ii*) *Purchases Book.* Purchase books are those books which record credit purchases of goods only. Any cash purchases or assets purchased on credit basis are not entered in this book.

(*iii*) *Sales Day Book.* This book is maintained in recording all credit sales made during a particular period. But any asset sold or cash sales are not recorded in this book.

(*iv*) *Purchase Returns (or returns outward) Book.* This book is maintained for recording the goods returned to the suppliers which had been already purchased on credit basis. And it will show the total purchase returns during the particular period.

(v) *Sales Returns Book.* This book records the goods returned by the customers which had already been sold to customers on credit basis. And it will show the total return inwards during the particular period.

(vi) *Bills Receivable Book.* It is the book for recording the bills received from customers for credit sales.

(vii) *Bills Payable Book.* It is the book for recording the acceptances (bills payable) given to the suppliers for the credit purchases.

(viii) *Journal Proper.* Those transactions which could not be recorded in any of the above books will be recorded in this book.

PREPARATION OF FINAL ACCOUNT

Final Account consists of three parts :

(i) Trading Account

(ii) Profit and loss A/c

(iii) Balance sheet

It should be prepared in the following way :

(i) Journalisation of transactions.

(ii) Postings of journal entry to ledger A/c.

(iii) Balancing of ledger (Find the debit or credit.)

(iv) Prepare Trial Balance with the help of balances which are found out from various ledgers.

(v) From the Trial Balance, now, we have to prepare the Final Account.

(vi) At the time of preparing Final Account, all the adjustments are taken care of at the appropriate places.

TEST QUESTIONS

1. What is meant by Subsidiary Books ?

2. What is Purchase Book ?

3. What is meant by Sales Return Book ?

4. Describe briefly important subsidiary books which are maintained by the large business organization.

5. What are the uses of Subsidiary Books ?

❑❑❑

3

Revenue Recognition and Measurement

For the purpose of preparing fair and true financial statement of the company, it has to take the correct decision about the revenue for the period. Suppose the revenue is overstated or understated it should affect the reality of the financial statement. Before we proceed to consider the problem of revenue recognition and measurement, it is useful to know the meaning of revenue for an accounting period.

According to the Financial Accounting Standards Board of USA. "Revenues are inflows or other enhancements of assets of an enterprise or settlements of its liabilities (or a combination of both) during a period from the delivering or producing goods, rendering services, or other activities that constitute the enterprises ongoing major or central operations".

The problems of revenue recognition could arise due to the following reasons :

(*i*) The seller agrees to sell his product at a particular point of time but the buyer takes delivery at a different point of time.

(*ii*) The seller receives the money from the buyer at a time different from the time of delivery of goods sold.

(*iii*) The buyer may pay money for the purpose of goods purchased at a point of time later than the date of billing.

(*iv*) Receipt of the sales price prior to the delivery of goods or billing.

Following are the methods exist as to when revenue could be recognised.

(*i*) Recognition at the time of sale.

(*ii*) Recognition at the time when the sales price is collected.

(*iii*) Recognition at the time when the product is completed.

(*iv*) Recognition proportionately over the period of performance of the contract.

METHODS FOR REVENUE RECOGNITION

(*i*) Percentage of completion method (*ii*) Completed contract method.

The above two methods are commonly followed by the contractors for the revenue recognition.

(*i*) *Percentage of Completion Method.* The percentage of completion method refers to the income earned by the contractor determined on the basis of progress of the contract. Under this method, current assets may include costs and recognized income not yet billed with respect to certain contracts.

(ii) *Completed Contract Method.* Under this method, incomes are recognized only when the contract is completed or substantially so.

MATCHING OF REVENUES AND EXPENSES

One of the most important concepts of the accounting is the matching concept. This concept provides the guidelines as to how the expenses be matched with revenues. Expenses incurred in an accounting year should be matched with the revenues recognised in that year. But at the same time only such expenses as incurred in creating revenues during the period should be deducted from those revenues for earning the income or profit during the period. The ultimate aim of the accounting is to construct the accounting record in such a manner so as to compare the cost with revenue.

Either the comparison of costs is not possible or it is likely to be difficult. Suppose these types of situations arise when the accounting system will be considered as unsatisfactory. In order to make a satisfactory accounting system a current matching of revenue as against the expenses will be followed *i.e.,* incurred expenses will be followed and matched against the realised income.

American Institute of Certified Public Accountants Committee on accounting procedure states that "it is plainly desirable to provide by charging in the current income statement, properly classified for all foreseeable costs and losses applicable against current revenues, to the extent that they can be measured and allocated to fiscal periods with reasonable approximation". Only current year expenses/incomes are taken into account. Suppose either previous year or subsequent year's expenses or incomes, paid or received should be adjusted properly *i.e.,* if any of the current year expenses are due, it should be added to the respective expenses or deducted if paid in advance.

And if any income of the current year is due but not received, it is added to the respective incomes. Suppose it should be received for the subsequent years, it means it is deducted from the respective income.

Based upon this principle only current year expenses are matched with the current year realised revenue. By application of this matching concept, proprietor can easily determine their firm's profit or loss and he can take additional effort to increase the earning capacity of the concern if necessary.

TEST QUESTIONS

1. What is meant by Revenue Recognition ?
2. Why the problems of revenue recognition could arise ?
3. Write short notes on Revenues and Expenses.
4. What are the methods employed to determine the revenue recognition ?

❑❑❑

4

Preparation of Final Accounts

The scope and importance of accounting is to provide variable information about a business enterprise to those persons who are directly or indirectly interested in the progress, performance and financial position of the concern.

Information is the basis for decision making in an organization. The efficiency and soundness of the management depends upon the availability of regular and correct information to those who exercise the managerial functions. Such persons may include owners, creditors, investors, employees, government, public, research scholars and the managers.

1. *Owners.* The owners of a business could contribute capital to be used for the purpose of starting and running the business. The ultimate aim of accounting is to provide necessary information to the owners relating to their business. They want to evaluate the past financial performance and also assess the future prospects through the accounting reports.
2. *Creditors.* Creditors, debenture holders, bankers and other financial institutions are interested in knowing about the short term as well as long term financial position of the company. Because, they want to find out the ability of the firm to pay interest and principal as and when it becomes due for payment.
3. *Potential Investors.* Any investor, before making investment in any particular company shares, wants to know not only the earning capacity of the organisation but also its solvency position. For this purpose, investors take information from accounting reports to a great extent in order to determine the relative merits of the available investment opportunities.
4. *Employees.* Employees are the backbone of the organisation. They are interested in the earning capacity of a concern because their salaries, bonus, and pension schemes are dependent on the size of the profit earned.
5. *Government.* Government is the sole authority for the country's economic development. For the purpose of finding out overall economic growth point of view, the government is very much interested in accounting statements and reports in order to see the financial position of a particular unit. With the help of the accounting information, government is not only to prepare national account but also to impose tax and excise duty.
6. *Public.* The public as consumers is interested in accounting information in order to testify whether the control is properly exercised on production, selling and distribution for the purpose of reducing the prices of the goods they buy. And also they are interested to know, whether all the available economic resources of the concern are being properly utilised for the benefit of the common man or not. And at the same time, they want to examine any of the aspects of the business which can be detrimental to the public interest.

7. *Research Scholars.* Financial statements are very helpful to the research scholars. Enormous information are available from the accounting reports. Depending upon their research area, the researcher could get the data for providing their thesis on which they are working and hence to complete their research projects.
8. *Regulatory Agencies.* In order to protect the public from the fraudulent activities of the business, various governments, voluntary service institutions, and other agencies use accounting information not only for the tax assessment purpose but also in evaluating how well various business concerns are operating under legal framework.
9. *Managers.* The foremost responsibility of the managers of the organisation is to obtain maximum return over the capital invested without causing any harm to the interest of the share holders. The manager would like to have a data regarding sales, expenses, assets, liabilities etc. relating to next year and also the flow of fund for the purpose of the activities of a business. He also takes a decision and alters the decision in best way. In all these aspects, relevant accounting information is needed.

RECORDING OF BUSINESS TRANSACTION - BASIS OF ACCOUNTING

There are three different Basis systems of accounting for recording of business transaction. They are *(i)* cash basis accounting, *(ii)* mercantile basis or Accrual basis of accounting, and *(iii)* mixed-basis of accounting.

(*i*) Cash Basis of Accounting

Under this system of accounting, actual cash received and actual cash payments are recorded. Credit transactions are not recorded at all until the cash is actually received or paid. Non trading concerns such as charitable institution, a club, a college etc and a professional man like a lawyer, a doctor, a chartered accountant etc maintains accounts under this system only. This basis of accounting is not a complete record of financial transactions of a trading period, because all outstanding transactions are not recorded.

(*ii*) Mercantile Basis of Accounting or Accrual Basis of Accounting

According to mercantile system of accounting, entries are made not only for actual receipt or payment of cash but also for the amount having been due for payment or receipt. Simply, both cash transactions and credit transactions are recorded and even non-trading concerns follow this type of accounting. Financial transaction discloses correct profit or loss for a particular period and also exhibits true financial position of the business on a particular day.

Normally, trading orgainsations, to prepare final account for the purpose of finding out profit or loss during a particular period, use the mercantile system of accounting.

(*iii*) Mixed System of Accounting

Under this basis of accounting, both cash system and mercantile system are followed. Simply, combination of cash system and mercantile system is called mixed system. Some of the records are maintained under the cash system and remaining others are maintained under mercantile system.

Apart from the basis of accounting, following are the methods of accounting to be followed in a normal practice. They are (*i*) Single entry method and (*ii*) Double entry method.

SINGLE ENTRY SYSTEM OF BOOK KEEPING

Under the single entry system, the principles of Double entry book keeping are not followed. Normally, every transaction has a two fold aspect. But in the single entry system of accounting only one aspect is recorded. So, it is called incomplete method of Book keeping. Trial Balance, Trading Account, Profit and Loss account, and Balance Sheet cannot be prepared with the help of the single entry system. This system is mainly followed by those organisations that have only limited number of transactions.

DOUBLE ENTRY SYSTEM OF BOOK KEEPING

Double entry system of book keeping refers to particular transactions which are entered in two aspects. It is based on the dual aspect concept. Posting of each transaction in two different accounts on opposite sides for equal value is known as the double entry system of book keeping. [Normally it is the most accurate, complete and scientific method of accounting].

Simply, every debit must have a corresponding credit and vice versa. Most of the trading organisations follow the double entry system of accounting.

Advantages of Double Entry System

(*i*) It provides a complete record of the financial transactions which is maintained.

(*ii*) It supplies complete information about the business.

(*iii*) It provides a check on the arithmetical accuracy of books of accounts by preparing a trial balance by taking balances of all ledger accounts.

(*iv*) It is helpful in ascertaining profit or loss of a particular period by preparing the trading and profit and loss account.

(*v*) It helps the businessman to evaluate the progress of his business through meaningful comparison of operating and financial performance over a period of time.

(*vi*) It helps in preventing frauds and errors.

(*vii*) It helps income tax and sales tax authorities.

(*viii*) It is helpful in preparing accurate claim for loss of stock as a result of fire to the insurance company.

Disadvantages of Double Entry System

(*i*) This system requires to maintain wider number of books of accounts, which is not convenient to small concerns.

(*ii*) There is no guarantee of absolute accuracy of the books of account which are maintained.

(*iii*) It requires more clerical labour, so the system is costly.

CLASSIFICATION OF ACCOUNTS

Normally, Accounts are classified into mainly two classes *viz.* (1) Personal accounts and (2) Impersonal accounts. These impersonal accounts are further subdivided into (*i*) Real account and (*ii*) Nominal account. But usually three types of accounts namely Personal Accounts, Real or Property Accounts and Nominal or Fictitious Accounts are opened to keep a complete record of business transactions.

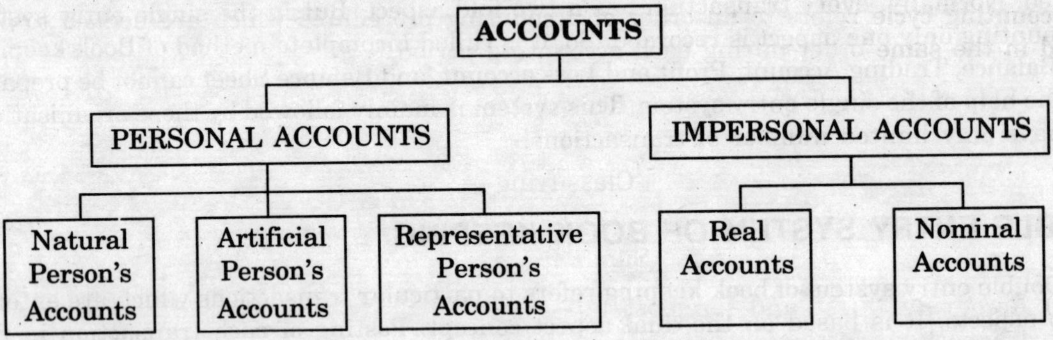

1. Personal Accounts

Personal Accounts are those which are related to persons. A separate account is prepared for each person, because the firm deals its transactions with a number of persons. Such accounts can take the following forms :

(*i*) Natural person's accounts *e.g.,* Kumar's account

(*ii*) Artificial persons' or body of persons' accounts *e.g.,* Bank account, any company's account

(*iii*) Representative person's accounts *e.g.,* salaries outstanding account, prepaid expenses account.

2. Impersonal Accounts

(*i*) *Real Accounts or Property Accounts.* Real Accounts are those accounts which can be related to a property, an asset or possession *e.g.,* plant account, machinery account, cash account etc. Separate account is prepared for each class of assets of the organisation.

(*ii*) *Nominal Accounts.* Nominal accounts are those which are related to the business expenses or losses and incomes or gains.

For example : Wages account, discount account, commission account.

RULES OF DOUBLE ENTRY (OR) ACCOUNTING RULES

Normally, most of the organisations follow the double entry system of accounting. The rules of double entry are as follows.

(*i*) **Personal Accounts**

Rules : Debit the Receiver
Credit the giver

(*ii*) **Real or property Accounts**

Rules : Debit what comes in
Credit what goes out.

(*iii*) **Nominal Accounts**

Rules : Debit all expenses and losses.

Credit all incomes and gains.

ACCOUNTING CYCLE

Accounting cycle refers to an order of accounting procedures which are needed to be repeated in the same order during each accounting period.

Recording
↓
Classifying
↓
Summarising

(*i*) *Recording.* First and foremost activity of accounting is recording of business transactions in the journal.

(*ii*) *Classifying.* Classifying the transactions in the journal by posting them to the appropriate ledger accounts to find out at a glance the total effect of such transactions in a particular account.

(*iii*) *Summarising.* Summarising simply refers to consolidation of one year transactions with the help of ledger Balances. Based upon these Balances, Trial Balance, and final accounts are to be prepared with a view to ascertaining profit or loss made during the particular financial year or trading period.

BOOKS OF ACCOUNTS : RECORDING, POSTING AND PREPARATION OF TRIAL BALANCE

Journal

Journal is derived from the French word "Jour" which means a day. Journal therefore means day to day transactions which are recorded in the books. It is in the form of debit and credit and is maintained with the help of accounting rules. The process of recording the transactions in a journal is called journalising.

A journal may be defined as the book of original or prime entry containing a chronological record of the business transactions.

Journal Format

1 Date		*2* Particulars	*3* L.F.	*4* Debit (Dr.) ₹	*5* Credit (Cr.) ₹
Year Month	*Date*	*Name of the Account to be debited* *Name of the Account to be credited* *To Narration*		*xx*	*xx*

Explanation

1. *Date.* The date on which the transaction takes place is entered in the journal.
2. *Particulars.* Under the particulars column, the names of the account to be debited is written in the first line, and in the second line, the account to be credited is written preceded by the word 'To Narration' which also explains briefly about the transaction.
3. *L.F.* It stands for ledger folio. It means the page number in the ledger in which the entry is posted.
4. *Debit.* Name of the account to be debited against the 'Dr' account is entered.
5. *Credit.* Name of the account to be credited against the 'Cr' account is entered.

Procedure for Journalising

In any particular transaction first of all we have to identify the receiving aspect and giving aspect of the transaction. All the transactions affect at least two of the basic accounting.

The rule for journalizing should be selected as follows.

Nature of Account	*Rule for debiting an account*	*Rule for Crediting an account*
1. Personal Account	Debit the Receiver	Credit the Giver
2. Real Account	Debit what comes in	Credit what goes out
3. Nominal Account	Debit all expenses and losses.	Credit all incomes and gains

TEST QUESTIONS

1. What is meant by Trading Account ?

2. Explain the meaning of Profit and Loss Account.

3. What is meant Balance Sheet ?

4. What is cash basis of Accounting ?

5. What is Mixed System of Accounting ?

6. Explain the meaning of Single Entry System of Book keeping.

7. What is meant by Double Entry System of Book keeping ?

8. What is book keeping ?

9. What are the classification of Accounts ?

10. Explain the concept of accounting rules with suitable illustration.

11. Explain the concept of accounting cycle. Give its Coverage.

12. What is meant by Trail Balance ? Explain the objectives of Trail Balance.

13. What are the methods available for preparing Trail Balance ?

14. What is meant by Final Accounts. Explain the procedure for preparation of Final Accounts.

15. What is accounting equation ? Illustrate its mechanism by imaginary figures to prove that the two sides equation are always equal.

16. Discuss briefly the relationship of accounting with other subjects.

17. Describe accounting as an information system.

18. Describe briefly the role of accountant in a society.

19. What do you mean by Journal ? Why is it called the book of original entry. Give the rules and advantages of Journalizing.

20. What do you mean by a postings ? How is posting made from the Journal to ledger ? Explain with suitable examples.

21. Define a ledger. Why is know as the principal book of accounts. Also give its rules.

22. Distinguish between Trading, Profit and Loss A/c and Balance Sheet.

23. Why is closing stock valued at cost or market price whichever is lower ?

24. Explain the concept of cost of goods sold.

25. What is Balance Sheet ? Why is it prepared ? Give a specimen of the Balance Sheet.

26. What are adjusting entries ? Why are these necessary for preparing final accounts.

27. How is the account relating to provision for doubtful debts kept ? What is the object of this account ? What it the influence of actual bad debts on it. How is it shown in the Balance Sheet ?

28. Discuss the various adjustment entries while preparing final accounts.

PROBLEMS AND SOLUTIONS

Problem 1. *Journalise the following transaction in the journal of Mr.T.R.Ramu.*

2003, Jan 1 Ramu commenced business with a capital of ₹ 50,000

↓ Personal A/c ↓ Real A/c

The above transaction has to affect the two accounts *i.e.,* (*i*) Real A/c and (*ii*) Personal A/c. After finding out the affected accounts, we have to apply the accounting rules as against the particular transaction. Here, cash is coming to the business and Ramu is the giver.

Date	*Particulars*	*L.F.*	*Dr.* ₹	*Cr.* ₹
2003, Jan. 1	Cash A/c Dr. To Ramu's Capital A/c (Being the amount invested in business)		50,000	50,000

2. Amount Deposited in Canara Bank ₹ 20,000

↓ Personal A/c ↓ Real A/c

Affected Accounts in the above transaction :

(*i*) Personal Account

(*ii*) Real Account.

In the above transaction, the Canara Bank is the artificial person to receive the money. It relates to Personal Accounts. As per the Personal Accounts rules, Debit the Receiver. Here, Canara Bank Account is debited and amount relates to real account. Amount goes out according to real account credit what goes out. Here, cash goes out. So, the Cash A/c is credited.

Date	Particulars		L.F.	Dr. ₹	Cr. ₹
2003, Jan. 2	Canara Bank A/c To Cash A/c (Being Cash paid to Canara Bank)	Dr.		20,000	20,000

3. Goods Purchased for cash ₹ 10,000

↓ Real A/c ↓ Real A/c

This is the cash transaction. The two aspects to be recorded are goods or purchase account and cash account. Both are related to Real Account. Now, we apply Real Account rules.

Date	Particulars		Amount Dr.	Amount Cr.
2003, Jan. 3	Purchase or goods A/c To Cash	Dr.	10,000	10,000

4. Purchase of goods worth ₹ 5,000 from Murali

↓ Real A/c ↓ Real A/c ↓ Personal A/c

This is the credit transaction. But, the above transaction affects three accounts.

Namely, (*i*) Good → Real Account
(*ii*) Amount → Real Account
(*iii*) Murali → Personal Account

Here, there is no need to give the effect on one Real Account [*i.e.*, Amount – Real Account]. Because, at the time of purchase, there is no settlement of money.

Goods Account relates to the Real Account. As per the Real Account rules, Goods Account is to be debited.

Murali is the Personal Account. As per the Personal Account rules Murali is the giver. So, his account is to be credited.

Date	Particulars		Amount Dr.	Amount Cr.
2003, Jan. 4	Goods or Purchase A/c To Murali Account	Dr.	5,000	5,000

Credit Transaction and Cash Transaction

If purchase and Sales Transaction bears a name means it is treated as credit transaction. And at the same time, even though there is a name, specifically mentioned cash means, it is treated as cash transaction.

5. Sold goods to Rajan Brothers for ₹ 10,000

↓ Real A/c ↓ Personal A/c ↓ Real A/c

This is a credit transaction for two reasons :

(*i*) Purchaser's name is given.

(*ii*) There is no mention that it is cash transaction.

The above transaction affects the three Accounts. *i.e.,*

(*i*) Real Account (goods)

(*ii*) Personal Account (Rajan Brothers)

(*iii*) Real Account (Amount).

In the three accounts, we have to give the effect on only two accounts *i.e.,* Goods account and Personal account.

Here, Rajan Brothers receives the goods, and goods go out from the business. So, the journal entry will be

Date	*Particulars*		*Amount Dr.*	*Amount Cr.*
2003, Jan. 4	Rajan Brothers A/c	Dr.	10,000	
	To Goods or Sales A/c			10,000

6. Sold goods worth ₹ 2,500

↓ ↓

Real A/c Real A/c

This is the cash transaction. The above transaction affects two accounts. *i.e.,*

(*i*) Real Account → goods

(*ii*) Real Account → Amount.

Amount of ₹ 2,500 is coming to the business. As per the Real Account rules, Debit when comes in. Here cash comes in. So, cash account is debited and goods go out from the business. It is also a real account. As per the Real Account rules, Credit what goes out. Here, goods go out from the business, so cash account is credited.

Date	*Particulars*		*Amount Dr.*	*Amount Cr.*
2003, Jan. 6	Cash A/c	Dr.	2,500	
	To Goods A/c			2,500

7. Amount of ₹ 9,000 Received from Rajan Brothers as full settlement

↓ ↓

Real A/c Personal A/c

This transaction directly affects two accounts.

(*i*) Real Account (Amount)

(*ii*) (Personal Account) Rajan Brothers

Indirectly, it affects one account *i.e.,* Nominal Account (Discount Account).

Actual sale of goods worth to Rajan Brothers	₹	10,000
Amount Received from Rajan Brothers	₹	9,000
The Amount treated as Discount A/c	₹	1,000

Here, we allow the discount to Rajan Brothers.

For receiving cash ₹ 9,000, Cash Account is to be debited. Discount is the Nominal Account. As per the Nominal Account rules Debit all expenses and losses. Here, Discount is the Expenses. So, Discount Account is to be debited in the value of ₹ 1,000. Rajan brother is the giver, so his account is to be credited. The journal entry will be

Date	*Particulars*		*Amount Dr.*	*Amount Cr.*
2003, Jan. 7	Cash A/c	Dr.	9,000	
	Discount A/c	Dr.	1,000	
	To Rajan Brothers A/c			10,000

8. Paid Salaries ₹ 25,000

↓ ↓

Nominal A/c Real A/c

The transaction has to affect the two accounts. *i.e.*, (*i*) Salaries account relates to Nominal Account. Its rule is debit all expenses and losses and accordingly it is to be debited. (*ii*) Cash account relates to real account. Its rule is credit what goes out. Accordingly it is to be credited. Therefore, the journal entry will be.

Date	*Particulars*		*Amount Dr.*	*Amount Cr.*
2003, Jan. 8	Salaries A/c	Dr.	25,000	
	To Cash A/c			25,000

9. Commission Received ₹ 3,500

↓ ↓

Nominal A/c Real A/c

The transaction is obviously by cash and is an income. So, the two important aspects are commission and cash. (*i*) Commission account relates to Nominal Account. As per the Nominal account rules credit all incomes and gains, accordingly it is to be credited. (*ii*) Cash account relates to Real Account. As per the Real account rules Debit what comes in. Accordingly cash account is to be debited. The journal entry will be

Date	*Particulars*		*Amount Dr.*	*Amount Cr.*
2003, Jan. 9	Cash A/c	Dr.	3,500	
	To Commission A/c			3,500

10. Entertainment expenses ₹ 1,000 paid

↓ ↓

Nominal A/c Real A/c

This is a cash transaction. Cash is going out and the entertainment is the expenditure. Cash relates to Real Account. As per Real Account Rules credit what goes out and accordingly it is to be credited. Entertainment relates to Nominal Account. Its rule is Debit all expenses and Losses. Accordingly, it is to be Debited. So, the journal entry will be.

Date	*Particulars*		*Amount Dr.*	*Amount Cr.*
2003, Jan. 10	Entertainment Expn. A/c To Cash A/c	Dr.	1,000	 1,000

Ledger

Ledger is a register having a number of pages which are numbered consecutively. Simply, ledger means consolidation of similar types of transactions under one head. In other words, a ledger may be defined as a summary statement of all the transactions relating to a person, asset, expenses or income which have taken place during a given period of time and show their net effect.

The process of preparation of accounts from the journal into ledger is called posting in the ledger. Examples of ledger accounts include sales account, purchase account, sales returns account, cash account, and so on.

Format of Ledger

Ledger can be divided into two parts (*i*) left hand side called debit side (Dr) and (*ii*) right hand side called credit side (Cr). Debit side starts with 'To' and credit side starts with 'By'. Most of the authors follow these practices.

Debit (Dr.)				*Ledger*			*Credit (Cr.)*
Date	*Particulars*	*Folio*	*Amount*	*Date*	*Particulars*	*Folio*	*Amount*

Posting of Journal Entry into Ledger

Problem 2. *Given the following journal entry, how do you post in into relevant ledger accounts.*

Date	*Particulars*		*L.F.*	*Dr.* ₹	*Cr.* ₹
2004, Jan. 1	*Cash A/c* *To Raju's Capital A/c* *[Being the business started]*	*Dr.*		*75,000*	 *75,000*

Solution :

Cash Account

Dr. *Cr.*

Date	*Particulars*	*Folio*	*Amount*	*Date*	*Particulars*	*Folio*	*Amount*
1.1.04	To Raju Capital A/c		75,000				

Capital Account

Dr. Cr.

Date	Particular	Folio	Amount	Date	Particular	Folio	Amount
				1.1.04	*By Cash A/c*		*75,000*

How to Balance an Account?

First we have to compute the total on each side separately. Next the side which has the highest value, should be put on both side. Then, we have to find the difference from the lower value side. This value is called Balance c/d. This is the closing balance for the end of the given period. This is called Balance Brought down.

Problem 3. *Journalise the following transaction in the books of Kumar and prepare necessary ledger accounts :*

2004, Jan.
1. Kumar started a Business with the capital of ₹ 60,000.
3. Amount Received from Bank ₹ 10,000.
4. Purchased goods from Ravi for ₹ 5,000.
5. Returned goods to Ravi for ₹ 1,000.
6. Sold goods for cash ₹ 5,000.
9. Sold goods to Lakshman for ₹ 3,500.
10. Amount of ₹ 3,750 paid to Ravi as full settlement.
12. Lakshman returned the goods worth ₹ 500. Complaint about damages.
20. Paid Salaries ₹ 2,500.
21. Dividend Received ₹ 1,000.
22. Amount paid to Mohan through a bank at ₹ 1,500.
24. Withdraw money from business for private use ₹ 1,000.
30. Withdraw money from Bank for Business use ₹ 3,000.

Solution : **Journalisation (*In the books of Kumar*)**

Date	Particulars		L.F.	Dr. ₹	Cr. ₹
2003, Jan. 1	Cash A/c To Kumar Capital A/c [Being the business started]	Dr.		60,000	60,000
3	Cash A/c To Bank A/c [Being the cash received from Bank]	Dr.		10,000	10,000
4	Goods A/c To Ravi A/c [Being Goods purchased from Ravi on credit basis]	Dr.		5,000	5,000

5	Ravi A/c Dr.		1,000	
	To Purchase Return A/c			1,000
	[Being the goods returned to Ravi on account of damages]			
6	Cash A/c Dr.		5,000	
	To Goods A/c			5,000
	[Being the goods sold for cash]			
9	Lakshman A/c Dr.		3,500	
	To Goods A/c			3,500
	[Being the goods sold to Lakshman on the credit Basis]			
10	Ravi A/c Dr.		4,000	
	To Cash A/c			3,750
	To Discount A/c			250
	[Being the payment of full Settlement]			
12	Sales Return A/c or Goods A/c Dr.		500	
	To Lakshman A/c			500
	[Being the goods returned to Lakshman]			
20	Salaries A/c Dr.		2,500	
	To Cash A/c			2,500
	[Being Salaries Paid]			
21	Cash A/c Dr.		1,000	
	To Dividend A/c			1,000
	[Being Dividend Received]			
22	Mohan A/c Dr.		1,500	
	To Bank A/c			1,500
	[Being amount paid to Mohan through bank]			
24	Drawing A/c Dr.		1,000	
	To Cash A/c			1,000
	[Being withdrawn money from Business for private use]			
30	Cash A/c Dr.		3,000	
	To Bank A/c			3,000
	[Being withdrawn money from bank for business use]			

Preparation of ledger Accounts

Cash Account

Dr. *Cr.*

Date	Particulars	Folio	Amount	Date	Particulars	Folio	Amount
1.1.04	To Capital A/c		60,000	20.1.04	By Salaries		2,500
3.1.04	To Bank A/c		10,000	24.1.04	By Drawings		1,000
6.1.04	To Goods A/c		5,000	31.1.04	By Balance c/d		79,250
10.1.04	To Ravi A/c		3,750				
21.1.04	To Dividend A/c		1,000				
30.1.04	To Bank A/c		3,000				
			82,750				82,750
1.2.04	To Balance b/d		79,250				

Kumar Capital Account

Date	Particulars	Folio	Amount	Date	Particulars	Folio	Amount
31.1.04	To Balance c/d		60,000	1.1.04	By Cash A/c		60,000
			60,000				60,000
				1.1.04	By Balance b/d		60,000

Bank Account

Date	Particulars	Folio	Amount	Date	Particulars	Folio	Amount
31.1.04	*To Balance c/d*		*14,500*	*3.1.04*	*By Cash A/c*		*10,000*
				22.1.04	By Mohan A/c		1,500
				30.1.04	By Cash A/c		3,000
			14,500				14,500
				1.2.04	By Balance b/d		14,500

Goods Account

Date	Particulars	Folio	Amount	Date	Particulars	Folio	Amount
4.1.04	*To Ravi A/c*		*5,000*	*6.1.04*	*By Cash A/c*		*5,000*
31.1.04	To Balance c/d		3,500	9.1.04	By Lakshman A/c		3,500
			8,500				8,500
				1.2.04	By Balance b/d		3,500

Ravi Account

Date	Particulars	Folio	Amount	Date	Particulars	Folio	Amount
5.1.04	To Purchase Return A/c		1,000	4.1.04	By Goods A/c		5,000
10.1.04	To Cash A/c		3,750				
	To Discount		250				
			5,000				5,000

Lakshman Account

Date	Particulars	Folio	Amount	Date	Particulars	Folio	Amount
9.1.04	*To Goods A/c*		*3,500*	*12.1.04*	*By Sales* Return A/c		500
				31.1.04	By Balance c/d		3,000
			3,500				3,500
1.2.04	By Balance b/d		3,000				

Discount Account

Date	Particulars	Folio	Amount	Date	Particulars	Folio	Amount
1.1.04	*To Balance c/d*		*250*	*10.1.04*	*By Ravi*		*250*
			250				*250*
				1.2.04	By Balance b/d		250

Sales Return Account

Date	Particulars	Folio	Amount	Date	Particulars	Folio	Amount
12.1.04	To Lakshman A/c		500	31.1.04	By Balance c/d		500
			500				500
1.2.04	To Balance b/d		500				

Salaries Account

Date	Particulars	Folio	Amount	Date	Particulars	Folio	Amount
20.1.04	To Cash A/c		2,500	31.1.04	By Balance c/d		2,500
			2,500				2,500
1.2.04	To Balance b/d		2,500				

Mohan Account

Date	Particulars	Folio	Amount	Date	Particulars	Folio	Amount
22.1.04	To Bank A/c		1,500	31.1.04	By Balance c/d		1,500
			1,500				1,500
1.2.04	To Balance b/d		1,500				

Drawing Account

Date	Particulars	Folio	Amount	Date	Particulars	Folio	Amount
24.1.04	To Cash A/c		1,000	31.1.04	By Balance c/d		1,000
			1,000				1,000
1.2.04	To Balance b/d		1,000				

Dividend Account

Date	Particular	Folio	Amount	Date	Particular	Folio	Amount
31.1.04	To Balance c/d		1,000	21.1.04	By Cash		1,000
			1,000				1,000
				1.2.04	By Balance b/d		1,000

From the above ledger accounts it can be noticed that

(*i*) Ravi Account is settled.

(*ii*) Some Accounts showing debit balances.

(*iii*) Some Accounts showing credit balances.

TRIAL BALANCE

Every transaction is recorded under double entry system. The fundamental Principle of Double entry system is that for every debit there must be a corresponding credit. All the ledger accounts are balanced. After arriving at the figures, total of all debit balances must be equaled to the total of credit balances if the accounts are arithmetically accurate.

At the end of the financial year, or at any time the balances of all the ledger accounts are extracted and written up, a statement is prepared which is known as Trial Balance.

Simply, Trial Balance is a settlement which is prepared in order to testify the arithmetical accuracy of entire financial transaction. Agreement of the Trial Balance exposes both the aspects of each transaction which have been recorded and that the books are arithmetically accurate. Suppose Trial Balance does not agree, it means there are errors which must be detected and rectified before preparing the final account. Trial Balance creates a link between ledger accounts and final accounts.

Aim of Trial Balance

1. To avoid unnecessary verification of all the pages of ledger.
2. It is a suitable and easy method of verifying the arithmetical accuracy of the entire transaction.
3. Trial Balance agrees only when the Debit side total is equal to credit side total. Otherwise, there are some errors.
4. It helps in the preparation of final Account. *i.e.,* Trading Accounts, Profit and Loss Account and Balance sheet.

Methods of preparing Trial Balance

There are two methods available for preparing Trial Balance.

1. Total Method　　2. Balances Method

Under the total method, without balancing the ledgers, Debit and credit totals of each account are shown in the two columns *i.e.,* debit side total in the debit column of Trial balance and credit side total is put in the credit column of Trial Balance.

Under the Balances method, the balances are extracted from various ledgers. Simply Debit side of the ledger balance is transferred to Debit side of trial balance; credit side of the ledger balance is transferred to credit side of Trial Balance. The nil balance accounts are not taken into account in this method. So, this method is more convenient to adopt and to be followed at regular practice.

Rules

Debit side = Either Asset Account balances or Expenses Account balances

Credit side = Either Liability Account balances or Income Account balances

Format of Trial Balance

Trial Balance of .... as on ....

S.No.	*Particulars*	*Debit Balance Amount (₹)*	*Credit Balance Amount (₹)*

NOTE : Generally, whenever we prepare the Trial Balance, if it tallies, it is an indication that all the transactions recorded in the books are correct. Suppose if the trial balance disagrees, beyond our attention the difference amount is placed as in the suspense Account. Do attempt suspense account only in few cases.

Problem 4. *Prepare Trial Balance as on 31.03.2002 from the following balances of Mr. Ravi.*

Capital *1,00,000*

Sales *1,50,000*

Plant & Machinery *60,000*

Purchases *50,000*

Sales Returns *5,000*

Wages	*10,000*
Sundry Creditors	*60,000*
Bad Debts	*7,000*
Bad Debts Provision	*3,000*
Land & Buildings	*1,00,000*
Debenture	*45,000*
Drawings	*10,000*
Commission Received	*7,500*
Auditor's Fees	*6,500*
Purchase Return	*10,000*
Bills Payable	*9,000*
Carriage Inwards	*2,000*
Goodwill	*10,000*
Reserve Fund	*25,000*
Wages & Salary	*5,500*
Carriage Outwards	*1,500*
Stock on 01.04.2001	*25,000*
Debtors	*49,000*
Interest Received	*4,000*
Travelling Expenses	*5,000*
Bank Overdraft	*3,000*
Trade Expenses	*3,400*
Motor Vehicle	*8,000*
Rent Received	*2,000*
Lease hold Property	*60,600*

Solution :

Trial Balance of Mr. Ravi as on 31st March 2002

Particulars	*Debit* (₹)	*Credit* (₹)
Capital	-	1,00,000
Sales	-	1,50,000
Plants & Machinery	60,000	-
Purchases	50,000	-
Sales Returns	5,000	-
Wages	10,000	-
Sundry Creditors	-	60,000
Bad Debts	7,000	-
Bad Debts Provision	-	3,000
Land & Buildings	1,00,000	-
Debentures	-	45,000

Drawings	10,000	-
Commission Received	-	7,500
Auditor's Fees	6,500	-
Purchase Return	-	10,000
Bills Payable	-	9,000
Carriage Inwards	2,000	-
Goodwill	10,000	-
Reserve Fund	-	25,000
Wages & Salary	5,500	-
Carriage Outwards	1,500	-
Stock 1.4.2001	25,000	-
Debtors	49,000	-
Interest Received	-	4,000
Travelling Expenses	5,000	-
Bank Overdraft	-	3,000
Trade Expenses	3,400	-
Motor Vehicle	8,000	-
Rent Received	-	2,000
Lease hold property	60,600	-
	4,18,500	4,18,500

Problem 5. *Prepare Trial Balance as on 31.03.2002 from the balances of Mr. Raju.*

Cash in Hand *1,70,000*
Building *1,60,000*
Stock on 01.04.2001 .... *70,000*
Purchases *3,20,000*
Sales Return *5,000*
Commission Received *7,000*
Interest on Drawings *5,000*
Director's Fees *2,000*
Carriage Inwards *4,000*
Carriage Outwards *3,000*
Wages *2,000*
Salaries Wages *3,000*
Investments *75,000*
Sales *7,30,000*
Preliminary Expenses *5,000*
Sundry Creditors *60,000*
Bills Payable *30,000*
Insurance *2,500*

Income from Investment	*3,500*
Printing & Advertisement	*15,000*
Bank Loan	*40,000*
Freight on Purchase	*5,000*
Furniture & Fittings	*18,000*
Drawings Accounts	*5,500*
Deposits	*86,000*
Sundry Debtors	*90,000*
Bills Receivables	*35,000*
Office Expenses	*3,000*
Motor Van	*63,000*
Loan on Mortgage	*1,02,000*
Interest on Loan	*4,500*
General Expenses	*6,500*
Dividend Received	*2,500*
Interest (Cr)	*1,000*

Solution : Trial Balance of Mr. Raju as on 31.03.2002

Particulars	*Debit (₹)*	*Credit (₹)*
Cash in Hand	1,70,000	-
Building	1,60,000	-
Stock 1.4.2001	70,000	-
Purchase	3,20,000	-
Sales Return	5,000	-
Commission Received	-	7,000
Interest on Drawings	-	5,000
Director's Fees	2,000	-
Carriage Inwards	4,000	-
Carriage Outwards	3,000	-
Wages	2,000	-
Salaries Wages	3,000	-
Investments	75,000	-
Sales	-	7,30,000
Preliminary Expenses	5,000	-
Sundry Creditors	-	60,000
Bills Payable	-	30,000
Insurance	2,500	-
Income from Investment	-	3,500
Printings and Advertisement	15,000	-
Bank Loan	-	40,000
Freight on Purchase	5,000	-

Furniture & Fittings	18,000	-
Deposits	-	86,000
Drawings Account	5,500	-
Sundry Debtors	90,000	-
Bills Receivables	35,000	-
Office Expenses	3,000	-
Motor Van	63,000	-
Loan on Mortgage	-	1,02,000
Interest on Loan	4,500	-
General Expenses	6,500	-
Dividend Received	-	2,500
Interest (Cr.)	-	1,000
	10,67,000	10,67,000

NOTE : Before the preparation of the Final Account, we have to know the following concepts and their specifications. Because these four concepts are the fundamentals to all the proceedings of Accounting, either for Trial Balance or for Final Account.

I. Income

Money earned by the concern due to rendering of services or sale of goods.

Example/Specifications :

Commission Received	Interest on Investment Received
Rent Received	Apprentice Premium Received
Dividend Received	Rent Received on sub letting
Interest on Drawings	Rent from Tenants
Sales	Income from any other sources
Bad Debts Recovered	Miscellaneous Revenue Receipt
Interest Received	Salary Received

II. Expenses

Expenses are those which can be incurred *i.e.,* amount paid for the purpose of purchasing of goods or those who render services in our organisation.

Wages paid	Carriage inwards
Salaries Paid	Carriage outwards
Commission Paid	Freight on purchases
Rent Paid	Customs Duty
Interest Paid	Advertisement Expenses paid
Oil, Water	Interest on Bank loan
Gas, Electricity Charges Paid	Interest on Capital.

Drawings Office Salaries Telephone Charges Legal Charges Audit Fees General Expenses Discount allowed Selling and Distribution Expenses	Discount on Bills Loss of Fire not covered by the Insurance company. Manager's remuneration Insurance Bad Debts Agents Commission

III. Assets

Anything which possesses certain monetary value is called Assets.

Example :

Current Assets	**Fixed Assets**	**Others**
Cash in hand and at Bank	Land & Buildings	Preliminary Expenses
Sundry Debtors	Machinery	Goodwill
Bills Receivable	Furniture & Fittings	Patents and Trade Mark
Stock in Trade	Loose tools and spares	Prepaid Expenses
Short Term Investments	Investments	
Marketable Securities	Motor van	
Accrued Incomes		
Prepaid Expenses		

IV. Liabilities

A Business organisation which is liable to pay a certain sum of money to the outsiders is called liabilities.

Example :

Capital	Bank overdraft
Reserve Fund	Outstanding expenses
Debenture	Deposits
Bank loan	Incomes received in advance
Mortgage loan	Expenses due but not paid
Sundry Creditors	Proposed Dividend
Bills Payable	Provision for Taxation

FINAL ACCOUNTS

Final Accounts are otherwise called Annual accounts. Normally Final Accounts are prepared at the end of the financial year or Accounting year. The purpose of preparing Final Accounts is to enable one to know the progress of the business, profit or loss and financial position of the firm at the right time.

The preparation of Final Account is not the first step of the Accounting process but it is the final product of the accounting process. It will give valuable information to the management and outsiders at the end of the Accounting period. Only after the preparation of Trial Balance it is possible to prepare Final Account. Final Account consists of the following parts.

1. Trading Account, 2. Profit and Loss Account, 3. Balance Sheet.

1. Trading Account

Trading Account is prepared to know the trading results or gross profit on trading of the business. Simply, it is to find out the gross profit from business due to buying and selling of goods or services during a particular period. In other words, Gross profit is the difference between the sales and the cost of goods sold.

In business, the expenditure and incomes are classified into Direct and Indirect. All the direct expenditure are debited into the debit side of the Trading Account and all the indirect incomes are credited into the credit side of the Trading Account. After transferring all the above details, we have to balance the Trading Account. If the balance is in the debit side it means the business is getting profit and named as Gross profit. Suppose the balance is in the credit side, it shows Loss and it is called Gross Loss. The Gross Profit or Gross Loss is transferred to the profit and Loss Account either on the Credit side or Debit side.

2. Profit and Loss Account

Profit and Loss Account is prepared to find out the net profit or net loss of the business. All the indirect incomes and expenditure are transferred to the Profit and Loss Account on the credit side and debit side respectively. After transferring all details to the Profit and Loss Account, we balance this account. If the balance is in debit side it is called Net profit. Suppose, the balance is in the credit side it is called as Net Loss. Net profit is transferred to the balance sheet Liabilities side and added to the capital. If it is Net Loss it will be deducted from the capital.

3. Balance Sheet

A Balance Sheet is a statement which is prepared for the purpose of finding out the Assets and liability position of the concern for the particular period. A Balance Sheet is also described as "Statement showing the sources and application of funds." It is a statement and not an account and prepared from real and personal Accounts. It has two sides. The left side of the balance sheet describes the Liabilities and Capital position. The right hand side of the balance sheet describes all the assets and investments.

Trading, Profit & Loss Account disclose the financial results of the concern at the end of the year. But the Balance Sheet discloses the Assets and Liability Position of the Concern as on the date.

Specimen form of Final Account Trading Account for the year ended ......31.3.

Dr. *Cr.*

Particulars	*Amount* ₹	*Amount* ₹	*Particulars*	*Amount* ₹	*Amount* ₹
To Opening Stock		xx	By Sales	xx	
To Purchase	xx		*Less* : Sales Return	xx	xx
Less : Purchase Return	xx	xx	By Closing Stock		xx
To Wages		xx	By Goods destroyed by fire		xx
To Carriage inward		xx	By Gross Loss [Transferred to P&L A/c debit side)		xx
To Manufacturing Expenses		xx			
To Fuel and Power		xx			
To Motive Power		xx			
To Coal, Water, Gas & Electricity		xx			
To Clearing Charges		xx			
To Import Duty		xx			
To Customs Duty		xx			
To Freight on Purchase		xx			
To Factory Rent and Insurance		xx			
To Works Managers Salary		xx			
To Gross Profit (B/f) (Transferred to P&L A/c Credit Side)		xx			
		xx			xx

Profit and Loss Account for the year ended 31.3

Dr. *Cr.*

Particulars	*Amount* ₹	*Amount* ₹	*Particulars*	*Amount* ₹	*Amount* ₹
To Gross Loss (Transferred from Trading A/c)		xx	By Gross Profit (Transferred from Trading A/c)		xx
To Advertisement Expenses		xx	By Rent received		xx
To Carriage outwards		xx	By Commission received		xx
To Bank Charges		xx	By Income from Investments		xx
To Salaries		xx	By Interest received		xx
To Rent and Taxes		xx	By Discount received		xx
To Stationeries		xx	By Income from another source		xx
To Insurance		xx	By Discount on creditors		xx
To Trade Expenses		xx	By Interest on Drawings		xx
To Interest on Capital		xx	By All Business income Other than that		
To Interest on Loan		xx			

To Establishment Expenses		xx	appeared in Trading Account credit side		xx
To Selling & Distribution Expn.		xx	By Net Loss		xx
To Sundry Expenses		xx	(Transferred to Balance sheet assets side)		
To Audit Fees		xx			
To Telephone Charges		xx			
To Depreciation		xx			
To Repair and Maintenance		xx			
To Bad Debts		xx			
To Bad Debts provision		xx			
To Loss on sale of fixed Assets		xx			
To Loss on stock by fire		xx			
To Agents Commission		xx			
To Discount on Debtors		xx			
To All Business Expenses (Other than that appeared in Trading Account debit side)					
By Net Profit (Transferred to Balance sheet Liability side)		xx			
		xx			xx

Balance Sheet as on 31.3

Dr. *Cr.*

Liabilities	*Amount* ₹	*Amount* ₹	*Assets*	*Amount* ₹	*Amount* ₹
Capital		xx	Cash in Hand		xx
Add : Net Profit		xx	Cash at Bank		xx
		xx	Sundry Debtors		xx
(–) *Less* : Drawings	xx				
+ Interest on Drawings	xx	xx	Investments		xx
		xx	Marketable Securities		xx
Add : Interest on Capital		xx	Bills Receivable		xx
Less : Income Tax		xx	Prepaid Expenses		xx
		xx	Machinery		xx
Sundry Creditors		xx	Building		xx
Bills Payable		xx	Furniture and Fittings		xx
Bank Overdraft		xx	Loose tools		xx
Outstanding expenses		xx	Motor Car		xx
Loan from Banks		xx	House & Carts		xx
Mortgage		xx	Goodwill Patents & Trade Mark		xx
Debenture		xx			
Reserve fund		xx	Preliminary Expenses		xx
Income Received in advance		xx	Profit & Loss A/c (Net Loss)		xx
			Closing Stock		xx

ADJUSTMENT

The ultimate aim of the Trading and Profit and Loss Account is to know the real Profit or Loss of the concern during a given period. The purpose of the Balance sheet is to know the financial position at a given period. True profit can be arrived at after adjusting all pending bills and outstanding expenses and incomes through entries. These entries which are passed at the end of the accounting period are called adjustment entries. The following important adjustments which are to be made at the end of the year are as follows.

Important Adjustments

1. Closing stock.
2. Outstanding expenses.
3. Prepaid or unexpired expenses.
4. Income earned but not received or Accrued income.
5. Income received in advance.
6. Depreciation.
7. Interest on capital.
8. Interest on drawings.
9. Interest on loan.
10. Bad debts.
11. Provision for bad and doubtful debts.
12. Provision for discount on debtors.
13. Provision for discount on creditors.
14. Goods distributed as free of sample.
15. Loss of stock by fire.

In the actual sense all the above adjustments are given outside the Trial Balance. While preparing the Final accounts all the adjustments are to be considered. Normally, all the adjustments will appear at two places in the final accounts *i.e.,* either

(*i*) Trading Account and Balance Sheet or

(*ii*) Profit & Loss Account and Balance Sheet.

Adjustment and their Treatment

1. *Closing Stock*

Trading Account	-	Credit side
Balance Sheet	-	Asset side

2. *Outstanding Expenses*

Trading or Profit & Loss A/c	-	Debit side
Balance Sheet	-	Liability side

3. *Prepaid Expenses*

Profit & Loss Account	-	Credit side
(subtract from respective expenses)		
Balance Sheet	-	Asset side

4. *Income Due but not Received*

Profit & Loss Account	-	Credit side
(Add with respective incomes)		
Balance Sheet	-	Asset side

5. *Income Received in Advance*
   Profit and Loss Account - Credit side
   (Subtract from respective incomes)
   Balance sheet - Liability side
6. *Depreciation*
   Profit and Loss Account - Debit side
   Balance Sheet - Liability side
   (Subtract from respective Assets)
7. *Interest on Capital*
   Profit and Loss Account - Debit side
   Balance Sheet - Liability side (Add the capital)
8. *Interest on Drawings*
   Profit and Loss Account - Credit side
   Balance Sheet - Liability side (Subtract from the capital)
9. *Interest on Loan*
   Profit and Loss Account - Debit side
   Balance Sheet - Liability side
   (Add with the respective loan)
10. *Bad Debts*
   Profit and Loss Account - Debit side
   Balance Sheet - Asset side
   (Subtract from the sundry debtors)
11. *Provision for Bad and Doubtful Debts*
   Regarding the Bad debts and provision for Bad and doubtful debts we have to apply the following formula.

   BD + NR – OR

   BD : It refers to the bad debts. It should be given either Trial Balance or Adjustments or both. The value of bad debts is transferred to formula for calculation. The calculated value should be transferred either to debit side or credit side of the P.L & A/c.

   Bad Debts (Adjustment)

   Treatment :

   (*i*) B/S Asset side [Subtract from Debtors], (*ii*) Transfer to formula [P.L & A/c]

   NR : It refers to New Reserve. Normally, it should be give in the adjustment, in the name of provision for doubtful debts or reserves on debtors and so on.

   Treatment :

   (*i*) Transfer to formula, (*ii*) Balance Sheet : Asset side (Subtract from the Debtors)

   OR : It represents old reserve. Normally, bad debts provision *i.e.,* old reserve is given in the Trial Balance. The treatment is that it should be transferred to the formula for calculating new bad debts provision.

   After finding the value, to apply the formula it should be transferred to P.L & A/c either debit side or credit side.
12. *Provision for Discount on Debtors*
   - Profit & Loss Accounts Debit Side
   - Balance Sheet Asset side [Deduct from sundry debtors]

13. *Provision for Discount on Creditors*
   - Profit & Loss Accounts Credit Side
   - Balance Sheet Liability side [Deduct from sundry creditors]

14. *Goods Distributed as free of samples*
   - Trading Accounts Debit Side [Deduct Purchases]
   - Profit & Loss Accounts Debit Side (treated as advertisement expenditure).

15. *Loss of Stock by fire*

   (*a*) **If Insurance Company admitted the full claim**

   Trading Account credit side (Total stock value destroyed by fire)

   Balance Sheet Asset side (Insurance Company Accounts)

   (*b*) **If Insurance Company admitted the part of the claim :** (for example 60%)

   Trading Account credit side (Total stock value Destroyed by fire) (100%)

   Profit and Loss Account Debit side (Loss by fire) (40%)

   Balance Sheet Asset side (Insurance Company Account) (60%)

16. *Managers Commission*

   In an organisation earn higher amount of profit it may given at certain percentage of commission on the net profit to their manager. It may calculated as follows :

$$\text{Commission payable} = \frac{\text{\% of Commission}}{100 + \text{Rate of Commission}} \times \text{Residual Profit}$$

   Treatment :

   — Profit and Loss Account Debit Side.

   — Balance Sheet Liabilities Side.

Problem 6. *The following figures are available relating to the business of Shri Vel for the year 2002.*

	₹
Opening stock	*25,000*
Purchases	*92,000*
Direct expenses	*4,000*
Closing stock	*29,600*
Sales	*1,38,000*

Calculate (i) Cost of goods sold and (ii) Gross Profit.

Solution :

(*i*) Cost of goods sold = Opening stock + Purchases + Direct Expen – Closing Stock

= ₹ 25,000 + 92,000 + 4,000 – 29,600

= **₹ 91,400**

(*ii*) Gross Profit = Sales – Cost of goods sold

= 1,38,000 – 91,400

= **₹ 46,600**

Problem 7. *Prepare Trading Account from the following Balances :*

	₹
Opening stock	*80,000*
Purchases	*3,00,000*
Sales	*4,50,000*
Purchase Returns	*10,000*

Sales Returns *20,000*
Wages *5,000*
Carriage & Freight *15,000*
Freight on purchases *12,000*

Solution : **Trading Account**

Dr. *Cr.*

Particulars	*Amount* ₹	*Amount* ₹	*Particulars*	*Amount* ₹	*Amount* ₹
To Opening Stock		80,000	By Sales	4,50,000	
To Purchases	3,00,000		*Less* : Sales Returns	20,000	4,30,000
Less : Purchase Returns	10,000	2,90,000			
To Wages		5,000			
To Carriage & Freight		15,000			
To Freight on Purchase		12,000			
To Gross Profit		28,000			
		4,30,000			4,30,000

Problem 8. *From the following balances extracted at the close of trading period ended on 31.3.2003, prepare profit and Loss Account as on that date.*

	₹		₹
Gross profit	*90,000*	*Discount Dr*	*1,000*
Carriage outward	*5,000*	*Apprentice Premium (Cr)*	*3,000*
Salaries	*11,000*	*Advertisement*	*1,000*
Rent & Taxes	*4,000*	*Travelling expenses*	*750*
Fire insurance premium	*3,000*	*Sundry Trade expenses*	*500*
Bad debts	*2,500*		

Solution : **Profit and Loss Account**

Dr. *Cr.*

Particulars	*Amount* ₹	*Amount* ₹	*Particulars*	*Amount* ₹	*Amount* ₹
To Carriage outwards		5,000	By Gross Profit		90,000
To Salaries		11,000	By Apprentice		
To Rent & Taxes		4,000	Premium		3,000
To Fire Insurance Premium		3,000			
To Bad Debts		2,500			
To Discount		1,000			
To Travelling Expenses		750			
To Sundry Trade Expenses		500			
To Advertisement		1,000			
To Net Profit		64,250			
		93,000			93,000

Problem 9. *From the following Trial balances of Mr. Ragunath for the year ending on 31.12.2003, prepare Final Accounts with the closing stock of ₹ 15,000.*

Particulars	*Debit* ₹	*Credit* ₹
Stock (1.1.2003)	*46,800*	-
Returns inwards	*10,000*	-
Purchases	*2,40,000*	-
Rents & Rates	*4,000*	-
Sales	-	*3,21,900*
Debenture	-	*25,000*
Reserve fund	-	*45,000*
Sundry Debtors	*60,000*	-
Salaries	*3,000*	-
Commission Received	-	*4,900*
Bad debts	*2,000*	-
Bad debts provision	-	*6,000*
Wages	*6,000*	-
Return outwards	-	*2,000*
Bills receivable	*25,000*	-
Investments	*60,000*	-
Sundry Creditors	-	*20,000*
Bank overdraft	-	*5,000*
Cash in hand	*11,000*	-
Goodwill	*26,000*	-
Capital	-	*63,000*
Furniture	*15,000*	-
General expenses	*2,000*	-
Discount (Cr)	-	*18,000*
	5,10,800	*5,10,800*

Solution : Trading Account for the year ended 31.12.2003

Particulars	₹	₹	*Particulars*	₹	₹
To Opening Stock		46,800	By Sales		3,21,900
To Purchases	2,40,000		*Less* : Sales Returns		10,000
Less : Return Outwards	2,000	2,38,000			3,11,900
To Wages		6,000	By Closing Stock		15,000
To Gross Profit		36,100			
		3,26,900			3,26,900

Profit and Loss Account for the year ended 31.12.2003

	₹	₹		₹	₹
To Rent & Rates		4,000	By Gross Profit		36,100
To Salaries		3,000	By Commission Received		4,900
To Bad Debts		2,000	By Discount (Cr.)		18,000
To General Expenses		2,000			
To Net Profit		48,000			
		59,000			59,000

Balance Sheet as on 31.12.2003

Liabilities	*Amount* ₹	*Amount* ₹	*Assets*	*Amount* ₹	*Amount* ₹
Capital		63,000	Sundry Debtors		60,000
Debenture		25,000	Bills Receivable		25,000
Reserve Fund		45,000	Investments		60,000
Bad Debts Provision		6,000	Cash in Hand		11,000
Sundry Creditors		20,000	Goodwill		26,000
Bank Overdraft		5,000	Furniture		15,000
Profit Loss A/c		48,000	Closing Stock		15,000
		2,12,000			2,12,000

Problem 10. *From the following Trial Balance of Mr.X, prepare the final accounts for the year ended on 31.12.1996.*

Debit Balance	₹	*Credit Balance*	₹
Land and Building	*50,000*	*Returns*	*2,500*
Purchases	*1,10,000*	*Discounts*	*1,200*
Stock	*40,000*	*Sales*	*2,05,000*
Returns	*1,500*	*Capital*	*1,15,000*
Wages	*10,000*	*Loan*	*15,000*
Salaries	*9,000*	*Commission*	*1,500*
Office Expenses	*2,400*	*Creditors*	*25,000*
Carriage	*3,200*	*Bills Payable*	*2,350*
Discounts	*750*		
Bad Debts	*1,200*		
Insurance	*1,500*		
Machinery	*50,000*		
Furniture	*10,000*		
Bills Receivable	*20,000*		
Sundry Debtors	*40,000*		
Cash	*6,000*		
Office Equipment	*12,000*		
	3,67,550		*3,67,550*

The following adjustments are to be made :

(a) Closing stock ₹ 60,000.

(b) Outstanding wages ₹ 2,000 and Rent ₹ 3,000.

(c) Depreciate land and buildings at 5%, Machinery at 10%, office equipment and furniture by 10%.

(d) Provide Reserve at 21/2% on debtors.

(e) Insurance prepaid ₹ 200.

(f) Calculate interest on capital at 5%. [MBA Nov. 1997, Madras]

Solution :

Trading Account of Mr. X for the year ended 31.12.1996

Particulars	₹	₹	*Particulars*	₹	₹
To Opening Stock		40,000	By Sales	2,05,000	
To Purchases	1,10,000		*Less* : Sales Returns	1,500	2,03,500
(–) Returns	2,500	1,07,500			
			By Closing Stock		60,000
To Wages	10,000				
(+) Outstanding	2,000	12,000			
To Carriage		3,200			
To Gross Profit		1,00,800			
		2,63,500			2,63,500

Profit and Loss Account of Mr. X for the year ended 31.12.1996

	₹	₹		₹	₹
To Salaries		9,000	By Gross Profit		1,00,800
To Office Expenses		2,400	By Commission		1,500
To Discounts		750	By Discounts		1,200
To Bad Debts Provision		2,200			
To Rent Outstanding		3,000			
To Insurance	1,500				
(–) Prepaid	200	1,300			
To Depreciation :					
5% on Land & Building	2,500				
10% on Machinery	5,000				
10% on Office Equipment	1,200				
10% on Furniture	1,000	9,700			
To Interest on capital		5,750			
To Net Profit (Transfer to Balance Sheet)		69,400			
		1,03,500			1,03,500

Balance Sheet of Mr. X as on 31.12.1996

Liabilities	*Amount* ₹	*Amount* ₹	*Assets*	*Amount* ₹	*Amount* ₹
Capital	1,15,000		Cash		6,000
+ Interest on Capital	5,750	1,20,750	Land & Building	50,000	
Loan		15,000	(–) Depreciation	2,500	47,500
Creditors		25,000	Machinery	50,000	
Bills Payable		2,350	(–) Depreciation	5,000	45,000
Outstanding Wages		2,000	Furniture	10,000	
Outstanding Rent		3,000	(–) Depreciation	1,000	9,000
Net Profit (P&L) A/c		69,400	Bills Receivable		20,000
			Sundry Debtors	40,000	
			(–) New Reserve	1,000	39,000
			Office Equipment	12,000	
			(–) Depreciation	1,200	10,800
			Closing Stock		60,000
			Prepaid Insurance		200
		2,37,500			2,37,500

NOTE : Bad Debts

BD + NR – OR
↓ ↓ ↓
1200 1000 0 = 2200

Problem 11. *The following balances are drawn from the books of M/s Arvind Mills as on 31.12.1997.*

Account	*Amount* ₹
Land	*1,00,000*
Building	*2,00,000*
Sales	*3,00,000*
Purchases	*1,75,000*
Sales returns	*10,000*
Purchase returns	*5,000*
Stock (1.1.97)	*25,000*
Debtors	*50,000*
Bank overdraft	*15,200*
Cash on hand	*5,000*
Creditors	*20,000*
Salaries	*10,000*
Wages	*12,000*
Goodwill	*15,000*
General Expenses	*5,000*

Selling expenses *12,000*
Bad debts *1,000*
Insurance *1,200*
Capital *2,81,000*

The following adjustments are to be made :

(a) Closing stock is ₹ 30,000.
(b) Provide depreciation at the rate of 10% on buildings.
(c) Write off further bad debts ₹ 1,000.
(d) Salaries yet to be paid ₹ 3,000.
(e) Insurance prepaid ₹ 300.

You are required to prepare a Trading and Profit and loss account and balance sheet of M/s Arvind Mills. [MBA April 1998, Madras]

Solution :

Trading Account of M/s. Arvind Mills for the year ended 31.12.1997

Particulars	₹	₹	*Particulars*	₹	₹
To Opening Stock		25,000	By Sales		3,00,000
To Purchase	1,75,000		(–) Sales Returns		10,000
(–) Purchase Returns	5,000	1,70,000			2,90,000
To Wages		12,000	By Closing Stock		30,000
To Gross Profit		1,13,000			
		3,20,000			3,20,000

Profit and Loss Account of M/s. Arvind Mills for the year ended 31.12.1997

Particulars	₹	₹	*Particulars*	₹	₹
To Salaries	10,000		By Gross Profit		1,13,000
(+) Outstanding	3,000	13,000			
To General Expenses		5,000			
To Selling Expenses		12,000			
To Bad Debts (1000 + 1000)		2,000			
To Insurance	1,200				
(–) Prepaid	300	900			
To Depreciation on Building 10%		20,000			
To Net Profit		60,100			
		1,13,000			1,13,000

Balance Sheet of M/s. Arvind Mills as on 31.12.1997

Liabilities	*Amount* ₹	*Amount* ₹	*Assets*	*Amount* ₹	*Amount* ₹
Capital	2,81,000		Cash on Hand		5,000
(+) Net Profit	60,100	3,41,100	Land		1,00,000
Bank Overdraft		15,200	Building	2,00,000	
Creditors		20,000	(–) Depreciation	20,000	1,80,000
Outstanding Salary		3,000	Debtors	50,000	
			(–) Further Bad debts	1,000	49,000
			Goodwill		15,000
			Closing Stock		30,000
			Prepaid Insurance		300
		3,79,300			3,79,300

Problem 12. *From the following Trial Balance, prepare the Trading and Profit and Loss Account of Mr. Kumaran for the year ended December 31, 1993 and the Balance Sheet as on that date.*

Particulars	*Debit* ₹	*Credit* ₹
Kumaran's Capital	—	*4,000*
Plant and Machinery	*5,000*	—
Office Furniture and fittings	*260*	—
Stocks on January1, 1993	*4,800*	—
Motor van	*1,200*	—
Sundry Debtors	*4,470*	—
Cash in hand	*40*	—
Cash at Bank	*650*	—
Wages	*15,000*	—
Salaries	*1,400*	—
Purchases	*21,350*	—
Sales	—	*48,000*
Bills Receivable	*720*	—
Bills Payable	—	*560*
Sundry Creditors	—	*5,200*
Returns Inwards	*930*	—
Provision for doubtful debts	—	*250*
Drawings	*700*	—
Returns outwards	—	*550*
Rent	*600*	—
Factory Lighting and heating	*80*	—
Insurance	*680*	—
General Expenses	*250*	—
Bad Debts	*200*	—
Discount	*650*	*420*
	58,980	*58,980*

The following adjustments are to be made :

(i) Stock on December 31, 1993 ₹ 5,200.

(ii) 3 months factory lighting and heating is due but not paid ₹ 30/-.

(iii) 5% depreciation to be written off on furniture.

(iv) Write off further bad debts ₹ 70.

(v) The provision for doubtful debts is to be increased to ₹ 300 and provision for discount on debtors be provided at 2%. [MBA Nov. 1995, Madras]

Solution :

Trading Account of Mr. Kumaran for the year ended 31.12.1993

Particulars	₹	₹	*Particulars*	₹	₹
To Opening Stock		4,800	By Sales	48,000	
To Purchases	21,350		*Less :* Sales Returns	930	47,070
Less : Return Outwards	550	20,800	By Closing Stock		5,200
To Wages		15,000			
To Factory lighting and heating	80				
Add : Outstanding	30	110			
To Gross Profit		11,560			
		52,270			52,270

Profit and Loss Account of Mr. Kumaran for the year ended 31.12.1993

Particulars	₹	₹	*Particulars*	₹	₹
To Salaries		1,400	By Gross Profit		11,560
To Rent		600	By Discount		420
To Insurance		680			
To General Expenses		250			
To Discount		650			
To Bad Debts & Provisions		320			
To Depreciation on Furniture		13			
To Discount on Debtors		82			
To Net Profit		7,985			
		11,980			11,980

Balance Sheet of Mr. Kumaran as on 31.12.1993

Liabilities	*Amount* ₹	*Amount* ₹	*Assets*	*Amount* ₹	*Amount* ₹
Capital	4,000		Cash in hand		40
(–) Drawings	700		Cash at Bank		650
	3,300		Plant & Machinery		5,000
(+) Net Profit	7,985	11,285	Office Furniture & Fittings	260	
Bills Payable		560	(–) Depreciation	13	247
Sundry Creditors		5,200	Motor Van		1,200
Outstanding Factory			Bills Receivable		720
Lighting and Heating		30	Closing Stock		5,200
			Sundry Debtors	4,470	
			(–) Bad Debts	70	
				4,400	
			(–) Provision for Doubtful Debts	300	
				4,100	
			(–) Discount on Debtors	82	4,018
		17,075			17,075

Note for bad debts : BD + NR – OR = $\frac{200}{70}$ + 300 – 250 = 320.

Problem 13. *From the following Trial Balance and given information, you are requested to prepare Final Account for the year ended on 31.12.1997.*

Dr.	₹	*Cr.*	₹
Purchases	*11,870*	*Capital*	*8,000*
Debtors	*7,580*	*Bad Debts recovered*	*250*
Return inwards	*450*	*Creditors*	*1,250*
Bank Deposit	*2,750*	*Return outwards*	*350*
Rent	*360*	*Bank Overdraft*	*1,570*
Salaries	*850*	*Sales*	*14,690*
Travelling Expenses	*300*	*Bills Payable*	*1,350*
Cash	*210*		
Stock	*2,450*		
Discount allowed	*40*		
Drawings	*600*		
	27,460		*27,460*

The following adjustments are to be made :

(a) *The closing stock on 31.12.1997 was ₹ 4,200.*

(b) *Write off ₹ 80 as bad debts and create a reserve for bad debts at 5% on sundry debtors.*

(c) *Three months rent is outstanding.*

(d) *Interest on Bank deposit ₹ 135 credited by the bankers and interest on overdraft ₹ 157 debited by them in the pass book have not been entered in the books.*

[MCA Dec. 1999]

Solution : Trading Account for the year ended 31.12.1997

Particulars	₹	₹	*Particulars*	₹	₹
To Opening Stock		2,450	By Sales	14,690	
To Purchases	11870		*Less* : Sales Returns	450	14,240
Less : Return Outwards	350	11,520			
			By Closing Stock		4,200
To Gross Profit		4,470			
		18,440			18,440

Profit and Loss Account for the year ended 31.12.1997

Particulars	₹	₹	*Particulars*	₹	₹
To Rent	360		By Gross Profit		4,470
(+) Outstanding (3x30)	90	450	By Bad Debts		
			Recovered		250
To Salaries		850	By Interest on Bank		
To Travelling Expenses		300	Deposit		135
To Discount Allowed		40			
To Bad Debts &					
Provisions (80+375)		455			
To Interest on Overdraft		157			
To Net Profit		2,603			
		4,855			4,855

Balance Sheet as on 31.12.1997

Liabilities	*Amount* ₹	*Amount* ₹	*Assets*	*Amount* ₹	*Amount* ₹
Capital	8,000		Cash		210
(–) Drawings	600		Debtors	7,580	
	7,400		(–) Bad Debts	80	
(+) Net Profit	2,603	10,003		7,500	
			(–) New Reserve	375	7,125
Creditors		1,250			
Bank Overdraft	1,570		Bank Deposit	2,750	
+ Interest Outstanding	157	1,727	+ Outstanding Interest	135	2,885
Bills Payable		1,350	Closing Stock		4,200
Rent Outstanding		90			
		14,420			14,420

Note for bad debts :	Drs :	7,580
	(–) Bad Debts	80
BD + NR – OR		7,500
	(–) NR (7500 × 5/100)	375
80 + 375 – 0 = 455		7,125

Problem 14. *From the following Trial Balance of Krishna Bros as on 31st December 1998, prepare Trading and Profit and Loss Account and a Balance sheet :*

	₹
Credit Balance	
Capital	*36,000*
Creditors	*8,720*
Bills payable	*2,528*
Sales	*78,182*
Loan	*12,000*
Debit Balance	
Debtors	*3,885*
Salaries	*4,000*
Discount	*1,000*
Postage	*273*
Bad debts	*287*
Interest	*1,295*
Insurance	*417*
Machinery	*10,000*
Stock on 1st January	*9,945*
Purchases	*62,092*
Wages	*4,300*
Buildings	*23,780*
Fixtures and fittings	*16,156*
Closing stock on 31st December 1998 was	*14,300*

[M.Sc., ISM May 2000]

Solution :

Trading Account of Krishna Brothers for the year ended 31.12.1998

Particulars	₹	₹	*Particulars*	₹	₹
To Opening Stock		9,945	By Sales		78,182
To Purchases		62,092	By Closing Stock		14,300
To Wages		4,300			
To Gross Profit		16,145			
		92,482			92,482

Profit and Loss Account of Krishna Brothers for the year ended 31.12.1998

Particulars	₹	₹	*Particulars*	₹	₹
To Salaries		4,000	By Gross Profit		16,145
To Discount		1,000			
To Postage		273			
To Bad Debts		287			
To Interest		1,295			
To Insurance		417			
To Net Profit		8,873			
		16,145			16,145

Balance Sheet of Krishna Brothers as on 31.12.1998

Liabilities	*Amount* ₹	*Amount* ₹	*Assets*	*Amount* ₹	*Amount* ₹
Capital		36,000	Debtors		3,885
Creditors		8,720	Machinery		10,000
Bills Payable		2,528	Buildings		23,780
Loan		12,000	Fixtures & Fittings		16,156
Profit & Loss A/c		8,873	Closing Stock		14,300
		68,121			68,121

Problem 15. *Following are the balances extracted from the books of Mohammad as on 31st December 1998. Prepare Final Account as on the date.*

	₹		₹
Capital	20,000	*Drawings*	5,000
Cash on Hand	5,000	*Cash at Bank*	8,000
Buildings	20,000	*Machinery*	6,000
Stock on 01.01.1998	3,000	*Sundry Debtors*	8,000
Sundry Creditors	6,000	*Repairs*	400
Commission paid	700	*Wages*	1,700
Rent and Rates	300	*Insurance Premium*	300
Purchases	60,000	*Sales*	96,000
Purchases Returns	750	*Sales Returns*	400
Furniture & Fixtures	1,600	*Carriage*	200
Loan to Ram	1,000	*Telephone Charges*	250
Discount allowed	50	*Salaries*	600
Bad Debts	350	*Discount earned*	100

[M.Sc.JTM Dec.1999]

Solution :

Trading Account of Mr. Mohammad for the year ended 31.12.1998

Particulars	₹	₹	Particulars	₹	₹
To Opening Stock		3,000	By Sales	96,000	
To Purchase	60,000		(–) Sales Returns	400	95,600
(–) Purchase Returns	750	59,250			
To Wages		1,700			
To Carriage		200			
To Gross Profit		31,450			
		95,600			95,600

Profit and Loss Account of Mr. Mohammad for the year ended 31.12.1998

Particulars	₹	₹	Particulars	₹	₹
To Repairs		400	By Gross Profit		31,450
To Commission Paid		700	By Discount earned		100
To Rent & Rates		300			
To Discount allowed		50			
To Bad Debts		350			
To Insurance Premium		300			
To Telephone Charges		250			
To Salaries		600			
To Net Profit		28,600			
		31,550			31,550

Balance Sheet of Mr. Mohammad as on 31.12.1998

Liabilities	Amount ₹	Amount ₹	Assets	Amount ₹	Amount ₹
Capital	20,000		Cash in Hand		5,000
(–) Drawings	5,000	15,000	Cash at Bank		8,000
			Buildings		20,000
Sundry Creditors		6,000	Machinery		6,000
Net Profit		28,600	Sundry Debtors		8,000
(Profit & Loss A/c)			Furniture Fixtures		1,600
			Loan to Ram		1,000
		49,600			49,600

Problem 16. *Following the balance has been extracted from the books of Mr. Ganesh on 31.12.1997.*

	₹		₹
Capital	*15,000*	*Loans Borrowed*	*20,000*
Drawings	*4,800*	*Stock (1.1.97)*	*7,500*
Machinery	*20,000*	*Purchases*	*60,000*
Furniture	*1,500*	*Sales*	*90,000*

Sundry Debtors	*20,000*	*Office Rent*	*1,000*
Sundry Creditors	*12,900*	*Insurance*	*240*
Interest (Dr.)	*1,250*	*Discount allowed*	*1,000*
Wages	*10,000*	*Discount earned*	*500*
Salaries	*7,500*	*General Expenses*	*1,200*
Carriage Inwards	*500*	*Cash on Hand*	*150*
Purchase Returns	*1,000*	*Bank balance*	*1,260*
Sales Returns	*1,500*		

The following adjustments are to be made :

(a) Closing stock ₹ 10,000.

(b) Outstanding rent ₹ 100. Salaries ₹ 900.

(c) Insurance prepaid ₹ 40 and interest on loans outstanding ₹ 250.

(d) Provide Depreciation 10% on machinery and 6% of furniture.

(e) Prepare Trading account, profit and loss account and Balance Sheet for the year ending 31st December 1997. [M.Sc. Dec. 1999]

Solution :

Trading Account of Mr. Ganesh for the year ended 31.12.1997

Particulars	₹	₹	*Particulars*	₹	₹
To Opening Stock		7,500	By Sales	90,000	
To Purchase	60,000		(–) Sales Returns	1,500	88,500
(–) Purchase Returns	1,000	59,000			
To Wages		10,000	By Closing Stock		10,000
To Carriage inwards		500			
To Gross Profit		21,500			
		98,500			98,500

Profit and Loss Account of Mr. Ganesh for the year ended 31.12.1997

Particulars	₹	₹	*Particulars*	₹	₹
To Interest (Dr.)		1,250	By Gross Profit		21,500
To Salaries	7,500		By Discount Earned		500
(+) Outstanding	900	8,400			
To Office Rent	1,000				
(+) Outstanding	100	1,100			
To Insurance	240				
(–) Prepaid	40	200			
To Discount allowed		1,000			
To General Expenses		1,200			
To Interest on Loan Outstanding		250			
To Depreciation on Machinery		2,000			
To Depreciation on Furniture		90			
To Net Profit		6,510			
		22,000			22,000

Balance Sheet of Mr. Ganesh as on 31.12.1997

Liabilities	*Amount* ₹	*Amount* ₹	*Assets*	*Amount* ₹	*Amount* ₹
Capital	15,000		Machinery	20,000	
(–) Drawings	4,800		(–) Depreciation	2,000	18,000
	10,200		Furniture	1,500	
(+) Net Profit	6,510	16,710	(–) Depreciation	90	1,410
			Sundry Debtors		20,000
Sundry Creditors		12,900	Cash on Hand		150
Outstanding Rent		100	Bank Balance		1,260
Outstanding Salaries		900	Closing Stock		10,000
Loans borrowed	20,000		Insurance Prepaid		40
(+) Interest on Loan					
Outstanding	250	20,250			
		50,860			50,860

Problem 17. *From the following trial balance extracted from the books of a merchant on 31.12.1998.*

	₹		₹
Furniture and Fittings	*640*	*Purchases*	*5,475*
Motor vehicles	*6,250*	*Sales*	*15,450*
Buildings	*7,500*	*Bank Overdraft*	*2,850*
Capital Account	*12,500*	*Sales Returns*	*200*
Provision for Bad Debts	*20*	*Purchase Returns*	*125*
Bad debts	*125*	*Advertising*	*450*
Sundry debtors	*3,800*	*Interest A/c (Dr.)*	*118*
Sundry creditors	*2,680*	*Commission (Cr.)*	*375*
Stock on 1.1.1998	*3,460*	*Cash*	*650*
General Insurance	*782*	*Taxes & Insurance*	*1,250*
Salaries	*3,300*		

The following adjustments are to be made :

(a) Closing stock was valued at ₹ 3250.

(b) Depreciate building @ 5%, furniture and fitting @ 10% and motor vehicle @ 20%.

(c) ₹ 85 is due for interest on Bank overdraft.

(d) Salaries ₹ 300 and Taxes ₹ 120 are outstanding.

(e) Insurance amounting to ₹ 100 is prepaid.

(f) One third of the commission received is in respect of work to be done next year.

(g) Write off further ₹ 100 as Bad debt and provision for bad debts is to be made equal to 5% on sundry Debtors.

Prepare Final Account for the year ended 31.12.1998.

Solution : Trading Account for the year ended 31.12.1998

Particulars	₹	₹	Particulars	₹	₹
To Opening Stock		3,460	By Sales	15,450	
To Purchase	5,475		(–) Sales Returns	200	15,250
(–) Purchase Returns	125	5,350	By Closing Stock		3,250
To Gross Profit		9,690			
		18,500			18,500

Profit and Loss Account for the year ended 31.12.1998

Particulars	₹	₹	Particulars	₹	₹
To Salaries	3,300		By Gross Profit		9,690
(+) Outstanding	300	3,600	By Commission	375	
To Insurance	782		(–) Received in		
(–) Prepaid	100	682	Advance	125	250
To Advertising		450			
To Bad Debts provisions		390			
To Interest	118				
(+) Outstanding	85	203			
To Taxes & Insurance	1,250				
(+) Outstanding	120	1,370			
To Depreciation :					
Building		375			
Furniture & Fittings		64			
Motor Vehicle		1,250			
Net Profit		1,556			
		9,940			9,940

Balance Sheet as on 31.12.1998

Liabilities	Amount ₹	Amount ₹	Assets	Amount ₹	Amount ₹
Capital	12,500		Cash		650
(+) Net Profit	1,556	14,056	Furniture & Fittings	640	
Sundry Creditors		2,680	(–) Depreciation	64	576
Bank Overdraft	2,850		Motor Vehicles	6,250	
(+) Interest Due	85	2,935	(–) Depreciation	1,250	5,000
			Buildings	7,500	
Outstanding Salary		300	(–) Depreciation	375	7,125
Outstanding Taxes			Sundry Debtors	3,800	
Insurance		120	(–) Bad Debts	100	
Commission received				3,700	
In advance		125	(–) Provision	185	3,515
			Closing Stock		3,250
			Prepaid Insurance		100
		20,216			20,216

NOTE : BD + NR – OR = 225 + 185 – 20 = 390.

Problem 18. *From the following Balance of Mr. Raju for the year ended on 31.3.2003, prepare Final Account.*

	₹
Capital	*1,00,000*
Drawings	*18,000*
Buildings	*15,000*
Furniture & fittings	*7,500*
Motor Van	*25,000*
Loan from Hari @ 12% interest	*15,000*
Interest paid on above	*900*
Sales	*1,00,000*
Purchases	*75,000*
Opening stock	*25,000*
Establishment expenses	*15,000*
Wages	*2,000*
Insurance	*1,000*
Commission Received	*4,500*
Sundry Debtors	*28,100*
Bank Balance	*20,000*
Sundry Creditors	*10,000*
Interest (Cr)	*3,000*

The following adjustments are to be made :

(a) The value of closing stock on 31.03.2003 was ₹ 32,000.

(b) Outstanding wages ₹ 500.

(c) Prepaid Insurance ₹ 300.

(d) Commission Received on advance ₹ 300.

(e) Allow interest on capital @ 10%.

(f) Depreciate Building 2½ %, Furniture's fittings 10%, Motor van 10%.

(g) Charge interest on Drawings ₹ 500.

(h) Accrued Interest ₹ 500/-.

Solution :

Trading Account of Mr. Raju for the year ended 31.12.2003

Particulars	₹	₹	*Particulars*	₹	₹
To Opening Stock		25,000	By Sales		1,00,000
To Purchases		75,000	By Closing Stock		32,000
To Wages	2,000				
(+) Outstanding	500	2,500			
To Gross Profit		29,500			
		1,32,000			1,32,000

Profit and Loss Account of Mr. Raju for the year ended 31.12.2003

Particulars	₹	₹	*Particulars*	₹	₹
To Interest Paid	900		By Gross Profit		29,500
(+) Due	900	1,800	By Interest on		
To Establishment Expn.		15,000	Drawings		500
To Insurance	1,000		By Interest	3,000	
(–) Prepaid	300	700	(+) Accrued Interest	500	3,500
To Interest on Capital		10,000			
To Depreciation :			By Commission		
Building		375	received	4,500	
Furniture & Fittings		750	(–) Commission		
Motor Van		2,500	received in advance	300	4,200
To Net Profit		6,575			
		37,700			37,700

Balance Sheet of Mr. Raju as on 31.12.2003

Liabilities	*Amount* ₹	*Amount* ₹	*Assets*	*Amount* ₹	*Amount* ₹
Capital		98,075	Bank Balance		20,000
Loan from Hari	15,000		Buildings	15,000	
(+) Interest outstanding	900	15,900	(–) Depreciation	375	14,625
Sundry Creditors		10,000	Furniture & Fittings	7,500	
Outstanding Wages		500	(–) Depreciation	750	6,750
Commission received			Motor Van	25,000	
In advance		300	(–) Depreciation	2,500	22,500
			Sundry Debtors		28,100
			Closing Stock		32,000
			Prepaid Insurance		300
			Accrued Interest		500
		1,24,775			1,24,775

NOTE :

Capital		1,00,000
(+) Interest on Capital		10,000
		1,10,000
(–) Drawings	18,000	
(+) Interest on Drawings	500	18,500
		91,500
(+) Net Profit		6,575
		98,075

Problem 19. *From the following balance, prepare Final Account of Mr. Kumar for the year ended on 31.12.1997.*

	₹	₹
Capital Account		*60,000*
Plant & Machinery	*18,000*	
Depreciation on Plant & Machinery	*2,000*	
Repair to Plant	*1,600*	
Wages	*28,000*	
Salaries	*4,000*	
Income Tax	*500*	
Cash in hand	*2,000*	
Furniture	*24,500*	
Depreciation on Motor car	*2,500*	
Purchase Less returns (Adjusted)	*93,500*	
Sales		*2,49,000*
Bank Overdraft		*13,800*
Accrued Income	*1,500*	
Salaries outstanding		*2,000*
Bills Receivable	*30,000*	
Bills Payable		*3,000*
Provisions for Bad debts		*6,000*
Bad debts	*1,000*	
Discount on Purchases		*4,000*
Sundry Debtors	*35,000*	
Sundry Creditors		*23,300*
Stock on Hand 01.01.1997	*37,000*	
Motor Car	*50,000*	
Stock on 31.12.1997	*30,000*	
	3,61,100	*3,61,100*

Write off ₹ 3,000 as bad debts and maintain a provision for bad debts at 5% Sundry Debtors. [MCA Nov. 1999]

Solution :

Trading Account of Mr. Kumar for the year ended 31.12.1997

Particulars	₹	₹	*Particulars*	₹	₹
To Opening Stock		37,000	By Sales		2,49,000
To Purchases (Adjusted)	93,500				
(–) Discount on Purchases	4,000	89,500			
To Wages		28,000			
To Gross Profit		94,500			
		2,49,000			2,49,000

Profit and Loss Account of Mr. Kumar for the year ended 31.12.1997

Particulars	₹	₹	Particulars	₹	₹
To Depreciation on Plant & Machinery		2,000	By Gross Profit		94,500
To Repairs		1,600	By Bad Debts & Provisions		400
To Salaries		4,000			
To Depreciation on Motor Car		2,500			
To Net Profit		84,800			
		94,900			94,900

Balance Sheet as on 31.12.2003

Liabilities	Amount ₹	Amount ₹	Assets	Amount ₹	Amount ₹
Capital Account	60,000		Plant & Machinery		18,000
(–) Income Tax	500	59,500	Cash in Hand		2,000
Bank overdraft		13,800	Furniture		24,500
			Accrued Income		1,500
Salaries outstanding		2,000	Bills receivable		30,000
Bills Payable		3,000	Sundry Debtors	35,000	
Sundry Creditors		23,300	(–) Bad debts	3,000	
Profit & Loss Account		84,800		32,000	
			(–) New Reserve	1,600	30,400
			Motor Car		50,000
			Closing Stock		30,000
		1,86,400			1,86,400

NOTE :

BD + NR – OR

$\left.\begin{array}{c}1,000\\ +\\ 3,000\end{array}\right\} + 1,600 - 6,000 = -400$

$= 5,600 - 6,000 = -400$

Debtors	35,000
(–) Bad Debts	3,000
	32,000

New Reserve $= 32,000 \times \frac{5}{100} =$ **1,600.**

Problem 20. *From the following data, prepare Trading, Profit and Loss Account and a balance sheet as on 31.3.96*

	₹		₹
Drawings	*10,000*	*Capital*	*30,000*
Purchases	*30,000*	*Purchase returns*	*1,000*
Sales returns	*5,000*	*Sales*	*60,000*
Carriage in	*2,000*	*Wages outstanding*	*2,000*
Carriage out	*3,000*	*Rent received*	*1,000*
Depreciation on plant	*4,000*	*Reserve for doubtful debts*	*1,000*

Plant Account	*20,000*	*Interest (cr)*	*5,000*
Wages and Salaries	*3,000*	*Sundry creditors*	*6,000*
Bad debts	*2,000*	*Loans*	*38,000*
Buildings	*20,000*		
Stock 1.4.95	*25,000*		
Interest	*5,000*		
Sundry Debtors	*15,000*		
	1,44,000		*1,44,000*

The following adjustments are to be made :

(a) Stock on 31.3.96 was ₹ 40,000. A fire broke out in the godown and destroyed stock worth ₹ 5,000 Insurance company had accepted and paid the claim in full.

(b) Provide for bad debts at the rate of 10 percent and provide for discount on debtors at the rate of 5 percent and on creditors at the rate of 10 percent.

(c) Depreciate buildings at the rate of 15 percent per annum.

(d) Rent outstanding amounted to ₹ 1,000.

(e) Closing stock includes samples worth ₹ 2,000.

(f) Provide interest on drawings at the rate of 10% and on capital @ 5%.

[MBA Madras Nov.1996]

Solution : Trading Account for the year ended 31.3.1996

Particulars	₹	₹	*Particulars*	₹	₹
To Opening Stock		25,000	By Sales	60,000	
To Purchase	30,000		(–) Returns	5,000	55,000
(–) Purchase Returns	1,000	29,000	By Loss of Stock		5,000
To Carriage inwards		2,000	By Closing Stock	40,000	
To Wages and Salaries		3,000	(–) Samples	2,000	38,000
To Gross Profit		39,000			
		98,000			98,000

Profit and Loss Account for the year ended 31.3.1996

Particulars	₹	₹	*Particulars*	₹	₹
To Goods sent as samples		2,000	By Gross Profit b/d		39,000
To Carriage outwards		3,000	By Rent Received	1,000	
To Depreciation on Buildings		3,000	(+) Rent outstanding	1,000	2,000
To Interest		5,000	By Interest on Drawings		1,000
To Bad debts & Provisions		2,500	By Interest		5,000
To Discount on debtors		675	By Discount on Creditors		600
To Interest on capital		1,500			
To Depreciation on plant		4,000			
To Net Profit		25,925			
		47,600			47,600

Balance Sheet as on 31.3.1996

Liabilities	*Amount* ₹	*Amount* ₹	*Assets*	*Amount* ₹	*Amount* ₹
Capital	30,000		Plant		20,000
(+) Interest on Capital	1,500		Debtors	15,000	
(+) Net Profit	25,925		(–) New Provision	1,500	
		57,425		13,500	
			(–) Discount	675	12,825
(–) Drawings	10,000				
(+) Interest on			Buildings	20,000	
Drawings	1,000	11,000	(–) Depreciation	3,000	17,000
		46,425			
Wages outstanding		2,000	Insurance Co. Account		5,000
Creditors	6,000		Closing Stock		38,000
(–) Discount on					
Creditors	600	5,400			
Loan		38,000			
Rent outstanding		1,000			
		92,825			92,825

NOTE : For Bad debts and provisions, BD + NR – OR = 2,000 + 1,500 – 1,000 = 2,500

Problem 21. *From the following balance extracted from the books of Shri Madhavan, prepare Final accounts for the year ended on 30th Sep. 1998 and a Balance Sheet as on that date.*

	₹		₹
Drawings	*6,480*	*Cash on hand*	*850*
Land & Building	*25,000*	*Cash at bank*	*13,000*
Investments	*30,000*	*Capital Account*	*1,20,000*
Sundry Debtors	*37,800*	*Bad Debts provision*	*2,470*
Plant & Machinery	*14,270*	*Sales*	*91,230*
Furniture & Fixtures	*1,250*	*Discount Account*	*120*
Carriage Inwards	*4,370*	*Purchase Returns*	*8,460*
Wages	*21,470*	*Sundry Creditors*	*12,170*
Salaries	*4,670*	*Apprentice premium*	*500*
Bank Charges	*140*	*Sales Returns*	*1,760*
Coal Gas & Water	*720*		
Rates and Taxes	*840*		
Purchases	*42,160*		
Bills Receivable	*1,270*		
Trade Expenses	*1,990*		
Stock (01.10.97)	*26,420*		
Fire Insurance	*490*		

The following adjustments are to be made :

(a) Charge Depreciation on land & building Account at 2½ %, plant and machinery at 10%, Furniture and fixtures at 10%.

(b) Make provision of 5% on Sundry Debtors for Doubtful Debts.

(c) Carry forward the unexpired amounts for fire insurance of ₹ 125, Rates and Taxes ₹ 240 and Apprentice premium ₹ 400.

(d) Charge 5% interest on capital and interest on Drawings is ₹ 300/-.

(e) The value of stock as on 30.09.1998 was ₹ 29,390/-.

(f) Outstanding wages are ₹ 530.

(g) Interest on investment ₹ 3,000 is accrued.

Solution :

Trading Account of Mr. Madhavan for the year ended 31.09.1998

Particulars	₹	₹	*Particulars*	₹	₹
To Opening Stock		26,420	By Sales	91,230	
To Purchases	42,160		(–) Sales Returns	1,760	89,470
(–) Purchase Returns	8,460	33,700	By Closing Stock		29,390
To Carriage inwards		4,370			
To Wages	21,470				
(+) Outstanding	530	22,000			
To Coal, Gas and Water		720			
To Gross Profit		31,650			
		1,18,860			1,18,860

Profit and Loss Account of Mr. Madhavan for the year ended 31.09.1998

Particulars	₹	₹	*Particulars*	₹	₹
To Salaries		4,670	By Gross Profit		31,650
To Bank Charges		140	By Discount		120
To Rate and Taxes	840		By Apprentice		
(–) Prepaid	240	600	Premium	500	
To Trade Expenses		1,990	(–) Received in		
To Fire Insurance	490		Advance	400	100
(–) Prepaid	125	365			
To Depreciation :			By Bad Debts		
Land & Building 2½%		625	Provision	2,470	
Plant & Machinery 10%		1,427	(–) New Provision	1,890	580
Furniture & Fixtures 10%		125			
To Interest on Capital		6,000	By Interest on		
To Net Profit			Drawings		300
(Transferred to Capital			By Accrued interest		
A/c)		19,808	Investments		3,000
		35,750			35,750

Balance Sheet of Mr. Madhavan as on 31.09.1998

Liabilities	*Amount* ₹	*Amount* ₹	*Assets*	*Amount* ₹	*Amount* ₹
Capital		1,20,000	Cash in hand		850
(+) Net Profit		19,808	Cash at bank		13,000
Interest on Capital		6,000	Bills Receivables		1,270
		1,45,808	Sundry Debtors	37,800	
(–) Drawings	6,480		(–) Provision for		
(+) Interest on			Bad Debts	1,890	35,910
Drawings	300	6,780	Investments		30,000
		1,39,028			
Sundry Creditors		12,170	Accrued Interest		3,000
Apprentice premium			Prepaid Insurance		125
Received in Advance		400	Prepaid Rates & Taxes		240
Outstanding Wages		530	Land & Building	25,000	
			(–) Depreciation	625	24,375
			Plant & Machinery	14,270	
			(–) Depreciation	1,427	12,843
			Furniture & Fixtures	1,250	
			(–) Depreciation	125	1,125
			Closing stock		29,390
		1,52,128			1,52,128

NOTE : BD + NR – OR = 0 + 1890 – 2470 = – 580.

Problem 22. *From the following Trial balance, prepare the Trading Account and Profit and Loss Account of Mr. Mugunthan for the year ended on 31.12.2000 and the Balance Sheet as on the date.*

Trial Balance

Particulars	*Debit*	*Credit*
Debtors and Creditors	*6,800*	*4,500*
Purchases and sales	*6,200*	*19,500*
Bills	*450*	*300*
Investment	*3,000*	-
Bad Debts & Reserve	*200*	*400*
Returns	*200*	*100*
Loose tools	*1,000*	-
Machinery	*9,600*	-
Furniture	*400*	-
Carriage inwards	*300*	-
Opening stock	*3,400*	-
Establishment charges	*250*	-
Wages	*2,500*	-

Coal and power	*1,300*	-
General Expenses	*2,300*	-
Rates and taxes	*2,500*	-
Drawings	*600*	-
Depreciation	*1,200*	-
Cash in hand	*100*	-
Discount	*100*	*100*
Bank overdraft		*2,500*
Capital		*15,000*
	42,400	*42,400*

The following adjustments are to be considered :

(a) Closing stock was valued at ₹ 3500.

(b) Coal unconsumed ₹ 200.

(c) Maintain 5% reserve for Bad debts.

(d) Liability for wages ₹ 300.

Solution : Trading Account for the year ended 31.12.2000

Particulars	₹	₹	*Particulars*	₹	₹
To Opening Stock		3,400	By Sales	19,500	
To Purchases	6,200		(–) Returns	200	19,300
(–) Returns	100	6,100	By Closing Stock		3,500
Carriage inwards		300			
To Coal and power	1,300				
(–) Unconsumed	200	1,100			
Wages	2,500				
(+) Liability	300	2,800			
Gross Profit		9,100			
		22,800			22,800

Profit and Loss Account for the year ended 31.12.2000

Particulars	₹	₹	*Particulars*	₹	₹
To Establishment Charges	100	250	By Gross Profit		9,100
			By Discount		100
To General Expenses		2,300			
To Rates and Tax		2,500			
To Depreciation		1,200			
To Bad Debts & Provision		140			
To Discount		100			
To Net Profit		2,710			
		9,200			9,200

Balance Sheet as on 31.12.2000

Liabilities	Amount ₹	Amount ₹	Assets	Amount ₹	Amount ₹
			Cash in hand		100
Capital	15,000		Furniture		400
(+) Net Profit	2,910		Machinery		9,600
	17,910		Loose Costs		1,000
(–) Drawings	600	17,310	Investments		3,000
			Sundry Debtors	6,800	
Sundry Creditors		4,000	(–) New Reserve	340	6,460
Bills Payable		800	Bills Receivable		450
Outstanding wages		300	Coal stock		200
Bank overdraft		2,500	Closing Stock		3,500
		24,710			24,710

NOTE : BD + NR – OR = 200 + 340 – 400 = 140.

Problem 23. *From the following Ledger Balances extracted at the close of trading year ended 31st March 2008. Prepare Trading and Profit and Loss account and Balance Sheet at that date, after giving effect to the under mentioned adjustments :*

	₹		₹
Capital on 1-4-2007	*50,000*	*Business Premises*	*55,000*
Stock on 1-4-2007	*8,000*	*Furniture and Fixtures*	*2,500*
Purchase	*20,000*	*Bills Receivable*	*3,500*
Sales	*80,000*	*Bills Payable*	*2,500*
Return Inwards	*1,500*	*Sundry Creditors*	*15,800*
Return Outwards	*400*	*Packing Machinery*	*4,500*
Wages	*6,900*	*Smith's Loan (Dr) @*	
Advertisement	*5,500*	*10% on 1-4-2007*	*5,000*
Apprenticeship Premium	*1,200*	*Investment*	*3,000*
Interest on Smith's Loan	*300*	*Cash-in-Hand*	*250*
Proprietor's Withdrawals	*3,000*	*Cash-at-Bank*	*3,500*
Office Expenses	*8,050*	*Sundry Debtors*	*20,000*

Adjustments to be made for the current period are :

(1) Stock-in-hand at 31st March 2008 ₹ 7,000; (2) Apprenticeship premium is for three years, paid advance on 1st April, 2007; (3) Interest on Capital to be allowed at 5% for the year; (4) Interest on Drawings to be charged to him as ascertained for the year ₹ 80; (5) ₹ 5,000 out of the Advertisement expenses are to be carried forward; (6) Stock valued at ₹ 3,000 destroyed by the fire on 25-3-2008 but the insurance company admitted a claim of ₹ 2,000 only and paid it in April 2008; (7) The manager is entitled to a commission of 10% of the Net profit calculated after charging such commission; (8) Included in sales is an amount of ₹ 10,000 representing goods on "sales or return". The customer still having the right to return the goods. The goods were invoiced charging a profit of 20% on sales; (9) The stock included material worth ₹ 1,000 for which bills had not been received and therefore, not yet accounted for.

Solution : **Trading and Profit and Loss Account**

For the year ended 31st March 2008

		₹			₹
To Opening Stock		8,000	By Sales	80,000	
To Purchases	20,000		*Less* : Sales Returns	1,500	
Less : Return	400			78,500	
	19,600		*Less* : Goods Sold on Return Basis	10,000	68,500
Add : Material not accounted for	1000	20,600	By closing stock	7,000	
To Wages		6,900	*Add* : Stock lying with customers sold on return basis	8,000	15,000
To Gross profit c/d		51,000	By Loss of stock by fire		3,000
		86,500			86,500
To Interest on capital		2,500	By Gross profit b/d		51,000
To Advertisement	5,500		By Apprentice Premium	1,200	
Less : Carried Forward	5,000	500	*Less* : Received in advance	800	400
To Loss of stock by fire		1,000	By Interest on drawings		80
To Office expenses		8,050	By Interest on Smith's loan	300	
		12,050	*Add* : Accrued Interest	200	500
To Manager's commission 1/11 of ₹ 39,930 *i.e.*, (51980–12,050)		3,630			
To Net profit transferred to capital account		36,300			
		51,980			51,980

Balance Sheet as on 31st March 2008

Liabilities		₹	*Assets*		₹
Sundry creditors	15,800		Cash-in-hand		250
Add : Purchase of material not accounted for	1,000	16,800	Cash-at-bank		3,500
			Investment		3,000
Bills payable		2,500	Sundry debtors	20,000	
Apprentice premium received in advance		800	*Less* : Goods sold on return basis	10,000	10,000
Manager's commission due		3,630	Insurance company A/c		2,000
Capital	50,000		Closing stock (7,000 + 8,000)		15,000
Add : Interest	2,500		Bills receivable		3,500
Add : Net profit	36,300		Smith's loan	5,000	
	88,800		*Add* : Accrued interest	200	5,200
Less : Drawings and Interest	3,080	85,720	Packing Machinery		4,500
			Furniture and Fittings		2,500
			Business Premises		55,000
			Advertisement (carried forward)		5,000
		1,09,450			1,09,450

Problem 24. *The following is the Trial Balance of Mr. Nandhu as on 31.12.2007. Prepare a Trading and Profit and Loss A/c for the year 2007 and Balance Sheet as at 31-12-2007 from it.*

	Dr.	Cr.
Purchases	2,80,000	
Opening Stock	10,000	
Salaries less P.F	5,400	
P.F. remittance including Proprietor's contribution @ 50%	1,200	
Rent @ ₹ 250 P.M.	2,750	
Machinery	29,000	
Wages	3,000	
Furniture and Fittings	5,000	
Electricity	550	
Trade Expenses	1,500	
Debtors	10,500	
Interest on Loan	900	
Commission	200	
Buildings	30,000	
Sales		3,05,000
Loan (10% Interest)		10,000
Creditors		15,000
Capital		55,000
Drawings	5,000	
	3,85,000	3,85,000

On 1.1.2007 Machinery worth ₹ 5,000 was sold for ₹ 4,000 and credited to machinery account. Wages include ₹ 1,000 paid for machinery erection charges. Purchases included cost of Scooter for ₹ 5,000. Proprietor has taken goods costing ₹ 1,000 for which no entry has been made. Sundry debtors include ₹ 500 which have become bad. Provide 10% for bad debts. Electricity bill is outstanding ₹ 50. Goods costing ₹ 5,000 were destroyed by fire, and insurance claim was received for ₹ 4,000. Provide depreciation at 10% on machinery, furniture and moped. Provide depreciation @ 5% on buildings. Closing stock is ₹ 12,000.

[MBA Anna]

Solution : Trading and Profit and Loss A/c of Mr. Nandhu

For the year ended 31st March Dec. 2007

		₹		₹
To Opening stock		10,000	By Sales	3,05,000
To Purchases	2,80,000		By Goods destroyed by fire	5,000
Less : Cost of Scooter	5,000		By Closing stock	12,000
	2,75,000			
Less : Goods taken away by the proprietor	1,000	2,74,000		
To Wages	3,000			
Less : Transferred to Machinery A/c	1000	2,000		
To Gross profit c/d		36,000		
		3,22,000		3,22,000
To salaries	5,400		By Gross Profit b/d	36,000
Add : Provident Fund (50% of ₹ 1,200)	600	6,000		
To Employer's contribution to provident fund		600		
To Rent	2,750			
Add : Rent outstanding	250	3,000		
To Electricity	550			
Add : Outstanding	50	600		
To Trade expenses		1,500		
To Interest on loan	900			
Add : Outstanding	100	1,000		
To Commission		200		
To Bad debts	500			
Add : Provision for bad debts (10% of ₹ 10,000)	1,000	1,500		
To Loss of stock of fire		1,000		
To Loss on sale of machinery		1,000		
To Depreciation on machinery		2,900		
To Depreciation on Buildings		1,500		
To Depreciation on Moped		500		
To Depreciation on furniture		500		
To Net profit transferred to Capital Account		14,200		
		36,000		36,000

Balance Sheet as on 31st December 2007

		₹			₹
Creditors		15,000	Bank (Insurance claim)		4,000
Loan	10,000		Debtors	10,500	
Add : Outstanding interest	100	10,100	*Less* : Bad debts	500	
Rent outstanding		250		10,000	
Electricity outstanding		50	*Less* : Provision for bad debts	1,000	9,000
Capital	55,000		Closing stock		12,000
Add : Net profit	14,200		Furniture	5,000	
	69,200		*Less* : Depreciation	500	4,500
Less : Drawings (5,000 flat)	6,000	63,200	Scooter	5,000	
			Less : Depreciation	500	4,500
			Machinery	29,000	
			Add : Erection charges	1,000	
				30,000	
			Less : Loss on sale	1,000	
				29,000	
			Less : Depreciation	2,900	26,100
			Buildings	30,000	
			Less : Depreciation	1,500	28,500
		88,600			88,600

Problem 25. *From the following Trial Balance of Mr. Subith prepare Profit and Loss A/c for the year 2007 and Balance Sheet as on 31.12.2007 after giving effect to the under mentioned adjustments.*

Debit Balance :

	₹		₹
Drawings	*3,250*	*Bad Debts*	*400*
Stock (1.1.2007)	*17,445*	*Patents*	*500*
Return Inwards	*554*	*Cash*	*62*
Carriage Inwards	*1,240*	*Discount Allowed*	*330*
Deposit with Anand Gupta	*1,375*	*Wages*	*754*
Carriage outwards	*725*	***Credit Balances :***	
Loan to Ashok @ 5%		*Capital*	*15,000*
giving on 1.1.2007	*1,000*	*Interest on loan to Ashok*	*25*
Rent	*820*	*Rent outstanding*	*130*
Purchases	*12,970*	*Creditors*	*3,000*
Goodwill	*1,730*	*Provision for Doubtful Debts*	*1,200*
Advertisement Expenses	*954*	*Sales*	*27,914*
Debtors	*4,000*	*Return*	*840*

Adjustments :

(1) The Manager of Mr. Subith is entitled to Commission 10% of the Net Profit calculated after charging such commission. (2) Increase Bad Debts by ₹ 600. Make Provision for Doubtful Debts @ 10% and provision for Discount on Debtors 5%. (3) Stock valued at ₹ 1,500 destroyed by fire on 25.12.2007 but the insurance co. admitted a claim for ₹ 950 only and paid it in 2008. (4) ₹ 200 out of the advertisement expenses are to be carried forward to the next year. (5) The value of Closing Stock is ₹ 18,792.

Solution : Trading and Profit and Loss A/c of Shri Subith

For the year ended 31st December 2007

		₹			₹
To Opening stock		17,445	By Sales	27,914	
To Purchases	12,970		*Less :* Returns	554	27,360
Less : Returns	840	12,130	By Stock in Trade [closing stock]		18,792
To Wages		754	By Stock destroyed by fire		1,500
To Carriage Inwards		1,240			
To Gross profit c/d		16,083			
		47,652			47,652
To Rent		820	By Gross profit b/d		16,083
To Advertisement exp	954		By Interest on Loan	25	
Less : Prepaid	200	754	*Add :* Accrued interest	25	50
To Bad Debts	400				
Add : Additional bad debts	600				
Add : New provision	340				
	1,340				
Less : Old provision	1,200	140			
To Loss on stock by fire		550			
To Carriage outwards		725			
To Discount		330			
To Provision for Discount on Debtors		153			
To Commission to Manager $\left(\frac{10}{110} / ₹\ 12{,}661\right)$		1,151			
To Net Profit transferred to Capital A/c		11,510			
		16,133			16,133

Balance Sheet of Shri Subith

As on 31st December 2007

Liabilities		₹	*Assets*		₹
Outstanding rent		130	Cash		62
Commission payable to Manager		1,151	Deposit with Anand Gupta		1,375
Creditors		3,000	Loan to Ashok		1,000
Capital	15,000		Interest accrued thereon		25
Add : Net profit	11,510		Insurance company		950
	26,510		Debtors	4,000	
Less : Drawings	3,250	23,260	*Less* : Further bad debts	600	
				3,400	
			Less : Provision for bad debts	340	
				3,060	
			Less : Provision for discount on debts	153	2,907
			Stock		18,792
			Prepaid advertisement		200
			Plant and patents		500
			Goodwill		1,730
		27,541			27,541

TEST PROBLEMS

1. From the following Trail Balance of mrs. Arun for the period of 31.03.2009.

Particulars	*Debit* ₹	*Credit* ₹
Capital	–	2,50,000
Machinery	1,60,000	–
Furniture	65,000	–
Sundry Creditors	–	74,000
Sundry Debtors	71,000	–
Bills Payable	–	10,000
Bills Receivable	30,000	–
Stock	61,000	–
Purchases	1,22,000	–
Sales	–	2,73,000
Bad Debts	2,000	–
Bad debts Provision	–	1,500
Wages	3,000	–

Salaries & Wages	2,000	–
Land & Buildings	66,000	–
Investments	70,000	–
Commission (Cr)	–	5,000
Cash in Hand	2,500	–
Cash at Bank	7,000	–
Bank Overdraft	–	25,000
Loan from Ramu @ 10% Interest	1,00,000	–
Interest Paid on above	5,000	–
Drawings	6,000	–
Manufacturing Expenses	2,000	–
Insurance	3,900	–
Trade Expenses	2,000	–
Advertisement	4,500	–
Goodwill	60,000	–
Carriage Inwards	2,900	–
Carriage Outwards	6,500	–
Returns	3,000	2,000
Interest (Cr)	–	4,500
Debentures	–	52,300
	8,57,300	**8,57,300**

The following adjustments are to be considered:

(*i*) The closing stock was valued at ₹ 52,000.

(*ii*) Wages due but not paid ₹ 1,000.

(*iii*) Insurance prepaid ₹ 900.

(*iv*) Commission earned but not received ₹ 600.

(*v*) Write off further bad debts ₹ 1,000 and create a reserve for bad debts @ 5% on sundry debtors.

(*vi*) Provide discount @ 2½ on sundry debotrs.

(*vii*) Allow discount @ 5% on sundry creditors.

(*viii*) Allow interest on capital @ 10%.

(*ix*) Charge interest on drawings ₹ 1,000.

(*x*) Charge depreciation on machinery at 5% and furniture 10%.

(*xi*) Interest on investment ₹ 2,500 is accorded.

(*xii*) Stock valued at ₹ 5,000 destroyed by fire on 25.3.2009, but the insurance company admitted only 80% of the claim and paid it on April 2009.

[Ans: Gross Profit: ₹ 1,37,100, Net Profit: ₹ 82,273, B/S Total: ₹ 5,70,873]

2. The following is the trial balance of M/s Krishna Agencies as on 31st March, 2009. Prepare Trading and Profit and Loss account for the year ended 31.3.2009 and a Balance Sheet on that date.

Particulars	Debit ₹	Credit ₹
Capital	–	1,00,000
Drawings	18,000	–
Buildings	15,000	–
Furniture and Fittings	7,500	–
Motor van	25,000	–
Loan from Hari @ 12% interest (1.4.2008)	–	15,000
Interest paid on above	900	–
Sales	–	1,00,000
Purchases	75,000	–
Opening stock	25,000	–
Establishment expenses	15,000	–
Wages	2,000	–
Insurance	1,000	–
Commission received	–	4,500
Sundry debtors	25,100	–
Bank balance	20,000	–
Sundry creditors		10,000
Interest	–	3,000
	2,32,500	2,32,500

Adjustments:

(*i*) The value of closing stock on 31st March, 2009 was ₹ 32,000.

(*ii*) Outstanding wages ₹ 500.

(*iii*) Prepaid insurance ₹ 300.

(*iv*) Commission received in advance ₹ 1,300.

(*v*) Depreciate: Building 2½ %, Furniture and Fittings 10%, Motor van 10%.

(*vi*) Charge interest on drawings ₹ 500.

(*vii*) Accrued interest ₹ 500. *[Periyar M.B.A, 2010]*

[Ans: Gross Profit: ₹ 29,500, Net Profit: ₹ 5,575, B/S Total: ₹ 1,24,775]

3. From the following Trial balance prepare the Trading and Profit & Loss A/c for the year ended Dec. 31, 2006 and Balance Sheet on that date.Trial Balance of A. Narain as on Dec.

Particulars	Debit ₹	Credit ₹
Capital	–	40,000
Sales	–	25,000
Purchases	15,000	–
Salaries	2,000	–
Rent	1,500	–
Insurance	300	–

Drawings	5,000	–
Machinery	28,000	–
Bank	4,500	–
Cash	2,000	–
Stock	5,200	–
Debtors	2,500	–
Creditors	–	1,000
Goodwill	3,000	–
Wages	23,600	–
General expenses	2,680	–
Motor car expenses	320	–
Bills Payable	–	3,000
Loan	–	20,000
Return	–	2,200
Discounts	–	4,400
	95,600	**95,600**

Adjustments:

(*i*) Stock on hand at Dec. 31, 2006, ₹ 4,900.

(*ii*) Salaries outstanding ₹ 300.

(*iii*) Rent paid in Advance ₹ 200.

(*iv*) Insurance paid in Advance ₹ 50.

(*v*) Depreciate Machinery by 10%.

(*vi*) During Dec. Narain took ₹ 100 in goods for his own use.

(*vii*) Commission earned but not received ₹ 3600.

[**Ans:** Gross Profit: ₹ 11,600, Net Profit: ₹ 13,250, B/S Total: ₹ 45,950]

❑❑❑

5

Fund Flow Statement

INTRODUCTION

The traditional concept of profit and loss account and balance sheet has a limited role to play in financial analysis. The profit and loss account reflects the results of the business operations for a specified period of time. It takes into account only the expenses incurred and income received during the accounting period. The balance sheet gives a summary of the assets and liabilities at a particular period of time. And at the same time, balance sheet does not explain the details about the movement of funds. In actual practice, a business concern receives funds from various sources and invested in various ways of investment. It is a continuous process. The ultimate aim of the financial management is to study and control these funds in order to maintain the solvency and financial soundness of the firm. For the purpose of complete study of sources and applications of funds over the accounting period, a separate statement is essential to find the periodical increase or decrease of such funds of an enterprise. This statement is called fund flow statement.

MEANING OF FUND FLOW STATEMENT

The fund flow statement is a statement which reveals the methods by which the business has been financed and how it has used its funds between two balance sheet dates.

In the words of Foulke : "A statement of sources and application of funds is a technical device, designed to analyse the changes in the financial conditions of a business enterprise between two balance sheet dates."

DIFFERENT NAMES OF FUND FLOW STATEMENT

A statement of sources and application of funds
A statement of sources and uses of funds
Where Got and where Gone statement
Inflow-outflow of fund statement
Statement of funds supplied and applied; funds received and disbursed statement

MANAGERIAL USES OF FUND FLOW STATEMENT

Fund flow statement is an invaluable analytical tool for a financial manager for the purpose of evaluating the employment of funds by a firm and also to assess sources of such funds. Following are the important managerial uses of fund flow statement.

1. The foremost use of the fund flow statement is to explain the reasons for changes in the assets and liabilities between two balance sheet dates.
2. Fund flow statement gives details about the funds obtained and used in past. Based upon this detail, manager can take correct actions at appropriate times.
3. Fund flow statement acts as a control device when compared with budgeted figures. It also gives guidance to the finance manager for taking remedial action if there is any deviation.
4. It helps the management to formulate various financial policies—viz dividend, bonus etc.
5. It gives guidance to the management with regard to working capital. Through fund flow statement, management can take proper steps for effective utilisation of surplus working capital or in case of inadequacy, suitable arrangement can be made for improving the working capital position.
6. It identifies the strong and weak financial areas of the firm.
7. It gives the answers for various financial intricate questions :
   - How much funds were generated ?
   - How were the funds used ?
8. Effective utilisation of available resources and scarce resources should be allocated according to the preferential needs.
9. With the help of the fund flow statement, financial and lending institutions can easily evaluate the credit worthiness and repaying capacity of the borrowing company.
10. It enables the management to reformulate the firm's financial activity on the basis of the statement.

LIMITATIONS OF FUND FLOW STATEMENT

1. In the real sense, the fund flow statement lacks originality, because it is only a rearrangement of data given in financial statements.
2. It indicates only the past year's performance and is not for the future. Even to prepare projected fund flow statement, it cannot show much accuracy.
3. It cannot reveal continuous changes. Because, only any particular two years are taken into account for analysis purpose.
4. Fund flow statement is not a substitute for a financial statement. It gives only some informations about changes in working capital alone.

STEPS IN PREPARATION OF FUND FLOW STATEMENT

(*i*) Preparation of fund flow statement.

(*ii*) Preparation of statement of changes in working capital.

(*iii*) Preparation of adjusted profits and loss account (to find out fund from operation or fund lost in operation).

(*iv*) Adjustment and their treatments.

(*v*) Preparation of separate ledger.

(*vi*) Treatment about the provision for taxation and proposed divider.

NOTE : Fund flow statement alone is a major part of the solution; remaining other things *i.e.*, working capital statement, P.L. A /c, preparation of ledger, treatment of provision for taxation and proposed dividend, adjustment etc were supported to work the fund flow statement.

I. Preparation Fund Flow Statement

Here, we have to prepare the fund flow statement in the T shape.

I. Fund Flow Statement : (Specimen form)

Sources of Funds	*Amount* ₹	*Applications of Funds*	*Amount* ₹
Issue of shares	xx	Redemption of redeemable	xx
Issue of debentures	xx	Preference shares	xx
Loan borrowed	xx	Redemption of debentures	xx
(Long term, medium term)		Repayment of loans	xx
Acceptance of deposits	xx	Repayment of deposits	xx
Sale of fixed assets	xx	Purchase of fixed assets	xx
Sale of investments (Long term)	xx	Purchase of long term	
Decrease in working capital	xx	investments	xx
(Transfer from working		Payment of dividend	xx
capital statements)		Income tax paid	xx
Fund from operation	xx	Increase in working capital	xx
(Transfer from P&L A/c		Fund loss in operation	xx
Working capital statement)		(Transfer from P&L A/c)	

II. Working Capital Statement

For the purpose of finding out increase or decrease in working capital, we have to prepare statement of changes in working capital. [TCA – TCL = WC]

Particulars	**Year I**	**Year II**
Current Assets		
Cash in hand	xx	xx
Cash at bank	xx	xx
Sundry debtors	xx	xx
Bills receivable	xx	xx
Marketable securities	xx	xx
Inventory	xx	xx
Prepaid expenses	xx	xx
Short term investment	xx	xx
Accrued incomes	xx	xx
Total Current Assets (TCA) (A)	xx	xx

Current Liabilities		
Sundry Creditors	xx	xx
Bills payable	xx	xx
Outstanding expenses	xx	xx
Bank overdraft	xx	xx
Income received in advance	xx	xx
Short term loans	xx	xx
Cash credit from bank	xx	xx
Provision for taxation	xx	xx
Proposed dividend	xx	xx
Provision against current assets	xx	xx
Provision for doubtful debts	xx	xx
Total Current Liabilities (TCL) (B)	xx	xx
Working Capital (A-B)	xx	xx
Increase or Decrease	xx	
[TAC – TCL = WC]		

After the computation of working capital, we have to find out the increase or decrease in working.

III. Fund from Operation : Fund from operation is found out by two methods

(*i*) Statement method.

(*ii*) Accounting method.

Normally, accounting method is easy and convenient. So, we have to adopt accounting method *i.e.,* profit and loss account is used to find out the fund from operation. Here, profit and loss account is prepared in a usual procedure.

Profits and Loss account for the year ended

Particulars	*Amount* ₹	*Particulars*	*Amount* ₹
To Goodwill written off	xx	By Balance b/d	xx
To Preliminary expenses written off	xx	By Profit on sale of fixed assets	xx
To Patents written off	xx		
To Depreciation	xx	By Interest sale of investment	xx
To Dividend paid	xx	By Any other non-operating incomes	xx
To Provision for taxation	xx		
To Loss on sale of fixed assets	xx	By Fund from operation	xx
To Discount on issue of shares	xx		
To Interim dividend paid	xx		
To Balance c/d	xx		
To Fund operation	xx		
	xx		xx

IV. Important adjustments and their treatments

All the adjustments appear in two places :

Adjustment		Treatment
1. Depreciation	-	P.L. A/c debit side Respective asset A/c credit side
2. Dividend paid	-	P.L. A/c debit side Fund flow statement—Application side
3. Income tax paid	-	Income tax A/c debit side Fund flow statement—Application side
4. Income tax provision	-	P.L. A/c debit side Income tax A/c credit side
5. Loss on sale of fixed Assets	-	P.L. A/c debit side Respective asset A/c credit side
6. Interim dividend paid	-	P.L . A/c debit side Fund flow statement—Application side

V. Preparation of separate ledger A/c, if necessary *i.e.,* about the non-current (either Assets or Liability) items related information given in the adjustment means we have to prepare separate ledger. Balances from this ledger can be transferred to fund flow statement means we have to prepare a separate ledger. Balances from this ledger can be transferred to fund flow statement.

VI. Treatment about the provision for taxation and proposed dividend

Provision for taxation and proposed dividend taken as current liability means it should appear under working capital statement.

Some times, regarding the provision for taxation, information is given in the adjustment. So, it should be treated as non current liability. Provision for taxation taken as non-current liability means proposed dividend is also taken as a non-current liability.

(*a*) Treatment of provision for taxation

(*i*) Income Tax provided given in the adjustment, we have to find the tax paid-
P.L. A/c debit side
Income Tax A/c credit
(Balancing figure of taxation A/c is called tax paid and then it is transferred to Applications side)

(*ii*) Income tax paid given in the adjustment, we have to find the income tax provision.
Fund flow statement – application side
Income tax A/c – debit side
(Balancing figure of taxation A/c is called tax provided and then it is transferred to P.L. A/c debit side)

(*b*) Treatment of proposed dividend

Whenever provision for taxation is treated as non-current liability, proposed dividend is also taken as non-current liability. At that time, the following rules will be applicable.

Last year amount – application side
Current year amount : profit & loss A/c debit side.

TEST QUESTIONS

1. What is meant by fund flow statement ?
2. Describe the various steps involved in preparation of fund flow statement.
3. What do you meant by funds from operation?
4. Explain the basic objectives of compiling a statement of sources and Application of Funds.
5. Explain the advantages and limitations of fund flow statement.

PROBLEMS AND SOLUTIONS

Problem 1. *The following are the summarised balance sheets of M/s.Krishna Ltd. as on 31.12.1999 and 2000.*

Liabilities	*1999* ₹	*2000* ₹
10% preference shares	*1,00,000*	*1,10,000*
Equity Shares	*2,20,000*	*2,50,000*
Share premium	*20,000*	*26,000*
Profit & Loss A/c	*1,04,000*	*1,34,000*
12% debentures	*70,000*	*64,000*
Creditors	*38,000*	*46,000*
Bills Payable	*5,000*	*4,000*
Provision for tax	*10,000*	*12,000*
Dividend Payable	*7,000*	*8,000*
	5,74,000	*6,54,000*

Assets	*1999* ₹	*2000* ₹
Machinery	*2,00,000*	*2,30,000*
Buildings	*1,50,000*	*1,76,000*
Land	*18,000*	*18,000*
Cash	*42,000*	*32,000*
Debtors	*38,000*	*38,000*
Bills receivable	*42,000*	*62,000*
Stock	*84,000*	*98,000*
	5,74,000	*6,54,000*

You are required to prepare a statement of sources and application of funds.

[BBM PU 2005]

Solution : **Fund Flow Statement**

Particulars	*Amount* ₹	*Particulars*	*Amount* ₹
Issue of preference shares	10,000	Purchase of machinery	30,000
Issue of Equity shares	30,000	Purchase of Building	26,000
Share premium received	6,000	Increase in working capital	14,000
Fund from operation	30,000	Redemption of debenture	6,000
	76,000		76,000

Workings : **(*i*) Statement of changes in working capital**

	1999	2000
	₹	₹
Current Assets :		
Cash	42,000	32,000
Debtors	38,000	38,000
Bills receivables	42,000	62,000
Stock	84,000	98,000
Total current assets	2,06,000	2,30,000
Current Liabilities :		
Creditors	38,000	46,000
Bills payable	5,000	4,000
Provision for Tax	10,000	12,000
Dividend payable	7,000	8,000
Total current liabilities	60,000	70,000
Working capital	1,46,000	1,60,000

Increase in working capital : ₹ 14000 (1,46,000 – 1,60,000)
[Transfer to Fund Flow Statement]

(*ii*) Profit and Loss Account

To Balance b/d (Closing)	1,34,000	By Balance c/d (Opening)	1,04,000
		By Fund from operation	30,000
	1,34,000		1,34,000

Problem 2. *From the following balance sheets, prepare schedule of changes in working capital.*

Liabilities	*Dec. 1980*	*Dec. 1981*	*Assets*	*Dec. 1980*	*Dec. 1981*
	₹	₹		₹	₹
Share capital	*2,00,000*	*2,50,000*	*Cash*	*30,000*	*47,000*
Creditors	*70,000*	*45,000*	*Debtors*	*1,20,000*	*1,15,000*
Retained Earnings	*10,000*	*23,000*	*Land*	*50,000*	*66,000*
			Stock	*80,000*	*90,000*
	2,80,000	*3,18,000*		*2,80,000*	*3,18,000*

[MBA April 2002 Madras University]

Solution : **Fund Flow Statement**

Source of funds	₹	*Application of funds*	₹
Issue of shares	50,000	Purchase of Land	16,000
Fund from operation	13,000	Increase in working capital	47,000
	63,000		63,000

Workings : (*i*) Statement of changes in working capital

	Dec. 1980 ₹	Dec. 1981 ₹
Current Assets :		
Cash	30,000	47,000
Debtors	1,20,000	1,15,000
Stock	80,000	90,000
Total current assets	2,30,000	2,52,000
Current liabilities :		
Creditors	70,000	45,000
Total current Liabilities	70,000	45,000
Working capital	1,60,000	2,07,000
Increase in working capital	(1,60,000 – 2,07,000)	47,000

(*ii*) Profit and Loss Accounts

To Balance b/d	23,000	By Balance c/d	10,000
		By Fund from operation (B/f)	13,000
	23,000		23,000

Problem 3. *The following are the summarised balance sheets of X Ltd., as on 31 December 1999 and 2000.*

Liabilities	*31st Dec. 1999* ₹	*31st Dec. 2000* ₹	*Assets*	*31st Dec. 1999* ₹	*31st Dec. 2000* ₹
Redeemable preference Shares	-	*10,000*	*Fixed Assets*	*41,000*	*40,000*
Equity shares	*40,000*	*40,000*	*Less : Depreciation*	*11,000*	*15,000*
General Reserve	*2,000*	*2,000*			
Profit & loss A/c	*1,000*	*1,200*		*30,000*	*25,000*
Debentures	*6,000*	*7,000*	*Debtors*	*20,000*	*24,000*
Creditors	*12,000*	*11,000*	*Stock*	*30,000*	*35,000*
Provision for Tax	*3,000*	*4,200*	*Prepaid exp.*	*300*	*500*
Proposed dividend	*5,000*	*5,800*	*Cash*	*1,200*	*3,500*
Bank overdraft	*12,500*	*6,800*			
	81,500	*88,000*		*81,500*	*88,000*

You are required to prepare :

1. *A statement showing changes in the working capital*
2. *A statement of sources and application of funds.*

[B.Com. Madras, Delhi, MBA Madras]

Solution : **Fund Flow Statement**

Source of funds	₹	*Application of funds*	₹
Issue of preference shares	10,000	Increase in working capital	16,200
Issue of Debentures	1,000		
Sale of fixed assets	1,000		
Fund from operation	4,200		
	16,200		16,200

Workings : **(*i*) Statement of changes in working capital**

	1999 ₹	*2000* ₹
Current assets :		
Debtors	20,000	24,000
Stock	30,000	35,000
Prepaid Expenses	300	500
Cash	1,200	3,500
Total Current Assets	51,500	63,000
Current liabilities :		
Creditors	12,000	11,000
Provision for tax	3,000	4,200
Proposed Dividend	5,000	5,800
Bank Overdraft	12,500	6,800
Total Current Liabilities	32,500	27,800
Working capital	19,000	35,200
Increase in working capital	16,200	(19,000 – 35,200)

Hint : Provision for taxation and proposed dividend taken as current liabilities.

(*ii*) Profit and Loss Account

To Balance b/d	1,200	By Balance c/d	1,000
To Depreciation	4,000	By Fund from operation	4,200
	5,200		5,200

Problem 4. *From the following balance sheets, prepare a statement showing changes in working capital during 1995.*

Balance sheet of Pioneer Ltd. as on 31st December.

Liabilities	*1994* ₹	*1995* ₹
Share capital	*5,00,000*	*6,00,000*
Reserves	*1,50,000*	*1,80,000*

P.L. A/c	*40,000*	*65,000*
Debentures	*3,00,000*	*2,50,000*
Creditors for goods	*1,70,000*	*1,60,000*
Provision for income tax	*60,000*	*80,000*
	12,20,000	*13,35,000*
Assets	*1994*	*1995*
	₹	*₹*
Fixed assets	*10,00,000*	*11,20,000*
Less : Depreciation	*3,70,000*	*4,60,000*
	6,30,000	*6,60,000*
Stock	*2,40,000*	*3,70,000*
Book debts	*2,50,000*	*2,30,000*
Cash in hand and at Bank Balance	*80,000*	*60,000*
Preliminary Expenses	*20,000*	*15,000*
	12,20,000	*13,35,000*

[B.Com. Bharathidasan Nov. 1986]

Solution : **Fund Flow Statement**

Source of funds	₹	*Application of funds*	₹
Issue of shares	1,00,000	Redemption of debentures	50,000
Fund from operation	1,50,000	Purchase of fixed assets	1,20,000
		Increase in working capital	80,000
	2,50,000		2,50,000

Workings : (i) Statement of changes in working capital

	1994	1995
	₹	₹
Current Assets :		
Stock	2,40,000	3,70,000
Book Debts	2,50,000	2,30,000
Cash in hand & Bank Balance	80,000	60,000
Total Current assets	5,70,000	6,60,000
Current liabilities :		
Creditors for goods	1,70,000	1,60,000
Provision for income tax	60,000	80,000
Total current liabilities	2,30,000	2,40,000
Working capital	3,40,000	4,20,000
Increase in working capital	80,000	(3,40,000 – 4,20,000)

(ii) Profit and Loss Account

	₹		₹
To Balance b/d	65,000	By Balance c/d	40,000
To Reserves	30,000	By Fund from operation	1,50,000
To Preliminary expenses written off	5,000		
To Depreciation	90,000		
	1,90,000		1,90,000

Problem 5. *Calculate fund from operation from the information given below as on 31.3.2000.*

1. *Net profit for the year ended 31.3.2000 ₹ 6,50,000.*
2. *Gain on sale of buildings ₹ 35,500.*
3. *Goodwill appears in the books at ₹ 1,80,000 out of that 10% has been written off during the year.*
4. *Old machinery worth ₹ 8,000 has been sold for ₹ 6,500 during the year.*
5. *₹ 1,25,000 have been transferred to reserve fund.*
6. *Depreciation has been provided during the year on machinery and furniture at 20% whose value is ₹ 6,50,000.* [B.Com. Madras]

Solution : Calculation of Fund from operation

	₹	₹
Net profit for the year ended 31.3.2000		6,50,000
Add : Non fund items : [P.L. A/c Debit side items]		
Goodwill written off (1,80,000 × 10/100)	18,000	
Loss on sale of machinery (8000 – 6500)	1,500	
Transferred to Reserve fund	1,25,000	
Depreciation (6,50,000 × 20/100)	1,30,000	
		2,74,500
		9,24,500
Less : Non fund items [P.L A/c credit side items]		
Gain on sale of Buildings		35,500
Fund from operation		8,89,000

Problem 6. *From the following balance sheets of a sole trader, prepare a fund flow statement.*

Liabilities	*1999* ₹	*2000* ₹	*Assets*	*1999* ₹	*2000* ₹
Capital	*63,000*	*1,00,000*	*Cash*	*15,000*	*20,000*
Long term loans	*50,000*	*60,000*	*Debtors*	*30,000*	*28,000*

Trade creditors	*42,000*	*39,000*	*Stock*	*55,000*	*72,000*
Bank overdraft	*35,000*	*25,000*	*Land & Building*	*80,000*	*1,00,000*
Outstanding expenses	*5,000*	*6,000*	*Furniture*	*15,000*	*10,000*
	1,95,000	*2,30,000*		*1,95,000*	*2,30,000*

[B.Com. Madras]

Solution : **Fund Flow Statement**

Source of funds	₹	*Application of funds*	₹
Loan borrowed	10,000	Purchase of Land & Buildings	20,000
Sale of Furniture	5,000	Increase in working capital	32,000
Fund from operation	37,000		
	52,000		52,000

Workings : ***(i)* Statement of changes in working capital**

	1999 ₹	*2000* ₹
Current Assets :		
Cash	15,000	20,000
Debtors	30,000	28,000
Stock	55,000	72,000
Total current assets	1,00,000	1,20,000
Current Liabilities :		
Trade creditors	42,000	39,000
Bank overdraft	35,000	25,000
Outstanding expenses	5,000	6,000
Total current liabilities	82,000	70,000
Working capital	18,000	50,000
Increase in working capital	32,000	(18,000 – 50,000)

***(ii)* Capital Account**

To Balance c/d	1,00,000	By Balance b/d	63,000
		By P.L.A/c	37,000
	1,00,000		1,00,000

***(iii)* Profit and Loss Account**

To Capital Account	37,000	By Fund from operation	37,000
	37,000		37,000

Problem 7. *Following are the comparative balance sheets of a HAL company for the year 1989 and 1990.*

Balance Sheet

Liabilities	*1989* ₹	*1990* ₹	*Assets*	*1989* ₹	*1990* ₹
Share capital	*70,000*	*74,000*	*Cash*	*9,000*	*7,800*
Debentures	*12,000*	*6,000*	*Debtors*	*14,900*	*17,700*
Creditors	*10,360*	*11,840*	*Stock*	*49,200*	*42,700*
Profit & loss A/c	*10,740*	*11,360*	*Goodwill*	*10,000*	*5,000*
			Land	*20,000*	*30,000*
	1,03,100	*1,03,200*		*1,03,100*	*1,03,200*

The following additional information is also available :

(i) Dividends were paid totalling ₹4,000.

(ii) Land was purchased for ₹ 10,000. You are required to prepare fund flow statement.

[B.Com. Madras 1993]

Solution : **Fund Flow Statement**

Source of funds	₹	*Application of funds*	₹
Issue of shares	4,000	Redemption of Debenture	6,000
Fund from operation	9,620	Dividend paid	4,000
Decrease in working capital	6,380	Purchase of Land	10,000
	20,000		20,000

Workings : (*i*) Statement of changes in working capital

	1989 ₹	*1990* ₹
Current Assets :		
Cash	9,000	7,800
Debtors	14,900	17,700
Stock	49,200	42,700
Total current assists	73,100	68,200
Current Liabilities :		
Creditors	10,360	11,840
Total current liabilities	10,360	11,840
Working capital	62,740	56,360
Decrease in working capital	(62,740 – 56,360)	6,380

(ii) Profit and Loss Account

To Balance c/d	11,360	By Balance b/d	10,740
To Goodwill written of	5,000	By Fund from operation	9,620
To Dividend Paid	4,000		
	20,360		20,360

(iii) Land Account

To Balance b/d	20,000	By Balance b/d	30,000
To Cash	10,000		
	30,000		30,000

Problem 8. *From the following balance sheets of AMB Ltd. as on 31.12.98 and 1999, prepare a schedule of changes in working capital and fund flow statement.*

Balance Sheet

Liabilities	*1998* ₹	*1999* ₹
Share capital	*1,00,000*	*1,00,000*
General reserve	*14,000*	*18,000*
P.L. A/c	*16,000*	*13,000*
Sundry creditors	*8,000*	*5,400*
Bills payable	*1,200*	*800*
Provision for Tax	*16,000*	*18,000*
Provision for doubtful debts	*400*	*600*
	1,55,600	*1,55,800*

Assets	*1998* ₹	*1999* ₹
Goodwill	*12,000*	*12,000*
Buildings	*40,000*	*36,000*
Plant	*37,000*	*36,000*
Investments	*10,000*	*11,000*
Stock	*30,000*	*23,400*
Bills receivable	*2,000*	*3,200*
Debtors	*18,000*	*19,000*
Cash at bank	*6,600*	*15,200*
	1,55,600	*1,55,800*

The following additional information is also available :

1. Depreciation charges on Plant & Buildings at ₹4,000 each.

2. Provision for taxation of ₹19,000 was made during the year 1999.

3. Interim dividend of ₹8,000 was paid during the year 1999.

[MCA Bharathidasan, M.Com. Madras] [M.Sc. PU 2000]

Solution : **Fund Flow Statement**

Source of funds	₹	*Application of funds*	₹
Fund from operation	36,000	Increase in working capital	7,000
		Interim dividend paid	8,000
		Tax paid	17,000
		Purchase of Plant	3,000
		Investments	1,000
	36,000		36,000

Workings : ***(i)* Statement of changes in working capital**

		1998	*1999*
Current Assets :			
Stock		30,000	23,400
Bills receivable		2,000	3,200
Debtors		18,000	19,000
Cash at Bank		6,600	15,200
Total current assets		56,600	60,800
Current Liabilities :			
Sundry creditors		8,000	5,400
Bills payable		1,200	800
Provision for Doubtful debts		400	600
Total current liabilities		9,600	6,800
Working capital		47,000	54,000
Increase in working capital		(47,000 – 54,000)	7,000

***(ii)* Profit and Loss Account**

To Balance c/d	13,000	By Balance b/d	16,000
To Depreciation on Buildings	4,000	By Fund from operation	36,000
To Depreciation on Plant	4,000		
To Income tax provided	19,000		
To Interim dividend paid	8,000		
To General reserve	4,000		
	52,000		52,000

***(iii)* Provision for Taxation Account**

To Balance b/d	18,000	By Balance b/d	16,000
To Cash (Tax Paid)	17,000	By PL A/c (Income Tax Provided)	19,000
	35,000		35,000

(iv) Building Account

To Balance b/d	40,000	By Balance b/d	36,000
		By Depreciation	4,000
	40,000		40,000

(v) Plant Account

To Balance b/d	37,000	By Balance b/d	36,000
To Cash (Purchase)	3,000	By Depreciation	4,000
	40,000		40,000

Problem 9. *From the following balance sheets of Exe Ltd. prepare*

(a) A statement of changes in working capital

(b) A fund flow statement

Liabilities	*1999* ₹	*2000* ₹	*Assets*	*1999* ₹	*2000* ₹
Equity share capital	*3,00,000*	*4,00,000*	*Good will*	*1,15,000*	*90,000*
Redeemable preference share capital	*1,50,000*	*1,00,000*	*Land & Building*	*2,00,000*	*1,70,000*
			Plant	*80,000*	*2,00,000*
General reserve	*40,000*	*70,000*	*Debtors*	*1,60,000*	*2,00,000*
Profit & Loss A/c	*30,000*	*48,000*	*Stock*	*77,000*	*1,09,000*
Proposed dividend	*42,000*	*50,000*	*Bills receivable*	*20,000*	*30,000*
Creditors	*55,000*	*83,000*	*Cash in hand*	*15,000*	*10,000*
Bills payable	*20,000*	*16,000*	*Cash at bank*	*10,000*	*8,000*
Provision for taxation	*40,000*	*50,000*			
	6,77,000	*8,17,000*		*6,77,000*	*8,17,000*

The following additional information is also available :

(a) Depreciation of ₹10,000 and ₹20,000 have been charged on plant and land buildings respectively in 2000.

(b) A dividend of ₹20,000 has been paid in 2000.

(c) Income tax of ₹35,000 has been paid during 2000.

[M.Com. Osmania B.Com. (Hons.) Delhi], [B.Com. PU 2004]

Solution : **Fund Flow Statement**

Source of funds	₹	*Application of funds*	₹
Issue of Equity shares	1,00,000	Redemption of Redeemable	50,000
Sale of Land & Buildings	10,000	Dividend paid	20,000
Fund from operation	2,18,000	Income tax paid	35,000
		Purchase of Plant	1,30,000
		Proposed dividend paid	42,000
		Increase in working capital	51,000
	3,28,000		3,28,000

Workings :(*i*) Statement of changes in working capital

	1999 ₹	*2000* ₹
Current Assets :		
Debtors	1,60,000	2,00,000
Stock	77,000	1,09,000
Bills receivable	20,000	30,000
Cash in hand	15,000	10,000
Cash at Bank	10,000	8,000
Total current assets	2,82,000	3,57,000
Current Liabilities :		
Creditors	55,000	83,000
Bills payable	20,000	16,000
Total current liabilities	75,000	99,000
Working capital	2,07,000	2,58,000
Increase in working capital	51,000	(2,58,000 – 2,07,000)

(*ii*) Profit and Loss Account

To General Reserve	30,000	By Balance c/d	30,000
To Goodwill written off	25,000	By Fund from operation	2,18,000
To Depreciation on Plant	10,000		
To Depreciation on Building	20,000		
To Dividend paid	20,000		
To Balance c/d	48,000		
To Income Tax provided	45,000		
To Proposed dividend	50,000		
	2,48,000		2,48,000

(*iii*) Provision for Taxation Account

To Cash (Tax paid)	35,000	By Balance b/d	40,000
To Balance c/d	50,000	By P.L. A/c	45,000
	85,000		85,000

(*iv*) Land & Building Account

To Balance b/d	2,00,000	By Depreciation	20,000
		By Balance c/d	1,70,000
		By Cash (Sale)	10,000
	2,00,000		2,00,000

(*v*) Plant Account

To Balance b/d	80,000	By Depreciation	10,000
To Cash	1,30,000	By Balance c/d	2,00,000
	2,10,000		2,10,000

Problem 10. *The following are the summarised Balance Sheets of Lucky Ltd. as on 31.12.96 and 1997.*

Liabilities	*1996* ₹	*1997* ₹	*Assets*	*1996* ₹	*1997* ₹
Share capital	*2,00,000*	*2,50,000*	*Land & Buildings*	*2,00,000*	*1,90,000*
General reserve	*50,000*	*60,000*	*Machinery*	*1,50,000*	*1,69,000*
P.L. A/c	*30,500*	*30,600*	*Stock*	*1,00,000*	*74,000*
Bank loan (Long term)	*70,000*	-	*Sundry debtors*	*80,000*	*64,200*
Sundry creditors	*1,50,000*	*1,35,200*	*Cash*	*500*	*600*
Provision for taxation	*30,000*	*35,000*	*Bank*	-	*8,000*
			Goodwill	-	*5,000*
	5,30,500	*5,10,800*		*5,30,500*	*5,10,800*

Additional information supplied during the year ended 31.12.97 :

(a) *Dividend of ₹23,000 was paid.*

(b) *Assets of another company were purchased for a consideration of ₹50,000 payable in shares.*

The following assets were purchased :

Machinery ₹25,000 : stock ₹20,000.

(c) *Machinery was further purchased for ₹8,000.*

(d) *Depreciation written off against machinery ₹12,000.*

(e) *Income tax paid during the year ₹33,000.*

(f) *Loss on sale of machinery ₹200 was written off to general reserve.*

(g) *Depreciation charged against land & buildings was ₹10,000.*

You are required to prepare fund flow statement. [M.Com. Madras adopted]

Solution : Fund Flow Statement

Source of funds	₹	*Application of funds*	₹
Sale of Machinery	1,800	Repayment of Bank loan	70,000
Fund from operation	93,300	Dividend paid	23,000
Decrease in working capital	18,900	Purchase of Machinery	8,000
Issue of shares (For stock)	20,000	Income Tax paid	33,000
	1,34,000		1,34,000

Workings : (*i*) Statement of changes in working capital

Current Assets :	*1996* ₹	*1997* ₹
Stock	1,00,000	74,000
Sundry Debtors	80,000	64,200
Cash	500	600
Bank	—	8,000
Total current assets	1,80,500	1,46,800

Current Liabilities :		
Sundry creditors	1,50,000	1,35,200
Total current liabilities	1,50,000	1,35,200
Working capital	30,500	11,600
Decrease in working capital	18,900	(30,500 – 11,600)

(*ii*) Profit and Loss Account

	₹		₹
To Dividend paid	23,000	By Balance b/d	30,500
To Depreciation on Machinery	12,000	By Fund from operation	93,300
To Depreciation on Land & Building	10,000		
To General Reserve	10,200		
To Income Tax (provided)	38,000		
To Balance c/d	30,600		
	1,23,800		1,23,800

(*iii*) Provision for Taxation Account

	₹		₹
To Cash	33,000	By Balance b/d	30,000
To Balance c/d	35,000	By Income (Tax provided) BF	38,000
	68,000		68,000

(*iv*) Machinery Account

	₹		₹
To Balance b/d	1,50,000	By Depreciation	12,000
To Shares	25,000	By General Reserve	200
To Cash (Purchase)	8,000	By Balance c/d	1,69,000
		By Cash	1,800
	1,83,000		1,83,000

(*v*) Goodwill Account

	₹		₹
To Balance b/d	Nil	By Balance c/d	5,000
To Shares	5,000		
	5,000		5,000

(vi) General Reserve Account

	₹		₹
To Balance c/d	60,000	By Balance b/d	50,000
To Loss on sale of Machinery	200	By Profit & Loss A/c	10,200
	60,200		60,200

(vii) Land & Buildings Account

	₹		₹
To Balance b/d	2,00,000	By Depreciation	10,000
		By Balance c/d	1,90,000
	2,00,000		2,00,000

(viii) Share Capital Account

	₹		₹
To Balance c/d	2,50,000	By Balance b/d	2,00,000
		By Machinery	25,000
		By Stock	20,000
		By Goodwill	5,000
	2,50,000		2,50,000

NOTE : Total shares issued to ₹50,000. Among this ₹25,000 as against machinery and ₹ 5,000 as against goodwill. Both are non current items. It should not affect the working capital. So, only ₹ 20,000 issued as against the stock. It should be treated as a source of funds. Because, it is a current asset.

Problem 11. *From the following summarised financial statement of Anxious Ltd as on 30.04.1998, prepare*

(a) Statement of changes in working capital for the year ended 30.04.1998 and

(b) A statement showing sources and applications of funds during the same period.

Liabilities	*1997* ₹	*1998* ₹	*Assets*	*1997* ₹	*1998* ₹
Share capital	*10,00,000*	*13,50,000*	*Fixed assets (Net)*	*18,00,000*	*20,50,000*
General reserve	*5,00,000*	*6,00,000*	*Investments*	*2,00,000*	*2,50,000*
Profit & loss A/c	*1,00,000*	*1,50,000*	*Inventories*	*5,00,000*	*7,00,000*
Debentures	*6,00,000*	*5,00,000*	*Debtors*	*5,85,000*	*6,40,000*
Sundry creditors	*9,00,000*	*10,50,000*	*Cash*	*15,000*	*10,000*
	31,00,000	*36,50,000*		*31,00,000*	*36,50,000*

During the year ended on 30.04.98 depreciation charged on fixed assets amounted to ₹2,50,000. The final dividend for the year ended 30.04.1997 amounted to ₹1,00,000 was paid on 08.01.98. [MCA Madras]

Solution : Fund Flow Statement

Source of funds	₹	*Application of funds*	₹
Issue of Shares	3,50,000	Purchase of fixed assets	5,00,000
Fund from operation	5,00,000	Purchase of Investments	50,000
		Dividend paid	1,00,000
		Increase in working capital	1,00,000
		Redemption of debenture	1,00,000
	8,50,000		8,50,000

Working : (*i*) Statement of changes in working capital

	1997	*1998*
Current Assets :	₹	₹
Inventors	5,00,000	7,00,000
Debtors	5,85,000	6,40,000
Cash	15,000	10,000
Total current assets	11,00,000	13,50,000
Current Liabilities :		
Sundry creditors	9,00,000	10,50,000
Total current liabilities	9,00,000	10,50,000
Working capital	2,00,000	3,00,000
Increase in working capital	1,00,000	(2,00,000 – 3,00,000)

(*ii*) Profit and Loss Account

	₹		₹
To General Reserve	1,00,000	By Balance b/d	1,00,000
To Dividend paid	1,00,000	By Fund from operation	5,00,000
To Depreciation	1,50,000		
To Balance c/d	2,50,000		
	6,00,000		6,00,000

(*iii*) Fixed Assets Account

To Balance b/d	18,00,000	By Depreciation	2,50,000
To Cash	5,00,000	By Balance c/d	20,50,000
	23,00,000		23,00,000

Problem 12. *From the following balance sheet you are required to prepare schedule of changes in working capital and fund flow statement.*

Balance Sheet

Liabilities	*31.3.1998*	*31.3.1999*	*Assets*	*31.3.1998*	*31.3.1999*
	₹	₹		₹	₹
Share capital	*50,000*	*50,000*	*Cash*	*20,000*	*10,000*
P.L. A/c	*80,000*	*1,10,000*	*Marketable securities*	*10,000*	-
12% debentures	-	*30,000*	*Inventories*	*60,000*	*1,00,000*
Sundry creditors	*20,000*	*25,000*	*Debtors*	*30,000*	*40,000*
Bills payable	*20,000*	*5,000*	*Gross block*	*1,00,000*	*1,40,000*
Other current liabilities	*10,000*	*15,000*	*(–) accumulated depreciation*	*(40,000)*	*(55,000*
	1,80,000	*2,35,000*		*1,80,000*	*2,35,000*

[MBA Madras 1997]

Solution : **Fund Flow Statement**

Source of funds	₹	*Application of funds*	₹
Issue of Debentures	30,000	Purchase of Gross block	40,000
Fund from operation	45,000	Increase in working capital	35,000
	75,000		75,000

Workings : ***(i)*** **Statement of changes in working capital**

	31.3.98	*31.3.99*
Current Assets :	₹	₹
Cash	20,000	10,000
Marketable securities	10,000	-
Inventories	60,000	1,00,000
Debtors	30,000	40,000
Total current assets	1,20,000	1,50,000
Current Liabilities :		
Sundry creditors	20,000	25,000
Bills payable	20,000	5,000
Other Current Liabilities	10,000	15,000
Total current Liabilities	50,000	45,000
Working capital	70,000	1,05,000
Increase in working capital	35,000	(70,000 – 1,05,000)

(ii) Profit and Loss Account

To Depreciation	15,000	By Balance b/d	80,000
To Balance c/d	1,10,000	By Fund from operation	45,000
	1,25,000		1,25,000

NOTE : Gross Block means total fixed assets.

Problem 13. *The following are the summarized balance sheets of KNP Ltd. on 31st December 2002 and 2003.*

Liabilities	*2002* ₹	*2003* ₹	*Assets*	*2002* ₹	*2003* ₹
Share capital	*12,00,000*	*16,00,000*	*Plant & Machinery*	*8,00,000*	*12,90,000*
Debentures	*4,00,000*	*6,00,000*	*Land & building*	*6,00,000*	*8,00,000*
Profit and loss A/c	*2,50,000*	*5,00,000*	*Stock*	*6,00,000*	*7,00,000*
Creditors	*2,30,000*	*1,80,000*	*Bank*	*40,000*	*80,000*
Provision for Bad & doubtful debts	*12,000*	*6,000*	*Preliminary Expenses*	*14,000*	*12,000*
Depreciation on land & buildings	*40,000*	*48,000*	*Debtors*	*1,38,000*	*1,22,000*
Depreciation on plant & machinery	*60,000*	*70,000*			
	21,92,000	*30,04,000*		*21,92,000*	*30,04,000*

The following adjustments are to be made :

1. *During the year a part of machinery costing ₹ 1,40,000 (accumulated depreciation there on ₹ 4,000) was sold for ₹ 12,000.*
2. *Dividend of ₹ 1,00,000 was paid during the year.*

Prepare : (a) Statement of changes in working capital, (b) Fund flow statement

Solution : **Fund Flow Statement**

Source of funds	₹	*Application of funds*	₹
Issue of shares	4,00,000	Dividend paid	1,00,000
Issue of Debentures	2,00,000	Purchase of Plant & Machinery	6,30,000
Sale of Machinery	12,000	Purchase of Land & Building	2,00,000
Fund from operation	4,98,000	Increase in working capital	1,80,000
	11,10,000		11,10,000

Workings : (i) Statement of changes in working capital

	2002	2003
Current Assets :	₹	₹
Stock	6,00,000	7,00,000
Bank	40,000	80,000
Debtors	1,38,000	1,22,000
Total current assets	7,78,000	9,02,000
Current Liabilities :		
Creditors	2,30,000	1,80,000
Provision for doubtful debts	12,000	6,000
Total current liabilities	2,42,000	1,86,000
Working capital	5,36,000	7,16,000
Increase in working capital	1,80,000	(5,36,000 – 7,16,000)

(ii) Profit and Loss Account

To Depreciation :		By Balance b/d	2,50,000
Plant & Machinery	14,000	By Fund from operation	4,98,000
Land & Buildings	8,000		
To Preliminary Expenses Written off	2,000		
To Dividend paid	1,00,000		
To Loss on sale of Machinery	1,24,000		
To Balance c/d	5,00,000		
	7,48,000		7,48,000

(iii) Plant and Machinery Account

To Balance b/d	8,00,000	By Cash	12,000
To Cash (Purchase)	6,30,000	By Accumulated Depreciation	4,000
		By Profit and Loss A/c	1,24,000
		By Balance c/d	12,90,000
	14,30,000		14,30,000

(iv) Accumulated Depreciation Account on Plant & Machinery

To Balance c/d	70,000	By Balance b/d	60,000
To Machinery A/c	4,000	By Profit & Loss A/c (Current year Depreciation)	14,000
	74,000		74,000

(v) Land & Buildings A/c

To Balance b/d	6,00,000	By Balance c/d	8,00,000
To Cash	2,00,000		
	8,00,000		8,00,000

(vi) Accumulated Depreciation Account on Land & Building

To Balance c/d	48,000	By Balance c/d By Profit & Loss A/c	40,000 8,000
	48,000		48,000

NOTE : Journal Entry for 1st Adjustment

Cash A/c	Dr.	12,000		[Sale of machinery]
Accumulated depreciation A/c	Dr.	4,000		[Depreciation]
Profit & Loss A/c	Dr.	1,24,000		[Loss on sale of machinery]
To machinery A/c			1,40,000	[Cost of machinery]

Problem 14. *From the following balance sheets of a Indian company Ltd. you are required to prepare fund flow statement.*

Balance Sheet

Liabilities	*Jan. 2002* ₹	*Dec. 2002* ₹	*Assets*	*Jan. 2002* ₹	*Dec. 2002* ₹
Current Liabilities	*30,000*	*32,000*	*Cash*	*40,000*	*44,400*
Bonds payable	*22,000*	*22,000*	*Accounts receivable*	*10,000*	*20,700*
Bonds payable discount	*(2,000)*	*(1,800)*	*Inventories*	*15,000*	*15,000*
Capital stock	*35,000*	*43,500*	*Land*	*4,000*	*4,000*
Retained earnings	*15,000*	*19,500*	*Buildings*	*20,000*	*16,000*
			Equipment	*15,000*	*17,000*
			Accumulated Depreciation	*(5,000)*	*(2,800)*
			Patents	*1,000*	*900*
	1,00,000	*1,15,200*		*1,00,000*	*1,15,200*

The following additional information is also available :

(a) Income for the period ₹ 10,000.

(b) A building that costs ₹ 4,000 and which had a book value of ₹ 1,000 was sold for ₹ 1,400.

(c) The depreciation charged for the period was ₹ 800.

(d) There was an issue of common stock ₹ 5,000.

(e) Cash dividend of ₹ 2,000 and ₹ 3,500 stock dividend were declared.

[M.Com. Madras]

Solution : **Fund Flow Statement**

Source of funds	₹	*Application of funds*	₹
Sale of Building	1,400	Purchase of equipment	2,000
Issue of common stock	5,000	Cash dividend paid	2,000
Fund from operation	10,700	Increase in working capital	13,100
	17,100		17,100

Workings : (i) Statement of changes in working capital

Current Assets :	*Jan. 2002* ₹	*Dec. 2002* ₹
Cash	40,000	44,400
Account receivable	10,000	20,700
Inventories	15,000	15,000
Total current assets	65,000	80,100
Current Liabilities :		
Current Liabilities	30,000	32,000
Total current liabilities	30,000	32,000
Working capital	35,000	48,100
Increase in working capital [48,100 – 35,000]	—	13,100

(ii) Profit and Loss Account

To Loss on Bonds Payable discount	200	By Balance b/d	15,000
To Patent written off	100	By Profit on sale of Building	400
To Cash dividend paid	2,000	By Fund from operation	10,700
To Depreciation	800		
To Stock dividend	3,500		
To Balance c/d	19,500		
	26,100		26,100

(iii) Capital Stock Account

To Balance c/d	43,500	By Balance c/d	35,000
		By Cash	5,000
		By Stock Dividend	3,500
	43,500		43,500

(iv) Accumulated Depreciation Account

To Balance c/d	2,800	By Balance b/d	5,000
To Buildings A/c	3,000	By Profit & Loss A/c	800
	5,800		5,800

(v) Building Account

To Balance b/d	20,000	By Cash	1,400
To Profit & Loss A/c (Profit on sale)	400	By Accumulated Depreciation	3,000
		By Balance c/d	16,000
	20,400		20,400

NOTE : Journal for IInd Adjustment

Cash A/c	Dr.	1400		[Sale of Building]
Accumulated Depreciation A/c	Dr.	3000		[Depreciation]
To Building A/c			4000	[Book value]
To Profit & Loss A/c			400	[Profit]

Problem 15. *From the following balance sheets of Kavin Ltd., prepare a statement of changes in working capital and fund flow statement for the year ended 31.3.2002.*

Liabilities	*2001* ₹	*2002* ₹	*Assets*	*2001* ₹	*2002* ₹
Share capital	*3,00,000*	*3,50,000*	*Goodwill*	*1,00,000*	*80,000*
Debentures	*1,50,000*	*2,50,000*	*Machinery*	*4,10,000*	*5,40,000*
General reserve	*1,00,000*	*1,50,000*	*Investment*	*30,000*	*80,000*
Profit & loss A/c	*60,000*	*70,000*	*Discount on issue of Debentures*	*5,000*	—
Provision for depreciation on machinery	*90,000*	*1,30,000*	*Cash at bank*	*1,20,000*	*1,30,000*
Sundry creditors	*75,000*	*1,10,000*	*Sundry debtors*	*80,000*	*1,90,000*
Bills payable	*10,000*	*15,000*	*Stock*	*40,000*	*55,000*
	7,85,000	*10,75,000*		*7,85,000*	*10,75,000*

During the year investments costing ₹ 30,000 were sold for ₹ 28,000 and a new machine was purchased for ₹ 45,000. The payment was made in fully paid shares.

[M.Com. Adapted]

Solution : **Fund Flow Statement**

Source of funds	₹	*Application of funds*	₹
Issue of shares	5,000	Purchase of Machinery (4)	85,000
Issue of Debentures	1,00,000	Increase in Working Capital (1)	95,000
Sale of investments	28,000	Purchase of Investment (6)	80,000
Fund from operation	1,27,000		
	2,60,000		2,60,000

Workings : **(*i*) Statement of changes in working capital**

Current Assets :	*1999* ₹	*2000* ₹
Cash at bank	1,20,000	1,30,000
Sundry Debtors	80,000	1,90,000
Stock	40,000	55,000
Total current assets	2,40,000	3,75,000

Current Liabilities :		
Sundry creditors	75,000	1,10,000
Bills payable	10,000	15,000
Total current liabilities	85,000	1,25,000
Working capital	1,55,000	2,50,000
Increase in working capital	95,000	(1,55,000 – 2,50,000)

(ii) Profit and Loss Account

To Goodwill written off	20,000	By Balance b/d	60,000
To General Reserve	50,000	By Fund from operation	1,27,000
To Discount issue of Debentures	5,000		
To Depreciation	40,000		
To Loss on Sale of Investments	2,000		
To Balance c/d	70,000		
	1,87,000		1,87,000

(iii) Share Capital Account

To Balance c/d	3,50,000	By Balance b/d	3,00,000
		By Machinery	45,000
		By Cash	5,000
	3,50,000		3,50,000

(iv) Machinery Account

To Balance b/d	4,10,000	By Balance c/d	5,40,000
To Shares	45,000		
To Cash (b/f)	85,000		
	5,40,000		5,40,000

(v) Provision for Depreciation on Machinery Account

To Balance c/d	1,30,000	By Balance b/d	90,000
		By Profit & Loss Account	40,000
	1,30,000		1,30,000

(vi) Investment Account

To Balance b/d	30,000	By Bank	28,000
To Purchase of Investment (b/f)	80,000	By Loss Sale of Investment	2,000
		By Balance c/d	80,000
	1,10,000		1,10,000

NOTE : Sale of Investment				
Cash A/c	Dr.	28,000		[Actual sale]
Profit & Loss A/c	Dr.	2,000		[Loss on sale]
To Investments			30,000	[Value of investment]

Problem 16. *From the following summarised balance sheets of Balaji & Co. as on 31.12.2003 and other information furnished, prepare fund flow statement.*

Balance sheet

Liabilities	*2003* ₹	*2002* ₹	*Assets*	*2003* ₹	*2002* ₹
Share capital	*2,00,000*	*50,000*	*Fixed assets*	*4,20,000*	*2,40,000*
Redeemable per shares	-	*1,00,000*	*Investments*	*15,000*	*18,000*
Profit & loss A/c	*3,50,000*	*1,20,000*	*Stock*	*1,60,000*	*58,500*
Debentures	-	*1,25,000*	*Bills receivable*	*92,000*	*1,37,000*
Sundry creditors	*1,90,000*	*2,25,000*	*Cash at bank*	*1,20,000*	*1,85,000*
Provision for Tax	*75,000*	*25,000*	*Prepaid expenses*	*8,000*	*6,500*
	8,15,000	*6,45,000*		*8,15,000*	*6,45,000*

The following additional information is also available :

(a) *On 31.12.2003 accumulated depreciation on fixed assets amounted to ₹ 1,20,000 and on 31st December 2002 ₹ 1,10,000*

(b) *Machinery costing ₹ 10,000 (accumulated depreciation thereon being ₹ 5,000) was discarded and written off during 2003.*

(c) *Depreciation written off during 2003 amounted to ₹ 15,000.*

(d) *During the year 2003 investments costing ₹ 6,000 were sold for ₹ 7,000.*

(e) *Dividend paid during the year was ₹ 45,000*

(f) *Redeemable preference shares were redeemed out of profits during the year at a premium of 5%.*

Solution :

Fund Flow Statement

Source of funds	₹	*Application of funds*	₹
Issue of shares	1,50,000	Repayment of Secured Loan	1,25,000
Sale of investments	7,000	Dividend paid	45,000
Decrease in working capital	22,000	Redemption of preference Shares	1,05,000
Fund from operation	2,99,000	Purchase of Investments	3,000
		Purchase of Fixed assets	2,00,000
	4,78,000		4,78,000

Workings : (i) Statement of changes in working capital

	2002	2003
Current Assets :	₹	₹
Stock	58,500	1,60,000
Sundry Debtors	1,37,000	92,000
Cash at Bank	1,85,000	1,20,000
Prepaid expenses	6,500	8,000
Total current assets	3,87,000	3,80,000
Current Liabilities :		
Sundry creditors	2,25,000	1,90,000
Provision for tax	25,000	75,000
Total current liabilities	2,50,000	2,65,000
Working capital	1,37,000	1,15,000
Decrease in working capital	22,000	(1,37,000 – 1,15,000)

(ii) Profit and Loss Account

	₹		₹
To Loss on sale of Machinery	5,000	By Balance b/d	1,20,000
To Dividend paid	45,000	By Profit on sale of Investments	1,000
To Premium on Redemption of Preference shares	5,000	By Fund from operation	2,99,000
To Depreciation	15,000		
To Balance c/d	3,50,000		
	4,20,000		4,20,000

(iii) Redeemable Preference Share Capital Account

To Cash	1,05,000	By Balance b/d	1,00,000
		By P&L A/c (premium)	5,000
	1,05,000		1,05,000

(iv) Fixed Assets Account

To Balance b/d (2,40,000 + 1,10,000)	3,50,000	By P&L A/c	5,000
To Cash	2,00,000	By Accumulated Depreciation	5,000
		By Balance c/d (4,20,000 + 1,20,000)	5,40,000
	5,50,000		5,50,000

(v) Accumulated Depreciation Account

To Fixed Assets	5,000	By Balance b/d	1,10,000
To Balance c/d	1,20,000	By P&L A/c (Current year Depreciation)	15,000
	1,25,000		1,25,000

(vi) Investment Account

To Balance b/d	18,000	By Cash	6,000
To Case	3,000	By Balance c/d	15,000
	21,000		21,000

NOTE :

(i) *Journal Entry for IInd Adjustment*

Profit & Loss A/c	Dr.	5,000		[Loss]
Accumulated depreciation A/c	Dr.	5,000		[Depreciation]
To machinery A/c			10,000	[Value of machinery]

(ii) *Journal Entry for IV transaction*

Cash A/c	Dr.	7,000	
To Profit and Loss A/c			1,000
To Investment A/c			6,000

(iii) Here, provisional for Taxation assumed to a current liability.

Problem 17. *From the following data of National Auto Ltd. for the year 2000 and 2001.*

Particulars	*2000* ₹	*2001* ₹
Cash	*2,000*	*2,500*
Account receivable	*2,400*	*2,700*
Inventories	*3,100*	*3,200*
Other current assets	*800*	*700*
Fixed assets	*5,000*	*5,800*
Accumulated depreciation	*2,100*	*2,500*
Accounts payable	*2,000*	*2,100*
Long term debt	*1,400*	*1,300*
Equity capital	*5,000*	*5,300*
Retained earnings	*2,800*	*3,700*

The following additional information is also available :

(a) *Fixed assets costing ₹1,200 were purchased for cash.*

(b) *Fixed assets [Original cost of ₹400 accumulated depreciation ₹150] were sold for ₹200.*

(c) *Depreciation for the year 2001 amounted to ₹550 and duly debited to profit & loss account.*

(d) *Dividend paid amounted to ₹300 in 2001.*

(e) *Reported income for 2001 was ₹2,400.* [M.Com. Adapted]

Solution : **Fund Flow Statement**

Source of funds	₹	*Application of funds*	₹
Issue of Equity Shares	300	Dividend paid	300
Sale of Fixed Assets	200	Purchase of Fixed Assets	1,200
Fund from operation	1,800	Repayment of Long term Debt	100
		Increase in working capital	700
	2,300		2,300

Workings : ***(i)* Statement of changes in working capital**

	2000	*2001*
Current Assets :	₹	₹
Cash	2,000	2,500
Accounts receivable	2,400	2,700
Inventories	3,100	3,200
Other current assets	800	700
Total current assets	8,300	9,100
Current Liabilities :		
Account payable	2,000	2,100
Total current liabilities	2,000	2,100
Working capital	6,300	7,000
Increase in working capital	700	(6300 – 7000)

***(ii)* Fixed Assets Account**

To Balance b/d	5,000	By Cash	200
To Cash	1,200	By Accumulated Depreciation	150
		By Profit & Loss A/c	50
		By Balance c/d	5,800
	6,200		6,200

***(iii)* Profit and Loss Account**

To Fixed Assets	50	By Balance c/d	2,800
To Depreciation	550	By Fund from operation	1,800
To Dividend paid	300		
To Balance c/d	3,700		
	4,600		4,600

***(iv)* Accumulated Depreciation Account**

To Fixed Assets	150	By Balance b/d	2,100
To Balance c/d	2,500	By Profit & Loss A/c	550
	2,650		2,650

NOTE :

(i) *Journal Entry for IInd Adjustment*

Cash A/c	Dr.	200		[Sale of fixed assets]
Accumulated depreciation A/c	Dr.	150		[Depreciation]
Profit and Loss A/c	Dr.	50		[Loss on sale]
To Fixed assets			400	

(ii) *Reported income*

It is included in the Retained Earnings. So, there is no need to give the effect of this Adjustment.

Problem 18. *From the following information, calculate funds from operations.*

Profit and Loss Account

	₹		₹
To expenses			
To Operating expenses	*1,00,000*	*By Gross profit*	*2,00,000*
To Depreciation	*40,000*	*By Gain on sale of building*	*20,000*
To loss on sale of machinery	*10,000*		
To advertisement expenses A/c	*5,000*		
To discount of debtors	*500*		
To discount on issue a shares	*500*		
To goodwill written off	*12,000*		
To preliminary expenses written off	*2,000*		
To Net profit	*50,000*		
	2,20,000		*2,20,000*

Solution :

Computation of fund from operation Profit and Loss Account

Expenses	₹	*Incomes*	₹
To Depreciation	40,000	By Balance b/d	Nil
To Loss on sale of Machinery	10,000	By Gain on sale of Buildings	20,000
To Goodwill written off	12,000	By Fund from operation	99,500
To Advertisement Expenses	5,000		
To Discount allowed	500		
To Preliminary Expenses Written off	2,000		
To Balance c/d	50,000		
	1,19,500		1,19,500

Problem 19. *Balance sheets of M/s Black and White as on Ist Jan. 2000 and 31st Dec 2000 were as follows :*

Liabilities	*Jan. 2000* ₹	*Dec. 2000* ₹	*Assets*	*Jan. 2000* ₹	*Dec. 2000* ₹
Creditors	*40,000*	*44,000*	*Cash*	*10,000*	*7,000*
White's loan	*25,000*	—	*Debtors*	*30,000*	*50,000*
Loan from bank	*40,000*	*50,000*	*Stock*	*35,000*	*25,000*
Capital	*1,25,000*	*1,53,000*	*Land*	*40,000*	*50,000*
			Building	*35,000*	*60,000*
			Machinery	*80,000*	*55,000*
	2,30,000	*2,47,000*		*2,30,000*	*2,47,000*

During the year machine costing ₹ 10,000 [accumulated depreciation ₹ 3,000] was sold for ₹ 5,000. The provision for depreciation against machinery as on Ist Jan 2000 was ₹ 25,000 and on 31st Dec 2000 ₹ 40,000. Net profit for the year 2000 amounted to ₹ 45,000. Prepare fund flow statement.

[M.Com. Madurai, MCA Bharathiar], [BBM PU 95]

Solution : **Fund Flow Statement**

Source of funds	₹	*Application of funds*	₹
Loan from PN Bank	10,000	Repayment of Mr.White's Loan	25,000
Sale of Machinery	5,000	Purchase of Land	10,000
Fund from operation	65,000	Purchase of Building	25,000
		Increase in working capital	3,000
		Drawings (Capital A/c)	17,000
	80,000		80,000

Working : **(*i*) Statement of changes in working capital**

	1.1.2000 ₹	*31.12.2000* ₹
Current Assets :		
Cash	10,000	7,000
Debtors	30,000	50,000
Stock	35,000	25,000
Total current assets	75,000	82,000
Current Liabilities :		
Creditors	40,000	44,000
Total current liabilities	40,000	44,000
Working capital	35,000	38,000
Increase in working capital	3,000	(35,000 – 38,000)

(ii) Profit and Loss Account

To Loss on sale of Machinery	2,000	By Fund from operation	65,000
To Depreciation	18,000		
To Balance c/d	45,000		
	65,000		65,000

(iii) Capital Account

To Balance c/d	1,53,000	By Balance b/d	1,25,000
To Cash (b/f)	17,000	By Profit & Loss A/c	45,000
	1,70,000		1,70,000

(iv) Machinery Account

To Balance c/d (80,000+25,000)	1,05,000	By Cash	5,000
		By P&L A/c	2,000
		By Accumulated Depreciation	3,000
		By Balance c/d	95,000
	1,05,000		1,05,000

(v) Accumulated Depreciation Account

To Machinery A/c	3,000	By Balance b/d	25,000
To Balance c/d	40,000	By P&L A/c (b/f)	18,000
	43,000		43,000

Journal Entry For 1st Adjustment :

Cash A/c	Dr.	5,000	
Accumulated depreciation A/c	Dr.	3,000	
Profit and Loss A/c	Dr.	2,000	
To Machinery A/c			10,000

Problem 20. *The Balance sheets of Dharan Ltd. as on 31.12.1999 and 31.12.2000 are as follows.*

Liabilities	*1999* ₹	*2000* ₹	*Assets*	*1999* ₹	*2000* ₹
Share capital	*2,00,000*	*2,50,000*	*Fixed assets*	*3,50,000*	*4,75,000*
Retained earnings	*1,60,000*	*3,00,000*	*Inventory*	*1,00,000*	*95,000*
Premium on share	—	*5,000*	*Accounts receivable*	*43,000*	*50,000*
Accumulated depreciation	*80,000*	*60,000*	*Prepaid expenses*	*4,000*	*5,000*
Debentures	*60,000*	—	*Cash*	*15,800*	*10,200*
Bank overdraft	*37,800*	*40,200*	*Commission on shares*	*25,000*	*20,000*
	5,37,800	*6,55,200*		*5,37,800*	*6,55,200*

The following additional information is also available :

(i) *Net profit for the year ₹ 1,40,000*

(ii) *Income tax was paid ₹ 40,000*

(iii) *Interim dividend paid during the year was ₹ 20,000.*

(iv) *An addition to the fixed asset was made during the year at a cost of ₹ 1,65,000 and fully depreciated machinery costing ₹ 40,000 was discarded, no salvage being realised.*

(v) *Depreciation for the year ₹ 20,000* [BBM, 2000]

Solution : **Fund Flow Statement**

Source of funds	₹	*Application of funds*	₹
Issue of shares	50,000	Redemption of debentures	60,000
Premium on shares received	5,000	Purchase of fixed assets	1,65,000
Fund from operation	2,25,000	Income Tax paid	40,000
Decreasing in working capital	5,000	Interim dividend paid	20,000
	2,85,000		2,85,000

Workings : **(*i*) Statement of changes in working capital**

	1999 ₹	*2000* ₹
Current assets :		
Inventories	1,00,000	95,000
Accounts receivable	43,000	50,000
Prepaid expenses	4,000	5,000
Cash	15,800	10,200
	1,62,800	1,60,200
Current Liabilities :		
Bank overdraft	37,800	40,200
Total current liabilities	37,800	40,200
Working capital	1,25,000	1,20,000
Decrease in working capital	5,000	[1,25,000 – 1,20,000]

(*ii*) Profit and Loss Account

	₹		₹
To Commission on shares Written off	5,000	By Balance b/d	1,60,000
To Depreciation	20,000	By Fund from operation (b/f)	2,25,000
To Income Tax paid	40,000		
To Interim dividend paid	20,000		
To Balance c/d	3,00,000		
	3,85,000		3,85,000

(*iii*) Fixed Assets Account

	₹		₹
To Balance c/d	3,50,000	By accumulated depreciation	40,000
To Cash (b/f)	1,65,000	By Balance c/d	4,75,000
	5,15,000		5,15,000

(*iv*) Accumulated Depreciation Account

	₹		₹
To Machinery A/c	40,000	By Balance b/d	80,000
(Fully Depreciated Machinery)		By Profit & Loss A/c (b/f)	20,000
To Balance c/d	60,000		
	1,00,000		1,00,000

Problem 21. *Following are the summarized Balance Sheet of XYZ Ltd. As on 31st Dec. 2002 and 2003.*

Liabilities	*2002* ₹	*2003* ₹	*Assets*	*2002* ₹	*2003* ₹
Share Capital	*1,00,000*	*1,25,000*	*Land and Building*	*1,00,000*	*95,000*
General Reserve	*25,000*	*30,000*	*Machinery*	*75,000*	*84,500*
Profit and Loss A/c	*15,250*	*15,300*	*Stock*	*50,000*	*37,000*
Bank loan (long-term)	*35,000*	-----	*Debtors*	*40,000*	*32,100*
Sundry Creditors	*75,000*	*67,600*	*Cash*	*250*	*300*
Provision for Taxation	*15,000*	*17,500*	*Bank*	----	*4,000*
			Goodwill	----	*2,500*
	2,65,250	*2,55,400*		*2,65,250*	*2,55,400*

Additional Information :

(*i*) *Dividend of ₹ 16,500/- was paid.*

(*ii*) *Assets of another company were purchased for a consideration of ₹ 25,000/- payable in shares.*

The following assets purchased

Stock 10,000

Machinery 12,500

(*iii*) *Machinery was further purchased for ₹ 4,000*

(*iv*) *Depreciation written off on machinery ₹ 6,000*

(*v*) *Income tax provided during the year ₹ 16,500/-*

(*vi*) *Loss on sale of machinery ₹ 100/- was written off to General Reserve. Prepare a statement of Funds Flow of XYZ Ltd.* [MBA Periyar]

Solution : **Fund Flow Statement**

Sources of Funds	₹	*Application Funds*	₹
Sale of land and buildings	5,000	Repayment of bank loan	35,000
Funds from operation	44,150	Dividend paid	16,500
Sale of machinery	900	Purchase of machinery	4,000
Decrease in working capital	9,450	Income tax paid	14,000
Issue of shares for stock	10,000		
	69,500		69,500

Workings :

1. Statement of changes in working capital :

Current Asset :

	2002 ₹	*2003* ₹
Stock	50,000	37,000
Debtors	40,000	32,100
Cash	250	300
Bank	---	4,000
Total current assets	90,250	73,400
Current Liabilities :		
Sundry creditors	75,000	67,600
Total current liabilities	75,000	67,600
Working capital	15,250	5,800
Decrease in working capital	9,450	

2. Share Capital A/c

	₹		₹
To Balance c/d	1,25,000	By Balance b/d	1,00,000
		By Stock	10,000
		By Machinery	12,500
		By Goodwill	2,500
	1,25,000		1,25,000

3. Profit and Loss A/c

	₹		₹
To Balance c/d	15,300	By Balance b/d	15,250
To Dividend paid	16,500	By FFO	44,150
To Depreciation (mach)	6,000		
To Income tax provision	16,500		
To General Reserves	5,100		
	59,400		59,400

4. Provision for Taxation A/c

	₹		₹
To Balance c/d	17,500	By Balance b/d	15,000
To Cash (Tax paid)	14,000	By P.L. A/c	16,500
	31,500		31,500

5. Machinery A/c

	₹		₹
To Balance b/d	75,000	By Balance c/d	84,500
To Shares	12,500	By Profit and loss A/c	6,000
To Cash	4,000	By General Reserve A/c	100
		By Cash	900
	91,500		91,500

6. Goodwill A/c

	₹		₹
To Balance b/d	Nil	By Balance c/d	2,500
To Shares	2,500		
	2,500		2,500

7. General Reserve A/c

	₹		₹
To Balance c/d	30,000	By Balance b/d	25,000
To Machinery	100	By Profit and Loss A/c	5,100
	30,100		30,100

TEST PROBLEMS

1. Babu & Co. presents the following Financial Statement for 1988 and 1989. Prepare a sources and application for funds statement.

Liabilities	*1988* ₹	*1989* ₹	*Assets*	*1988* ₹	*1989* ₹
Bill Payable	4,52,000	6,28,000	Cash	1,06,000	62,000
Creditors	8,26,000	12,54,00	Investment	1,74,000	–
Loan from bank	2,00,000	4,70,000	Debtors	6,92,000	10,56,000
Resaves & Surplus	13,84,000	17,28,000	Stock	8,64,000	13,66,000
Share capital	12,00,000	12,00,000	Net fixed assets	22,26,000	27,96,000
	40,62,000	**52,80,000**		**40,62,000**	**52,80,000**

Depreciation of ₹ 3,78,000 was written off for the year 1989 on fixed assets.

[Madras, B.A. Corp. C&M, March 1990]

[Ans: Increase in working capital ₹ 2,18,000]

2. Balance Sheets of M/s. Raman and Krishnan as on 1st January, 1998 and 31st December 1998 were as follows:

Balance Sheet

Liabilities	*1.1.98* ₹	*31.12.98* ₹	*Assets*	*1.1.98* ₹	*31.12.98* ₹
Bill Payable	80,000	88,000	Cash	25,000	22,000
Mrs. Krishnan's loan	50,000	–	Debtors	30,000	80,000
Loan, Secured on Building	80,000	80,000	Stock	75,000	40,000
Creditors	30,000	60,000	Bills Receivable	25,000	30,000
Capitals:			Building	1,00,000	90,000
Raman	40,000	50,000	Furniture	1,05,000	86,000
Krishnan	80,000	70,000			
	3,60,000	**3,48,000**		**3,60,000**	**3,48,000**

During 1998, furniture costing 10,000 (accumulated depreciation ₹ 6,000) was sold for ₹ 3,000. Net profit for the year was ₹ 80,000, divided equally to the partners. Prepare a statement of sources and uses of funds for the year 1998.

[Ans: Decrease in working capital ₹ 21,000]

3. Balance Sheet of Ganesh Mills Ltd.

Liabilities	*1992* ₹	*1993* ₹	*Assets*	*1992* ₹	*1993* ₹
Equity share capital	3,00,000	4,00,000	Building	2,50,000	3,00,000
10% Redeemable per share capital	2,00,000	--	Machinery	3,00,000	3,20,000
			Furniture	20,000	18,000
Capital Redemption Reserve	–	1,00,000	Investments	1,00,000	1,50,000
			Stock	3,00,000	2,50,000
Reserve Fund	2,00,000	1,20,000	Debtors	1,40,000	2,00,000
Share Premium	30,000	30,000	Cash at bank	20,000	32,000
Profit & Loss A/c	1,20,000	1,80,000			
12% Debentures	2,00,000	3,00,000			
Creditors	80,000	1,40,000			
	11,30,000	**12,70,000**		**11,30,000**	**12,70,000**

The following transactions took place during the year 1993:

(*a*) Preference shares were redeemed at 10% premium.

(*b*) ₹ 20,000 was transferred to Reserve Fund from P & L A/c.

(*c*) Investments (book value ₹ 40,000) were sold for ₹ 70,000.

(*d*) Depreciation provided on Building, Machinery and Furniture ₹ 20,000, ₹ 30,00 and ₹ 2,000 respectively.

(*e*) Dividends paid ₹ 50,000 and income tax paid ₹ 45,000. Prepare a funds flow statement showing change in working capital.

[Madras, B.Com. Nov.2004; Bangalore. B.Com. April 1994]

[**Ans:** Decrease in working capital ₹ 38,000]

4. From the following prepare a statement showing changes in working capital during 2002

Balance Sheet of Premier Ltd.
as on 31st December

Liabilities	*2001* ₹	*2002* ₹	*Assets*	*2001* ₹	*2002* ₹
Share capital	5,00,000	6,00,000	Fixed Assets	10,00,000	11,20,000
Reserves	150000	1,80,000	Less: Depreciation	3,70,000	4,60,000
P&L Account	40,000	65,000		6,30,000	6,60,000
Debentures	3,00,000	2,50,000	Stock	2,40,000	3,70,000
			Book debts	2,50,000	2,30,000
Creditors for good	1,70,000	1,60,000	Cash in hand and at bank	80,000	60,000
Provision for Income tax	60,000	1,80,000	Preliminary exp.	20,000	15,000
	12,20,000	**13,35,000**		**12,20,000**	**13,35,000**

[Madras, B.C.S. (ICE) Oct. 2002; B.Com., March 1996]

[**Ans:** Increase in working capital ₹ 1,00,000]

5. Prepare a statement of changes in working capital from the following details of 'R' Ltd.

Liabilities	*31.12.99* ₹	*31.12.2000* ₹	*Assets*	*31.12.99* ₹	*31.12.2000* ₹
Equity capital	5,00,000	5,00,000	Fixed Assets	6,00,000	7,00,000
Debentures	3,70,000	4,50,000	Long-term		
Tax payable	77,000	43,000	Investments	2,00,000	1,00,000
Creditors	96,000	1,92,000	Work-in-progress	80,000	90,000
Dividend payable	87,000	80,000	Stock	1,50,000	2,25.,000
			Debtors	70,000	1,40,000
			Cash	30,000	10,000
	11,30,000	**12,65,000**		**11,30,000**	**12,65,000**

[Madras, B.Com., B.B.A, B.Com. (CS) April 2008; B.Com., Nov.1993]

[Ans : Increase in working capital ₹ 80,000]

6. Finds funds from operations from the following data:

Opening balance of P& L A/c ₹ 60,000

Closing balance of P& L A/c ₹ 30,000

The following items appeared in P& L A/c:

Interium divided paid ₹ 20,000, proposed divided ₹ 30,000, depreciation ₹ 50,000, Preliminary expenses ₹ 1,000, loss on sale of machinery ₹ 3,000, General Reserve ₹, 5,000, sinking fund ₹ 10,000, salaries paid ₹, 3,000, profit on sale of car ₹ 4,000, and tax paid ₹ 5,000.

[Bharathiar, B.B.M., April 1994]

[Ans: Funds from operation ₹ 90,000]

7. From the following, compute the funds from operation

Trading and Profit and Loss Account

	₹		₹
To cash Purchases	50,000	By Sales	60,000
To Gross Profit c/d	10,000		
	60,000		60,000
To Salaries	8,000	By Gross Profit b/d	10,000
To Rent	7,000	By Dividends received	3,000
To Depreciation	2,000	By Interest Investments	3,000
To Goodwill written off	1,000	By Net Loss	4,000
To Preliminary expenses written off	500		
To Discount on issue of Debentures	1,500		
	20,000		**20,000**

[Madras, BBA (old) April 1994]

[Ans: Funds outflow account of operation. ₹ 5,000]

8. From the following details, calculate funds from operations.

Particulars	₹
Salaries	5,000
Rent	3,000
Depreciation on Plant	5,000
Provision for tax	4,000
Loss on sale of Plant	2,000
Opening balance of P&L A/c	25,000
Transfer to General Reserve	1,000
Goodwill written off	2,000
Dividend Received	5,000
Refund of tax	3,000
Profit on sale of building	5,000
Closing balance of P&L A/c	60,000
Discount on issue of debentures	2,000
Provision for bad debts	1,000
Prelinary expenses written off	3,000
Proposed divided	6,000

[Madras, 1st M.Com. (CA2A)April 2008; Nov. 2006; B.Com., (Non sem) April 2006; B.Com. March 1994]

[**Ans.** Funds from operation ₹ 47,000]

9. The following is the comparative Balance Sheet of A Ltd. Prepare a funds Flow statement:

Balance Sheet

Liabilities	*31.12.05* ₹	*31.12.05* ₹	*Assets*	*31.12.05* ₹	*31.12.05* ₹
Share capital	8,000	8,500	Land	5,000	5,000
P&L Appn. A/c	1,450	2,450	Plant	2,400	3,400
Creditors	900	500	Debtors	1,650	1,950
Mortgage loan	–	500	Stock	900	700
			Cash at Bank	400	900
	10,350	**11,950**		**10,350**	**11,950**

[Madras, B.Com. (sem) April 2006; 1st M.Com., (CA2A) April 2005; (10 Times) MBA Apil 2003; B.A., Corp. C&M, March 1995; M.Com., April 1995]

[**Ans.** Increase in working capital: ₹ 1,000; Total sources: ₹ 2,000; Applications: ₹ 1,000; Funds from operations: ₹ 1000]

10. From the following Balance Sheets of Arun Ltd. Prepare a sources and uses of funds statement for 2005.

	31.12.05 ₹	31.12.04 ₹
Assets		
Cash	75,000	35,000
Debtors	90,000	98,000
Stock and work-in-progress	1,20,000	87,000
Long term investments	10,000	15,000
Land	30,000	20,000
	3,25,000	**2,55,000**
Liabilities		
Accounts payable	45,000	50,000
Notes payable (short-term)	35,000	20,000
Notes payable (due Dec. 2006)	20,000	–
Capital Stock	1,50,000	1,25,000
Retained earnings	75,000	60,000
	3,25,000	**2,55,000**

[Madras, BBA April 2005; B.C.S ICE, May 2003; B.Com., Mar. 1997; B.A. Crop., C&M Sep. 1995]

[**Ans.** Increase in working capital: ₹ 35,000; Total sources: ₹ 45,000; Applications: ₹ 10,000; Funds from operations: ₹ 15,000]

11. The Balance Sheet of Swatantra Bharat Co. Ltd. As at 31st December 1991 and 1992 are given below:

	1991 ₹	1992 ₹
Assets		
Freehold land	1,00,000	1,00,000
Plant at cost	1,04,000	1,00,000
Furniture at cost	7,000	9,000
Investments at cost	60,000	80,000
Debtors	30,000	70,000
Stock	60,000	65,000
Cash	30,000	45,000
	3,91,000	**4,69,000**
Liabilities		
Share capital	1,00,000	1,50,000
Share premium	–	5,000
General reserve	50,000	60,000
Profit & Loss A/c	10,000	17,000
6% Debentures	70,000	50,000
Provision for depreciation on plant	50,000	56,000
Provision for depreciation on furniture	5,000	6,000
Provision for taxation	20,000	30,000
Sundry creditors	86,000	95,000
	3,91,000	**4,69,000**

A plant purchase for ₹ 4,000 (depreciation ₹ 2,000) was sold for cash ₹ 800 on 30th Sep. 1992. On 30th June 1992, an item of furniture was purchased for ₹ 2,000. These were the only transitions concerning fixed assets during 1992. Depreciation on plant was provided at 8% on cost (the sold item is not taken into consideration) and on furniture at 12½ % on average cost. A dividend of 22½% on original shares was paid.

Prepare a schedule of changing in working capital and statement of sources and application of funds during 1992.

[Madras, B.Com., Nov. 1993]

[**Ans.** Increase in working capital: ₹ 51,000; Total sources of funds: ₹ 1,35,500; Applications of funds: ₹ 84,500; Funds from operation: ₹ 79,700; Loss on sale of plant: ₹ 1,200; Depreciation of plant for 1992; ₹ 8,000; Opening Balance of provision for tax is to be assumed as paid *i.e.*, ₹ 20,000; Closing balance of ₹ 30,000 is the provision for 1992; Dividend ₹ 22,500.]

❑❑❑

6
Cash Flow Statement

INTRODUCTION

Cash contributes significant role in the entire economic activities of the business world. And at the same time, cash is not only essential for business, but is also essential for each and every activity of human life. What blood is to human body, cash is to a business firm. The firm receives cash from various sources like issue of shares, sale of assets etc. It needs cash to make payments for various purposes like payment to suppliers and to meet out the day to day expenses. The foremost responsibility of the financial manager is to determine cash planning activities and to maintain adequate cash balances. At this juncture cash flow statement is an important tool of cash planning and control. The term cash is used to refer to cash in hand and bank balance.

MEANING

Cash flow statement is a statement which is prepared from the historical data showing the inflow and outflow of cash. It shows the sources and uses of cash between the two balance sheet dates. It clearly explains the causes for changes in cash position between two periods. Simply, it is a receipts and payments account in a summary form.

USES OF CASH FLOW STATEMENT

Cash flow statement is an important tool of financial analysis. It is vital to financial management. Its main uses are as follows :

(i) It gives guidance to the management in taking and implementing short-term financial policies.

(ii) It helps to strengthen the borrowing capacities of the firms. The financial institutions can easily assess the repaying capacities of the firms through the cash flow analysis.

(iii) It contributes significant role for the capital budgeting decisions.

(iv) It helps in short term financial decisions relating to liquidity.

(v) In order to find out the variation and take necessary remedial measures with the help of the comparison of actual cash flow statements with the projected cash flow statements.

(vi) To overcome the problem of meeting deficit cash or investment of surplus cash with the help of the projected cash flow statement. Thus, projected cash flow

statement is usually prepared on the basis of past year's experience.

(*vii*) It explains the causes for poor cash position in spite of huge profits or surplus cash balance in spite of low profits.

(*viii*) It explains the major sources and uses of cash for the business concern during a particular period of time.

LIMITATIONS OF CASH FLOW ANALYSIS

Cash flow statement is a systematic tool of financial analysis. However, it suffers from some limitations which are as follows :

1. A cash flow statement cannot be equated with the income statement. An income statement considers both cash and non-cash items. So, cash does not mean net income of business.
2. The cash flow statement may not represent the real liquid position of the concern. Due to this aspect, postponing of purchases and payments could be developed.
3. Cash flow statement cannot replace the income statement or fund flow statement. Each and every statement has a separate function to perform.
4. Due to inflation, economic depression and other external factors, projected cash flow statement may not achieve its results.

DIFFERENCE BETWEEN CASH FLOW ANALYSIS AND FUND FLOW ANALYSIS

1. Cash flow statement starts with the opening cash balance and ends with the closing cash balance by processing through various sources and uses. But, there are no opening and closing balances in fund flow statement.
2. Cash from operation can be found out under the cash flow statement. But, fund from operation can be found out under the fund flow statement.
3. Separate statements are prepared for the purpose of finding out increase or decrease in working capital under the fund flow statement. But, no separate statements for increase or decrease in working capital are prepared in cash flow analysis.
4. A cash flow statement explains the causes for the changes in cash and bank balances *i.e.,* cash receipts and cash payments alone. But, fund flow statement indicates the causes for the changes in net working capital.
5. Cash flow statement is suitable for short term financial planning and decision, while fund flow statement is appropriate for long term financial planning and decisions.
6. Cash flow analysis deals with the movement of actual or notional cash. But, fund flow statement deals with not only cash but also the items constituting working capital. Cash is one of the components of working capital.
7. Whenever, wherever there is inflow of cash there will definitely be inflow of funds. But, sound fund position need not be a sound cash position.

STEPS IN PREPARATION OF CASH FLOW STATEMENT

Cash flow statement can be prepared on the same pattern on which fund flow statement is prepared. But, here statement of changes in working capital does not need to be prepared. Remaining all other procedures were same in fund flow statement.

Cash flow statement is prepared on any one of the following assumptions :

— When all transactions are taken as cash transactions.

— When all transactions are not cash transactions.

Here, we have to proceed with all the problems by treating all the transactions as cash transactions.

Steps

1. No need to prepare working capital statement
2. Preparation of cash flow statement
3. Preparation of profit & loss account-computation of cash from operation
4. Preparation of separate ledger if necessary
5. Treatment of adjustments

1. *No need to prepare the working capital statement*

Changes in current assets and current liabilities are adjusted in the cash flow statement itself. So, separate statement is not necessary for the changes in working capital.

2. Cash Flow Statement (Proforma)

Inflow of cash	*Amount* ₹	*Outflow of cash*	*Amount* ₹
Opening Cash Balance (including bank balance)	xx	Redemption of preference shares	xx
		Repayment debenture holders	xx
Issue of Shares	xx	Repayment of Loans	xx
Issue of Debentures	xx	Purchase of fixed assets	xx
Raising of loans	xx	Dividend paid	xx
Sale of fixed assets	xx	Income Tax paid	xx
Dividends received	xx	Cash from Operation (Lost in operation) Transfer from P&L A/c	xx
Share premium received	xx		
Cash from operation (Transfer from P&L A/c)		Closing balance (including bank balance)	
	xx		xx

3. *Preparation of Profit & Loss Account - Computation of cash from operation*

Cash from operations can be found out in two methods. One is statement form another one is preparation of profit and loss account. Normally, cash from operation can be found out with the help of the preparation of profit and loss account because it is an easy and convenient method. Here, profit and loss account is prepared in usual procedure.

Profit and Loss A/c

Dr.	Amount ₹		Amount ₹ Cr.
To Goodwill written off	xx	By Opening Balance b/d	xx
To General reserve	xx	By Dividends received	xx
To Preliminary expenses written off	xx	By Interest on investments	xx
To Depreciation	xx	By Profit on sale of assets	xx
To Loss on sale of fixed assets	xx	By Cash from operation *(Balancing figure)*	xx
To Loss on sale of Investments	xx		
To Patents & Trade mark written off	xx		
To Income tax provided	xx		
To Interim dividend paid	xx		
To Closing balance c/d	xx		
To Cash from operation *(Balancing figure)*	xx		
	xx		xx

4. *Preparation of Separate Ledger*

If information of any particular assets or liabilities are given in the adjustment, we have to prepare separate asset or liabilities account. Balances from this ledger can be transferred to cash flow statement.

5. *Treatment of adjustments*

The additional information which are given apart from the balance sheet are, simply called as adjustment. All the adjustments will appear in two places. The following are the important adjustments and their treatment.

(*a*) Dividend paid	-	Cash flow statement - outflow side
	-	Profit & loss A/c - Debit side
(*b*) Depreciation	-	P.L.A/c - Debit side
		Respective asset A/c - credit side
(*c*) Loss on sale of assets	-	P.L.A/c - Debit side
		Respective asset A/c - credit side
(*d*) Income Tax provision	-	P.L.A/c - Debit side
	-	Income Tax - Credit side.

NOTE : The adjustments applicable for fund flow statements will also be applicable for cash flow statements.

TEST QUESTIONS

1. What is meant by cash flow statement ?
2. How will you prepare the cash flow statement ?
3. What is the purpose of preparing cash flow statement ?
4. What are the differences between cash flow and fund flow statement ?
5. Explain the advantages of cash flow statement.
6. What are the limitations of cash flow statement ?

PROBLEMS AND SOLUTIONS

Problem 1. *From the following profit and loss account, compute the case from operations.*

Profit and Loss account for the year ended 31.3.2001

	Amount ₹		*Amount* ₹
To Salaries	*25,000*	*By Gross Profit*	*1,25,000*
To Rent	*3,000*	*By Profit on sale of land*	*15,000*
To Depreciation	*10,000*	*By Income tax refund*	*13,000*
To Loss on Sale of plant	*4,000*		
To Goodwill written off	*10,000*		
To Proposed dividend	*15,000*		
To Provision for Tax	*12,000*		
To Net Profit	*74,000*		
	1,53,000		*1,53,000*

Solution :

	Computation of cash from operation		
	Net profit earned during the year		74,000
Add :	Non-cash and Non-operating expenses		
	Depreciation	10,000	
	Loss on sale of plant	4,000	
	Goodwill written off	10,000	
	Proposed dividend	15,000	
	Provision for tax	12,000	
			51,000
			1,25,000
Less :	Non-cash and Non-operating income		
	Profit on sale of land	15,000	
	Income tax refund	13,000	
			28,000
	Cash from operation		97,000

Problem 2. *Statement of financial position of Mr.Arun is given below.*

Liabilities	*01.1.2000* ₹	*31.12.2000* ₹	*Assets*	*01.1.2000* ₹	*31.12.2000* ₹
Account Payable	*29,000*	*25,000*	*Cash*	*40,000*	*30,000*
Capital	*7,39,000*	*6,15,000*	*Debtors*	*20,000*	*17,000*
			Stock	*8,000*	*13,000*
			Building	*1,00,000*	*80,000*
			Other fixed Assets	*6,00,000*	*5,00,000*
	7,68,000	*6,40,000*		*7,68,000*	*6,40,000*

The following additional information is also available :

(a) There were no drawings.

(b) There were no purchases or sale of either building or other fixed assets. Prepare a statement of case flow. [BBM, MBA Anna]

Solution : **Cash Flow Statement**

Inflow of cash	*Amount* ₹	*Outflow of cash*	*Amount* ₹
Opening Cash Balance	40,000	Decrease in accounts payable	4,000
Decrease in Debtors	3,000	Increase in stock	5,000
		Cash from operation (1)	4,000
		Closing cash balance	30,000
	43,000		43,000

Workings : **1. Profit and Loss Account**

	Amount ₹		*Amount* ₹
To Depreciation on Building	20,000	By Capital Account (Loss)	1,24,000
To Depreciation on Plant	1,00,000		
To Cash from operation (Loss on operation)	4,000		
	1,24,000		1,24,000

2. Capital Account of Mr.Arun

To Profit & Loss A/c (Loss)	1,24,000	By Balance b/d	7,39,000
To Balance c/d	6,15,000		
	7,39,000		7,39,000

3. Building Account

To Balance b/d	1,00,000	By Depreciation (P&L A/c)	20,000
		By Balance c/d	80,000
	1,00,000		1,00,000

4. Other Fixed Assets Account

To balance b/d	6,00,000	By Depreciation (P&L A/c)	1,00,000
		By Balance c/d	5,00,000
	6,00,000		6,00,000

Problem 3. *From the following particulars of Mrs.Ragu, prepare cash flow statements.*

	1.1.99	31.12.99
Liabilities :	₹	₹
Creditors	36,000	41,000
Mrs.A's Loan	—	20,000
Capital	1,48,000	1,49,000
Bank Loan	30,000	25,000
	2,14,000	2,35,000
Assets :		
Cash	4,000	3,600
Debtors	35,000	38,400
Stock	25,000	22,000
Land	20,000	30,000
Buildings	50,000	55,000
Machinery	80,000	86,000
	2,14,000	2,35,000

During the year Mrs.Ragu had drawn ₹ 26,000 for personal use. The provision for depreciation against machinery as on 1.1.99 was ₹ 27,000 and as on 31.12.99 ₹ 36,000.

Solution : **Cash Flow Statement**

Inflow of cash	*Amount* ₹	*Outflow of cash*	*Amount* ₹
Opening cash balance	4,000	Repayment of Bank loan	5,000
Loan borrowed from Mrs. A	20,000	Increase in Debtors	3,400
Decrease in stock	3,000	Purchase of Land	10,000
Cash from operation (1)	36,000	Purchase of Buildings	5,000
Increase in creditors	5,000	Capital Account (Drawings)	26,000
		Purchase of machinery (3)	15,000
		Closing Cash Balance	3,600
	68,000		68,000

Workings : **1. Profit and Loss Account**

	Amount ₹		*Amount* ₹
To Depreciation (4)	9,000	By Cash from operation	36,000
To Capital Account	27,000		
	36,000		36,000

2. Capital Account

To Cash (Drawings)	26,000	By Balance b/d	1,48,000
To Balance c/d	1,49,000	By Profit & Loss A/c (Transfer to P&L A/c)	27,000
	1,75,000		1,75,000

3. Machinery Account

To Balance b/d (80,000+27,000)	1,07,000	By Balance c/d (86,000+36,000)	1,22,000
To Cash (b/f)	15,000		
	1,22,000		1,22,000

4. Accumulated Depreciation Account

To Balance c/d	36,000	By Balance b/d	27,000
		By P&L A/c (b/f)	9,000
	36,000		36,000

Problem 4. *The Balance sheet of Super Computers Ltd. as on 31.12.1992 and 31.12.1993 respectively are given below.*

Liabilities	*1992* ₹	*1993* ₹	*Assets*	*1992* ₹	*1993* ₹
Share capital	*1,00,000*	*1,60,000*	*Fixed assets at cost*	*1,52,000*	*2,00,000*
Retained earnings	*70,250*	*85,300*	*Inventory*	*93,400*	*89,200*
Accumulated Depreciation	*60,000*	*40,000*	*Sundry Debtors*	*30,800*	*21,100*
6% Debentures	*50,000*	—	*Prepaid expenses*	*3,950*	*3,000*
Sundry creditors	*28,000*	*48,000*	*Bank*	*28,100*	*20,000*
	3,08,250	*3,33,300*		*3,08,250*	*3,33,300*

The following additional information for the year 1993 is also available.

(i) *Net profit ₹ 27,050.*

(ii) *Depreciation charged ₹ 10,000.*

(iii) *Cash dividend declared during the period ₹ 12,000.*

(iv) *An addition to the building was made during the year at a cost of ₹ 78,000 and fully depreciated equipment costing ₹ 30,000 was discarded, no salvage value being realised. Prepare a cash flow statement.* [BE Anna 2004]

Solution : **Cash Flow Statement**

Inflow of cash	*Amount* ₹	*Outflow of cash*	*Amount* ₹
Opening cash balance	28,100	Redemption of debentures	50,000
Decrease in inventory	4,200	Cash dividend paid	12,000
Decrease in debtors	9,700	Purchase of building	78,000
Decrease in prepaid expenses	950	Closing cash balance	20,000
Issue of shares	60,000		
Cash from operation	37,050		
Increase in creditors	20,000		
	1,60,000		1,60,000

Workings : **1. Profit and Loss Account**

	Amount ₹		*Amount* ₹
To Cash dividend paid	12,000	By balance b/d	70,250
To Depreciation (Current Year)	10,000	By Cash from Operation (b/f)	37,050
To Balance c/d	85,300		
	1,07,300		1,07,300

2. Accumulated Depreciation Account

To Fixed Assets (Discarded Equipment)	30,000	By Balance b/d	60,000
		By P&L A/c	10,000
To Balance c/d	40,000		
	70,000		70,000

3. Fixed Assets Account

To Balance b/d	1,52,000	By Depreciation	30,000
To Cash (Purchase)	78,000	By Balance c/d	2,00,000
	2,30,000		2,30,000

Problem 5. *The following are the summarised balance sheets of South Computers Ltd. as on 31.12.2000 and 31.12.2001.*

Liabilities	*2000* ₹	*2001* ₹	*Assets*	*2000* ₹	*2001* ₹
Share Capital	*2,00,000*	*2,50,000*	*Land & Buildings*	*2,00,000*	*1,90,000*
General Reserve	*50,000*	*60,000*	*Machinery*	*1,50,000*	*1,69,000*
P&L A/c	*30,500*	*30,600*	*Stock*	*1,00,000*	*74,000*
Bank loan	*70,000*	—	*Sundry Debtors*	*80,000*	*64,200*
Sundry Creditors	*1,50,000*	*1,35,200*	*Cash*	*500*	*600*
Provision for Taxation	*30,000*	*35,000*	*Bank*	—	*8,000*
			Goodwill	—	*5,000*
	5,30,500	*5,10,800*		*5,30,500*	*5,10,800*

The following additional information for the the year 2001 is also available :

(i) Dividend of ₹ 23,000 was paid.

(ii) The following assets of another company were purchased for a consideration of ₹ 50,000 paid in shares.

(a) Stock ₹ 20,000 and (b) Machinery ₹ 25,000

(iii) Machinery was further purchased for ₹ 8,000.

(iv) Depreciation written off machinery ₹ 12,000.

(v) Income Tax provided during the year ₹ 33,000.

(vi) Loss on sale of machinery ₹ 200 was written off to general reserve.

(vii) Prepare cash flow statement. [M.Com. Madurai]

Solution : **Cash Flow Statement**

Inflow of cash	*Amount* ₹	*Outflow of cash*	*Amount* ₹
Opening cash balance	500	Repayment of Bank Loan	70,000
Sale of Land & Building	10,000	Decrease in Sundry Creditors	14,800
Decrease in Sundry Debtors	15,800	Dividend paid	23,000
Sale of Machinery	1,800	Purchase of Machinery	8,000
Sale of Stock	46,000	Income Tax paid	28,000
Cash from operation	78,300	Closing cash balance (8,000 + 600)	8,600
	1,52,400		1,52,400

Workings : **1. Share Capital Account**

-	*Amount* ₹		*Amount* ₹
To Balance c/d	2,50,000	By Balance b/d	2,00,000
		By Stock	20,000
		By Machinery	25,000
		By Goodwill	5,000
	2,50,000		2,50,000

2. General Reserve Account

To Loss on sale of Machinery	200	By Balance b/d	50,000
To Balance c/d	60,000	By Profit & Loss A/c	10,200
	60,200		60,200

3. Provision for Taxation Account

To Cash (Tax paid)	28,000	By Balance b/d	30,000
To Balance c/d	35,000	By P & L A/c	33,000
	63,000		63,000

4. Profit and Loss Account

To Dividend Paid	23,000	By Balance b/d	30,500
To Depreciation on Machinery	12,000	By Cash from operation	78,300
To Income tax provided	33,000		
To Transfer to General Reserve	10,200		
To Balance c/d	30,600		
	1,08,800		1,08,800

5. Machinery Account

To Balance b/d	1,50,000	By Depreciation	12,000
To Shares	25,000	By Loss on sale of Machinery	200
To Cash	8,000	By Cash (b/f)	1,800
		By Balance c/d	1,69,000
	1,83,000		1,83,000

6. Stock Account

To Balance b/d	1,00,000	By Cash (b/f)	46,000
To Shares	20,000	By Balance c/d	74,000
	1,20,000		1,20,000

7. Goodwill Account

To Balance b/d	Nil	By Balance c/d	5,000
To Shares	5,000		
	5,000		5,000

NOTE : In the absence of direction, the differences in the Land & Building value (*i.e.,* 2,00,000 – 1,90,000 = 10,000) are treated as sale of Land & Building and not as depreciation. If any specific direction is given in the problem, we proceed with the problem according to the direction.

Problem 6. *Balance Sheets of M/s.Black and White as on 1st Jan.2000 and 31st Dec. 2000 were as follows.*

Liabilities	*Jan.2000* ₹	*Dec.2000* ₹	*Assets*	*Jan.2000* ₹	*Dec.2000* ₹
Creditors	*40,000*	*44,000*	*Cash*	*10,000*	*7,000*
White loan	*25,000*	—	*Debtors*	*30,000*	*50,000*
Loan from bank	*40,000*	*50,000*	*Stock*	*35,000*	*25,000*
Capital	*1,25,000*	*1,53,000*	*Land*	*40,000*	*50,000*
			Building	*35,000*	*60,000*
			Machinery	*80,000*	*55,000*
	2,30,000	*2,47,000*		*2,30,000*	*2,47,000*

During the year machine costing ₹ 10,000 (accumulated depreciation ₹ 3,000) was sold for ₹ 5,000. The provision for depreciation against machinery as on 1st Jan.2000 was ₹ 25,000 and on 31st Dec.2000 ₹ 40,000. Net profit for the year 2000 amounted to ₹ 45,000. Prepare cash flow statement. [M.Com. Madurai, MCA Bharathiar, BBM PU95]

Solution : **Cash Flow Statement**

Inflow of cash	*Amount* ₹	*Outflow of cash*	*Amount* ₹
Opening cash balance	10,000	Increase in Debtors	20,000
Decrease in stock	10,000	Purchase of Land	10,000
Increase in Creditors	4,000	Purchase of Buildings	25,000
Loan from Bank	10,000	Repayment of Mr.White's Loan	25,000
Sale of Machinery	5,000	Capital Account (3)(Drawings)	17,000
Cash from Operation (1)	65,000	Closing Cash Balance	7,000
	1,04,000		1,04,000

Workings : **1. Profit and Loss Account**

	Amount ₹		*Amount* ₹
To Loss on sale of Machinery	2,000	By Balance b/d	Nil
To Depreciation (4)	18,000	By Cash from operation	65,000
To Balance c/d	45,000		
	65,000		65,000

2. Machinery Account

To Balance b/d (80,000 + 25,000)	1,05,000	By Cash	5,000
		By P&L A/c	2,000
		By Accumulated Depreciation	3,000
		By Balance c/d (55,000 + 40,000)	95,000
	1,05,000		1,05,000

3. Capital Account

To Cash	17,000	By Balance b/d	1,25,000
To Balance c/d	1,53,000	By P&L A/c	45,000
	1,70,000		1,70,000

4. Accumulated Depreciation Account

To Machinery A/c	3,000	By Balance b/d	25,000
To Balance c/d	40,000	By P&L A/c	18,000
	43,000		43,000

Journal for Ist Adjustment :

Cash A/c	Dr.	5,000		(Sale of Machinery)
Accumulated Depreciation A/c	Dr.	3,000		(Depreciation)
P.L A/c	Dr.	2,000		(Loss on Sale of Machinery)
To Machinery A/c			10,000	

Problem 7. *From the following balance sheet of Exe Ltd., prepare cash flow statement*

Liabilities	*1999* ₹	*2000* ₹
Equity share capital	3,00,000	4,00,000
Redeemable preference Share capital	1,50,000	1,00,000
General Reserve	40,000	70,000
Profit & Loss A/c	30,000	48,000
Proposed dividend	42,000	50,000
Creditors	55,000	83,000
Bills Payable	20,000	16,000
Provision for taxation	40,000	50,000
	6,77,000	8,17,000

Assets	*1999* ₹	*2000* ₹
Goodwill	1,15,000	90,000
Land & Buildings	2,00,000	1,70,000
Plant	80,000	2,00,000
Debtors	1,60,000	2,00,000
Stock	77,000	1,09,000
Bills Receivable	20,000	30,000
Cash in hand	15,000	10,000
Cash at bank	10,000	8,000
	6,77,000	8,17,000

The following additional information is also available :

(a) Depreciation of ₹ 10,000 and ₹ 20,000 have been charged on Plant and Land and Buildings in 2000.

(b) A dividend of ₹ 20,000 has been paid in 2000.

(c) Income tax of ₹ 35,000 has been paid during 2000. [B.Com. PU 2004]

Solution : **Cash Flow Statement**

Inflow of cash	*Amount* ₹	*Outflow of cash*	*Amount* ₹
Opening Cash Balance	25,000	Redemption of preference Shares	50,000
Issue of Shares	1,00,000	Dividend paid	42,000
Increase in Sundry Creditors	28,000	Decrease in Bills Payable	4,000
Sale of Land & building	10,000	Increase in Debtors	40,000
Cash from operation	2,18,000	Increase in Stock	32,000
		Increase in bills receivable	10,000
		Purchase of Plant	1,30,000
		Interim dividend paid	20,000
		Income Tax paid	35,000
		Closing Cash balance (10,000 + 8,000)	18,000
	3,81,000		3,81,000

Workings : **1. Profit and Loss Account**

	Amount ₹		*Amount* ₹
To General Reserve	30,000	By Balance c/d	30,000
To Proposed dividend	50,000	By Cash from operation	2,18,000
To Goodwill written off	25,000		
To Depreciation of Plant	10,000		
To Depreciation of Land & Buildings	20,000		
To Interim dividend paid	20,000		
To Income Tax provided (2)	45,000		
To Balance c/d	48,000		
	2,48,000		2,48,000

2. Provision for Taxation Account

To Cash (Tax paid)	35,000	By Balance b/d	40,000
To Balance c/d	50,000	By P&L A/c (Tax Provisions)	45,000
	85,000		85,000

3. Land & Buildings Account

To Balance b/d	2,00,000	By Depreciation A/c	20,000
		By Balance c/d	1,70,000
		By Cash (b/f)	10,000
	2,00,000		2,00,000

4. Plant Account

To Balance b/d	80,000	By Depreciation	10,000
To Cash (b/f)	1,30,000	By Balance c/d	2,00,000
	2,10,000		2,10,000

Problem 8. *From the following comparative Balance Sheet of ABC Ltd. as on 31.12.2002 and 2002.*

Liabilities	*2001* ₹	*2002* ₹	*Assets*	*2001* ₹	*2002* ₹
Share Capital	*70,000*	*74,000*	*Cash*	*9,000*	*7,800*
Debentures	*12,000*	*6,000*	*Trade Debtors*	*14,900*	*17,700*
Creditors	*10,360*	*11,840*	*Marketable Securities*	*49,200*	*42,700*
Provision for Doubtful debts	*700*	*800*	*Land*	*20,000*	*30,000*
Profit & Loss A/c	*10,040*	*10,560*	*Goodwill*	*10,000*	*5,000*
	1,03,100	*1,03,200*		*1,03,100*	*1,03,200*

The following additional information is also available :

(i) *Dividend of ₹ 3,500 was paid during the year 2002.*

(ii) *Land was purchased for ₹ 10,000 and amount provided for the amortization of goodwill of ₹ 5,000.*

(iii) *Debentures was repaid ₹ 6,000.*

Prepare cash flow statement. [B.Com. Madurai]

Solution :

Cash Flow Statement

Inflow of cash	*Amount* ₹	*Outflow of cash*	*Amount* ₹
Opening cash balance	9,000	Increase in debtors	2,800
Issue of Shares	4,000	Dividend paid	3,500
Increase in Creditors	1,480	Purchase of land	10,000
Decrease in Marketable Securities	6,500	Redemption of debentures	6,000
Cash from operation	9,120	Closing cash balance	7,800
	30,100		30,100

Workings :

1. Profit and Loss Account

	Amount ₹		*Amount* ₹
To Provision for Doubtful debts	100	By Balance b/d	10,040
To Dividend Paid	3,500	By Cash from operation	9,120
To Goodwill written off	5,000		
To Balance c/d	10,560		
	19,160		19,160

2. Debentures Account

To Cash (b/f)	6,000	By Balance b/d	12,000
To Balance c/d	6,000		
	12,000		12,000

3. Land Account

To Balance b/d	20,000	By Balance c/d	30,000
To Cash	10,000		
	30,000		30,000

4. Goodwill Account

To Balance b/d	10,000	By P&L A/c	5,000
		By Balance c/d	5,000
	10,000		10,000

Problem 9. *From the following Balance Sheet of Gristol Ltd., make out the statement of sources and uses of case.*

Liabilities	*1998* ₹	*1999* ₹	*Assets*	*1998* ₹	*1999* ₹
Capital	*1,15,000*	*1,15,000*	*Cash & Bank*		
Sundry Creditors	*51,500*	*48,000*	*Balance*	*45,000*	*45,000*
Outstanding Expn.	*6,500*	*6,000*	*Sundry Debtors*	*33,500*	*21,500*
8% Debentures	*45,000*	*35,000*	*Temporary*		
Depreciation Fund	*20,000*	*22,000*	*Investment*	*55,000*	*37,000*
Reserve for			*Prepaid Expenses*	*500*	*1,000*
Contingencies	*30,000*	*30,000*	*Stock in Trade*	*41,000*	*53,000*
Profit & Loss A/c	*8,000*	*11,500*	*Land & Buildings*	*75,000*	*75,000*
			Machinery	*26,000*	*35,000*
	2,76,000	*2,67,500*		*2,76,000*	*2,67,500*

The following additional information is also available :

(i) *10% dividend was paid in cash.*

(ii) *New machinery for ₹ 15,000 was purchased but old machinery costing ₹ 6,000 was sold for ₹ 2,000; accumulated depreciation was ₹ 3,000.*

(iii) *₹ 10,000 8% debentures were redeemed by purchase from open market @ ₹ 96 for a debenture of ₹ 100.*

(iv) *₹ 18,000 investments were sold at book value.* [M.Com. Bombay]

Solution : **Cash Flow Statement**

Inflow of cash	Amount ₹	Outflow of cash	Amount ₹
Opening Cash balance	45,000	Decrease in Sundry Creditors	3,500
Decrease in Sundry debtors	12,000	Decrease in Outstanding Expenses	500
Sale of Machinery	2,000	Increase in prepaid expenses	500
Sale of Investments	18,000	Redemption of debentures	9,600
Cash from operation	20,600	Increase in Stock in Trade	12,000
		Payment of dividend	11,500
		Purchase of Machinery	15,000
		Closing Stock balance	45,000
	97,600		97,600

Workings : **1. Profit and Loss Account**

	Amount ₹		Amount ₹
To Payment of dividend	11,500	By Balance b/d	8,000
To Loss on sale of Machinery	1,000	By Profit on Redemption of Debentures (10,000-9,600)	400
To Depreciation	5,000	By Cash from operation	20,600
To Balance c/d	11,500		
	29,000		29,000

2. Accumulated Depreciation Account

To Machinery	22,000	By Balance b/d	20,000
To Balance c/d	3,000	By P&L A/c (b/f)	5,000
	25,000		25,000

3. Machinery Account

To Balance b/d	26,000	By Cash	2,000
To Cash (b/f)	15,000	By P&L A/c	1,000
		By Accumulated Depreciation	3,000
		By Balance c/d	35,000
	41,000		41,000

4. Debenture Account

To Cash	9,600	By Balance b/d	45,000
To Profit on Redemption	400		
To Balance c/d	35,000		
	45,000		45,000

5. Investment Account

To Balance b/d	55,000	By Cash	18,000
		By Balance c/d	37,000
	55,000		55,000

NOTE : Redemption of debenture $\frac{96}{100} \times 10{,}000 = 9{,}600$

Actual value of debenture	=	10,000
Amount paid	=	9,600
Profit on Redemption of debenture	=	400

Problem 10. *The Comparative Balance Sheets of Mr. Hitler for the two years are as follows.*

Liabilities	*2002* ₹	*2003* ₹	*Assets*	*2002* ₹	*2003* ₹
Loan from wife	—	*20,000*	*Cash*	*11,000*	*15,000*
Bills Payable	*12,000*	*8,000*	*Debtors*	*40,000*	*35,000*
Creditors	*25,000*	*52,000*	*Stock*	*25,000*	*30,000*
Loan from Bank	*43,000*	*60,000*	*Machinery*	*20,000*	*14,000*
Capital	*66,000*	*34,000*	*Land & Buildings*	*50,000*	*80,000*
	1,46,000	*1,74,000*		*1,46,000*	*1,74,000*

The following additional information is also available :

(i) Net Loss for the year 2003 amounted to ₹ 13,000.

(ii) During the year machine costing ₹ 5,000 (accumulated depreciation ₹ 2,000) was sold for ₹ 2,500. The provision for depreciation against machinery as on 31.12.2002 was ₹ 6,000 and on 31.12.2003 was ₹ 7,000. [MBA Anna 2005]

Solution : **Cash Flow Statement**

Inflow of cash	*Amount* ₹	*Outflow of cash*	*Amount* ₹
Opening Cash Balance	11,000	Decrease in bills payable	4,000
Loan borrowed from wife	20,000	Increase in Stock	5,000
Increase in Creditors	27,000	Purchase of Land & Buildings	30,000
Loan borrowed from bank	17,000	Drawings (2) (Capital A/c)	19,000
Decrease in Debtors	5,000	Cash from operation	9,500
Sale of Machinery	2,500	Closing cash balance	15,000
	82,500		82,500

Workings :

1. Profit and Loss Account

	Amount ₹		Amount ₹
To Loss on sale of Machinery	500	By Balance b/d	13,000
To Depreciation A/c	3,000		
To Cash from operation	9,500		
	13,000		13,000

2. Capital Account

To Profit & Loss A/c (Net Loss)	13,000	By Balance b/d	66,000
To Balance c/d	34,000		
To Cash (b/f)	19,000		
	66,000		66,000

3. Machinery Account

To Balance b/d (20,000 + 6,000)	26,000	By Cash	2,500
		By Profit & Loss A/c	500
		By Accumulated Depreciation	2,000
		By Balance c/d (14,000 + 7,000)	21,000
	26,000		26,000

4. Accumulated Depreciation Account

To Machinery A/c	2,000	By Balance b/d	6,000
To Balance c/d	7,000	By P&L A/c	3,000
	9,000		9,000

NOTE :

Journal Entry for IInd Adjustment

Cash A/c	Dr.	2,500		(Sale price)
Accumulated Depreciation	Dr.	2,500		(Depreciation)
Profit & Loss A/c	Dr.	500		(Loss)
To Machinery			5,000	(Value of machinery)

Problem 11. *From the comparative balance sheets of Serial Engineering Ltd. As at 31.12.1998 and other information furnished, prepare a cash flow statement for the year ended on 31.12.1998.*

Liabilities	*1997* ₹	*1998* ₹	*Assets*	*1997* ₹	*1998* ₹
Equity Share Capital	*50,000*	*2,00,000*	*Fixed Assets*	*2,40,000*	*4,20,000*
			Investments	*18,000*	*15,000*
Redeemable Pref. Share Capital	*1,00,000*	—	*Stock*	*58,500*	*1,60,000*
			Sundry Debtors	*1,37,000*	*92,000*
Retained Earning	*1,20,000*	*3,50,000*	*Cash at Bank*	*1,85,000*	*1,20,000*
Unsecured Loan	*1,25,000*	—	*Prepaid expenses*	*6,500*	*8,000*
Bills payable	*2,25,000*	*1,90,000*			
Provision for Tax	*25,000*	*75,000*			
	6,45,000	*8,15,000*		*6,45,000*	*8,15,000*

The following additional information is also available :

(i) On 31.12.1998 accumulated depreciation on fixed assets amounted to ₹ 1,20,000 and on 31st December 1997 to ₹ 1,10,000.

(ii) Machinery costing ₹ 10,000 (Accumulated depreciation thereon being ₹ 5,000) was discarded and written off during 1998.

(iii) Depreciation written off during 1998 amounted to ₹ 15,000.

(iv) During the year 1998 investments costing ₹ 6,000 were sold for ₹ 7,000.

(v) Dividend paid during the year was ₹ 45,000.

(vi) Redeemable preference shares were redeemed out of profile during the year at a premium of 5%.

Solution : **Cash Flow Statement**

Inflow of cash	*Amount* ₹	*Outflow of cash*	*Amount* ₹
Opening Cash Balance	1,85,000	Repayment unsecured loan	1,25,000
Issue of Shares	1,50,000	Decrease in bills payable	35,000
Increase in provision for taxation	50,000	Increase in stock	1,01,500
Decrease in Sundry Debtors	45,000	Increase in prepaid expenses	1,500
		Dividend paid	45,000
Sale of Investments	7,000	Purchase of fixed assets (3)	2,00,000
Cash from operation	2,99,000	Redemption of preference Shares	1,05,000
		Purchase of investment (4)	3,000
		Closing Cash balance	1,20,000
	7,36,000		7,36,000

Workings : **1. Profit and Loss Account**

	Amount ₹		Amount ₹
To Loss on Machinery (Discarded)	5,000	By Balance b/d	1,20,000
		By Profit on sale of Investment	1,000
To Dividend paid	45,000	By Cash from Operation	2,99,000
To Premium on Redemption of Preference shares	5,000		
To Depreciation	15,000		
To Balance c/d	3,50,000		
	4,20,000		4,20,000

2. Redeemable Preference Share Capital Account

To Cash	1,05,000	By Balance b/d	1,00,000
		By Premium	5,000
	1,05,000		1,05,000

3. Fixed Assets Account (Machinery)

To Balance b/d	3,50,000	By Profit & Loss A/c	5,000
To Cash	2,00,000	By Accumulated Depreciation	5,000
		By Balance c/d (4,20,000 + 1,20,000)	5,40,000
	5,50,000		5,50,000

4. Investment Account

To Balance b/d	18,000	By Cash	6,000
To Cash	3,000	By Balance c/d	15,000
	21,000		21,000

5. Accumulated Depreciation Account

To Balance c/d	1,20,000	By Balance b/d	1,10,000
To Machinery	5,000	By P&L A/c	15,000
	1,25,000		1,25,000

NOTE : Journal Entry for Adjustment (*ii* & *iv*)

(*ii*)	Profit & Loss A/c	Dr.	5,000	
	Accumulated Depreciation A/c	Dr.	5,000	
	To Machinery A/c			10,000
(*iv*)	Cash A/c	Dr.	7,000	
	To Profit & Loss A/c			1,000
	To Investment A/c			6,000

Problem 12. *Prepare a cash flow statement from the balance sheets of TTD & Co. as on 31.3.2000 and 31.3.2001. (₹ In thousands)*

Liabilities	*2000* ₹	*2001* ₹	*Assets*	*2000* ₹	*2001* ₹
Capital	*140*	*140*	*Fixed Assets (Net)*	*90*	*87*
Reserves	*74*	*105*	*Cash*	*75*	*97*
Creditors	*32*	*35*	*Debtors*	*43*	*40*
Outstanding			*Inventory*	*49*	*58*
Wages	*3*	*4*	*Prepaid Expenses*	*3*	*5*
Expenses					
Outstanding	*11*	*3*			
	260	*287*		*260*	*287*

Accumulated depreciation was ₹ 16,000 and ₹ 19,000 respectively at the beginning and end of the year 2001.

Other information Sales ₹ 3,00,000, Wages ₹ 23,000, Operating Expenses ₹ 47,000, Cost of goods ₹1,90,000, Rent ₹ 6,000 and Depreciation ₹ 3,000. [MBA Madras]

Solution : **Cash Flow Statement**

Inflow of cash	*Amount* ₹	*Outflow of cash*	*Amount* ₹
Opening cash balance	75,000	Increase in inventory	9,000
Increase in creditors	3,000	Decrease in Miscellaneous	
Increase in wages outstanding	1,000	Expenses outstanding	8,000
Decrease on debtors	3,000	Increase in prepaid expenses	2,000
Cash from operation (1)	34,000	Closing cash balance	97,000
	1,16,000		1,16,000

Workings : **1. Profit and Loss Account**

	Amount ₹		*Amount* ₹
To Depreciation	3,000	By Balance b/d	74,000
To Balance c/d	1,05,000	By Cash operation	34,000
	1,08,000		1,08,000

2. Fixed Assets Account

To Balance b/d (90,000 + 16,000)	1,06,000	By Balance c/d (87,000 + 19,000)	1,06,000
	1,06,000		1,06,000

3. Accumulated Depreciation Account

To Balance c/d	19,000	By Balance b/d	16,000
		By P&L A/c (Current year Depreciation)	3,000
	19,000		19,000

Problem *13. Kapin Ltd. furnishes you the following balance sheet for the year ending on 31.12.2002 and 2003. You are required to prepare cash flow statement of the year ended on 31.12.2003.*

Liabilities	*2002* ₹	*2003* ₹	*Assets*	*2002* ₹	*2003* ₹
Equity Share Capital	*10,000*	*10,000*	*Goodwill*	*1,200*	*1,200*
General Reserve	*1,400*	*1,800*	*Land*	*4,000*	*3,600*
Profit & Loss A/c	*1,600*	*1,300*	*Building*	*3,700*	*3,600*
Sundry Creditors	*800*	*540*	*Equipment*	*1,000*	*1,100*
Bills payable	*120*	*80*	*Stock*	*3,000*	*2,340*
Provision for Taxation	*1,600*	*1,800*	*Accounts Receivable*	*2,000*	*2,220*
Provision for Bad Debts	*40*	*60*	*Bank Balance*	*660*	*1,520*
	15,560	*15,580*		*15,560*	*15,580*

The following additional information is also available :

(i) A piece of land has also been sold for ₹ 800.

(ii) Depreciation amounting to ₹ 600 has been charged on building.

(iii) Provision for taxation has been made for ₹ 1,700 during the year.

[B.Com. Adapted]

Solution : **Cash Flow Statement**

Inflow of cash	*Amount* ₹	*Outflow of cash*	*Amount* ₹
Opening Cash balance	660	Decrease in Sundry Creditors	260
Decrease in stock	660	Decrease in Bills payable	40
Sale of land	800	Purchase of equipment	100
Cash from operation	2,420	Increase in account receivables	220
		Tax paid	1,500
		Purchase of building	500
		Land purchased	400
		Closing Cash balance	1,520
	4,540		4,540

Workings :

1. Profit and Loss Account

	Amount ₹		Amount ₹
To General Reserve	400	By Balance b/d	1,600
To Provision for Doubtful debts	20	By Cash from Operation	2,420
To Depreciation on Building	600		
To Income Tax Provision	1,700		
To Balance c/d	1,300		
	4,020		4,020

2. Provision for Taxation Account

To Cash (Tax paid)	1,500	By Balance b/d	1,600
To Balance c/d	1,800	By Profit & Loss A/c (Income Tax provision)	1,700
	3,300		3,300

3. Land Account

To Balance b/d	4,000	By Cash	800
To Cash	400	By Balance c/d	3,600
	4,400		4,400

4. Building Account

To Balance b/d	3,700	By Depreciation (P&L A/c)	600
To Cash	500	By Balance c/d	3,600
	4,200		4,200

Cash Flow (AS 3) Revised Format

Under the revised format, cash flow statement should be prepared in such a way as to report the cash flows during the periods separately for operating, investing and financing activities.

I Cash Flows from Operating Activities

Net profit earned during the year	xx
Add : Depreciation	xx
Loss on sale of machinery	xx
Preliminary expenses written off	xx
Goodwill written off	xx
Patents and copy right written off	xx
Operating profit before working capital changes	xx

	Adjustment of working capital		
	(Add cash flow, less cash outflows)		
	Decrease in current assets	xx	
	Decrease in current liabilities	xx	
	Increase in current assets	xx	
	Increase in current liabilities	xx	
	Cash flows from operating activities		xx
II	**Cash Flows from Investing Activities**		
	Purchase of machinery	xx	
	Purchase of land & building	xx	
	Purchase of goodwill	xx	
	Purchase of furniture	xx	
	Sale of machinery	xx	
	Sale of land & building	xx	
	Sale of furniture	xx	
	Interest on investment received	xx	
	Cash flows from investing activities		xx
III	**Cash Flows from Financing Activities**		
	Issue shares	xx	
	Issue debentures	xx	
	Loan borrowed	xx	
	Redemption of shares	xx	
	Redemption of debentures	xx	
	Loan repaid	xx	
	Dividend paid	xx	
	Interim dividend paid	xx	
	Drawings	xx	
	Net cash flows from financing activities		xx
	Net increase or decrease in cash and cash equivalent		xx
	Add : Opening cash balance		
	(Adjust BOD if any given the problem)		xx
	Closing cash Balance		xx
	(Adjust BOD if any given the problem)		

NOTE : In the question will specifically mention for the applying revised methods only, we follow the revised format otherwise better to follow Existing format.

Problem 14. *Prepare cash flow statement under Revised format from the following balance sheets of Tiruchengodu Traders Ltd.*

Liabilities	*2000* ₹	*2001* ₹	*Assets*	*2000* ₹	*2001* ₹
Share Capital	*17,00,000*	*18,35,000*	*Buildings*	*8,00,000*	*10,00,000*
Reserves	*40,000*	*83,700*	*Plant and Machinery*	*2,50,000*	*3,70,000*
P & LAPP. A/c	*1,00,000*	*1,30,000*	*Furniture*	*5,000*	*6,000*
Provision for dividends	*70,000*	*50,000*	*Cash*	*2,000*	*2,200*
Creditors	*1,00,000*	*95,000*	*Debtors*	*1,00,000*	*45,000*
Bank overdraft	*8,000*	*18,000*	*Bills receivable*	*8,000*	*9,000*
Bills payable	*14,000*	*13,000*	*Stock*	*4,00,000*	*3,43,700*
Mortgage Loan	*10,000*	*70,000*	*Prepaid expenses*	*3,000*	*3,100*
			Investments	*1,64,000*	*1,70,000*
			Goodwill	*3,00,000*	*3,43,700*
			Preliminary Expenses	*10,000*	*2,000*
	20,42,000	*22,94,700*		*20,42,000*	*22,94,700*

The following additional information is also available :

(a) *Depreciation is charged on buildings at 3% of cost of ₹ 9,00,000 on plant and machinery at 8% of cost of ₹ 4,00,000; Furniture at 5% of cost ₹ 8,000.*

(b) *Investments were purchased and interest was received ₹ 3,000 which was used in writing down the book value of investment.*

(c) *The declared dividends for 70,000 were paid and interim dividend for ₹ 20,000 was paid out of P & L App. A/c.*

Solution : Cash Flow Statement (Revised Method)

		₹	₹
I	Cash flow from operating activities :		
	Net profit before tax and extraordinary item	1,43,700	
	Adjustment for depreciation for furniture	400	
	Adjustment for depreciation for plant and machinery	32,000	
	Adjustment for depreciation on buildings	27,000	
	Preliminary expenses written off	8,000	
	Operating profit before working capital changes	2,11,100	
	Decrease in debtors	55,000	
	Decrease in stock	56,300	
	Decrease in creditors	(5,000)	
	Increase in bills receivable	(1,000)	
	Decrease in bills payable	(1,000)	
	Increase in prepaid expenses	(100)	
	Net cash flow from investing activities		3,15,300
II	Cash flow from investing activities :		
	Interest on investments	3,000	
	Purchase of investment	(9,000)	
	Purchase of buildings	(2,27,000)	
	Purchase of machinery	(1,52,000)	
	Purchase of furniture	(1,400)	
	Purchase of goodwill	(43,700)	
	Net cash flow from investing activities		4,30,100

III	Cash flow from financing activities :		
	Issue of shares	1,35,000	
	Mortgage loan	60,000	
	Dividend paid for 2000	(70,000)	
	Interim dividend paid	(20,000)	
	Net cash flows from financing activities		1,05,000
	Net increase (decrease) in cash and cash equivalents		(9,800)
	Cash and cash equivalents opening balance (Bank O/D-cash)		(6,000)
	Cash and cash equivalents closing balance (Bank O/D -cash)		(15,800)

Workings :

1. Profit and Loss A/c

To Balance c/d	1,30,000	By Balance b/d	1,00,000
To Transfer reserves	43,700		
To Provision for dividend	50,000	By	1,43,700
To Interim dividend paid	20,000		
	2,43,700		2,43,700

2. Buildings A/c

To Balance b/d	8,00,000	By Balance c/d	10,00,000
To Purchase (Bf)	2,27,000	By Depreciation (9,00,000 × 3/100)	27,000
	10,27,000		10,27,000

3. Plant and Machinery A/c

To Balance b/d	2,50,000	By Balance c/d	3,70,000
To Purchase (Bf)	1,52,000	By Depreciation (4,00,000 × 8/100)	32,000
	4,02,000		4,02,000

4. Furniture A/c

To Balance b/d	5,000	By Balance c/d	6,000
To Purchase (Bf)	1,400	By Depreciation (8,000 × 5/100)	400
	6,400		6,400

5. Investment A/c

To Balance b/d	1,64,000	By Balance c/d	1,70,000
To Purchase Investment (Bf)	9,000	By Bank (Interest)	3,000
	1,73,000		1,73,000

TEST PROBLEMS

1. From the following Balance Sheet of Arvind Ltd., you are required to prepare a cash flow statement:

Liabilities	*1989* ₹	*1990* ₹	*Assets*	*1989* ₹	*1990* ₹
Share Capital	4,00,000	5,00,000	Cash	60,000	94,000
Trade Creditors	1,40,000	90,000	Debtors	2,40,000	2,30,000
Profit & Loss A/c	20,000	46,000	Stock	1,60,000	1,80,000
			Land	1,00,000	1,32,000
	5,60,000	**6,36,000**		**5,60,000**	**6,36,000**

[**Ans:** Closing balance of cash ₹ 94,000, Total cash available ₹ 1,60,000, CFO ₹ 34,000]

2. From the following Balance Sheet as on 31.12.93 and 31.12.92, prepare a Cash Flow Statement:

Liabilities	*1993* ₹	*1992* ₹	*Assets*	*1993* ₹	*1992* ₹
Share Capital	1,50,000	1,00,000	Fixed assets	1,50,000	1,00,000
Profit & Loss A/c	80,000	50,000	Goodwill	40,000	50,000
General Reserve	40,000	30,000	Stock	80,000	30,000
6% Debentures	60,000	50,000	Debtors	80,000	50,000
Creditors	40,000	30,000	Bills Receivable	20,000	30,000
Outstanding exp.	15,000	10,000	Bank	15,000	10,000
	3,85,000	**2,70,000**		**3,85,000**	**2,70,000**

[Manonmaniam Sundarnar, B.Com., Nov. 1994]

[**Ans:** Total cash available ₹ 70,000, Closing balance at bank ₹ 15,000, CFO ₹ 5,000]

3. The summarized Balance Sheet of Kandan Ltd., as on 31.12.91 and 31.12.92 are as following:

Liabilities	*1991* ₹	*1992* ₹	*Assets*	*1991* ₹	*1992* ₹
Share capital	4,50,000	4,50,000	Fixed assets	4,00,000	3,20,000
General reserve	3,00,000	3,10,000	Investment	50,000	60,000
P&L A/c	56,000	68,000	Stock	2,40,000	2,10,000
Creditors	1,68,000	1,34,000	Debtors	2,10,000	4,55,000
Tax provision	75,000	10,000	Bank	1,49,000	1,97,000
Mortgage loan	-	2,70,000			
	10,49,000	**12,42,000**		**10,49,000**	**12,42,000**

Additional Details

(1) Investments costing ₹ 8,000 were sold for ₹ 8,500.

(2) Tax provision made the year was ₹ 9,000.

(3) During the year part of the fixed assets costing ₹ 10,000 was sold for ₹ 12,000 and the profit was included in P&L Account. You are required to prepare cash flow statement for 1992.

[Madras, B.Com., (CS) (SY6A) April 2007; M.Com., April 1993]

[**Ans:** Total cash available ₹ 4,39,500, Closing balance at bank 1,97,000, CFO ₹ 1,50,500. Note: Investments and tax provision are treated as 'non current' items]

4. The following shows the balance in condensed from of Pavitra Ltd. At the beginning as well as at the end of the year 1987:

Liabilities	*1.1.87* ₹	*31.12.87* ₹	*Assets*	*1.1.87* ₹	*31.12.87* ₹
Creditors	52,000	47,500	Cash & Bank balance	45,000	45,000
Outstanding exp.	6,000	6,500	Debtors	38,500	26,500
8% Debentures	45,000	35,000	Investments	50,000	32,000
Depreciation fund	20,000	22,000	Prepaid expenses	500	1,000
Reserve for contingencies	30,000	30,000	Stock-in-trade	41,000	53,000
			Land & Building	77,000	77,000
P&L A/c	8,000	11,500	Machinery	24,000	33,000
Share capital	1,15,000	1,15,000			
	2,76,000	**2,67,500**		**2,76,000**	**2,67,500**

The following information is also available

(*a*) 10% dividend was paid in cash.

(*b*) New Machinery for ₹ 15,000 was purchased but old machinery costing ₹ 6,000 was sold for ₹ 2,000 on which accumulated depreciation was ₹ 3,000.

(*c*) ₹ 10,000 Debentures were redeemed by purchase from open market at ₹ 96 for a debenture of ₹ 100.

(*d*) Investments were sold at book value.

Prepare a Cash Flow statement

[Madras, 1st M.Com., (CA2A) AP 2005, M.Com., April 1988]

[**Ans.** Total cash available ₹ 81,100, closing cash and bank balance ₹ 45,000, CFO ₹ 16,100]

5. From the following balance you are required to calculate cash from operations:

	31.12.89 ₹	31.12.90 ₹
P & L. A/c balance	50,000	3,10,000
Debtors	90,000	84,000
Creditors	40,000	52,000
Bills Receivable	24,000	30,000
Prepaid expenses	3,200	2,800
Bills Payable	30,000	32,000
Outstanding expenses	2,400	3,200
Outstanding Income	1,600	1,800
Income received in advance	500	600

[Madras, M.Com., Sep 1991; B.Com., Nov.1991 (1/2 figures)]

[**Ans.** Cash from operations ₹ 2,75,100 (2,60,000 + 21,300 – 6,200)]

6. From the following Balance Sheets as on 31st December, prepare a Cash Flow statement and Adjusted P & L A/c.

Liabilities	*31.12,2000* ₹	*31.12.2001* ₹	*Assets*	*31.12.2000* ₹	*31.12.2001* ₹
Share Capital	1,00,000	1,50,000	Fixed assets	1,00,000	1,50,000
P & L A/c	50,000	80,000	Goodwill	50,000	40,000
General Reserve	30,000	40,000	Inventories	50,000	80,000
16% Bonds	50,000	60,000	Debtors	50,000	80,000
Sundry creditors	30,000	40,000	Bill Receivable	10,000	20,000
Expenses outstanding	10,000	15,000	Bank	10,000	15,000
	2,70,000	**3,85,000**		**2,70,000**	**3,85,000**

[Madras, 1st M.Com. (CA2A) April 2007; B.Com., (C&M) Oct. 2001; B.A. Corp. C&M, May 1998; March 1989; M.Com., Sep 1985]

[**Ans:** Funds from operations ₹ 50,000; Cash Outflow on account of operation: ₹ 5,000; Sources of cash: ₹ 60,000; Applications of cash: ₹ 55,000 (including cash outflow on account of operations).

7. The Comparative Balance Sheet of Mr. Wheldon for the two years were as follows:

Liabilities	*1988* ₹	*1989* ₹	*Assets*	*1988* ₹	*1989* ₹
Capital	1,50,000	1,75,000	Land & Buildings	1,10,000	1,50,000
Loan from Bank	1,60,000	1,00,000	Machinery	2,00,000	1,40,000
Creditors	90,000	1,00,000	Stock	50,000	45,000
Bills Payable	50,000	40,000	Debtors	70,000	80,000
Loan from IFC	-	25,000	Cash	20,000	25,000
	4,50,000	**4,40,000**		**4,50,000**	**4,40,000**

Additional Information :

Net profit of the year 1989 amounted to ₹ 60,000. During the year a machine costing ₹ 25,000 (accumulated depreciation ₹ 10,000) was sold for ₹ 13,000. The provision for depreciation against machinery as on 31-12-88 was ₹ 50,000 and on 31-12-89 ₹ 85,000. You are required to prepare a Cash Flow Statement. *[Bharathiyar, B.B.M. (CA) Nov. 2007; Madras, B.Com., Sep. 1990]*

[**Ans:** Cash from operations: ₹ 1,02,000; Funds from operations: ₹ 1,07,000; Drawing: ₹ 35,000; Sources of Cash: ₹ 1,40,000; Applications of Cash: ₹ 1,35,000; Current year's depreciation: ₹ 45,000]

8. The Balance Sheet of Thiruganananam Ltd., for the year 1989 and 1990 were as follows:

Liabilities	*1989* ₹	*1990* ₹	*Assets*	*1989* ₹	*1990* ₹
Share capital	1,50,000	1,75,000	Buildings	1,10,000	1,50,000
Profit & Loss A/c	1,20,000	80,000	Plant	2,00,000	1,40,000
Loan from bank	1,40,000	20,000	Stock	50,000	45,000
Creditors	85,000	93,000	Debtors	70,000	80,000
Outstanding exp.	5,000	7,000	Cash	15,000	22,000
Bills payable	50,000	40,000	Prepaid expenses	5,000	3,000
Loan from IFC	-	25,000			
	4,50,000	**4,40,000**		**4,50,000**	**4,40,000**

Additional Information

(*a*) Net profit for the year 1990 ₹ 60,000.

(*b*) During the year a plant costing ₹ 25,000 (accumulated depreciation ₹ 10,000) was sold for ₹ 13,000.

(*c*) The provision for depreciation against plant as on 31-12-89 was ₹ 50,000 and on 31-12-90 was ₹ 85,000.

You are required to prepare a Cash Flow Statement. *[Madras B.Com., Oct. 1993]*

[**Ans:** Cash from operations ₹ 1,04,000; Funds from operations: ₹ 1,07,000; Sources of cash: ₹ 1,67,000; Uses: ₹ 1,60,000; Depreciation on machinery for 1990: ₹ 45,000]

9. The following are the Balance Sheet of Velavan Brothers Ltd., as on 31st, March 1986 and 1987.

Balance sheet

Liabilities	*31.3.87* ₹	*31.3.86* ₹	*Assets*	*31.3.87* ₹	*31.3.86* ₹
Share capital	5,000	4,000	Fixed assets	4,000	4,100
Profit and Loss A/c	320	300	*Less:* Depreciation	4,000	4,000
Debentures	700	600		1,500	1,100
				2,500	3,000
Creditors	1,400	1,700	Debtors	2,400	2,000
Provision of tax	420	300	Prepaid expenses	50	30
Proposed dividend	580	500	Preliminary exp.	300	500
Bank Overdraft	680	1,250	Cash	350	120
			Stock	3,500	3,000
	9,100	**8,650**		**9,100**	**8,650**

Additional Information:

1. Tax paid during the year ending 31.3.87 ₹ 350.
2. Dividend proposed during the year ending 31.3.87 ₹ 400.
3. Fixed assets coasting ₹ 700, accumulated depreciation thereon ₹ 300 were sold at book value.

You are required to prepare a cash flow statement.

[Madras, B.Com., B.Com. (CS) etc Nov. 2008; Madurai, B.Com., April 1993 adapted]

[**Ans:** Cash from operations: ₹ 570; Funds from operations: ₹ 1,790; Sources of Cash: ₹ 2,070; Uses of Cash : ₹ 1,270; Purchase of Fixed Assets: ₹ 600; Depreciation for the year ending 31-3-86 : ₹ 700; Provision made for Tax : ₹ 470; Dividend paid : ₹ 320; Opening balance (OD–Cash) + Sources–Applications = Closing balance (OD–Cash) (1,250–120) = –1,130 O.D + 2070 = 330 O.D. (380–350)]

❑❑❑

7
Ratio Analysis

MEANING

Ratio is simply a number expressed in terms of another. It refers to the numerical or quantitative relationship between two variables that are comparable. It is a comparison of the numerator with the denominator.

In other words, the ratio means relationship between two figures expressed mathematically. It can be expressed in terms of percentage proportions and quotient too.

SIGNIFICANCE OF RATIO ANALYSIS

Ratio analysis is an effective and suitable tool of financial analysis. Analysis of financial statement with the support of ratios would guide the management in important decision making, implementation and control. Ratio analysis is an instrument for diagnosing the financial health of an enterprise. The usefulness of the ratio analysis is not only for the financial manager, but also to various parties who are interested to know different purposes of financial information. In the real sense, ratio analysis is based on the accounting data contained in the financial statements. Various classifications of ratios are used for different purposes.

ADVANTAGES OF RATIO ANALYSIS

1. *Simplifies financial statement.* Financial Statement contains the summary of one year's financial activities that is, application of Ratio as against the financial statements. The interested people can know the information without any difficulty because the entire financial statement is simplified in an easy manner.
2. *Facilitates intra-firm comparison.* Analysis and interpretation of a particular firm over a period of year can be made. And also comparison among different divisions of the organisation is made easy with the help of various ratios.
3. *Planning and Forecasting.* Actually ratios are derived from the past financial statements. Ratios give suitable guidance to management for formulating various budgets and construct relevant policies and also to prepare the future plan of action etc.
4. *Aid to inter firm comparison.* Comparison between two or more firms is more essential. In this regard, absolute figures are not sufficient to determine the correct comparison of firms. With the help of the ratios, one firm is able to compare with another firm and also find out their position.

5. *Facilitates decision making.* Ratios throw light on the degree of efficiency of the management and utilisation of the assets. That is why it is called surveyor of efficiency. They help the management in the aspect of decision making.
6. *Helps in corrective action.* Ratio analysis facilitates the inter-firm comparison. It exposes the successful and unsuccessful firms. At the time of comparison, if any of the unfavourable variations are identified, immediately the corrective actions should be taken.
7. *Aid to co-ordination.* The management wants to establish harmonious and cordial relationship among all the departments in the organisation. Meanwhile, the strength and weakness of the organisation should be communicated in an easily understandable manner. This type of quick and clear communication can achieve better co-ordination.

LIMITATIONS OF RATIO ANALYSIS

1. *Limitations of financial statements.* Ratios are usually calculated on the past year's financial data contained in the financial statement. In the real sense, financial statements suffer a number of limitations. When ratios are derived from the financial statements, they also suffer from the same limitations.
2. *Differences in Definition.* There is no clear cut formula for computing ratios. Each and every company follows a separate formula for computing different ratios. Due to these different types of formulas, comparison of different industries becomes difficult.
3. *Ratios alone are not adequate.* Various tools are available for evaluating the financial performance of a company. Under this aspect, ratios are tools of quantitative analysis only. Normally qualitative factors which may generally influence the arrival of conclusion are ignored while computing ratios.
4. *Problems of price level changes.* Even though there are certain limitations, inflation is utmost important for industrial and economic development of the country. Due to this aspect, price fluctuation could not be eliminated. Ratios fail to reflect the price level changes as they are based on Historical data. Hence, they may give misleading results when inflationary conditions are ignored.
5. *It is not substitute for personal judgement.* It is only a beginning and gives limited information for decision making. It is just an aid and cannot replace thinking and personal judgement employed in the decision making aspect.
6. *Ratios can be manipulated.* There will be a great demand for goods during the festival season when compared to previous periods. Suppose this inventory turnover ratio is considered for decision making, the results get distorted. It is necessary to take the average inventories to present a fair view of the business activity.

   Despite certain limitations, ratio analysis continues to be a powerful tool for analysis and interpretation of financial statements.

CLASSIFICATION OF RATIOS

For the purpose of financial performance analysis, ratios are classified into the following categories.

A. Liquidity (Short-term Solvency) Ratios

Formula

1. $\textit{Current Ratio} = \dfrac{\text{Current Assets}}{\text{Current Liabilities}}$

   Current Assets

   Cash in hand and Bank, Stock, sundry Debtors, bills receivable, short term investments, marketable securities, accrued incomes, prepaid expenses.

   Current Liabilities

   Sundry creditors, bills payable, Bank overdraft, outstanding expenses, income received in advance, income tax provisions, bad debts provisions, dividend payable, any other account which is payable in short period.

2. Quick Ratio or Liquid Ratio or Acid test ratio

   $$\textit{Acid Test Ratio} = \frac{\text{Quick Assets}}{\text{Quick Liabilities}} \text{ (or) } \frac{\text{Liquid Assets}}{\text{Liquid Liabilities}} \text{ (or) } \frac{\text{LA}}{\text{CL}}$$

   Quick assets or liquid assets = All current assets except stock

   Quick Liabilities or liquid liabilities = All current liabilities except bank overdraft

3. $\textit{Cash Position Ratio} = \dfrac{\text{Cash + Marketable Securities}}{\text{Current Liabilities}}$

4. $\textit{Net working Capital Ratio} = \dfrac{\text{Net working Capital}}{\text{Net Assets}}$

   Net working capital = Current assets – Current liabilities

5. $\textit{Solvency Ratio} = \dfrac{\text{Outside Liabilities}}{\text{Total Assets}}$

B. Long-term Solvency Ratios

1. $$\textit{Debt-Equity Ratio} = \frac{\text{Debt}}{\text{Equity}} \text{ (or) } \frac{\text{External Equities}}{\text{Internal Equities}} \text{ (or) } \frac{\text{Outsider's Fund}}{\text{Shareholder's Fund}}$$

   External Equities refer to the total outside liabilities. The term internal equities refers to all claims of preference shareholders and equity share holders such as share capital reserves and surplus. Outsider's fund refers to all short term debts like mortgage, bills etc.

   Computation of long term financial ratios, the term debt, like debentures are to be considered.

   Acceptable norm for this ratio is considered to be 2:1.

2. $$\textit{Proprietary Ratio} = \frac{\text{Shareholder's Fund}}{\text{Total Assets}} \text{ (or) } \frac{\text{Shareholder's Fund}}{\text{Total Tangible Assets}}$$

   Shareholder's fund includes preference share capital, Equity share capital, Reserves surplus, Profit & Loss Account Balance if any.

Total Assets

Total assets represent all assets including goodwill. But total tangible assets means total assets minus goodwill, Profit & Loss A/c (Debit) Balance, Preliminary Expenses.

3. *Ratio of fixed assets to proprietor's fund* $= \dfrac{\text{Fixed Assets}}{\text{Proprietor's Fund}}$

[Fixed assets are valued at original cost of the assets less depreciation].

4. *Current assets to proprietor's fund Ratio* $= \dfrac{\text{Current Assets}}{\text{Proprietor's Fund}}$

C. Profitability Ratios

1. *Gross Profit Ratio* $= \dfrac{\text{Gross Profit}}{\text{Sales}} \times 100$

2. *Net Profit Ratio* $= \dfrac{\text{Net Profit}}{\text{Sales}} \times 100$

3. *Operating Ratio* $= \dfrac{\text{Cost of Goods Sold + Operating Expenses}}{\text{Sales}} \times 100$

Cost of Goods Sold = Sales – Gross Profit

Operating Expenses = All the expenses debited in the profit & Loss A/c except financial expenses *i.e.,* Administrative Expenses, Selling & Distribution Expenses, Financial Expenses.

Financial expenses may or may not include the operating expenses.

4. *Return on Capital Employed* $= \dfrac{\text{Return}}{\text{Capital Employed}} \times 100$

Return : Net profit

Capital employed : Share holders fund + long term liabilities

(*or*)

Fixed assets + Current Assets – Current Liabilities

$$\frac{\text{Profit Before Tax and Interest}}{\text{Capital Employed}}$$

5. *Operating Profit Ratio* $= \dfrac{\text{Operating Profit}}{\text{Net Sales}} \times 100$

Operating Profit = Net Profit + Non-Operating Expenses-Non-Operating Income

6. *Return on Total Assets* $= \dfrac{\text{Return}}{\text{Total Assets}} \times 100$

[Return = PAT]

7. *Return on Shareholder Return* $= \dfrac{\text{Return}}{\text{Shareholder's Fund}} \times 100$

8. *Dividend Payout Ratio* $= \dfrac{\text{Dividend Per Share}}{\text{Earning Per Share}}$

9. $\textit{Dividend Per Share} = \dfrac{\text{Dividend paid to Equity Shareholders}}{\text{No. of Equity Shares}}$

10. $\textit{Earning Per Equity Share} = \dfrac{\text{Profit Available to Equity Shares}}{\text{No. of Equity Shares}}$

11. $\textit{Dividend Yield} = \dfrac{\text{Dividend Per Share}}{\text{Market Price Per Share}}$

12. $\textit{Price Earning Ratio} = \dfrac{\text{Market Price of a Share}}{\text{Earning Per Share}}$

13. $\textit{Fixed Interest Coverage} = \dfrac{\text{Operating Income}}{\text{Annual Interest Expenses}}$

14. $\textit{Interest Coverage Ratio} = \dfrac{\text{EBIT}}{\text{Fixed Interest Expenses}}$

D. Activity or Turnover Ratios

1. $\textit{Stock Turnover Ratio} = \dfrac{\text{Cost of Goods Sold}}{\text{Average Stock}}$

2. *Debtors Turnover Ratio or Debtors Velocity*

$$= \frac{\text{Debtors + Bills Receivable}}{\text{Credit Sales}} \times \text{No. of Working Days}$$

3. $\textit{Creditors Turnover Ratio} = \dfrac{\text{Creditors + Bills Payable}}{\text{Credit Purchase}} \times 365$

4. $\textit{Average Payment Period} = \dfrac{\text{Account Payable}}{\text{Net Credit Purchase}} \times 365$

5. $\textit{Working Capital Turnover Ratio} = \dfrac{\text{Cost of Sales}}{\text{Net Working Capital}}$

6. $\textit{Fixed Assets Turnover Ratio} = \dfrac{\text{Cost of Sales}}{\text{Net Fixed Assets}}$

7. $\textit{Total Capital Turnover Ratio} = \dfrac{\text{Cost of Sales}}{\text{Total Capital Employed}}$

8. $\text{Capital Turnover Ratio} = \dfrac{\text{Cost of Sales}}{\text{Net Working Capital}}$

9. $\textit{Current Assets Turnover Ratio} = \dfrac{\text{Cost of Sales}}{\text{Current Assets}}$

10. $\textit{Sales to Net worth Ratio} = \dfrac{\text{Cost of Sales}}{\text{Net worth}}$

11. $\textit{Expenses Ratio} = \dfrac{\text{Individual Expenses}}{\text{Sales}}$

E. Leverage or Capital Structure Ratios

1. $$\textit{Debt – Equity Ratio} = \frac{\text{Debt}}{\text{Equity}}$$

2. $$\textit{Proprietary Ratio} = \frac{\text{Shareholder's Fund}}{\text{Total Assets}}$$

3. $$\textit{Capital Gearing Ratio} = \frac{\text{Fixed Interest Bearing Securities}}{\text{Equity Share Capital}}$$

(*or*)

$$= \frac{\text{Pre Share Capital + Debentures + Other Borrowed Funds}}{\text{Equity}}$$

4. $$\textit{Reserves to Equity Capital Ratio} = \frac{\text{Revenue Reserve}}{\text{Equity Capital}}$$

5. $$\textit{Fixed Assets to Net worth Ratio} = \frac{\text{Fixed Assets}}{\text{Net worth}}$$

6. $$\textit{Current Assets to Net worth Ratio} = \frac{\text{Current Assets}}{\text{Net worth}}$$

7. $$\textit{Current Liabilities to Net worth Ratio} = \frac{\text{Current Liabilities}}{\text{Net worth}}$$

8. $$\textit{Fixed Assets to Current Assets Ratio} = \frac{\text{Fixed Assets}}{\text{Current Assets}}$$

9. $$\textit{Fixed Assets Ratio} = \frac{\text{Fixed Assets}}{\text{Long – Term Funds}}$$

TEST QUESTIONS

1. What is meant by Ratio Analysis ?
2. List out the Liquidity Ratios.
3. What are Turnover Ratios ?
4. What do you understand by Operating Ratios and Stock Turnover Ratio ?
5. Briefly explain the objectives of Ratio Analysis.
6. What are the Limitations Ratio Analysis ?
7. Discuss some of the important ratios usually worked from the financial statements showing how they would be useful to top level management.
8. "Ratio analysis is a tool to examine the health of a business with a view to make the financial results more intelligible".
9. Discusses the significance of various accounting ratios in the analysis of financial statements.

PROBLEMS AND SOLUTIONS

Type I : Final Account to Ratio

Problem 1. *From the data calculate :*

(i) Gross Profit Ratio (ii) Net Profit Ratio (iii) Return on Total Assets
(iv) Inventory Turnover (v) Working Capital Turnover (vi) Net worth to Debt

Sales	*25,20,000*	*Other Current Assets*	*7,60,000*
Cost of sale	*19,20,000*	*Fixed Assets*	*14,40,000*
Net profit	*3,60,000*	*Net worth*	*15,00,000*
Inventory	*8,00,000*	*Debt.*	*9,00,000*
		Current Liabilities	*6,00,000*

[B.Com. Madurai, BBM PU May 2005]

Solution :

(i) $$\text{Gross Profit Ratio} = \frac{\text{GP}}{\text{Sales}} \times 100 = \frac{6,00,000}{25,20,000} \times 100 = 23.81\%$$

Sales – Cost of Sales = Gross Profit

25,20,000 – 19,20,000 = 6,00,000

(ii) $$\text{Net Profit Ratio} = \frac{\text{NP}}{\text{Sales}} \times 100 = \frac{3,60,000}{25,20,000} = 14.28\%$$

(iii) $$\text{Inventory Turnover Ratio} = \frac{\text{Turnover}}{\text{Inventory}} \times 100 = \frac{19,20,000}{8,00,000} = 2.4 \text{ times}$$

Turnover Refers Cost of Sales

(iv) $$\text{Return on Total Assets} = \frac{\text{NP}}{\text{Total Assets}} = \frac{3,60,000}{30,00,000} \times 100 = 12\%$$

FA + CA + inventory [14,40,000 + 7,60,000 + 8,00,000] = 30,00,000

(v) $$\text{Net worth to Debt} = \frac{\text{Net worth}}{\text{Debt}} = \frac{15,00,000}{9,00,000} \times 100 = 1.66 \text{ times}$$

(vi) $$\text{Working Capital Turnover} = \frac{\text{Turnover}}{\text{Working Capital}}$$

Working Capital = Current Assets – Current Liabilities

= 8,00,000 + 7,60,000 – 6,00,000

15,60,000 – 6,00,000 = 9,60,000

$$\text{Working Capital Turnover Ratio} = \frac{19,20,000}{9,60,000} = 2 \text{ times.}$$

Problem 2. *Perfect Ltd. gives the following Balance sheet. You are required to compute the following ratios.*

(a) Liquid Ratio *(c) Debt–Equity Ratio*

(b) Solvency Ratio *(d) Stock of Working Capital Ratio*

Balance Sheet

	₹		₹
Equity share capital	*15,00,000*	*Fixed Assets*	*14,00,000*
Reserve fund	*1,00,000*	*Stock*	*5,00,000*
6% Debentures	*3,00,000*	*Debtors*	*2,00,000*
Overdraft	*1,00,000*	*Cash*	*1,00,000*
Creditors	*2,00,000*		
	22,00,000		*22,00,000*

Solution :

(*a*) $$\text{Liquid Ratio} = \frac{\text{Liquid Assets}}{\text{Liquid Liabilities}} \text{ (or) } \frac{\text{Liquid Assets}}{\text{Current Liabilities}}$$

LA Debtors = 2,00,000 *i.e.,* $\frac{3,00,000}{2,00,000} = 1.5$

Cash = 1,00,000

= 3,00,000

Liquid Liabilities : Creditors = 2,00,000

(*b*) $$\text{Debt – Equity Ratio} = \frac{\text{External Equities}}{\text{Internal Equities}}$$

External Equities :

All outsiders loan Including current liabilities

3,00,000 + 1,00,000 + 2,00,000 = 6,00,000

Internal Equities :

It Includes share holders fund + Reserves

15,00,000 + 1,00,000 = 16,00,000

$$\text{Debt – Equity Ratio} = \frac{6,00,000}{16,00,000} = 0.375$$

(*c*) $$\text{Solvency Ratio} = \frac{\text{Outside Liabilities}}{\text{Total Assets}}$$

Outside Liabilities = Debenture + Overdraft + Creditors

= 3,00,000 + 1,00,000 + 2,00,000 = 6,00,000

$$\therefore \quad \text{Solvency Ratio} = \frac{6,00,000}{22,00,000} \times 100 = 27.27\%$$

(*d*) $$\text{Stock of Working Capital Ratio} = \frac{\text{Stock}}{\text{Working Capital}}$$

$$\text{Working Capital} = \text{Current Assets} - \text{Current Liabilities}$$
$$= 8,00,000 - 3,00,000 = 5,00,000$$

$$\text{Stock of Working Capital Ratio} = \frac{5,00,000}{5,00,000} \times 100 = 100\%$$

Problem 3. *Calculate the following ratios from the balance sheet given below :*

(i) Debt – Equity Ratio *(ii) Liquidity Ratio*

(iii) Fixed Assets to Current Assets *(iv) Fixed Assets Turnover*

Balance Sheet

Liabilities	₹	*Assets*	₹
Equity shares of ₹ 10 each	*1,00,000*	*Goodwill*	*60,000*
Reserves	*20,000*	*Fixed Assets*	*1,40,000*
P.L. A/c	*30,000*	*Stock*	*30,000*
Secured loan	*80,000*	*Sundry Debtors*	*30,000*
Sundry creditors	*50,000*	*Advances*	*10,000*
Provision for taxation	*20,000*	*Cash Balance*	*30,000*
	3,00,000		*3,00,000*

The sales for the year were ₹ 5,60,000. [MBA adapted]

Solution :

(i) $$\text{Debt – Equity Ratio} = \frac{\text{Long – Term Debt}}{\text{Shareholders Fund}}$$

$$\text{Long-term Debt} = \text{Secured loan ₹ } 80,000$$
$$\text{Shareholder's Fund} = \text{Equity Share Capital + Reserves + P.L.A/c}$$
$$= 1,00,000 + 20,000 + 30,000 = 1,50,000$$

$$\text{Debt-Equity Ratio} = \frac{80,000}{1,50,000} = .53$$

(ii) $$\text{Liquidity Ratio} = \frac{\text{Liquid Assets}}{\text{Liquid Liabilities}}$$

$$\text{Liquid Assets} = \text{Sundry Debtors + Advances + Cash Balance}$$
$$= 30,000 + 10,000 + 30,000 = 70,000$$
$$\text{Liquid Liabilities} = \text{Provision for Taxation + sundry creditors}$$
$$= 20,000 + 50,000 = 70,000$$

$$\text{Liquid Ratio} = \frac{70,000}{70,000} = 1$$

(iii) Fixed Assets to Current Assets

$$= \frac{\text{Fixed Assets}}{\text{Current Assets}} = \frac{1,40,000}{1,00,000} = 1.4$$

(iv) $$\text{Fixed Assets Turnover} = \frac{\text{Turnover}}{\text{Fixed Assets}} = \frac{5,60,000}{1,40,000} = 4$$

Problem 4. *The Balance sheet of Naronath & Co. as on 31.12.2000 shows as follows :*

Liabilities	₹	*Assets*	₹
Equity capital	*1,00,000*	*Fixed Assets*	*1,80,000*
15% Preference shares	*50,000*	*Stores*	*25,000*
12% Debentures	*50,000*	*Debtors*	*55,000*
Retained Earnings	*20,000*	*Bills Receivable*	*3,000*
Creditors	*45,000*	*Bank*	*2,000*
	2,65,000		*2,65,000*

Comment on the Financial position of the Company i.e., Debt - Equity Ratio, Fixed Assets Ratio, Current Ratio, Liquidity. [M.Com., Bhopal]

Solution :

(*i*) $$\text{Debt – Equity Ratio} = \frac{\text{Debt – Equity Ratio}}{\text{Long – Term Debt}}$$

$$\text{Long-term Debt} = \text{Debentures}$$
$$= 50{,}000$$
$$\text{Shareholder's Fund} = \text{Equity + Preference + Retained Earnings}$$
$$= 1{,}00{,}000 + 50{,}000 + 20{,}000$$
$$= \frac{50{,}000}{1{,}70{,}000} = .29$$

(*ii*) $$\text{Fixed Assets Ratio} = \frac{\text{Fixed Assets}}{\text{Proprietor's Fund}} = 1{,}80{,}000$$

$$\text{Proprietor's Fund} = \text{Equity Share Capital + Preference Share Capital + Retained Earnings}$$
$$= 1{,}00{,}000 + 50{,}000 + 20{,}000 = 1{,}70{,}000$$
$$\text{Fixed Assets Ratio} = \frac{1{,}80{,}000}{1{,}70{,}000} = 1.05$$

(*iii*) $$\text{Current Ratio} = \frac{\text{Current Assets}}{\text{Current Liabilities}}$$

$$\text{Current Assets} = \text{Stores + Debtors + BR + Bank}$$
$$= 25{,}000 + 55{,}000 + 3{,}000 + 2{,}000 = 85{,}000$$
$$\text{Current Liabilities} = 45{,}000$$
$$\text{Current Ratio} = \frac{85{,}000}{45{,}000} = 1.88$$

(*iv*) $$\text{Liquid Ratio} = \frac{\text{Liquid Assets}}{\text{Liquid Liabilities}}$$

$$\text{Liquid Assets} = \text{Debtors + Bill Receivable + Cash}$$
$$= 55{,}000 + 3{,}000 + 2{,}000 = 60{,}000$$
$$\text{Liquid Liabilities} = 45{,}000$$
$$\text{Liquid Ratio} = \frac{60{,}000}{45{,}000} = 1.33$$

Problem 5. *From the following particulars pertaining to Assets and Liabilities of a company calculate :*

(a) Current Ratio *(b) Liquidity Ratio* *(c) Proprietary Ratio*
(d) Debt-equity Ratio *(e) Capital Gearing Ratio*

Liabilities	₹	*Assets*	₹
5000 equity shares ₹ 10 each	*5,00,000*	*Land & Building*	*6,00,000*
8% 2000 pre shares ₹ 100 each	*2,00,000*	*Plant & Machinery*	*5,00,000*
9% 4000 Debentures of ₹ 100 each	*4,00,000*	*Debtors*	*2,00,000*
Reserves	*3,00,000*	*Stock*	*2,40,000*
Creditors	*1,50,000*	*Cash and Bank*	*55,000*
Bank overdraft	*50,000*	*Prepaid expenses*	*5,000*
	16,00,000		*16,00,000*

[M.Sc. ITM Dec. 1999]

Solution :

(i)

$$\text{Current Ratio} = \frac{\text{Current Assets}}{\text{Current Liabilities}}$$

Current Assets = Stock + Cash + Prepaid Expenses + Debtors
= 2,40,000 + 55,000 + 5,000 + 2,00,000 = 5,00,000

Current Liabilities = Creditors + Bank Overdraft
= 1,50,000 + 50,000 = 2,00,000

$$= \frac{5,00,000}{2,00,000} = 2.5 : 1$$

(ii)

$$\text{Liquid Ratio} = \frac{\text{Liquid Assets}}{\text{Liquid Liabilities}}$$

Liquid Assets = Cash and Bank + Debtors
= 55,000 + 2,00,000 = 2,55,000

Liquid Liabilities : Creditors = 1,50,000

$$\text{Liquid Ratio} = \frac{2,55,000}{1,50,000} = 1.7 : 1$$

(iii)

$$\text{Proprietary Ratio} = \frac{\text{Proprietor's Fund}}{\text{Total Tangible Assets}}$$

Proprietor's Funds = Equity Share Capital + Preference Share Capital + Reserves and Surplus
= 5,00,000 + 2,00,000 + 3,00,000

$$\text{Proprietary Ratio} = \frac{10,00,000}{16,00,000} = 0.625 : 1$$

(iv) $$\text{Debt – Equity Ratio} = \frac{\text{External Equities}}{\text{Internal Equities}}$$

$$\text{External Equities} = \text{Long-term Liabilities + Short-term Liabilities}$$
$$= 4,00,000 + 2,00,000 = 6,00,000$$
$$\text{Internal Equities} = \text{Proprietor's funds}$$
$$= \frac{6,00,000}{10,00,000} = 0.6 : 1$$

(v) $$\text{Capital Gearing Ratio} = \frac{\text{Fixed Interest Bearing Securities}}{\text{Equity Share Capital + Reserves}}$$

Fixed Interest Bearing Securities = Preference Shares 2,00,000
Debentures 4,00,000
6,00,000

$$= \frac{6,00,000}{8,00,000} = 0.75 : 1$$

Problem 6. *From the following details of a trader you are required to calculate :*

(i) Purchase for the year.
(ii) Rate of stock turnover
(iii) Percentage of Gross profit to turnover

Sales ₹	*33,984*	*Stock at the close at cost price*	*1,814*
Sales Returns	*380*	*G.P. for the year*	*8,068*
Stock at the beginning at cost price	*1,378*		

Solution :

Trading Account

To Opening stock	1,378	By Sales	33,984
To Purchase (Bf)	25,972	(–) Sales Returns	380
			33,604
To gross profit	8,068	By Closing stock	1,814
	35,418		35,418

(i) Purchase for the year ₹ 25,972

(ii) $$\text{Stock Turnover} = \frac{\text{Cost of Goods Sold}}{\text{Average Stock}}$$

$$\text{Cost of Goods Sold} = \text{Sales} - \text{GP} = 33,984 - 8,068 = 25,916$$

$$\text{Average Stock} = \frac{\text{Opening Stock + Closing Stock}}{2}$$

$$= \frac{1,372 + 1,814}{2} = 1,596$$

$$= \frac{25,916}{1,596} = 16.23 \text{ times}$$

(*iii*) Percentage of Gross Profit to Turnover

$$= \frac{\text{Gross Profit}}{\text{Sales}} \times 100 = \frac{8,068}{33,984} \times 100 = 23.74\%.$$

Problem 7. *Calculate stock turnover ratio from the following information :*

Opening stock	*58,000*
Purchases	*4,84,000*
Sales	*6,40,000*

Gross Profit Rate - 25% on Sales. [M.Sc., Dec.1999]

Solution :

$$\text{Stock Turnover Ratio} = \frac{\text{Cost of Goods Sold}}{\text{Average Stock}}$$

$$\text{Cost of Goods Sold} = \text{Sales} - \text{G.P}$$

$$= 6,40,000 - 1,60,000 = 4,80,000$$

$$\text{Stock Turnover Ratio} = \frac{4,80,000}{58,000} = 8.27 \text{ times } \textbf{Ans.}$$

Here, there is no closing stock. So, there is no need to calculate the average stock.

Problem 8. *Calculate the operating Ratio from the following figures.*

Items	*(₹ in Lakhs)*
Sales	*17,874*
Sales Returns	*4*
Other Incomes	*53*
Cost of Sales	*15,440*
Administration and Selling Exp.	*1,843*
Depreciation	*63*
Interest Expenses (Non-operating)	*456*

Solution :

$$\text{Operating Ratio} = \frac{\text{Cost of Goods Sold + Operating Expenses}}{\text{Sales}} \times 100$$

$$= \frac{15,440 + 1,843}{17,870} \times 100 = 97\%$$

Problem 9. *The following is the Trading and Profit and loss account of Mathan Bros Private Limited for the year ended June 30,2001.*

	₹		₹
To Stock in hand	*76,250*	*By Sales*	*5,00,000*
To Purchases	*3,15,250*	*By Stock in hand*	*98,500*
To Carriage and Freight	*2,000*		
To Wages	*5,000*		
To Gross Profit	*2,00,000*		
	5,98,500		*5,98,500*

To Administration Expenses		*1,01,000*	*By Gross profit*		*2,00,000*
To Finance Expenses :			*By Non-operating Incomes*		
Interest	*1,200*		*Interest on Securities*	*1,500*	
Discount	*2,400*		*Dividend on Shares*	*3,750*	
Bad Debts	*3,400*	*7,000*	*Profit on Sale of Shares*	*750*	*6,000*
To Selling Distribution Expenses		*12,000*			
To Non-operating expenses					
Loss on sale of securities	*350*				
Provision for legal suit	*1,650*	*2,000*			
To Net profit		*84,000*			
		2,06,000			*2,06,000*

You are required to calculate :

(i) Gross profit Ratio *(ii) Expenses Ratio (individual)*
(iii) Net profit Ratio *(iv) Operating profit Ratio*
(v) Operating Ratio *(vi) Stock turnover Ratio*

Solution :

(*i*) $$\text{Gross Profit Ratio} = \frac{\text{Gross Profit}}{\text{Sales}} \times 100 = \frac{2,00,000}{5,00,000} \times 100$$

(*ii*) $$\text{Expenses Ratio} = \frac{\text{Individual Expenses}}{\text{Sales}}$$

(*a*) $$\frac{\text{Administration Expenses}}{\text{Sales}} \times 100 = \frac{1,01,000}{5,00,000} \times 100 = 2.02\%$$

(*b*) $$\frac{\text{Finance Expenses}}{\text{Sales}} \times 100 = \frac{7,000}{5,00,000} \times 100 = 1.40\%$$

(*c*) $$\frac{\text{Selling and Distribution Expenses}}{\text{Sales}} \times 100 = \frac{12,000}{5,00,000} \times 100 = 2.40\%$$

(*d*) $$\frac{\text{Non - Operating Expenses}}{\text{Sales}} \times 100 = \frac{2,000}{5,00,000} \times 100 = 0.4\%$$

(iii) Net Profit Ratio :

$$\frac{\text{Net Profit}}{\text{Sales}} \times 100 = \frac{84,000}{5,00,000} \times 100 = 16.8\%$$

(*iv*) $$\text{Operating Profit Ratio} = \frac{\text{Operating Profit}}{\text{Sales}} \times 100$$

$$\text{Operating Profit} = \text{Net Profit} + \text{Non-Operating Expenses} - \text{Non Operating Incomes}$$

$$= 84,000 + 2,000 - 6,000 = 80,000$$

$$= \frac{80,000}{50,00,000} \times 100 = 16\%$$

(v) $$\text{Operating Ratio} = \frac{\text{Cost of Goods Sold + Operating Expenses}}{\text{Sales}} \times 100$$

$$\text{Cost of Goods Sold} = \text{Sales} - \text{Gross profit}$$

i.e., $5,00,000 - 2,00,000 = 3,00,000$

Operating Expenses

All Expenses Debited in the Profit & Loss A/c Except Non-operating Expenses [including Finance expense]

$$1,01,000 + 7,000 + 12,000 = 1,20,000$$

$$\text{Operating Ratio} = \frac{3,00,000 + 1,20,000}{5,00,000} \times 84\%$$

(vi) $$\text{Stock Turnover Ratio} = \frac{\text{Cost of Goods Sold}}{\text{Average Stock}}$$

$$\text{Costs of Goods Sold} = 3,00,000$$

$$\text{Average Stock} = \frac{\text{Opening Stock + Closing Stock}}{2}$$

$$= \frac{76,250 + 95,500}{2} = 85,875$$

$$\therefore \quad = \frac{3,00,000}{85,875} = 3.49 \text{ times}$$

Problem 10. *Suraj & Co. sells goods on cash as well as credit (though not on deferred instalment terms). The following particulars are extracted from their books of account for the calendar year 2004.*

Total Gross sales	=	*1,00,000*
Cash sales (included in above)	=	*20,000*
Sales Returns	=	*7,000*
Total Debtors for Sales on 31.12.2004	=	*9,000*
Bills Receivable on 31.12.2004	=	*1,000*
Provision for Doubtful Debts on 31.12.2004	=	*1,000*
Total Creditors 31.12.2004	=	*10,000*

Calculate the Average Collection Period. [MCA Madras]

Solution :

Average Collection Period

$$= \frac{\text{Debtors + Bills Receivable + Provision for Doubtful Debts}}{\text{Net Credit Sales}} \times 365$$

$$= \frac{9,000 + 1,000 + 1,000}{73,000} \times 365 = 55 \text{ days}$$

Workings :

Net Credit Sales = Total Gross Sales – Cash Sales – Sales Returns
= 1,00,000 – 20,000 – 7,000 = 73,000

Problem 11. *The following is the Trading account of M/s SKC Ltd. You are required to calculate the stock turnover Ratio.*

To Opening Stock	*7,960*	*By Sales*	*39,000*
To Purchases	*19,500*	*By closing stock*	*7,200*
To Carriage inwards	*500*		
To gross profit	*18,240*		
	46,200		*46,200*

Solution :

$$\text{Stock Turnover Ratio} = \frac{\text{Cost of Goods Sold}}{\text{Average Stock}}$$

$$\text{Cost of Goods Sold} = \text{Sales} - \text{Gross Profit}$$

$$= 39{,}000 - 18{,}240 = 20{,}760$$

$$\text{Average Stock} = \frac{\text{Opening Stock} + \text{Closing Stock}}{2}$$

$$= \frac{7{,}960 + 7{,}200}{2}$$

$$= 7{,}580$$

$$= \frac{20{,}760}{7{,}580} = 2.73 \text{ times}$$

Problem 12. *The Balance Sheet of Lal and Co. on 31.12.2000 shows the following details :*

	₹
Cash	*9,500*
Marketable Securities	*15,000*
Inventories	*1,00,000*
Debtors	*85,000*
Prepaid Expenses	*5,000*
Long-term Loans	*1,06,000*
Trade Creditors	*64,000*
Income Tax Payable	*9,000*
Accrued Expenses	*12,000*

You are required to compute

(i) Current Ratio *(ii) Acid-Test Ratio.* [MCA Madras]

Solution :

(*i*) $$\text{Current Ratio} = \frac{\text{Current Assets}}{\text{Current Liabilities}}$$

Current Assets = Cash + Marketable Securities + Inventories + Debtors + Prepaid Expenses

= 9,500 + 15,000 + 1,00,000 + 85,000 + 5,000 = 2,14,500

Current Liabilities = Trade Creditors + Income Tax Payable + Accrued Expenses

= 64,000 + 9,000 + 12,000 = 85,000

$$\text{Current Ratio} = \frac{\text{Current Assets}}{\text{Current Liabilities}}$$

$$\therefore \quad \frac{2,14,500}{85,000} = 2.52 : 1$$

(*ii*) $$\text{Acid Test Ratio} = \frac{\text{Liquid Assets}}{\text{Liquid Liabilities}}$$

Liquid Assets = Cash + Marketable Securities + Debtors + Prepaid Expenses

= 9,500 + 15,000 + 85,000 + 5,000 = 1,14,500

Liquid Liabilities = Trade Creditors + Income Tax Payable + Accrued Expenses

= 64,000 + 9,000 + 12,000 = 85,000

$$\therefore \quad \frac{1,14,500}{85,000} = 1.34 : 1$$

Problem 13. *From the following figures calculate the creditors turnover ratio and the average age of accounts payable.*

	₹
Credit Purchases During the Year 1998	*1,00,000*
Creditors on 01.01.1998	*20,000*
Creditors on 31.12.1998	*10,000*
Bills Payable on 01.01.1998	*4,000*
Bills Payable on 31.12.1998	*6,000*

[B.Com., Dec. 2003 Periyar]

Solution :

$$\text{Creditor's Turnover Ratio} = \frac{\text{Net Credit Purchase}}{\text{Average Account Payable}} = \frac{1,00,000}{20,000} = 5 \text{ times}$$

$$\text{Average Payment Period} = \frac{\text{Months}}{\text{Creditors Turnover}} = \frac{12}{5} = 2.4 \text{ months}$$

Problem 14. *From the data given below compute :*

(a) Working Capital *(b) Net Capital Employed* *(c) Current Ratio*
(d) Acid Test Ratio *(e) Debt-Equity Ratio* *(f) Fixed Assets Ratio*

Balance Sheet of Butterfly Ltd. as on 31st December

Liabilities	₹	*Assets*	₹
Equity Share Capital	25,000	*Fixed Assets*	30,000
Preference Share Capital	5,000	*Current Assets : Stores*	2,000
Reserve and Surplus	4,000	*Sundry Debtors*	1,000
Debentures	8,000	*Cash*	500
Bank loan	4,000	*Bank*	2,500
Sundry creditors	1,000	*preliminary expenses*	8,000
Proposed Dividends	1,000	*Brokerage on shares*	2,000
Provision for Taxation	2,000	*Stock*	4,000
	50,000		50,000

[B.Com. Madurai]

Solution :

Working Capital = Current Assets – Current Liabilities

Current Assets = Stores + Sundry Debtors + Cash + Bank + Stock

= 2,000 + 1,000 + 2,500 + 4,000 + 500 = 10,000

Current Liabilities = Sundry Creditors + Proposed Dividends + Provision for Taxation

= 1,000 + 1,000 + 2,000 = 4,000

(*a*) Working Capital = 10,000 – 4,000 = 6,000

(*b*) Net Capital Employed

All assets excluding fictitious assets – Current liabilities *i.e.,*

₹ 40,000 - 4,000 = 36,000

(*c*)
$$\text{Current Ratio} = \frac{\text{Current Assets}}{\text{Current Liabilities}} = \frac{10,000}{4,000} = 2.5 : 1$$

(*d*)
$$\text{Acid Test Ratio} = \frac{\text{Liquid Assets}}{\text{Liquid Liabilities}}$$

Liquid Assets = 2,500 + 500 + 1,000 = *i.e.,* 4,000

Liquid Liabilities = 2,000 + 1,000 + 1,000 = *i.e.,* 4,000

$$= \frac{4,000}{4,000} = 1$$

(*e*)
$$\text{Debt – Equity Ratio} = \frac{\text{Outsider's Fund}}{\text{Shareholder's Fund}} = \frac{16,000}{34,000} = .47 : 1$$

Outsider's Fund 16,000

Outsider's Fund = Debentures + Bank Loan + Sundry Creditors + Proposed Dividends + Provision for Taxation

= 8,000 + 4,000 +1,000 + 1,000 + 2,000 = 16,000

Shareholder's Fund = Equity Share Capital + Preference Share Capital + Reserves and Surplus

= 25,000 + 5,000 + 4,000 = 34,000

Debt-Equity Ratio = 0.47 :1

(*f*) Fixed Assets Ratio = $\frac{\text{Fixed Assets}}{\text{Long - term Funds}} = \frac{30,000}{46,000}$ = .65 : 1

Long-term Funds = Equity Share Capital, Preference Share Capital, Reserves and Surplus, Debentures, Bank Loan.

= 25,000 + 5,000 + 4,000 + 8,000 + 4,000 = 46,000

Problem 15. *You have been asked by the management of a firm to project a Trading, Profit and Loss A/c and the Balance Sheet on the basis of the following estimated figures and ratios, for the next financial year.*

Ratio to gross profit	*20%*
Stock turnover ratio	*5 times*
Average debt collection period	*3 Months*
Creditors	*3 Months*
Current ratio	*2*
Proprietary ratio (fixed assets to capital employed)	*75%*
Capital gearing ratio (Preference shares and debentures to equity)	*30%*
Net profit to issued equity capital	*10%*
General Reserve and Profit and Loss to issued equity capital	*25%*
Preference share capital to debentures	*2*
Cost of sales consists of 50% for materials	
Gross profit	*₹ 6,25,000*

[MBA Periyar]

Solution : Projected Trading and Profit Loss Account

Expenses	*Amount* ₹	*Incomes*	*Amount* ₹
To Cost of materials	12,50,000	By Sales	31,25,000
To Direct expenses	12,50,000		
To Gross profit	6,25,000		
	31,25,000		31,25,000
To Indirect expenses (Balancing figure)	4,81,500	By Gross profit	6,25,000
To Net Profit	1,43,500		
	6,25,000		6,25,000

Projected Balance Sheet

Liabilities	₹	*Assets*	₹
Preference Share Capital	5,12,500	Fixed Assets	19,21,875
Equity Share Capital	14,35,000	Current Assets :	
Debentures	2,56,250	Stock	5,00,000
General Reserve	2,15,250	Debtors	7,81,250
Profit and Loss A/c	1,43,500		
Current Liabilities :			
Overdraft	3,28,125		
Creditors	3,12,500		
	32,03,125		32,03,125

Workings :

(1) Sales :

$$\text{Gross Profit Ratio} = \frac{\text{Gross Profit}}{\text{Sales}} \times 100$$

$$(i.e.)\ 20 = \frac{₹\ 6,25,000}{\text{Sales}} \times 100$$

$$20 \text{ Sales} = ₹\ 6,25,000 \times 100$$

$$\text{Sales} = \frac{₹\ 6,25,000}{20} \times 100$$

$$= \mathbf{₹\ 31,25,000}$$

(2) Cost of Sales :

$$\text{Cost of Sales} = \text{Sales} - \text{Gross Profit}$$
$$= ₹\ 31,25,000 - ₹\ 6,25,000$$
$$= \mathbf{₹\ 25,00,000}$$

(3) Materials :

$$50\% \text{ of Cost of Sales} = 50\% \text{ of } ₹\ 25,00,000$$
$$= \mathbf{₹\ 12,50,000}$$

(4) Direct Expenses :

$$\text{Direct Expenses} = \text{Cost of Sales} - \text{Cost of Materials}$$
$$= ₹\ 25,00,000 - ₹\ 12,50,000$$
$$= \mathbf{₹\ 12,50,000}$$

(5) Stock :

$$\text{Stock Turnover Ratio} = \frac{\text{Cost of Sales}}{\text{Stock}} = 5$$

$$i.e.\ 5 = \frac{₹\ 25,00,000}{\text{Stock}}$$

$$\mathbf{Stock = ₹\ 5,00,000\ (25,00,000/5)}$$

(6) Debtors :

$$\text{Debtors Turnover} = \frac{\text{Debtors}}{\text{Credit Sales}} \times 12$$

$$(i.e.)\ 3 = \frac{\text{Debtors}}{₹\ 31,25,000} \times 12$$

$$\textbf{Debtors} = \textbf{₹ 7,81,250}$$

(7) Total Current Assets = Stock + Debtors

= ₹ 5,00,000 + ₹ 7,81,250

= **₹ 12,81,250**

(8) Current Liabilities :

$$= \frac{\text{Current Assets}}{\text{Current Liabilities}} = 2$$

(*i.e.*) 2 Current Liabilities = Current Assests

$$\text{Current Liabilities} = \frac{₹\ 12,81,250}{2}$$

= **₹ 6,40,625**

(9) Creditors :

$$\text{Creditors Turnover Ratio} = \frac{\text{Creditors}}{\text{Credit Purchases}} \times 12 = 3$$

$$(i.e.)\ 3 = \frac{\text{Creditors}}{₹\ 12,50,000} \times 12$$

Creditors = **₹ 3,12,500**

(Materials have been purchased on credit)

(10) Overdraft :

Overdraft = Current Liabilities – Creditors

= ₹ 6,40,625 – ₹ 3,12,500

= **₹ 3,28,125**

(11) Fixed Assets :

$$\frac{\text{Fixed Assets}}{\text{Capital Employed}} = \frac{75}{100}$$

$$\frac{\text{Working Capital}}{\text{Capital Employed}} = \frac{25}{100}$$

Working Capital = Current Assets – Current Liabilities

= ₹ 12,81,250 – ₹ 6,40,625

= **₹ 6,40,625**

Fixed Assets = ₹ 6,40,625 × 3

= **₹ 19,21,875**

(12) Capital Employed :

Capital Employed = Fixed Assets + Current Assets – Current Liabilities

= ₹ 19,21,875 + ₹ 12,81,250 – ₹ 6,40,625

= **₹ 25,62,500**

(13) Capital Gearing Ratio :

$$= \frac{\text{Pref. Share Capital + Debenture}}{\text{Total Capital Employed}} = 30\%$$

Pref. Share Capital + Debentures = 30% of ₹ 25,62,500

= **₹ 7,68,750**

Equity Shareholders' Fund = Capital Fund – (Pref. Share Capital and Debentures)

= ₹ 25,62,500 – ₹ 7,68,750

= **₹ 17,93,750**

Preference Share Capital = ₹ 7,68,750 × $\frac{2}{3}$ = **₹ 5,12,500**

Debentures = ₹ 7,68,750 × $\frac{1}{3}$ = **₹ 2,56,250**

(14) General Reserve and Profit and Loss :

25% of Equity Share Capital = ₹ 17,93,750 × $\frac{25}{125}$ = **₹ 3,58,750**

(Shareholders Fund include General Reserve and Profit)

(15) Equity Share Capital :

Equity Shareholders Fund – (Reserve and Profit)

₹ 17,93,750 – ₹ 3,58,750 = **₹ 14,35,000**

(16) Profit :

10% of Equity Share Capital

10% of ₹ 14,35,000 = **₹ 1,43,500**

(17) General Reserve :

General Reserve and Profit – Profit

₹ 3,58,750 – ₹ 1,43,500 = **₹ 2,15,250**

Type II : Ratio to Balance Sheet

Problem 1. *From the following details find out*

(i) Current Assets (ii) Current Liabilities (iii) Liquid Assets (iv) Stock

Current Ratio	*2.5*
Liquidity Ratio	*1.5*
Working Capital	*₹ 60,000*

[MBA Madras]

Solution :

(1) Current Assets	–	Current Liabilities	=	Working Capital
↓		↓		↓
2.5	–	1.0	=	1.5
↓		↓		↓
1,00,000	–	40,000	=	60,000

(2) Liquid Ratio : Liquid Assets : Liquid Liabilities

Liquid Assets	↓	Liquid Liabilities	↓
1.5		=	1.00
↓			↓
60,000		=	40,000

	₹
Current Assets	1,00,000
Current Liabilities	40,000
Liquid Assets	60,000
Stock	40,000

NOTE :

(i) Here, all Current Liabilities have been taken as Liquid Liabilities.

(ii) Difference between Current Assets and Liquid Assets is the stock.

Problem 2. *From the following details, prepare Balance sheet of Moorthy Ltd., with as many details as possible.*

(i) Stock Velocity : 6.

(ii) Capital Turnover Ratio : 2.

(iii) Fixed Asset Turnover Ratio : 4.

(iv) Gross Profit Turnover Ratio : 20%.

(v) Debtor's Velocity : 2 months.

(vi) Creditors Velocity : 73 days.

(vii) Gross Profit was ₹ 60,000.

(viii) Reserves and Surplus ₹ 20,000.

(ix) Closing Stock was ₹ 5,000 in Excess of Opening Stock. [B.Com. 2003 PU]

Solution :

Workings :

(i)

Cost of Goods Sold	+	GP	=	Sales
↓		↓		↓
80%		20%		100%
2,40,000	+	60,000	=	3,00,000

(ii) $$\text{Stock turnover} = \frac{\text{Cost of Goods Sold}}{\text{Average Stock (X)}} = \text{Stock Velocity (6)}$$

$$X = \frac{2,40,000}{6}$$

Average Stock = 40,000

Total Stock value = 40,000 × 2 = 80,000

Less : Excess = 5,000

75,000

Opening Stock = 37,500

Closing Stock = 37,500 + 5,000 = 42,500

(*iii*) Debtor's Velocity = 2 months

$$\frac{\text{Debtors (X)}}{\text{Sales}} \times 12 = 2 \text{ i.e., } X = 3,00,000 \times \frac{2}{12}$$

Debtors = ₹ 50,000

(*iv*) Creditor's Velocity = 73 days.

$$\frac{\text{Creditors (X)}}{\text{Purchase}} \times 365 = 73$$

$$X = 2,45,000 \times \frac{73}{365} = 49,000$$

NOTE : Purchase = Cost of Sales + Increase in Stock = 2,40,000 + 5,000 = 2,45,000

(*v*) Fixed Assets Turnover Ratio $= \frac{\text{Turnover}}{\text{Fixed Assets (X)}}$

$$X = \frac{2,40,000}{4} = 60,000$$

(*vi*) Capital Turnover Ratio = 2

$$\frac{\text{Turnover}}{\text{Capital (X)}} = 2$$

$$X = \frac{2,40,000}{2} = 2 \qquad 1,20,000$$

(*vii*)	Total Capital =	1,20,000
	Creditors =	49,000
	Total Liabilities =	1,69,000
	All Assets (42,500 + 50,000 + 60,000) =	1,52,500
	Cash (1,69,000 – 1,52,500) =	16,500
		1,69,000

Statement of Proprietary Funds :

Fixed Assets =		60,000
Working Capital		
(Current Assets – CL)		
Closing Stock	42,500	
Debtors	50,000	
Cash	16,500	
	1,09,000	
Less : Creditors	49,000	
		60,000
Proprietor's Fund		1,20,000

It consists of share capital and Reserves and Surplus.

Share Capital	1,00,000
Reserves and Surplus	20,000
	1,20,000

Problem 3. *Calculate the current assets of a company from the following information :*

(i) Stock Turnover 5 times

(ii) Stock at the end is ₹ 5,000; more than the stock in the beginning

(iii) Sales (all credit) ₹ 2,00,000

(iv) Gross Profit Ratio 20%

(v) Current Liabilities ₹ 60,000

(vi) Quick Ratio 0.75.

Solution :

(1) Cost of Goods Sold + G.P. = Sales

↓ ↓ ↓

80% + 20% = 100

↓ ↓ ↓

1,60,000 + 40,000 = 2,00,000

(2) Stock Turnover Ratio = 5 times

$$\frac{\text{Cost of Goods Sold}}{\text{Average Stock (X)}} = 5 \text{ times}$$

$$X = \frac{1,60,000}{5} = 32,000$$

Average Stock = ₹ 32,000

Full Stock Value = 32,000 × 2 = 64,000

Less : Excess Value = 5,000

59,000

$$\frac{59,000}{2} = 29,500$$

Opening Stock = 29,500

Closing Stock = 29,500 + 5,000 = 34,500

(3) Quick Ratio

Quick Assets : Quick Liabilities

↓ ↓

0.75 : 1.00

↓ ↓

45,000 : 60,000

Current Assets

Closing Stock	=	34,500
Quick Assets	=	45,000
		79,500

Problem 4. *From the following information, prepare a Balance sheet as on 31.3.2003 :*

(i) Working Capital ₹ 1,20,000
(ii) Reserves and Surplus 80,000
(iii) Bank Overdraft 20,000
(iv) Assets (Fixed) – Proprietary Ratio 0.75 : 1
(v) Liquid Ratio 1.5
(vi) Current Ratio 2.5.

Solution :

(1) Current Assets – Current Liabilities = Working Capital

Current Assets	–	Current Liabilities	=	Working Capital
↓		↓		↓
2.5	–	1.00	=	1.5
↓		↓		↓
2,00,000	–	80,000	=	1,20,000

(2) Proprietor's Fund – Fixed Assets = Working Capital

Proprietor's Fund	–	Fixed Assets	=	Working Capital
↓		↓		↓
1.00	–	.75	=	.25
↓		↓		↓
4,80,000	–	3,60,000	=	1,20,000

(3) Liquid Ratio

Liquid Assets	:	Liquid Liabilities
1.5	:	1.00
90,000	:	60,000

Current Liabilities	80,000	Current Assets	2,00,000
Less : BOD	20,000	Liquid Assets	90,000
Liquid Liabilities	60,000	Stock	1,10,000

Balance Sheet

Liabilities	₹	*Assets*	₹
Share Capital (4,80,000 – 80,000)	4,00,000	Fixed Assets	3,60,000
Reserves and Surplus	80,000	Stock	1,10,000
Bank Overdraft	20,000	Other Current Assets	90,000
Sundry Creditors	60,000		
	5,60,000		5,60,000

Problem 5. *From the following information prepare a Balance sheet and show the working.*

(i) Working Capital ₹ 75,000
(ii) Reserves and Surplus ₹ 1,00,000
(iii) Bank Overdraft ₹ 60,000
(iv) Current Ratio : 1.75.
(v) Liquid Ratio : 1.15
(vi) Long-term Liabilities Nil
(vii) Fixed Assets to Proprietor's Fund : 0.75

[MCA, MBA, Madras]

Solution :

(1) Current Assets – Current Liabilities = Working Capital

1.75	– 1.00	= .75
↓	↓	↓
1,75,000	– 1,00,000	= 75,000

(2) Proprietor's Fund – Fixed Assets = Working Capital

↓	↓	↓
1.00	– .75	= .25
↓	↓	↓
3,00,000	– 2,25,000	= 75,000

(3) Liquid Ratio

Liquid Assets : Liquid Liabilities

1.15	– 1.00
↓	↓
46,000	– 40,000

Current Liabilities	1,00,000	Current Assets	1,75,000
Less : BOD	60,000	Liquid Assets	46,000
Liquid Liabilities	40,000	Stock	1,29,000

Balance Sheet

Liabilities	₹	*Assets*	₹
Share Capital (3,00,000 – 1,00,000)	2,00,000	Fixed Assets	2,25,000
Reserves and Surplus	1,00,000	Stock	1,29,000
Bank Overdraft	60,000	Other Current Assets	46,000
Sundry Creditors (1,00,000 – 60,000)	40,000		
	4,00,000		4,00,000

Problem 6. *From the following particulars prepare the balance sheet of ABC Limited.*

(i) Sales for the year ₹ 20,00,000

(ii) Gross Profit Ratio 25%

(iii) Current Ratio : 1.50

(iv) Quick (cash Drs) Ratio : 1.25

(v) Stock Turnover Ratio : 15

(vi) Debt Collection Period · 1 ½ months

(vii) Turnover to Fixed Assets : 1.5

(viii) Fixed Assets to Networth : 5/6 (.83)

(ix) Ratio of Reserves to Share Capital 1/3 (0.33) [The term turnover refers to cost of sales and stock refers to closing stock].

[B.Com. Madras, MCA Bharathidasan, MBA Madras].

Solution :

(*i*) Cost of Goods Sold + Gross Profit = Sales

↓ ↓ ↓

75% + 25% = 100%

↓ ↓ ↓

1,50,000 + 5,00,000 = 20,00,000

(*ii*) Stock Turnover Ratio

$$\frac{\text{Cost of Goods Sold}}{\text{Average Stock (X)}} = 15 \qquad \frac{15,00,000}{X} = 15$$

$$X = \frac{15,00,000}{15}$$

$$\text{Average Stock} = 1,00,000$$

(*iii*) Current Ratio	: 1.50	6,00,000
Quick Ratio	: 1.25	5,00,000
Stock	.25	1,00,000

(*iv*) Current Ratio

Current Assets : Current Liabilities

↓ ↓

1.50 1.00

6,00,000 4,00,000

(*vi*) Debt Collection Period : 1½ months

$$\frac{\text{Debtors}}{\text{Sales}} \times 12 = 1.5 \qquad \frac{X}{20,00,000} \times 12 = 1.5$$

$$X = 20,00,000 \times \frac{1.5}{12}$$

$$\text{Debtors} = 2,50,000$$

(*vii*) Turnover to Fixed Assets : 1.5

$$\frac{\text{Cost of Goods Sold}}{\text{Fixed Assets (X)}} = 1.5$$

$$X = \frac{15,00,000}{1.5}$$

$$\text{Fixed Assets} = 10,00,000$$

(*viii*) Fixed Assets to : Networth = 5/6

↓ ↓

5 : 6

10,00,000 : 12,00,000

$$\left[\frac{10,00,000}{5} \times 6 = 12,00,000\right]$$

(*ix*) Ratio of Reserves to Share Capital = 1/3

Reserves	+	Share Capital	=	Net Worth
1	+	3	=	4
3,00,000	+	9,00,000	=	12,00,000

$$\left[\frac{12,00,000}{4} \times 3 = 9,00,000\right]$$

Balance Sheet

Liabilities	₹	*Assets*	₹
Share Capital	9,00,000	Fixed Assets	10,00,000
Reserves	3,00,000	Current Assets	6,00,000
Current Liabilities	4,00,000		
	16,00,000		16,00,000

Problem 7. *From the following information you are required to prepare a balance sheet :*

Current Ratio	– *1.75*
Liquid Ratio	– *1.25*
Stock Turnover Ratio (Cost of Sales / Closing Stock)	– *9*
Gross Profit Ratio	– *25%*
Debt Collection Period	– *1 ½ months*
Reserves and Surplus to Capital	– *0.2*
Turnover of Fixed Assets	– *1.2*
Capital Gearing Ratio	– *0.6*
Fixed Assets to Net worth	– *1.25*
Sales for the year	– *₹ 12,00,000*

[B.Com. Madras]

Solution :

(*i*)

Cost of Goods Sold	+	Gross Profit	=	Sales
↓		↓		↓
75%	–	25%	=	100%
9,00,000	+	3,00,000	=	12,00,000

(*ii*) Stock Turnover Ratio = 9

$$\frac{\text{Cost of Goods Sold}}{\text{Average Stock (X)}} = 9 \qquad \frac{9,00,000}{X} = 9$$

$$X = \frac{9,00,000}{9}$$

$$\text{Stock} = 1,00,000$$

(*iii*)

Current Ratio	1.75	3,50,000
Quick Ratio	1.25	2,50,000
Stock	0.50	1,00,000

(*iv*) Debt Collection Period = 1 ½ months

$$\frac{\text{Debtors}}{\text{Sales}} \times 12 = 1.5$$

Debtors = 1,50,000

$$X = 12,00,000 \times \frac{1.5}{12}$$

Debtors = 1,50,000

(*v*) Turnover of Fixed Assets 1.2

$$\frac{\text{Turnover}}{\text{(X) Fixed Assets}} = 1.2 = \frac{9,00,000}{X} = 1.2$$

$$X = \frac{9,00,000}{1.2}$$

Fixed Assets = 7,50,000

(*vi*) Fixed Assets to : Networth = 1.25 :1

↓ ↓

1.25 : 1.00

7,50,000 : 6,00,000

(*vii*) Reserves and Surplus to Capital : 0.2 : 1

Reserves	+	Share Capital	=	Net worth
0.2	+	1.00	=	1.2
↓		↓		↓
1,00,000	+	5,00,000	=	6,00,000

$$\left[\frac{6,00,000}{1.2} \times 1 = 5,00,000\right]$$

(*viii*) Capital Gearing Ratio

$$\frac{\text{(X) Fixed Interest Bearing}}{\text{Equity Share Capital}} = 0.6$$

X = 5,00,000 × 0.6

Long-term Debt = ₹ 3,00,000

Balance Sheet

Liabilities	₹	*Assets*	₹
Equity Share Capital	5,00,000	Fixed Assets	7,50,000
Long-term Debt	3,00,000	Current Assets	3,50,000
Reserves	1,00,000		
Current Liabilities	2,00,000		
	11,00,000		11,00,000

NOTE : Current Ratio

Current Assets	:	Current Liabilities
1.75		1.00
3,50,000		2,00,000

Problem 8. *Using the information and the form given below compute the balance sheet items for a firm having a sale of ₹ 36 lakhs.*

Sales / Total Assets	3	*Sales / Debtors*	15
Sales / Fixed Assets	5	*Current Ratio*	2
Sales / Current Assets	7.5	*Total Assets / Net worth*	2.5
Sales / Inventories	20	*Debt Equity*	1

Balance Sheet

Liabilities	₹	*Assets*	₹
Networth	***	*Fixed Assets*	***
Long-term Debt	***	*Inventories*	***
Current Liabilities	***	*Debtors*	***
		Liquid Assets	***
		Current Assets	***

Solution :

(1) Sales : Total assets = 3
↓ ↓
3 : 1
36,00,000 : 12,00,000

(2) Sales : Fixed assets = 5
5 : 1
36,00,000 : 7,20,000

(3) Sales : Current assets = 7.5
7.5 : 1.00
36,00,000 : 4,80,000

(4) Sales : Inventories
20 : 1
36,00,000 : 1,80,000

(5) Sales : Debtors
15 : 1.00
36,00,000 : 2,40,000

(6) Current Ratio : $\frac{\text{Current Assets}}{\text{Current Liabilities}}$
2 : 1.00
4,80,000 : 2,40,000

(7) Total Assets : Net worth = 2.5
↓ ↓
2.5 : 1.00
12,00,000 : 4,80,000

(8) Debt	:	Equity
1.0	:	1.0
4,80,000	:	4,80,000

Balance Sheet

Liabilities	₹	*Assets*	₹
Net worth	4,80,000	Fixed Assets	7,20,000
Long-term Debt	4,80,000	Inventories	1,80,000
Current Liabilities	2,40,000	Debtors	2,40,000
		Liquid Assets	60,000
	12,00,000		12,00,000

Current Assets		4,80,000
Debtors	2,40,000	
Stock	1,80,000	
		4,20,000
Liquid Assets		60,000

Problem 9. *From the following information compute the Balance sheet*

Total Assets/Net worth	=	*3.5*
Sales to fixed Assets	=	*6*
Sales to current Assets	=	*8*
Sales to inventory	=	*15*
Sales to Debtors	=	*18*
Current Ratio	=	*2.5*
Annual sales	=	*₹ 25,00,000*

[MBA Madras]

Solution :

(*i*) Sales to Fixed Assets = 6 : 1

↓ ↓

25,00,000 4,16,667

(*ii*) Sales to Current Assets = 8

$$\frac{\text{Sales}}{\text{(X) Current Assets}} = 8$$

$$X = \frac{25,00,000}{8}$$

Current Assets = 3,12,500

(*iii*) $$\text{Debtors} = \frac{\text{Sales}}{\text{(X) Debtors}} = 18$$

$$X = \frac{25,00,000}{18} = 1,38,889$$

(*iv*) Sales	:	Inventory = 15 :1
15	:	1
↓		↓
25,00,000	:	1,66,667
(*v*) Current Ratio		
Current Assets	:	Current Liabilities
2.5	:	1.0
↓		↓
3,12,500	:	1,25,000
(*vi*) Total Assets	:	Net worth = 3.5
3.5	:	1.00
↓		↓
7,29,167	:	2,08,333

$$\left[\frac{7,29,167}{3.5} \times 1.00 = 2,08,333\right]$$

Total Assets	=	Fixed Assets	4,16,667
		Current Assets	3,12,500
			7,29,167

Long Term Debt :

Total Assets = [Net worth + Current Liabilities)

7,29,167 = [1,78,667 + 1,25,000]

Long-term Debt = ₹ 4,25,500

Balance Sheet

Liabilities	₹	*Assets*	₹
Net worth	1,78,667	Fixed Assets	4,16,667
Long-term Debt	4,25,500	Current Assets	3,12,500
Current Liabilities	1,25,000		
	7,29,167		7,29,167

Current Assets :

Inventory	1,66,667
Debtors	1,38,889
Liquid Assets	6,944
Current Assets	3,12,500

Problem 10. *Following are the ratios to the trading activities of Indian Traders Ltd.*

Debtor's Velocity	*3 months*
Stock Velocity	*8 months*
Creditors Velocity	*2 months*
Gross Profit Ratio	*25%*

Gross Profit for the year ended 31.12.2001 amounts to ₹ 4,00,000. Closing stock of the year is ₹ 10,000 above the opening stock. Bills receivable are worth ₹ 25,000 and bills payable ₹ 10,000.

Find out (a) Sales (b) Sundry Debtors (c) Closing Stock and (d) Sundry Creditors.

[B.Com., Madras 1991]

Solution :

(1) Cost of Goods Sold + GP = Sales

75% + 25% = 100%

↓ ↓ ↓

12,00,000 + 4,00,000 = 16,00,000

(2) Debtor's Velocity : 3 months

$$\frac{\text{Debtors}}{\text{Sales}} \times 12 = 3, \textit{ i.e., } \frac{X}{16,00,000} \times 12 = 3$$

= 4,00,000

Less : Bills receivable = 25,000

Sundry Debtors = 3,75,000

(3) Stock Velocity : 8 months

$$\frac{\text{Cost of Goods Sold}}{\text{Average Stock (X)}} \times 12 = 8 = \frac{12,00,000}{X} \times 12 = 8$$

$$X = 12,00,000 \times \frac{8}{12}$$

Average Stock = 8,00,000

Total Stock Value 8,00,000 × 2 = 16,00,000

Excess Stock = 10,000

15,90,000

Opening Stock = 7,95,000   7,95,000

Closing Stock = 7,95,000

Excess Value = 10,000   8,05,000

16,00,000

(4) Sundry Creditors

Opening Stock	+	Purchase – Closing Stock	=	Cost of Goods Sold
7,95,000	+	x – 8,05,000	=	12,00,000
x = 12,00,000	+	8,05,000 – 7,95,000	=	12,10,000

(5) Creditor's Velocity = 2 months

$$\frac{\text{Creditors + Bills Payable}}{\text{Purchase}} \times 12 = 2, \textit{ i.e.}, \frac{X}{12,00,000} \times 12 = 2$$

Account Payable = 2,01,667

Less : Bills Payable = 10,000

Creditors = 1,91,667

Problem 11. *From the following information prepare a Balance Sheet with as many details as possible.*

Gross Profit	*₹ 80,000*	*Current Assets*	*₹ 1,50,000*
Gross Profit to Cost of Goods Sold Ratio	*1/3*	*Account Payable Velocity*	*90 days*
		Bills Receivable	*₹ 20,000*
Stock Velocity	*6 times*	*Bills Payable*	*₹ 5,000*
Opening Stock	*₹ 36,000*	*Fixed Assets Turnover Ratio*	*8 times*
Account Receivable Velocity	*72 days*		
(Year 360 days)			

***Note** : Turnover refers to Cost of Sales.*

[M.Com Madras Nov. 1978] [B.Com. Madras Nov.1978 PU 2004]

Solution :

(1)

Cost of Goods Sold	+	GP	=	Sales
↓		↓		↓
3	+	1	=	4
2,40,000	+	80,000	=	3,20,000

(2) Stock Velocity = 6 times

$$\frac{\text{Cost of Goods Sold}}{\text{Average Stock (X)}} = \frac{2,40,000}{X} = 6$$

∴ Average Stock = 40,000

(3) Average Stock = ₹ 40,000

Full Stock Value = 40,000 × 2 = 80,000

Less : Opening Stock = 36,000

Closing Stock = 44,000

(4) Debtors Velocity

$$\frac{\text{Debtors + Bill Receivable}}{\text{Sales}} \times 360 = 72$$

$$X = 3,20,000 \times \frac{72}{360} = 64,000$$

$$\therefore \quad \text{Drs + Bills Receivable} = 64,000$$
$$\textit{Less}: \text{Bills Receivable} = 20,000$$
$$\text{Debtors} = 44,000$$

(5) **Creditor's Velocity or Accounts Payable Velocity**

$$\frac{\text{Creditors + Bills Payable}}{\text{Purchase}} \times 360 = 90, \; i.e., \; \frac{X}{12,48,000} \times 360 = 90$$

$$X = 2,48,000 \times \frac{90}{360}$$

$$\text{Bills Payable + Creditors} = 62,000$$
$$\textit{Less}: \text{Bills payable} = 5,000$$
$$\text{Creditors} = 57,000$$

Find out the Purchases

Opening Stock + Purchase – Closing Stock = Cost of Goods Sold

↓ ↓ ↓ ↓

36,000 + x – 44,000 = 2,40,000

x = 2,40,000 + 44,000 – 36,000

Purchase ₹ = 2,48,000

(6) **Fixed Assets Turnover Ratio**

$$\frac{\text{Turnover}}{\text{Fixed Assets (X)}} = 8, \; i.e., \; X = \frac{2,40,000}{8}$$

$$\text{Fixed Assets} = 30,000$$

Balance Sheet

Liabilities	₹	*Assets*	₹
Capital (B/F)	1,18,000	Fixed Assets	30,000
Creditors	57,000	Closing Stock	44,000
Bills Payable	5,000	Debtors	44,000
		Bills Receivable	20,000
		Other Current Assets	42,000
	1,80,000		1,80,000

Total Current Assets given :		1,50,000
Stock	44,000	
Debtors	44,000	
B.R.	20,000	1,08,000
Other Current Assets		42,000

Problem 12. *From the following information presented by a firm for the year ended 31st December, find out :*

(i) Net worth *(ii) Current Liabilities*
(iii) Total Debt to Net worth *(iv) Long-term Debt*
(v) Current Assets *(vi) Stock*
(vii) Debtors and *(viii) Fixed Assets*

Sales to Net worth	:	*5 times*
Current Liabilities to Net worth	:	*50%*
Total Debts to Net worth	:	*60%*
Current Ratio	:	*2*
Sales to Stock	:	*10 times*
Debtor's Velocity	:	*9 times*
Annual Sales	:	*₹ 15,00,000*
Cash Sales	:	*40% of Sales*

[M.Com. (CA) May 2004 PU]

Solution :

(*i*) Sales to Net worth : 5 times

Sales	:	Net worth
5	:	1
15,00,000	:	3,00,000

$$\left[\frac{15,00,000}{5} \times 1 = 3,00,000\right]$$

(*ii*) Current Liabilities to Net worth

Current Liabilities = 50% of ₹ 3,00,000
= 1,50,000

(*iii*) Total Debt to Net worth = 60%

Total Debt is 60% of 3,00,000 = 1,80,000 (or)

Total Debt	:	Net worth
60%	:	100%
↓		↓
1,80,000	:	3,00,000

(*iv*) Long-term Debt

Long term Debt = Total Debt – Current Liabilities
= 1,80,000 – 1,50,000 = 30,000

(*v*) Current Assets

Current Ratio

Current Assets	:	Current Liabilities
2.0	:	1.00
3,00,000	:	1,50,000

(*vi*) Stock

Sales to Stock = 10 times

Sales	:	Stock
10.0	:	1.00
15,00,000	:	1,50,000

(*vii*) Debtor's Velocity : 9 times

$$\text{Credit Sales} = 15{,}00{,}000 \times \frac{60}{100}$$

$$= 9{,}00{,}000$$

$$\text{Debtor's Turnover Ratio} = \frac{\text{Debtors (X)}}{\text{Sales}} = 9,\ i.e.,\ \frac{X}{9{,}00{,}000} = 9$$

$$X = \frac{9{,}00{,}000}{9}$$

$$\text{Debtors} = 1{,}00{,}000$$

(*viii*) Fixed Assets

Fixed Assets to Net worth Ratio = 60%

$$\left[\frac{3{,}00{,}000}{100} \times 60 = 1{,}80{,}000\right]$$

i.e., Fixed Assets	:	Net worth
↓		↓
60%	:	100%
1,80,000	:	3,00,000

Problem 13. *With the help of the following Ratios regarding Narmatha Tex, draw the Trading, Profit and Loss A/c and Balance Sheet of the company for the year 2004.*

(*i*)	*Current Ratio*	: *2.5*
(*ii*)	*Liquidity Ratio*	: *1.5*
(*iii*)	*Net working capital*	: *₹ 3,00,000*
(*iv*)	*Stock Turnover Ratio*	: *6 times (Cost of Sales/Closing Stock)*
(*v*)	*Gross Profit Ratio*	: *20%*
(*vi*)	*Fixed Assets Turnover Ratio (on Cost of Sales)*	: *2 times*
(*vii*)	*Debt Collection Period*	: *2 months*
(*viii*)	*Fixed Assets to Shareholder's Net worth*	: *0.80*
(*ix*)	*Reserves and Surplus to Capital*	: *0.5*

[M.Com. Bharathiar 1991]

Solution :

(1) Current Assets	–	Current Liabilities	=	Working Capital
↓		↓		↓
2.5	–	1.00		1.5
↓		↓		↓
5,00,000	↓	2,00,000	=	3,00,000

(2) Current Ratio 2.5 → 5,00,000

Liquidity Ratio 1.5 → 3,00,000

Stock 1.0 → 2,00,000

(3) Stock Turnover Ratio : 6 times

$$\frac{\text{(X) Cost of Goods Sold}}{\text{Closing Stock}} = 6, \textit{ i.e., } \frac{X}{2,00,000} = 6$$

Cost of Goods Sold = 12,00,000

(4) Cost of Goods Sold + GP = Sales

80% + 20% = 100%

12,00,000 + 3,00,000 = 15,00,000

$$\left[\frac{12,00,000}{80} \times 20\right] = 3,00,000$$

(5) Debt Collection Period = 2 months

$$\frac{\text{X Drs + BR}}{\text{Sales}} \times 12 = 2, \textit{ i.e., } \frac{X}{15,00,000} \times 12 = 2$$

$$X = 15,00,000 \times \frac{2}{12}$$

Debtors + BR = 2,50,000

(6) Fixed Assets Turnover Ratio

$$\frac{\text{Turnover}}{\text{Fixed Assets}} = 2, \textit{ i.e., } \frac{12,00,000}{X} = 2$$

$$X = \frac{12,00,000}{2} = 6,00,000$$

(7) Fixed Assets to Shareholder's Net worth = .80

$$\frac{\text{Fixed Assets (6,00,000)}}{\text{Shareholder's Net worth (X)}} = .80$$

$$X = \frac{6,00,000}{.80}$$

Shareholder's Net worth = 7,50,000

(8) Reserves and Surplus to capital : 0.5

Reserves	+	Share Capital	=	Net worth
.50	+	1.00	=	1.50
↓		↓		↓
2,50,000	+	5,00,000	=	7,50,000

Balance Sheet

Liabilities	₹	*Assets*	₹
Share Capital	5,00,000	Fixed Assets	6,00,000
Reserves and Surplus	2,50,000	Current Assets	5,00,000
Current Liabilities	2,00,000		
Long-term Loan	1,50,000		
	11,00,000		11,00,000

Total Current Assets given :		5,00,000
Stock	2,00,000	
Debtors	2,50,000	4,50,000
Cash		50,000

Problem 14. *From the following figures and ratios draw out trading, profit and loss account and balance sheet.*

Share capital = *1,80,000*
Working capital = *63,000*
Bank overdraft = *10,000*

There is no fictitious asset. In current assets there is no asset other than Stock debtors and cash. Closing stock is 20% higher than the opening stock.

Current Ratio : *2.5*
Proprietary Ratio : *0.7*
Stock Velocity : *4*
Net Profit Ratio : *10% (to average Capital employed)*
Quick Ratio : *1.5*
Gross Profit Ratio : *20% to Sales*
Debtor's Velocity : *365 days*

Answer : Gross Profit ₹ 38,500, NP 23,950, B/s total 2,22,000.

Problem 15. *With the following Ratios and further information given below, prepare Trading, Profit and Loss A/c and a Balance Sheet of Shri Surjit & Co.*

(i) Gross Profit Ratio	: *25%*	*(vi) Fixed Assets/Capital : 5/4*	
(ii) Net Profit/Sales	: *20%*	*(vii) Fixed Assets/Total Current Assets : 5/7*	
(iii) Stock Turnover Ratio	: *10*	*(viii) Fixed Assets*	: *₹ 10,00,000*
(iv) Net Profit Capital	: *1/5*	*(ix) Closing Stock*	: *₹ 1,00,000*
(v) Capital to Total Liabilities	: *1/2*		

Solution :

(*i*) Capital

Fixed Assets	:	Capital
5	:	4
10,00,000	:	8,00,000

$$\left[\frac{5}{10,00,000}\times 4\right] = 8,00,000$$

(*ii*) Net Profit Ratio

Net Profit	:	Capital
1.00	:	5.00
↓		↓
1,60,000		8,00,000

(*iii*) Net Profit/Sales : 20%

$$\frac{\text{Net Profit (1,60,000)}}{\text{Sales (X)}} \times 100 = 20$$

$$X = 1,60,000 \times \frac{100}{20}$$

$$\text{Sales} = ₹\ 8,00,000$$

(*iv*)

Cost of Goods Sold	+	GP	=	Sales
75%	+	25%		100%
6,00,000	+	2,00,000		8,00,000

(*v*) Stock Turnover Ratio

$$\frac{\text{Cost of goods sold (6,00,000)}}{\text{Average Stock (X)}} = 10$$

$$X = \frac{6,00,000}{10}$$

Average stock = 60,000

Actual/Full stock value 60,000 × 2	1,20,000
Less : Closing Stock	1,00,000
Opening Stock	20,000

(*vi*) Total Liabilities : Capital to total liabilities $\frac{1}{2}$

$$\frac{\text{Capital}}{\text{(X) Total Liabilities}} = \frac{1}{2}$$

$$\frac{8,00,000}{\text{Total Liabilities}}$$

$$X = 8,00,000 \times 2 = 16,00,000$$

(*vii*) Total Current Assets

Fixed Assets to Total Current Assets : 5/7

Fixed Assets = ₹ 10,00,000

$$\frac{\text{Fixed Assets}}{\text{(X) Total Current Assets}} = 5/7$$

$$X = 10,00,000 \times \frac{7}{5}$$

$$= 14,00,000$$

Less : Closing Stock = 1,00,000

Current Assets = 13,00,000

Trading and Profit and Loss Account for the year ended

	₹		₹
To Opening Stock	20,000	By Sales	8,00,000
To Purchases	6,80,000	By Closing Stock	1,00,000
To Gross Profit	2,00,000		
	9,00,000		9,00,000
To Expenses	40,000	By Gross Profit	2,00,000
To Net Profit	1,60,000		
	2,00,000		2,00,000

Balance Sheet

Liabilities	₹	*Assets*	₹
Share Capital (8,00,000 – 1,60,000)	6,40,000	Fixed Assets	10,00,000
Net Profit	1,60,000	Stock	1,00,000
Current Liabilities	16,00,000	Other Current Assets	13,00,000
	24,00,000		24,00,000

Problem 16. *You are given the following information pertaining to the Financial Statements of Reliance Ltd as on 31.12.2004. On the basis of the information supplied, you are required to prepare Trading, Profit and Loss Account for the year ended and a Balance Sheet as on the date.*

Net Current Assets	:	*2,00,000*
Issued Share Capital	:	*6,00,000*
Current Ratio	:	*1.8*
Quick Ratio [Ratio of Debtors and Bank Balance to Current Liabilities]	:	*1.35*
Fixed Assets to Shareholder's Equity	:	*80%*
Ratio of Gross Profit on Turnover	:	*25%*
Net Profit to Issued Share Capital	:	*20%*
Stock Turnover Ratio	:	*5 times*
Average of Outstanding for the year	:	*36 ½ days*

On 31.12.2004, the Current Assets consisted only of Stock Debtors and Bank Balance Liabilities consisted of Share Capital, Current Liabilities and Assets consisted of Fixed Asset and Current Assets.

Solution :

(1) Current Assets – Current Liabilities = Working Capital

1.8		1.00		.8
4,50,000	–	2,50,000	=	2,00,000

(2) Quick Ratio

Quick Assets	:	Current Liabilities
1.35		1.00
3,37,500		2,50,000

(3) Stock

Current Assets – Quick Assets = Stock

4,50,000 – 3,37,500 = 1,12,500

(4) Stock Turnover

$$\frac{\text{Cost of Goods Sold (X)}}{\text{Closing Stock (1,12,500)}} = 5$$

$$X = 1,12,500 \times 5 = 5,62,500$$

(5) Ratio of Gross Profit on Turnover 25%

Cost of Goods Sold	+	GP	=	Sales
75%	+	25%		100%
5,62,500	+	1,87,500		7,50,000

(6) Debtor's Turnover Ratio (Here, there are no Bills Receivable)

$$\frac{\text{Drs}}{\text{Sales}} \times 365 = 36.5, \textit{ i.e., } \frac{X}{7,50,000} \times 365 = 36.5$$

$$X = 7,50,000 \times \frac{36.5}{365}$$

Debtors = ₹ 75,000

(7)

Quick Assets (Debtors + Bank)	=	3,37,500
Less : Debtors	=	75,000
Cash in hand	=	2,62,500

(8) Net Profit to Issued Share Capital : 20%

20% : 100

↓ ↓

1,20,000 : 6,00,000

$$\left[\frac{6,00,000}{100} \times 20\right] = 1,20,000$$

(9) Fixed Assets

Fixed Assets to Shareholder's Equity, change into

Shareholder's equity	–	Fixed Assets	=	Net Current Assets
↓		↓		↓
100%	–	80%	=	20
↓		↓		↓
10,00,000	–	8,00,000	=	2,00,000

$$\left[\frac{2,00,000}{20} \times 80\right] = 8,00,000$$

Trading and Profit and Loss Account for the year ended

	₹		₹
To Cost of Goods Sold	5,62,500	By Sales	7,50,000
To Gross Profit	1,87,500		
	7,50,000		7,50,000
To Expenses	67,500	By Gross Profit	1,87,500
To Net Profit	1,20,000		
	1,87,500		1,87,500

Balance Sheet

Liabilities	₹	*Assets*	₹
Share Capital	6,00,000	Fixed Assets	8,00,000
Reserves and Surplus (B/F)	2,80,000	Current Assets :	
		Stock	1,12,500
		Debtors	75,000
		Bank	2,62,500
Profit for the year	1,20,000		
Current Liabilities	2,50,000		
	12,50,000		12,50,000

Problem 17. *The following are the Ratios and other details of Rubix Ltd. :*

Debtor's velocity	:	*3 months*
Creditor's velocity	:	*2 months*
Stock turnover	:	*8 times*
Capital - turnover Ratio	:	*2.5 times*
Fixed Assets - Turnover Ratio	:	*8 times*
Gross profit Turnover Ratio	:	*25%*

Gross Profit in a year amounts to ₹ 80,000. There is no Long-term Loan or Overdraft. Reserves and Surplus amount to ₹ 28,000. Liquid Assets are ₹ 97,333. Closing Stock of the year is ₹ 2,000 more than the Opening Stock. Bills Receivable amount to ₹ 5,000 and Bills Payable to ₹ 2,000.

Find out :

(i) Sales *(ii) Sundry Debtors* *(iii) Sundry Creditors*

(iv) Closing Stock *(v) Fixed Assets* *(vi) Proprietor's Fund*

Construct the Balance Sheet with as many details as possible. [M.Com., 2004]

Solution :

(*i*) Sales

Cost of Goods Sold	+	G.P.	–	Sales
75%		25%		100%
2,40,000		80,000		3,20,000

(*ii*) **Sundry Debtors**

$$\text{Debtor's Velocity} = \frac{\text{Debtors + Bill Receivable (X)}}{\text{Sales (3,20,000)}} \times 12 = 3$$

$$X = 3{,}20{,}000 \times \frac{3}{12} = 80{,}000$$

$$\text{Debtors + Bills Receivable} = 80{,}000$$

$$\textit{Less}: \text{Bills Receivable} = 5{,}000$$

$$\text{Debtors} = 75{,}000$$

(*iii*) **Sundry Creditors**

$$\frac{\text{Creditors + Bills Payable}}{\text{Purchase (Credit)}} \times 12 = 2$$

$$X = 2{,}42{,}000 \times \frac{2}{12} = 40{,}333$$

$$\textit{Less}: \text{Bills Payable} = 2{,}000$$

$$\text{Creditors} = 38{,}333$$

Find out the Purchase

Opening Stock	+	Purchase – Closing Stock	=	Cost of Goods Sold
29,000	+	X – 31,000	=	2,40,000
X = 2,40,000	+	31,000 – 29,000		
X = 2,42,000	*i.e,*	Purchase = ₹ 2,42,000		

(*iv*) **Closing Stock**

$$\frac{\text{Cost of Goods Sold}}{\text{Average Stock (X)}} = 8 \text{ times}$$

$$X = \frac{2{,}40{,}000}{8}$$

$$\text{Average Stock} = 30{,}000$$

$$\text{Total Stock Value } 30{,}000 \times 2 = 60{,}000$$

$$\textit{Less}: \text{Excess} = 2{,}000$$

$$58{,}000$$

$$\text{Opening Stock} = 29{,}000$$

$$\text{Closing Stock } 29{,}000 + 2{,}000 = 31{,}000$$

(*v*) **Fixed Assets**

$$X = \frac{3{,}20{,}000}{8} = 40{,}000$$

Fixed Assets Turnover Ratio = 8

(*vi*) Proprietor's Fund

Proprietor's Fund = Fixed Assets + Stock + Liquid Assets – Current Liability

= 40,000 + 31,000 + 97,333 – 40,333 = ₹ 1,28,000

Cash and Bank Balance

Quick Assets		97,333
Less : Bills Receivable	5,000	
Debtors	75,000	80,000
Cash at Bank		17,333

Balance Sheet

Liabilities	₹	*Assets*	₹
Share Capital	1,00,000	Fixed Assets	40,000
Reserves and Surplus	28,000	Stock	31,000
Bills Payable	2,000	Debtors	75,000
Sundry Creditors	38,333	Bills Receivable	5,000
		Cash and Bank	17,333
	1,68,333		1,68,333

Problem 18. *From the following information of a Textile Company complete the Proforma balance Sheet if Sales are worth ₹ 28,00,000.*

Sales to Net worth	=	*2.3 times*
Current Debt to Net worth	=	*42%*
Total Debt to Net worth	=	*75%*
Current Ratio	=	*2.9 times*
Net Sales to Inventory	=	*4.7 times*
Average Collection Period	=	*64 days*
Fixed Assets to Net worth	=	*53.2%*

Proforma Balance Sheet

Net worth	?	*Fixed Assets*	?
Long-term Debt	?	*Cash*	?
Current Debt	?	*Stock*	?
		Sundry Debtors	?

[M.Com. Annamalai 1982]

Solution :

(1) Sales to Net worth : 2.3 times

$$\frac{\text{Sales (23,00,000)}}{\text{Net worth (X)}} = 2.3 \text{ times}$$

$$X = \frac{23,00,000}{2.3} = 10,00,000$$

Net worth = ₹ 10,00,000

(2) Current Debt

Current Debt : Net worth

↓ ↓

42% : 100%

↓ ↓

4,20,000 10,00,000

$$\frac{10,00,000}{100} \times 42 = 4,20,000$$

(3) Total Debt

Total Debt to Net worth = 75%

Total Debt : Net worth

75% : 100

7,50,000 : 10,00,000

[*i.e.,* Total debt is 75% of net worth $10,00,000 \times \frac{75}{100} = 7,50,000$]

(4) Long-term Debt

Long-term Debt = Total Debt – Current Debt

= 7,50,000 – 4,20,000

= 3,30,000

(5) Current Assets

Current Ratio : 2.9

Current Assets : Current Liabilities

2.9 1.0

12,18,000 4,20,000

$$\frac{4,28,000}{10} \times 2.9 = 12,18,000$$

(6) Inventory

Net Sales to Inventory

$$\frac{\text{Sales } (23,00,000)}{\text{Inventory } (X)} = 4.6 \text{ tonnes}$$

$$X = \frac{23,00,000}{4.6}$$

Inventory = 5,00,000

(7) Debtors

Average Collection Period

Here, there is no bill receivable. Hence, the formula

$$\frac{\text{Debtors } (X)}{\text{Sales } (23,00,000)} \times 360 = 90$$

$$X = 23,00,000 \times \frac{90}{360}$$

Debtors = 5,75,000

(8) Fixed Assets

Fixed Assets to Net worth

$$\frac{\text{Fixed Assets}}{\text{Net worth}} = 53.2\%$$

Fixed Assets	Net worth
↓	↓
53.2%	100%
5,32,000	10,00,000

$$\frac{10,00,000}{100} \times 53.2$$

(9) Find out the Cash

Total Current Assets		12,18,000
Less Stock	5,00,000	
Debtors	5,75,000	10,75,000
Cash		1,43,000

Balance Sheet

Liabilities	₹	*Assets*	₹
Net worth	10,00,000	Fixed Assets	5,32,000
Long-term Debt	3,30,000	Debtors	5,75,000
Current Debt	4,20,000	Stock	5,00,000
		Cash	1,43,000
	17,50,000		17,50,000

Problem 19. *Srinivasan Cotton Company's Stock Turnover is 5 times stock at the end is ₹ 20,000 which is more than at the beginning. Sales (all Credit) are ₹ 8,00,000. Rate of Gross Profit on Cost is 1/4. Current Liabilities ₹ 1,20,000. Quick Ratio is 0.75. Calculate Current Assets.* [MBA Madras]

Solution :

$$\text{Stock Turnover Ratio} = \frac{\text{Cost of Goods Sold (6,00,000)}}{\text{Average Stock (X)}} = 5$$

$$X = \frac{6,00,000}{5} = 1,20,000$$

Average Stock = 1,20,000

NOTE :

Cost of Goods Sold	= Sales	–	Gross Profit	
	= 8,00,000	–	2,00,000	= 6,00,000
Total Stock Value :	1,20,000 × 2		2,40,000	
Less : Excess Value			20,000	
			2,20,000	

Opening Stock = ₹ 1,10,000

Closing Stock = ₹ 20,000 + 1,10,000 = 1,30,000

Quick Ratio :

Quick Assets	:	Current Liabilities
↓		↓
.75		1.00
↓		↓
90,000		1,20,000

Current Assets :

Quick Assets = ₹ 90,000
Closing Stock = ₹ 1,30,000

Current Assets = ₹ 2,20,000

Problem 20. *Calculate Stock Turnover Ratio from the following details :*
(i) Opening Stock ₹ 29,000 *(ii) Closing Stock ₹ 31,000*
(iii) Sales ₹ 3,20,000 *(iv) Gross Profit – Ratio 25% on Sales*

[B.Com. 2003 PU]

Solution :

$$\text{Stock Turnover Ratio} = \frac{\text{Cost of Goods Sold}}{\text{Average Stock}}$$

$$= \frac{2,40,000}{30,000} = 8 \text{ times}$$

$$\text{Average Stock} = \frac{29,000 + 31,000}{2} = 30,000$$

Cost of Goods Sold	+	G.P.	–	Sales
75%	+	25%		100%
2,40,000		80,000		3,20,000

TEST PROBLEMS

1. The following information is extracted from the book of Confident Co. Ltd. You are required to rearrange the information for Financial Analysis and calculate (1) Return on investment (ROI) (2) Return on capital employed (3) Return on shareholders' funds (4) Return on equity shareholders' funds (5) Return on total assets.

Particulars	₹	*Particulars*	₹
Net Sales	10,00,000	Profit & Loss Account	2,00,000
Cost of goods sold	6,00,000	Debentures	2,50,000
Interest on debentures	25,000	Sundry creditors	50,000
Loss on sale of furniture	5,000	Equity share capital	3,00,000
Interest on govt. securities	5,000	10% pref. share capital	2,00,000
Fixed assets less depreciation	10,75,000	Operating expenses	1,50,000
Investment in govt. securities	50,000	Provision for tax	75,000
Current assets	5,00,000		
Reserves	4,00,000		

[**Ans.** (1) 17.24%, (2) 12%, (3) 12.62%, (4) 10.77%]

2. Calculate the earnings per share from the following information:

Net Profit before tax	₹ 10,00,000
Tax on profit	₹ 50%
15% preference share capital (₹ 10 each)	₹ 2,00,000
Equity share capital 4,700 shares of ₹ 10 each	₹ 4,70,000

[**Ans,** ₹ 100 per share]

3. Profit and Loss Account of X Ltd., is given below

Profit and Loss Account

Particulars	₹	*Particulars*	₹
To Opening stock	2,00,000	By sales	16,00,000
To Purchases	12,00,000	By Closing stock	3,20,000
To Administration expenses	1,20,000	By Dividend	4,000
To Selling expenses	80,000		
To Financial expenses	40,000		
To Loss on sale of assets	5,000		
To Net profit	2,79,000		
	19,24,000		**19,24,000**

Calculate the Profitability Ratios

[**Ans.** (1) G.P: 32.5%, (2) N.P: 17.44%, (3) OP: 20%, (4) OP Ratio: 80%]

4. (*a*) From the following details of a trader you are required to calculate stock turnover ratio.

	₹
Sales	39,984
Sales returns	380
Opening stock at cost	1,378
Closing stock at cost	1,814
Total Gross profit for the year	8.068

(*b*) Calculate stock turnover ratio and Stock turnover period from the following sales ₹ 10,000,000; Gross profit ratio 20%; Stock at the beginning of the year ₹ 1,75,000; Stock at the end of the year ₹ 1,45,000.

[Madras, B.Com. Nov. 2004; Madurai Kamaraj, B.Com.]

[**Ans.** (1) 19.76 Times (2) 2.4 months]

5. Ganesh Bros. sells goods on cash and credit terms and also purchased goods on cash and credit terms. The following particulars are obtained from their books.

	₹
Total sales	5,00,000
Cash sales	40,000
Sales returns	20,000
Debtors at the end	80,000
Bills receivable at the end	20,000
Reserve for doubtful debts	1,000

Total purchases	3,00,000
Cash Purchases	50,000
Purchase returns	10,000
Creditors at the end	60,000
Bills payable at the end	20,000
Reserve for discount on creditors	2,000
Opening stock	50,000
Closing stock	40,000
Gross profit	1,00,000
Fixed assets	10,00,000

Calculate activity ratios (turnover ratio)

[**Ans.** (1) 8.44 Stock Turnover Ratio; (2) 0.48 Times Fixed Asset Turnover Ratio; (3) 4.4 Debtors Turnover Ratio; (4) 83 Debtors Collection Period; (5) 2 Times A/c Payable; (6) 122 A/c Payable Period]

6. You are given the following information

	₹
Cash	18,000
Debtors	1,42,000
Closing Stock	1,80,000
Bills Payable	27,000
Creditors	50,000
Outstanding expenses	15,000
Tax payable	75,000

Calculate: (*a*) Current ratio (*b*) Liquidity ratio (c) Absolute liquidity ratio.

[Madras, B.Com., BBA, April 2008; Madurai Kamaraj, B.Com., April 1993]

[**Ans.** (1) 2.036 Times, (2) 0.96, (3) 0.11]

7. From the following Balance Sheet of Balaji Industries Ltd., you are required to calculate debt equity ratio.

Balance Sheet

As at 31.12.1999

Liabilities	₹	*Assets*	₹
Share capital		Fixed assets	1,20,000
10,000 shares of ₹ 10 each	1,00,000	Current assets	80,000
General reserve	12,000		
P & L A/c	8,000		
Debentures	30,000		
Current liabilities	50,000		
	2,00,000		**2,00,000**

[**Ans.** 0.67]

8. Balance Sheet of Rama Ltd. as at 31.12.1993 is as follows:

Liabilities	₹	*Assets*	₹
Equity capital	2,00,000	Fixed assets	3,60,000
9% Preference share capital	1,00,000	Stock	50,000
8% Debentures	1,00,000	Debtors	1,10,000
Profit and Loss A/c	40,000	Bills Receivable	6,000
Creditors	90,000	Bank balance	4,000
	5,30,000		**5,30,000**

Find out: (1) Fixed assets ratio and (2) Capital gearing ratio.

[Madurai Kamaraj, B.Com., April 1994]

[Ans. (1) 0.81 (2) 0.833]

9. Given below is the summarized Balance Sheet and Profit and Loss of Ragunath Sugar Mills Ltd. as on 31.12.2007. You are required to calculate.

1. Current ratio
2. Quick ratio
3. Fixed assets ratio
4. Debt equity ratio
5. Proprietary ratio
6. Stock turnover ratio
7. Fixed assets turnover ratio
8. Return on capital employed
9. Debtors turnover ratio
10. Creditors turnover ratio
11. Net profit ratio
12. Operating ratio

Balance Sheet
as on 31.12.2007

Liabilities	₹	*Assets*	₹
Share capital		Land and building	30,00,000
40,000 shares of ₹ 10 each	40,00,000	Plant and Machinery	16,00,000
Reserves	18,00,000	Stock	29,60,000
Creditors	26,00,000	Debtors	14,20,000
Profit and Loss Account	6,00,000	Cash at bank	6,20,000
6% Debentures	6,00,000		
	96,00,000		**96,00,000**

Profit and Loss Account for the Year Ended on 31.12.2007

Particulars	₹	*Particulars*	₹
To Opening stock	19,90,000	By sales	1,70,00,000
To Purchases	1,09,05,000	By Closing stock	29,80,000
To Direct expenses	2,85,000		
To Gross profit	68,00,000		
	1,99,80,000		**1,99,80,000**
To Administration expenses	30,00,000	By Gross profit b/d	68,00,000
To Selling & Distribution exp.	6,00,000	By Non-operating income	1,80,000
To Financial expenses	3,00,000		
To Other non-operating exp.	80,000		
To Net profit	30,00,000		
	69,80,000		**69,80,000**

[**Ans.** (1) 1.92, (2) 0.78, (3) 0.66, (4) 0.094, (5) 0.67, (6) 4.10 times, (7) 3.69 times, (8) 45.71%, (9) 11.97 times, (10) 4.19 times (11) 17.64%, (12) 81.17%]

10. Find out fixed assets and gross profit from the following information:

Sales ₹ 10,00,000

Gross profit ratio 25%

Fixed assets turnover (on cost of sales) 5 times

[Madras, M.Com., Nov. 2008]

[**Ans:** ₹ 1,50,000]

11. Given:

Current assets	=	2.8
Acid–test ratio	=	1.5
Working capital	=	₹ 1,62,000

Calculate:

1. Current
2. Current liabilities
3. Liquid assets
4. Stock

[Madras, BCA, Nov. 2008; M.Com., April 1994]

[**Ans:** (1) ₹ 2,52,000, (2) ₹ 90,000, (3) ₹ 1,35,000, (4) ₹ 1,17,000]

12. Following are the ratios relating to the trading activities of Nagul Traders Ltd., Madras

Receivables turnover	=	90 days
Inventory turnover	=	3 times
Payables turnover	=	3 months
Gross profit ratio	=	25%

Gross profit for the amounted to ₹ 18,000, closing inventory of the year is ₹ 2,000 above the opening inventory. Bills Receivable amount to ₹ 2,500 and Bills Payable ₹ 1,00. Ascertain the following:

1. Sales
2. Debtors
3. Closing inventory and
4. Sundry creditors.

[Madras, M.Com., Sep. 1986]

[**Ans.** (1) ₹ 72,000, (2) ₹ 1550 Debtors, (3) 19,000, (4) 13,000]

13. The following figures are extracted from the Balance Sheet of X Ltd. As on 31st December:

Particulars	*1992* ₹	*1993* ₹
Stock	25,000	40,000
Debtors	10,000	16,000
Cash at Bank	5,000	4,000
Creditors	8,000	15,000
Bills Payable	2,000	3,000
Provision for Taxes	5,000	7,000
Bank Overdraft	5,000	15,000

Calculate the Current ratio and Quick ratio for two years.

[Periyar, B.Com., April/May 2007; Madras B.Com., (CS) (old) Nov. 2008; B.C.S.Oct. 2000]

[**Ans.** (1) Current ratio, (2) Quick ratio 1992 – 2 times, 1992 – 0.75
1993 – 1.5 times, 1993 – 0.50]

14. From the following particulars, pertaining to assets and liabilities of a company calculate (*a*) liquid ratio, (*b*) proprietary ratio, (*c*) debt equity ratio, and (*d*) capital gearing ratio.

Liabilities	₹	*Assets*	₹
5,000 equity shares of ₹ 50 each	2,50,000	Building	3,00,000
1,000 8% preference shares of ₹ 100 each	1,00,000	Machinery	2,50,000
2,000 9% Debentures of ₹ 100 each	2,00,000	Stock	1,20,000
Reserves	1,50,000	Debtors	1,00,000
Creditors	75,000	Cash at Bank	27,500
Bank Overdraft	25,000	Prepaid expenses	2,500
	8,00,000		**8,00,000**

[Madras, BCA, Nov. 2007 (2 Times), B.C.S (ICE) Oct. 2003; BCA/B.Sc (ICE) May 2003; April 2002; B.Com. (old) Oct. 2002; B.Com. March 1989; B.A. Corp. C&M, March 1997]

[**Ans:** (1) Current ratio (2) Quick ratio
1992 — 2 times 1992 — 0.75
1993 — 1.5 times 1993 — 0.50

15. Following is the Balance Sheet of Kovalan & Co.Ltd.

Liabilities	₹	*Assets*	₹
Equity shares capital	1,00,000	Cash	2,000
6% Preference share capital	1,00,000	Bank	10,000
7% Debentures	40,000	Bills Receivable	30,000
8% Public debt	20,000	Investments	20,000
Bank overdraft	40,000	Debtors	70,000
Creditors	60,000	Stock	40,000
Outstanding creditors	7,000	Furniture	30,000
Proposed dividend	10,000	Machinery	1,00,000
Reserves	1,50,000	Land & Building	2,20,000
Reserves for taxation	20,000	Goodwill	35,000
P & L Account	20,000	Preliminary expenses	10,000
	5,67,000		**5,67,000**

During the year provision for taxation was ₹ 20,000. Dividend was proposed at ₹ 10,000. Profit carried from the last year was 15,000. You are required to calculate.

(*i*) Current ratio

(*ii*) Liquidity ratio

(*iii*) Debt-equity ratio

(*iv*) Fixed assets ratio and

(*v*) Fixed charges cover ratio

[Madras, B.C.S (ICE) Oct. 2002; B.Com., March 1990; B.A. Corp. C&M. Sep 1996; B.Sc. C&M. Oct. 1999]

[Ans: (1) 1.26, (2) 0.96, (3) 0.17, (4) 0.83, (5) 8.95 (Profit before interest and tax ₹ 39400, Fixed charges 2,800 + 1,600 = 4400)]

16. From the following given ratios and figures, prepare a summarized Balance Sheet of XYZ Co. Ltd., for the year ended 31.12.2005.

(*a*) Working capital	= ₹ 60,000
(*b*) Reserves and surplus	= ₹ 40,000
(*c*) Bank overdraft	= ₹ 10,000
(*d*) Asset (fixed) proprietorship ratio	= 0.75
(*e*) Current ratio	= 2.50
(*f*) Liquid ratio	= 1.50

[Madras, BBA (Sem) April 2006; B.C.S. (PYE) April 2005; B.C.S (ICE) May 2004; (2 Times); M.Com., 1st Year April 2003; Double Figs.; B.Com., April 2001 (old) double figures, B.Com., April 1999]

[Ans: Assets – Total: ₹ 2,80,000; Fixed assets: ₹ 1,80,000; Stock : ₹ 40,000; Other current assets: ₹ 60,000; Liabilities – Total : ₹ 2,80,000; Capital: ₹ 2,00,000; Reserves and surplus: ₹ 40,000; Bank overdraft: ₹ 10,000; Other current liabilities: ₹ 30,000]

17. From the following details prepare statement of Proprietary funds with as many details as possible.

(*i*) Stock velocity	= 6
(*ii*) Capital turnover ratio	= 2
(*iii*) Fixed assets turnover ratio	= 4
(*iv*) Gross profit turnover ratio	= 20 percent
(*v*) Debtors velocity	= 2 months
(*vi*) Creditors velocity	= 73 days

The Gross profit was ₹ 60,000. Reserves and surplus amount to ₹ 20,000. Closing stock was ₹ 5,000 in excess of opening stock

[Madras B.Com. (CS) April 2007; M.Com. (ICE) May 2007; B.Com. (old) April 2007; BBA (MG3B) Nov 2004; 1st Year M.Com. (ICE) Oct 2002; B.Com., April 2002 (old); B.Com. April 2000; B.A., Corp, Oct. 2003; March 1994; B.B.A., Nov. 2004; B.C.S., Oct. 2003; M.Com., Sep. 1993]

[Ans: Proprietary funds : ₹ 1,20,000; Capital : ₹ 1,00,000; Reserves : ₹ 20,000; Current liabilities : ₹ 49,000; Debtors ₹ 50,000; Closing stock : ₹ 42,500; Other current assets: ₹ 16,500; (Bal. fig. in Balance Sheet) fixed assets ₹ 60,000]

❑❑❑

8

Fixed Assets and Depreciation

FIXED ASSETS

At the time of commencement of business, the owner of the organisation can invest money into the concern as assets. These assets may be current asset and/or fixed asset. Current assets are those which can be converted into cash quickly. But, fixed assets are those assets which cannot be converted into cash quickly. Both assets are essential for the successful running of the business. But, current assets are maintained in the business in order to operate the fixed assets and carry on the business activities. It is otherwise called as working capital. In the actual sense, fixed assets can be classified into Tangible fixed assets and Intangible fixed assets. Normally fixed assets are utilised for the productive purpose of the organisation. For the purpose of utilisation of fixed assets to the production purpose, certain values of fixed assets are to be reduced. Such reduced value is called depreciation. So, depreciation is treated as admissible business expenditure upto a prescribed limit. At the same time, depreciation can be Tangible fixed assets which include a physical form of asset such as plant and machinery, land and buildings, furniture and fittings, replacement of tools, vehicles etc. and Intangible fixed assets which include goodwill, patents, copyright, trademark etc.

MEANING OF DEPRECIATION

The concept of depreciation is related to fixed assets only. Current assets are never depreciated rather these are valued. Simply, Depreciation means it is a permanent and gradual shrinkage in the book value of fixed asset. Depreciation is charged on the book value only. Once,Depreciation is charged, it should gradually reduce the value of fixed assets.

The Institute of Chartered Accountants of India defines depreciation as "a measure of the wearing out, consumption or other loss of value of a depreciable asset arising from use, affluxion of time or obsolescence through technology and market changes. Depreciation is allocated so as to charge a fair proportion of the depreciable amount in each accounting period during the expected useful life of the asset. Depreciation includes amortisation of assets whose useful life is predetermined".

According to the International Accounting Standard Committee "depreciation is the allocation of the depreciable amount of an asset over its estimated useful life. Depreciation for the accounting period is charged to income either directly or indirectly".

CAUSES OF DEPRECIATION

The following are the main causes of depreciation :

(*i*) *Physical Cause.* It is caused mainly from the wear and tear due to friction, pull, impact, fatigue, twisting etc. And also it includes lack of maintenance and repairs in time.

(*ii*) *Time Factors.* Some assets lose its value simply with passage of time in the practical business life. There are certain assets with a fixed period of legal life such as lease, patents and copyrights. Here, instead of depreciation, provision for the consumption of these assets is created. This is called amortisation.

(*iii*) *Economic Factors.* Depreciation arises due to the changes in Fashion and Technology. In the real sense, new model and new technology may make the asset become obsolete even if it is in good physical condition. Some times, due to organisational growth, usage of assets are to be stopped or inadequacy of existing equipment due to the expansion of the business.

(*iv*) *Abnormal Occurrences.* The value of asset may be decreased because of accidents due to some wrong operations or some loose component which may result in heavy damages to the industry. Inferior quality of materials also decreases the value of asset.

(*v*) *Depletion.* Certain assets are of wasting character perhaps due to the extraction of raw materials from them. In lieu of writing off depreciation to provide for the consumption or utilisation of an asset of a wasting character is called provision for depletion.

OBJECTIVES OR NEED FOR PROVIDING DEPRECIATION

(*i*) To ascertain correct profits of the organisation

(*ii*) To show the accurate financial position of the organisation

(*iii*) To make provision for replacement of assets

(*iv*) To determine the correct tax liability

(*v*) To provide guidance to the management for important financial matters

(*vi*) To keep the capital intact

(*vii*) To provide depreciation is a statutory need - statutory obligation.

BASIC FACTORS FOR CALCULATING DEPRECIATION

(*i*) The cost of the asset

(*ii*) The estimated number of years of its life

(*iii*) The estimated residual or scrap value at the end of its life.

METHODS FOR PROVIDING DEPRECIATION

(*i*) Fixed Instalment or Straight Line Method.

(*ii*) Fixed Percentage on Diminishing Balance Method.

(*iii*) Sum of the years Digits Method.
(*iv*) Annuity Method.
(*v*) Depreciation Fund Method.
(*vi*) Insurance Policy Method.
(*vii*) Revaluation Method.
(*viii*) Machine Hour Rate Method.
(*ix*) Depletion Method.
(*x*) Repairs Provision Method.

(*i*) *Fixed Instalment or Straight Line or Fixed Percentage on Original Cost.* Under this method, the Depreciation is calculated on the basis of either a fixed percentage of the original value of the asset or divide the original value of asset by the number of years of its estimated life. Every year, the same amount is written off as Depreciation so as to reduce the asset account to nil.

Depreciation =

$$\frac{\text{Cost of the Asset + Installation Charges − Scrap Value + Removal Cost}}{\text{Estimated useful Life of the Asset}}$$

(*ii*) *Diminishing Balance Method.* Under the diminishing Balance method, depreciation is calculated at a fixed percentage on the opening balance of each year. Each year the opening balance may be decreasing in value. This decreasing book value is commonly known as written down value of the asset. While applying the depreciation rate both salvage or scrap value and removal costs are ignored. There are no possibilities to reduce the book value to zero.

(*iii*) *Sum of the Years Digits Method.* It gives decreasing depreciation charge year by year. For the purpose of obtaining yearly depreciation diminishing percentages to the cost of the asset, less salvage value is applied. Under this method, the rate of depreciation is a fraction having the sum of the digits representing the useful life of the asset as its denominator and individual year as its numerator.

(*iv*) *Annuity Method.* Under the Annuity method, the annual depreciation charges would be ascertained with the help of Annuity table. This method gives importance to interest factor. Other methods do not take into account the interest factor while investing the assets. Fixed interest rate is charged on the opening balance of each year and then cost of asset together with interest thereon is written off equally over the life of the asset.

(*v*) *Depreciation Fund Method.* Depreciation fund method provides an adequate financial requirement for the replacement of the asset when the asset is replaced by a new one. Depreciation fund account is opened and the amount of depreciation is credited to that account. The asset account stands year after year at its original cost. At the end of each year, the amount of depreciation is debited and depreciation fund account is credited and the corresponding amount is invested in securities of some reputed companies, for the purpose of mobilising funds for replacement.

(*vi*) *Insurance Policy Method.* Under this method, an insurance policy is taken from the insurance company for the purpose of replacement of an asset. At the end of the definite period, the insurance company will pay the assured sum with the help of which asset can be repurchased.

(*vii*) *Revaluation Method.* This method is suitable for small and diverse items of asset such as bottles, corks, trade marks, loose tools, livestock etc. Under this method the amount of depreciation is ascertained to find the difference between the book value of the asset and the real value of the asset. At the end of the year the difference is taken as depreciation.

(*viii*) *Machine Hour Rate Method.* The Economic Life of the asset is estimated in terms of working hours. Hourly rate is determined by dividing total cost of the asset by total number of hours to be operated in its life time. The annual depreciation charge is calculated by applying this rate to the actual number of hours operated in the particular accounting period.

$$\text{Machine hour rate} = \frac{\text{Cost} - \text{Scrap Value}}{\text{Total hours (whole lifetime)}}$$

Depreciation for the year = Machine Hour value × Estimated Hours in a year.

(*ix*) *Depletion Method.* The Economic Life of the asset is determined by geographical survey methods in terms of total units of resource deposits. The depletion rate per unit is calculated by dividing the total cost of the asset by the estimated available number of units.

(*x*) *Repairs Provision Method.* Under this method, first the total repair and renewal costs are determined for the whole life of the asset and then it is added to the capital cost to get a total value. Then, this value is divided by its estimated life. The resultant value is treated as Repair, Renewals and depreciation. It has to be charged to the profit and loss Account each year. The corresponding Credit is given to provision for depreciation and Repairs account.

TEST QUESTIONS

1. What is meant by Depreciation ?
2. Define Depreciation.
3. What is meant by Fixed Assets ?
4. What are the causes of providing Depreciation ?
5. Briefly explain the various objectives of Depreciation.
6. Describe the basic factors for calculating Depreciation.
7. Describe the various methods for providing Depreciation.
8. What is meant by straight line method of calculating Depreciation ?
9. Depreciation is an apportionment of cost. Discusses and give the main problems which are faced in calculating the amount of Depreciation.
10. Discusses the merits and demerits of various methods of calculating Depreciation.
11. Depreciation is a source of fund. Explain.
12. 'Depreciation Accounting is a process of allocation and not of valuation' – Comment.

PROBLEMS AND SOLUTIONS

Problem 1. *On 1.1.1998 X Ltd. purchased a machinery for ₹ 58,000 and spent ₹ 2,000 on its execution. On 1.7.1998 an additional ₹ 20,000 worth of machinery was purchased. On 1.7.2000 the machine was purchased and on 1.1.1998 was sold for ₹ 28,600 and on the same date a new machine was purchased at a cost of ₹ 40,000. Show the machinery account for the first four calendar years according to written down value method taking the rate of depreciation @ 10%.* [MBA Anna Dec. 2003]

Solution : **Machinery Account**

Date	*Particulars*	*Amount* ₹	*Date*	*Particulars*	*Amount* ₹
1.1.98	To Cash	60,000	31.12.98	By Depreciation	6,000
1.7.98	To Cash	20,000	31.12.98	By Depreciation $\left[20{,}000 \times \frac{10}{100} \times \frac{6}{12}\right]$	1,000
			31.12.98	By Balance c/d	73,000
		80,000			80,000
1.1.99	To Balance b/d	73,000	31.12.99	By Depreciation	7,300
			31.12.99	By Balance c/d	65,700
		73,000			73,000
1.1.00	To Balance b/d	65,700	1.7.00	By Depreciation for 6 months	2,430
1.7.00	To Cash	40,000	1.7.00	By P&L A/c (Loss on sale)	17,570
			1.7.00	By Cash	28,600
			31.12.00	By Depreciation on Balance machinery (80,000 – 60,000 = 20,000)	1,710
			31.12.00	By Depreciation $\left[40{,}000 \times \frac{10}{100} \times \frac{6}{12}\right]$	2,000
			31.12.00	By Balance c/d	53,390
		1,05,700			1,05,700
1.1.01	To Balance b/d	53,390	31.12.01	By Depreciation	5,339
			31.12.01	By Balance c/d	48,051
		53,390			53,390

1. Workings :

Value of Machinery on the date of purchase 1.1.98	60,000
Less : Depreciation for 1.1.98 to 31.12.98	6,000
	54,000
Less : Depreciation for 1.1.99 to 31.12.99	5,400
	48,600
Less : Depreciation for 6 months 1.1.2000 to 1.7.2000 (48,600 × 10/100 × 6/12)	2,430
Value of Machinery as on the date of sale	46,170
Sale price of the machinery	28,600
Loss on sale of Machinery	17,570

2. Depreciation on Balance Machinery :

Total	80,000
Sold	60,000
Balance Machinery	20,000

Value of Machinery on 1.7.98	20,000
Depreciation for 6 months 1.7.98 to 31.12.98	1,000
	19,000
Less : Depreciation for 1.1.99 to 31.12.99	1,900
	17,100
Less : Depreciation for 1.1.2000 to 31.12.2000	1,710
	15,390
Less : Depreciation for 1.1.2001 to 31.12.2001	1,539
	13,851

3. Total Depreciation for 2001

Depreciation for new machinery *i.e.,* purchased on 1.7.2000 (40,000 – 2,000 = 38,000 × 10/100)	3,800
Depreciation on old machinery	1,539
	5,339

Problem 2. *X Ltd purchased a machine for ₹ 60,000 on 1.1.1998. Depreciation is provided @ 10% p.a. on diminishing Balance method. Prepare machinery account for the year 2000 in each of the following alternative cases.*

(i) *If the machine is sold on 1.7.2000 for ₹ 28,600.*

(ii) *If a new machine costing ₹ 60,000 is purchased on 1.7.2000 after surrendering the old one and paying cash ₹ 35,000.*

[MBA Anna Dec. 2002]

Solution : (*i*) If the machine is sold on 1.7.2000 for ₹ 28,600

Machinery Account

Date	*Particulars*	*Amount* ₹	*Date*	*Particulars*	*Amount* ₹
1.1.1998	To Bank	60,000	31.12.1998	By Depreciation	6,000
			31.12.1998	By Balance c/d	54,000
		60,000			60,000
1.1.1999	To Balance b/d	54,000	31.12.1999	By Depreciation	5,400
			31.12.1999	By Balance c/d	48,600
		54,000			54,000
1.1.2000	To Balance b/d	48,600	1.7.2000	By Depreciation (48,600 × 10/100 × 6/12)	2,430
				By Cash	28,600
				By Loss on Sale of machinery	17,570
		48,600			48,600

Workings :

	₹
Cost of the Machinery	60,000
Less : Depreciation [6,000 + 5,400 + 2,430]	13,830
Value of Machinery as on the date of Sale	46,170
Sale Price of the machinery	28,600
Loss on Sale of machinery	17,570

(*ii*) If the new machine costing ₹ 60,000 is purchased on 1.7.2000 after surrendering the old one and paying cash ₹ 35,000.

Date	*Particulars*	*Amount* ₹	*Date*	*Particulars*	*Amount* ₹
1.1.1998	To Cash	60,000	31.12.1998	By Depreciation	6,000
			31.12.1998	By Balance c/d	54,000
		60,000			60,000
1.1.1999	To Balance b/d	54,000	31.12.1999	By Depreciation	5,400
			31.12.1999	By Balance	48,600
		54,000			54,000

Machinery Account

Date	Particulars	Amount ₹	Date	Particulars	Amount ₹
1.7.2000	To Cash (35,000 cash 25,000 adjustment from old machine)	60,000		By Depreciation on old machine (49,600 × 10/100 × 6/12)	2,430
				By Depreciation on new machine (60,000 × 10/100 × 6/12)	3,000
				By Balance c/d	54,570
		60,000			60,000

Problem 3. *Mr. Kumar purchased a machine for ₹ 1,60,000 on 1.1.2000. Its probable working life was estimated as 10 years and its probable scrap value at the end of that time is ₹ 10,000. You are required to prepare necessary accounts based on straight line method of depreciation for three years.*

Solution :

$$\text{Annual Depreciation} = \frac{\text{Cost of the Asset} - \text{Scrap Value}}{\text{Life of the Asset}}$$

$$= \frac{\text{Rs. } 1{,}60{,}000 - 10{,}000}{10 \text{ years}} = \frac{1{,}50{,}000}{10 \text{ years}} = ₹\ 15{,}000.$$

Machinery Account

Date	Particulars	Amount ₹	Date	Particulars	Amount ₹
1.1.2000	To Cash	1,60,000	31.12.2000	By Depreciation	15,000
			31.12.2000	By Balance c/d	1,45,000
		1,60,000			1,60,000
1.1.2001	To Balance b/d	1,45,000	31.12.2001	By Depreciation	15,000
			31.12.2001	By Balance c/d	1,30,000
		1,45,000			1,45,000
1.1.2002	To Balance b/d	1,30,000	31.12.2002	By Depreciation	15,000
			31.12.2002	By Balance c/d	1,15,000
		1,30,000			1,30,000

Depreciation Account

Date	Particulars	Amount ₹	Date	Particulars	Amount ₹
31.12.2000	To Machinery A/c	15,000	31.12.2000	By P.L A/c	15,000
		15,000			15,000
31.12.2001	To Machinery A/c	15,000	31.12.2001	By P.L A/c	15,000
		15,000			15,000
31.12.2002	To Machinery A/c	15,000	31.12.2002	By P.L A/c	15,000
		15,000			15,000

Problem 4. *On 1.1.1999 machinery was purchased by Mr. X for ₹ 50,000. On 1.7.2000 additions were made to the extent of ₹ 10,000. On 1.4.2001 further additions were made to the extent of ₹ 6,400.*

On 30.6.2002 machinery, the original value of which was ₹ 8,000 on 1.1.1999 was sold for ₹ 6,000. Depreciation is charged at 10% p.a. on original cost.

Show the machinery account for the years from 1999 to 2002 in the books of Mr. X. Closes his books on 31st December every year. [ICWA Inter]

Solution :

Machinery Account

Date	Particulars	Amount ₹	Date	Particulars	Amount ₹
1.1.1999	To Cash	50,000	31.12.1999	By Depreciation	5,000
			31.12.1999	By Balance c/d	45,000
		50,000			50,000
1.1.2000	To Balance b/d	45,000	31.12.2000	By Depreciation	5,500
1.7.2000	To Cash	10,000		(50,000 × 10/100 = 5,000)	
				(10,000 × 10/100 × 6/12 = 500)	
			31.12.2000	By Balance c/d	49,500
		55,000			55,000
1.1.2001	To Balance b/d	49,500	31.12.2001	By Depreciation	6,480
1.4.2001	To Cash	6,400	31.12.2001	By Balance c/d	49,420
		55,900			55,900
1.1.2002	To Balance b/d	49,420	30.6.2002	By Bank	6,000
30.6.2002	To Profit on Sale		31.12.2002	By Depreciation	6,240
	of Machinery	800	31.12.2002	By Balance c/d	37,980
		50,220			50,220
1.1.2003	To Balance c/d	37,980			

Workings :

(*i*) Depreciation for 2001

10% on ₹ 50,000 for one year 50,000 × 10/100	=	5,000
10% on ₹ 10,000 for one year 10,000 × 10/100	=	1,000
10% on ₹ 64,000 for 9 months (6,400 × 10/100 × 9/12)	=	480
		6,480

(*ii*) Depreciation for 2002

10% on ₹ 42,000 for one year 42,000 × 10/100 (*i.e.,* 50,000 – 8,000)	=	4,200
10% on ₹ 10,000 for one year 10,000 × 10/100	=	1,000
10% on ₹ 6,400 for one year 6,400 × 10/100	=	640
10% on ₹ 8,000 for 6 months 8,000 × 10/100 × 6/12	=	400
		6,240

(*iii*) Computation of Profit on Sale of Machinery

Original value of Machinery	8,000
Less : Depreciation for 3½ years @ 10% *i.e.,* 800 × 3.5	2,800
Written down value of machinery on 30.6.2002	5,200
Amount realised on Sale	6,000
Profit on Sale of Machinery	800

Problem 5. *On 1.1.1999 ABC Ltd. purchased five machines for ₹ 20,000 each. Depreciation is charged at the rate of 10% p.a on cost. The accounting year ends on 31st December each year. On 31.3.2000 one machine was sold for ₹ 16,000 and on 30.9.2001 another machine was sold for ₹ 15,000. A new machine was purchased on 30.6.2002 for ₹ 24,000. Prepare machinery account and provision for depreciation account for four years.*

Solution :

Machinery Account

Date	*Particulars*	*Amount* ₹	*Date*	*Particulars*	*Amount* ₹
1.1.1999	To Cash	1,00,000	31.12.1999	By Cash	16,000
				By Provision for Depreciation A/c	2,500
				By P & L A/c	1,500
			31.12.1999	By Balance c/d	80,000
		1,00,000			1,00,00
1.1.2000	To Balance B/d	80,000	30.9.2000	By Bank A/c	15,000
30.9.2000	To P.L A/c	500		By Provision for Depreciation A/c	5,500
			30.12.2000	By Balance c/d	60,000
		80,500			80,500

1.1.2001	To Balance B/d	60,000	31.12.2001	By Balance c/d	84,000
30.6.2001	To Bank A/c	24,000			
		84,000			84,000
1.1.2002	To Balance B/d	84,000			

Provision for Depreciation Account

Date	*Particulars*	*Amount* ₹	*Date*	*Particulars*	*Amount* ₹
31.12.1998	To Balance c/d	10,000	31.12.1998	By Depreciation	10,000
		10,000			10,000
			1.1.1999	By Balance B/d	10,000
31.3.1999	To Machinery A/c	2,500	31.3.1999	By Depreciation (on 20,000 for 3 months)	500
31.12.1999	To Balance c/d	16,000	31.12.1999	By Depreciation (on 80000 for one year)	8,000
		18,500			18,500
30.9.2000	To Machinery A/c	5,500	1.1.2000	By Balance B/d	16,000
31.12.2000	To Balance c/d	18,000	30.9.2000	By Depreciation (on 20,000 for 9 months)	1,500
			31.12.2000	By Depreciation	6,000
		23,500			23,500
31.12.2001	To Balance c/d	25,200	1.1.2001	By Balance B/d	18,000
			31.12.2001	By Depreciation (on 60,000 for one year)	6,000
				By Depreciation (on 24,000 for 6 months)	1,200
		25,200			25,200

Problem 6. *India Ltd. charges depreciation on plant and machinery under Reducing Balance System @ 15% per annum. On 1.4.1998, the Balance in Ledger stood at ₹ 4,60,000. The following particulars are given relating to plant and machinery during the four years ended 31.3.2002.*

	Date		**Particulars**
(1)	*1.9.1998*	:	*A machine Purchased for ₹ 20,000 (Installation Expenses ₹ 1,000) on 1.5.96 was fully destroyed in an accident.*
(2)	*1.7.1999*	:	*Purchased a new machine costing ₹ 50,000 (Installation Expenses ₹ 2,500). A sum of ₹ 30,000 was paid on the same date and the Balance was paid in May 2000.*

(3) 31.8.2000 : *Plant purchased on 1.4.97 for ₹30,000 (Installation Expenses ₹1,500) was disposed off for ₹ 36,000.*

(4) 1.11.2001 : *Some old machineries (Book value on 1.4.98 at ₹ 10,000) were sold for ₹ 4,000.*

Show the plant & machinery Account as would appear in the books of the company for the four years ended 31.3.2002 assuming depreciation is charged proportionately even if the asset is sold or destroyed. [M.Com. Madras]

Solution : **Plant and Machinery Account**

Date	Particulars	Amount ₹	Date	Particulars	Amount ₹
1.4.1998	To Balance B/d	4,60,000	1.1.1998	By Profit & Loss Account	14,434
			31.3.1999	By Depreciation for 5 months (1)	962
			31.3.1999	By Depreciation Account @ 15% on ₹ 4,44,604	66,691
			31.3.1999	By Balance c/d	3,77,913
		4,60,000			4,60,000
1.4.1999	To Balance B/d	3,77,913	31.3.2000	By Depreciation A/c (56,687 + 5,906)	62,593
1.7.1999	To Bank	32,500			
1.7.1999	To Creditors	20,000	31.3.2000	By Balance c/d	3,67,820
		4,30,413			4,30,413
1.4.2000	To Balance B/d	3,67,820	31.8.2000	By Bank A/c (Sale)	36,000
31.8.2000	To P & L A/c (2) (Profit on sale of machinery)	17,864	31.3.2001	By Depreciation (2)	1,209
			31.3.2001	By Depreciation A/c 15% on 3,48,475 (*i.e.*, 3,67,820 – 19,345)	52,271
				By Balance c/d	2,96,204
		3,85,684			3,85,684
1.4.2001	Balance B/d	2,96,204	1.11.2001	By Bank A/c (Sale)	4,000
			1.11.2001	By Depreciation (for 7 months on ₹ 6,141)	537
			1.11.2001	By P & L A/c (3) (Loss)	1,604
			31.3.2002	By Depreciation A/c (15% 2,90,063 full year)	43,509
			31.3.2002	By Balance c/d	2,46,554
		2,96,204			2,96,204

Working Notes :

1. *Calculation of Loss on Accident*

		₹
	Cost on 1.5.1996	21,000
Less :	Depreciation for 11 months in 1996-97	2,887
	Value on 1.4.1997	18,113
Less :	Depreciation for 1997-98	2,717
	Value on 1.4.98	15,396
Less :	Depreciation for 5 months	962
	Loss on accident	14,434

2. *Calculation of Profit on Sale for Machinery on 31.8.2000*

		₹
	Cost on 1.4.1997	31,500
Less :	Depreciation for 11 months in 1997-98	4,725
	Value on 1.4.1998	26,775
Less :	Depreciation for 1998-99	4,016
	Value on 1.4.99	22,759
Less :	Depreciation for 1999-2000	3,414
	Value on 1.4.2000	19,345
Less :	Depreciation for 5 months	1,209
	Value on 31.8.2000	18,136
Less :	Amount realised on Sale	36,000
	Profit on Sale of Machinery	17,864

3. *Calculation of Loss on Sale of Machinery on 1.11.2001*

		₹
	Book value on 1.4.98	10,000
Less :	Depreciation for 1998-99	1,500
	Value on 1.4.99	8,500
Less :	Depreciation for 1999-2000	1,275
	Value on 1.4.2000	7,225
Less :	Depreciation for 2000-2001	1,084
	Value on 1.4.2001	6,141
Less :	Depreciation for 7 months	537
	Value on 1.11.2001	5,604
Less :	Amount realised on Sale	4,000
	Loss on Sale of Machinery	1,604

Problem 7. *A firm purchases a 5 year lease for ₹ 30,000. It is decided to write off depreciation on the annuity method, presuming the rate of interest to be 5% per annum. If annuity of ₹ 1 for 5 years at 5% is 0.230975. Show the lease account for the full period of 5 years.*

Solution :

The amount of depreciation to be charged every year

$$= 0.230975 \times 30{,}000 = ₹\ 6{,}929.25$$

Lease Account

Date	Particulars	Amount ₹	Date	Particulars	Amount ₹
1st year	To Bank	30,000.00	1st year	By Depreciation	6,929.25
	To Interest			By Balance c/d	24,570.75
	(30,000 × 5/100)	1,500.00			
		31,500.00			31,500.00
2nd year	To Balance B/d	24,570.75	2nd year	By Depreciation	6,929.25
	To Interest			By Balance c/d	18,870.04
	(24,570.75 × 5/100)	1,228.54			
		25,799.29			25,799.29
3rd year	To Balance B/d	18,870.04	3rd year	By Depreciation	6,929.25
	To Interest			By Balance c/d	12,884.29
	(18,870.04 × 5/100)	943.50			
		19,813.54			19,813.54
4th year	To Balance B/d	12,884.29	4th year	By Depreciation	6,929.25
	To Interest	644.21		By Balance c/d	6,599.25
	(12,884.29 × 5/100)				
		13,528.50			13,528.50
5th year	To Balance B/d	6,599.25	5th year	By Depreciation	6,929.25
	To Interest	330.00			
	(6,599.25 × 5/100)				
		6,929.25			6,929.25

Problem 8. *Ramu & Co., purchased a machine at a cost of ₹ 99,600. It was expected to last for 6 years with a scrap value of ₹ 3,000. Find out the depreciation for each of the six years under*

(i) Production units method and

(ii) Machine Hour Rate method.

Total estimated life in units of production is 87,380 units and total estimated life in machine is 20,900 hours.

Additional Data are :

Year	*1*	*2*	*3*	*4*	*5*	*6*	*Total*
Units produced	*11,900*	*14,000*	*13,000*	*12,500*	*16,250*	*19,730*	*87,380*
Working Hours	*3,400*	*3,800*	*3,000*	*2,800*	*3,900*	*4,000*	*20,900*

Solution :

Production Units method :

$$\text{Depreciation Rate per unit} = \frac{\text{Cost} - \text{Salvage Value}}{\text{Estimated Life in Hours}} = \frac{99{,}600 - 3{,}000}{87{,}380}$$

$$= \frac{96{,}600}{87{,}380} = ₹\ 1.10$$

Computation of Annual Depreciation

Year	*Units Produced*	*Rate Per Unit*	*Annual Depreciation (₹) (Units Produced × Rate Per Unit)*
1	11,900	1.10	13,090
2	14,000	1.10	15,400
3	13,000	1.10	14,300
4	12,500	1.10	13,750
5	16,250	1.10	17,875
6	19,730	1.10	21,703

Machine Hours or Working Hours Method :

$$\text{Depreciation Rate Per Hour} = \frac{\text{Cost} - \text{Scrap value}}{\text{Estimated life in hours}} = \frac{99{,}600 - 3{,}000}{20{,}900}$$

$$= ₹\ 4.62$$

Computation of Annual Depreciation

Year	*Working Hours*	*Rate Per Hour ₹*	*Depreciation (Working Hour × Rate Per Hour) ₹*
1	3400	4.62	15,708
2	3800	4.62	17,556
3	3000	4.62	13,860
4	2800	4.62	12,936
5	3900	4.62	18,018
6	4000	4.62	18,480

Problem 9. *ABC Ltd. purchased a car at a cost of ₹ 3,00,000 and its estimated life is 60,000 running hours. The car runs for 2000 miles in the first year. 3,000 miles for the second year, 2,500 miles for the third year. Compute per mile and yearly Depreciation.*

Solution :

$$\text{Depreciation} = \frac{\text{Cost} - \text{Scrap}}{\text{Estimated Life in Running Miles}} = \frac{3{,}00{,}000}{60{,}000} = ₹\ 5$$

Computation of Annual Depreciation

Year	*Running Miles*	*Depreciation (Running Miles × Rate Per Running Miles)*
1	2000	10,000
2	3000	15,000
3	2500	12,500

Problem 10. *KLP Ltd. leased a manganese ore mine on 30th June 2000 for a sum of ₹6,00,000. It is estimated that the total Quantity of ore in the mine is 60,000 tonne of which 80% may be raised. The annual output is as follows.*

Year	*2000*	*2001*	*2002*	*2003*	*2004*
Output (Tonnes)	*2,500*	*7,500*	*5,000*	*9,000*	*10,000*

Solution :

Depreciation charge per tonne = Total cost/Effective production [80% of 60,000]

i.e., $\frac{6,00,000}{48,000}$ [60,000 × 80/100 = 48,000]

= ₹ 12.5

Mine Account

Date	*Particulars*	*Amount* ₹	*Date*	*Particulars*	*Amount* ₹
30.6.2000	To Cash	6,00,000	31.12.2000	By Depreciation (2,500 × 12.5)	31,250
				By Balance c/d	4,68,750
		6,00,000			6,00,000
1.1.2001	To Balance B/d	4,68,750	31.12.2001	By Depreciation (7,500 × 12.5)	93,750
			31.12.2001	By Balance c/d	3,75,000
		4,68,750			4,68,750
1.1.2002	To Balance B/d	3,75,000	31.12.2002	By Depreciation (5,000 × 12.5)	62,500
			31.12.2002	By Balance c/d	3,12,500
		3,75,000			3,75,000
1.1.2003	To Balance B/d	3,12,500	31.12.2003	By Depreciation (9,000 × 12.5)	1,12,500
			31.12.2003	By Balance c/d	2,00,000
		3,12,500			3,12,500

1.1.2004	To Balance B/d	2,00,000	31.12.2004	By Depreciation (10,000 × 12.5)	1,25,000
			31.12.2004	By Balance c/d	75,000
		2,00,000			2,00,000
1.1.2005	To Balance B/d	75,000			

Problem 11. *On 1.1.2002 Rahim Ltd. had a stock of bottles valued at ₹ 12,000. On 1.7.2002 the company purchased additional bottles for ₹ 4,000. On 31.12.2002 the entire stock of bottles was revalued at ₹ 15,000. Calculate the amount of Depreciation.*

Solution : **Bottles Account**

Date	*Particulars*	*Amount* ₹	*Date*	*Particulars*	*Amount* ₹
1.1.2002	To Balance B/d	12,000	31.12.200	By Depreciation (16,000 – 15,000)	1,000
1.7.2002	To Cash	4,000	31.12.2002	By Balance c/d	15,000
		16,000			16,000
1.1.2003	To Balance B/d	15,000			

Problem 12. *On 1.1.99 Nasma Ltd. purchased a machine for ₹ 60,000 which was expected to last for 4 years. The repairs and maintenance charges were estimated to be ₹ 19,000 during the life time of the asset. Actual expenses for repair and maintenance during 1999, 2000, 2001, 2002, had been ₹ 2,000, ₹ 5,000, ₹ 6,500, ₹ 7,000 respectively. At the end of the fourth year, the machine is sold at ₹ 11,500. Prepare necessary accounts using an equitable method of charging depreciation and maintenance expenses.*

Solution :

Provision for Depreciation and Repair Account

Date	*Particulars*	*Amount* ₹	*Date*	*Particulars*	*Amount* ₹
31.12.1999	To Repair & maintenance	2,000	31.12.1999	By P.L Account	17,500
	To Balance c/d	15,500			
		17,500			17,500
31.12.2000	To Repairs & maintenance A/c	5,000	1.1.2000	By Balance B/d	15,500
	To Balance c/d	28,000	31.12.2000	By P.L A/c	17,500
		33,000			33,000

31.12.2001	To Repair & maintenance A/c	6,500	1.1.2001	By Balance B/d	28,000
	To Balance c/d	39,000	31.12.2001	By P.L A/c	17,500
		45,500			45,500
31.12.2002	To Repair & maintenance	7,000	1.1.2002	By Balance c/d	39,000
	To Balance c/d	49,500	31.12.2003	By P.L A/c	17,500
		56,500			56,500

Machinery Account

Date	*Particulars*	*Amount* ₹	*Date*	*Particulars*	*Amount* ₹
1.1.1999	To Bank	60,000	31.12.1999	By Balance c/d	60,000
1.1.2000	To Balance B/d	60,000	31.12.2000	By Balance c/d	60,000
1.1.2001	To Balance B/d	60,000	31.12.2001	By Balance c/d	60,000
1.1.2002	To Bank B/d	60,000	31.12.2002	By Cash	11,500
31.12.2002	To P.L. A/c	1,000	31.12.2002	By Provision for Depreciation & Repairs	49,500
		61,000			61,000

Workings :

Cost of the Machine	60,000
Less : Scrap Value	9,000
	51,000
Add : Estimated Repairs and Maintenance Expenses	19,000
Composite Cost	70,000

Annual Cost of Depreciation and Repairs

$$\frac{\text{Composite cost}}{\text{Number of years}} = \frac{70{,}000}{4} = ₹\ 17{,}500$$

Problem 13. *KRN & Co. purchased a machinery at a cost of ₹ 80,000 on 1.1.1997. On 1.1.1998 additions were made to the amount of ₹ 40,000. On 31.3.1999 machinery purchased on 1.1.1998 costing ₹ 12,000 was sold for ₹ 11,000 and on 30.6.1999 machinery purchased on 1.1.1997 costing ₹ 32,000 was sold for ₹ 26,700. On 1.10.1999 additions were made to the amount of ₹ 20,000. Depreciation was provided at 10% p.a. on Diminishing Balance method. Show the machinery account for the three years from 1997 to 1999. [Year ended on Dec. 31]*

[B.Com. Madras]

Solution : **Machinery Account**

Date	Particulars	Amount ₹	Date	Particulars	Amount ₹
1.1.1997	To Bank A/c	80,000	31.12.1997	By Depreciation	8,000
			31.12.1997	Balance c/d	72,000
		80,000			80,000
1.1.1998	To Balance B/d	72,000	31.12.1998	By Depreciation	11,200
1.1.1998	To Bank A/c	40,000	31.12.1998	By Balance c/d	1,00,800
		1,12,000			1,12,000
1.1.1999	To Balance B/d	1,00,800	31.3.1998	By Depreciation	270
	To P & L A/c			By Bank A/c	11,000
	(Profit Transferred)	470		By Depreciation	1,296
	To P & L A/c			By Bank A/c	26,700
	(Profit Transferred)	2,076	31.12.1999	By Depreciation	6,908
1.10.1999	To Bank A/c	20,000		By Balance c/d	77,172
		1,23,346			1,23,346
1.1.2000	To Balance B/d	77,172			

Working Notes :

		₹
1.	Machinery Purchased on 1.1.1998	12,000
Less :	Depreciation for 1998 @ 10%	1,200
	Balance as on 1.1.99	10,800
	Depreciation for 3 months in 1999	270
	Book Value as on 31.3.99	10,530
	Profit (Balancing Figure)	470
	Amount realised	11,000
2.	Cost of Machinery on 1.1.1997	32,000
Less :	Depreciation for 1997	3,200
	Balance on 1.1.1998	28,800
Less :	Depreciation for 1998	2,880
	Balance on 1.1.1999	25,920
Less :	Depreciation for 6 months in 1999	1,296
	Book Value on 30.6.99	24,624
	Profit (Balancing Figure)	2,076
	Sold for	26,700

3. Depreciation for the Remaining Machines

Book value of machines on 1.1.99	1,00,800
Book value of machines on 1.1.99 sold in 1999	36,720
	64,080
Depreciation for 1999 on 64,080 @ 10%	6,408
Depreciation for New Machine for 3 months on ₹ 20,000	500
Total	6,908

Problem 14. *On 1.4.1995 a firm purchased a machinery worth ₹3,00,000. On 1.10.1997 it buys additional machinery worth ₹ 60,000/- and spends ₹ 6,000 on its erection. The accounts are closed each year on 31st March. Assuming the annual depreciation to be 10%, show the machinery account for 5 years under straight line method and written down value method.*

Solution : **Straight Line Method : Machinery Account**

Date	*Particulars*	*Amount ₹*	*Date*	*Particulars*	*Amount ₹*
1.4.1995	To Cash	3,00,000	31.3.1996	By Depreciation	30,000
			31.3.1996	By Balance c/d	2,70,000
		3,00,000			3,00,000
1.4.1996	To Balance B/d	2,70,000	31.3.1997	By Depreciation	30,000
			31.3.1997	By Balance c/d	2,40,000
		2,70,000			2,70,000
1.4.1997	To Balance B/d	2,40,000	31.3.1998	By Depreciation	
1.10.1997	To cash	66,000		(30,000 + 3,300)	33,300
			31.3.1998	By Balance c/d	2,72,700
		3,06,000			3,06,000
1.4.1998	To Balance B/d	2,72,700	31.3.1998	By Depreciation	36,600
			31.3.1998	By Balance c/d	2,36,100
		2,72,700			2,72,700
1.4.1999	To Balance B/d	2,36,100	31.3.1999	By Depreciation	36,600
			31.3.1999	By Balance c/d	1,99,500
		2,36,100			2,36,100
1.4.2000	To Balance B/d	1,99,500			

Written Down Value Method : Machinery Account

Date	*Particulars*	*Amount* ₹	*Date*	*Particulars*	*Amount* ₹
1.4.1995	To Cash	3,00,000	31.3.1996	By Depreciation	30,000
			31.3.1996	By Balance c/d	2,70,000
		3,00,000			3,00,000
1.4.1996	To Balance B/d	2,70,000	31.3.1997	By Depreciation	27,000
			31.3.1997	By Balance c/d	2,43,000
		2,70,000			2,70,000
1.4.1997	To Balance B/d	2,43,000	31.3.1998	By Depreciation	27,300
1.10.1997	To Cash	60,000	31.3.1998	By Balance c/d	2,75,700
		3,03,000			3,03,000
1.4.1998	To Cash	2,75,700	31.3.1998	By Depreciation	27,570
			31.3.1999	By Balance c/d	2,48,130
		2,75,700			2,75,700
1.4.1999	To Balance B/d	2,48,130	31.3.2000	By Depreciation	24,813
			31.3.2000	By Balance c/d	2,23,317
		2,48,130			2,48,130
1.4.2000	To Balance B/d	2,23,317			

Depreciation for 1997 :

Depreciation on ₹ 2,43,000 @ 10% for one year	24,300
Depreciation on 60,000 @ 10% for 6 months	3,000
	27,300

Problem 15. *From the following data find out the depreciation for period of 5 years. The cost of machine is ₹ 2,00,000. The scrap value after a period of 5 years is estimated at ₹ 40,000. Using the sum of the digits method, calculate the depreciation for every year.*

Solution :

The sum of the years digits = 5 + 4 + 3 + 2 + 1 = 15

Cost of the machine = 2,00,000

Scrap value = 40,000

Therefore, cost of machine – scrape value = 2,00,000 – 40,000 = 1,60,000

Now, Depreciation charge for each year can be calculated as follows :

Depreciation charge for the I year = 5/15 × 1,60,000 = 53,334

Depreciation charge for the IInd year = 4/15 × 1,60,000 = 42,667

Depreciation charge for the IIIrd year = 3/15 × 1,60,000 = 32,000

Depreciation charge for the IVth year = 2/15 × 1,60,000 = 21,334

Depreciation charge for the Vth year = 1/15 × 1,60,000 = 10,667

TEST PROBLEMS

1. Vijay & Co. purchased a Grinding machine on 1st January 1995 for ₹ 9,250 and immediately spent ₹ 750 on 1st July, 1996, it purchased another machine for ₹ 2,500 and on 1st July, 1997, it sold off the first machine purchased in 1995 for ₹ 7,000 and on the same date it purchased another machine for ₹ 6,250. On 1st July, 1998, the second machine purchased for ₹ 2,500 was also sold off for ₹ 500. Depreciation was provided on the machinery on written down value basis at 10% p.a. Give the machinery account for four years commencing from Jan. 1, 1995. Calculations are to be made to the nearest rupee.

[**Ans:** Machinery A/c Closing Balance 1995: ₹ 10,000
Machinery A/c Closing Balance 1996: ₹ 11,500
Machinery A/c Closing Balance 1997: ₹ 16,725
Machinery A/c Closing Balance 1998: ₹ 8,075]

2. A firm purchases a 5 years lease for ₹ 1,60,000 on 1st January 1995. It decides to write off depreciation on the Annuity Method, presuming the rate of interest to be 5% per annum. the annuity table shows that a sum of ₹ 36,956 should be written off every year. Show the Lease Account for five years. Calculations are to be made to the nearest rupee.

[**Ans:** Lease A/c Closing Balance 1995: ₹ 1,68,000
Lease A/c Closing Balance 1996: ₹ 1,37,596
Lease A/c Closing Balance 1997: ₹ 1,05,672
Lease A/c Closing Balance 1998: ₹ 72,152
Lease A/c Closing Balance 1999: ₹ 36,956]

3. A company purchased a 3 years lease on January 1995 for ₹ 1,00,000. It is decided to provide for the replacement of lease at the end of 3 years by setting up a sinking fund. It is expected that the investments will fetch interest at 5%. Sinking Fund Table shows that to provide the requisite sum at 5% at the end of 3 years an investment at ₹ 31,728,88 is required every year. Investments are made to nearest rupee. On 31st December, 1997, the investments were sold for ₹ 61,000. On 1st January 1998, the same lease was renewed for a further period of 3 years by paying ₹ 1,20,000.

Show the journal entries and give the lease account, depreciation account, depreciation fund account, depreciation fund investment account and new lease account.

[**Ans:** Lease A/c Closing Balance: ₹ 1,00,000
Sinking Fund A/c Closing Balance: ₹ 1,04,045.00
Depreciation: ₹ 31,728.88
Sinking Fund A/c Closing Balance: ₹ 1,04,045.00
Sinking Fund Investment A/c Closing Balance: ₹ 65,045
Interest on Sinking Fund Investment A/c Closing Balance: ₹ 3,252.25
New Lease A/c Closing Balance: ₹ 1,20,000]

❑❑❑

SECTION II : COST ACCOUNTING

9

Cost Accounting : Cost Sheet, Accounting for Manufacturing Cost

INTRODUCTION

Financial Accounting concentrates in the preparation of Trading Account, Profit and Loss Account and Balance Sheet. Profit and Loss Account shows the net profit of the organisation. And Balance Sheet shows the true financial position of the organisation. But the financial accounting does not concentrate on the operational efficiency of the organisation. Financial Accounting serves several functions to the organisation such as finance, administration, production but the operational efficiency of those functions is lacking. Apart from these activities, Financial Accounting has certain limitations. In order to overcome these limitations and to obtain more efficient operations of the organisation the cost accounting system is developed.

CONCEPT OF COST ACCOUNTING

Cost

The term cost is very often used in day to day activities. The cost is the amount of resources given up in exchange for some goods or services.

American Institute of Certified Public Accountants defined cost as expanded or other property transferred, capital, stock issued, services performed or liability incurred in consideration of goods or services received or to be received.

Costing

Costing may be referred "as classifying, recording and appropriate allocation of expenditure for the determination of costs of products or services".

Cost Accounting

The Institute of Cost and Works Accountants (ICWA) (UK) defines cost accounting as "the process of accounting for cost from the point at which expenditure is incurred or committed to the establishment of its ultimate relationship with cost centres and cost units". In its widest usage, it embraces the preparation of statistical data, the application of cost control methods and the ascertainment of the profitability of activities carried out or planned.

According to Wheldon "cost accounting is the application of accounting and costing principle methods are techniques in the ascertainment of costs and the analysis of saving or excess cost incurred as compared with previous experience or with standards".

Cost Accountancy is the application of costing and cost accounting principles, methods and techniques to the science, art and practice of cost control and the ascertainment of profitability.

OBJECTIVES OF COST ACCOUNTING

1. It enables the management to ascertain the unit cost of product, service, job or department, and also to estimate the profit or loss of each operation.
2. To guide the management on future expansion programmes and proposed capital projects.
3. To provide necessary guidance to fix the accurate selling price of the product.
4. To co-ordinate cost reduction programme along with the different departmental heads.
5. To assist the management in preparing Budgets and necessary steps which are to be taken for the implementation of budgeting control.
6. To collect and supply relevant data to the management for taking important financial decisions.
7. To interpret and present data to the management for planning, evaluation of performance and control.
8. To provide specialised services of cost audit.
9. To assist the management in the future production policies.

ADVANTAGES OF COST ACCOUNTING

(*i*) To disclose the profitable and unprofitable activities of the organisation.
(*ii*) It supplies information upon which estimates and tenders are based.
(*iii*) To facilitate the introduction of suitable plans of wage payment to reward efficiency and to provide adequate incentive to the less efficient workers.
(*iv*) Helpful to the Government.
(*v*) Installation of Costing System will strengthen confidence in the minds of the public about the fairness of the prices charged.

LIMITATIONS OF COST ACCOUNTING

The following are the main limitations of cost accounting :

(*i*) *It is Expensive.* The installation of costing system in the industry requires huge amount of capital. Because, double set of account books has to be maintained. And at the same time it requires the persons who have specialised knowledge in costing. They require higher amount of salary and other benefits.

(*ii*) *Failure of Costing System.* Cost accounting system has failed to bring expected results in many cases. Under this background, it is treated as a defective system. However, it is not a faulty system.

(*iii*) *It Ignores a Uniform Procedure.* In the practical sense of cost accounting in a particular situation, two competent cost accountants may arrive at different results from the same information. Because of this, we can say, there is no uniform procedure for cost accounting.

(iv) *Matter of Routine Forms and Statements.* Sending of costing information to the management requires large number of forms and statements. Simply says, introduction of costing system involves additional and unnecessary paper work.

(v) *It is an Unnecessary Application.* Cost Accounting is only recently developed and installed in many industries. They have been progressing tremendously. And at the same time, some of the organisations can successfully run without the applications of cost accounting.

GENERAL PRINCIPLES OF COST ACCOUNTING

The following are some of the principles of costing :

(i) Cost accounting should ignore the convention of prudence.

(ii) Cause effect relationship.

(iii) Past costs should not form part of future costs.

(iv) Exclusion of abnormal costs from cost accounts.

(v) Principle of double entry should be followed preferably.

ELEMENTS OF COST

In order to implement the effective cost control for the sound managerial decisions, the management may be provided with adequate data. For the purpose of achieving the above objectives, the total cost of the product is analysed by the elements of cost *i.e.,* nature of expenses. Actually, the product cost is divided into three elements *i.e.,* Material, Labour, and Overheads.

The elements of cost show the following graphical form.

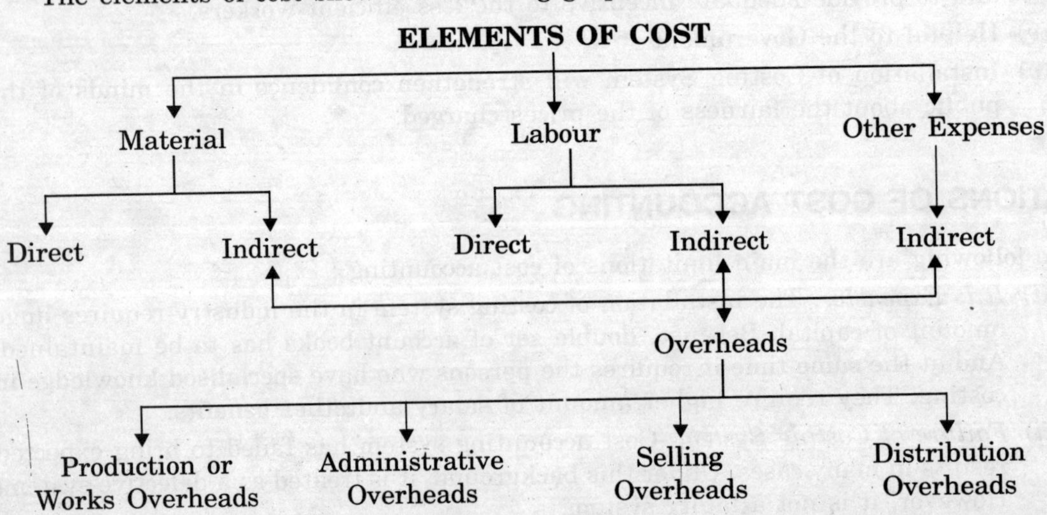

By Grouping the above elements of cost, the following divisions of costs are obtained.

(*i*) Direct Material + Direct Labour	=	Prime Cost
(*ii*) Prime Cost + Works or Factory Overheads	=	Works or Factory Cost
(*iii*) Cost Production + Selling and Distribution Overhead	=	Total Cost (Cost of Sales)
(*iv*) Work cost + Administration Overhead	=	Cost of Production

Strictly Speaking the Elements of Cost can be classified into :

- Direct Material
- Direct Labour
- Overheads.

Direct Material

Direct materials are those materials which can be directly identified with each unit of the finished product. It directly enters the production process and forms a part of the finished product. Direct materials can be classified in the following forms :

(*i*) All raw materials

(*ii*) Raw Materials specifically purchased for specific job

(*iii*) Parts purchased or produced

(*iv*) Packing materials.

Direct Labour

Direct wages refer to all labour expenses in altering the construction, composition, confirmation of the product. Simply, it is that labour which can be conveniently identified or attributed wholly to a particular job or converting raw material into finished goods. Wages of such labour force are known as direct wages.

Overheads

It may be defined as the aggregate of the cost of indirect materials, indirect labour and some other expenses including services which cannot conveniently be charged to particular cost unit or cost centre. Generally overheads may be sub divided into the following categories :

(*i*) Production overhead or factory overhead or manufacturing overhead

(*ii*) Administrative overhead

(*iii*) Selling overhead

(*iv*) Distribution overhead.

COST SHEET

Cost sheet is a statement which has to be prepared for the purpose of finding out total cost of the particular product. In other words, it is a statement to show the product manufactured during a particular accounting period along with the break-up of costs.

Bigg defines, "The expenditure, which has been incurred upon production for a period, is extracted from the financial books, and stores records, and set out in a memorandum or a statement. If this statement is confined to the disclosure of the cost of the units produced during the period, it is termed as cost sheet".

Important Purposes of Cost Sheet

(*i*) It shows the total cost and cost per unit of the products manufactured during a particular period.

(*ii*) It facilitates the comparative study of various elements of current cost with previous results and estimated costs.

(*iii*) It helps to formulate a concrete production policy.

(*iv*) It helps in fixing selling price.

(*v*) It guides the businessmen to minimise the cost of production.

Specimen Form of Cost Sheet

	Opening stock of Raw material	xx	
Add :	Purchase of Raw materials	xx	
			xx
Less :	Closing stock of Raw materials		xx
	Cost of Raw materials consumed		xx
Add :	Direct wages		xx
	Prime cost		xx
Add :	Factory overhead [*i*]		xx
	Total factory cost incurred during the year		xx
Add :	Opening stock of work in progress		xx
Less :	Closing stock of work in progress		xx
	Works cost		xx
Add :	Administration overhead [*ii*]		xx
	Cost of production		xx
Add :	Opening stock of finished goods		xx
Less :	Closing stock of finished goods		xx
	Cost of goods sold		xx
Add :	Selling and Distribution overhead [*iii*]		xx
	Cost of sales		xx
Add :	Profit for the period		xx
	Sales		xx

Details about the various Overheads

(*i*) Factory Overheads

Wages of Foremen

Factory Lighting

Consumable Stores

Lubricants

Electric Power

Oil and Water

Factory Manager's Salary

Time Keeper's Salary

Material Transportation Expenses

Factory Rent, Factory Lighting, Employees State Insurance Contribution, Depreciation – Factory Plant
Electric Power
Heat and Lighting
Insurance and Taxes
Miscellaneous Expenses – Factory
Plant maintenance – Stationery in Factory

(*ii*) Administrative Overheads

Office Rent
Bank Charges
Telephone Charges
Salaries of Office Staff
Repairs and Renewals – Office
Depreciation on Office Building
Manager's Salary
Director's Fees
Office Stationery
Postage and Telegrams
Insurance
Lighting of the Office
Rates and Taxes

(*iii*) Selling and Distribution Overheads

Expenses on Packing Materials
Salaries of Sales Staff
Sales Manager's Salary
Carriage Outward
Travelling Expenses
Advertising
Delivery Van Expenses
Godown Rent
Distribution Department - Salaries and Expenses
Sales Commission
Sales Promotion
Depreciation of Delivery Van.

NOTE : The following expenses are excluded from cost accounts. Even though it should be given in the problem, it should not appear anywhere in the cost sheet. Because, it is purely financial nature rather than costing nature.

(*i*) Transfer to Reserves
(*ii*) Income-tax Paid
(*iii*) Dividend Paid
(*iv*) Discount on Shares Written Off

Simplified form of Cost Sheet

Particulars	Total Cost ₹	Cost Per Unit ₹
Direct Material	xx	xx
Direct Labour	xx	xx
Prime Cost	xx	xx
Add : Works Overhead or factory Overhead	xx	xx
Works Cost	xx	xx
Add : Administrative Overhead	xx	xx
Cost of Production	xx	xx
Add : Selling and Distribution Overheads	xx	xx
Total Cost or Cost of Sales	xx	xx
Add : Profit	xx	xx
Sales	xx	xx

TEST QUESTIONS

1. What is meant by Cost Accounting ?
2. Define Cost Accounting.
3. What is Cost ?
4. What are the elements of cost ?
5. Briefly explain the objectives of cost accounting.
6. Describe the advantages of cost accounting.
7. What are the limitations of cost accounting ?
8. What are the principles of cost accounting ?
9. Prepare a chart showing the different elements of cost.
10. What is meant by cost sheet ? Explain the purpose of preparing cost sheet.

PROBLEMS AND SOLUTIONS

Problem 1. *From the following details calculate prime cost, factory cost, cost of production, cost of sales and profit from the following particulars :*

	₹		₹
Direct Materials	*1,20,000*	*Depreciation :*	
Direct Wages	*40,000*	*Factory Plant*	*1,000*
Wages of Foremen	*5,000*	*Office Premises*	*2,500*
Electric Power	*1,000*	*Consumable Stores*	*5,000*
Lighting : Factory	*3,000*	*Manager's Salary*	*10,000*
Office	*1,000*	*Director's Fees*	*2,500*
Store Keeper's Wages	*2,000*	*Office Stationery*	*1,000*
Oil and Water	*1,000*	*Telephone Charges*	*250*
Rent: Factory	*10,000*	*Postage and Telegrams*	*5,000*

Office	*2,500*	*Salesmen's Salaries*	*2,500*
Repairs and Renewals:		*Travelling Expenses*	*1,000*
Factory Plant	*3,500*	*Advertising*	*3,000*
Office Premises	*1,000*	*Warehouse Charges*	*1,000*
Transfer to Reserve	*2,000*	*Sales*	*3,80,000*
Dividend Paid	*1,000*	*Carriage Outward*	*800*
		Income-tax	*15,000*

Solution : **Statement of Cost and Profit**

Particulars	₹	₹
Direct Materials		1,20,000
Direct Wages		40,000
Prime Cost		1,60,000
Add : Factory Overheads :		
Wages of Foreman	5,000	
Electric Power	1,000	
Storekeeper's Wages	2,000	
Oil and Water	1,000	
Factory Rent	10,000	
Repairs and Renewals – Factory Plant	3,500	
Factory Lighting	3,000	
Depreciation – Factory Plant	1,000	
Consumable Stores	5,000	
		31,500
Factory Costs		1,91,500
Add : Administration Overheads :		
Office Rent	2,500	
Repairs and Renewals – Office Premises	1,000	
Office Lighting	1,000	
Depreciation : Office Premises	2,500	
Manager's Salary	10,000	
Director's Fees	2,500	
Office Stationery	1,000	
Telephone Charges	250	
Postage and Telegrams	500	
		21,250
Cost of Production		2,12,750
Add : Selling and Distribution Overheads		
Carriage Outward	800	
Salesmen's Salaries	2,500	
Travelling Expenses	1,000	
Advertising	3,000	
Warehouse Charges	1,000	
		8,300
Cost of Sales		2,21,050
Profit		1,58,950
Sales		3,80,000

Problem 2. *The following information has been obtained from the records of Narmatha Corporation Ltd. for the period from January 1 to June 30, 2003.*

	1.1.2003 ₹	*30.6.2003* ₹
Cost of Raw Materials	*30,000*	*25,000*
Cost of Work in Progress	*12,000*	*15,000*
Cost of Stock of finished Goods	*60,000*	*55,000*
Transactions during six months are :		
Purchase of Raw Materials	*1,50,000*	-
Wages Paid	*3,30,000*	-
Factory Overheads	*92,000*	-
Administration Overheads	*60,000*	-
Selling and Distribution Overhead	*30,000*	-
Sales	*12,50,000*	

Prepare Cost Sheet.

Solution : **Statement of Cost**

	₹
Opening Stock of Raw Materials	30,000
Add : Purchase of Raw Materials	5,50,000
	5,80,000
Less : Closing Stock of Raw Materials	25,000
Cost of Materials Consumed	5,55,000
Direct Wages	3,30,000
Prime Cost	8,85,000
Add : Factory Overheads	92,000
Factory Cost Incurred	9,77,000
Add : Opening Work-in-progress	12,000
	9,89,000
Less : Closing Work-in-progress	15,000
Factory (*or*) Manufacturing or Works Cost	9,74,000

Income Statement

Particulars	₹	₹
Sales		12,50,000
Less : Cost of Goods Sold :		
Opening Stock of Finished Goods	60,000	
Add : Factory Cost of the year	9,74,000	
	10,34,000	
Less : Closing Stock of Finished Goods	55,000	
		9,79,000
Gross Profit		2,71,000

Less : Indirect Expenses :		
Administration Expenses	60,000	
Selling and Distribution Expenses	30,000	
		90,000
Net Profit		1,81,000

Problem 3. *Suriyat & Co. Ltd. requires a statement showing the result of its production, operation for Sep. 2002. Cost records give the following information.*

	1.9.2002 ₹	*30.9.2002* ₹
Raw Materials	*1,00,000*	*1,23,500*
Finished Goods	*71,500*	*42,000*
Work in Progress	*31,000*	*34,500*

Transactions during the month of Sep. 2002 :

	₹
Purchase of Raw Materials	*88,000*
Direct Wages	*70,000*
Works' Expenses	*39,500*
Administration Expenses	*13,000*
Sale of Factory Scrap	*2,000*
Selling and Distribution Expenses	*15,000*
Sales	*2,84,000*

Solution : Statement of Cost

	₹	₹
Opening Stock of Raw Materials		1,00,000
Add : Purchase of Raw Materials		88,000
		1,88,000
Less : Closing Stock of Raw Materials		1,23,500
Value of Material Consumed		64,500
Add : Direct Wages		70,000
Prime Cost		1,34,500
Add : Factory Overhead :		
Works Expenses	39,500	
Less : Sale of Factory Scrap	2,000	37,500
Total Factory Cost		1,72,000
Add : Opening Stock of Work-in-progress		31,000
		2,03,000

Less : Closing Stock of Work-in-progress	34,500
Works Cost	1,68,500
Add : Administration Expenses	13,000
Cost of Production	1,81,500
Add : Opening Stock of Finished Goods	71,500
	2,53,000
Less : Closing Stock of Finished Goods	42,000
Cost of Goods to be sold	2,11,000
Add : Selling and Distribution Expenses	15,000
Cost of Sales	2,26,000
Profit	58,000
Sales	2,84,000

Problem 4. *Mr. Gopal furnishes the following data related to the manufacturing of a product during the month of April 2004.*

	₹
Raw Materials Consumed	*15,000*
Direct Labour Charges	*9,000*
Machine Hours Worked	*900*
Machine Hour Rate (₹)	*5*
Administrative Overheads	*20% on works cost*
Selling Overheads	*Res.0.50 per unit*
Units Produced	*17,100*
Units Sold	*16,000*

@ ₹ 4 per unit

You are required to prepare a cost sheet from the above showing (i) the cost of production per unit (ii) profit per unit sold and profit for the period. [B.Com.]

Solution : **Cost Sheet**

Particulars	*Amount* ₹	*Cost per Unit* ₹
Raw Material Consumed	15,000	
Direct Labour	9,000	
Direct Expenses	Nil	
Prime Cost	24,000	
Add : Factory Overheads 900 × 5 =	4,500	
Works Cost of 17,100 units	28,500	
Add : Admn. Overhead 20% on Works Cost	5,700	
Cost of Production 17,100 units (₹ 34,200/17,100 units = ₹ 2 per unit)	34,200	2.00

Add : Opening Stock of Finished Goods	Nil	
Less : Closing Stock of Finished Goods 1,100 units at ₹ 2	2,200	
Cost of Goods Sold 16,000 units	32,000	
Add : Selling Overheads 16,000 × 0.50 =	8,000	0.50
Cost of Sales 16,000 units	40,000	2.50
Sales 16,000 × 4 =	64,000	
Profit on 16,000 units	24,000	

Problem 5. *The following extracts of costing information relate to product z for the year ending 31.3.2003.*

	₹
Purchase of Raw Materials	*48,000*
Direct Wages	*40,000*
Stock of Raw Materials on 1.4.2002	*8,000*
Stock of Finished Goods on 1.4.2002 (1,600 units)	*6,400*
Stock of Raw Material on 31.3.2003	*8,800*
Stock of Finished Goods [3200 units] at Current Cost of Production	*12,840*
Works Overheads	*16,800*
Work in Progress on 1.4.2002	*1,920*
Work in Progress on 31.3.2003	*6,400*
Office on Cost	*3,200*
Sales (Finished Product)	*1,20,000*

Selling and Distribution Cost is 40 paise per unit. During the year 25,600 units were produced. Calculate the cost of production and extend the cost sheet to show the profit also.

Solution : **Cost Sheet for the year ended 31.3.2003**

Particulars	*TC* ₹	₹
Raw Material Used :		
Opening Stock	8,000	
Add : Purchases	48,000	
	56,000	
Less : Closing Stock	8,800	
	47,200	
Add : Direct Wages	40,000	
Prime Cost	87,200	
Add : Factory Overheads	16,800	
Factory Cost	1,04,000	
Add : Opening stock of work in progress (1.4.2002)	1,920	
	1,05,920	

Less :	Closing Stock of Work in Progress (31.3.2003)	6,400	
	Works Cost	99,520	3.89
Add :	Office on Cost	3,200	0.12
	Cost of Production (25,600 units)	1,02,720	4.01
Add :	Opening Stock (1,600 units)	6,400	
	(27,200 units)	1,09,120	-
Less :	Closing Stock 3,200 units	12,840	-
	Cost of Goods Sold	96,280	4.01
Add :	Selling cost @ 40 paise per unit	9,600	0.40
	(24,000 × .40)	1,05,880	4.41
	Profit	14,120	0.59
	Sales	1,20,000	5.00

Problem 6. *RCH Ltd. is manufacturing refrigerators. The following details are furnished in respect of its factory operations for the year ended 31.12.2002.*

Work in Progress 1.1.2002	*61,000*	
At Prime Cost	*20,000*	*81,000*
Manufacturing Expenses		
Work in Progress 31.12.2002		
At Prime Cost	*54,000*	
Manufacturing Expenses	*9,000*	*63,000*
Opening Stock of Raw Materials		*3,25,000*
Purchase of Raw Material		*5,00,000*
Direct Labour		*2,31,000*
Manufacturing Expenses		*96,000*
Closing Stock of Raw Material		*2,24,000*

On the basis of above data, prepare a statement showing the cost of production. Also indicate separately the amount of manufacturing expenses which enter the cost of production.

Solution : **Cost Sheet**

		₹	₹
	Raw Material		
	Opening Stock	3,25,000	
Add :	Purchases	5,00,000	
		8,25,000	
Less :	Closing Stock of Raw Material	2,24,000	
	Value of Raw Material Consumed		6,01,000
Add :	Direct Labour		2,31,000
			8,32,000
Add :	Work in Progress in the beginning		61,000
			8,93,000

Less : Work in Progress at the end		54,000
Prime Cost		7,17,000
Add : Manufacturing Expenses :		-
Relating to Opening Work in Progress	20,000	-
Add : Relating to 2002	96,000	
	1,16,000	
Less : Relating to Closing Work in Progress	9,000	1,07,000
Cost of Production		8,24,000

Problem 7. *The following details are available from the costing records of Himalaya & Co. Ltd.*

Stock of Raw Materials on 1.1.2003	*12,800*
Stock of Finished Goods on 1.1.2003	*28,000*
Purchases during the year	*2,92,000*
Productive Wages	*1,98,000*
Sale of Finished Goods	*5,92,000*
Stock of Finished Goods on 31.12.2003	*30,000*
Stock of Raw Materials on 31.12.2003	*13,600*
Works Overheads	*43,736*
Office and General Expenses	*35,524*

The Company is about to send a tender for plant. The costing department estimates that the materials required would cost ₹ 20,000 and wages for making the plant would cost ₹ 12,000. Tender is to be made keeping a net profit of 20% on selling price. State what would be the amount of the tender if based on the percentages. [B.Com. Madras]

Solution : Cost sheet for the year ended 31.12.2003

	₹	₹
Opening Stock of Raw Materials	12,800	
Add : Purchases during the year	2,92,000	
	3,04,800	
Less : Closing Stock of Materials	13,600	
Value of Material Consumed		2,91,200
Productive Wages		1,98,000
Prime Cost		4,90,000
Add : Works Overheads		43,735
Factory Cost		5,33,736
Add : Office and General Overheads		35,524
Cost of Production		5,69,260
Add : Opening Stock of Finished Goods		28,000
		5,97,260
Less : Closing Stock of Finished Goods		30,000
Cost of Goods Sold		5,67,260
Profit		24,740
Sales		5,92,000

Workings :

(*i*) Percentage of factory overheads to productive wages

$$\frac{43,736}{1,98,000} \times 100 = 22\%$$

(*ii*) Percentage of office on cost to factory cost

$$\frac{35,524}{5,33,736} \times 100 = 6.66\%$$

Materials	20,000
Productive wages	12,000
Prime Cost	32,000
Factory Overheads (22% on Wages)	2,640
Factory Cost	34,640
Office on Cost (6.66% on Factory Cost)	2,307
Total Cost	36,947
Profit (20% on Selling Price)	9,237
Tender price	46,184

Problem 8. *The following is the trading profit and loss A/c and other details. You are required to prepare a cost sheet showing the price at which the coolers should be marketed in order to earn a profit of 10% on selling price.*

Trading Account

	₹		₹
To Cost of Materials	*80,000*	*By Sales*	*4,00,000*
To Direct Wages	*1,20,000*	*(1000 Coolers)*	
To Other Manufacturing Cost	*50,000*		
To Gross Profit	*1,50,000*		
	4,00,000		*4,00,000*
To Office Salaries	*60,000*	*By Gross Profit*	*1,50,000*
To Rent and Insurance	*10,000*		
To Selling Expenses	*30,000*		
To General Expenses	*20,000*		
To Net Profit	*30,000*		
	1,50,000		*1,50,000*

For the year ending 31.12.2003 it is estimated that

(*i*) *Output and sales will be 1,200 coolers.*

(*ii*) *Prices of material will rise by 20% on the 2002 level.*

(*iii*) *Wages will increase by 5%.*

(*iv*) *Manufacturing cost will rise in proportion to the prime cost.*

(*v*) *Selling expenses per unit remain unaffected.*

(*vi*) *Other expenses will remain constant.*

Solution : Cost sheet for the year ending 31.12.2003

Output for 1,000

Particulars	*CPU* ₹	*Total Cost* ₹
Cost of Materials	80.00	80,000
Direct Wages	120.00	1,20,000
Prime Cost	200.00	2,00,000
Manufacturing Expenses	50.00	50,000
Factory Cost	250.00	2,50,000
Office Salaries	60.00	60,000
Rent and Insurance	10.00	10,000
General Expenses	20.00	20,000
Cost of Production	340.00	3,40,000
Selling Expenses	30.00	30,000
Cost of Sales or Total Cost	370.00	3,70,000
Profit	30.00	30,000
Sales	400.00	4,00,000

Estimated cost sheet for the year ending 31.12.2004

[Estimated output of 1,200 coolers]

Particulars		*CPU* ₹	*Total Cost* ₹
Materials	80.00		
Add : 20% increase	16.00	96.00	1,15,200
Wages	120.00		
Add : 5% increase	6.00	126.00	1,51,200
Prime Cost		222.00	2,66,400
Manufacturing Expenses (25% on Prime Cost)		55.50	66,600
Works Cost		277.50	3,33,000
Add : Administration Overheads			
Office Salaries		50.00	60,000
Rent and Insurance		8.33	10,000
Other Expenses (Constant)		16.67	20,000
Cost of Production		352.50	4,23,000
Selling Expenses (Constant per unit)		30.00	36,000
Cost of Sales or Total Cost		382.50	4,59,000
Profit (10% on selling Price)		42.50	51,000
Sales		425.00	5,10,000

Workings :

Computation of Profit 10% on Selling Price

If selling price is ₹ 100 then profit is ₹ 10 and cost is ₹ 90 (100-10) if cost is ₹ 90 then profit is ₹ 10.

If Cost is ₹ 382.50, then profit is 382.50/90 × 10 = 42.50

Total Profit = ₹ 42.50 × 12,00 = **₹ 51,000.**

Problem 9. *Compute works cost from the following where indirect wages are 50% of direct wages; indirect materials are 50% of direct materials and indirect expenses are 100% of direct expenses.*

Direct Expenses	*₹ 10,000*
Direct Wages	*₹ 30,000*
Direct Materials	*₹ 10,000*

[B.Com., Osmania Oct. 1993]

Solution : **Cost Sheet**

Particulars	₹	₹
Direct Materials		10,000
Direct Wages		30,000
Direct Expenses		10,000
Prime Cost		50,000
Indirect materials	5,000	
Indirect Wages	15,000	
Indirect Expenses	10,000	30,000
Works Cost		80,000

Problem 10. *From the following information calculate cost of production :*

Raw Materials Consumed	*30,000*
Productive Wages	*18,000*
Machine Hours Worked	*900*
Administrative Overheads :	
20% on Works Cost	
Machine Hour Rate ₹ 10	

[B.Com., Nagpur, March 1989]

Solution : **Cost Sheet**

Calculation of Cost of Production :

	₹
Raw Material Consumed	30,000
Productive Wages	18,000
Factory Overheads :	
Machine hours worked 900 at ₹ 10	9,000
Works cost	57,000
Add : Admn. overheads 20% on works cost	11,400
Cost of Production	68,400

Problem 11. *From the following data, prepare a statement showing cost and profit per unit for the month of January 1988.*

Raw Material used	*₹ 40,000*
Direct Wages	*₹ 22,400*
Man Hours Worked	*9500 hours*
Man Hour Rate	*₹ 4 per unit*
Office Overhead	*20% on works cost*
Units Produced and Sold	*20,000*
Selling Price	*₹ 10 per unit*
Selling overhead or Re 1 per unit	

[B.Com., Calicut, Oct. 1989]

Solution : **Cost Sheet**

Particulars	*Amount* ₹	*Cost Per Unit* ₹
Raw Materials used	40,000	2.00
Direct Wages	22,400	3.12
Direct Expenses	-	-
Prime Cost	62,400	3.10
Add : Factory Overhead : Indirect Wages	15,600	0.78
Works Cost	78,000	3.90
Add : Office overhead at 20% on works cost	15,600	0.78
Cost of Production	93,600	4.68
Add : Selling Overhead at ₹ 1 per unit	20,000	1.00
Total Cost1,13,600	5.68	
Sales at ₹ 10 per unit	2,00,000	10.00
Less : Total Cost	1,13,600	5.68
Profit	86,400	4.32

Workings :

Man Hours Worked	=	9500 hours
Man Hour Rate	=	₹ 4 per hour
Total Wages 9500 × 4	=	38,000
Less : Direct Wages	=	22,400
Indirect Wages		15,600 (Treated as Factory Overhead)

Problem 12. *Prepare a Cost Sheet :*

Labour ₹ 1,50,000, Prime Cost ₹ 3,50,000, Factory Expenses ₹ 98,000, Office expenses ₹ 85,000, 10% of the output is in stock and the sales total upto ₹ 5,10,000. [B.A. Madras]

Solution :

Particulars	₹
Materials	2,00,000
Labour	1,50,000
Prime Cost	3,50,000
Factory Expenses :	98,000
Works Cost	4,48,000
Office Expenses	85,000
Cost of Production	5,33,000
Less : Closing Stock of Finished Goods (10% of Cost of Production)	53,300
Cost of Goods Sold	4,79,700
Profit	30,300
Sales	5,10,000

Problem 13. *The Southern Traders Ltd., manufactured and sold 800 cookers in the year ending 31st March 2002. The summarised Trading and Profit and Loss Account is given below.*

	₹		₹
To Cost of Materials	*64,000*	*By Sales*	*3,20,000*
Direct Wages	*96,000*		
Manufacturing Expenses	*40,000*		
Gross Profit c/d	*1,20,000*		
	3,20,000		*3,20,000*
To Office Salaries	*48,000*	*By Gross Profit B/d*	*1,20,000*
Rent, Rates & Taxes	*8,000*		
Selling Expenses	*16,000*		
General Expenses	*24,000*		
Net Profit	*24,000*		
	1,20,000		*1,20,000*

For the year ending 31st March 2003 it has been estimated that

(a) Output and sales will be 1,000 cookers.

(b) Price of materials will rise by 25% on the previous year's level.

(c) Wages will rise by 12 ½%.

(d) Manufacturing cost will rise in proportion to the combined cost of materials and wages.

(e) Selling cost per unit will remain unchanged.

(f) Other expenses will remain unaffected by the rise in output.

Prepare a cost statement showing the price at which cookers would be marketed so as to show a profit of 12% on the selling price.

Solution : **Cost Sheet**

Particulars	*Total Cost* ₹	*Per Unit Cost* ₹
Cost of Materials	64,000	80.00
Direct Wages	96,000	120.00
Prime Cost	1,60,000	200.00
Manufacturing Expenses	40,000	50.00
Factory Cost	2,00,000	250.00
Add : Office Overheads : Office Salaries	48,000	60.00
Rent, Rates & Taxes	8,000	10.00
General Expenses	24,000	30.00
Cost Production	2,80,000	350.00
Add : Selling Expenses	16,000	20.00
Total Cost	2,96,000	370.00
Profit	24,000	30.00
Sales	3,20,000	400.00

Calculation of percentage of manufacturing expenses on combined cost of materials and wages.

$$\frac{\text{Manufacturing Expenses}}{\text{Cost of Material \& Wages}} \times 100 \quad i.e., \quad \frac{40,000}{1,60,000} \times 100 = 25\%$$

Cost Statement for 1000 Cookers

Particulars		*Total Cost* ₹	*Cost Per Unit* ₹
Materials 64,000/800 × 1,000	80,000		
Add : Increase 25%	20,000		
		1,00,000	100.00
Direct Wages 96,000/800 × 1,000	1,20,000		
Add : Increase 12 ½ %	15,000		
		1,35,000	135.00
Prime Cost		2,35,000	235.00
Manufacturing Wages : 25% on Prime Cost		58,750	58.75
Works Cost		2,93,750	293.75
Add Office Overheads :			
Office Salaries		48,000	48.00
Rent, Rates & Taxes		8,000	8.00
General Expenses		24,000	24.00
Cost of Production		3,73,750	373.75
Selling Expenses		20,000	20.00
Total Cost		3,93,750	393.75
Profit 12% on Selling Price		53,693	53.69
Sales		4,47,443	447.44

Problem 14. *The following data related to the manufacture of a standard product during the 4 weeks of Feb. 2003.*

	₹
Raw Materials Consumed	*20,000*
Direct Wages	*12,000*
Machine Hours Worked	*1,000*
Machine Hour Rate	*₹ 2*
Office Overhead	*15% on works cost*
Selling Overhead	*37 paise per unit*
Units Sold	*18,000 at ₹ 2.50 each*

You are required to prepare a cost sheet in respect of the above, showing (a) cost per unit (b) The profit for the 4 weekly period.

Solution : **Cost Sheet**

Period 4 weeks ended 28th Feb. 2003 **Output : 18,000 units**

Particulars	*Total Cost* ₹	*Per Unit Cost* ₹
Raw Materials Consumed	20,000	1.11
Direct Wages	12,000	0.67
Prime Cost	32,000	1.78
Factory Overheads @ ₹ 2 per machine hour for 1,000 hours	2,000	0.11
Factory Cost	34,000	1.89
Office Overhead @ 15% on factory cost	5,100	0.28
Cost of Production	39,100	2.17
Selling overhead @ 37 paise per unit for 18,000 unit	6,600	0.37
Total Cost	45,760	2.54
Loss	– 760	– 0.04
Sales	45,000	2.50

TEST PROBLEMS

1. From the following information calculate the cost of production:

	₹
Raw materials consumed	30,000
Productive wages	18,000
Machine hours worked	900
Administrative overhead 20% on works cost	
Machine hour rate ₹ 10.	

[B.Com., Nagpur, March 1989]

[**Ans.** Cost of production = 68,400]

2. The following extracts of costing information relate to commodity X for the year ending 31.12.1992:

	Year ₹
Purchase of raw materials	6,000
Direct wages	5,000
Rent Rates and Insurance	2,000
Carriage inwards	100
Stock (1.1.1992): Raw materials	1,000
Finished products-200 tonnes	800
Stock (31.12.1992): Raw materials	
Finished products- 400 tonnes	
Cost of factory supervision	400
Sale of finished products	15,000

Advertising and selling cost is 40 paise per tonne sold 3,000 tonnes of the commodity was sold during the year. Prepare a Cost Sheet.

[Ans. Profit: 1,275], [B.Com. (Pass) Delhi 1993]

❑❑❑

10

Job Costing

Most industries may be broadly classified into two major heads.

(*i*) Job order industries.

(*ii*) Mass production industries.

Normally, job order industries engage in production based upon the customers' orders. Each and every job has its own features and requires a special attention.

The ICMA terminology defines job costing as "that form of specific order costing which applies where the work is undertaken to customers' requirements and each order is of comparatively short duration. The work is usually carried out within a factory or workshop and moves through processes or operations as a continuously identifiable unit".

ADVANTAGES OF JOB ORDER COSTING

(*i*) It enables the organisation to find which jobs are more profitable and those which are unprofitable.

(*ii*) It helps the management to determine the operating efficiency of the various factors of production and some of the functional units.

(*iii*) It helps in determining the cost of similar jobs taken up in future and thus helps in formulation of future production planning.

(*iv*) Accurate identification of wastage, spoilage and defectives with respect to the production orders may assist the management to take effective steps in reducing these to minimum extent.

(*v*) By employing predetermined overhead rates in job costing, all the advantages of budgetory control can be obtained.

LIMITATIONS

(*i*) Cost comparison among different jobs becomes difficult or meaningless because there may be major economic changes.

(*ii*) Job costing is a historical costing in nature, so it may not be useful for future planning and control.

(*iii*) Job costing system cannot be operated effectively without having a sound production control system.

(*iv*) Job costing is expensive.

(*v*) It requires more clerical work for cost collection of each job.

BATCH COSTING

Batch costing is forming a part of job costing. Batch costing is done when production consists of a certain specified number of articles or production involves limited repetition work. Normally, under the job costing, production is carried out on the basis of specific orders. But, in Batch costing products are manufactured and retained as stock and sold on demand.

The total of batch cost can be found out by totalling each order number. The cost of production per unit can be ascertained by dividing the total cost by total batch quantity.

TEST QUESTIONS

1. What is meant by job costing ?
2. Explain the meaning of Batch costing.
3. What are the advantages of job costing ?
4. List out the limitations of job costing.

PROBLEMS AND SOLUTIONS

Problem 1. *The details given below have been taken from the cost records of an engineering works in respect of the job No 303.*

Material ₹ 4,010

Wages : Department A : 60 hours @ ₹ 3 per hour
Department B : 40 hours @ ₹ 2 per hour
Department C : 20 hours @ ₹ 5 per hour

The overhead expenses are as follows.

Variable : Department A : ₹ 5,000 for 5000 hours.
Department B : ₹ 3,000 for 1500 hours.
Department C : ₹ 2,000 for 500 hours.

Fixed expenses ₹ 20,000 for 10,000 working hours.

Calculate the cost of the job No 303 and the price for the job to give a profit of 25% on the selling price. [B.Com. Madurai]

Solution :

Job Cost Sheet (Job No. 303)

Particulars	₹	₹
Materials		4,010
Wages : Dept A (60 × ₹ 3)	180	
Dept B (40 × ₹ 2)	80	
Dept C (20 × ₹ 5)	100	360
Overhead Expenses :		
Variable		
Dept A = $\frac{5,000}{5,000}$ = ₹ 1 × 60 =	60	

Dept B = $\frac{3,000}{1,500}$ = ₹ 2 × 40 =	80	
Dept C = $\frac{2,000}{500}$ = ₹ 4 × 20 =	80	220
Fixed Expenses :		
$\frac{20,000}{10,000}$ = 2 × (60 + 40 + 20)		240
Cost of job		4,830
Add : Profit 25% on Selling Price		1,610
Selling Price		6,440

Problem 2. *Printwell Ltd. took up two jobs during the 1st week of April 1992. The following details are available.*

Particulars	*Job 101* ₹	*Job 102* ₹
Material Supplied	*2,000*	*1,400*
Wages Paid	*900*	*600*
Direct Expenses	*100*	*—*
Material Transferred from 101 to 102	*100*	*100*
Material Returned to Stores	*—*	*50*
Find the Cost of each job.		

[B.Com. Osmania April, 1993]

Solution : **Job Account**

Particulars	*Job 101* ₹	*Job 102* ₹	*Particulars*	*Job 101* ₹	*Job 102* ₹
To Materials	2,000	1,400	By Materials trans-		
To Wages	900	600	ferred to job 102	100	-
To Direct Expenses	100	-	By Materials returned		
To Materials transferred			to Stores	-	50
from job 101		100	By Balance c/d	2,900	2,050
	3,000	2,100		3,000	2,100

Cost of each job :

Job 101 : ₹ 2,900

Job 102 : ₹ 2,050

Problem 3. *A worker takes 9 hours to complete a job on daily wages and 6 hours on scheme of payment by results. His day rate is 75 paise per unit. The material cost of the product is ₹ 4 and the works overheads are recovered at 15% of the total direct wages. Calculate the factory cost of the product under (a) Halsey plan and (b) Rowan plan.*

[B.Com. Osmania Oct. 1995]

Solution : **Under Halsey Plan**

Time Taken × Hourly Rate + (50% of time Saved × Hourly Rate)

= 6 hours × 0.75 + (50% of 3 hours × 0.75)

= 4.5 + 1.12 = ₹ 5.62

Time saved : 9-6 = 3 Hours

Under Rowan Plan

$$\text{Time Taken} \times \text{Hourly Rate} + \left[\frac{\text{Time Taken}}{\text{Standard Time}} \times \text{Time Saved} \times \text{Hourly Rate}\right]$$

= 6 hours × 0.75 + [6/5 × 3 × 0.75]

= 4.50 + 1.50 = ₹ 6.00

Statement of Factory Cost

Particulars	(*a*) ₹	(*b*) ₹
Materials	4.00	4.00
Direct Wages	5.62	6.00
Prime Cost	9.62	10.00
Add : Factory overheads : (15% of wages)	0.84	0.90
Factory Cost	10.46	10.90

Problem 4. *A company has to submit a tender for the manufacture of a machine in 1988. The estimate of the costing department indicates that the materials and wages would cost ₹ 40,000 and ₹ 50,000 respectively. Percentage of factory on cost to wages and percentage of office on cost to works cost would be 20% and 10% respectively.*

[B.Com., Nagpur 1989]

Solution : **Estimate for Tender Price**

	₹
Materials	40,000
Wages	50,000
Prime cost	90,000
Factory on cost 20% on wages	10,000
Works cost	1,00,000
Office on cost 10% on works cost	10,000
Cost of production	1,10,000
Profit 20% on selling price *i.e.,* 25% on cost	27,500
Selling price for tender	1,37,500

Problem 5. *From the following particulars of KRG Ltd. find out the value of the tender*

	₹
Material used	*3,000*
Production Wages	*2,300*
Direct Expenses	*250*

Provide 60% of productive wages for works on cost and 12½% on works cost for office on cost. Profit to be realised 15% on the tender price. [B.Com., Nagpur 1988]

Solution : Statement of Value of Tender

Particulars	₹
Materials	3,000.00
Productive Wages	2,300.00
Direct Expenses	250.00
Prime Cost	5,550.00
Works on cost 60% of productive wages	1,380.00
Works Cost	6,930.00
Office on cost 12½% on the works cost	866.25
Cost of production	7,796.25
Profit 15% on the tender price *i.e.,* 15/85 of the cost	1,375.81
Value of the Tender	9,172.06

Problem 6. *What is the cost of a job consuming materials worth ₹ 8,000, wages for 200 Labour hours at ₹ 5 per hours in Dept. A and 100 Labour hours at ₹ 4 per hour in Dept. B. The overheads of the factory amounted to ₹ 15,000 for 7,500 total working hours of all the departments.* [B.Com. Osmania Oct. 1993]

Solution : Cost Sheet

	Amount ₹	*Amount* ₹
Materials		8,000
Wages : Dept A 200 × 5	1,000	
Dept B 100 × 4	400	1,400
Overhead Expenses :		
$\left[\frac{15,000}{7,500} = \text{Rs. 2 per hour}\right]$		
i.e., 300 hours × ₹ 2.00		600
Total cost of a job		10,000

TEST PROBLEMS

1. The following figures have been extracted from the books of manufacturing company. All jobs pass through the company's two departments;

	Working Department ₹	Finishing Department ₹
Materials used	6,000	500
Direct labour	3,000	1,500
Factory overheads	1,800	1,200
Direct labour hours	12,000	5,000
Machine hours	10,000	2,000

The following information relates to job No 17:

	Working Department ₹	Finishing Department ₹
Materials used	120	10
Direct labour hours	65	25
Direct labour hours	265	70
Machine hours	255	25

You are required to enumerate four methods of absorbing factory overhead by Jobs showing the each department under the methods quoted.

[B.Com., Calicut, Sept/Oct. 1988]

[**Ans.** Four methods of absorbing factory overhead : Rates for each Dept.]

Methods of Absorption (basic)	*Rate of working dept*	*Rate of finishing dept*
1. Materials used	30%	240%
2. Direct labour	60%	80%
3. Direct labour	0.15	0.24
4. Machine hours	0.18	0.60

❑❑❑

11

Process Costing

Process costing is one of the important methods of costing. This method of costing is normally applicable to the different processes involved while converting a raw material into finished product when the raw material has passed through different stages before completion. With the help of the process costing, the manufacturer can find out the cost of each process and the cost of the product.

Simply, it refers to find out the cost at different stages of process and cost of product to industries is known as process costing.

DEFINITION

Operation costing is "the category of basic costing methods applicable, where standardised goods or services result from a sequence of repetitive and more or less continuous operations or processes to which cost are charged before being averaged over the units produced during the period".

[ICMA Definition]

ICMA defines process costing as "that form of operation costing which applies, where standardised goods are produced".

APPLICATION OF PROCESS COSTING

The following are some of the industries, where process costing system is normally applied.

Paper mills Biscuit works Oil refining Chemical works Soap making Distillation process Sugar mills	Paint, Ink and Varnishing etc. Meat Products Factory Milk Dairy Textile, Weaving, Spinning etc. Food Products Coke Works Gas Manufacturing

In the real sense, process costing may be adopted in organisations producing a single commodity in bulk or a group of products of different types.

FEATURES OF PROCESS COSTING

(*i*) Production is a continuous flow and the final product is the result of sequence of processes.

(*ii*) Clearly defined process cost centres.

(*iii*) Different types of products with or without by-products are simultaneously produced at one or more stages of manufacture.

(*iv*) Under the method of process costing normal and abnormal losses or gains are to be treated properly.

(*v*) The output of one process becomes the raw material of another process.

(*vi*) All the finished products are uniform and all units are exactly identical during one or more processes.

(*vii*) To calculate the effective units of production is possible under this method, even all the inputs may not be converted into finished goods.

ELEMENTS OF PRODUCTION COST

The following are the important elements of production cost under process costing :

(*i*) Material

(*ii*) Labour

(*iii*) Production overhead.

(*i*) Material

The material required for production is issued to the first process, then offer processing. Then it can be transferred to next process and so on. In some situations, material may pass from the first process to the next process where an additional material is to be added; it may continue until completion. Normally, material requisitioned in the prescribed form only may be issued. Cost incurred for this operation is treated as material cost.

(*ii*) Labour

Some of the Labour Forces are directly engaged in manufacturing of a product. But, generally employees are utilised continuously on one process and time spent by them is debited to the process account. Amount paid for the utilisation of Labour force is treated as labour cost. Normally, the cost of direct labour constitutes a very small part of the cost of production in industries. Because more number of automatic machineries are installed in the industry.

(*iii*) Production Overhead

Any expenses incurred for the production other than the material and labour come under the head of production overhead. Normally, the overhead element of total constitutes generally a very huge portion in the process costing. So, appropriate decision is required to ensure that reasonable share of production is charged to each process.

Material cost, Labour cost, and Production Overhead cost, these three elements taken together are called the cost of production of the product.

ADVANTAGES OF PROCESS COSTING

(*i*) To find out the cost of each process in an easy manner without any difficulty and of the final product at short intervals.

(*ii*) To find out the cost in simple and economical ways than job costing.

(*iii*) To adopt the standard costing principles effectively in process costing.

(*iv*) Appropriate allocation of the expenses can be made easily and the costs in each process accurately determined.

(*v*) Enables to determine the correct valuation of closing inventories.

LIMITATIONS OF PROCESS COSTING

(*i*) It is based on the historical cost system. So, the available cost information may not be useful for further important organisational decision making.

(*ii*) The entire process costing system is based on the average cost methods. But, average costs do not always reflect the true costs.

(*iii*) Any of the unfinished products which are available in any process at the end of the period are expressed in equivalent production units. It develops subjective element in scientific cost determination.

(*iv*) Frequently it is very difficult to estimate the normal quantity loss in process.

(*v*) Process costing system does not evaluate the efforts of individual workers or supervisors.

DIFFERENCES BETWEEN PROCESS COSTING AND JOB COSTING

Process Costing

Process costing means finding out the cost of product at each process or stages of the production.

Job Costing

Job costing is a method of cost ascertainment in industries engaged in different jobs. Under this method, costs are collected and accumulated for each job or operation or project separately.

Process Costing	*Job Costing*
In the process costing, the production is a continuous flow and the products are being homogenous.	Under job costing, production is carried out as against the specific orders.
Each and every process is related to another process. So, products lose their individuality.	Each job is separate and independent.
Costs are calculated at the end of the specific cost period.	Costs are calculated when a particular job is completed.

Cost of one process being transferred to the next process is a usual feature.	Here, there is no transfer of costs from one job to another.
Normally, the production is continuous so there is work in progress at the beginning and at closing.	There may or may not be work in progress at opening or closing in an accounting period.
Production is standardized and stable, therefore control is easier.	Cost control is comparatively more difficult because each job needs more managerial attention.

Process Cost Accounting Procedure

(*i*) Prepare separate account for each process. It is called process account.

(*ii*) All the direct and indirect expenses are debited to the respective processes.

(*iii*) Input (Raw material) introduced are entered in the first process account.

(*iv*) The total cost of one process is transferred to the next process as an initial cost till the production is completed.

(*v*) If any Normal Loss, Abnormal Loss, Normal Gain and Abnormal Gain arises, it should be treated properly.

Specimen Form of Process I A/c

Particulars	*Cost Per Unit* ₹	*Total Cost* ₹	*Particulars*	*Cost Per Unit* ₹	*Total Cost* ₹
To input (Raw Material Introduce)	xx	xx	By Transfer to Process II A/c	xx	xx
To Direct Wages		xx			
To Direct Expenses		xx			
To Production Overheads		xx			
	xx	xx		xx	xx

Specimen Form of Process II A/c

Particulars	*Cost Per Unit* ₹	*Total Cost* ₹	*Particulars*	*Cost Per Unit* ₹	*Total Cost* ₹
To Transfer from process I A/c	xx	xx	By Loss of weight (Normal Loss)	xx	xx
To Direct Material		xx	By Sale of Scrap	xx	xx
To Direct Wages		xx	By Abnormal Loss	xx	xx
To Abnormal Gain		xx	By Transfer to Process III A/c	xx	xx
	xx	xx		xx	xx

Specimen Form of Process III A/c

Particulars	*Cost Per Unit* ₹	*Total Cost* ₹	*Particulars*	*Cost Per Unit* ₹	*Total Cost* ₹
To Transfer from process II A/c	xx	xx	By Normal Loss	xx	xx
To Material		xx	By Abnormal Loss	xx	xx
To Direct Labour		xx	By Finished Stock	xx	xx
To Manufacturing Expenses		xx			
	xx	xx		xx	xx

Process Losses

The Process Losses can be classified into (*i*) Normal process Loss, (*ii*) Abnormal process Loss.

Normal Process Loss. The amount of loss which is unavoidable on account of inherent nature of production. This loss is quite expected under normal conditions.

Normal Loss is generally calculated as a certain percentage of input. But, sometimes, such a loss is due to loss of weight, say due to evaporation or other action. In this regard, such wastage is not physically present, obviously it cannot have any value. But, anyhow, normal loss is physically present in the form of scrap; it may have some value, so it should be credited to the process account.

Abnormal Process Loss. Any loss arising due to any of the unforeseen factors, which is over and above the Normal Loss is termed as Abnormal Loss. It arises due to carelessness, machine breakdown, use of defective material and so on.

Simply, Actual Loss is more than the estimated normal loss and the difference may be categorised as Abnormal Loss. Abnormal Loss account is debited with the quantity and the cost therefore process account is credited.

(*i*) *Formula For Abnormal Loss*

$$\frac{\text{Normal Cost of Normal Production}}{\text{Normal Output}} \times \text{Units of Abnormal Loss}$$

(*ii*) *Abnormal Gain*

Abnormal gain arises when the actual loss is less than the estimated normal loss and the difference may be treated as abnormal gain.

$$\frac{\text{Normal Cost of Normal Output}}{\text{Units of Normal Output}} \times \text{Units of Abnormal Gain}$$

(*iii*) *Value of Abnormal Wastage*

$$\frac{\text{Normal Cost of Normal Output}}{\text{Normal Output}} \times \text{Abnormal Loss}$$

TEST QUESTIONS

1. What is meant by process costing ?
2. Define process costing.
3. Explain the applications of process costing in different industries.
4. Describe the features of process costing.
5. Briefly explain the advantages of process costing.
6. What are the limitations of process costing?
7. What are the differences between process costing and job costing ?
8. List out any five industries in which process costing is use.
9. Name the four important aspects of process costing.
10. What is Normal loss ? How is it treated in cost accounts?
11. What does abnormal loss/gain arises ? How will you treat on these in cost accounts ?
12. Give the main objectives of inter-process profit.

PROBLEMS AND SOLUTIONS

Problem 1. *A product passes through two distinct processes A and B and then to finished stock. The output of A, passes direct to B and that of B passes to finished stock. From the following information you are required to prepare process account.*

Particulars		*Process A*	*Process B*
Material Consumed	(₹)	*12,000*	*6,000*
Direct Labour	(₹)	*14,000*	*8,000*
Manufacturing Expenses	(₹)	*4,000*	*4,000*
Input in Process A		*10,000 (units)*	—
Input in Process A	(₹)	*10,000 (value)*	—
Output (units)		*9,400*	*8,300*
Normal Wastage		*5%*	*10%*
Value of Normal Wastage (per 100 units)	(₹)	*8*	*10*

No opening or closing stock is held in the process.

[MBA Anna Dec. 2003] [B.Com., Madurai]

Solution :

Process A Account

Particulars	*Units*	*Amount* ₹	*Particulars*	*Units*	*Amount* ₹
To Input	10,000	10,000	By Normal Wastages	500	40
To Material Consumed		12,000	By Abnormal Wastage	100	421
To Director Labour		14,000	By Transfer to Process B A/c	9,400	39,539
To Manufacturing Expenses		4,000			
	10,000	40,000		10,000	40,000

$$\left[\text{Rs. } 40{,}000 - 40 = \frac{39{,}960}{9{,}500} \times 100 = \text{Rs. } 420.6\right] \textit{ i.e., } ₹\ 421$$

Process B Account

Particulars	*Units*	*Amount* ₹	*Particulars*	*Units*	*Amount* ₹
To Process A A/c	9,400	39,539	By Normal Wastages	940	94
To Material Consumed		6,000	By Abnormal Wastage	160	1,087
To Director Labour		8,000	By Finished stock A/c @ ₹6.80	8,300	56,358
To Manufacturing Expenses		4,000			
	9,400	57,539		9,400	57,539

Problem 2. *50 units are introduced into process at a cost of ₹ 50. The total additional expenditure incurred by the process is ₹ 30. Of the units introduced 10% are normally spoilt in the course of manufacture but these possess a scrap value of ₹ 0.25 each. Owing to an accident, only 40 units are produced. You are required to prepare process account.*

[MBA Anna Dec. 2002] [B.Com. Kerala May 1986]

Solution :

Process Account

	Units	*Amount* ₹		*Units*	*Amount* ₹
To Material Introduced @ Re 1 per unit	50	50	By Normal Loss 50 × 10/100 = 5 × 0.25	5	1.25
To Additional Direct Expenditure	-	30	By Abnormal Loss (5 × 1.75)	5	8.75
			By Output Transferred to next process (40 × 1.75)	40	70.00
	50	80		50	80.00

Workings :

(*i*) Normal output 50 – 5 = 45
Actual output 40
Abnormal Loss 5 Units

(*ii*) Cost per unit = $\frac{80-1.25}{45}$ = ₹ 1.75

Problem 3. *In process A, 100 units of raw materials were introduced at a cost of ₹ 1,000. The other expenditure incurred by the process is ₹ 600. Of the units introduced, 10% are normally scraped in the course of manufacture and they possess a scrap value of ₹ 7 per unit. The output of process A was only 75 units. Calculate the value of abnormal loss.*

[MBA Anna Jan. 2005]

Solution : **Process A Account**

Particulars	*Units*	*Amount* ₹	*Particulars*	*Units*	*Amount* ₹
To Materials	100	1,000	By Normal Loss	10	70
To Other Expenses		600	By Abnormal Loss	15	255
			By Process B A/c @ ₹17	75	1,275
	100	1,600		100	1,600

Workings :

$$\text{Value of Abnormal Wastage} = \frac{\text{Normal Cost of Normal Output}}{\text{Normal Output}} \times \text{Abnormal Loss}$$

Normal Cost = ₹ 1,600 – 70 = ₹ 1,530

$$\text{Amount of Abnormal Units} = \frac{1,530}{90} \times 15 = 255$$

$$\text{Amount of Normal Units} = \frac{1,530}{90} \times 75 = 1,275$$

Problem 4. *In process A, 100 units of raw materials were introduced at a cost of ₹ 1,000. The other expenditure incurred by the process was ₹ 602. Of the units introduced, 10% are normally lost in the course of manufacture and they possess a scrap value of ₹ 3 each. The output of process A was only 75 units. Prepare process A Account and Abnormal Loss account.*

[B.Com. Madras]

Solution : **Process A Account**

Particulars	*Units*	*Amount* ₹	*Particulars*	*Units*	*Amount* ₹
To Raw Materials	100	1,000	By Normal Loss 10% of 100 units @ ₹3 each	10	30
To Other Expenses		602	By Abnormal Loss	15	262
			By Process B (output)	75	1,310
	100	1,602		100	1,602

Working Notes :

	Units entered	100
Less :	Normal loss	10
	Normal output	90
	Actual output	75
	Units of Abnormal loss	15

Value of Abnormal Loss

$$= \frac{\text{Normal Cost of Normal Output}}{\text{Normal Output}} \times \text{Units of Abnormal Loss}$$

$$= \frac{1,572}{90} \times 15 = 262 \quad \left[\frac{1,602-30}{100-10} \times 15\right]$$

Abnormal Loss Account

Particulars	*Units*	*Amount* ₹	*Particulars*	*Units*	*Amount* ₹
To Process	15	262	By Cash (Scrap value of Loss @ ₹ 3)	15	45
			By Costing P.L A/c		217
	15	262		15	262

Problem 5. *The following details have been extracted from the costing records of an oil mill for the year ended 30.6.1996. The product passes through two distinct processes A and B and then to finished stock. It is known from the past experience that wastage occurs in the process as under.*

In process A 5% of the units entering and in process B, 10% of the units entering.

The scrap value of the wastage in process A is ₹ 8 per 100 units and in process B is ₹ 10 per 100 units.

The process figures are as follows.

	A ₹	B ₹
Material	25,000	10,000
Wages	30,000	20,000
Manufacturing Expenses	10,000	10,000
Factory Lighting	5,000	5,000
Sundry Expenses	5,000	-
5,000 units were introduced into process A costing	25,000	-

The output were

From process A : 4,700 units

From process B : 4,150 units

Prepare process cost – Accounts showing cost of output per unit.

[B.Com. Bangalore May 1987]

Solution :

Process A Account

	Units	TC ₹		Units	TC ₹
To Units Introduced	5,000	25,000	By Wastage 5% of 5,000 tonnes	250	20
To Materials		25,000	By Abnormal Loss	50	1,052
To Wages		30,000	By Output Transferred to B	4,700	98,928
To Manufacturing exp.		10,000			
To Factory Lighting		5,000			
To Sundry Expenses		5,000			
	5,000	1,00,000		5,000	1,00,000

NOTE :

(*i*) Normal Output 5,000 – 250 units = 4,750

Actual Output = 4,700

Abnormal Loss 50 units

(*ii*) Cost per unit

$$\frac{\text{Total Cost} - \text{Value of Normal Wastage}}{\text{Normal Output}}$$

$$\frac{1,00,000 - 20}{4,750} = \frac{99,980}{4,750} = ₹\ 21.0484$$

Abnormal Loss = 50 × 21.0484 = 1,052

Output = 4,700 × 21.0484 = 98,928

Process B Account

	Units	TC ₹		Units	TC ₹
To Output from Process A	4,700	98,928	By Normal Wastage 10% of 4,700 tonnes	470	47
To Materials		10,000	By Abnormal Loss	80	2,721
To Wages		20,000	By Finished Stock	4,150	1,41,160
To Sundry expenses		5,000			
To Manufacturing Expenses		10,000			
	4,700	1,43,928		4,700	1,43,928

Workings :

(*i*) Normal output 4700 – 470 = 4,230

But, Actual output 4,150

Abnormal Loss 80

(*ii*) Cost per unit = $\frac{1,43,928 - 47}{4,230} = \frac{1,43,881}{4,230}$

= ₹ 34.0144 per unit

Abnormal Loss = 80 × 34.0144

= 2,721

(*iii*) Value of Finished Stock

Output × Cost per unit = 4,150 × 34.0144

= 1,41,160

Problem 6. *2,000 units costing ₹ 4 per unit were introduced to process I. Labour costs and other expenses were ₹ 1,080 and ₹ 120 respectively. Its output was 1,900 units. The normal scrap was 10% of the input and had a realisable value of ₹ 1 per unit. Prepare process I Account, Normal Loss Account and Abnormal Gain Account.* [B.Com. Delhi 1994]

Solution :

Process I Account

	Units	*TC* ₹		*Units*	*TC* ₹
To Raw Materials	2,000	8,000	By Normal Loss	200	200
To Labour		1,080	By Transfer to		
To Other Costs		120	Process II	1,900	9,500
To Abnormal Gain	100	500			
	2,100	9,700		2,100	9,700

Cost per unit = $\frac{9,200 - 200}{2,000 - 200}$ = 5.00

Value of Output = 1,900 × 5 = 9,500

Value of Abnormal Gain = 100 × 5 = 500

Normal Loss Account

Particulars	*Units*	*Amount*	*Particulars*	*Units*	*Amount*
To Process	200	200	By Sale of Scrap	100	100
			By Abnormal Gain (Short fall in Scrap Value)	100	100
	200	200		200	200

Abnormal Gain Account

Particulars	*Units*	*Amount*	*Particulars*	*Units*	*Amount*
To Normal Loss	100	100	By Process I	100	500
To P & L A/c	-	400			
	100	500		100	500

Problem 7. *Make out the necessary accounts from the following details :*

		Process A	*Process B*
Materials	(₹)	*30,000*	*3,000*
Labour	(₹)	*10,000*	*12,000*
Overheads	(₹)	*7,000*	*8,600*
Input (units)		*20,000*	*17,500*
Normal Loss		*10%*	*4%*
Sale of wastage per unit		*₹ 1*	*₹ 2*

There was no opening or closing stock or work in progress. Final output from process B was 17,000 units. [B.Com. Calcutta]

Solution :

Process A Account

Particulars	*Units*	*Amount* ₹	*Particulars*	*Units*	*Amount* ₹
To Material	20,000	30,000	By Normal Loss (10%)	2,000	2,000
To Labour	—	10,000	By Abnormal Loss	500	1,250
To Overheads	—	7,000	By Process B A/c @ ₹ 2.50	17,500	43,750
	20,000	47,000		20,000	47,000

Workings :

$$\text{Cost per unit} = \frac{\text{Total Process Cost} - \text{Scrap Value from Normal Loss}}{\text{Input} - \text{Normal Loss}}$$

$$= \frac{47{,}000 - 2{,}000}{20{,}000 - 2{,}000} = 2.50$$

Abnormal Wastages (in units)

Input = 20,000

Less : Normal Wastage 10% = 2,000

Normal Output = 18,000

Less : Actual Output = 17,500

Abnormal Wastage = 500

Process B Account

Particulars	*Units*	*Amount* ₹	*Particulars*	*Units*	*Amount* ₹
To Process A A/c	17,500	43,750	By Normal Loss 4%	700	1,400
To Materials		3,000			
To Labour	-	12,000	By Finished stocks	17,000	66,735
To Overheads	-	8,600			
To Abnormal Gain	200	785			
	17,700	68,135		17,700	68,135

$$\text{Cost of Abnormal Gain} = \frac{65,950}{16,800} \times 200 = 785$$

$$\text{Cost of Finished Stocks} = \frac{65,950}{16,800} \times 17,000 = 66,735$$

$$\begin{aligned}\text{Abnormal Gain} &= \text{Actual Output} - \text{Normal Output}\\ &= 17,000 - (17,500 - 4\% \text{ of } 17,500)\\ &= 17,000 - 16,800 = 200 \text{ units}\end{aligned}$$

Normal Loss Account

Particulars	*Units*	*Amount* ₹	*Particulars*	*Units*	*Amount* ₹
To Process A A/c	2,000	2,000	By Sale (Process A : 2000 × ₹ 1 + Process B 500 × ₹ 2)	2,500	3,000
To Process B A/c	700	1,400	By Abnormal Gain A/c	200	400
	2,700	3,400		2,700	3,400

Abnormal Loss Account

Particulars	*Units*	*Amount* ₹	*Particulars*	*Units*	*Amount* ₹
To Process A A/c	500	1,250	By Sales (500 × ₹ 1)	500	500
			By Costing P.L & A/c.	-	750
	500	1,250		500	1,250

Abnormal Gain Account

Particulars	*Units*	*Amount* ₹	*Particulars*	*Units*	*Amount* ₹
To Normal Loss A/c	200	400	By Process B A/c	200	785
To Costing P&L A/c	-	385			
	200	785		200	785

Costing Profit and Loss Account

Particulars		*Amount.* ₹	*Particulars*		*Amount* ₹
To Abnormal Loss A/c		750	By Abnormal Gain A/c		385

Problem 8. *Product x is obtained after it passes through distinct processes. You are required to prepare process accounts from the following information.*

	Total ₹	*Process*		
		I	*II*	*III*
Materials	*15,084*	*5,200*	*3,960*	*5,924*
Direct Wages	*18,000*	*4,000*	*6,000*	*8,000*
Production Overheads	*18,000*	—	—	—

1,000 units @ ₹ 6 per unit were introduced in process I. Production overheads are to be distributed as 100% on direct wages.

Actual Output	*Unit*	*Normal Loss*	*Value of Scrap per unit ₹*
Process I	*950*	*5%*	*4*
Process II	*840*	*10%*	*8*
Process III	*750*	*15%*	*10*

[B.Com. Delhi]

Solution : **Process I Account**

Particulars	*Units*	*Amount*	*Particulars*	*Units*	*Amount*
To Materials Introduced @ ₹6 per unit	1,000	6,000	By Normal Loss	50	200
To Materials	-	5,200	By Transferred to process II @ ₹ 20 per unit	950	19,000
To Direct Wages		4,000			
To Production Overheads		4,000			
	1,000	19,200		1,000	19,200

Process II Account

Particulars	*Units*	*Amount*	*Particulars*	*Units*	*Amount*
To Transferred from Process I A/c	950	19,000	By Normal Loss	95	760
To Materials		3,960	By Abnormal Loss	15	600
To Direct Wages		6,000	By Transferred to the next process @ 40 per unit	840	33,600
To Production Overheads		6,000			
	950	34,960		950	34,960

Workings : $\left[\text{Abnormal Loss} = \frac{34,960 - 760}{950 - 95} \times 15 = 600 \right]$

Process III Account

Particulars	*Units*	*Amount*	*Particulars*	*Units*	*Amount*
To Transferred from Process II	840	33,600	By Normal Loss	126	1,260
To Materials		5,924	By Transferred to finished goods @ 76 per unit	750	57,000
To Direct Wages		8,000			
To Production Overheads		8,000			
To Abnormal Gain @ ₹ 76 per units	36	2,736			
	876	58,260		876	58,260

Workings : Abnormal Gain = $\frac{55,524 - 1,260}{840 - 126}$ = ₹ 76 × 36 units = ₹ 2,736.

Abnormal Loss Account

Particulars	*Amount*	*Particulars*	*Amount*
To Process II A/c	600	By Cash (Sale of Scrap of Abnormal Loss of unit)	120
		By Costing P & L A/c	480
	600		600

Abnormal Gain Account

Particulars	₹	*Particulars*	₹
To Process III	360	By Process III	2,736
To costing Profit and Loss Account	2,376		
	2,736		2,736

Workings :

Loss of units : 90. On sale of 90 units amount recovered is ₹ 900.

Therefore, 1,260 – 900 = ₹ 360 is debited.

Problem 9. *A product passes through three processes A, B and C. 10,000 units at a cost of ₹1 were issued to process A. The other direct expenses were :*

	Process A ₹	*Process B* ₹	*Process C* ₹
Sundry Materials	*1,000*	*1,500*	*1,480*
Direct Labour	*5,000*	*8,000*	*6,500*
Direct Expenses	*1,050*	*1,188*	*1,605*

The wastage of Process A was 5% and Process B 4%. The wastage of process A was sold at ₹ 0.25 per unit and that of B at ₹ 0.50 per unit and that of C at ₹ 1.00 per unit. The overhead charges were 168% of direct labour. The final product was sold at ₹ 10 per unit, fetching a profit of 20% on sales. Find the percentage of wastage in process C.

[B.Com. Andhra]

Solution :

Process A Account

Particulars	*Units*	*Amount* ₹	*Particulars*	*Units*	*Amount* ₹
To Units introduced	10,000	10,000	By Normal Wastage	500	125
To Sundry Materials		1,000	By Process B	9,500	25,325
To Direct Labour		5,000			
To Direct Expenses		1,050			
To Overheads		8,400			
	10,000	25,450		10,000	25,450

Process B Account

Particulars	*Units*	*Amount* ₹	*Particulars*	*Units*	*Amount* ₹
To Process A	9,500	25,325	By Normal Wastage	380	190
To Sundry Materials		1,500	By Process C	9,120	49,263
To Direct Labour		8,000			
To Direct Expenses		1,188			
To Overheads		13,440			
	9,500	49,453		9,500	49,453

Process C Account

Particulars	*Units*	*Amount* ₹	*Particulars*	*Units*	*Amount* ₹
To Process B	9,120	49,263	By Normal Wastage	456	456
To Sundry Materials		1,480	By Sales ₹ 10	8,664	86,640
To Direct Labour		6,500			
To Direct Expenses		1,605			
To Overheads		10,920			
	9,120	69,768		9,120	87,096

Normal Wastage is Computed as follows :

Total cost in process C = ₹ 69,768

Suppose, No.of Normal Wastage units = x

Sales Value of Waste one is = ₹ 1 *i.e.,* x units @ ₹ 1 per unit

Total Cost – Sales Value of Normal Wastage

= ₹ 69,768 – ₹ x *i.e.,* Total Cost – No.of units produced × cost per unit.

When selling price is ₹ 10 per unit, the cost per unit is

₹ 10–20% = ₹8 per unit

Thus total cost = (9,120 – x) × ₹ 8

= 72,960 – ₹ $8x$

$$69,768 - x = 72,960 - 8x$$

$$8x - x = 72,960 - 69,768$$

$$7x = 3,192$$

$$x = 456$$

Therefore percentage of Normal wastage

$$= \frac{456}{9,120} \times 100 = 5\%.$$

TEST PROBLEMS

1. The following details have been extracted from the costing records of an oil mill for the year ended 30th June, 1986. The products passes through two distinct processes A and B and then to finished stock. It is known from the past experience that wastage occurs in the processes as under:

In process A, 5% of the units entering and in process B, 10% of the units entering, The Scrap value of the wastage in process A is ₹ 8 per 100 units and process B is ₹ 10 per 100 units. The process figures are as following:

	A ₹	B ₹
Materials	25,000	10,000
Wages	30,000	20,000
Manufacturing expenses	10,000	10,000
Factory lighting	5,000	5,000
Sundry expenses	5,000	-

5,000 units were introduced into process A costing ₹ 25,000

The outputs were:

From process A-4,700 units.

From process B-4,150 units.

Prepare process cost accounts showing cost of output per units.

[B.Com., Bangalore, April/May 1987]

[**Ans:** Process A A/c = 4700 units, 98,928

Process B A/c = 4150 units, 141160]

2. A certain product passes through three processes before it is transferred to finished stock The following information is obtained for the month of December:

Items	*Process I* ₹	*Process II* ₹	*Process III* ₹	*Finished stock* ₹
Opening stock	2,000	12,000	10,000	25,000
Direct materials	13,000	20,000	40,000	
Direct wages	10,000	10,500	50,000	
Production overhead	10,000	25,000	25,000	
Closing stock	5,000	6,000	32,000	32,000
Profit percent on transfer	20%	25%	10%	
Price to the next process;				
Inter-process profit for				
Opening Stock	-	2,000	2,800	10,000

Stock-in-process is valued at prime cost and finished stock has been valued at the price at which it was received from process III. Sales during the period were ₹ 8,00,000.

Prepare Process Accounts, showing profit element at each stage.

[B.Com., Gandhiji, April/May 1988]

[**Ans:** Process I A/c = Total = 37,500, cost = 30,000, profit = 7,500

Process II A/c = Total = 1,32,000, cost = 90,213, profit = 41,787

Process III A/c = Total = 2,50,000, cost = 1,86,563, profit = 63,437]

3. Prepare the Process Cost accounting from the following:

		Process X	**Process Y**
Material used	tonnes	100	140
Cost per ton	₹	120	200
Sent from process X to Y		75%	–
Loss in weight		2%	2%
Scrap in tonnes		10%	10%
Scrap realisation per tonnes	₹	100	200
Wages	₹	30,000	35,0000

[B.Com., Osmania Oct. 1993]

[**Ans:** Process X = 22 tonnes @ ₹ 465.90 = 10250 10,250:

Process Y = 18,128 tons@ 494.43 = 89,630]

❑❑❑

12

Activity Based Costing

Activity Based Costing is the new approach of cost accounting. Under the Activity Based Costing costs are first found out to the activities and then to products. It focuses on activities performed to produce products.

Under the traditional costing, there is an absence of appropriate basis of allocation of cost and that should be left to the decision of the cost accountant to select appropriate basis for allocation. In accurate cost information, thus provided by the traditional costing, methods may lead to wrong decisions if used for control purposes or determination of selling price.

Professor Vipul pointed out, "Activity Based Costing had its genesis in the increasing importance of indirect Costs in the manufacturing operations. The direct processing costs which are easier to handle are being relegated to the background with each passing day due to automation. In this modern scenario, where indirect costs for outweighing the direct processing costs in many a situations, one cannot be content with rough and ready methods of yester years in dealing with the indirect costs."

The present industrial organisation follows an advanced manufacturing technology in the allocation. Because, the traditional costing system will not be suitable for the present high tech manufacturing industries.

The CIMA official Terminology defines Activity Based Costing as "Cost attribution to cost units on the basis of benefit received from indirect activities *e.g.,* ordering, setting up, assuring quality".

CONCEPT OF ACTIVITY BASED COSTING

In the present globalisation era, each and every organisation will successfully compete its products in the international market only with the efficient application of Activity Based Costing. An organisation, to hold itself on the market, has to manage properly the value chain at each stage. Value added at all the stages are to be compared with the costs associated and on that basis decisions are implemented, which enables cutting of the unnecessary activities and adding the new activities. In order to improve the quality of managerial decisions, Activity Based Costing supplies exact cost information to the management.

IMPLEMENTATION OF ACTIVITY BASED COSTING

The following are the important steps involved in implementing Activity based Costing to achieve the desired results.

(*i*) Identifying the functional areas involved in the organisation.

(*ii*) To determine the key activities involved in all the functional areas.
(*iii*) Allocating the common indirect cost to various activities at all the functional areas.
(*iv*) To determine the most suitable cost driver in each activity under the functional areas of management.
(*v*) To prepare activity wise expenditure statement.

FUNCTIONAL AREAS OF THE ORGANISATION

(*i*) Production Management
(*ii*) Personnel Management
(*iii*) Sales management
(*iv*) Repairs maintenance
(*v*) Administration
(*vi*) Public Relation and
(*vii*) Quality Control Management.

Some of the cost drivers in Activity Based costing system are as follows :

(*i*) Number of receiving orders for the receiving department
(*ii*) Number of despatch orders for the despatch department
(*iii*) Number of units
(*iv*) Amount of Labour cost incurred
(*v*) Value of materials in a product
(*vi*) Number of inspections
(*vii*) Number of parts received per month
(*viii*) Number of direct Labour hours
(*ix*) Number of purchasing and ordering hours
(*x*) Number of Labour transactions
(*xi*) Number of Customers orders processed
(*xii*) Number of employees

The following factors are to be considered while selecting cost drivers :

(*i*) Cost of measurement and
(*ii*) Degree of correlation between cost drivers and the actual consumption of overhead.

CLASSIFICATION OF ACTIVITIES

Under the production process, activities are identified and classified into different categories or segments. Basically, activities are classified into the following four activity categories.

(*i*) Unit level activities
(*ii*) Batch level activities
(*iii*) Product level activities
(*iv*) Facility level activities

BENEFITS OF IMPLEMENTING ACTIVITY BASED COSTING

The following are the important benefits of implementing activity based costing :

(*i*) Activity Based Costing provides valuable information to the management to identify the areas of cost reduction. If a company's financial position is not satisfactory, it advises the management to go for lay off measures.

(*ii*) Now-a-days non-manufacturing costs play a prominent role in the constituent of total cost. Activity Based Costing provides appropriate guidance for the allocation of non-manufacturing cost.

(*iii*) Activity Based Costing provides accurate cost information which is essential for most of the recent productivity approaches. With the help of these activities overall performance of the organisation will be improved.

(*iv*) It assists the management to formulate an effective pricing policy.

(*v*) Activity Based Costing helps the manager to take decisions whether he should get the activity done within the firm or sub contract the same to an outside agency.

(*vi*) With the help of the Activity Based Costing, cost of each activity is to be determined accurately. It enables the manager to evaluate the performance of transferor and transferee departments.

TEST QUESTIONS

1. What is meant by Activity Based costing ?
2. Define Activity Based costing.
3. What are the steps involved in implementing the Activity based costing ?
4. What are the functional areas of the organization ?
5. List out the classification of activities.
6. Describe the benefits of implementing Activity based costing.

❑❑❑

13

Inventory Pricing and Valuation

The term inventory generally refers to stock or stock in trade. Inventory includes (*i*) stock of finished goods (*ii*) work in progress (*iii*) raw materials and components. In a trading organisation inventory refers to goods meant for resale or unsold stock. In case of manufacturing organisation, inventory consists of raw materials, semi-finished goods, finished goods and stores.

The Institute of Chartered Accountants of India (ICAI) defines in accounting standard number 2. Inventories as tangible properties held.

(*i*) Enable to make a sale in the ordinary course of the business.

(*ii*) In the process of production for such sale.

(*iii*) To be consumed in the production of goods or services for sale including maintenance supplies and consumables other than machinery spares.

Inventory valuation is more essential for the organisation, in order to assess the operating performance and financial position of the company. Normally, inventory valuation is done at the end of the financial year.

OBJECTIVES OF INVENTORY VALUATION

(*i*) The ultimate object of the inventory valuation is the determination of the true profit earned by the organisation during a particular accounting period.

(*ii*) To determine the correct financial position of the concern because inventory is shown as the current asset in the Balance sheet. Suppose, it could not be properly valued means it is difficult to determine the correct financial position.

BASES OF INVENTORY VALUATION

(*i*) *Historical Cost.* Under the historical cost, cost accounting provides a certain rule that the inventory should be valued at cost.

(*ii*) *Either the Cost or Market Price : Whichever is lower.* Under this method, the inventory is valued at cost or market price whichever is lower.

(*iii*) *Net Realizable Method.* Net realizable value represents the estimated selling price less cost of the completion. But, under this method, the stock is valued at historical cost as the selling price will be lower to a certain extent.

(*iv*) *Replacement Cost Method.* Under this method inventories are valued at a replacement value. It may be taken as either the market value or reproduction value.

TECHNIQUES OF INVENTORY CONTROL

The following are the important techniques of inventory control normally followed in practice :

(i) Level setting
(ii) JIT (Just in time) inventory system
(iii) Economic ordering quantity
(iv) ABC (Always better control) analysis
(v) VED analysis [Vital, Essential, Desirable]
(vi) Perpetual inventory system
(vii) Inventory turnover ratio
(viii) Inventory cost report
(ix) FNSD analysis
F : Fast moving items
N : Normal moving items
S : Slow moving items
D : Dead items.

METHODS OF VALUATION OF INVENTORIES

The following methods for pricing material issues are generally followed :

(i) First in first out method
(ii) Last in first out method
(iii) Average cost method
(iv) Inflated price method
(v) Specific price method
(vi) Highest in first out method
(vii) Base stock method
(viii) Replacement price method
(ix) Realisable value method
(x) Current standard price method
(xi) Market price method

TEST QUESTIONS

1. What is meant by Inventory ?
2. Explain the concept of inventory valuation.
3. What are the objectives of inventory valuation ?
4. Describe the various bases of inventory valuation.
5. List out the eight methods of valuing material issues.
6. State briefly the different methods of pricing material issues and indicate their impact on the ascertainment of profits.
7. Describe the Techniques of inventory control.
8. What factors have to be considered for adopting a method for pricing of materials ?

PROBLEMS AND SOLUTIONS

Problem 1. *The stock of material in hand as on 1st September was 500 units @ ₹ 10 per unit. The following purchases and issues were subsequently made. Prepare the stores ledger account showing how the value of the issues would be recorded under FIFO method.*

Purchases :	*6th Sep.*	*100 units*	*at*	*₹ 11*
	20th Sep.	*700 units*	*at*	*₹ 12*
	27th Sep.	*400 units*	*at*	*₹ 13*
	13th Oct.	*1000 units*	*at*	*₹ 14*
	20th Oct.	*500 units*	*at*	*₹ 15*
	17th Nov.	*400 units*	*at*	*₹ 16*
Issues :	*9th Sep.*	*500 units*		
	22nd Sep.	*500 units*		
	30th Sep.	*500 units*		
	15th Oct.	*500 units*		
	22nd Oct.	*500 units*		
	11th Nov.	*500 units*		

[B.Com., Andhra, Madurai]

Solution :

		Stores ledger Account						*FIFO*		
		Receipts			*Issues*			*Balance*		
Date	*Particulars*	*Qty.*	*CPU*	*TC*	*Qty.*	*CPU*	*TC*	*Qty.*	*CPU*	*TC*
Sep. 1	Balance B/d	—	—		—	—	—	500	10.00	5000
Sep. 6	Goods received	100	11	1100	—	—	—	500	10.00	5000
								100	11.00	1100
Sep. 9	Requisition slip. No of Issues	—	—	—	500	10.00	5000	100	11.00	1100
Sep. 20	Goods Received	700	12	8400	—	—	—	100	11.00	1100
								700	12.00	8400
Sep. 22	Goods issued	—	—	—	100	11.00	1100			
					400	12.00	4800	300	12.00	3600
Sep. 27	Goods Received	400	13	5200	—	—	—	300	1200	3600
								400	13.00	5200
Sep. 30	Goods issued	—	—	—	300	12.00	3600	—	—	—
					200	13.00	2600	200	13.00	2600
Oct. 13	Goods received	1000	14	14,000	—	—	—	200	13.00	2600
								1000	14.00	14000
Oct. 15	Requisition Slip	—	—	—	200	13.00	2600	—	—	—
					300	14.00	4200	700	14.00	9800
Oct. 20	Goods received	500	15	7,500	—	—	—	700	14.00	9800
								500	15.00	7500
Oct. 22	Requisition Slip No	—	—	—	500	14.00	7000	200	14.00	2800
								500	15.00	7500
Nov. 11	Requisition slip No	—	—	—	200	14..00	2800	—	—	—
					300	15.00	4500	200	15.00	3000
Nov. 17	Goods Received	400	16	6,400	—	—	—	200	15.00	3000
								400	16.00	6400

Value of the stock in hand ₹ 9,400

i.e., 200 × 15 + 400 × 16 = ₹ 9,400

Problem 2. *Prepare stores ledger account from the following transaction under FIFO method :*

(1) Jan. 1	*Received*	*1000 units*	*at ₹ 20*	*per unit*
(2) Jan. 10	*Received*	*260 units*	*at ₹ 21*	*per unit*
(3) Jan. 20	*Issued*	*700 units*		
(4) Feb. 4	*Received*	*400 units*	*at ₹ 23*	*per unit*
(5) Feb. 21	*Received*	*300 units*	*at ₹ 25*	*per unit*
(6) Mar. 16	*Issued*	*620 units*		
(7) Mar. 18	*Issued*	*240 units*		
(8) Mar. 21	*Received*	*500 units*	*at ₹ 22*	*per unit*
(9) Mar. 29	*Issued*	*380 units*		

[B.Com. PU May 2002]

Solution :

		Stores ledger FIFO method								
		Receipts			*Issues*			*Balance*		
Date	*Particulars*	*Qty.*	*CPU*	*TC*	*Qty.*	*CPU*	*TC*	*Qty.*	*CPU*	*TC*
Jan. 1	Goods received	1000	20.00	20,000	—	—	—	1000	20.00	20,000
Jan. 12	Goods received	260	21.00	5,460	—	—	—	1000 260	20.00 21.00	20,000 5,460
Jan. 20	Requisition Slip No	—	—	—	700	20.00	14,000	300 260	20.00 21.00	6,000 5,460
Feb. 4	Goods received	400	3.00	1,200	—	—	—	300 260 400	20.00 21.00 3.00	6,000 5,460 1,200
Feb. 21	Goods received	300	25.00	7,500	—	—	—	300 260 400 300	20.00 21.00 3.00 25.00	6,000 5,460 1,200 7,500
Mar. 16	Goods issued	—	—	—	300 260 60	20.00 21.00 3.00	6000 5460 180	340 300	3.00 25.00	1020 7500
Mar. 18	Requisition slip No.	—	—	—	240	3.00	720	100 300 240	3.00 25.00 3.00	300 7500 720
Mar. 21	Goods received	500	22.00	11,000	—	—	—	100 300 240 500	3.00 25.00 3.00 22.00	300 7500 720 11000
Mar. 29	Requisition slip No.	—	—	—	100 280	3.00 25.0	300 7000	20 240 500	25.0 3.00 22.00	500 720 11000

Value of the stock in hand = 20 × 25 + 240 × 3 + 500 × 22 = 12,220

Problem 3. *From the following transaction, prepare separate stores ledger accounts using the following pricing methods.*

(i) FIFO and (ii) LIFO

January 1	*Opening balance*	*100 units*	*@ ₹ 6 each*
January 5	*Received*	*500 units*	*@ ₹ 6 each*
January 20	*Issued*	*300 units*	
February 5	*Issued*	*200 units*	
February 6	*Received*	*500 units*	*@ ₹ 5 each*
March 10	*Issued*	*300 units*	
March 12	*Issued*	*250 units*	

[B.A. (Corp) PU 2002]

Solution :

		Stores ledger (FIFO)								
		Receipts			*Issues*			*Balance*		
Date	*Particulars*	*Qty.*	*CPU*	*TC*	*Qty.*	*CPU*	*TC*	*Qty.*	*CPU*	*TC*
Jan. 1	Balance B/d	—	—	—	—	—	—	100	5	500
Jan. 5	Goods received	500	6	3,000	—	—	—	100	5	500
								500	6	3,000
Jan. 20	Requisition slip	—	—	—	100	5	500	—	—	—
					200	6	1,200	300	6	1,800
Feb. 5	Requisition slip	—	—	—	200	6	1,200	100	6	600
Feb. 6	Goods received	500	5	2,500	—	—	—	100	6	600
								500	5	2,500
Mar. 10	Goods issued	—	—	—	100	6	600	300	5	1,500
					200	5	1000			
Mar. 12	Goods issued				250	5	1250	50	5	250

Value of stock in hand is ₹ 250 *i.e.,* [50 × 5 = 250].

		Stores ledger (LIFO)								
		Receipts			*Issues*			*Balance*		
Date	*Particulars*	*Qty.*	*CPU*	*TC*	*Qty.*	*CPU*	*TC*	*Qty.*	*CPU*	*TC*
Jan. 1	Blance B/d	—	—	—	—	—	—	100	5	500
Jan. 5	Goods received	500	6	3,000	—	—	—	100	5	500
								500	6	3,000
Jan. 20	Requisition slip	—	—	—	200	6	1,200	100	5	500
								300	6	1,800
Feb. 5	Goods requisition	—	—	—	200	6	1,200	100	5	500
								100	6	600
Feb. 6	Goods received	500	5	2,500	—	—	—	100	6	600
								100	5	600
								500	5	2,500
Mar. 10	Goods requisition	—	—	—	300	5	1,500	100	5	500
								100	6	600
								200	5	1,000
Mar. 12	Goods requisition	—	—	—	200	5	1,000			
					50	6	300	100	5	500
								50	6	300

Value of Stock in hand is ₹ 800 [100 × 5 + 50 × 6 = 800]

Problem 4. *The following is an extract of the record of receipts and issues of sulphur in a chemical factory during Feb. 1998.*

1998 Feb. 1 Opening balance 500 tonnes @ ₹ 200
3 Issue : 70 tonnes
4 Issue : 100 tonnes
8 Issue : 80 tonnes
13 Received from suppliers 200 tonnes @ ₹ 190
14 Returned from dept 15 tonnes
16 Issue : 250 tonnes
20 Received from suppliers 240 tonnes @ ₹ 190
24 Issue : 300 tonnes
25 Received from suppliers 320 tonnes @ ₹ 190
26 Issue : 115 tonnes
27 Returned from dept. 35 tonnes
28 Received from supplier 100 tonnes @ ₹ 190

Issues are to be priced on the principle of FIFO. The stock verifier of the factory had found a shortage of 10 tonnes on the 22nd and left a note accordingly. Prepare the stores ledger account. [M.Com., Periyar May 2003]

Solution :

		Stores ledger (FIFO)								
		Receipts			Issues			Balance		
Date	Particulars	Qty.	CPU	TC	Qty.	CPU	TC	Qty.	CPU	TC
Feb. 1	Balance B/d	—	—	—	—	—	—	500	200	1,00,000
Feb. 3	Issued	—	—	—	70	200	14,000	430	200	86,000
Feb. 4	Issued	—	—	—	100	200	20,000	330	200	66,000
Feb. 8	Issued	—	—	—	80	200	16,000	250	200	50,000
Feb. 13	Goods received	200	190	38,000	—	—	—	250	200	50,000
								200	190	38,000
Feb. 14	Returns	15	10	2,850	—	—	—	250	200	50,000
								200	190	38,000
								15	190	2,850
Feb. 16	Issued	—	—	—	250	200	50,000	200	190	38,000
								15	190	2,850
Feb. 20	Goods Received	240	190	45,600	—	—	—	200	190	38,000
								15	190	2,850
								240	190	45,600
Feb. 22	Shortage	—	—	—	10	200	2,000	190	190	36,100
								15	190	2,850
								240	190	45,600
Feb. 24	Issued	—	—	—	190	190	36,100	—	—	—
					15	190	2,850			
					95	190	18,050	145	190	27,550
Feb. 25	Goods Received	320	190	60,800	—	—	—	145	190	27,550
								320	190	60,800

Feb. 26	Issued	—	—	—	115	190	21,850	30	190	5,700
								320	190	60,800
Feb. 27	Returned	35	190	6650	—	—	—	30	190	5,700
								320	190	60,800
								35	190	6,650
Feb. 28	Goods Received	100	190	19,000	—	—	—	30	190	5,700
								320	190	60,800
								35	190	6,650
								100	190	19,000

Value Stock in hand is ₹ 92,150 [5700 + 60,800 + 6650 + 19000].

Problem 5. *Balaji Industries had an opening stock of 300 units of materials valued at ₹ 600. Receipts and Issues during August 1998 were as follows.*

	Units	*Value (₹)*
August 2 Received	*200*	*440*
August 4 Issued	*150*	—
August 6 Received	*200*	*460*
August 11 Issued	*150*	—
August 19 Issued	*200*	—
August 22 Received	*200*	*480*
August 31 Issued	*250*	—

Show the stores ledger account using LIFO Method. [M.Com. (CA) Periyar May 2004]

Solution :

		Stores ledger (LIFO)								
		Receipts			*Issues*			*Balance*		
Date	*Particulars*	*Qty.*	*CPU*	*TC*	*Qty.*	*CPU*	*TC*	*Qty.*	*CPU*	*TC*
Aug. 1	Balance B/d	—	—	—	—	—	—	300	2.00	600
Aug. 2	Goods Received	200	2.20	440	—	—	—	300	2.00	600
								200	2.20	440
Aug. 4	Goods issued	—	—	—	150	2.20	330	300	2.00	600
								50	2.20	110
Aug. 6	Goods Received	200	2.30	460	—	—	—	300	2.00	600
								50	2.20	110
								200	2.30	460
Aug. 11	Goods issued	—	—	—	150	2.30	345	300	2.00	600
								50	2.20	110
								50	2.30	115
Aug. 19	Goods issued	—	—	—	50	2.30	115	—	—	—
					50	2.20	110			
					100	2.00	200	200	2.00	400
Aug. 22	Goods received	200	2.40	480	—	—	—	200	2.00	400
								200	2.40	480
Aug. 31	Goods issued	—	—	—	200	2.40	480			
					50	2.00	100	150	2.00	300

Value of stock in hand ₹ 300.

Problem 6. *Prepare stores ledger Account from the following information*

Jan. 1	*Purchased*	*500 kg*	*at ₹ 20 per kg*
Jan. 10	*Purchased*	*300 kg*	*at ₹ 21 per kg*
Jan. 15	*Issued*	*600 kg*	—
Jan. 20	*Purchased*	*400 kg*	*at ₹ 22 per kg*
Jan. 25	*Issued*	*300 kg*	—
Jan. 27	*Purchased*	*500 kg*	*at ₹ 21 per kg*
Jan. 31	*Issued*	*200 kg*	—

Adopt the Base stock method of issue and ascertain the value of closing stock. Assume Base stock 200 kg. [B.Com. Madurai]

Solution :

		Stores ledger (FIFO) – Base stock								
		Receipts			*Issues*			*Balance*		
Date	*Particulars*	*Qty.*	*CPU*	*TC*	*Qty.*	*CPU*	*TC*	*Qty.*	*CPU*	*TC*
Jan. 1	Balance B/d	500	20	10,000	—	—	—	500	20	10,000
Jan. 10	Goods received	300	21	6,300	—	—	—	500	20	10,000
								300	21	6,300
Jan. 15	Requisition slip No.	—	—	—	300	20	6000	200	20	4,000
					300	21	6300			
Jan. 20	Goods received	400	22	8,800	—	—	—	200	20	4,000
								400	22	8,800
Jan. 25	Requisition slip No.	—	—	—	300	22	6600	200	20	4,000
								100	22	2,200
Jan. 27	Goods received	500	21	10,500	—	—	—	200	20	4,000
								100	22	2200
								500	21	10500
Jan. 31	Issued	—	—	—	100	22	2200			
					100	21	2100	200	20	4000
								400	21	8400

Value of closing stock of 600 kg is ₹ 12400
[200 kg × ₹ 20 + 400 kg × ₹ 21 = 12,400]

Problem 7. *The following transaction took place in respect of an item of material.*

Date	*Receipts Quantity*	*Rate (₹)*	*Issue Quantity*
2.09.2000	*200*	*2.00*	—
10.9.2000	*300*	*2.40*	—
15.9.2000	—	—	*250*
18.9.2000	*250*	*2.60*	—
20.9.2000	—	—	*200*

Record the above transaction in the stores ledger pricing issues at Simple average method.

Solution :

		Stores Ledgers Simple Average Method							
		Receipts			*Issues*			*Balance*	
Date	*Particulars*	*Qty.*	*CPU*	*TC*	*Qty.*	*CPU*	*TC*	*Qty.*	*TC*
2.9.2000	Goods received	200	2.00	400	—	—	—	200	400
10.9.2000	Goods received	300	2.40	720	—	—	—	500	1120
15.9.2000	Issue of material	—	—	—	250	2.20	550	250	570
18.9.2000	Goods received	250	2.60	650	—	—	—	500	1220
20.9.2000	Issue of material	—	—	—	2000	2.50	500	300	720

Problem 8. *You have been asked to calculate the following levels for part No.96867 from the following information given there under.*

(a) Re-ordering level *(b) Maximum level*

(c) Minimum level *(d) Danger level* *(e) Average stock level*

The re-ordering quantity is to be calculated from the following data :

(i) Total cost of purchasing relating to the order = ₹ 20.

(ii) Number of units to be purchased during the year = 5000.

(iii) Purchase price per unit including transportation cost = ₹ 50.

(iv) Annual cost of storage of one unit = ₹ 5.

Lead times : Average : 11days

Average : 11 days

Maximum : 16 days

Minimum : 7 days

Max. for emergency purchases 5 days

Rate of consumption Average : 15 units per day

Maximum : 20 units per day

Answer. *a* – 300 units, *b* = 440 units, *c* = 150 units, *d* = 60 units, *e* = 250 units

Re order quantity 200 units.

Problem 9. *A publishing house purchases 2000 units of a particular item per year at a unit cost of ₹ 20.*

The ordering cost per order is ₹ 50 and the inventory carrying cost is 25%.

Find the optimal order quantity and the minimum total cost including purchase cost.

If 3% discount is offered by the supplier for the purchase in lots of 1000 or more, should the publishing house accept the offer ? [CS Inter]

Solution :

$$\text{Optimal order quantity on EOQ} = \sqrt{\frac{2CO}{I}}$$

C = Annual consumption *i.e.,* 2000 units

O = Cost of placing an order *i.e.,* ₹ 50/-; Annual carrying cost per unit = ₹ 5 [*i.e.,* 25% of ₹ 20]

$$= \left[\frac{25}{100} \times 20 = 5\right]$$

$$= \sqrt{\frac{2 \times 2000 \text{ units} \times ₹\,50}{₹\,5}} = 200 \text{ units.}$$

(*i*) Computation of Total cost (without discount)

Number of orders to be placed for getting 2000 units @ 200 units per order 2000/200	=	10 orders
Average inventory $\left(\frac{200 \text{ units per order}}{2}\right)$	=	100 units
Purchase price of 2000 units @ ₹ 20	₹	40,000
Ordering cost (10 orders @ ₹ 50)	₹	500
Carrying cost for 100 units (100 × 5)	₹	500
Total cost	₹	41,000

(*ii*) Computation of total cost with 3% Discount (Purchase order quantity is of 1000 units)

Unit cost	₹	20.00
Less : Discount 3%	₹	0.60
	₹	19.40
Lot size 1000 units		
No. of orders for 2000 units @ 1000 units		2 orders
Average inventory $\left(\frac{1000 \text{ units}}{2}\right)$		500 units
Purchase cost for 2000 units × ₹ 19.40	₹	38,800
Ordering cost for 2 orders @ ₹ 50	₹	100
Carrying cost for average inventory 500 units of ₹ 19.40 $\left(500 \times 19.40 \times \frac{25}{100}\right)$	₹	2,425
Total cost	₹	41,325

Based on the above calculation the supplier's offer of 3% discount should not be accepted because it will increase cost by ₹ 325/- as compared to the economic order quantity of 200 units.

Problem 10. *From the following Data find out Economic ordering quantity*

Annual usage	:	*8000 units*
Cost of material per unit	:	*₹ 20*
Cost of placing and receiving one order	:	*₹ 60*
Annual carrying cost of one unit	:	*10% of inventory value*

Solution :

Formula for the calculation of economic ordering quantity : $EOQ = \sqrt{\frac{2CO}{I}}$

C = Annual usage of material *i.e.,* 8000 units

O = Cost of placing one order *i.e.,* ₹ 60/-

I = Annual carrying cost per unit $\frac{20 \times 10}{100} = 2$

$$EOQ = \sqrt{\frac{2 \times 8,000 \times 60}{2}}$$

= 692 units.

Problem 11. *Find out the economic ordering quantity from the following particulars :*

Annual usage : *₹ 2,40,000*

Cost of placing and receiving one order : *₹ 120*

Annual carrying cost 10% of inventory value

Solution :

Formula for the calculation of economic ordering quantity : $EOQ = \sqrt{\frac{2CO}{I}}$

C = Annual requirement of material in Rupees 2,40,000

O = Cost of placing one order *i.e.,* ₹ 120/-

I = 10% carrying cost

$$EOQ = \sqrt{\frac{2 \times 2,40,000 \times 120}{10/100}}$$

$$= \sqrt{\frac{2 \times 2,40,000 \times 120 \times 100}{10}}$$

= ₹ 24,000/-

Problem 12. *Following information relating to a type of material is available :*

Annual Demand : *2400 units*

Unit price : *₹ 2.40*

Ordering cost per order : *₹ 4.00*

Carrying cost : *12% p.a*

Interest rate : *10% p.a*

Lead time : *Half month*

Calculate Economic order quantity and total annual inventory cost in respect of the particular raw material.

Solution :

$$EOQ = \sqrt{\frac{2CO}{I}}$$

C = Annual Demand *i.e.,* 2400 units

O = Ordering cost ₹ 4.00/-

I = Carrying cost 12% of unit price

$$\text{EOQ} = \sqrt{\frac{2 \times 2400 \times \text{Rs. } 4}{\text{Rs. } 2.40 \times 12/100}}$$

$= 258$ units

Calculation of total inventory cost

Purchase price of 2400 units @ ₹ 2.40 per unit	₹ 5760.00
Add : Carrying cost $\frac{1}{2} \times 258$ units $\times 2.40 \times \frac{12}{100}$	37.15
Add : Ordering cost of 10 orders @ ₹ 4 per order	40.00
Total Inventory cost	5837.15

NOTE :

$$\text{No. of orders} = \frac{\text{Annual Demand}}{\text{EOQ}}$$

$$= \frac{2400 \text{ units}}{258 \text{ units}}$$

$= 10$ orders

□□□

14

Standard Costing

The standard cost is a predetermined cost which determines what each product or service should cost under given operational conditions. Simply speaking standard cost is an expected cost of producing one unit.

The efficiency of the management depends upon the effective control of costs. If there is a difficulty to control the costs, it means the organisation automatically invites the risk. So, the system of standard costing is the most appropriate way of controlling costs.

DEFINITION

Standard

According to **Prof. Eric. L. Kohler,** *"Standard is a desired attainable objective, a performance, a goal, a model".*

Standard Cost

The Institute of Cost and Management Accountants, England defines standard cost is "a predetermined cost which is calculated from management's standard of efficient operation and the relevant necessary expenditure".

Standard Costing

The Institute of Cost and Management Accountants, England defines standard costing as "The preparation and use of standard costs and the analysis of variances of their causes and the points of incidence".

Historical Costing

Historical costing is the process of accumulating costs after they are incurred in an orderly manner. Costing of actual costs in a systematic manner is known as historical costing.

The ICMA defines historical cost as "the actual cost of acquiring assets, goods and services and historical costing as a "system of accounting in which all values are based on the historical costs incurred. This is the basis prescribed in the Companies Act for published accounts".

Limitations on historical costing are :

(*i*) It is a post-mortem examination of the actual cost.

(*ii*) It is not suitable for cost comparison.

(*iii*) Inaccurate cost determination.

STANDARD COST VS BUDGETARY CONTROL

In an organisation the ultimate aim of both standard costing and budgetary control is to maximise the efficiency and managerial control. Both the costing techniques have the predetermined costs and this should be compared with the actual performance and to find out the variance and to take corrective actions. Without standard cost, either preparation of budget or the system of practical budgeting control cannot be achieved.

Similarity between Standard Cost and Budgetary Control

(*i*) The ultimate object of both techniques is the determination of cost in advance.

(*ii*) For both of them, certain standards are fixed.

(*iii*) In both the cases, comparison will be carried out.

(*iv*) In both the situations, variations are identified and corrective actions are taken care of.

Differences between Budgetary Control and Standard Costing

Budgetary Control	Standard Costing
(*i*) It is more extensive in its application because it deals with the operations of the entire business.	It is intensive as it is applied to manufacturing of a product or contributing a service.
(*ii*) Budgets are prepared for sales, production, cash etc.	Standard costing is determined by classifying recording and apportionment expenses to respective cost unit.
(*iii*) Budgetary control is related to financial accounts.	It is related to cost accounts.
(*iv*) It can be operated without standards.	It cannot be operated without budget.
(*v*) It does not require standardisation of products.	It requires standardisation of products.
(*vi*) Budgets are expressed in total amounts.	Standards are for unit of production.
(*vii*) Variances are not normally revealed through the accounts.	Variances are revealed through different accounts.

ADVANTAGES OF STANDARD COSTING

(*i*) It guides the management in formulating price and production policy.

(*ii*) It facilitates the reduction in clerical and accounting cost and management time.

(*iii*) It helps to generate profit at higher level, through the comparison of actual cost to the standard costs. If any of the differences are identified, the corrective actions are taken immediately.

(*iv*) It helps to determine the accurate profit in future.

(*v*) The principle of management by exception can be made applicable in the business for concentrating its attention on below or above the standards set.

(*vi*) It helps in effective application of delegation of authority and responsibility. As a result, executives become more responsible as it clearly shows who is responsible for the cost centres.

(*vii*) It helps to minimise the wastages and losses. Through this higher level productivity can be achieved.

(*viii*) It creates an atmosphere of cost consciousness among the executives, workers and foremen because the variance analysis fixes responsibility for favourable or unfavourable performances.

(*ix*) It helps in budgetary control and in decision making.

(*x*) It facilitates timely cost reports to management and a forward looking aspect is encouraged at all levels of management.

LIMITATIONS OF STANDARD COSTING

(*i*) Standard costing is an expensive technique for a small level organisation.

(*ii*) It is costly as the fixing of standards needs advanced professional skills.

(*iii*) Distinction may not be always possible between controllable and uncontrollable variances, because of responsibility to a particular person or process becomes very difficult.

(*iv*) The effective utilisation of variances analysis depends mostly on the basis of standards set. And at the same time, setting of correct standards is also very difficult.

(*v*) Standard costing is not suitable for the industries which produce non-standardized products.

(*vi*) In the real sense, whenever the organisation fixes the standards, it should affect the freedom of the managers. So, they strongly oppose this system.

DETERMINATION OF STANDARDS COSTS

The following preliminary steps are to be taken into account before setting standards for different elements of costs :

(*i*) Establishment of cost centre

(*ii*) Classification and codification of accounts

(*iii*) Types of standards or period of use

(*iv*) Setting the standards

I. Establishment of Cost Centre

Setting of cost centres is the very first step required before setting of standards. According to The Chartered Institute of Management Accountants, London cost centre is defined as "a location, person or item of equipment (or group of these) for which cost may be ascertained and used for the purpose of cost control". When the organisation establishes the cost centre, the standards are fixed and the variances are analysed. Cost centre is necessary because fixing of responsibility and defining the lines of authority becomes easier.

II. Classification and Codification of Accounts

In a business organisation various kinds of expenses are incurred. However, the actual expenses are classified under suitable heads for the purpose of establishment of codes and symbols. Coding is useful for speedy collection, analysis of cost information and mechanical devices.

III. Period of Use

After the classifying and coding of accounts, the next step for the establishment of standard cost is the length of the operating period for which standards are to be used. The different types of standards are normally taken into account while determining the standards.

(*a*) *Basic Standards.* ICMA, London defines basic standard as "an underlying standard from which a current standard can be developed". Basic standard is set up for some base year and is not changed as material prices and labour rate change.

(*b*) *Ideal Standard.* Ideal standard is set up under ideal conditions. ICMA defines it as "the standard which can be attained under the most favourable condition possible". It indicates the higher level efficiency of the manufacturing process in the organisation.

(*c*) *Current Standard.* ICMA, London, defines it as "a standard which is established for use over a short period of time and is related to current conditions". Current standard is a short term standard as it is modified at regular intervals.

(*d*) *Expected Standard.* Expected standard is otherwise termed as practical standard. ICMA defines the expected standard as "the standard which is anticipated, can be attained during a future specified budget period". Whenever the organisation is setting this type of standards, due weightage is given for all the expected conditions.

(*e*) *Activity Level.* The quantum of output or the level of activity to be obtained in forthcoming period must be divided clearly before establishing any standards. In this regard the sales potential and production capacity decide the quantum of output to be manufactured within a specified future period. Any of the idle capacity, unutilised capacity, and other key factors should be considered before determining the attainable level of output.

(*f*) *Organisation for Standard Costing.* For the purpose of achieving successful standard costing system, the organisation should appoint a separate committee. The committee consists of marketing manager, production manager, purchase manager, human resource manager, chief engineer and cost accountant. The committee may supply all information to different departments. They may revise the standards if necessary and finally approve the standards according to the current price level of the economy.

IV. Setting of Standards

After approval of the standards from the committee, the standard cost is determined for each and every element of cost such as direct material, direct labour and overheads. Cost accountant act as a coordinator of these activities and also he ensures that the setting of standards is accurate.

VARIANCE ANALYSIS

Variance means difference. The term variance has been derived from the verb 'to vary' meaning to differ. The real picture of the standard costing to the management is the presentation of variances. In the practical sense, some times standard costing is meaningless because without the predetermination and analysing the variances of cost. In standard costing, variance analysis means investigating the differences between the standard cost and the actual cost. ICWA, London defines variance as "difference between a standard cost and the comparable actual cost incurred during a period".

Simply variance analysis is the process of examining the variances by sub dividing the total variance. Through this way, the organisation can fix responsibility for off-standard performance.

Favourable and Unfavourable Variances

When the actual cost incurred is less than the standard cost, the differences is known as favourable variance. It is also known as positive variance.

When the actual cost incurred is more than the standard cost, the difference is known as unfavourable or adverse variance. It is also known as negative or debit variance.

Controllable and Uncontrollable Variances

Variances are classified into controllable and uncontrollable variances.

Controllable variances are those which arise due to inefficiency of a cost centre *i.e.* individual or department. For example, excess usage of materials, excess time taken by worker etc is the relevant examples of controllable variance.

Uncontrollable variances are those variances which arise due to factors beyond the control of the management or concerned person or department of the organisation. Uncontrollable variances normally arise due to the external factors only. For example, government restrictions, change in the market price etc. Whenever uncontrollable variance arises, no particular individual can be held responsible for it.

The ultimate aim of the standard costing is the effective cost control.

COMPUTATION OF VARIANCES

Normally, the following are the common variances which are computed by the management.

(*a*) Material variances

(*b*) Labour variances

(*c*) Overhead variances

(*d*) Sales variances.

Computation of the above variances with the help of the following formula.

(*a*) Material Variances

(*i*) MCV = (SQ × SP) – (AQ × AP)

(*ii*) MPV = (SP – AP) × AQ

(*iii*) MUV or MQV = (SQ – AQ) × SP

(*iv*) MMV = (RSQ – AQ) × SP

(*v*) MYV or MSUV = (SQ – RSQ) × SP

$$\text{RSQ} = \frac{\text{Individual of SQ}}{\text{Total of SQ}} \times \text{Total of AQ}$$

Abbreviations used :

MCV : Material Cost Variance
MPV : Material Price Variance
MUV OR MQV : Material Usage Variance or Material Quantity Variance
MMV : Material Mix Variances or
MYV : Material Yield Variance
MSUV : Material Sub Usage Variance

(*b*) Labour Variances

(*i*) Labour cost variance = (SH × SR) – (AH × AR)

(*ii*) Labour rate variance = (SR – AR) × AH

(*iii*) Labour efficiency variance = (SH – AH) × SR

(*iv*) Labour mix variance = (RSH – AH) × SR

$$\text{RSH} = \frac{\text{Individual of SH}}{\text{Total of SH}} \times \text{Total of AH}$$

(*v*) Labour sub efficiency variance or Labour yield variance = (SH – RSH) × SR

Abbreviations used :

SH : Standard Hours SR : Standard Rate
AH : Actual Hours AR : Actual Rate

(*c*) Overhead Variances

Under the overhead variances the following variances are normally applied.

1. *Overhead Cost Variance*

   Standard cost of actual output – Actual cost.

   $$\text{Standard cost of actual output} = \frac{\text{SC} \times \text{AO}}{\text{SO}}$$

2. *Overhead Budget or Expenditure Variance*

   Standard cost – Actual cost

3. *Overhead Volume Variance*

   (Actual output – Std output) x Std rate per unit.

4. *Overhead Efficiency Variance*

   (Actual output – Std output in actual hours worked) × Std rate per unit.

   Standard output in actual hours

   $$\text{Worked} = \frac{\text{Standard output} \times \text{Actual hours}}{\text{Standard hours}}$$

5. *Overhead Capacity Variances*

   (Standard output in actual hours worked – Std output) × Std rate per unit.

6. *Overhead Calendar Variance (If number of days given in the problem only)*

   (Std output in actual days worked – Std output) × SR per unit.

   $$\text{Standard output in Actual days} = \frac{\text{SO} \times \text{A days}}{\text{S days}}$$

(d) Sales Variances

1. Sales value variance : (AQ × AP) – (SQ × SP)
2. Sales price variance : (AP – SP) × AQ
3. Sales volume variance : (AQ – SQ) × SP
4. Sales mix variance : (AQ – RSQ) × SP
5. Sales sub volume variance : (RSQ – SQ) × SP

Abbreviations Used :

AQ : Actual Quantity SQ : Standard Quantity

AP : Actual Price SP : Standard Price

RSQ : Revised Standard Quantity

$$\left[\text{RSQ} = \frac{\text{SQ}}{\text{Total SQ}} \times \text{Total AQ} \right]$$

TEST QUESTIONS

1. What is meant by standard costing ?
2. Define standard costing.
3. What is meant by historical costing ?
4. What are the limitations of historical costing ?
5. Difference between standard costing and budgetary control.
6. What are the advantages of standard costing ?
7. List out the limitations of standard costing.
8. What is standard costing ? Bring out clearly the relationship between standard costs and budgetary control.
9. Cost standards indicate what cost should be incurred under desirable operating conditions while budgeted costs indicate what costs are expected to be recognizing limitations posed by less than optimal operating conditions. Explain.
10. Define standard cost. At what level standards should be set ? Do standard cost represent a separate type of cost system ?

PROBLEMS AND SOLUTIONS

Material Variances

Problem 1. *From the following information compute material variances :*

	Standard			Actual		
	Qty.	*CPU*	*Tot*	*Qty.*	*CPU*	*TC*
Material A	10	2	20	5	3	15
B	20	3	60	10	6	60
C	20	6	120	15	5	75
	50		200	30		150

Solution :

(*i*) *MCV : (SQ × SP) – (AQ × AP)*

Material	A	(10 × 2) – (5 × 3)	=	5	(F)
	B	(20 × 3) – (10 × 6)	=	0	
	C	(20 × 6) – (15 × 5)	=	45	(F)
				50	(F)

(*ii*) *Material Price Variance : (SP – AP) × AQ*

A	(2 – 3) × 5	=	5	(A)
B	(3 – 6) × 10	=	30	(A)
C	(6 – 5) × 15	=	15	(F)
			20	(A)

(*iii*) *Material Usage Variances : (SQ – AQ) × SP*

A	(10 – 5) × 2	=	10	
B	(20 – 10) × 3	=	30	
C	(20 – 15) × 6	=	30	
			70	(F)

(*iv*) *Material Mix Variance*

A	(6 – 5) × 2	=	2	(F)
B	(12 – 10) × 3	=	6	(F)
C	(12 – 15) × 6	=	18	(A)
			10	(A)

(*v*) *Material Yield Variances*

(SQ – RSQ) × SP

A	(10 – 6) × 2	=	8	(F)
B	(20 – 12) × 3	=	24	(F)
C	(20 – 12) × 6	=	48	(F)
			80	(F)

NOTE : $RSQ = \frac{\text{Individual of SQ}}{\text{Total of SQ}} \times \text{Total of AQ}$

$$A = \frac{10}{50} \times 30 = 6$$

$$B = \frac{20}{50} \times 30 = 12$$

$$C = \frac{20}{50} \times 30 = 12$$

Problem 2. *From the following particulars compute (a) material cost variance, (b) material price variance, (c) material usage variance.*

Quantity of materials purchased	*3000 units*
Value of materials purchased	*₹ 9000*
Standard quantity of materials required per tonne of output 30 units	
Standard rate of material	*₹ 2.50 per unit*
Opening stock of material	*Nil*
Closing stock of material	*500 units*
Output during the period	*80 tonnes*

[MBA, MCA Madras]

Solution :

(*i*) MCV (SQ × SP) – (AQ × AP)
(2000 × 2) – (2500 × 3)
4000 – 7500 = 3500 (A)

(*ii*) MPV (SP – AP) × AQ
(2 – 3) × 2500 = 2500 (A)

(*iii*) MUC (SQ – AQ) × SP
(2000 – 2500) × 2 = 1000 (A)

AP = 9000/3000 = ₹ 3
SQ = 80 × 25 = 2000 units
SP = ₹ 2 per unit
AQ = Material purchased + O.P Stock – Closing Stock
= 3000 + 0 – 500
= 3000 – 500 = **2500 units.**

Problem 3. *The standard material cost for 100 kg of chemical D is made up of :*
Chemical A – 30 kg @ ₹ 4 per kg
Chemical B – 40 kg @ ₹ 5 per kg
Chemical C – 80 kg @ ₹ 6 per kg.
In a batch 500 kg of chemical D were produced over a mix of
Chemical A – 140 kg @ a cost of ₹ 588
Chemical B – 220 kg @ a cost of ₹ 1056
Chemical C – 440 kg @ a cost of ₹ 2860.
How do the yield mix and the price factors contribute to the variance in the actual cost per 100 kg of chemical D over the standard cost ? [B.Com. Calicut]

Solution :

Chemical	*Standard*		*Actual*	
	Qty.	*Rate (per kg (₹))*	*Qty.*	*Rate (per kg (₹))*
A	30 kg	4.00 per kg	28	4.20
B	40 kg	5.00 per kg	44	4.80
C	80 kg	6.00 per kg	88	6.50
	150 kg		160	

Actual price = $\frac{588}{140} \times 1 = 4.20$

$= \frac{1056}{220} \times 1 = 4.80$

$= \frac{2860}{440} \times 1 = 6.50$

(i) *MCV : (SQ × SP) – (AQ × AP)*

Chemical	A	(30 × 4) – (28 × 4.20)	=	2.40	(F)
	B	(40 × 5) – (44 × 4.80)	=	11.20	(A)
	C	(80 × 6) – (88 × 6.50)	=	92.00	(A)
Total material cost variance			=	100.80	(A)

(ii) *MPV : (SP – AP) × AQ*

Chemical	A	(4 – 4.20) × 28	=	5.60	(A)
	B	(5 – 4.80) × 44	=	8.80	(F)
	C	(6 – 6.50) × 88	=	44.00	(A)
Total material price variance				40.80	(A)

(iii) *MUV = (SQ – AQ) × SP*

Chemical	A	(30 – 28) × 4	=	8	(F)
	B	(40 – 44) × 5	=	20	(A)
	C	(80 – 88) × 6	=	48	(A)
Total material price variance				60	(A)

(iv) *MMV (RSQ – AQ) × SP*

Chemical	A	(32.00 – 28.00) × 4		16	(F)
	B	(42.66 – 44.00) × 5	=	6.65	(A)
	C	(85.33 – 88.00) × 6	=	16.00	(A)
Total material mix variance				6.65	(A)

NOTE : Computation of RSQ = [Individual of SQ/Total of SQ] × Total of AQ

Chemical A = [30/150] × 160 = 32

B = [40/150] × 160 = 42.66

C = [80/150] × 160 = 85.33

(v) MYV (SQ – RSQ) × SP

Chemical	A	(30 – 32) × 4	=	8.00	(A)
Chemical	B	(40 – 42.66) × 5	=	13.35	(A)
Chemical	C	(80 – 85.33) × 6	=	31.98	(A)
Total material yield variance			=	53.33	(A)

Problem 4. *From the following particulars calculate*

(i) Material cost variance

(ii) Material price variance

(iii) Material usage variance.

Material	Standard		Actual	
	Units	Price ₹	Units	Price ₹
A	4040	4	4320	4.80
B	1640	6	1520	7.20
C	1400	8	1520	7.60

[B.Com. Delhi]

Solution :

(i) *Material Cost Variance : (SQ × SP) – (AQ × AP)*

Material	A	(4040 × 4) – (4320 × 4.80)	=	4576	(A)
		(1640 × 6) – (1520 × 7.20)	=	1104	(A)
		(1400 × 8) – (1520 × 7.60)	=	352	(A)
Total material cost variance			=	6032	(A)

(ii) *Material Price Variance : (SP – AP) × AQ*

Material	A	(4 – 4.80) × 4320	=	3456	(A)
		(6 – 7.20) × 1520	=	1824	(A)
		(8 – 7.60) × 1520	=	608	(F)
Total material price variance			=	4672	(A)

(iii) *Material Usage Variance : (SQ – AQ) × SP*

Material	A	(4040 – 4320) × 4	=	1120	(A)
	B	(1640 – 1520) × 6	=	720	(F)
	C	(1400 – 1520) × 8	=	960	(A)
Total material usage variance			=	1360	(A)

Problem 5. *The Standard mix of product is :*

Product x 600 units at 15 paise per unit

Product y 800 units at 20 paise per unit

Product z 1000 units at 25 paise per unit

The Consumption was :

x 640 units at 20 paise per unit

y 960 units at 15 paise per unit

z 840 units at 30 paise per unit

Calculate the material variances. [B.Com.]

Solution :

	Standard		Actual	
	Qty.	*Price*	*Qty.*	*Price*
Product X	600	.15	640	.20
Product Y	800	.20	960	.15
Product Z	1000	.25	840	.30
	2400		2440	

(*i*) *Material Cost Variance (MCV) : (SQ × SP) – (AQ × AP)*

Product	A	(600 × .15) – (640 × .2)	=	38	(A)
Product	B	(800 × .2) – (960 × .15)	=	16	(F)
Product	C	(1000 × .25) – (840 × .30)	=	2	(A)
		Total MCV	=	24	(A)

(*ii*) *Material Price Variance : (SP – AP) × AQ*

Product	A	(.15 – .20) × 640	=	32	(A)
Product	B	(.20 – .15) × 960	=	48	(F)
Product	C	(.25 – .30) × 840	=	42	(A)
		Total MPC	=	26	(A)

(*iii*) *Material Price Variance : (SP – AP) × AQ*

Product	A	(600 – 640) × .5	=	6	(A)
Product	B	(800 – 960) × .20	=	32	(A)
Product	C	(1000 – 840) × .25	=	40	(F)
		Total MPV		2	(F)

(*iv*) *MMV : (RSQ – AQ) × SP*

Computation of RSQ

Individual of SQ/Total of AQ × Total of SQ

$$A = \frac{600}{2400} \times 2440 = 610$$

$$B = \frac{800}{2400} \times 2440 = 813.33$$

$$C = \frac{1000}{2400} \times 2440 = 1016.67$$

MMV :

Product A	:	(610 – 640) × .15	=	4.5	(A)
Product B	:	(813.33 – 960) × .20	=	29.33	(A)
Product C	:	(1016.67 – 840) × .25	=	44.16	(F)
		Total MMV	=	10.33	(F)

(v) *MYV : (SQ – RSQ) × SP*

Product A	:	(600 – 610) × .15	=	1.5	(A)
Product B	:	(800 – 813.33) × .20	=	2.67	(A)
Product C	:	(1000 – 1016.67) × .25	=	4.17	(A)
		Total MYV		8.34	(A)

Problem 6. *The standard material cost to produce one tonne of chemical x is*

300 kg of material A @ ₹ 10 per kg.

400 kg of material B @ ₹ 5 per kg.

500 kg of material C @ ₹ 6 per kg.

During a period 100 tonnes of mixture X were produced from the usage of

35 tonnes of material A at a cost of ₹ 9000 per tonne

42 tonnes of material B at a cost of ₹ 6000 per tonne.

53 tonnes of material C at a cost of ₹ 7000 per tonne.

Calculate material variances. [B.Com. Delhi]

Solution :

	Standard		*Actual*	
	Qty. (Tonnes)	*Price (₹)*	*Qty. (Tonnes)*	*Price per tonnes (₹)*
Chemical A	30	10,000	35	9,000
Chemical B	40	5,000	42	6,000
Chemical C	50	6,000	53	7,000
	120		130	

NOTE : Here, the standard data are converted on the basis of actual details.

(i) *Material Cost Variances : (SQ × SP) – (AQ × AP)*

Chemical	A	(30 × 10,000) – (35 × 9000)			
		3,00,000 – 3,15,000	=	15,000	(A)
Chemical	B	(40 × 5000) – (42 × 6000)			
		2,00,000 – 2,52,000	=	52,000	(A)
Chemical	C	(50 × 6000) – (53 × 7000)			
		3,00,000 – 3,71,000	=	71,000	(A)
Total material cost variance			=	1,38,000	(A)

(ii) *Material Price Variance : (SP – AP) × AQ*

Chemical	A	(10000 – 9000) × 35	=	35,000	(F)
Chemical	B	(5000 – 6000) × 42	=	42,000	(A)
Chemical	C	(6000 – 7000) × 53	=	53,000	(A)
Total material price variance			=	60,000	(A)

(*iii*) *Material Quantity Variance : (SQ – AQ) × SP*

Chemical	A	(30 – 35) × 10000	=	50,000	(A)
Chemical	B	(40 – 42) × 5000	=	10,000	(A)
Chemical	C	(50 – 53) × 6000	=	18,000	(A)
Total material Quantity variance			=	78,000	(A)

(*iv*) *Material Mix Variance (MMV) : (RSQ – AQ) × SP*

Computation of RSQ :

[Individual of SQ/Total of SQ] × Total of AQ

A = 30/120 × 130 = 32.5

B = 40/120 × 130 = 43.33

C = 50/120 × 130 = 54.17

Chemical	A	(32.5 – 35) × 10,000	=	25,000	(A)
Chemical	B	(43.33 – 42) × 5,000	=	6,650	(F)
Chemical	C	(54.17 – 53) × 6,000	=	7,020	(F)
Total material mix variance			=	11,330	(A)

(*v*) *Material Yield Variance (MYV) : (SQ – RSQ) × SP*

Chemical	A	(30 – 32.5) × 10,000	=	25,000	(A)
Chemical	B	(40 – 43.33) × 5,000	=	16,650	(A)
Chemical	C	(50 – 54.17) × 6,000	=	25,020	(A)
Total material yield variance			=	66,670	(A)

Problem 7. *The standard cost of a certain chemical mixture*

40% materials A at ₹ 25 per kg

60% materials B at ₹ 36 per kg

A standard loss of 10% is expected in production. During a period there is used

150 kgs of material A at ₹ 27 per kg

260 kgs of material B at ₹ 34 per kg

The actual output was 360kgs. Compute all materials variances.

[M.Com. Nov. 2004 PU]

Solution :

	Standard		Actual	
	Qty. (kg)	*Price (per kg) (₹)*	*Qty. (kg)*	*Price (per kg) (₹)*
Material A	160	25	150	27
Material B	240	36	260	34
	400		410	
Less : Standard loss 10%	10		Actual loss 50	
	390		360	

(i) *Material Cost Variance (SQ×SP) – (AQ×AP)*

Material	A	(160 × 25) – (150 × 27)	=	50	(A)
Material	B	(240 × 36) – (260 × 34)	=	200	(A)
Total material cost variance			=	250	(A)

(ii) *Material Price Variance (SP – AP) × AQ*

Material	A	(25 – 27) × 150	=	300	(A)
Material	B	(36 – 34) × 260	=	520	(F)
Total material price variance			=	220	(F)

(iii) *Material Usage Variance : (SQ – AQ) × SP*

Material	A	(160 – 150) × 25	=	250	(F)
Material	B	(240 – 260) × 36	=	720	(A)
Total material usage variance			=	470	(A)

(iv) *Material Mix Variance : (RSQ – AQ) × SP*

RSQ = (Individual SQ/Total of SQ) × Total of AQ

RSQ for Material A	: 160/400 × 410	=	164	Kg
RSQ for Material B	: 240/400 × 410	=	246	Kg
MMV for A	= (164 – 150) × 25	=	350	(F)
MMV for B	= (246 – 260) × 36	=	504	A)
Total material mix variance		=	154	(A)

(v) *Material yield variance : (SQ – RSQ) × SP*

Material A	: (160 – 164) × 25	=	100	(A)
Material B	: (240 – 246) × 36	=	216	(A)
Total material yield variance		=	316	(A)

Problem 8. *From the following information calculate material mix variance.*

Material	*Standard Quantity*	*Actual Quantity*	*Price per unit ₹*
X	*50*	*45*	*14*
Y	*40*	*35*	*12*
Z	*30*	*40*	*11*

Due to shortage of X, it was decided to reduce its consumption by 10 and increase the consumption of Y and Z by 6 and 4 respectively. [MBA Madras]

Solution :

Material mix variance : (RSQ – AQ) × SP

RSQ = (Individual of SQ/Total of SQ) × Total of AQ

	Material X : $\frac{50}{120} \times 120$	=	50 units
Less :	Reduction in consumption	=	10 units
		=	40 units
	Material Y : $\frac{40}{120} \times 120$	=	40 units
Add :	Increase in consumption	=	6 units
		=	46 units
	Material Z : $\frac{30}{120} \times 120$	=	30 units
Add :	Increase in consumption	=	4 units
			34 units

Material Mix Variance

Material X (40 – 45) × 14	=	70 (A)
Material Y (46 – 35) × 12	=	132 (F)
Material Z (34 – 40) × 11	=	66 (A)
Total material mix variance	=	4 (A)

Problem 9. *From the following information calculate the material mix variance.*

Material	*Standard*	*Actual*
A	*200 units @ ₹ 12*	*160 units @ ₹ 13*
B	*100 units @ ₹ 10*	*140 units @ ₹ 10*

Due to shortage of material A, it was decided to reduce consumption of A by 15% and increase that of material B by 30%. [M.Com. (CA) 2004 PU, MBA Madras]

Solution :

Material mix variance : (RSQ – AQ) × SP

RSQ = (Individual of SQ/Total of SQ) × Total of AQ

Material A : $\frac{200}{300} \times 300$	=	200 units
Less : Reduction in consumption by 15%	=	30 units
$200 \times \frac{15}{300}$	=	170 units
Material B : $\frac{100}{300} \times 300$	=	100 units
Add : Increase in consumption by 30%	=	30 units
	=	130 units

Material mix variance for	A (170 – 160) × 12	=	120 F)
	B (130 – 140) × 10	=	100 (A)
Total material mix variance		=	20 (F)

Problem 10. *Rubix Ltd. is engaged in producing a standard using 60 kg of chemical X and 40 kg of chemical Y. The standard loss of production is 30%. The standard price X is ₹5 per kg and of Y is ₹ 10 per kg.*

The actual mixture and yield were as follows :

X 80 kg @ ₹ 4.50 per kg and Y 70 kg @ ₹ 8.00 per kg.

Actual yield 115 kg.

Calculate material variances [Price, usage, yield, mix]. [CS Final]

Solution :

	Standard		Actual		
	Quantity	*Price (₹)*		*Quantity*	*Price (₹)*
Chemical X	60	5.00		80	4.50
Chemical Y	40	10.00		70	8.00
	100			150	
Less : Standard loss 30%	30		Actual loss	35	
	70			115	

Conversion Table :

X = 60/70 × 115 = 98.57

Y = 40/70 × 115 = 65.71

	Standard		Actual	
	Quantity	*Price (₹)*	*Quantity*	*Price (₹)*
X	98.57	5.00	80.00	4.50
Y	65.71	10.00	70.00	8.00
	164.28		150.00	

(*i*) *Material Cost Variance : (SQ × SP) – (AQ × AP)*

X	(98.57 × 5.00) – (80.00 × 4.50)	=	132.85	(F)
Y	(65.71 × 10.00) – (70.00 × 8.00)	=	97.1	(F)
Total material cost variance		=	229.95	(F)

(*ii*) *Material Price Variance (MPV) : (SP – AP) × AQ*

Product X :	(5.00 – 4.50) × 80	=	40	(F)
Product Y :	(10.00 – 8.00) × 70	=	140	(F)
Total material price variance		=	180	(F)

(*iii*) *Material Quantity Variance (MQV) : (SQ – AQ) × SP*

Product X :	(98.57 – 80) × 5	=	92.85	(F)
Product Y :	(65.71 – 70) × 10	=	42.90	(A)
Total material quantity variance		=	49.95	(F)

(*iv*) *Material Mix Variance (MMV) : (RSQ – AQ) × SP*

RSQ = (Individual of SQ/Total of SQ) × Total of AQ

Product X =	(98.57/164.28) × 150	=	90	
Product Y =	(65.71/164.28) × 150	=	60	
MMV :				
Product X =	(90 – 80) × 5	=	50	(F)
Product Y =	(60 – 70) × 10	=	100	(A)
Total material mix variance		=	50	(A)

(*v*) *Material Yield Variance (MYV) : (SQ – RSQ) × SP*

Product A :	(98.57 – 90) × 5	=	42.85	(F)
Product B :	(65.71 – 60) × 10	=	57.10	(F)
Total material yield variance		=	99.95	(F)

Problem 11. *The standard mix of a product P is shown below :*

Raw material X 30 units @ ₹ 2 each.

Raw material Y 70 units @ ₹ 3 each.

Standard loss is 10% of input. Actual mix is 34 units of X and 66 units of Y. Rates are the same.

The actual loss is 15% of input. Calculate the material variances. [CS. Inter]

Solution :

	Standard			*Actual*	
	Quantity	*Price* (₹)		*Quantity*	*Price* (₹)
Raw material X	30	2		34	2
Raw material Y	70	3		66	3
	100			100	
Standard loss 10%	10		Actual loss 5%	15	
	90			85	

Conversion Table :

X : 30/90 × 85 = 28.33

Y : 70/90 × 85 = 66.11

	Standard		Actual	
	Quantity	Price (₹)	Quantity	Price (₹)
Raw material X	28.33	2	34	2
Raw material Y	66.11	3	66	3
	94.44		100	

(i) *Material Cost Variance : (SQ × SP) – (AQ × AP)*

X	(28.33 × 2.00) – (34 × 2.00)			
	(56.66 – 68)	=	11.34	(A)
Y	(66.11 × 3.00) – (66 × 3.00)			
	198.33 – 198.00	=	.33	(F)
Total material cost variance		=	11.01	(A)

(ii) *Material Price Variance : (SP × AP) × AQ*

X	(2 – 2) × 34	=	0	
Y	(3 – 3) × 66	=	0	
Total price variance		=	0	

(iii) *Material Quantity Variance (SQ – AQ) × SP*

Material	X	(28.33 – 34.00) × 2.00	=	11.34	(A)
Material	Y	(66.11 – 66.00) × 3.00	=	.33	(F)
Total material quantity variance			=	11.01	(A)

(iv) *Material Mix Variance : (RSQ – AQ) × SP*

RSQ = (Individual of SQ/Total of SQ) × Total of AQ.

Material X : $\frac{28.33}{94.44} \times 100 = 29.99$ *i.e.* 30

Material Y : $\frac{66.11}{94.44} \times 100 = 70$

MMV of material	X = (30 – 34) × 2.00	=	8.00	(A)
	Y = (70 – 66) × 3.00	=	12.00	(F)
Total material mix variance		=	4.00	(F)

(v) *MYV : (SQ – RSQ) × SP*

X	(28.33 – 30) × 2.00	=	3.34	(A)
Y	(66.11 – 70) × 3.00	=	11.66	(A)
Total material yield variance		=	15.00	(A)

NOTE : Standard loss and actual loss given in the problem means we have to prepare the conversion table for our convenience.

Problem 12. *A manufacturing concern which has adopted standard costing furnishes the following information.*

Standard :

Material for 70kg finished products : 100 kg

Price of material ₹ 1 per kg.

Actual :

output : 2,10,000 kg

Material used : 2,80,000 kg

Cost of materials : ₹ 2,52,000

Calculate :

(i) Material cost variance

(ii) Material price variance

(iii) Material usage variance. **[B.Com. Kerala]**

Solution :

SQ = For 70 kg of finished product, it requires 100 kg of raw material. So, for 2,10,000 kg of output, what is the raw material requirement ?

SQ = (100/70) × 2,10,000 = 3,00,000 kg

SP = ₹ 1.00

Actual price per kg = cost/output, *i.e.,* $\frac{2,52,000}{2,80,000} = 0.90$

Actual quantity = 2,80,000 kg

SQ = 3,00,000 AQ = 2,80,000

SP = 1.00 AP = 0.90

(i) Material Usage Variance

(SQ – AQ) × SP

(3,00,000 – 2,80,000) × 1.00 = 20,000 (F)

(ii) Material Price Variance

(SP – AP) × AQ

(1.00 – .90) × 2,80,000 = 28,000 (F)

(iii) Material Cost Variance

(SQ × SP) – (AQ × AP)

(3,00,000 × 1.00) – (2,80,000 × .90) = 48,000 (F)

Problem 13. *From the following particulars calculate.*

(i) Material Cost Variance
(ii) Material Price Variance
(iii) Material Usage Variance

Standard output	*100 units*
Standard material per unit	*3 kg*
Standard price	*₹ 2.00*
Actual output	*80 units*
Actual price	*₹ 2.50*
Actual material used	*250 kg*

[MBA Madras]

Solution :

SQ = 240 SP = 2.00

AQ = 250 AP = 2.50

(i) Material Cost Variance : (SQ × SP) – (AQ × AP)

Standard material for actual output = 80 × 3 = 240

i.e., MCV = (SQ × SP) – (AQ × AP)

= (240 × 2.00) – (250 × 2.50)

= 480 – 625 = 145 (A)

(ii) Material Price Variance

(SP – AP) × AQ

(2.00 – 2.50) × 250 = 125 (A)

(iii) Material Usage Variance

(SQ – AQ) × SP

(240 – 250) × 2 = 20 (A)

Problem 14. *The standard material required to manufacture one unit of product X is 10 kg and the standard price per kg of material is ₹ 2.50. The cost accounts record however reveals that 11,500 kg of material costing ₹ 27,600 was used for manufacturing 1000 units of product X. Calculate :*

(i) Material cost variance
(ii) Material price variance
(iii) Material usage variance.

Solution :

Standard price of material per kg = ₹ 2.50

Standard material requirement to manufacture one unit of product x is = 10 kg

Standard material for actual output = 1000 × 10 = 10,000 kg.

Actual usage of material = 11,500 kg

Actual cost of material = ₹ 27,600

$$\text{Actual price of material per kg} = \frac{27,600}{11,500}$$

= ₹ 2.40

SQ = 10,000 AQ = 11,500
SP = 2.50 AP = 2.40

(i) *Material Cost Variance*
(SQ × SP) – (AQ × AP)
(10,000 × 2.50) – (11,500 × 2.40)
25000 – 27600 = 2600 (A)

(ii) *Material Price Variance*
(SP – AP) × AQ
(2.50 – 2.40) × 11500 = 1150 (F)

(iii) *Material Usage Variance*
(SQ – AQ) × SP
(10,000 – 11500) × 2.50 = 3750 (A)

Problem 15. *The standard quantity and standard price of raw material used for one unit of product A are given below.*

Material	*Quantity*	*Standard Price*
X	*2 kgs*	*₹ 3 per kg*
Y	*4 kgs*	*₹ 2 per kg*

The actual production and relevant data are as follows. Output 500 units of product A.

Material	*Total quantity for 500 units*	*Total cost ₹*
X	*1200 kgs*	*₹ 3900*
Y	*1800 kgs*	*₹ 4000*

Calculate : (i) MCV (ii) MPV (iii) MUV.

Solution :

Standard quantity means standard quantity for actual production.
For one unit of product A, 2 kg of material X is required.
For 500 units of product A, 1000 kg of raw material X is required.
For one unit of product A, 4 kg of material Y is required.
For 500 units of product A, 4 × 500 = 2000 kg of raw material Y is required.

(i) *MCV : (SQ × SP) – (AQ × AP)*

Material	X	(1000 × 3) – (1200 × 3.25)		
		3000 – 3900	900	(A)
Material	Y	(2000 × 2) – (1800 × 2.50)	500	(A)
		Total MCV	1400	(A)

(ii) *Material Price Variance : (SP – AP) × AQ*

Material	X	(3 – 3.25) × 1200	=	300	(A)
Material	Y	(2 – 2.50) × 1800	=	900	(A)
Total material price variance			=	1200	(A)

(*iii*) *Material Usage Variance* : *(SQ – AQ) × SP*

Material	X	(1000 – 1200) × 3	=	600	(A)
Material	Y	(2000 – 1800) × 2	=	400	(F)
Total material usage variance			=	200	(A)

B. Labour Variances

Problem 1. *The standard labour component and the actual labour component engaged in a week for a job are as follows.*

Particulars	*Skilled Workers*	*Semi Skilled Workers*	*Unskilled Workers*
Standard number of workers in the gang	*32*	*12*	*6*
Standard wage rate per hour (₹)	*3*	*2*	*1*
Actual number of workers employed in the gang during the week	*28*	*18*	*4*
Actual wage rate per hour ₹	*4*	*3*	*2*

During the 40 hour working week, the gang produced 1800 standard labour hours of work.

Calculate the different labour variances. [MBA Madras]

Solution :

Category of workers	*Standard*		*Actual*	
	Hours	*Rate (₹)*	*Hours*	*Rate (₹)*
Skilled	1280	3.00	1120	4.00
Semiskilled	480	2.00	720	3.00
Unskilled	240	1.00	160	2.00
	2000		2000	
Loss	Nil		200	
Total Hours	2000	Hours Produced	1800	

(*i*) 1280/2000 × 1800 = 1152

(*ii*) 480/2000 × 1800 = 432

(*iii*) 240/2000 × 1800 = 216

Category of workers	Standard		Actual	
	Hours	Rate (₹)	Hours	Rate (₹)
Skilled	1152	3.00	1120	4.00
Semiskilled	432	2.00	720	3.00
Unskilled	216	1.00	160	2.00
	1800		2000	
Loss	Nil		(–) 200	
	1800		1800	

Labour Variance

(i) *Labour Cost Variance : (SH × SR) – (AH × AR)*

Skilled	(1152 × 3.00) – (1120 × 4.00)	=	1,024	(A)
Semiskilled	(432 × 2.00) – (720 × 3.00)	=	1,296	(A)
Unskilled	(216 × 1.00) – (160 × 2.00)	=	104	(A)
Total labour cost variances		=	2,424	(A)

(ii) *Labour Rate Variance : (SR – AR) × AH*

Skilled	(3.00 – 4.00) × 1120	=	1,120	(A)
Semiskilled	(2.00 – 3.00) × 720	=	720	(A)
Unskilled	(1.00 – 2.00) × 160	=	160	(A)
Total labour rate variance		=	2,000	(A)

(iii) *Labour Efficiency Variance : (SH – AH) × SR*

Skilled	(1152 – 1120) × 3.00	=	96	(F)
Semiskilled	(432 – 720)	=	576	(A)
Unskilled	(216 – 160)	=	56	(F)
Total labour efficiency variance		=	424	(A)

(iv) *Labour Mix Variance : (RSH – AH) × SR*

Skilled	(1280 – 1120) × 3.00	=	480	(F)
Semiskilled	(432 – 720) × 2	=	576	(A)
Unskilled	(240 – 160) × 1.00	=	80	(F)
Total labour mix variance		=	16	(A)

NOTE : RSH (Individual of std Hrs/Total of std Hrs × Total of Actual Hrs

Skilled :	1152/1800 × 2000	=	1,280
Semiskilled :	432/1800 × 2000	=	480
Unskilled :	216/1800 × 2000	=	240

(v) *Labour Yield Variance : (SH – RSH) × SR*

Skilled	(1152 – 1280) × 3.00	=	384	(A)
Semiskilled	(432 – 480) × 2.00	=	96	(A)
Unskilled	(216 – 240) × 1	=	24	(A)
Total labour yield variance		=	504	(A)

Problem 2. *The details regarding the composition and the weekly wage rates of labour force engaged on a job scheduled to be completed in 30 weeks are as follows.*

Category of workers	*Standard*		*Actual*	
	No. of labours	*Weekly wage rate per labourer (₹)*	*No. of labourer*	*Weekly wage rate per labourer (₹)*
Skilled	*75*	*60*	*70*	*70*
Semiskilled	*45*	*40*	*30*	*70*
Unskilled	*60*	*30*	*80*	*20*

The work actually has been completed in 32 weeks. Calculate the various labour variances.

Solution :

Category of workers	*Standard*		*Actual*	
	Hours	*Rate (₹)*	*Hours*	*Rate (₹)*
Skilled	2,250	60	2,240	70
Semiskilled	1,350	40	960	50
Unskilled	1,800	30	2,560	20
	5,400		5,760	

(i) *Labour Cost Variance : (SH × SR) – (AH × AR)*

			₹	
Skilled	(2250 × 60) – (2240 × 70)	=	21,800	(A)
Semiskilled	(1350 × 40) – (960 × 50)	=	6,000	(F)
Unskilled	(1800 × 30) – (2560 × 20)	=	2,800	(F)
Total labour cost variances		=	13,000	(A)

(ii) *Labour Rate Variances : (SR – AR) × AH*

Skilled	(60 – 70) × 2240	=	22,400	(A)
Semiskilled	(40 – 50) × 960	=	9,600	(A)
Unskilled	(30 – 20) × 2560	=	25,600	(F)
Total labour rate variance		=	6,400	(A)

(*iii*) *Labour Efficiency Variance : (SH – AH) × SR*

Skilled	(2250 – 2240) × 60	=	600	(A)
Semiskilled	(1350 – 960) × 40	=	15,600	(F)
Unskilled	(1800 – 2560) × 30	=	22,800	(A)
Total labour efficiency variance			7,800	(A)

(*iv*) *Labour Mix Variances : (RSH – AH) × SR*

RSH :	Skilled	2250/5400 × 5760	=	2,400
	Semiskilled	1350/5400 × 5760	=	1,440
	Unskilled	1800/5400 × 5760	=	1,920

Skilled	(2400 – 2240) × 60	=	9,600	(F)
Semiskilled	(1440 – 960) × 40	=	19,200	(F)
Unskilled	(1920 – 2560) × 30	=	19,200	(A)
Total labour mix variance		=	9,600	(F)

(*v*) *Labour Yield Variance : (SH – RSH) × SR*

Skilled	(2250 – 2400) × 60	=	9,000	(A)
Semiskilled	(1350 – 1440) × 40	=	3,600	(A)
Unskilled	(1800 – 1920) × 30	=	3,600	(A)
Total labour efficiency variance		=	16,200	(A)

Problem 3. *Calculate the labour variances from the following information.*

Standard wages

Grade X : 90 labourers at ₹ 2 per hour

Grade Y : 60 labourers at ₹ 3 per hour

Actual wages

Grade X : 80 labourers at ₹ 2.50 per hour

Grade Y : 70 labourers at ₹ 2.00 per hour

Budgeted hours 1000; Actual hours 900

Budgeted Gross production 5000 units, Standard loss 20%; Actual loss 900 units.

Solution :

Category of workers		*Standard* *Hours*	*Rate* (₹)		*Actual* *Hours*	*Rate* (₹)
Grade X	(90 × 1000)	90,000	2	900 × 80	72,000	2.50
Grade Y	(60 × 1000)	60,000	3	900 × 70	63,000	2.00
		1,50,000			1,35,000	

Production units	5,000		5,000
Loss 20%	1,000	Actual Loss	900
	4,000		4,100

In order to adjust this standard loss and actual loss we have to prepare another table called Conversion Table.

Grade X : 90,000/4000 × 4100 = 92,250

Grade Y : 60,000/4000 × 4100 = 61,500

Conversion Table

	Standard		Actual	
	Hours	*Rate (₹)*	*Hours*	*Rate (₹)*
Grade X	92,250	2.00	72,000	2.50
Grade Y	61,500	3.00	63,000	2.00
	1,53,750		1,35,000	

(*i*) *Labour Cost Variance : (SH × SR) – (AH × AR)*

Grade X : (92,250 × 2.00) – (72,000 × 2.50)	=	4500	(F)
Grade Y : (61,500 × 3.00) – (63,000 × 2.00)	=	58,500	(F)
Total labour cost variance	=	63,000	(F)

(*ii*) *Labour Rate Variance : (SR – AR) × AH*

Grade X : (2 – 2.5) × 72,000	=	36,000	(A)
Grade Y : (3 – 2) × 63,000	=	63,000	(F)
Total labour cost variance	=	27,000	(F)

(*iii*) *Labour Efficiency Variance : (SH – AH) × SR*

Grade X : (92,250 – 72,000) × 2	=	40,500	(F)
Grade Y : (61,500 – 63,000) × 3	=	4,500	(A)
Total labour efficiency variance	=	36,000	(F)

(*iv*) *Labour Mix Variance : (RSH – AH) × SR*

RSH Grade X = 92,250/1,53,750 × 1,35,000	=	81,000
Grade Y = 61,500/1,53,750 × 1,35,000	=	54,000

LMV Grade X = (81,000 – 72,000) × 2	=	18,000	(F)
Y = (54,000 – 63,000) × 3	=	27,000	(A)
Total mix variance	=	9,000	(A)

(v) *Labour Yield Variance : (SH – RSH) × SR*

Grade X :	(92,250 – 18,000) × 2	=	22,500	(F)
Grade Y :	(61,500 – 54,000) × 3	=	22,500	(F)
Total LYV		=	45,000	(F)

Problem 4. *From the data given below calculate labour variances for the two departments*

	Dept. A	*Dept. B*
Actual gross wages (Direct) (₹)	*2,000*	*1,800*
Standard hours produced	*8,000*	*6,000*
Standard rate per hours	*.30 paise*	*.35 paise*
Actual hours worked	*8,200*	*5,800*

[ICWA Int]

Solution :

	Standard		*Actual*	
	Hours	*Rate* (₹)	*Hours*	*Rate* (₹)
Department A	8,000	.30	8,200	—
Department B	6,000	.35	5,800	—
	14,000		14,000	

NOTE : Here, actual rates are not given directly. It should be given in indirect way. When we need the actual rate at that place we apply the following techniques. Instead of actual rate, actual gross wages are given *i.e.,* (AH × AR).

(i) *Labour Cost Variances : (SH × SR) – (AH × AR)*

Department A	(8000 × .30) – (2000)	=	400	(F)
Department B	(6000 × .35) – (1800)	=	300	(F)

(ii) *Labour Rate Variance : (SR – AR) × AH*

Here, actual rate is not given in the problem, so we apply the following formula :

(SR – AR) × AH : (SR × AH) – (AR × AH)

Department A	(.30 × 8200) – 2000	=	460	(F)
Department B	(.35 × 5800) – 1800	=	230	(F)

(iii) *Labour Efficiency Variance : (SH – AH) × SR*

Department A	(8000 – 8200) × .30	=	60	(A)
Department B	(6000 – 5800) × .35	=	70	(F)

(iv) *Labour Mix Variance : (RSH – AH) × SR*

RSH : For A :	8000/14000 × 14000	=	8000	
RSH : For B :	6000/14000 × 14000	=	6000	
Department A	(8000 – 8200) × .30	=	60	(A)
Department B	(6000 – 5800) × .35	=	70	(F)

(v) *Labour Yield Variance : (SH – RSH) × SR*

Department A	(8000 – 8000) × .30	=	0
Department B	(6000 – 6000) × .35	=	0

(No need to apply LMV, LYV)

Problem 5. *ABC Ltd. furnishes you the following particulars.*

Product X requires 20 hours per unit.

Standard Rate per hour is ₹ 2

Units produced : 4000

Hours taken 76,000 (including 200 hours for power failure) at ₹ 2.10 per hour.

Calculate :

(i) Direct labour cost variance

(ii) Direct labour rate variance

(iii) Direct labour efficiency variance

(iv) Direct labour idle time variance. [M.Com. Madras]

Solution :

Standard hours	:	80.000
Standard rate	:	₹ 2.00
Actual hours	:	76000 (– 200)
Actual rate	:	2.10

(i) LCV	:	SH × SR – AH × AR		
		(80.000 × 2.00) – (76000 × 2.10)	=	400 (F)
(ii) LRV	:	(SR – AR) × AH		
		(2.00 – 2.10) × 76000	=	7600 (A)
(iii) LEV	:	(SH – AH) × SR		
		(80,000 – 75800) × 2	=	8400 (F)

NOTE :

Actual hours	=	76000
Less : Idle time for power failure	=	200
		75800

(iv) LITV	:	(Labour idle time variance)		
		Idle time × SR		
		200 × 2	=	400 (A)

C. Overhead Variances

Problem 1. *In department A the following data is submitted for the week ended on 31st December.*

Standard output for 40 hours per week	*1400 units*
Standard fixed overhead	*1400*
Actual output	*1200 units*

Actual hours worked	*32 hours*
Actual fixed overhead	*1500*

Calculate overhead variances. [CA Inter & MBA]

> **NOTE :** Before attempting to apply formula better we have to prepare following type of table for all the overhead problems.

Solution :

	Budget	*Actual*
Output (units)	1400	1200
Cost/Overhead (₹)	1400	1500
Hours	40	32

Overhead Variances

(*i*) *Overhead Cost Variance*

Standard cost of actual output – Actual cost

1200 – 1500 = 300 (A)

[SCAC = SC × AO/SO, *i.e.,* 1400 × 1200/1400 = 1200]

(*ii*) *Overhead Budget Variance*

SC – AC

1400 – 1500 = 100 (A)

(*iii*) *Overhead Volume Variance*

(Actual output – Std output) × Std rate per unit

(1200 – 1400) × 1.00 = 200 (A)

Std Rate per unit = SC/So

[*i.e.,* 1400/1400 = ₹ 1.00]

(*iv*) *Overhead Efficiency Variance*

(Actual Output – Std output in actual hours worked) × SR per unit

(1200 – 1120) × 1 = 80 (F)

SO in A.Hrs worked = SO × A.Hrs/SHrs = 1400 × 32/40 = 1120

(*v*) *Overhead Capacity Variances*

(Std output in actual hrs worked – Std output) × Std rate per unit

(1120 – 1400) × 1 = 280 (A)

> **NOTE :** If number of days are given in the problem only we have to apply the calendar variance, otherwise there is no need to calculate calendar variance.

Problem 2. *Calculate overhead variances from the following data :*

Particulars	*Budget*	*Actual*
Fixed overhead for July	*₹ 5000*	*₹ 6000*
Production in July (Units)	*1000*	*1050*
Standard time for 1 unit	*10 hours*	
Actual hours worked	—	*11,000 hrs.*

Solution :

	Budget	Actual
Cost/Overhead (₹)	5000	6000
Production in units *i.e.,* output	1000	1050
Hours (1000 × 10)	10,000	11000

Overhead Variances

(i) *Overhead Cost Variances*

Std cost of actual output – Actual cost

5250 – 5000 = 750 (A)

[SC of AO = SC × AO/SO = 5000/1050/1000 = 5250]

(ii) *Overhead Budget Variance*

= (Std cost – Actual cost)

(5000 – 6000) = 1000 (A)

(iii) *Overhead Volume Variance*

(Actual output – Std output) × Std rate per unit

= (1050 – 1000) × 5 = 250 (F)

[Std Rate per unit = SC/SO = 5000/1000 = ₹ 5]

(iv) *Overhead Efficiency Variances*

(Act output – Std output in actual hours worked) × SR per unit

= (1050 – 1100) × 5 = 250 (A)

[Std output in actual hours worked : SO × AHRS/SHRS = 1000 × 11000/10,000 = 1100]

(v) *Overhead Capacity Variance*

(Std output in actual hrs worked – Std output) × SR per unit

(1100 – 1000) × 5 = 500 (F)

Problem 3. *RAC Ltd. has furnished you the following data :*

	Budget	*Actual Scp. 1998*
No. of working days	*25*	*27*
Production in units	*20,000*	*22,000*
Fixed overheads (₹)	*30,000*	*31,500*

Budgeted fixed overhead rate is ₹1 per hour. In Sep. 1998 the actual hours worked were 31,500. Calculate the overhead variances.

Solution :

	Budget	Actual
Number of working days	25	27
Production in units (*i.e.,* output)	20,000	22,000
Cost (₹)	30,000	31,000
Hours	30,000	31,500

(i) *Overhead Variance :* (Std cost of AO – AC)

= (33,000 – 31,000) = 2000 (F)

[SCAO = SC × AO/SO = 30,000 × 22,000/20,000 = 33000]

(*ii*) *Overhead Budget Variance :* (SC – AC)

= (30,000 – 31,000) = 1000 (A)

(*iii*) *Overhead Volume Variance :* (AO – SO) × SR per unit

= (22,000 – 2,000) × 1.5 = 3000 (F)

[SR per unit = SC/SO = 30,000/20,000 = 1.5]

(*iv*) *Overhead Efficiency Variance :* (AO – SO in actual hours worked) × SR per unit

= (22,000 – 21,000) × 1.5 = 1500 F

[So, in Actual worked = SO × AHrs/SHrs = 20,000 × 31,500/30,000 = 21000]

(*v*) *Overhead Capacity Variance :* (SO in actual hours worked – SO) SR per unit

= (21,000 – 20,000) × 1.5 = 1500 F

(*vi*) *Overhead Calendar Variance :* [Number of days given in the problem]

(SO in actual days worked – SO) × SR per unit

= (21,600 – 20,000) × 1.5 = 2400 F

[So, in actual days worked = SO × A. days/S.days = 20,000 × 27/25 = 21600]

Problem 4. *Calculate overhead variances :*

Particulars	*Budget*	*Actual*
No. of working days	*20*	*22*
Man hours per day	*8000*	*8400*
Output per man hour in unit	*1.0*	*.90*
Overhead cost	*1,60,000*	*1,68,000*

Solution :

Particulars	*Budget*	*Actual*	
Number of working days	20	22	
Cost	₹ 1,60,000	₹ 1,68,000	
Hours	8,000	8,400	
Output (8000 × 20 × 1)	1,60,000	1,66,320	(8400 × 22 × 0.90)

Overhead Cost Variance

(*i*) *Overhead Cost Variance :* (SC of AO – AC)

= (1,66,320 – 1,68,000) = 1680 (A)

NOTE : [SC of AO = SC × AO/SO = 1,60,000 × 1,66,320/1,60,000 = 1,66,320]

(*ii*) *Overhead Budget Variance :* (SC – AC)

= (1,60,000 – 1,68,000) = 8000 (A)

(*iii*) *Overhead Volume Variance :* (AO – SO) × SR per unit

= (1,66,320 – 1,60,000) × 1

= 6320 (F)

SR per unit = SC/SO = 1,60,000/1,60,000 = 1.00

(*iv*) *Overhead Efficiency Variance :* (AO – SO in actual hours worked) × SR per unit

= (1,66,320 – 1,68,000) × 1 = 1680 (A)

SO in A.Hrs worked = SO × A.Hrs/S.Hrs = 1,60,000 × 8400/8000 = 1,68,000

(v) *Overhead Capacity Variance :* (SO in Actual Hrs worked – SO) × SR per unit
= (1,68,000 – 1,60,000) × 1
= 8000 (F)

(vi) *Overhead Calendar Variance :* (SO in actual days worked – SO) × SR per unit
= (1,76,000 – 1,60,000) = 16,000 F
[SO in A.days worked = SO × A.days/S.days = 1,60,000 × 22/20 = 1,76,000]

D. Sales Variances

Problem 1. *The budgeted sales for one month and the actual results achieved are as under.*

Product	Budget Qty.	Budget Rate (₹)	Budget Amount (₹)	Actual Qty.	Actual Rate (₹)	Actual Amount (₹)
A	1000	100	1,00,000	1200	125	1,50,000
B	700	200	1,40,000	800	150	1,20,000
C	500	500	1,50,000	600	300	1,80,000
D	300	500	1,50,000	400	600	2,40,000
	2500		5,40,000	3000		6,90,000

Calculate sales variances in respect of each product. [MBA 2005 Anna]

Solution :

(i) *Sales Value Variance : (AQ × AP) – (SQ × SP)*

Product A	:	(1200 × 125) – (1000 × 100)	=	50,000	(F)
Product B	:	(800 × 150) – (700 × 200)	=	20,000	(A)
Product C	:	(600 × 300) – (500 × 500)	=	7,000	(A)
Product D	:	(400 × 600) – (300 × 500)	=	9,000	(F)
		Total sales value variance	=	32,000	(F)

(ii) *Sales Price Variance : (AP – SP) × AQ*

Product A	:	(125 – 100) ×1200	=	30,000	(F)
Product B	:	(150 – 200) × 800	=	40,000	(A)
Product C	:	(300 – 500) × 600	=	1,20,000	(A)
Product D	:	(600 – 500) × 400	=	40,000	(F)
		Total sales price variance	=	90,000	(A)

(iii) *Sales Volume Variance : (AQ – SQ) × SP*

Product A	:	(1200 – 1000) × 100	=	20,000	(F)
Product B	:	(800 – 700) × 200	=	20,000	(F)
Product C	:	(600 – 500) × 500	=	50,000	(F)
Product D	:	(400 – 300) × 500	=	50,000	(F)
		Total Sales volume variance	=	1,40,000	(F)

(*iv*) *Sales mix variance : (SQ – RSQ) × SP (RSQ : Revised std Qty.)*

RSQ

Product A	:	1000/2500 × 3000	=	1,200
Product B	:	700/2500 × 3000	=	840
Product C	:	500/2500 × 3000	=	600
Product D	:	300/2500 × 3000	=	360

Sales Mix Variance

Product A	:	(1200 – 1200) × 100	=	0000	
Product B	:	(800 – 840) × 200	=	8,000	(A)
Product C	:	(600 – 600) × 500	=	0000	
Product D	:	(400 – 360) × 500	=	20,000	(F)
		Total sales mix variance	=	12,000	(F)

(*v*) *Sales Sub Volume Variance : (RSQ – SQ) × SP*

Product A	:	(1200 – 1000) × 100	=	20000	(F)
Product B	:	(840 – 700) × 200	=	28000	(F)
Product C	:	(600 – 500) × 500	=	50000	(F)
Product D	:	(360 – 300) × 500	=	30000	(F)
		Total sales sub volume variance	=	1,28,000	(F)

Problem 2. *From the following details find out the sales quantity variances.*

Product	*Standard*		*Actual*	
	Quantity	*Price (₹)*	*Quantity*	*Price (₹)*
R	*400*	*12*	*300*	*10*
S	*400*	*15*	*500*	*16*

[MBA Madras]

Solution :

(*i*) *Sales Value Variance : (AQ × AP) – (SQ × SP)*

Product A	:	(300 × 10) – (400 × 12)	=	1,800	(A)
Product S	:	(500 × 16) – (400 × 15)	=	2,000	(F)
		Total sales value variance	=	200	(F)

(*ii*) *Sales Price Variance : (AP – SP) × AQ*

Product R	:	(10 – 12) × 300	=	600	(A)
Product S	:	(16 – 15) × 500	=	500	(F)
		Total sales price variance	=	100	(A)

(*iii*) *Sales Volume Variance (AQ – SQ) × SP*

Product R	:	(300 – 400) × 12	=	1,200	(A)
Product S	:	(500 – 400) × 15	=	1,500	(F)
		Total sales volume variance	=	300	(F)

(*iv*) *Sales Mix Variance : (AQ – RSQ) × SP*

RSQ for product R = 400/800 × 800 = 400

S = 400/800 × 800 = 400

Sales Mix Variance

Product R	:	(300 – 400) × 12	=	1,200	(A)
Product S	:	(500 – 400) × 15	=	1,500	(F)
		Total sales mix variance	=	300	(F)

(*v*) *Sales Sub Volume Variance : (RSQ – SQ) × SP*

Product R	:	(400 – 400) × 12	=	0
Product S	:	(400 – 400) × 15	=	0
		Total sales sub volume variance	=	0

Problem 3. *Calculate sales variances from the following data*

Product	*Budget*		*Actual*	
	Quantity	*Price per unit*	*Quantity*	*Price per unit*
A	*500*	*40*	*600*	*41*
B	*300*	*25*	*200*	*24*
C	*200*	*20*	*400*	*22*
D	*600*	*30*	*400*	*25*

Solution :

(*i*) *Sales Value Variance : (AQ × AP) – (SQ × SP)*

Product A	:	(600 × 41) – (500 × 40)	=	4600	(F)
Product B	:	(200 × 24) – (300 × 25)	=	2700	(A)
Product C	:	(400 × 22) – (200 × 20)	=	4800	(F)
Product D	:	(400 × 25) – (600 × 30)	=	8000	(A)
		Total sales value variance	=	1300	(A)

(*ii*) *Sales Price Variance : (AP – SP) × SQ*

Product A	:	(41 – 40) × 600	=	600	(F)
Product B	:	(24 – 25) × 200	=	200	(A)
Product C	:	(22 – 20) × 400	=	800	(F)
Product D	:	(25 – 30) × 40	=	2000	(A)
		Total sales price variance	=	800	(A)

(iii) Sales Volume Variance : (AQ – SQ) × SP

Product A	=	(600 – 500) × 40	=	4000	(F)
Product B	=	(200 – 300) × 25	=	2500	(A)
Product C	=	(400 – 200) × 20	=	4000	(F)
Product D	=	(400 – 600) × 30	=	6000	(A)
		Total sales volume variance	=	500	(A)

Problem 4. *Harikan Ltd. furnishes the following information relating to budgeted sales and actual sales for March 2002.*

Product	*Budget*		*Actual*	
	Quantity	*Price per unit*	*Quantity*	*Price per unit*
A	*1200*	*15*	*880*	*18*
B	*800*	*20*	*880*	*20*
C	*2000*	*40*	*2640*	*38*

[CA Inter] [M.Com. CA]

Solution :

(i) Sales Value Variance (AQ × AP) – (SQ × SP)

Product A	:	(880 × 18) – (1200 × 15)	=	2,160	(A)
Product B	:	(880 × 20) – (800 × 20)	=	1,600	(A)
Product C	:	(2640 × 28) – (2000 × 40)	=	20,320	(F)
		Total sales value variance	=	16,560	(F)

(ii) Sales Price Variance : (AP – SP) × AQ

Product A	:	(18 – 15) × 880	=	2,640	(F)
Product B	:	(20 – 20) × 880	=	0	
Product C	:	(38 – 40) × 2640	=	5,280	(A)
		Total sales volume variance	=	2,640	(A)

(iii) Sales Volume Variance : (AQ – SQ) × SP

Product A	:	(880 × 1200) × 15	=	4,800	(A)
Product B	:	(880 × 800) × 20	=	1,600	(F)
Product C	:	(2640 – 2000) × 40	=	25,600	(F)
		Total sales volume variance	=	22,400	(F)

(iv) Sales Mix Variance : (AQ – RSQ) × SP

RSQ for A 1200/3200 × 4400 = 1650

B 800/3200 × 4400 = 1100

C 2000/3200 × 4400 = 2750

Product A	:	(880 – 1650) × 15	=	11,550	(A)
Product B	:	(880 – 1100) × 20	=	4,400	(A)
Product C	:	(2640 – 2750) × 40	=	4,400	(A)
		Total sales mix variance	=	20,350	(A)

(*v*) *Sales sub volume variance : (RSQ – SQ) × SP*

Product A	:	(1650 – 1200) × 15	=	6,750	(F)
Product B	:	(1100 – 800) × 20	=	6,000	(F)
Product C	:	(2750 – 2000) × 40	=	30,000	(F)
		Total sales sub volume variance	=	42,750	(F)

TEST PROBLEMS

1. Eskay Ltd., produces an article by blending two basic raw materials. The following standards have been set up for raw materials.

Material	Standard Mix	Standard price per kg.
A	40%	₹ 4.00
B	60%	₹ 3.00

The standard loss processing is 15%. During September, 1990, the company produced 1,700 kg of finished output.

The position of stock and purchase for the month of September, 1990, is as under:

Material	Stock on 1-9-90 Kg	Stock on 30-9-90 Kg	Purchased during Kg	September, 90 cost ₹
A	35	5	800	3,400
B	40	50	1,200	3,400

Calculate the following variances:

(A) Material price variance

(B) Materials usage variance

(C) Materials yield variance

(D) Materials mix variance

(E) Total materials cost variance

[B.Com., (Hons) Delhi! 1994. C.S. (Inter) Dec. 1995 & Dec. 1991]

[**Ans.**

(A) Material price variance = ₹ 376.25F

(B) Materials usage variance = ₹ 90A

(C) Materials yield variance = ₹ 68A

(D) Materials mix variance = ₹ 22A

(E) Total materials cost variance = ₹ 286.25F]

2. The standard mix and actual mix for producing an article is given below:

Standard	*Actual*
A- 60 units at ₹ 10 per unit	80 units at ₹ 12 per unit
B- 90 units at ₹ 20 per unit	60 units at ₹ 25 per unit

Calculate the Material price variance and Material mix variance.

[B.Com., Gandhiji, April/May 1988]

[**Ans.** A = ₹ 460A, B = ₹ 240F]

3. A contract job is scheduled to be completed in 30 weeks with a labour gang of 100 skilled and 40 semi-skilled and 60 unskilled workers. The standard weekly wages of each type of workers are: skilled ₹ 60, semi-skilled ₹ 36 and unskilled ₹ 24. The work is actually completed in 32 weeks with a labour gang of 80 skilled, 50 semi-skilled and 70 unskilled workeres and actual weekly wage rates–average ₹ 65 for skilled. ₹ 40 of semi-skilled and ₹ 20 for unskilled workers. Analyse the variance in the labour cost due to various reasons.

[B.Com., Rajasthan 1983.]

[**Ans.** Labour cost variance = ₹ 8,800A, Labour rate variance = ₹ 10,240A,
Labour efficiency variance = ₹ 1,440F, Labour mix variance = ₹ 1440F]

4. A gang of workers normally consists of 30 men, 15 women and boys. They are paid at standard rates as under.

Men	₹ 0.80
Women	₹ 0.60
Boys	₹ 0.40

In a normal working week of 40 hours, the gang is expected to produce 2000 units of output. During the week ended 31st, March 1993, the gang consisted of 40 men, 10 women and 5 boys. The actual wages paid were at the rate of ` 0.70. ` 0.65 and ` 0.30 responsibility. 4 hours were lost due to abnormal idle time and 1.60 units were produced. Calculate:

(I) Labour cost variance, (II) Labour rate variance, (III) Labour efficiency variance, (IV) Labour mix variance, (V) Labour idle time variance.

[B.Com., (Hons) Delhi 1993.]

[**Ans.** LCV = ₹ 256 (adverse), LRV = ₹ 160 (F), LEC = ₹ 416 (A),
LMV = ₹ 108 (A), LITV = ₹ 160A]

❑❑❑

SECTION III : MANAGEMENT ACCOUNTING

15

Management Accounting

INTRODUCTION

Financial accounting had started at an earlier times along with the development of trade activities. The ultimate aim of the financial accounting is to supply financial information to the outsiders and also to prepare final account. But, it could not supply the valuable information to the management. The development of company type of organisation has resulted in a wider economic activity and separation of ownership and management. At present, our life style has become faster, technological changes taking place day by day, economic and social values being obsolete within a day. Under this situation, the management is not ready to wait upto the end of the one financial year regarding the problems arising from day-to-day transactions. The accurate information regarding the business transaction must be collected from week to week or month to month. In order to fulfill the above activities in an efficient manner, a separate system of accounting is developed. It is popularly known as Management Accounting.

MEANING

The term Management Accounting refers to accounting for the management *i.e.,* accounting which provides necessary information to the management for discharging its functions. In other words, any system of accounting which helps the management to carry out the operational activities of a concern more effectively is termed as Management Accounting.

The term Management Accounting is of recent origin even in the USA. Management Accounting has developed into a full fledged subject, distinct from accounting in the present commercial and financial world. It is otherwise known as management-oriented accounting or accounting for management.

DEFINITION OF MANAGEMENT ACCOUNTING

Some definitions of Management Accounting are as follows.

"Any form of accounting which enables a business to be conducted more efficiently can be regarded as Management Accounting."

—Institute of Chartered Accountants of England

"Such of its techniques and procedures by which accounting mainly seeks to aid the management collectively have come to be known as Management Accounting."

—Institute of Chartered Accountants of India

"Management Accounting is the adaptation and analysis of accounting information and its diagnosis and explanation in such a way as to assist the management."—**T.G. Rose**

"Management Accounting is concerned with accounting information that is useful to management."

—Robert N. Anthony

SCOPE OF MANAGEMENT ACCOUNTING

The scope of Management Accounting is very wide as to comprise an investigation of all the aspects and branches of business operations. The following are some of the areas of specialisation included within the orbit of Management Accounting.

(*i*) Financial Accounting
(*ii*) Cost Accounting
(*iii*) Budgeting and Forecasting
(*iv*) Statistical Data
(*v*) Cost Control Technique
(*vi*) Taxation
(*vii*) Methods and Procedure
(*viii*) Internal Financial Control
(*ix*) Office services

OBJECTIVES OF MANAGEMENT ACCOUNTING

The ultimate objective of the Management Accounting is to help the management in order to maximise profits or at least minimise expenses and control the losses. The foremost objective of management accounting is to assist the management to carry on an effective functioning of the overall managerial activities. A few objectives of the management accounting can be summarised as follows.

(*i*) *To assist in planning and formulating future policy.* Planning is one of the important functions of the business management. It includes proper analysis of available data and forecast on the basis of available information. It facilitates the preparation of statement in the light of past result and gives future estimation.

(*ii*) *To guide the interpretation of financial statements.* Management accounting provides guidance for analysing and interpreting the various financial statements. Through this way, business executives, investors, creditors, and employees of the organisation are enabled to obtain required information.

(*iii*) *Helps in decision making.* Management accounting assists in decision making process in an efficient manner with the help of the various alternative information which are available with regard to cost and revenue. Under this aspect, all the available data are analysed and correct decision may be taken with the help of the management accounting.

(iv) *Assists in organising.* Management accounting emphasizes on budgetary control, marginal costing, standard costing, cash flow, and fund flow analysis. All the above areas require an intensive study of the firm. It assists in rationalising the organisational structure of the business concern in an efficient manner.

(v) *To assist in controlling.* Some of the control techniques such as standard costing, budgetary control are helpful in controlling performance. Management accounting is one of the tools for managerial control.

(vi) *To help in effective communication of information.* Management accounting provides a means of communicating management plans and programmes through the organisation. It is a vital part of the organisation's management information system.

(vii) *Helps motivating employees.* Management accounting assists the management by providing a continuous motivation to their employees.

(viii) *Assistance in co-ordination.* Co-ordination refers to a Co-ordial and harmonious relationship maintained by the manager in an organisation. Management accounting is concerned with the efficiency of various phases of management. It helps in overall control and effective co-ordination of business operations.

LIMITATIONS OF MANAGEMENT ACCOUNTING

Management accounting suffers from some limitations. They can be summarised as follows :

(i) *Limitations of basic records.* Management accounting is generally concerned with the rearrangement of data. The correctness of management accounting depends upon some of the accounting records such as financial accounting records, cost accounting and other records. Normally, they have their own limitations which are also the limitations of management accounting.

(ii) *It is only a tool.* Management accounting is a mere tool for management. At any time, any of the important decisions, and corrective steps or measures are taken by the management itself and not by the management accountant.

(iii) *Personal bias.* Personal prejudices and bias affect the objectivity of decisions.

(iv) *Expensive.* The installation of management accounting systems in an organisation requires a huge amount of capital. So, it is not suitable for the small scale organisation.

(v) *Supplies only data.* The important function of the management accounting is to supply only data and not to influence the decisions. It can only give the information and not the prescription.

(vi) *Evolutionary stage.* Management Accounting is only at a developmental stage. It could not reach the final stage. So, the decision at the developmental stage is not a standardised one.

DIFFERENCES BETWEEN FINANCIAL ACCOUNTING AND MANAGEMENT ACCOUNTING

Some of the differences between financial accounting and management accounting are summarised as follows.

(i) *Objectives.* The main objective of the financial accounting is to make a periodical report to owners, creditors, investors, employees, and general public with regard to the financial position of a business at the end of the period. On the other hand, the objective of the management accounting is to assist internal management.

(ii) *Nature.* Financial accounting is concerned with past data whereas the Management accounting stresses on the future. And also it deals with the future plans and policies.

(iii) *Legal provisions.* As per the provisions of the law, financial accounting is compulsory for all the business concerns. But, the management accounting is followed on voluntary basis to increase the operational efficiency of the business organisations.

(iv) *Accounting principle.* Financial accounting is governed by the generally accepted accounting principles and conventions. But, no such set of principles are followed in management accounting.

(v) *Methodology.* In financial accounting, records are maintained in the form of revenue, income and expenditure, personal accounts, real accounts, and nominal accounts etc. But, in the case of management accounting, costs and revenue are usually reported by responsibility centres or profit centres.

(vi) *Publication.* Financial statements like trading, profit and loss A/c and Balance sheet are published for the use of all concerned *i.e.,* investors, creditors, employees, and general public. These statements are duly audited by the practising chartered accountants. These provisions are not there in management accounting.

(vii) *Coverage.* Financial accounting covers entire business activity specifically for the whole financial transaction. But, management accounting considers only the activity relevant to the management for decision making purpose.

(viii) *Periodicity of reporting.* In management accounting, immediate and prompt communication of data is essential. In real practice, if the data are received too late or not upto date, it would not be useful for the management decision making purpose. Under financial accounting, quick communication of information is not required unless otherwise stated.

DIFFERENCES BETWEEN FINANCIAL ACCOUNTING AND COST ACCOUNTING

The following are some of the differences between financial accounting and cost accounting.

(i) *Purpose.* Financial accounting provides information about the financial position of the company to its owners and other related parties.

But, cost accounting provides information about the costing aspect of the management. And also provides information about the cost per unit of the product manufactured by the concern.

(ii) *Compulsory.* All the business organisations keep the financial accounting in order to meet the requirements of Partnership Act, Companies Act and Income Tax Act. But, cost accounting is kept in the organisation according to its willingness.

(*iii*) *Overall analysis of profit.* Financial accounting concentrates on the whole business and overall analysis of profit is possible. It discloses the profit or loss of the business as a whole for the one year transaction through the financial statements.

But, the cost accounting has to disclose the profit or loss of a particular product during a particular period of time. Under the costing, overall analysis of profit is not possible.

(*iv*) *Reporting of costs.* In the financial accounting, costs are reported in a consolidated manner in the financial statements. But, under cost accounting, costs are divided on a unit basis in cost accounts.

(*v*) *Mode of transaction.* Financial accounting is concerned with the external transaction. Normally, it deals with the monetary transaction on the basis of payment or receipt of cash. But, cost accounting is related to the internal transactions only. It could not deal with the monetary transaction.

(*vi*) *Price fixation.* Cost accounting provides sufficient information for price fixation of a product. With the help of the cost accounting only, the concern fixes the price of its product.

But, financial accounting could not provide any assistance with regard to price fixation.

(*vii*) *Stock valuation.* Under financial accounting, stocks are valued at cost or market price whichever is less. But, in the case of cost accounting, stocks are valued at cost.

(*viii*) *Nature of dealings.* Financial accounting is concerned with only actual facts and figures. But, cost accounting is concerned partly with the actual facts and figures and partly with estimates.

(*ix*) *Science.* Financial accounting is a positive science. But, cost accounting is sometimes positive science and sometimes normative science.

DIFFERENCES BETWEEN COST ACCOUNTING AND MANAGEMENT ACCOUNTING

Cost accounting and management accounting both have more or less same objectives for the management. In spite of the similarities, there are certain differences between these two accountings.

Some of the differences between cost accounting and management accounting are summarised as follows :

(*i*) *Base.* Cost accounting develops a strong base for management accounting. But, the management accounting is developed from both financial accounting and cost accounting.

(*ii*) *Purpose.* Cost accounting takes necessary steps for collecting data in order to help the management. But, management accounting supplies all accounting information to the management for solving all business problems.

(*iii*) *Nature of data used.* Under cost accounting only quantitative aspect is recorded. But, in the management accounting, both quantitative and qualitative informations are to be recorded.

(*iv*) *Object.* The primary objective of cost accounting is to ascertain the cost of producing a product or providing a service. But, the aim of the management accounting is to provide information to the management for the overall operational activities of the business.

(*v*) *Tools techniques.* Standard costing, variance analysis, break even analysis etc, are the important tools and techniques of cost accounting.

But, in the case of management accounting not only the standard costing, variance analysis, break even analysis but also fund flow statement, cash flow statements, ratio analysis etc. are the tools and techniques of this accounting.

(*vi*) *Installation of the system.* Cost accounting can be installed without the support from management accounting.

When the organisation decides to install management accounting, it should obtain some basic details from the cost accounting and financial accounting.

But, management accounting can be installed in the organisation to obtain some of the basic support from the financial accounting and cost accounting.

TEST QUESTIONS

1. What is meant by Management Accounting ?
2. Define Management Accounting.
3. Explain the scope of Management Accounting.
4. What are the objectives of Management Accounting ?
5. State the limitations of Management Accounting.
6. What are the differences between Financial Accounting and Management Accounting ?
7. Differences between Financial Accounting and Cost Accounting.
8. What are the differences between Cost Accounting and Management Accounting ?
9. "Management Accounting provides immense help in management decision making". Discusses.
10. "Management Accounting is an extension of Financial Accounting". Discusses.

❑❑❑

16

Marginal Costing

INTRODUCTION

Marginal costing is one of the techniques of costing just like other methods of costing *viz.* job or process costing. It helps the management to take important decisions specifically for the price fixation and assessment of profitability. It reveals the inter-relationship between cost, volume of sales and profit. It classifies cost into two parts *viz* fixed and variable cost. Variable cost is considered only to find the cost of production. But, fixed costs are not included. So, a special technique of costing is developed to find out the cost of production known as marginal costing. Marginal Costing is also used to find out the cost per unit upto a particular level or output. Marginal Costing is otherwise called as direct costing, differential costing, incremental costing, or comparative costing.

DEFINITION OF MARGINAL COST AND MARGINAL COSTING

The Institute of Cost and Works Accountants of India defined marginal cost as "the amount at any given volume of output by which aggregate costs are changed, if the volume of output is increased or decreased by one". In order to find out the marginal cost, we need the following elements of cost.

(*i*) Direct material.

(*ii*) Direct labour.

(*iii*) Other direct expenses.

(*iv*) Total variable overheads.

i.e., marginal cost = prime cost + total variable overheads.

Marginal costing is defined by the ICWA as *"the ascertainment by differentiating between fixed cost and variable costs of marginal costs and of the effect on profit of changes in volume of type of output"*.

Batty defines marginal costing as *"a technique of cost accounting which pays special attention to the behaviour of costs with changes in the volume of output"*.

MAIN FEATURES OF MARGINAL COSTING

1. All costs are classified into fixed and variable.
2. When evaluation of finished goods and work-in-progress are taken into account, they will be only variable costs.

3. Marginal costing is a method of costing which is used in other methods of costing.
4. Fixed cost should be subtracted/deducted from the contribution for the purpose of finding out net profit or loss.
5. Total fixed cost remains constant irrespective of the level of production but fixed cost per unit cannot be uniform.
6. Selling price per unit and variable cost per unit remain the same.
7. To employ the cost volume profit relationship the firm has to determine its profitability at various levels of activity possible.
8. Contribution is otherwise called as income or profit.
9. Normally, Fixed Costs are charged to the profit and loss account in which year it was actually incurred and they are not adjusted in the income of the subsequent years.
10. In all the stages, fixed and variable costs are to be segregated. Apart from this, semi variable costs are also segregated into fixed and variable.

ADVANTAGES

1. *Helps to fix selling price.* Fixation of selling price is an important task of the manufacturer. Because, depending upon the price level of the product, profit of the organisation is to be determined. The differentiation between fixed costs and variable costs is very helpful in fixing the selling price of the products.
2. *Budgetary Control.* Through the preparation of flexible budget, we have to find the total fixed cost and variable cost under different levels of activity. Without the flexible budget, it is difficult to find the total cost at various stages of activity.
3. *Make or buy decisions.* Sometimes the organisation has to take decision to manufacture a product itself or buy a product from outside suppliers. It would take the decision to purchase from outside if the price paid recovers some of the fixed expenses.
4. *Helps in production planning.* Through the break even chart, each and every stage of profit is to be determined clearly. So, unprofitable products can be removed from product line. Profitable products should be increased according to the required level.
5. *Effective results.* The comparison of other systems of costing like process, job etc gives better results for the operations.
6. *Benefits of overheads simplification.* Fixed overheads are segregated from the production cost. With the help of this function, the problem of over absorption or under absorption is totally eliminated.
7. *Constant in nature.* Variable costs fluctuate from time to time. But, in the long run, marginal costs are stable irrespective of the level of production.
8. *Simplicity.* Marginal costing is simple to understand and easy to compute. So, it does not require more time for computation, and its application.
9. *Cost control.* Marginal costing is combined with standard costing and budgetary control which makes the cost control mechanism more effective.

DISADVANTAGES

1. *Difficult to analyse overhead.* It is difficult to segregate fixed and variable costs accurately. In real sense, a major technical difficulty arises on drawing a sharp line of demarcation between fixed and variable costs.

2. *Time factor ignored.* Normally, in short run periods, both fixed and variable costs were constant. But, in the long run all costs are variable including fixed costs. So, comparison of performance between two periods is not possible.
3. *Inaccurate price fixation.* Price fixation and comparison between two jobs cannot be done in an accurate manner because selling price is fixed on the basis of contribution. Suppose cost plus contract means, it is very difficult to fix the price.
4. *Limited Role.* Marginal costing in no way, explains the reasons for the increase or decrease in production or sales because it is difficult to combine it with other techniques like standard costing and budgetary control.
5. *Claim for loss of stock.* In any business organisation, to follow a marginal costing technique for the stock valuation, in case of goods destroyed by fire, full loss cannot be recovered from the insurance company.
6. *Problem of variable overheads.* In most of the situations, marginal costing smoothly solves the problem of over and under absorption of fixed overheads. But, there is a problem of variable overhead and semi variable overheads.
7. *Unsuitability for certain industries.* Marginal costing is found unsuitable in industries where the value of work in progress is high level as compared to its turnover. It is specifically for the ship industries and contract work. This type of industries have more work in progress. At the time of valuation of work in progress, fixed cost is ignored, so it shows manipulation in its profit.
8. *Objection by income tax authorities.* A concern or industry, which adopts marginal costing techniques for the valuation of inventories and profit estimation, is objected by the income tax authorities because it does not show an accurate profit.

Specimen form of marginal cost statement

Particulars	*Products*		*Total*
	A	*B*	
Net Sales	xx	xx	xx
Less : Variable Cost	xx	xx	xx
Prime Cost + All			
Variable overheads	xx	xx	xx
Contribution	xx	xx	xx
Less : Fixed Cost	xx	xx	xx
Profit	xx	xx	xx

ABSORPTION COSTING

Absorption costing, in actual practice, is charging of all the costs both fixed and variable to the production, processes and treats all costs as product costs. In real sense, in absorption costing, fixed overhead can never be absorbed exactly because of difficulty in determining costs and volume of output.

The Institute of Cost and Management Accountants (U.K) defines it as "the practice of charging all costs both variables and fixed to operations, processes or products".

Absorption costing is otherwise called as total or full cost method.

Practical Applications of Marginal Costing

Marginal costing technique may be applied with various aims and purposes. The important purposes are as follow.

Profit Planning

In order to determine the profit level of the firm in future period is absolutely important. Profit planning is therefore a part of operational planning. Marginal costing assists the management in the profit planning through computation of contribution ratio. In the real sense, profits are affected by various factors such as the marginal cost per unit, total fixed cost, selling price and volume of sales. Hence, the organisation can achieve its profit by modifying one or more of the above variables.

Profit Volume Ratio

The ratio of contribution to sales is the p/v ratio or profit volume ratio. It may be expressed in percentage. It is one of the effective tools for studying the profitability of business.

Break Even Point

BEP may be defined as that level or point of sales volume at which the total revenue is equal to total costs. Simply, it is a no-profit, no loss point. This is also a minimum point of production where total costs are recovered. If sales exceeds the Break Even Point, organisation earns a profit. If sales are below the Break Even Point, the organisation incurs a loss. In other words, this is a point at which loss ceases and profit starts.

[Talk about the BEP in single word; it is the point, where income is exactly equal to expenditure.]

Break	Means	Divide
Even	Means	Equally
Point	Means	Position or place [sale/produced units]

1. *Margin of safety.* Margin of safety may be defined as the excess of actual sales or production at the selected activity over Break even sales or production. Simply, margin of sales is excess sales over the break even sales. It is abbreviated as M.O.S.
2. *Level of activity planning.* Now a days, business concerns face the problems of finding the level of activity which is optimum for a business to adopt. In this respect, the management wants to take right decision from the different levels of production or selling activities available. The marginal costing technique helps the management to determine the optimum level of activity.
3. *Fixation of selling price.* One of the important functions of the cost accountant is the ascertainment of cost for the purpose of fixation of selling price. At the time of price fixation, raw material cost, direct labour cost plus other overheads are also taken into account to find the total cost of the product. Apart from this, a certain percentage of profit is added to the total cost to arrive at the selling price. Marginal Costing of a product represents the minimum price for that product and any sales below marginal cost would entail a loss of cash.

4. *Decision to make or buy.* Some time, a firm may buy certain products or parts or tools from outside, which may be made by the firm itself. The management must decide which one is most profitable to the firm. If the marginal cost of the product is lower than the price of buying from outside sources, it is better for the firm to manufacture the product by itself.
5. *Introduction of a new product.* Existing firm may add additional products in its products line without any difficulty, with the help of its available production capacity. The new product is sold in the market at a reasonable price with large quantities. If it is a reputed company, the sales may increase. So, total cost would come down and automatically profit will be increased.
6. *Evaluation of performance.* With the help of the marginal costing, the management can measure the operational efficiency of all the departments or sales division. Those departments or divisions which have a highest P/V ratio indicate the highest performance efficiency.
7. *Decision making.* In normal practice, price must not be less than total cost. So, marginal costing acts as a price fixer and contributes profit. But, this principle cannot be successful at all times. If in any situation price is equal to marginal cost, there will be a loss. Some times, the firm has to face a loss when (*i*) competitors cannot be driven out (*ii*) there is cut-throat competition and so on. Marginal costing guides the management to take correct decisions whenever faced with this type of situations.
8. *Maintaining a desired level of profit.* Some times, an industry has to reduce its price due to competition and government regulation. But, the ultimate aim of the management is to maintain the same level of profit. For this purpose, marginal costing technique can assist the management to determine how many units have to be sold to maintain the same level of profit.
9. *Alternative methods of production.* Management has to select a method of production among so many alternatives. Marginal cost gives the marginal contribution under each of the proposed methods which are worked out and the method which gives the maximum contribution is normally adopted. And also with the help of the marginal costing, the management should compare the alternative method of manufacture : either machine work or hand work and one machine or more machines.
10. *Decision to accept bulk order or foreign order.* Some times, organisation has to receive both bulk order and foreign order for supplying the goods. A decision has to be taken now whether to accept both orders or reject them. In this respect, marginal costing technique gives the correct direction to the management for accepting or rejecting the order.

Cost Volume Profit Analysis

Cost volume profit analysis is one of the analytical tool used for studying the relationship between volume, cost, prices and profits. In cost volume profit analysis, an attempt is made to measure variations of costs and profits and volume. In the words of Heiser, "The most significant single factor in profit planning of the average business is the relationship between the volume of business costs and profits".

From time to time the management is very much interested to know and evaluate the profitability of the product or product mix. And also to analyse the effect of change in the volume of output, will have on the cost of production and profits.

To understand the cost volume profit relationship in a detailed manner, we have to study the following :

(i) Break even analysis
(ii) Marginal cost formula
(iii) Profit volume ratio
(iv) Profit graph
(v) Key factor
(vi) Sales mix etc.

Break Even Analysis

It is a tool for analysing the financial aspect whereby the impact on profit, of the changes in volume, price costs and sales mix can be estimated with higher level accuracy.

Profit Volume Ratio

It is an important tool in decision making. It is used for the calculation of BEP and in problems regarding profit and sales relationship. A higher P/V ratio indicates the greater profitability and vice versa. So, the organisation makes necessary effort to obtain higher P/V ratio.

Margin of Safety

Margin of safety may be defined as the excess of actual sales or production at the selected activity over Break even sales or production. Simply, margin of sales is excess sales over the break even sales. It is abbreviated as M.O.S.

Break Even Chart

Break even point should be computed with the help of the graphical representation or applying mathematical formula. Graphical representation of break-even point is known as break even chart. Dr. Vance is of the opinion that "It is a graph showing the amounts of fixed variable costs and the sales revenue at different volumes of operation. It shows at what volume the firm first covers all costs with revenue of break-even."

From the following data, draw break even chart. Fixed cost ₹ 8000, variable cost ₹ 4.00 percentage, selling price per unit ₹ 6.00. Units produced and sold 4,000, 6,000, 8,000 and 12,000.

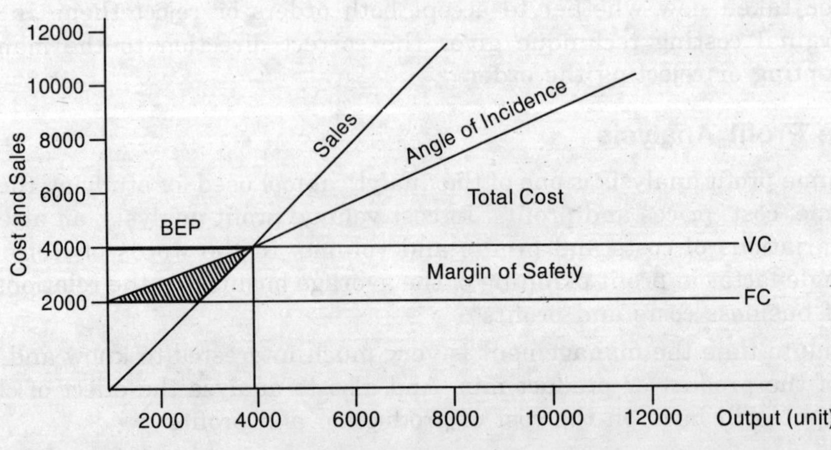

Fig. 1.

Angle of Incidence

Angle of incidence indicates the profit earning capacity. The angle is formed at the break even point where the sales line cuts the total cost line. The angle may be large or small. Large angle of incidence indicates higher profit rate and vice versa.

Assumptions of Break Even Analysis

(*i*) All costs are segregated into fixed and variable cost.

(*ii*) Total fixed costs are constant at all levels of output.

(*iii*) Production and sales figures are same.

(*iv*) Variable costs vary proportionately with the level of volume of output.

(*v*) Selling price per unit and operational efficiency remains unchanged.

(*vi*) Production and sales are same.

(*vii*) Volume of sales and volume of production are equal hence there is no unsold stock.

(*viii*) There is only one product.

(*ix*) If there are multiple products, sales mix remains constant.

(*x*) There will be no change in the general price level.

(*xi*) Cost and revenue depend only on volume of production or output and not on any other factor.

Advantages of Break Even Analysis and Chart

1. Enables to provide more detailed information and easily understandable than those of profit & loss account and balance sheet information.
2. To determine the total cost, fixed cost and variable cost.
3. Product planning.
4. Inter-firm comparison is possible.
5. To select the best product mix.
6. Choosing the best promotion mix
7. To take the make or buy decisions.
8. Preparation of flexible budget.
9. Formulation of price policy.
10. It provides guidance for cost control.
11. To find out the profitability of different levels of activity and various products.
12. Total profit could be calculated accurately.

Limitations

1. Fixed cost does not always remain constant.
2. It ignores economies of scale in production.
3. Variable costs do not always vary proportionately.
4. No importance is given to the opening and closing stocks.
5. Only limited information is provided by the break even point.
6. Study concentrates only on sales mix or product mix.
7. Sales revenue does not always change proportionately.

Formula : Computation of BEP

First type :

1. *Problem given in values :*

$$\text{BEP} = \frac{\text{Fixed Cost} \times \text{Sales}}{\text{Sales} - \text{Variable Cost}}$$

2. *Problem given in unit :*

$$\text{BEP} = \frac{\text{Fixed Cost}}{\text{Selling price per unit} - \text{Variable cost per unit}}$$

3. *Problem given in values :*

$$\text{BEP} = \frac{\text{Fixed Cost}}{\text{P/V Ratio}}$$

$$\text{Computation of P/V ratio} = \frac{\text{Contribution}}{\text{Sales}} \times 100$$

$$\text{Contribution} = \text{Sales} - \text{Variable Cost}$$

Second type : Only two periods' details are given in the problem, we have to find the following :

1. P/V ratio
2. BEP
3. Fixed Cost
4. Find the profit with the help of given sales.
5. Find the sales with the help of given profit.
6. MOS
7. Variable cost.

The above should be calculated with the help of the following formula

1. $$P/V\ Ratio = \frac{\text{Difference of Profit}}{\text{Difference of Sales}} \times 100$$

2. $$BEP = \frac{\text{Fixed Cost}}{\text{P/V Ratio}}$$

3. *Fixed Cost*

Given Sales × P/V =	Contribution	xx	[FC + Profit]
	Less : Profit	xx	
	Fixed Cost	xx	

4. *Find the profit with the help of given sales*

Given Sales × P/V =	Contribution	xx
	Less : FC	xx
	Profit	xx

5. *Find the sales with the help of given profit*

$$\frac{\text{FC} + \text{Desired Profit}}{\text{P/V Ratio}}$$

6. *Margin of safety*

(i) Margin of safety = Actual Sales – BEP Sales

(or)

(ii) If desired profit given in the problem $= \dfrac{\text{Desired Profit}}{\text{P/V Ratio}}$

or

(iii) Margin of safety in units $= \dfrac{\text{Profit}}{\text{Contribution per unit}}$

7. *Variable Cost*

Sales	xx
Less : Value of P/V ratio	xx
Variable Cost	xx

Example :

Sales 100%	50,000
Less : Value of P/V Ratio $\left(50{,}000 \times \dfrac{40}{100}\right)$	20,000
Variable Cost	30,000

Sales – P/V Ratio = Vc

8. *Sales in units required to maintain the present level of profit*

$= \dfrac{\text{Total Contribution required}}{\text{New Contribution per unit}}$

Marginal Cost Statement

Sales	xx
Less : Variable Cost	xx
Contribution	xx
Less : Fixed Cost	xx
Profit	xx

TEST QUESTIONS

1. What is marginal cost ?
2. What is meant by marginal costing ?
3. Describe the main features of marginal costing.
4. Explain the advantages and limitations of marginal costing.
5. What is meant by Absorption costing ?
6. What is contribution ?
7. What is P/V ratio ?

8. Give marginal cost equation.

9. Define angle of incidence.

10. What is meant by cost volume profit analysis ?

11. What is meant by Break-even point ?

12. How is margin of safety calculated ?

13. "The effect of Price reduction is always to reduce the P/v ratio, to raise break-even point and to the margin of safety". Explain and illustrate by numerical examples.

14. What do you understand by the term cost volume profit relationship ? Why is this relationship important in business management ?

15. "The technique of marginal costing can be valuable aid to Management". Discuss.

16. What is meant by break-even analysis ? Discuss the assumptions and the limitations of this technique.

17. What do you understand by contribution ? How does it helps the management to solving various problems ?

PROBLEMS AND SOLUTIONS

Problem 1. *From the following particulars you are required to calculate BEP.*

(a) Fixed cost ₹ 2,00,000, selling price per unit ₹ 40, variable cost per unit ₹ 1.5.

(b) Fixed cost ₹ 40,000, sales ₹ 1,00,000, variable cost ₹ 30,000.

Solution :

(*a*) $$\text{Computation of BEP} = \frac{\text{Fixed Cost}}{\text{Selling price per unit} - \text{Variable cost per unit}}$$

$$\text{Fixed Cost} = ₹\ 2,00,000$$

$$\text{Selling price per unit} = ₹\ 40 \text{ per unit}$$

$$\text{Variable cost per unit} = ₹\ 15 \text{ per unit}$$

$$= \frac{2,00,000}{40-15}$$

$$\text{BEP in units} = 8,000$$

$$\text{BEP in value} = \text{BEP units} \times \text{Selling price per unit}$$

$$= 8,000 \times 40$$

$$= ₹\ 3,20,000$$

(*b*) $$\text{BEP} = \frac{\text{Fixed Cost} \times \text{Sales}}{\text{Sales} - \text{Variable Cost}}$$

$$= \frac{40,000 \times 1,00,000}{1,00,000 \times 30,000}$$

$$= \frac{4,00,000}{7} = ₹\ 57,142.$$

Problem 2. *From the following data calculate break even point expressed in terms of units and also the new BEP if selling price is reduced by 10%.*

Fixed Expenses	₹
Depreciation	*2,00,000*
Salaries	*2,00,000*
Variable Expenses	
Materials	*₹ 6 per unit*
Labour	*₹ 4 per unit*
Selling Price	*₹ 20 per unit*

Solution :

$$\text{BEP} = \frac{\text{Fixed Cost}}{\text{Selling price per unit} - \text{Variable cost per unit}}$$

$$= \frac{4,00,000}{20-10}$$

BEP in units = 40,000 units

New break even point if selling price is reduced by 10%

Fixed Cost	= ₹	4,00,000
Material	= ₹	6.00
Labour	= ₹	4.00
	₹	10.00

New Selling price :

Selling Price	= ₹	20.00
Less : 10% Reduction	= ₹	2.00
	₹	18.00

$$\text{BEP} = \frac{\text{Fixed Cost}}{\text{Selling price per unit} - \text{Variable cost per unit}}$$

$$= \frac{4,00,000}{8}$$

BEP in units = 50,000 units

Problem 3. *From the following particulars find out the BEP, what will be the selling price per unit if BEP is to be brought down to 9,000 units.*

	₹
Variable cost per unit	*₹ 75*
Fixed expenses	*₹ 2,70,000*
Selling price per unit	*₹ 100*

Solution :

$$\text{BEP} = \frac{\text{Fixed Cost}}{\text{Selling price per unit} - \text{Variable cost per unit}}$$

Fixed Cost = ₹ 2,70,000

Selling price = ₹ 100

Variable cost = ₹ 75

$$= \frac{2,70,000}{100 - 75}$$

BEP in units = 10,800 units

BEP in value = 10,800 units × Selling price

= *i.e.,* 10,800 × 100

= ₹ 10,80,000

If BEP is brought down to 9,000 units

$$\text{BEP} = \frac{\text{Fixed Cost (2,70,000)}}{\text{Contribution per unit (X)}}$$

Contribution per unit is treated as X

$$X = \frac{2,70,000}{9,000} = 30$$

Therefore, New Selling price is ₹ 105 *i.e.,* (₹ 75 + ₹ 30 = ₹ 105)

Problem 4. *The following information relating to a company is given to you : Calculate BEP.*

	₹
Sales	*7,00,000*
Fixed cost	*1,80,000*
Variable cost	*4,00,000*

Solution :

$$\text{BEP} = \frac{\text{Fixed Cost}}{\text{Contribution}} \times \text{Sales}$$

Contribution = Sales – Variable cost

= 4,00,000 – 2,50,000

= 1,50,000

$$\text{BEP} = \frac{1,80,000}{1,50,000} \times 4,00,000$$

BEP Sales = 4,80,000

Present Sales = 4,00,000

80,000

Based upon the above calculation, sales are to be increased only by ₹ 80,000 to break even.

Problem 5. *From the following data you are required to calculate the break-even point and net sales value at this point.*

Selling price per unit	*₹ 25*
Direct material cost per unit	*₹ 8*
Direct labour cost per unit	*₹ 5*
Fixed overhead	*₹ 24,000*

Variable overheads @ 60% on Direct Labour.

Trade discount 4%

If sales are 15% and 20% above the break even volume determine the net profits.

Solution :

(*i*)

$$\text{BEP} = \frac{\text{Fixed Cost}}{\text{Selling price per unit} - \text{Variable cost per unit}}$$

$$= \frac{24{,}000}{24-16}$$

$$= \frac{24{,}000}{8}$$

BEP in units = 3000 units

BEP in value = BEP Units × Selling price

= 3000 units × ₹ 24

= ₹ 72,000

Workings :

(*a*) Selling Price :

Selling price per unit	= ₹ 25.00	
Less : Trade discount 4%	= ₹ 1.00	$\left[25.00 \times \frac{4}{100}\right]$
Selling Price	= ₹ 24.00	

(*b*) Variable Cost :

Direct Material cost per unit	= ₹ 8.00	
Direct labour cost per unit	= ₹ 5.00	
Variable overhead 60% on Direct Labour	= ₹ 3.00	$\left[5 \times \frac{60}{100}\right]$
Variable Cost	= ₹ 16.00	

(*ii*) **If sales are 15% above the break even volume, find out the profit.**

Formula :

Given Sales × P/V ratio	=	xx
Less : Fixed Cost	=	xx
Profit	=	xx

BEP Sales is	=	72,000		
15% above the break even sales	=	10,800		
Increased sale volume	=	82,800		
Therefore, $82{,}800 \times \frac{33.33}{100}$	=	27,597	*i.e.,*	27,600
Less : Fixed cost	=	24,000		24,000
Profit	=	3,597		3,600

NOTE : Find the P/V ratio

$$\text{P/V ratio} = \frac{\text{Contribution}}{\text{Sales}}$$

$$\text{Contribution} = \text{Sales} - \text{Variable cost}$$

$$= 24 - 16 = ₹\,8$$

$$= \frac{8}{24} \times 100$$

$$= 33.33\%$$

(*iii*) **If sales are 20% above the break even, determine the profit.**

Break even sales	=	₹ 72,000		
20% increase	=	₹ 14,400		
Increased sales volume	=	₹ 86,400		
$82{,}800 \times \frac{33.33}{100}$	=	28,797	*i.e.,*	28,800
Less : Fixed cost	=			24,000
Profit	=			4,800

Problem 6 :

(*i*) *From the following details you are required to determine the break even point.*

Direct Labour	*₹ 100 per unit*
Direct Material	*₹ 40 per unit*
Variable overhead	*100% of direct labour*

Fixed overheads ₹ *60,000*

Selling price ₹ *400 per unit*

(ii) In order to increase the efficiency in production, the concern installs improved machinery, which results in fixed overhead of ₹ *20,000, but the variable overhead is reduced by 40%.*

Solution :

(i) Computation of Break even point

$$\text{BEP} = \frac{\text{Fixed Cost}}{\text{Selling price per unit} - \text{Variable cost per unit}}$$

Fixed Cost = ₹ 60,000

Variable Cost

Direct Material	= ₹	40
Direct Labour	= ₹	100
Variable overhead 100% on direct labour	= ₹	100
	₹	240

$$\text{BEP} = \frac{60,000}{400 - 240}$$

$$= \frac{60,000}{160}$$

BEP in units = 375 units

BEP in value = BEP Unit × Selling price

= 375 units × ₹ 400

= ₹ 1,50,000

(ii) In order to increase the production : The New BEP

Fixed overhead	= ₹	60,000
(+) Additional	= ₹	20,000
Total fixed cost	= ₹	80,000

Variable overhead is reduced by 40%

Variable Cost

Direct Material	= ₹	40
Direct Labour	= ₹	100
Variable overhead $100 \times \frac{60}{100}$	= ₹	60
Total Variable Cost	₹	200

$$\text{Revised BEP} = \frac{\text{Fixed Cost}}{\text{Selling price per unit} - \text{Variable cost per unit}}$$

$$= \frac{80,000}{400-200}$$

BEP in units = 400 units

BEP in value = 400 × 400

= ₹ 1,60,000

Problem 7. *The P/V ratio of a firm dealing in Electrical equipment is 50% and the margin of safety is 40%. Find out BEP and the net profit, if sales volume is ₹ 50,00,000.*

[MBA Anna, MCA 2000 PU]

Solution :

(*i*) Contribution

Given Sales × P/V ratio = Contribution

$$50,00,000 \times \frac{50}{100} = ₹\ 25,00,000$$

(*ii*) Break even sales = (Actual Sales – BEP Sales = M.O.S. (or)

Actual Sales – M.O.S. = BEP Sales

Sales = ₹ 50,00,000

Less : Margin of safety 40% on sales = ₹ 20,00,000

Break even sales = ₹ 30,00,000

(*iii*) Fixed cost

$$\text{BEP (30,000)} = \frac{\text{Fixed Cost (X)}}{\text{P/V Ratio (50\%)}}$$

$$X = 30,00,000 \times \frac{50}{100}$$

Fixed Assets = ₹ 15,00,000

(*iv*) **Find out profit :**

Contribution = Fixed cost + Profit or Fixed cost – Loss

Contribution = ₹ 25,00,000

Less : Fixed Cost = ₹ 15,00,000

Profit = ₹ 10,00,000

Problem 8. *Assuming that the cost structure and selling prices remain the same in both the periods. Compute the following :*

(a) Profit volume Ratio

(b) BEP for sales

(c) Profit when sales are ₹ 1,00,000

(d) Sales required to earn a profit of ₹ 20,000

(e) Safety margin in both the periods

Periods	*Sales ₹*	*Profit ₹*
I	*1,20,000*	*9,000*
II	*1,40,000*	*13,000*

[B.Com. PU 2004]

Solution :

(*a*) $$\text{Profit Volume Ratio} = \frac{\text{Difference of Profit}}{\text{Difference of Sales}} \times 100$$

$$= \frac{13{,}000 - 9{,}000}{1{,}40{,}000 - 1{,}20{,}000} \times 100$$

$$= \frac{4{,}000}{20{,}000} \times 100$$

$$\text{P/V Ratio} = 20\%$$

(*b*) $$\text{BEP for sales} = \frac{\text{Fixed Cost}}{\text{P/V Ratio}}$$

$$= \frac{15{,}000}{20/100}$$

$$\text{BEP Sales} = ₹\ 75{,}000$$

NOTE : $$\text{Fixed Cost} = \text{Contribution} - \text{Profit}$$

$$= 1{,}20{,}000 \times \frac{20}{100} - 9{,}000$$

$$= 24{,}000 - 9{,}000 = 15{,}000$$

[therefore, Contribution = Given sales × P/V Ratio]

(*c*) Profit when sales are ₹ 1,00,000

$$\text{Profit} = \text{Contribution} - \text{Fixed cost}$$

$$= 1{,}00{,}000 \times \frac{20}{100} - 15{,}000$$

$$= 20{,}000 - 15{,}000 = 5{,}000$$

(*d*) Sales required to earn a profit of ₹ 20,000

$$= \frac{\text{Fixed Cost + Desired Profit}}{\text{P/V Ratio}}$$

$$= \frac{15{,}000 + 20{,}000}{20/100} = ₹\ 1{,}75{,}000$$

(*e*) Safety margin in both the periods

	Actual Sales	– BEP Sales	= Margin of safety
(*i*)	1,20,000	– 75,000	= 45,000
(*ii*)	1,40,000	– 75,000	= 65,000

Problem 9. *Find out profit from the following data*

Sales	₹ *8,00,000*
Marginal cost	₹ *6,00,000*
Break-even sales	₹ *6,00,000*

[SAS Commercial 1982]

Solution :

(*i*) $$\text{P/V Ratio} = \frac{\text{Contribution}}{\text{Sales}} \times 100$$

$$= \frac{2,00,000}{8,00,000} \times 100 = 25\%$$

(*ii*) Fixed Expenses

$$\text{BED (60,00,000)} = \frac{\text{Fixed Expenses (X)}}{\text{P/V Ratio (25\%)}}$$

$$X = 6,00,000 \times \frac{25}{100} = 1,50,000$$

Fixed Expenses = ₹ 1,50,000

(*iii*) Find out profit

Contribution = ₹ 2,00,000

Less : Fixed Expenses = ₹ 1,50,000

Profit = ₹ 50,000

Problem 10. *P/V ratio is 30% and margin of safety is 40%. Find out the fixed cost and net profit if the actual sales is ₹ 5,00,000.*

Solution :

Sales = ₹ 5,00,000

Less : Margin of safety 40% = ₹ 2,00,000

BEP = ₹ 3,00,000

NOTE : BEP = (Actual Sales – Margin of safety) 3,00,000

Find the Fixed Cost.

$$\text{BEP (3,00,000)} = \frac{\text{Fixed Cost (X)}}{\text{P/V Ratio (30\%)}}$$

$$X = 3,00,000 \times \frac{30}{100} = ₹\ 90,000$$

Profit or Loss = Contribution – Fixed Cost

= 1,50,000 – 90,000 = ₹ 60,000

NOTE : Contribution = Given sales × P/V ratio

$$= 5,00,000 \times \frac{30}{100} = 1,50,000$$

Problem 11. *An analysis of Digital manufacturing Co. Ltd., submits the following information :*

Cost Element	*Variable Cost (% Sales)*	*Fixed Cost (₹)*
Direct Material	*32.8*	—
Direct Labour	*28.4*	—
Factory overheads	*12.6*	*1,89,900*
Distribution overheads	*4.1*	*58,400*
General Administration overheads	*1.1*	*66,700*

Budgeted sales are ₹ 18,50,000. You are required to determine.

(a) The break even sales volume.

(b) Profit at the budgeted sales value

(c) The profit if actual sales

(i) Drop by 10%

(ii) Increase by 5% from budgeted sales. [M.Com. Adopted]

Solution :

(*a*) *Break Even Sales Volume*

$$\text{BEP} = \frac{\text{Fixed Cost}}{\text{P/V Ratio}}$$

$$= \frac{3{,}15{,}000}{21/100}$$

$$\text{BEP} = ₹\ 15{,}00{,}000$$

Workings :

(*i*) Fixed Cost

Factory overheads = ₹	1,89,900
Distribution overheads = ₹	58,400
General administration overheads = ₹	66,700
Total Fixed Cost = ₹	3,15,000

(*ii*) $$\text{P/V Ratio} = \frac{\text{Contribution}}{\text{Sales}} \times 100$$

$$\text{Contribution} = \text{Sales} - \text{Variable Cost}$$

$$= 100 - 79$$

$$= 21\%$$

(Here, sales are assumed to be 100%)

(*iii*) Variable Cost

Direct Material = 32.8% of sales

Direct Labour = 28.4% of sales

Factory overheads = 12.6% of sales

Distribution overheads = 4.1% of sales

General administration overheads = 1.1% of sales

Total = 79.0%

(*b*) Profit at the budgeted sales volume of ₹ 18,50,000

Profit = Contribution – Fixed Cost

$$= 18,50,000 \times \frac{21}{100} - 3,15,000$$

$$= 3,88,500 - 3,15,000 = 73,500$$

NOTE : Contribution = Given Sales × P/V Ratio

(*c*) The profit, if actual sales

(*i*) Drop by 10%

Sales =	₹	18,50,000
Less : 10% =	₹	1,85,000
Sales (at 10% Reduction) =	₹	16,65,000

Profit = Contribution – Fixed Cost

$$= 16,65,000 \times \frac{21}{100} - 3,15,000$$

$$= 3,49,650 - 3,15,000 = 34,650$$

(*ii*) Increase by 5% from budgeted sales

Sales =	₹	18,50,000
+ 5% =	₹	92,500
Sales at 5% increase =	₹	19,42,500

Profit = Contribution – Fixed Cost

$$= 19,42,500 \times \frac{21}{100} - 3,15,000$$

$$= 4,07,925 - 3,15,000 = 92,925$$

Problem 12. *Raj Corporation Ltd. has prepared the following estimates for the year 1994–95.*

Sales Units	₹	*15,000*
Fixed Expenses	₹	*34,000*
Sales Value	₹	*1,50,000*
Variable Cost ₹ 6 per unit		

You are required to

(i) Find P/V ratio, break even point, and margin of safety.

(ii) Calculate the revised P/V ratio, break even point and margin of safety in each of the following cases.

(a) *Decrease of 10% in selling price.*

(b) *Increase of 10% of variable costs.*

(c) *Increase of sale volume by 2000 units.*

(d) *Increase of ₹ 6,000 in fixed cost.* [MCA 2000]

Solution :

(*i*)

$$\text{Selling price per unit} = \frac{1,50,000}{15,000} = ₹\ 10$$

$$\text{Variable cost per unit} = ₹\ 6$$

$$\text{Contribution per unit} = ₹\ 4$$

$$\text{P/V Ratio} = \frac{C}{S} \times 100$$

$$= \frac{4}{10} \times 100 = 40\%$$

$$\text{BEP in units} = \frac{\text{Fixed Cost}}{\text{Selling price per unit} - \text{Variable cost per unit}}$$

$$= \frac{34,000}{4} = 8,500 \text{ units}$$

$$\text{BEP in sales} = 8,500 \text{ units} \times ₹\ 10 = 85,000$$

$$\text{Margin of safety} = \text{Actual Sales} - \text{BEP Sales}$$

$$= 1,50,000 - 85,000 = 65,000$$

(*ii*)

Particulars	*P/V Ratio*	*BEP Value*	*Margin of Safety*
(*a*) Decrease in selling price $10 \times \frac{10}{100} = 1$, *i.e.,* $10 - 1 = 9$	$\frac{9-6}{9} \times 100$ $= 33\frac{1}{3}\%$	$\frac{34,000}{33\frac{1}{3}/100}$ = 1,02,000	= 9 × 15,000 = 1,35,000 – 1,02,000 = 33,000
(*b*) Increase of 10% in variable cost $6 \times \frac{10}{100} = .60$ 6 + .60 = 6.60	$\frac{10-6.60}{10} \times 100$ = 34%	$\frac{34,000}{34/100}$ = 1,00,000	1,50,000 – 1,00,000 = 50,000
(*c*) Increase of Sales Volume by 2000 units	No change *i.e.,* 40%	No change *i.e.,* 85,000	Sales 1,50,000 + 2000 × 10 20,000 1,70,000 1,70,000 – 85,000 = 85,000
(*d*) Increase of ₹ 6,000 in fixed cost	No change *i.e.,* 40%	$\frac{40,000}{40/100}$ = 1,00,000	1,50,000 – 1,00,000 = 50,000

Problem 13. *You are given the following information in respect of a company.*

	₹
(i) Fixed cost	*13,000*
(ii) Variable cost	*15,000*
(iii) Total cost	*28,000*
(iv) Net profit	*2,000*
(v) Net sales	*30,000*

(a) Find out the break-even point.

(b) Forecast the profit for sales volume ₹ 50,000.

(c) Estimate the volume of sales turnover to make a net profit of ₹ 10,000.

[ACS Final]

Solution :

(a) *Break even Point*

Find the P/V ratio

NOTE : Sales − Variable Cost = Contribution

$$30{,}000 - 14{,}000 = 16{,}000$$

$$\text{P/V Ratio} = \frac{\text{Contribution}}{\text{Sales}} \times 100$$

$$= \frac{16{,}000}{30{,}000} \times 100 = 53\frac{1}{3}\%$$

$$\text{BEP} = \frac{\text{F}}{\text{P/V Ratio}} = \frac{13{,}000}{53\frac{1}{3}/100}$$

$$= ₹\ 24{,}375$$

(b) *Find the profit when sales are ₹ 50,000*

$$\text{Given sales} \times \text{P/V ratio} = \text{Contribution}$$

$$50{,}000 \times \frac{53\frac{1}{3}}{100} = 26{,}667 \text{ (FC + Profit)}$$

Less : Fixed cost = 13,000

Profit = 13,667

(c) *Sales to earn a profit of ₹ 10,000*

$$= \frac{\text{Fixed Cost + Profit}}{\text{P/V Ratio}}$$

$$= \frac{13{,}000 + 10{,}000}{53\frac{1}{3}/100}$$

$$= 13{,}000 + 10{,}000 \times \frac{100}{53} = ₹\ 43{,}125$$

Problem 14. *Sale of a product amounts to 200 units per month at ₹ 10 per unit. Fixed overheads ₹ 400 per month and variable cost is ₹ 6 per unit. There is a proposal to reduce prices by 10%. Calculate the present and future status by applying P/V ratio to find how many units must be sold to maintain total profit.* [MBA Madras]

Solution : Profitability Statement

Number of Units	*At Present*	*10% Reduction in selling price*
	₹	₹
Number of units	200	200
Selling price	10.00	9.00
Sales value	2000	1800
Less : Variable cost (200 × 6)	1200	(200 × 6) 1200
Contribution	800	600
Less : Fixed cost	400	400
Profit	400	200

$$\text{Computation of P/V ratio} = \frac{\text{Contribution}}{\text{Sales}} \times 100$$

$$= \frac{800}{1000} \times 100 = 40\%$$

$$= \frac{600}{1800} \times 100 = 33\frac{1}{3}\%$$

Number of units to be sold

$$\frac{\text{Fixed Cost + Profit}}{\text{P/V Ratio}} = \frac{400+400}{33\frac{1}{3}/100}$$

$$= 800 \times \frac{100}{33\frac{1}{3}}$$

$$= ₹\ 2,402$$

$$= \frac{2,402}{9} = ₹\ 266$$

Result : To maintain the total profit of ₹ 800 sales of 266 units are to be achieved.

Problem 15. *The sales and turnover during two periods are given below :*

Period I : sales ₹ 20 Lakhs, profit ₹ 2.00 Lakhs

Period II : sales ₹. 30 Lakhs, profit ₹ 4.00 Lakhs

Compute (i) P/V ratio (ii) The sales required to earn a profit of ₹ 5 Lakhs (iii) The profit when sales are ₹ 10,00 Lakhs. [MBA Madras]

Solution :

(*i*) $$\text{P/V ratio} = \frac{\text{Differences of Profit}}{\text{Differences of Sales}} \times 100$$

$$= \frac{2,00,000}{10,00,000} \times 100$$

$$= 20\%$$

(*ii*) **Sales required to earn a profit of ₹ 5,00,000 lakhs.**

$$\frac{\text{FC + Desired Profit}}{\text{P/V Ratio}} = \frac{2,00,000 + 5,00,000}{20/100}$$

$$= ₹\ 35,00,000$$

Now we find out fixed cost

$$\text{Given sales} \times \text{P/V ratio} = \text{Contribution}$$

$$20,00,000 \times \frac{20}{100} = 4,00,000 \text{ (FC + Profit)}$$

(Any one period sales assumed)

Less : Profit =	2,00,000
Fixed Cost =	2,00,000

(*iii*) **Find the profit**

$$\text{Given sales} \times \text{P/V ratio} = \text{Contribution (FC + Profit)}$$

$$10,00,000 \times \frac{20}{100} = 2,00,000$$

Less : Fixed Cost =	2,00,000
Profit =	0

Problem 16. *From the following data calculate :*

(*i*) *Break even point expressed in amount of sales in rupees.*

(*ii*) *Number of units that must be sold to earn a profit of ₹ 1,20,000 per year.*

(*iii*) *How many units are to be sold to earn a net income of 15% of sales ?*

Selling price per unit	*₹ 40*
Variable manufacturing cost per unit	*₹ 22*
Variable selling cost per unit	*₹ 3*
Fixed selling cost	*₹ 20,000*
Fixed factory overheads	*₹ 1,60,000*

Solution :

(*i*) $$\text{BEP} = \frac{\text{Fixed Cost}}{\text{Selling price per unit} - \text{Variable cost per unit}}$$

$$= \frac{1,80,000}{40 - 25}$$

$$= \frac{1,80,000}{15} = 12,000 \text{ units.}$$

BEP in value 12000 units × ₹ 40 = ₹ 4.80.000

NOTE : *Fixed cost*

Fixed factory overheads	= ₹	1,60,000
Fixed selling costs	= ₹	20,000
		1,80,000

Variable cost

Variable manufacturing cost per unit	= ₹	22
Variable selling cost per unit	= ₹	3
		25

(*ii*) Units to be sold to earn a profit of ₹ 1,20,000

$$\frac{\text{FC + Desired Profit}}{\text{Contribution per unit}}$$

$$\frac{1,80,000 + 1,20,000}{15} = 20,000 \text{ units}$$

(*iii*) Units are to be sold to earn a net income of 15% of sales

Number of units to be sold = N

$$N = \frac{\text{FC + Desired Profit}}{\text{Contribution per unit}}$$

$$N = \frac{1,80,000 + \frac{15}{100}(N \times \text{Rs. } 40)}{15}$$

$$15\ N = 1,80,000 + 6\ N$$

$$9\ N = 1,80,000$$

$$N = \frac{1,80,000}{9}$$

$$= 20,000 \text{ units}$$

Problem 17. *A factory engaged in manufacturing buckets is working at 40% capacity and produces 10,000 buckets per annum. The present cost break up for one bucket is as under*

	₹
Materials	*10*
Labour cost	*3.00*
Overheads	*5 (60% fixed)*

The selling price is ₹ 20 per bucket. It is decided to work the factory at 50% capacity. The selling price falls by 3%. At 90% capacity the selling price falls by 5% accompanied by a similar fall in the prices of materials.

You are required to calculate the profit at 50% and 90% capacities and also calculate the break even point for the same capacity productions. [BBM 2000]

Solution : **Profitability Statement**

Capacity level / *Number of Units*	*50%* / *12,500*		*90%* / *22,500*	
	Cost per unit (₹)	*Total cost (₹)*	*Cost per unit (₹)*	*Total cost (₹)*
Sales	19.40	2,42,500	19.00	4,27,500
Less : Variable Cost				
Material	10.00	1,25,000	9.50	2,13,750
Labour (Wages)	3.00	37,500	3.00	67,500
Variable Overheads	2.00	25.000	2.00	45,000
Total Variable Costs	15.00	1,87,500	14.50	3,26,500
Contribution (Sales – VC)	4.40	55,000	4.50	1,01,250
Less : FC	2.40	30,000	1.33	30,000
Profit	2.00	25,000	3.17	71,250
BEP in Units = $\frac{\text{FC}}{\text{Contribution per unit}}$		$\frac{30,000}{4.40}$		$\frac{30,000}{4.50}$
		6818 units		6667 units
BEP in value BEP units × Selling price		6818 units × ₹ 19.40		6667 units × ₹ 19.00
		₹ 1,32,270		₹ 1,26,373

Workings : At 50%

(*i*) Selling Price	₹	20.00
Less : 3%		.60
Selling Price at 50%		19.40

At 90%

(*ii*) Selling Price	₹	20.00
Less : 5%		1.00
Selling Price at 90%		19.00

At 90%

(*iii*) Material Cost	₹	10.00
Less : 5%		0.50
Material Cost at 90%		9.50

Problem 18. *From the following data calculate :*

(i) P/V ratio

(ii) Profit when sales are ₹ 20,000

(iii) New break even point if selling price is reduced by 20%.

Fixed expenses	*₹ 4,000*
Break even point	*₹ 10,000*

[MBA Anna]

Solution :

(*i*) P/V ratio

$$\text{BEP } (10{,}000) = \frac{\text{Fixed Cost } (4{,}000)}{\text{P/V Ratio } (X)}$$

$$X = \frac{4{,}000}{10{,}000} \times 100$$

$$= 40\%$$

(*ii*) Profit when sales are ₹ 20,000

Given sales × P/V ratio = Contribution

$$20{,}000 \times \frac{40}{100} = 8{,}000$$

Less : Fixed cost = 4,000

Profit = 4,000

(*iii*) New Break even point : Selling price is reduced by 20%

Assume selling price was = ₹ 100

Less : 20% = ₹ 20

Now, new selling price is = ₹ 80

Contribution = Sales – Variable cost

= 80 – 60

= 20

Find variable cost :

Sales = 100

Less : P/V ratio = 40 (Taken only old P/V ratio)

60

$$\text{New P/V ratio} = \frac{\text{Contribution}}{\text{Sales}} \times 100$$

$$= \frac{20}{80} \times 100$$

$$= 25\%$$

$$\text{Break even point} = \frac{\text{Fixed Cost}}{\text{P/V Ratio}}$$

$$= \frac{4{,}000}{25/100}$$

$$= 4{,}000 \times \frac{100}{25}$$

$$= ₹\ 16{,}000$$

Problem 19. *The particulars of two plants producing an identical product with the same selling price are as under.*

Capacity utilization	*Plant A* 70% (*₹ in Lakhs*)	*Plant B* 60% (*₹ in Lakhs*)
Sales	*150*	*90*
Variable cost	*105*	*75*
Fixed cost	*30*	*20*

It has been decided to merge the plant B with plant A. The additional fixed expenses involved in the merger amount to ₹ 2 lakhs.

(i) *Find the Break Even point of plant A and Plant B before merger and the Break Even point of the merger plant.*

(ii) *Find the capacity utilisation of the integrated plant required to earn a profit of ₹ 18 lakhs.* [M.Com. MKU]

Solution : **Statement of Cost**

Particulars	*Plant A* (₹)	*Plant B* (₹)	*Merge Plant*
Sales	150	90	240
Variable cost	105	75	180
Contribution	45	15	60
Fixed cost	30	20	52
P/V Ratio = $\frac{C}{S} \times 100$	$\frac{45}{150} \times 100$ = 30%	$\frac{15}{90} \times 100$ = 16.7%	$\frac{60}{240} \times 100$ = 25%
BEP = $\frac{F}{P/V\ Ratio}$	$\frac{30}{30/100}$ 100 Lakhs	$\frac{20}{16.7/100}$ 120 Lakhs	$\frac{52}{25/100}$ 208 Lakhs

$$\text{Sales of integrated plant at a profit } \frac{F + P}{P/V} = \frac{52+18}{25/100}$$

$$= 280 \text{ lakhs.}$$

Conversion of Sales into 100% capacity at both the plants

$$\text{Plant A 100\% Capacity sales} = \frac{150}{70} \times 100 = 214.29 \text{ lakhs}$$

$$\text{Plant B 100\% Capacity sales} = \frac{90}{60} \times 100 = 150.00 \text{ lakhs}$$

100% capacity of integrated plant = 214.29 + 150 = 364.29

$$\text{Capacity : Sales of 280 lakhs} = \frac{280}{364.29} \times 100 = 76.86\%$$

Thus, the plant operates at 76.86% capacity to earn a profit of ₹ 18.00 lakhs.

Problem 20. *S Ltd. furnishes you the following information relating to the half year ended on 30th June 2000.*

Fixed expenses	*₹ 45,000*
Sales value	*₹ 1,50,000*
Profit	*₹ 30,000*

During the second half of the year, the company has a projected loss of ₹ 10,000. Calculate :

(i) The break even point and margin of safety for six months ending on 30th June 2000.

(ii) Expected sales volume for second half of the year assuming that P/V ratio and fixed expenses remain constant in the second half year also.

(iii) The break even point and margin of safety for the whole year 2000.

[M.Com. 2004 PU]

Solution :

(i) Calculation of BEP

$$\text{BEP} = \frac{\text{Fixed Expenses}}{\text{P/V Ratio}}$$

$$\text{Find the P/V ratio} = \frac{\text{Contribution}}{\text{Sales}} \times 100$$

$$\text{Contribution} = \text{Fixed expenses} + \text{Profit}$$

$$= 45{,}000 + 30{,}000 = 75{,}000$$

$$\text{P/V ratio} = \frac{\text{Contribution}}{\text{Sales}} \times 100$$

$$= \frac{75{,}000}{1{,}50{,}000} \times 100$$

$$= 50\%$$

$$\text{BEP} = \frac{45{,}000}{50/100}$$

$$= 45{,}000 \times \frac{100}{50} = 90{,}000$$

$$\text{Margin of Safety} = \text{Actual Sales} - \text{BEP Sales}$$

$$= 1{,}50{,}000 - 90{,}000 = 60{,}000$$

(ii) Expected Sales for the second half of year

$$\frac{\text{Fixed Cost} + \text{Desired Profit}}{\text{P/V Ratio}}$$

But, here the company has a projected loss for second half year. So, the following changes in formula

$$\frac{\text{Fixed Cost} - \text{Loss}}{\text{P/V Ratio}}$$

$$\frac{45{,}000 - 10{,}000}{50/100} = \frac{35{,}000}{50/100} = 35{,}000 \times \frac{100}{50}$$

Expected Sales = ₹ 70,000

(*iii*) BEP for the whole year

Fixed expenses for the first half year = ₹ 45,000

Fixed expenses for the whole year (45,000 × 2) = ₹ 90,000

$$\text{BEP} = \frac{\text{Fixed Expenses}}{\text{P/V Ratio}}$$

$$= \frac{90{,}000}{50/100} = 1{,}80{,}000$$

Sales for the whole year :

First half = 1,50,000

Second half = 70,000

Sales for the whole year = 2,20,000

Margin of Safety

Actual Sales – BEP Sales = MOS

2,20,000 – 1,80,000 = 40,000

Problem 21. *The R & S. Co. furnishes you the following information :*

	First half	*Second half*
Sales (₹)	*8,10,000*	*10,26,000*
Profit earned (₹)	*21,600*	*64,800*

From the above information, you are required to compute the following, assuming that the fixed cost remains the same in both the periods.

(*i*) *P/V ratio*

(*ii*) *Fixed cost*

(*iii*) *The amount of profit or loss where sales are ₹ 6,48,000*

(*iv*) *The amount of sales required to earn a profit of ₹ 1,08,000.*

[M.Com. CA,2004 PU]

Solution :

(*i*) *P/V ratio*

$$= \frac{\text{Differences of Profit}}{\text{Differences of Sales}} \times 100$$

$$= \frac{43{,}000}{2{,}16{,}000} \times 100$$

$$= 20\%$$

(*ii*) *Fixed cost*

$$\text{Given sales} \times \text{P/V ratio} = \text{Contribution}$$

$$8{,}10{,}000 \times \frac{20}{100} = 1{,}62{,}000$$

$$\textit{Less}: \text{Profit} = 21{,}600$$

$$\text{Fixed cost} = 1{,}40{,}400$$

(*iii*) *Amount of profit or loss : Sales are ₹ 6,48,000*

$$\text{Given sales} \times \text{P/V ratio} = \text{Contribution}$$

$$6{,}48{,}000 \times \frac{20}{100} = 1{,}29{,}600$$

$$\textit{Less}: \text{Fixed cost} = 1{,}40{,}400$$

$$\text{Loss} = 10{,}800$$

(*iv*) *Amount of Sales*

$$\frac{\text{FC + Given Profit}}{\text{P/V Ratio}} = \frac{1{,}40{,}400 + 1{,}08{,}000}{20/100}$$

$$= ₹\ 12{,}42{,}000$$

Problem 22. *You are given the following data for the year 1998 of the company.*

Variable cost	₹	*6,00,000*
Fixed cost	₹	*4,00,000*
Net profit	₹	*2,00,000*
Sales	₹	*12,00,000*

Find (i) P/V ratio (ii) BEP (iii) Profit when sales amounted to ₹ 14,00,000 (iv) sales required to earn a profit of ₹ 6,00,000.

Solution : **Marginal Cost Statement**

$$\text{Sales} = 12{,}00{,}000$$

$$\textit{Less}: \text{Variable cost} = 6{,}00{,}000$$

$$\text{Contribution} = 6{,}00{,}000$$

$$\textit{Less}: \text{Fixed cost} = 4{,}00{,}000$$

$$\text{Profit} = 2{,}00{,}000$$

(*i*)

$$\text{P/V Ratio} = \frac{\text{Contribution}}{\text{Sales}} \times 100$$

$$= \frac{6{,}00{,}000}{12{,}00{,}000} \times 100 = 50\%$$

(*ii*)

$$\text{BEP} = \frac{\text{Fixed Cost}}{\text{P/V Ratio}}$$

$$= \frac{4{,}00{,}000}{50/100} = 8{,}00{,}000$$

(*iii*) Profit, when sales amounted to ₹ 14,00,000

Given sales × P/V ratio = Contribution

$$= 14,00,000 \times \frac{50}{100}$$

Contribution = 7,00,000 [FC + Profit]

Less : Fixed cost = 4,00,000

Profit = 3,00,000

(*iv*) Sales, required to earn a profit of ₹ 6,00,000

$$= \frac{\text{Fixed Cost + Desired Profit}}{\text{P/V Ratio}}$$

$$= \frac{3,00,000 + 6,00,000}{50/100}$$

$$= 9,00,000 \times \frac{100}{50}$$

= ₹ 18,00,000

Problem 23. *Royal hotel has annual fixed costs applicable to rooms of ₹ 15,00,000 for a 300 room hotel with average daily room rates of ₹ 40 and average variable costs of ₹ 6 for each room rented. The hotel operates 365 days a year. Income tax rate is 30%. You are required to find the number of rooms the hotel must rent to earn a net income after tax of ₹ 10,00,000 and compute the break even point in terms of number of rooms rented.*

[MCA Madras]

Solution : **Profitability Statement**

Desired profit after tax = ₹ 10,00,000

Less : Tax rate 30%

$\left[10,00,000 \times \frac{30}{70}\right]$ = 4,28,571

Total expected profit = 14,28,571

Fixed cost = 15,00,000

Contribution = 29,28,571

(FC + Expected profit)

Contribution per unit = Sales – Variable cost

= 40 – 6 = 34

Number of rooms in the hotel must be rented to earn a net income

$$= \frac{\text{Total contribution}}{\text{Contribution per unit}}$$

$$= \frac{29,28,571}{34} = 86,134 \text{ room days.}$$

$$\text{Break even point in units} = \frac{\text{FC}}{\text{Contribution per unit}}$$

$$= \frac{15,00,000}{34}$$

= 44,118 room days

Problem 24. *Rams & Co. manufactures and sells chairs, tables and cabinets. The cost and sales data of the company are*

Product	*Selling price per unit (₹)*	*Variable cost per unit (₹)*	*% of sales value of each product to total*
Chairs	*90*	*70*	*20*
Table	*110*	*90*	*30*
Cabinet	*150*	*110*	*50*

The annual fixed cost is ₹ 20,000. The maximum production and sales capacity is ₹ 1,50,000. At present the company is operating at 80% of its capacity.

(a) Calculate the BEP of the company.

(b) Calculate the present annual profit.

(c) What would be the effect on profit if it utilizes its full capacity.

(d) What would be the net effect on the profit if it operates only at 50% capacity assuming the product mix remains unchanged. [MBA Madras]

Solution :

Workings : *Calculation of Sales and Variable costs*

(*i*) *Sales* ₹

Chairs = 1,50,000 × 20/100 = 30,000

Tables = 1,50,000 × 30/100 = 45,000

Cabinets = 1,50,000 × 50/100 = 75,000

(*ii*) *Variable cost*

Chairs = 30,000 × 70/100 = 23,333

Tables = 45,000 × 90/110 = 36,818

Cabinets = 75,000 × 110/150 = 55,000

	Chairs	*Tables*	*Cabinets*	*Total*
Sales	30,000	45,000	75,000	1,50,000
Less : VC	23,334	36,818	55,000	1,15,152
Contribution	6,667	8,182	20,000	34,849
Less : Fixed cost	—	—	—	20,000
Present profit				14,849

$$BEP = \frac{\text{Fixed Cost}}{\text{Contribution}} \times \text{Total Sales}$$

$$= \frac{20,000}{34,848} \times 1,50,000 = ₹\ 86,088$$

Profitability Statement of different capacity operations

	50%	*100%*	*80%*
Sales	93,750	1,87,500	1,50,000
Less : VC	57,576	1,43,940	1,15,152
Contribution	36,174	43,560	34,848
Less : Fixed cost	20,000	20,000	20,000
Profit	16,174	23,560	14,848

If the firm works at 100% capacity, the net profit will be ₹ 23,560.

If the firm works at 50% capacity the profit will be ₹ 16,174.

Problem 25. *A company produces and markets industrial containers and packing cases. Due to competition the company proposes to reduce the selling price. If the present level of profit is to be maintained, indicate the number of units to be sold if the proposed reduction in selling price is (i) 5% (ii) 10% (iii) 15%.*

The following additional information is available

Present sales (30,000 units)	*3,00,000*
Variable cost (30,000 units)	*1,80,000*
Contribution	*1,20,000*
Less : fixed cost	*70,000*
Profit	*50,000*

Solution :

Present sales = 3,00,000

$$\text{Selling Price} = \frac{\text{Sale Value}}{\text{Number of Units}}$$

$$= \frac{3,00,000}{30,000} = ₹\ 10$$

Present selling price is ₹ 10.

(*i*) $5\%\ \text{Reduction} = 10 - \left[\frac{5}{100} \times 10\right] = 9.50$

(*ii*) $10\%\ \text{Reduction} = 10 - \left[\frac{10}{100} \times 10\right] = 9.00$

(*iii*) $15\%\ \text{Reduction} = 10 - \left[\frac{15}{100} \times 10\right] = 8.50$

Contribution at various levels of selling price :

Percentage of reduction at	5%	10%	15%
Selling price	10.00	10.00	10.00
Less : Reduction	.50	1.00	1.50
Present selling price	9.50	9.00	8.50
Less : Variable cost	6.00	6.00	6.00
Contribution	3.50	3.00	2.50

Find the total contribution in order to maintain the present level of profit :

Present sales = ₹ 3,00,000

Less : Variable cost = ₹ 1,80,000

Total Contribution = 1,20,000

Number of units to be sold to earn a total contribution of ₹ 1,20,000 to maintain the present level of profits.

(*a*) At 5% Reduction $= ₹\ \frac{1,20,000}{3.50} = 34,286$ units.

(*b*) At 10% Reduction $= ₹\ \frac{1,20,000}{3} = 40,000$ units.

(*c*) At 15% Reduction $= ₹\ \frac{1,20,000}{2.50} = 48,000$ units.

Problem 26. *The following information is given about the Kasturi Rangas & Co. as on December 31 1999.*

Particulars	₹
Cost of goods sold	20,00,000
Sales	1,40,00,000
Advertising expenses	70,00,000
Warehousing expenses	10,00,000
Transportation expenses	10,00,000

The company has two products. Super which sells for ₹ 100 per unit and Grand, which sells for ₹ 50 per unit. During the year, sales were as follows : Super 80,000 units and Grand 1,20,000 units. Production costs (Cost of goods sold) were as follows : Super ₹ 20 per unit; and Grand ₹ 3.33 per unit. Advertising expenses were approximately 50% of the sales of each product. Warehousing expenses is a variable based on the number of units sold. Transportation costs were incurred equally for each product. You are required to

(i) Compute the contribution to net earnings for Super.

(ii) Compute the contribution to net earnings for Grand.

(iii) Compute the total unit cost (production and marketing costs) of Super.

(iv) Compute the total unit cost (production and marketing costs) of Grand.

[MBA Madras]

Solution :

Profitability Statement or Statement of Contribution to Net Earnings

(*i*), (*ii*)

Particulars	*Super* (₹)	*Grand* (₹)
Sales (*i*)	80,00,000	60,00,000
Less : Variable cost :		
Production cost of goods sold	16,00,000	4,00,000
Warehousing expenses	4,00,000	6,00,000
Total variable cost (*ii*)	20,00,000	10,00,000
Contribution (*iii*) [S – V.C.] (*i*) – (*ii*)	60,00,000	50,00,000
Less : Fixed cost		
Advertising Expenses	40,00,000	30,00,000
Transport Expenses	5,00,000	5,00,000
Total Fixed cost (*iv*)	45,00,000	35,00,000
Profit [Contribution – TFC]	15,00,000	15,00,000
Contribution to Net earnings :	400%	333.33%
Formula = $\frac{\text{Contribution}}{\text{Net earnings}} \times 100$		

Workings :

Super Grand

(*a*) Production cost : 80,000 × 20 = 16,00,000 – 4,00,000 = [1,20,000 × 3.33]

(*b*) Warehousing cost :

Total units = 2,00,000

$$\text{Super} = \frac{10,00,000}{2,00,000} \times 80,000$$

$$= ₹\ 4,00,000$$

$$\text{Grand} = \frac{10,00,000}{2,00,000} \times 1,20,000 = 6,00,000$$

(*c*) Advertising Expenses :

Super 50% of Sales

$$80,00,000 \times \frac{50}{100} = 40,00,000$$

Grand 50% of Sales

$$60,00,000 \times \frac{50}{100} = 30,00,000$$

Total Advertising expenses = 70,00,000

(*d*) Transport Expenses : (Distributed equally to both the products)

Super = 5,00,000
Grand = 5,00,000

Total = 10,00,000

Statement of Cost per unit

Particulars	*Super (₹)*	*Grand (₹)*
Sales units	80,000	1,20,000
Sales (₹)	80,00,000	60,00,000
Costs		
Production cost	16,00,000	4,00,000
Advertising expenses	40,00,000	30,00,000
Warehouse expenses	4,00,000	6,00,000
Transport expenses	5,00,000	5,00,000
Total cost	65,00,000	45,00,000

(*iii*), (*iv*) Cost per unit

$$\frac{\text{Total Cost}}{\text{Number of Units}} \qquad \frac{65,00,000}{80,000 \text{ Units}} \qquad \frac{45,00,000}{1,20,000 \text{ Units}}$$

₹ 81.25 ₹ 37.50

Problem 27. *Coimbatore Computers Ltd. decides to effect a 10% reduction in the price of its product because it is felt that such a step may lead to greater volume of sales. It is anticipated that there are no prospects of a change in total fixed costs and variable cost per unit. The directors wish to maintain net profits at the present level.*

The following information has been obtained from its books :

Sales : 10,000 units ₹ 2,00,000
Variable cost : ₹ 15 per unit
Fixed cost : ₹ 40,000

How does the management proceed to implement this decision ? [MCA 1998 Madras]

Solution :

Marginal Cost Statement

Particulars	*Per unit* ₹	*Total* ₹
Sales (10,000 units)	20.00	2,00,000
Less : Variable cost	15.00	1,50,000
Contribution	5.00	50,000
Less : Fixed cost		40,000
Profit		10,000

$$\text{P/V ratio} = \frac{\text{Contribution}}{\text{Sales}} \times 100$$

$$= \frac{5}{20} \times 100 = 25\%$$

$$\text{BEP} = \frac{\text{Fixed Cost}}{\text{P/V Ratio}}$$

$$= \frac{40,000}{25/100} \times 1,60,000$$

Effect of change of 10% reduction in selling price

Selling Price =	20.00
Less : 10% =	2.00
Selling price after reduction =	18.00
Less : Variable cost =	15.00
Contribution =	3.00

$$\text{P/V ratio} = \frac{\text{Contribution}}{\text{Sales}} \times 100$$

$$= \frac{3}{18} \times 100 = 16.67\%$$

$$\text{BEP} = \frac{\text{Fixed Cost}}{\text{P/V Ratio}}$$

$$= \frac{40,000}{16.67/100} \times ₹\ 3,00,000$$

Sales to earn present level of profit of ₹ 10,000

$$= \frac{\text{Fixed Cost + Desired Profit}}{\text{P/V Ratio}}$$

$$= \frac{40,000 + 10,000}{16.67/100}$$

$$= ₹\ 3,00,000$$

The management decided to implement this decision because the break even sales will be increased to ₹ 2,40,000. If the company wants to maintain the present level of profit *i.e.*, ₹ 10,000, it should take steps to increase the sales amounting to ₹ 3,00,000.

TEST PROBLEMS

1. The following figures are extracted from the books of Vijay Irons Ltd. for the years 1989 and 1990 whose capacity is 10,000 irons p.a

	Per unit.
	₹
Direct material	3.50
Direct labour	0.50
Fixed overhead	2.00
Selling price	8.00

Production in 1989 was 10,000 units and in 1990 also it was 10,000 units. Sales was 8,000 units in 1989 and 12,000 units in 1990.

Prepare cost statement assuming that the company uses:

(*a*) absorption costing (*b*) Marginal costing

[Madras B.Com. March 1987]

[Ans.

Income statement (under absorption costing)

	1989		*1990*	
Particulars	*Units*	*Total ₹*	*Units*	*Total ₹*
Cost of sales	8000	48000	12000	72000
Profit	8000	16000	12000	24000
Sales	**8000**	**64000**	**12000**	**96000**

Income statement (under marginal costing)

	1989		1990	
Particulars	*Units*	*Total ₹*	*Units*	*Total ₹*
Profit	–	12000	–	28000

2. A company is considering expansion. Fixed costs amount to ₹ 4,20,000 and are expected to increase by ₹ 1,25,000 when plant expansion is completed. The present plant capacity is 80,000 units a year. Capacity will increase by 50% with the expansion. Variable costs, currently ₹ 680 per unit, are expected to go down by ₹ 0.40. per unit with the expansion. The current selling price is ₹ 16 per unit and is expected to remain the same under each alternative.

What are the break even points under either alternative? Which alternative is better and why.

[Madras, M.com., May 1989]

[Ans. Current Break-even point (in rupees) ₹ 7,30,435,
(2) Break-even point after expansion ₹ 9,08,333]

3. Raviraj Ltd. manufactures and sells four types of products under the brand names A, B, C and D. The sales mix in value comprises 33 1/3 %, 41 2/3%, 16 2/3% and 8 1/3% of products A, B, C and D respectively. The total budgeted sales (100%) are ₹ 60,000 per month.

Operating costs are

Variable cost:

Product	A 60% of Selling price
	B 68% of Selling price
	C 80% of Selling price
	D 40% of Selling price

Fixed cost: ₹ 14,700 per month

Calculate the break-even point for the products on an overall basis and also the B.E. Sales of individual products. Show the proof for your answer.

[Madras, B.Com(ICEO) May 2003; B.Com., Sep. 1989]

[Ans. B.E.P = ₹ 42,000, Sales = Nil]

4. From the following information relating to palani Bros. Ltd., you are required to find out (*a*) P/V Ratio (*b*) Break-even point, (*c*) Profit, (*d*) Margin of safety (*e*) Volume of sales to earn profit of ₹ 6,000.

	₹
Total fixed costs	4,500
Total variable cost	7,500
Total Sales	15,000

[Madras, B.Com. (AF), B.Com(CS), B.Com(Gen) April 2008; B.Com., B.B.A., etc. nov. 2007; 1st M.Com. Nov. 2006; Nov. 2005; B.B.A. (old) Nov, 2006; B.Com. (CS) April 2006; B.Com. Oct. 2000; M.Com. May 1995 (ICE)]

[Ans. (1) P/V Ratio = 50%, (2) BEP = ₹ 9000, (3) Profit = ₹ 3000, (4) Margin of Cost ₹ 6000 (5) Volume of Sales ₹ 21000]

5. A toy manufacturer earns an average net profit of ₹ 3 per piece in a selling price of ₹ 15 by producing and selling 60,000 pieces at 60% of the potential capacity. Composition of his cost of sales is:

Direct materials	–	₹ 4
Direct wages	–	₹ 1
Works overhead	–	₹ 6 [50% fixed]
Sales overhead	–	₹ 1 [25% varying]

During the current year, he intends to produce the same number but anticipates that:

1. His fixed charge will go up by 10%
2. Rates of direct labour will increase by 20%
3. Rates of direct material will increase by 5%
4. Selling price cannot be increased.

Under these circumstances he obtains an order for a further 20% of his capacity. What minimum price will you recommend for accepting the order to ensure the manufacturer an overall profit to ₹ 1,80,500?

[Madras, B.Com., B.B.A., (etc) Nov. 2007; M.Com., (ICE) (PBF) Oct. 2005; M.Com. II year Oct. 2001; M.Com., May 1998 (ICE); October 1989]

[Ans: (1) Calculation of cash and profit of current year, with increased costs, on 60,000 units: profit = 1,33,500 (2) Calculation of required profit from new order = 47,000] (3) Calculation of minimum price to be charged for the new order = ₹ 11 per unit]

6. From the following details, prepare a marginal cost statement and income statement as per absorption costing technique.

	A ₹	B ₹	C ₹
Direcct materials	2,500	10,000	1,000
Direct labour	3,000	3,000	500
Factory overhead:			
Fixed	1,000	500	500
Variable	1,300	3,000	1,500
Selling overhead:			
Fixed	500	300	200
Variable	700	2,000	1,000
Sales	10,000	20,000	5,000

[Madras, B.A. Corp, C&M March 1991]

[**Ans.** 1. Marginal Cost – A: ₹ 7,500; B: ₹ 18,000 C: ₹ 4,000;
2. Contribution – A: ₹ 2,500; B: ₹ 2,000 C: ₹ 1,000;
Total fixed cost – ₹ 3,000; Total profit; ₹ 2,500]

Absorption costing	A	B	C
Total	₹ 9,000	₹ 18,800	₹ 4,700
Profit	₹ 1,000	₹ 1,200	₹ 300

7. The following information is given by the companies ABC and XYZ.

Particulars	*ABC* ₹	*XYZ* ₹
Units produced and sold	85,000	85,000
Revenues	1,70,000	1,70,000
Fixed Costs	80,000	34,000
Operating income	51,000	51,000
Variable Costs	34,000	85,000

Find the break-even point of each company both in units as well as in value.

[Madras, B.C.S. (ICE) May 2003]

[**Ans.** (1) Breakeven units : ABC : 50,000 units; XYZ : 34,000 units
(2) Breakeven value : ABC : ₹ 1,00,000; XYZ : ₹ 68,000]

8. From the following data find out the break-even point and break-even sale. If the selling price is reacted to ₹ 18 per unit what will be the break-even point and new break-even sales?

Budgeted output	–	1,00,000 units
Fixed expenses	–	₹ 5,00,000

Variable expenses	–	₹ 10 per unit
Selling price	–	₹ 20 per unit

[Madras B.A, Corp. C&M (ICE) May, 1998]

[**Ans.** BEP : 50,000 units; BE Sales : ₹ 10,00,000; If selling price is reduced to ₹ 18; BEP: 62,500 units; BE sales: ₹ 11,25,000]

9. ABC & Co. has just been formed. The owners have a special process which will enable them to produce a unique product 'Z' the demand for which is uncertain. Their estimated costs are.

	₹
Material per unit	2
Labour per unit	6
Variable manufacturing expenses per unit	3
Variable selling expenses per unit	1
Fixed manufacturing expenses	24,000
Fixed administration and selling expenses	72,000

(*a*) If the selling price is ₹ 20 per unit how many units they have to sell to:

1. break even, 2. make a profit of ₹ 32,000

(*b*) If the demand for the product is 10,000 units what selling price must they charge in order to :

1. break-even 2. make a profit of ₹ 24,000

[Madras, M.Com., (ICE) (PBFO) Oct. 2004; B.A. Corp., May 1996; C&M (ICE)]

[**Ans:** (1) (*a*) 12,000 units,(*b*) 16,000 units (2) (*a*) ₹ 21.6 per unit (*b*) 24 per unit]

❑❑❑

17

Relevant Cost for Decision Making

DECISION MAKING

Decision making is the process of choosing the best course of action among the various alternative courses since if there is no choice, there is no decision to take. Generally, a decision always focuses on the future prediction. The aim of the decision maker is therefore to select the best course of action for the future.

Relevant Costs

A cost that is relevant to a decision is called relevant cost. In an organisation the decision maker just makes use of relevant costs. In other words, costs are relevant if they guide the executive towards the decision that harmonises with top management's objectives.

Differential Cost

Differential cost means the change in costs due to change in the level of activity or pattern or method of production. Simply, differential cost is the result of an alternative course of action.

COST CONCEPTS IN DECISION MAKING

Certain concepts which are generally used in the analysis of cost for decision making are listed below.

(*i*) Marginal cost
(*ii*) Out of pocket cost
(*iii*) Differential costs
(*iv*) Sunk costs
(*v*) Opportunity costs
(*vi*) Replacement cost
(*vii*) Avoidable and unavoidable costs
(*viii*) Imputed costs
(*ix*) Relevant costs and irrelevant costs.

STEPS INVOLVED IN DECISION MAKING

The following steps are involved in decision making process.

(*i*) Problem identification
(*ii*) Identifying alternatives
(*iii*) Evaluating Quantitative factors

(*iv*) Examining Qualitative factors
(*v*) Obtaining further details if necessary
(*vi*) Selection of the best alternative.

AREAS OF DECISION MAKING

The executives of the organisation or the decision maker of the concern has to adopt the above steps in the following important areas of decision.

(*i*) Make or buy decisions
(*ii*) Sell or process decisions
(*iii*) Special order decisions
(*iv*) Incremental analysis
(*v*) Decision regarding further processing of joint/by products
(*vi*) Sales mix decisions
(*vii*) Additional shift decisions
(*viii*) Adding or dropping product line decisions
(*ix*) Plant closing down decisions

(*i*) *Make or Buy Decisions.* A firm may be producing some products, or tools or parts by itself. The same products or tools may be available from the outside suppliers. The management can take decision in this regard comparing the price that has to be paid and the saving that can be effected on cost.

(*ii*) *Sell or Process Decisions.* An organisation can sell its product when it has been partly processed or it is sent for further processing before selling it. When a product passes various stages of manufacturing operation, it may be a marketable product at a number of different points along the way. Under this type of industrial sector, the company has an option to sell the product at various stages of completion. Under the sell or process decisions, incremental analysis guides the management to take correct decisions.

(*iii*) *Special Order Decisions.* Large Scale purchasers may place huge orders at a price less than the customer's sale price on receiving a bulk order from the foreign companies. A decision has to be taken now whether to accept the order or to reject it. Such an order can prove beneficial to the company when it is working below full production capacity and the price offered results in incremental revenue which is higher than the differential costs.

(*iv*) *Incremental Analysis.* Incremental analysis refers to the changes in costs or revenue due to changes in the level of activity or pattern or method of production. Under the incremental analysis, the organisation has to get either incremental revenue and cost or decremental revenue and cost. Based upon the incremental revenue only, the management can take a decision.

(*v*) *Decision Regarding Further Processing of Joint or By-product.* Certain industries produce two or more products of almost more or less equal value which are simultaneously produced from the same manufacturing process and from the same raw material. They are known as joint products.

The term by-product refers to one or more products of relatively small value that are produced simultaneously with a product of greater value.

Generally, the management has to take decision regarding further processing of joint products or by-products after the split off. This type of decision is taken on the basis of comparison of differential cost and incremental revenue.

(*vi*) *Sales Mix Decisions.* Sales mix is the ratio in which various products are produced and sold. Generally when an industry manufactures more than one product, it has to face the problem of which product mix gives maximum profit. The best product mix is that which yields the maximum profit. Those products which give maximum contribution are to be retained and their production increased. Automatically sales is also increased. Based upon the results of p/v ratio and break even points only the organisation can take sales mix decisions.

(*vii*) *Additional Shift Decisions.* Any organisation, if it wants to go for the introduction of additional shift, incurs some additional cost. In this aspect, the additional cost should be compared with the additional revenue. So, the management can take decision on the basis of the net effect on the profit earned by the company due to this additional shift.

(*viii*) *Adding or Dropping Product Line Decisions.* Some time, a manufacturing company may decide to add some new product or delete the existing product from the production line. In order to arrive at the correct decision in this regard, management has to find the profitable position of the company based upon the comparative analysis of differential cost and incremental revenue.

(*ix*) *Plant Closing Down Decisions.* Sometimes a manufacturing organisation should decide to close its business either on temporary basis or permanent basis. Closing down of business arises because closing is better than operating business at loss. In this situation, marginal costing assists the management to take suitable actions.

TEST QUESTIONS

1. What is meant by Decision making ?
2. What is Differential Costs ?
3. What is meant by Relevant Costs ?
4. What do you understand by relevant cost for Decision making ?
5. Describe the various steps involved in Rational Decision making.
6. "The role of Management Accountant in deciding among alternative counsel action is crucial". Explain this statement with special reference to special order acceptance.
7. What factors would you take into consideration in closing or suspending the business activity ?
8. Discuss the basic differences between differential costing and marginal costing. State the applications of differential costing.

PROBLEMS AND SOLUTIONS

Problem 1. *HR Ltd., makes a single product which sells for ₹ 30 per unit and there is a great demand for the product. The variable cost of the product is ₹ 16 as detailed below.*

	₹
Direct material	*8*
Direct Labour (2 Hrs)	*4*
Variable overhead	*4*
Total cost	*16*

The labour force is currently working at full capacity and no extra time can be made available. Mr. Goyal, a customer has approached the company with a request for the manufacture of a special order at ₹ 8,000. The cost of the order would be ₹ 3,000 for direct material and 600 labour hours will be required and variable overhead per hour should be ₹2. Should the order be accepted or not. [MBA Madras]

Solution :

Sales Price = ₹ 30

Order amount = ₹ 8,000

No. of unit $\left[\dfrac{8{,}000}{30}\right] = 267$

Cost details per unit

Direct material $\dfrac{3{,}000}{267} = 11.23$

Direct labour $\left(\dfrac{4}{2}\times 600 = 1{,}200\right)\dfrac{1{,}200}{267} = 4.49$

Variable Expenses (600 × 2 = 1,200) = 4.49

Total variable cost per unit = 20.21

Total variable cost for 267 units × ₹ 20.21 = ₹	5,396
Sales value at special order = ₹	8,000
Less : variable cost = ₹	5,396
Contribution = ₹	2,604

₹ 2,604 is treated as an Additional Contribution and it will be an income to the concern. So, the order may be accepted.

Problem 2. *A Company has a capacity of producing 1,00,000 units of a certain product in a month. The sales department reports that the following schedule of sales price is possible.*

Volume of production	*Selling price per unit*
60%	*0.90*
70%	*0.80*
80%	*0.75*
90%	*0.67*
100%	*0.61*

The variable cost of manufacture between these levels is ₹ 0.15 per unit. Fixed cost is ₹ 40,000.

You are required to prepare a statement showing incremental revenue and differential cost at each stage. At which volume of production, will the profit be maximum ?

If there is a bulk order at ₹ 0.40 per unit for the balance capacity over the maximum profit volume for export and the price quoted will not affect the internal sale. Will you advise to accept this bid and why ? [MBA Anna]

Solution :

(*a*) **Statement of incremental revenue and differential cost**

Capacity level %	*Units Nos.*	*Variable Cost* ₹	*Fixed Cost* ₹	*Total Cost* ₹	*Differential Cost* ₹	*Sales or Revenue* ₹	*Incremental Revenue* ₹
60	60,000	9,000	40,000	49,000	—	54,000	—
70	70,000	10,500	40,000	50,500	1,500	56,000	2,000
80	80,000	12,000	40,000	52,000	1,500	60,000	4,000
90	90,000	13,500	40,000	53,500	1,500	60,300	300
100	1,00,000	15,000	40,000	55,000	1,500	61,000	700

Based upon the above calculation 80% capacity level is the maximum profit.

(*b*) **Income from the bulk order :**

20,000 units @ .40 paise per unit	**8,000**
***Less :* Additional Variable cost (20,000 × .15)**	**3,000**
Additional Net Profit	**5000**

It is decided to accept the bulk order. But, fixed costs are not considered because fixed cost will be constant upto the production level of 1,00,000 units. This is the budgeted production.

Problem 3. *The Chennai Machinery & Co. manufactured and sold 1000 calculators last year at a price of ₹ 800 each. The cost structure of a calculator is as follows.*

	₹
Material	*200*
Labour	*100*
Variable cost	*50*
Marginal cost	*350*
Factory overhead (Fixed)	*200*
Total cost	*550*
Profit	*250*
Sale price	*800*

Due to heavy competition, price has to be reduced to ₹ 750 for the coming year. Assuming no change in costs, state the number of calculators that would have to be sold at the new price to ensure the same amount of total profits as that of the last year.

[B.Com., Madras]

Solution :

Profit for 1,000 calculators 1000 × 250 = ₹ 2,50,000

$$\text{Computation of P/V ratio} = \frac{\text{Contribution}}{\text{Sales}} \times 100$$

$$\text{Contribution} = \text{Sales} - \text{V.C.}$$

$$= 750 - 350 = 400$$

$$\text{P/V ratio} = \frac{400}{750} \times 100 = \mathbf{53.33\%}$$

Sales required to earn a profit of ₹ 2,50,000

$$= \frac{\text{Fixed Cost + Profit}}{\text{P/V Ratio}}$$

$$= \frac{2,00,000 + 2,50,000}{53.33/100}$$

$$= ₹8,43,802$$

$$\text{Sales in units} = \frac{8,43,802}{750} = 1125 \text{ calculator.}$$

If the company is to sell 1,125 calculators only, it will earn the last year's total profit of 2,50,000 even in the reduction of selling price at ₹ 750/-.

Problem 4. *Following information has been made available from the records of KRS Ltd, manufacturing spare parts.*

	Cost per unit
Direct material	₹
X	8.00
Y	6.00
Direct wages	
X	24 hours @ 25 paise per hour
Y	16 hours@ 25 paise per hour.
Variable overheads	150% of wages
Fixed overheads	₹ 750
Selling price of X	₹ 25
Selling price of Y	₹ 20

The directors want to be acquainted with the desirability of adopting any one of the following alternative sales mixes in the budget for the next period.

(a) 250 units of X and 250 units of Y.

(b) 400 units of Y only.

(c) 400 units of X and 100 units of Y.

(d) 150 units of X and 350 units of Y.

State which of the alternative sales mixes you would recommend to the management.

[MBA, Anna Dec. 2003] [B.Com. Madurai]

Solution : **Marginal Cost Statement**

Particulars	*Product X*	*Product Y*
	₹	₹
Direct Material	8	6
Direct wages	6	4
Variable overheads	9	6
Total variable cost	23	16
Selling price	25	20
Less : Variable cost	23	16
Contribution	2	4

Alternative Sales Mix Decisions

(*a*) 250 units of X and 250 units of Y

		₹
Contribution :	Product X, 250 × ₹ 2 =	500
	Product Y, 250 × ₹ 4 =	1,000
		1,500
	Less : Fixed cost =	750
	Profit	750

(*b*) 400 units of product Y

Contribution :	Product Y : 400 × ₹4 =	1,600
	Less : Fixed cost =	750
	Profit	850

(*c*) 400 units of product X and 100 units of Product Y

Contribution :	Product X : 400 × ₹ 2 =	800
	Product Y : 100 × ₹ 4 =	400
		1,200
	Less : Fixed cost =	750
	Profit	450

(*d*) 150 units of Product X and 350 units of Product Y

Contribution :	Product X : 150 × ₹ 2 =	300
	Product Y : 350 × ₹ 4 =	1,400
		1,700
	Less : Fixed cost =	750
	Profit	950

Result and Decision :

Among the four different sales mixes, (*d*) is the most profitable since it gives the maximum profit of ₹ 950/-. So, it should be recommended.

Problem 5. *The management of a company finds that the cost of making a component part is ₹ 10. While the same is available in the market at ₹ 9 with an assurance of continuous supply.*

Give a suggestion whether to make or buy this part. Give also your view in case the supplier reduces the price from ₹ 9 to 8.00.

The cost information is as follows

Material	*₹ 3.50*
Direct Labour	*₹ 4.00*
Other variable expenses	*₹ 1.00*
Fixed expenses	*₹ 1.50*
Total	*10.00*

Solution :

In order to take decision regarding the making or buying the component part, fixed cost should not be considered. Because these will be incurred even if the part is produced or not. But, if the part is produced, the following additional costs should be incurred.

	₹
Material	3.50
Direct Labour	4.00
Other variable Expenses	1.00
Total cost	8.50

It is available in the market for ₹ 9.00. But, the production cost of the part is ₹ 8.50. So, the company gets contribution of .50 paise per part (9.00 – 8.50) even if it manufactures by itself.

If the same is available in the market at ₹ 8.00, the company should not manufacture the part. It is better to buy the part in the market. As per the above calculation it is better if the company manufacture the part itself.

Problem 6. *The management of a company is thinking whether it should drop one item from the product line and replace it with another. Given below are present cost and output data.*

Product	*Price*	*Variable Costs Per unit*	*Percentage of sales*
	₹	₹	₹
Book shelf	*60*	*40*	*30%*
Table	*100*	*60*	*20%*
Bed	*200*	*120*	*50%*

Total fixed costs per year ₹ 7,50,000

Sales ₹ 25,00,000

The change under consideration consists in dropping the line of Tables and adding the line of cabinets. If this change is made, the manufacturer forecasts the following costs and output data.

Product	*Price*	*Variable Costs Per unit (A)*	*Percentage of sales*
	₹	₹	₹
Book shelf	*60*	*40*	*15%*
Cabinet	*160*	*60*	*10%*
Bed	*200*	*120*	*40%*

Total fixed costs per year ₹ 7,50,000

Sales ₹ 26,00,000

Should this proposal be accepted or not ? comment. [M.Com. Adapted]

Solution : Comparative Profitability Statement

	Book Shelves	*Tables* ₹	*Beds* ₹	*Total* ₹	*Book Shelf*	*Cabinets* ₹	*Beds* ₹	*Total* ₹
Sales	7,50,000	5,00,000	12,50,000	25,00,000	13,00,000	2,60,000	10,40,000	26,00,000
Less Variable cost	5,00,000	3,00,000	7,50,000	15,50,000	8,66,667	97,500	62,4,000	15,88,166
Contribution	2,50,000	2,00,000	5,00,000	9,50,000	4,33,333	1,62,500	4,16,000	10,11,833
Less fixed cost				7,50,000				7,50,000
Profit (Contribution - fixed cost)				2,00,000				2,16,000

Comments : Based on the above calculation, the manufacturer will stand to gain in case he drops the production of tables in preference to cabinets. But, the demand for cabinets should not be a temporary period.

Workings :

Existing Situation — *Sales* — *Variable costs*

Book shelve $25{,}00{,}000 \times \frac{30}{100}$ = ₹ 7,50,000 ; $7{,}50{,}000 \times \frac{40}{60}$ = ₹ 5,00,000

Tables $25{,}00{,}000 \times \frac{20}{100}$ = ₹ 5,00,000 ; $5{,}00{,}000 \times \frac{60}{100}$ = ₹ 3,00,000

Beds : $25{,}00{,}000 \times \frac{50}{100}$ = ₹ 12,50,000 ; $12{,}50{,}000 \times \frac{120}{200}$ = ₹ 7,50,000

Proposed Situation — *Sales* — *Variable Costs*

Book shelves $26{,}00{,}000 \times \frac{50}{100}$ = ₹ 13,00,000 ; $13{,}00{,}000 \times \frac{40}{60}$ = ₹ 8,66,667

Cabinets $26{,}00{,}000 \times \frac{10}{100}$ = ₹ 2,60,000 ; $26{,}00{,}000 \times \frac{60}{100}$ = ₹ 97,500

Beds : $26,00,000 \times \frac{40}{100}$ $10,40,000 \times \frac{120}{200}$

= ₹ 10,40,000 = ₹ 6,24,000

Problem 7. *Modern Cutting Machines & Co manufactures hand operated cutting machines. Prepare a schedule showing the differential costs and incremental revenue at each stage from the following data. At what volume the company should set its level of production ?*

Output (No. in lakhs)	*Selling price (per machine)*	*Total semifixed cost (₹ in lakhs)*	*Total variable cost (₹ in lakhs)*	*Total fixed cost (₹ in lakhs)*
0.60	*240*	*30*	*83.6*	*28.4*
1.20	*220*	*30*	*163.6*	*28.4*
1.80	*200*	*34*	*255.6*	*28.4*
2.40	*180*	*34*	*315.6*	*28.4*
3.00	*160*	*40*	*355.6*	*28.4*
3.60	*140*	*40*	*380.6*	*28.4*

[MBA Anna]

Solution :

Schedule showing the differential costs and incremental revenues

Output (No. in lakhs)	*Selling Price Per Machine (₹)*	*Sales Value ₹ (in Lakhs)*	*Incremental Revenue ₹ (in Lakhs)*	*Semi Fixed Cost ₹ (in Lakhs)*	*Variable Cost ₹ (in Lakhs)*	*Fixed Cost ₹ (in Lakhs)*	*Total Cost ₹ (in Lakhs)*	*Differential Cost ₹ (in Lakhs)*
0.60	240	144	—	30.0	83.6	28.4	142.0	—
1.20	220	264	120	30.0	63.6	28.4	222.0	80.0
1.80	200	360	96	34.0	255.6	28.4	318.0	96.0
2.40	180	432	72	34.0	315.6	28.4	378.0	60.0
3.00	160	480	48	40.0	355.6	28.4	424.0	46.0
3.60	140	504	24	40.0	380.6	28.4	449.0	25.0

Comments : The company should set its level of output at 3,00,000 units. Because up to this level incremental revenue exceeds differential cost.

Problem 8. *KKS Ltd having installed capacity of 1,00,000 units of a product is currently operating at 70% utilisation. At current levels of input prices, the FOB unit costs (after taking credit for applicable export incentives) work out as follows.*

Capacity utilisation	*FOB unit costs*
%	*(₹)*
70	*97*
80	*92*
90	*87*
100	*82*

The company has received three foreign offers from different sources as under.

Source K 5000 units at ₹ 55 per unit FOB.

Source L 10,000 units at ₹ 52 per unit FOB.

Source C 10,000 units at ₹ 51 per unit FOB.

Advise the company as to whether any or all the export orders should be accepted or not.
[B.Com. Hons. Delhi 2000]

Solution :

Statement showing differential cost of different capacity levels

Capacity %	*Production units*	*FOB unit Cost (₹)*	*Total Cost (₹)*	*Differential Cost*	*Per unit Differential Cost*
70	70,000	97	67,90,000	—	—
80	80,000	92	73,60,000	5,70,000	57
90	90,000	87	78,30,000	4,70,000	47
100	1,00,000	82	82,00,000	3,70,000	37

Statement showing Gain or Loss on accepting the various Export order

Export order source	*Export order (units)*	*Capacity utilisation %*	*Differential cost per unit ₹*	*Total (₹)*	*FOB Price per unit*	*Sales revenue from export*	*Profit or Loss*
K	5,000	75%	57	2,85,000	55	2,75,000	10,000
L	10,000	85%	5000 57 5000 47	5,20,000	52	5,20,000	Nil
C	10,000	95%	5000 57 5000 37	4,20,000	51	5,10,000	90,000
Total	25,000	155%		12,25,000		13,05,000	1,00,000

Comment : The Company should accept all the three export orders.

Problem 9. *A company manufactures three products A, B and C. There are no common processes and the sale of one product does not affect prices or volume of sale of any other.*

The company's budgeted profit/Loss for 1998 has been abstracted thus.

	Total ₹	*A* ₹	*B* ₹	*C* ₹
Sales	3,00,000	45,000	2,25000	30,000
Production costs				
Variable :	1,80,000	24,000	1,44,000	12,000
Fixed :	60,000	3,000	48,000	9,000
Total Factory cost :	2,40,000	27,000	1,92,000	21,000

Selling admi, costs				
Variable :	*24,000*	*8,100*	*8,100*	*7,800*
Fixed :	*6,000*	*2,100*	*1,800*	*2,100*
Total cost	*2,70,000*	*37,200*	*2,01,900*	*30,900*
Profit	*30,000*	*7,800*	*23,100*	*– 900*
[Sales – Total Cost]				

On the basis of the above, the board had almost decided to eliminate product C, on which a loss was budgeted. Meanwhile, they have sought your opinion. As the company's Cost Accountant, what would you advise ? Give reasons for your answer.

Solution : **Profitability Statement**

	₹	*A*	₹	*B*	₹	*C*	*Total*
Sales		45,000		2,25,000		30,000	3,00,000
Less : Variable cost							
Production cost	24,000		1,44,000		12,000		
Sell Adm. Cost	8,100	32,100	8,100	1,52,100	7,800	19,800	2,04,000
		12,900		72,900		10,200	96,000
Less : Fixed cost (60,000 + 6,000)							66,000
Profit							30,000
P/V Ratio C/S × 100		28.67%		32.4%		34.%	

Based upon the above computation product C is contributing ₹ 10,200 towards the fixed expenses of the company. If the product C is discontinued the profit of the company will be reduced to ₹ 19,800 [*i.e.,* 30,000 – 10,200]. And the P/V ratio of product C is higher as compared to other products. Under this background it is advisable to continue the product C.

Problem 10. *A radio manufacturing company finds that it costs ₹ 6.25 to make each component x 6640, while the same is available in the market at ₹ 4.85 each, with an assurance of continuous supply. The break up of cost is as follows :*

Materials	*₹ 2.75 each*
Labour	*₹ 1.75 each*
Other variable cost	*₹ 0.50 each*
Depreciation and other fixed cost	*₹ 1.25 each*
	6.25

should you make or buy ?

Solution :

Variable cost of manufacturing is ₹ 5.00.

i.e., (6.25 – 1.25)

But, the market price is ₹ 4.85

If the fixed cost of ₹ 1.25 is added, it is not profitable to make the component.

Better to procure it from outside supply, because, if it purchases from outside supply it can get a profit of .15 paise.

Assignment Problem

Problem 11. *Due to industrial depression, a plant is running at present only 50% of its capacity. The following details are available.*

Particulars	*Cost of production per unit*
	(₹)
Direct material	2
Direct Labour	1
Variable overhead	3
Fixed overhead	2
	8
Production per month	*20,000 units*
Total cost of production	₹ *1,60,000*
Sales price	₹ *1,40,000*
	Loss ₹ *20,000*

An exporter offer to buy 5000 units per month at the rate of ₹ 6.50 per unit and the company hesitates to accept the offer for the fear of increasing its already operating losses. Advise whether the company should accept or decline this offer. [B.Com. Adapted]

Answer. Loss reduced from ₹ 20,000 to ₹ 15,000. So, the firm must accept the offer.

Problem 12. *The Managing Director of Ranbaxy Ltd., ask for your assistance in arriving at a decision as to continue manufacturing a component X or to buy it from an outside supplier. The component X is used in finished products of the company. The company data are supplied.*

The annual requirement of component X is 10,000 units. The lowest Quotation from an outside supplier is ₹ 8.00 per unit.

The component X is manufactured in the machine shop. If the component X is bought out, certain machinery will be sold at its book value and the residual capacity of the machine shop will remain idle.

The total expenses of the Machine shop for the year ended 31.3.2004 are as follows. During that year the shop manufactured 10,000 units of X.

	₹
Material	*1,35,000*
Direct Labour	*1,00,000*
Indirect Labour	*40,000*
Power and Fuel	*6,000*
Repairs and Maintenance	*11,000*
Rates, Taxes, Insurance	*16,000*
Depreciation	*20,000*
Other Overhead Expenses	*29,600*

The following expenses of the Machine shop apply to Manufacturing of component X :

	₹
Materials	*35,000*
Direct Labour	*56,000*

Indirect Labour *12,000*

Power and Fuel *600*

Repairs and Maintenance *1,000*

The sale of machinery used for the manufacture of component X would reduce depreciation by ₹4,000 and insurance by ₹2,000. If the component X is bought out, the following additional expenses would be incurred.

Freight ₹ 1.00 per unit.

Inspection ₹ 10,000 pa.

You are required to prepare a report to the Managing Director showing the comparison of expenses of Machine shop.

(1) When the component X is made and

(2) When bought out. [MBA Anna. 2005]

Solution : Comparative Cost Statement

Particulars	*To make component (X) (₹)*	*To buy component (X) (₹)*
Direct Material	35,000	
Direct Labour	56,000	
Indirect Labour	12,000	
Power and Fuel	600	
Repairs and Maintenance	1,000	
Depreciation	4,000	
Insurance	2,000	
Total variable cost	1,10,600	
Variable cost per unit	11.06	
Purchase price per unit	---	8.00
Freight charges per unit	---	1.00
Inspection charges per unit	---	1.00
Cost per unit	11.06	10.00

Comments :

Manufacturing cost of the component is	₹	11.06
Purchase price of the component is	₹	10.00
Cost savings	₹	1.06

The component is buying outside actually it will get a cost of savings of ₹ 1.06 per unit. Only variable cost is to be considered. In both the situation fixed constant. Costs would remain Even if the production component X is discontinued fixed cost cannot be saved. In this situation the capacity which would remain Ideal on account of buying this component from the outside market can be utilized for some other purpose in near future.

TEST PROBLEMS

1. A company which sells 5,000 units at ₹ per unit has the following cost structure:

Direct material	₹ 30 per unit
Direct wages	₹ 20 per unit
Overhead	₹ 30 per unit (60% fixed)

On this basis of detailed discussions the following suggestions have emerged to improve the profit:

(A) Increase the selling price by 20% and increase the product quality by using superior material which increase material cost per unit by 30%. It is expected to result in sales of 4,800 units of the improved product.

(B) Decrease the selling price by 10% and spend additional amount on advertising up to ₹ 1,00,000. It is estimated to improve the sales by an additional 4,000 units.

(C) Reduce the sellings price by 15% and reduce the product quality by savings of 20% in material per unit, 25% on wages per unit and ₹ 30,000 on fixed overhead. The sales volume is not expected to be affected.

You are required to suggest the most profitable alternative.

[**Ans:** Profit: Current position ₹ 1,00,000, A = ₹ 1,45,200, B = ₹ 62,000, C = ₹ 1,10,000 Conclusion; Alternative (A) is recommended because it gives the more profit]

2. Gifts Land Ltd. is considering hiring a machine at an annual charge of ₹ 12,000 to increase the output of a product from its present level of 6000 units. It is anticipated that with the introduction of the machine the variable cost per unit well be reduced by ₹ 1.00 due to savings in labour cost. The new machine will not affect fixed cost in total, apart from the hiring charges. The selling price of the product is ₹ 12 per unit. The present cost structure of the product is Variable cost ₹ 9 per unit and Fixed cost ₹ 1 per unit.

You are required to calculate the number of extra units which must be produced and sold to justify hiring the machine (*i.e.,* the break-even point for the new machine).

[Madras B.Com., C&M., Oct. 1993]

[**Ans:** Extra units to be produced 1,500; Total units: 7,500; Present S: 6,000 × 12 = 72,000; V : 6,000 × 9 = 54,000; C : 18,000; F : 6,000; P = 12,000; Future S : 7,500 × 12 = 90,000; V: 7,500 × 8 = 60,000; C: 30,000; F = 18,000; P = 12,000; So, break-even point for new machine = 7,500 – 6,000 = 1,500 units]

3. A company is considering expansion. Fixed costs amount to ₹ 4,20,000 and are expected to increase by ₹ 1,25,000 when plant expansion is completed. The present plant capacity is 80,000 units a year. The Capacity will increase by 50% with the expansion. Variable costs are currently ₹ 680 per unit are expected to go down by ₹ 0.40 per unit with expansion. The current selling price is ₹ 16 per unit and is expected to remain same under both alternatives. What are the break-even points under either alternative? Which alternative is better and why?

[Madras 1st M.Com. (ICE) (PBF) May 2005]

*[**Ans:** Current BEP: ₹ 7,30,435 or 45652 units, Future BEP: ₹ 9,08,333 or 56771 units.*

4. An umbrella manufacturer makes average net profit of ₹ 5 per piece on a selling price of ₹ 28.60 by producing and selling 60,000 pieces at 60% of the potential capacity. His cost of sales (per unit) is:

	₹
Direct material	7.00
Direct wages	2.50
Works overhead (50% fixed)	12.50
Selling overhead (75% fixed)	1.60

During the current year he intends to produce the same number of units but anticipates that his fixed charges will go up by 100%, while rates of direct labour and direct material will increase by 8% and 6% respectively. But, he has no option of increasing the selling price. Under this situation he obtains an offer for a further 20% of his capacity. What minimum price would you recommend for acceptance to ensure the manufacturer an overall profit for ₹ 1,67,300? Reason out your recommendations.

[Madras, M.Com., Sep. 1992; Oct. 1997 (Double Figures):

M.Com., (ICE), Oct. 1998 (Double Figures)]

[**Ans** : Minimum price for new offer of 20% of capacity *i.e.,* 20,000 units = ₹ 34.345 (or) ₹ 6,86,900 (sale value); New material cost: ₹ 7.42; Wages : ₹ 2.70; Variable works overheads: ₹ 16.77; (old ₹ 16.15); Expected-loss on 60,000 units = ₹ 1,84,200; Total new fixed cost: ₹ 8,94,000 (old) 4,47,000; New total variable cost: ₹ 13,41,600; Total cost: ₹ 22,35,600; Profit : ₹ 1,67,300; Sales: ₹ 24,02,900]

❑❑❑

18

Budget and Budgetary Control

NEED FOR BUDGETING

Budget is not only essential for government and various business organisations but also for the individuals. So, every one is very familiar with the budgeting. Without the budget or predetermined objectives no one can achieve its targets and go for performance evaluation. Whenever the organisation fixes its targets, it is necessary to evaluate its performance. *i.e.,* the actual performance can be compared to the targeted one. If any deviation arises, the organisation can take a suitable action for correcting the deviation in future with the help of budgeting.

BUDGETING AND BUDGETARY CONTROL

Introduction

Modern industrial world faces stiff competition, uncertainty and it is exposed to different types of risks. Apart from the competition, modern era is the age of technology where fast changes are taking place. Due to this fast changes, automatic competition is generated at higher level and reactions of competitors are unknown and it is difficult to determine the consumer preferences in the context of too many products are available in the market. Planning is very important function of management. It relates to what is to be done, how, when and where it is to be done. Thus planning is related to the future course of events. Ultimate aim of efficient management is that all types of operations should be predetermined in advance. So, cost can be controlled at all levels. If management is effective, it accomplishes the objective with minimum effort and cost.

Budget is not a new term. Everyone is familiar with the idea of budget because it is essential in every movement of our life—individual, institution or industry, State Government or Central Government.

Definition

The word budget is derived from a French term "Bougette" which denotes a leather pouch fund allocated for meeting anticipated expenses.

According to ICMA, England, a budget is *"a financial and or quantitative statements prepared and approved prior to a defined period of time, of the policy to be pursued during the period for the purpose of attaining a given objective".*

It is also defined as *"a blue print of a projected plan of action of a business for a definite period of time".*

Budgetary Control

The Chartered Institute of Management Accountants, London, defines budgetary control "as the establishment of budgets relating to the responsibilities of executives to the requirements of a policy and the continuous comparison of actual with budgeted results either to secure by individual action the objective of that policy or to provide a basis for its revision".

Meaning of budget, budgeting and budgetary control, according to Rowland and William H. Harris, is that

"Budgets are the individual objectives of a department etc., where as budgeting may be said to be the act of building budgets. Budgetary control embraces all this and in addition includes the science of planning the budgets themselves and the utilisation of such budgets to effect on overall management tool for the business planning and control.

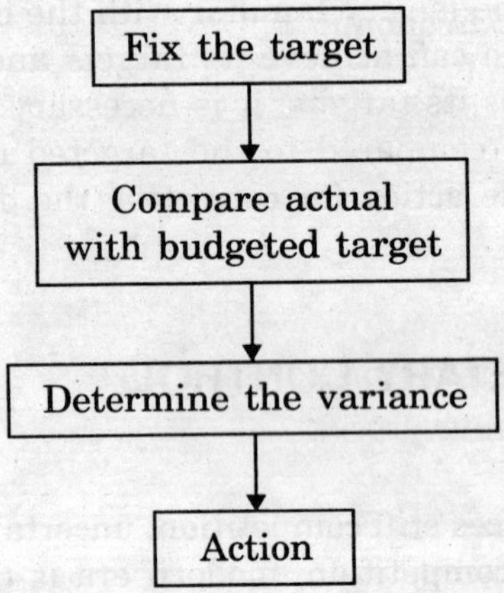

Process of Budgetary control

Advantages of Budgetary Control

The advantages and benefits of budgetary control are summarised below.

1. It brings efficiency and economy in the work of the whole enterprise. Simply it is an impersonal policeman that generates ordered effort and brings about the efficiency in results.
2. It establishes divisional and departmental responsibilities so back passing is not possible.
3. It secures proper co-ordination among various functional activities of the organisation. And also it promotes mutual co-operation and team spirit among the persons involved.
4. Reduction in cost and elimination of inefficiency is achieved automatically. As a result, decrease in cost of production by increasing the volume of output.
5. It enables the management to decentralise responsibility without losing control of entire business operations since it pin-points inefficiency.
6. It facilitates to receive great favour from credit agencies. *i.e.,* if the organisation has a well developed budget and operates accordingly, it receives more amount of bank credit.
7. It aims at maximisation of profit through cost control and proper utilisation of resources.

8. Budget provides advance information, not only for the elimination of financial crisis but also for the efficent use of available capital.
9. It provides adequate guidance to the field of research and development in future.
10. It enables to evaluate the performance.
11. It allows to achieve the balanced capital structure *i.e.,* it avoids over capitalisation or under capitalisation.
12. Budgets fix the goals and targets without which operation lacks direction.

Disadvantages of Budgetary Control

1. Opposition against the spirit of budgeting.
2. The success of the budgetary control depends upon the degree of accuracy of the estimates. Forecasting is essential for budgeting. But, there are no possibilities for hundred percent accuracy in forecasts and estimates.
3. Inflation, Deflation, Economic & Government policies will affect the success of the budgetary control.
4. Effectiveness of the budgetary control depens upon the willing co-operation or team work of all concerned. If there is no co-operation the system will be ineffective.
5. Budgetary control is essentially a tool of decision making and helps the management to take various decisions. But, it cannot replace the management.
6. It is not suitable for small concerns because it requires huge amount of money and professional staff for preparing budget.
7. It is a time consuming process.

Essentials of a Sound Budgetary Control

For an effective and efficient system of Budgetary control certain pre-requisites must be needed. These are :

1. The system should have full support from top management.
2. There should be a true delegation of authority and responsibility with the well planned organisational setup.
3. Staff should be strongly and properly motivated towards budgeting.
4. Budgets should actually work as a co-ordinating device rather than control device.
5. The accounting system should provide accurate and timely information.
6. Deviations from the standard targets should be reported promptly and clearly to all levels of management.
7. The budget should lay down the targets which are easily attainable.
8. Sufficient operational freedom should be given to the concerned executives within the overall framework.
9. Past experience is a very useful guide for the future. So, important points revealed by past experience should be taken into account while preparing budget in future.

Objectives of Budgeting

1. To determine organisational objectives.
2. To minimise waste and control expenses.

3. To plan and control the income and expenditure of the firm.
4. To fix responsibilities in different departments or heads.
5. To ensure the availability of working capital.
6. To centralize the control system.
7. Increase profitability through elimination of waste.
8. To take remedial action in order to correct deviations from established standards.
9. To find in which area action is needed and to solve the problem without delay.
10. To provide long term and short term plans for attaining organisational goals.

Installations of Budgetary Control

The organisation which has to achieve an effective system of budgetary control, will need the following steps.

1. *Organisation Chart.* A concern must have a well defined organisation chart for budgetary control. It is essential in order to have clear determination of authority and responsibility of each individual. Determination of authorities helps to minimise conflict among the personnel.
2. *Objectives.* It requires a clearly defined objective in terms of both quantity and quality that are sought to be achieved by the system of budgetary control.
3. *Budget Centre.* A budget centre is a part of the organisation for which budget is prepared to cover entire operational activities of the organisation. It is necessary for cost control purposes. With the help of the different budget centres, performance should be evaluated in an easy manner.
4. *Budget Committee.* Budget committee should be established for the purpose of incorporation and execution of plans. In small organisations, either the Cost Accountant or Chartered Accountant prepares the budget. In case of big companies a separate committee is formed for this task. The committee consists of various section heads, the chief executive and the budget controller. The ultimate aim of budget committee is to prepare a master budget with the help of the department wise budget which has already been prepared by the departmental executives.
5. *Budget Manual.* It is a written document which sets out the authorities and responsibilities of persons engaged in regular operational activities. It clearly lays down objectives of the organisation and the procedure to be followed by the executives concerned. It is the responsibility of the budget officer to prepare and maintain this manual.
6. *Budget Period.* The length of time for which the budget is prepared and employed is called budget period. It may be different for different industries or even it may differ among the same industry or business. The budget period will depend upon the following factors.
   - The type of business
   - Length of the trade cycle
   - Nature of the product
7. *Key Factor.* Key factor is also known as limiting factor or governing factor or principal budget factor. Simply, if these factors are not available in sufficient quantity, that should be referred as limiting or key factor. It may arise due to

shortage of material, labour, hours, capital, plant capacity. It is essential for other budgets. So, the concern will have to first prepare key factor related aspects and then other budgets are prepared.

Classification of Budget

Different types of budgets have been developed keeping in view the different purposes they serve. Some of the important classifications of the budgets are discussed below.

A. Classification According to Time

Based on the time factor, budgets are broadly classified in the following three types.

(*i*) *Long term Budgets.* The budgets are prepared to show the long term planning of the organisation. This budget is prepared normally for a period of 5 to 10 years. *Example :* Capital expenditure budget, research and development, long term finances etc.

(*ii*) *Short term Budgets.* Short term budgets are those which have to be prepared for a period of one or two years. *Example :* Cash Budget, Material Budget etc.

(*iii*) *Current Budget.* Current budget is one which has to be prepared for a very short period say a month or a quarter year and is related to the current conditions.

B. Classification According to Function

A functional budget is a budget which relates to any of the functions of an organisation. The following are the functional budgets commonly used.

(*i*) *Sales Budget.* Sales budget is a forecast of total sales (volume) during the budget period. It may contain the information regarding the sales, month wise, product wise, and area wise. This budget is prepared by the sales manager.

(*ii*) *Production Budget.* Production budget is prepared by the production manager. Its preparation depends upon the sales budget. The objective of this budget is to determine the quantity of production for a budgeted period. In other words, it is a quantity of units to be produced during a budget period.

Production units may be calculated in the following way : budgeted sales + desired closing stock – opening stock

(*iii*) *Materials Budget.* Material procurement budget is an estimate of quantities of raw materials to be purchased for production during the budget period. It helps the organisation to formulate effective purpose policy of raw materials. Materials budget should be prepared normally taking into account the following factors *i.e.*, availability of finance, storage facilities, price trends in the markets.

(*iv*) *Labour Budget.* Labour budget is a budget which is prepared by the personnel department of the organisation. It shows the total hours required to complete the production target. And also it shows the cost incurred for the labour used for the production.

(*v*) *Factory Overhead Budget.* This budget indicates the estimated costs of indirect materials, indirect labour and indirect factory expenses incurred during the budget period. This budget is classified into fixed, variable and semi-variable.

(*vi*) *Administrative Expenses Budget.* In order to estimate the amount required to meet the administrative and operational activities of the organisation, the administrative expenses budget is prepared. This budget will provide proper guidance and estimation for the expenses incurred in the budget period.

(*vii*) *Selling and Distribution Overhead Budget.* This budget is prepared by the sales manager of each territory. It indicates an estimate of administrative expenses to be incurred in the budget period. Preparation of selling and distribution overhead budget depends upon the sales budget.

(*viii*) *Capital Expenditure Budget.* Capital expenditure budget is a long term planning for the proposed capital outlay and its financing. Capital expenditure is an expenditure which has to be incurred for the purpose of acquiring benefit not only for the particular year but also for the subsequent period of 5 to 10 years. Capital budgeting is the most important and complicated problem of managerial decisions. Capital budgeting is also known as investment decision making.

(*ix*) *Cash Budget.* Cash budget is prepared by the chief accountant of the organisation. It may be prepared either monthly or weekly. Cash budget is a statement to show the estimated amount of cash receipts and payment and balance during the budget period. Simply, it represents the estimated cash receipts and payments over the specific future period.

(*x*) *Master Budget.* Master budget is a budget which has to incorporate all functional budgets. The definition of this budget given by the Chartered Institute of Management Accountant, England is as follows. "The summary budget, incorporating its component functional budgets and which is finally approved, adopted, and employed." It is otherwise called as finalised profit plan. Normally, it has to be approved by the board of directors before it is put into operational activities.

C. Classification According to Flexibility

(*i*) *Fixed Budget.* A fixed budget is drawn for a fixed level of activity and a prescribed set of conditions. It has been defined as "a budget which is designed to remain unchanged irrespective of the volume of output or level of activity actually attained". In the real sense, it does not consider any change in expenditure arising out of changes in the level of activity.

(*ii*) *Flexible Budget.* Flexible budget is otherwise called as variable budget. The Chartered Institute of Management Accountants, England, defines a flexible budget "as a budget which by recognising the difference in behaviour between fixed and variable costs in relation to fluctuations in output, turnover or other variable factors such as number of employees is designed to change appropriately with such fluctuations".

Normally, the flexible budget is prepared in any of the following cases :

1. Where there are general changes in sales.
2. Where the business is a new one and it is difficult to forecast the demand.
3. In an industry which has to be influenced by changes in fashion.

ZERO BASE BUDGETING

The zero base budgeting, as a managerial tool, has become increasingly popular since the early 1970's. The main aim of the zero base budgeting is the cost reduction and optimum utilisation of resources. It first came into being when former president Jimmy Carter of the United States of America, then Governor of the state of Georgia, introduced it as a means of controlling state expenditure.

Definition of Zero base Budgeting

Zero base budgeting is defined as *"a planning and budgeting process which requires each manager to justify his entire budget request in detail from scratch (hence zero base) and shifts the burden of proof to each manager to justify why he should spend money at all. The approach requires that all activities be analysed in decision packages which are evaluated by systematic analysis and ranked in the order of importance"*.

Steps in Zero Base Budgeting

1. Determination of objectives.
2. Determination of extent of application.
3. Identification of decision making units.
4. Through the cost-benefit analysis.
5. Preparation of budgets.

PERFORMANCE BUDGETING

Any type of budgeting, in order to be successful, must provide performance appraisal as well as follow-up measures. Without performance appraisal and follow-up measures, the budget will not be successful. In this regard, responsibility centre and a programme of expected performance in physical units of that centre must be established.

According to the National Institute of Bank Management, Mumbai, performance budgeting technique is the process of analysing, identifying, simplifying and crystallising specific performance objectives of a job to be achieved over a period in the framework of the organisational objectives. The technique is characterised by its specific direction towards the business objectives of the organisation.

TEST QUESTIONS

1. What is meant by budget ?
2. Define budget.
3. Compare budget, budgeting and budgetary control.
4. What is budget period.
5. Define budgetary control.
6. What is budget manual ?
7. What are operating budgets ?
8. What do you understand by flexible budgeting ?
9. List out the importance of budgetary control.
10. What is meant by cash budget ?
11. Write short note on performance budgeting.
12. What is zero base budgeting ?
13. Programme Budgeting Vs Performance Budgeting.
14. Explain the advantages and limitations of Budgetary Control System.
15. Describe the essential steps of a Budgetary Control System.
16. "Budgetary control means worrying before work rather than after. Its keynotes are planning co-ordination and control." Explain this statement.

17. What is meant by the term Budgeting ? Mention the type of budgets normally prepared by a big industrial undertakings.

18. What are the steps involved in zero base Budgeting ?

PROBLEMS AND SOLUTIONS

I. Production Budget

Problem 1. *Prepare a production budget for three months ending on March 31, 2001 for a factory producing four products on the basis of the following information.*

Type of Product	*Estimated Stock on 1.1.2001 (units)*	*Estimated sales during Jan. March 2001 (units)*	*Desired closing Stock on March 31, (2001 units)*
A	*2,000*	*10,000*	*3,000*
B	*3,000*	*15,000*	*5,000*
C	*4,000*	*13,000*	*3,000*
D	*3,000*	*12,000*	*2,000*

[M.Com., Bharathiyar]

Solution :

Formula for production Budget : Sales + closing stock – Opening stock

Production Budget for three months from Jan. to March

		₹	
Product A :	Estimated sales	10,000	
Add :	Closing stock	3,000	
		13,000	
Less :	Estimated Opening stock	2,000	
			11,000
Product B :	Estimated sales	15,000	
Add :	Closing stock	5,000	
		20,000	
Less :	Estimated Opening stock	3,000	
			17,000
Product C :	Estimated sales	13,000	
Add :	Closing stock	3,000	
		16,000	
Less :	Estimated Opening stock	4,000	
			12,000
Product D :	Estimated sales	12,000	
Add :	Closing stock	2,000	
		14,000	
Less :	Estimated Opening stock	3,000	
			11,000
	Total Production units		51,000

Problem 2. *RSP Ltd., manufactures two products A and B. A forecast of the number of units to be sold in first seven months of the year is given below. (units)*

Month	*Product MP*	*Product ST*	*Product B*
January	*2,000*	*1,000*	*2,800*
February	*2,400*	*1,200*	*2,800*
March	*3,200*	*1,600*	*2,400*
April	*4,000*	*2,000*	*2,000*
May	*4,800*	*2,400*	*1,600*
June	*4,800*	*2,400*	*1,600*
July	*4,000*	*2,000*	*1,800*

It is anticipated that (1) there will be no work in progress at the end of any month (2) finished units equal to half the sales for the next month will be in stock at the end of each month (including the previous December). Prepare production budget.

Solution :

Production Budget [for six months ending 30th June] (units)

Product – MP	*Jan.*	*Feb.*	*March*	*April*	*May*	*June*
Sales	1,000	1,200	1,600	2,000	2,400	2,400
Add closing stock (half the Sales for next Month)	600	800	1,000	1,200	1,200	1,000
	1,600	2,000	2,600	3,200	3,600	3,400
Less : Opening stock (half the sales for current Month)	500	600	800	1,000	1,200	1,200
Budgeted production	1,100	1,400	1,800	2,200	2,400	2,200

Total Budgeted production for Six Months

1,100 + 1,400 + 1,800 + 2,200 + 2,400 + 2,200 = 11,100 units

Product – ST (units)	*Jan.*	*Feb.*	*March*	*April*	*May*	*June*
Product : Sales	2,800	2,800	2,400	2,000	1,600	1,600
Add closing stock	1,400	1,200	1,000	800	800	900
	4,200	4,000	3,400	2,800	2,400	2,500
Less : Opening stock	1,400	1,400	1,200	1,000	800	800
Budgeted production	2,800	2,600	2,200	1,800	1,600	1,700

Total Budgeted production for Six Months

2,800 + 2,600 + 2,200 + 1,800 + 1,600 + 1,700 = 12,700 units

Summarised Production cost Budget

	Product MP		Product ST		
	Output 11,100 (Units)		*Output 12,700 (Units)*		
	Per unit	*Amt (₹)*	*Per unit*	*Amt (₹)*	*Total*
Direct material	10.00	1,11,000	15.00	1,90,000	3,01,500
Direct Labour	5.00	55,500	10.00	1,27,000	1,82,500
Prime Cost	15.00	1,66,500	25.00	3,17,500	4,84,000
Factory overheads	4.00	44,400	3.00	38,100	82,500
	19.00	2,10,900	28.00	3,55,600	5,66,500

NOTE :

Factory overheads per unit = Annual overhead/Annual output

Product MP = 88,000/22,000 = ₹ 4.00

ST = 72,000/24,000 = ₹ 3.00

Problem 3. *The sales director of a Narmadha Manufacturing Company reports that next year he expects to sell 50,000 units of a particular product.*

The production manager consults the storekeeper and casts his figures as follows.

Two kinds of raw materials A and B are required for manufacturing the product. Each unit of the product requires 2 units of A and 3 units of B. The estimated opening balances at the commencement of the next year are

Finished products 10,000 units

Raw materials A : 12,000 units; B 15,000 units.

The desirable closing balances at the end of the next are finished products : 14,000units; A : 13,000 units; B 16,000 units.

Draw up a quantitative chart showing materials purchase budget for the next year.

Solution :

Formula : The units to be produced

Formula = Sales + Desired closing stock – opening stock

50,000 + 14,000 – 10,000 = 54,000 units

Material Procurement Budget

	Finished Products	*Materials*	
		A	*B*
	Units	*Units*	*Units*
As per the production budget Requirement	54,000	1,08,000	1,62,000
Estimated opening Balance	+ 10,000	– 12,000	– 15,000
	64,000	96,000	1,47,000
Closing Balance	– 14,000	13,000	16,000
Estimated sales of Product	50.000	—	—
Estimated purchase of materials	—	1,09,000	1,63,000

Problem 4. *Draw a materials procurement (Quantitative) Budget from the following information. Estimated sales of a product 40,000 units. Each unit of the product requires 3 units of materials A and 5 units of B.*

Estimated opening balances at the commencement of the next year.

Finished product	*5,000 units*
Materials A	*12,000 units*
Materials B	*20,000 units*
Materials on order	
Materials A	*7,000 units*
Materials B	*11,000 units*

The desirable closing balances at the end of the next year.

Finished product	*7,000 units*
Material A	*15,000 units*
Material B	*25,000 units*
Materials on order	
Material A	*8,000 units*
Material B	*10,000 units*

[B.Com. Madurai]

Solution :

	Production Budget (in units)
Estimated Sales	40,000
Add : Desired Closing Stock	7,000
	47,000
Less : Opening Stock	5,000
Estimated production	42,000

Material Procurement Budget (in units)

		Material A		Material B
Estimated Consumption				
42,000 × 3		1,26,000		
Add : 42,000 × 5				2,10,000
Desired Closing Stock		15,000		25,000
Material on order (Closing)		8,000		10,000
		1,49,000		2,45,000
Less : Opening Stock	12,000		20,000	
Materials on order (Opening)	7,000	19,000	11,000	31,000
Estimated Purchases		1,30,000		2,14,000
Total purchase	3,44,000 units			

Sales Budget

Problem 5. *Ram Lal & Co. sells two products A and B which are manufactured in one plant. During the year 1985, it plans to sell the following quantities of each product.*

	Ist Quarter	*IInd Quarter*	*IIIrd Quarter*	*IVth Quarter*
Product A	*90,000*	*2,50,000*	*3,00,000*	*80,000*
Product B	*80,000*	*75,000*	*60,000*	*90,000*

Each of these two products is sold on a seasonal basis. Ram Lal plans to sell product A throughout the year at a price of ₹ 10 a unit and product B at a price of ₹ 20 a unit.

A study of the past experience reveals that Ram Lal has lost about 3% of its billed revenue each year, because of returns (constituting 2% of Loss of revenue) allowances and bad debts (1% loss).

Prepare a Sales budget incorporating the above information.

Solution : **Sales Budget of Ram Lal and Co**

	First Quarter ₹	*Second Quarter* ₹	*Third Quarter* ₹	*Fourth Quarter* ₹	*Total* ₹
Product A	9,00,000	25,00,000	30,00,000	8,00,000	72,00,000
Product B	16,00,000	15,00,000	12,00,000	18,00,000	61,00,000
Total	25,00,000	40,00,000	42,00,000	26,00,000	1,33,00,000
Less : Deductions :					
(*i*) Returns	50,000	80,000	84,000	52,000	2,66,000
(*ii*) Allowances and Bad debts	25,000	40,000	42,000	26,000	1,33,000
Total Deduction	75,000	1,20,000	1,26,000	78,000	3,99,000
Net sales (Sales – Total Deductions)	24,25,000	38,80,000	40,74,000	25,22,000	1,29,01,000

Problem 6. *Jayam & Co. manufactures two products A and B and sells them through two divisions East and West. For the purpose of submission of sales budget to the budget committee, the following information has been made available.*

Budgeted sales for the current year were

Product	*East*	*West*
X	*400 @ ₹ 9*	*600 @ ₹ 9*
Y	*300 @ ₹ 21*	*500 @ ₹ 21*

Actual sales for the current year were

Product	*East*	*West*
X	*500 @ ₹ 9*	*700 @ ₹ 9*
Y	*200 @ ₹ 21*	*400 @ ₹ 21*

Adequate market studies reveal that product X is popular but under priced. It is observed that if price of X is increased by ₹ 1 it will find a ready market. On the other hand, Y is overpriced to customers and market could absorb more if sales price of Y be reduced by ₹ 1. The management had agreed to give effect to the above price changes.

From the information based on these, price changes and reports from salesman, the following estimates have been prepared by divisional managers.

Percentage increase in sales over current budget is

Product	*East*	*West*
X	*+ 10%*	*+ 5%*
Y	*+ 20%*	*+ 10%*

With the help of an intensive advertisement campaign the following additional sales above the estimated sales of divisional managers are possible.

Product	*East*	*West*
X	*60*	*70*
Y	*40*	*50*

You are required to prepare Budget for sales incorporating the above estimates and also show the budgeted and actual sales of the current year.

Solution : **Sales Budget of Jayam & Co.**

Division	*Product*	*Budget for future period*			*Budget for current period*			*Actual sales for current period*		
		Qty.	*Price* ₹	*Value* ₹	*Qty.*	*Price* ₹	*Value* ₹	*Qty.*	*Price* ₹	*Value* ₹
East	X	500	10	5,000	400	9	3,600	500	9	4,500
	Y	400	20	8,000	300	21	6,300	200	21	4,200
Total		900		13,000	700		9,900	700		8,700
West	X	700	10	7,000	600	9	5,400	700	9	6,300
	Y	600	20	12,000	500	21	10,500	400	21	8,400
Total		1,300		19,000	1,100		15,900	1,100		14,700
Total	X	1,200	10	12,000	1,000	9	9,000	1,200	9	10,800
	Y	1,000	20	20,000	800	21	16,800	600	21	12,600
Total		2,200		32,000	1,800		25,800	1,800		23,400

Factory Overhead Budget

Problem 7. *Rexin Ltd. supplies you the following average figures of previous quarters. Prepare a manufacturing overhead budget for the quarter ending on March 31,2002. The budgeted output during this quarter is 5,000 units.*

Fixed overheads	*₹ 40,000*
Variable overheads	*₹ 20,000 (varying @ ₹ 5 per unit)*
Semi-variable overheads	*₹ 20,000 (40% fixed and 60% varying @ 3 per unit)*

Solution : **Manufacturing Overhead Budget**

Fixed overheads		₹ 40,000
Variable overheads		₹ 25,000
Semi Variable overheads		
Fixed	8,000	
Variable @ ₹ 3 per unit	15,000	
		23,000
Total overhead costs		88,000

Selling and Distribution Overhead Budget

Problem 8. *You are requested to prepare sales overhead budget from the estimation given below.*

Advertisement	₹ *2,500*
Salaries of Sales Department	*5,000*
Expenses of Sales Department	*1,500*
Counter Salesman's salaries and dearness allowance	*6,000*
Commission to counter salesman at 1% on their sales	

Travelling salesmen's commission at 10% on their sales and expenses at 5% on their sales. The sales during the period were estimated as follow.

Counter sales	*Travelling Salesman's*
₹	₹
80,000	*10,000*
1,20,000	*15,000*
1,40,000	*20,000*

[B.Com., BBM]

Solution : **Sales overhead Budget**

Estimated Sales

Fixed Overheads	₹ 90,000	₹ 1,35,000	₹ 1,60,000
Advertisement	2,500	2,500	2,500
Expenses of Sales department	1,500	1,500	1,500
Salaries of Sales department	5,000	5,000	5,000
Counter Salesmen's salaries and dearness allowance	6,000	6,000	6,000
Total Fixed cost	15,000	15,000	15,000
Variable Cost			
Counter Salesman's Commission @1% on their sales	800	1,200	1,400
Travelling Salesman's Commission @ 10% on their sales	1,000	1,500	2,000
Expenses on Travelling Salesmen's sales @ 5%	500	750	1,000
Total variable cost	2,300	3,450	4,400
Total Sales overheads (FC + VC)	17,300	18,450	19,400

Problem 9. *From the following particulars prepare a production budget of a company for the year ended on 30th June 2002.*

Product	*Sales in units*	*Estimated stock 1.7.2001*	*Stock (units) 30.6.2002*
X	*18000*	*1680*	*1860*
Y	*12000*	*600*	*1740*
Z	*8400*	*960*	*960*

[B.Com. PU 2004]

Solution : **Production Budget (Units)**

	Product X	*Product Y*	*Product Z*
Sales (units)	18,000	12,000	8,400
Add : Closing stock	1,860	1,740	960
	19,860	13,740	9,360
Less : Estimated opening stock	1,860	1,740	960
Production	18,000	12,000	8,400

Total Units to be produced 18,000 + 12,000 + 8,400 = 38,400 units

Problem 10. *From the following figures prepare a raw material purchase budget for January.*

	Materials A (Units)	*Materials B (Units)*
Estimated stock on 1st Jan.	*16,000*	*6,000*
Estimated stock on 31st Jan.	*20,000*	*8,000*
Estimated consumption	*1,20,000*	*44,000*

[BCA 2000 PU]

Solution :

	Raw material A	*Raw material B*
Estimated Consumption (units)	1,20,000	44,000
Add : Estimated stock on 31st Jan.	20,000	8,000
	1,40,000	52,000
Less : Estimated stock on 1st Jan.	16,000	6,000
Estimated Purchase (units)	1,24,000	46,000

II. Cash Budget

Problem 1. *A company expects to have ₹37,500 cash in hand on 1.4.1995. And requires you to prepare an estimate of cash position during the three months April to June 1995. The following information is supplied to you.*

Months	*Sales*	*Purchases*	*Wages*	*Factory Expenses*	*Office Expenses*	*Selling Expenses*
	₹	₹	₹	₹	₹	₹
Feb.	*75,000*	*45,000*	*9,000*	*7,500*	*6,000*	*4,500*
March	*84,000*	*48,000*	*9,750*	*8,250*	*6,000*	*4,500*
April	*90,000*	*52,500*	*10,500*	*9,000*	*6,000*	*5,250*
May	*1,20,000*	*60,000*	*13,500*	*11,250*	*6,000*	*6,570*
June	*1,35,000*	*60,000*	*14,250*	*14,000*	*7,000*	*7,000*

Other Information :

1. *The period of credit allowed by suppliers—2 months.*
2. *20% sales is for cash and period of credit allowed to customers for credit sale is one month.*
3. *Delay in payment of all expenses—1 month.*
4. *Income Tax of ₹ 57,500 is due to be paid on June 15, 1995.*
5. *The company is to pay dividends to shareholders and bonus to workers which is ₹ 15,000 and ₹ 22,500 respectively in the month of April.*
6. *Plant has been ordered and is expected to be received and paid in May. It will cost ₹ 1,20,000.* [B.Com. Madras]

Solution :

Cash Budget

Particulars	*April*	*May*	*June*
	₹	₹	₹
Opening cash balance	37,500	11,700	(–) 91,050
Receipts :			
Amount received from cash sales (20%)	18,000	24,000	27,000
Amount received from credit sales [80% of previous months sales]	67,200	72,000	96,000
Total Receipts	1,22,700	1,07,700	31950
Payments :			
Amount paid to creditors [2 months previous month purchase]	45,000	48,000	52,500
Wages [previous month]	9,750	10,500	13,500
Factory expenses [previous month]	8,250	9,000	11,250
Office expenses [previous month]	6,000	6,000	6,000
Selling expenses [previous month]	4,500	5,250	6,570
Income Tax paid	-	-	57,500
Dividend to shareholders	15,000	-	-
Bonus to workers	22,500	-	-
Amount paid for purchase of plant	-	1,20,000	-
Total Payment	1,11,000	1,98,750	1,47,320
Closing balance [TR – TP]	11,700	– 91,050	–1,15,370

NOTE :

In order to meet the cash deficiency of ₹ 91,050 and 1,15,370 in the month of May and June the company will arrange the overdraft facilities over and above the cash deficiency.

If direction is given in the problem only, we arrange the overdraft facilities, otherwise no need to arrange the overdraft facilities.

Problem 2. *Prepare cash Budget for 3 months ended on 30th Sep. 1999 :*

Cash at Bank on 1.7.1999 ₹ 25,000

Salaries and wages monthly ₹ 10,000

Interest payable ₹ 5,000 (August)

Particulars	*June* ₹	*July* ₹	*Aug.* ₹	*Sep.* ₹
Cash sales	-	*1,40,000*	*1,52,000*	*1,21,000*
Credit sales	*1,00,000*	*80,000*	*1,40,000*	*1,20,000*
Purchases (₹)	*1,60,000*	*1,70,000*	*2,40,000*	*1,80,000*
Other expenses	-	*20,000*	*22,000*	*21,000*

Credit sales are collected 50% in the month in which sales are made, and 50% in the month following. Collection from credit sales are subject to 5% discount if payment is received during the month of sales and 2 ½% if payment is received in the month following.

Creditors are paid either on a prompt category or 30 days basis. It is estimated that 10% of creditors are in the prompt category.

Solution : Cash Budget for three months ended 30.9.1994

Particulars	*July* ₹	*Aug.* ₹	*Sep.* ₹
Opening Cash	25,000	60,750	1,04,250
Receipts			
Cash Sales	1,40,000	1,52,000	1,21,000
Amount received from credit sales	86,750	1,05,500	1,25,250
Total Receipts	2,51,750	3,18,250	3,50,500
Payments			
Amount paid to creditors (10% prompt category)	17,000	24,000	18,000
Amount paid to creditor (90% on 30 day basis)	1,44,000	1,53,000	2,16,000
Other expenses	20,000	22,000	21,000
Salaries and wages	10,000	10,000	10,000
Interest payable	-	5,000	-
Total payment	1,91,000	2,14,000	2,65,000
Closing balance [TR – TP]	60,750	1,04,250	85,500

Workings :

	July ₹	Aug. ₹	Sep. ₹
Collection of credit sales			
(*i*) 50% in the month of sales are made	40,000	70,000	60,000
Less : Discount 5%	2,000	3,500	3,000
	38,000	66,500	57,000
(*ii*) 50% in the month following months Sales	50,000	40,000	70,000
Less : Discount 2½%	1,250	1,000	1,750
	48,750	39,000	68,250

July = 38,000 + 48,750 = 86,750
August = 66,500 + 39,000 = 1,05,500
September = 57,000 + 68,250 = 1,25,250.

Problem 3. *Sarathi & Co. wishes to arrange overdraft facilities with its bankers during period April to June, when it will be manufacturing mostly for stock. Prepare cash budget for the above period from the following data. Including the extent of bank facilities the company will require at the end of each month.*

(*a*)

Months	*Sales* ₹	*Purchases* ₹	*Wages* ₹
Feb.	*1,80,000*	*1,24,800*	*12,000*
March	*1,92,000*	*1,44,000*	*14,000*
April	*1,08,000*	*2,43,000*	*11,000*
May	*1,74,000*	*2,46,000*	*10,000*
June	*1,26,000*	*2,68,000*	*5,000*

(*b*) *50% of credit sales is realised in the month following the sale and the remaining 50% in the second month following. Creditors are paid in the month following the month of purchase.*

(*c*) *Cash at Bank on 1st April (estimated) ₹ 25000.*

[M.Com., Madras] [B.Com. Nov. 95 Bharathiar]

Solution : **Cash budget**

Particulars	*April*	*May*	*June*
Opening Cash balance	25,000	56,000	3,000
Receipts			
Amount collected from credit sales	1,86,000	1,50,000	1,41,000
Total Receipts	2,11,000	2,06,000	1,44,000
Payments			
Amount paid to creditors	1,44,000	2,43,000	2,46,000

Wages paid	11,000	10,000	5,000
Total Payments	1,55,000	2,53,000	2,51,000
Balance	56,000	–47,000	–1,07,000
Bank Overdraft	–	OD + 50,000	1,20,000
Closing balance	56,000	3,000	13,000

Workings :

Credit sales Collection :

April = 50% of March + 50% of Feb.
96,000 + 90,000 = 1,80,000
May = 50% April + 50% March
54,000 + 96,000 = 1,50,000
June = 50% of May + 50% April
87,000 + 54,000 = 1,41,000

NOTE :

(*i*) Wages are assumed to be paid in the same month.

(*ii*) Overdraft facilities are arranged to meet out the cash deficiency in the month of May and June.

Problem 4. *Prepare cash Budget for the month of May, June and July 1989 on the basis of the following information.*

I.

Months	*Credit Sales* ₹	*Credit Purchases* ₹	*Wages* ₹	*Manufacturing Expenses* ₹	*Office Expenses* ₹	*Selling Expenses* ₹
March	*60,000*	*36,000*	*9,000*	*4,000*	*2,000*	*4,000*
April	*62,000*	*38,000*	*8,000*	*3,000*	*1,500*	*5,000*
May	*64,000*	*33,000*	*10,000*	*4,500*	*2,500*	*4,500*
June	*58,000*	*35,000*	*8,500*	*3,500*	*2,000*	*3,500*
July	*56,000*	*39,000*	*9,500*	*4,000*	*1,000*	*4,500*
August	*60,000*	*34,000*	*8,000*	*3,000*	*1,500*	*4,500*

II. Cash Balance on Ist May 1989 is ₹ 8,000.

III. Plant costing ₹ 16,000 is due for delivery in July. Payable I0% on delivery and the balance after 3 months.

IV. Advance Tax of ₹ 8,000 each is payable in March and June.

V. Period of credit allowed (I) by suppliers – 2 months and (II) to customers one month.

VI. Lag in payment of manufacturing expenses – 1/2month

VII. Lag in payment of office and selling expenses – one month. [M.Com. Adapted]

Solution : **Cash budget**

ParticularsMay (₹)	*June (₹)*	*July (₹)*	
Opening Cash balance	8,000	13,750	12,250
Receipts			
Amount received from credit sales	62,000	64,000	58,000
Total Receipts	70,000	77,750	70,250
Payments			
Wages paid	10,000	8,500	9,500
Amount paid to purchase of plant	–	–	1,600
Advance Tax	–	8,000	–
Amount paid to creditors	36,000	38,000	33,000
Manufacturing expenses paid	3,750	4,000	3,750
Office expenses	1,500	2,500	2,000
Selling expenses	5,000	4,500	3,500
Total Payments	56,250	65,500	53,350
Closing Balance	13,750	12,250	16,900

Workings :

Manufacturing expenses

(*i*) May $= \frac{1}{2}$ of May + $\frac{1}{2}$ of April

2250 + 1500 = **3750**

(*ii*) June $= \frac{1}{2}$ of June + $\frac{1}{2}$ of May

1750 + 2250 = **4000**

(*iii*) July $= \frac{1}{2}$ of July + $\frac{1}{2}$ of June

2000 + 1750 = **3750**

Problem 5. *Prepare cash Budget for the three months ending on 30.6.1998 from the information given below.*

I.

Month	*Sales* ₹	*Material* ₹	*Wages* ₹	*Overheads* ₹
Feb.	*14,000*	*9,600*	*3,000*	*1,700*
March	*15,000*	*9,000*	*3,000*	*1,900*
April	*16,000*	*9,200*	*3,200*	*2,000*
May	*17,000*	*10,000*	*3,600*	*2,200*
June	*18,000*	*10,400*	*4,000*	*2,300*

II. ***Credit terms***

Sales /Debtors – 10% sales are on cash, 50 % of the credit sales are collected next month, and the balance in the following month.

Creditors : Materials 2 Months
Wages ¼ Month
Overheads ½ Month

III. Cash and Bank Balance on 1.4.1998 is expected to ₹ 6,000.

IV. Other relevant information are :

(a) Plant and machinery will be installed in Feb. 1998 at a cost of ₹ 96,000. The monthly instalment of ₹ 2,000 is payable from April onwards.

(b) Dividend @ 5% on preference share capital of ₹ 2,00,000 will be paid on Ist June.

(c) Advance to be received for sale of vehicles ₹ 9,000 in June.

(d) Dividend from investments amounting to ₹, 1,000 are expected to be in June.

(e) Income Tax (advance) to be paid in June is ₹ 2,000. [ICWA (Int)]

Solution :

Cash Budget for the period of three months ending on 30.6.1998

	April ₹	*May* ₹	*June* ₹
Opening balance (Cash)	6,000	3,950	3,000
Receipts			
Amount received from cash sales	1,600	1,700	1,800
Credit sales	13,050	13,950	14,850
Dividend	—	—	1,000
Advance received for sale of vehicles	—	—	9,000
Total Receipts	20,650	19,600	29,650
Payments			
Dividend paid on preference shares	—	—	10,000
Income tax paid	—	—	2,000
Capital expenditure	2,000	2,000	2,000
Amount paid to creditors [previous 2 months purchase]	9,600	9,000	9,200
Wages	3,150	3,500	3,900
Overheads	1,950	2,100	2,250
Total payments	16,700	16,600	29,350
Closing Balance	3,950	3,000	300

Workings :

(*i*) *Collection of credit sales*

April = 50% of March + 50% of Feb.
6,750 + 6,300 = 13,050

May = 50% of April + 50% of March
7,200 + 6,750 = 13,950

June = 50% of May + 50% April

7,650 + 7,200 = 14,850

(*ii*) *Wages*

$$\text{April} = \frac{1}{4} \text{ of March} + \frac{3}{4} \text{ of April}$$

750 + 2,400 = 3,150

$$\text{May} = \frac{1}{4} \text{ of April} + \frac{3}{4} \text{ of May}$$

$$3{,}200 \times \frac{1}{4} + 3{,}600 \times \frac{3}{4}$$

800 + 2,700 = 3,500

$$\text{June} = \frac{1}{4} \text{ of May} + \frac{3}{4} \text{ of June}$$

$$3{,}600 \times \frac{1}{4} + 4{,}000 \times \frac{3}{4}$$

900 + 3,000 = 3,900

(*iii*) *Overheads*

$$\text{April} = \frac{1}{2} \text{ of April} + \frac{1}{2} \text{ of March}$$

1,000 + 950 = 1950

$$\text{May} = \frac{1}{2} \text{ of May} + \frac{1}{2} \text{ of April}$$

1,100 + 1,000 = 2,100

$$\text{June} = \frac{1}{2} \text{ of June} + \frac{1}{2} \text{ of May}$$

1,150 + 1,100 = 2,250

Problem 6. *From the following forecasts of income and expenditure prepare a cash budget for three months commencing Ist June when the bank balance was ₹ 1,00,000/-*

Months	*Sales*	*Purchases*	*Wages*	*Factory Expenses*	*Ad. Sell Expenses*
	₹	₹	₹	₹	₹
April	*80,000*	*41,000*	*5,600*	*3,900*	*10,000*
May	*76,500*	*40,500*	*5,400*	*4,200*	*14,000*
June	*78,500*	*38,500*	*5,400*	*5,100*	*15,000*
July	*90,000*	*37,000*	*4,800*	*5,100*	*17,000*
August	*95,000*	*35,000*	*4,700*	*6,000*	*13,000*

A sales commission of 5% on sales, due two months after sales, is payable in addition to selling expenses, plant valued at ₹ 65,000 will be purchased and paid for in August and the dividend for the last financial year of ₹ 15,000 will be paid in July. There is 2 months credit period allowed to customers and received from suppliers.

[ICWA] [M.Com. Madras]

Solution : Cash Budget for the period of three months

	June	July	August
	₹	₹	₹
Opening balance	1,00,000	1,11,400	1,03,075
Receipts :			
Amount received from credit sales	80,000	76,500	78,500
Total Receipts	1,80,000	1,87,900	1,81,575
Payments :			
Amount paid to creditors	41,000	40,500	38,500
Wages paid	5,400	5,400	4,800
Factory expenses	4,200	5,100	5,100
Adms Selling expenses	14,000	15,000	17,000
Sales commission	4,000	3,825	3,925
Payment of dividend	-	15,000	-
Purchase of Plant	-	-	65,000
Total Payments	68,600	84,825	1,34,325
Closing Balance [TR – TP]	1,11,400	1,03,075	47,250

NOTE :

(1) Assumed that wages, factory, administration and selling expenses are payable in the following month.

(2) Sales Commission

June	July	Aug
80,000 × 5/100	76,500 × 5/100	78,500 × 5/100
= 4,000	= 3,825	= 3,925

Problem 7. *Reliance India Ltd., A newly started company wishes to prepare cash budget from January. Prepare a cash budget for the first six months from the following estimated revenue and expenses.*

Months	*Total sales*	*Materials*	*Wages*	*Overheads*	
				Production	*Selling & Distribution*
	₹	₹	₹	₹	₹
January	*20,000*	*20,000*	*4,000*	*3,200*	*800*
February	*22,000*	*14,000*	*4,400*	*3,300*	*900*
March	*28,000*	*14,000*	*4,600*	*3,400*	*900*
April	*36,000*	*22,000*	*4,600*	*3,500*	*1,000*
May	*30,000*	*20,000*	*4,000*	*3,200*	*900*
June	*40,000*	*25,000*	*5,000*	*3,600*	*1,200*

Cash balance on 1st January was ₹ 10,000. A new machinery is to be installed for ₹20,000 on credit to be repaid by two equal installments in March and April.

Sales commission @ 5% on total sales is to be paid within a month following actual sales.

₹ 10,000, being the amount of IInd call, may be received in March. Share premium amounting to ₹ 2000 is also obtainable with the IInd call.

Period of credit allowed by suppliers	*2 months*
Period of credit allowed to customers	*1 month*
Delay in payment of overheads	*1 month*
Delay in payment of wages	$\frac{1}{2}$ *month*

Assume cash sales to be 50% of total sales.

Solution :

Cash Budget

Particulars	*Jan.* ₹	*Feb.* ₹	*March* ₹	*Apr.* ₹	*May* ₹	*June* ₹
Opening balance	10,000	18,000	29,800	27,000	24,700	33,100
Receipts						
Second call money received	-	-	10,000	-	-	-
Share Premium received			2,000			
Amount received from customers	-	10,000	11,000	14,000	18,000	15,000
Cash Sales	10,000	11,000	14,000	18,000	15,000	20,000
Total Receipts (A)	20,000	39,000	66,800	59,000	57,700	68,100
Payments						
Amount paid to Purchase of Machinery	-	-	10,000	10,000	-	-
Sales Commission paid	-	1,000	1,100	1,400	1,800	1,500
Amount paid to creditors	-	-	20,000	14,000	14,000	22,000
Payment of overheads (production + selling and distri)	-	4,000	4,200	4,300	4,500	4,100
Payment of wages	2,000	4,200	4,500	4,600	4,300	4,500
Total Payments (B)	2,000	9,200	39,800	34,300	24,600	32,100
Closing Balance (A – B)	18,000	29,800	27,000	24,700	33,100	36,000

Workings :

(1) Sales Commission

Jan. 20,000 × 5/100 = 1,000
Feb. 22,000 × 5/100 = 1,100
March 28,000 × 5/100 = 1,400
April 36,000 × 5/100 = 1,800
May 30,000 × 5/100 = 1,500
June 40,000 × 5/100 = 2,000

(2) Material suppliers treated as creditors.

(3) Cash Sales is 50% of total sales.

	Cash Sales	*Credit sales*
	₹	₹
January	10,000	10,000
February	11,000	11,000
March	14,000	14,000
April	18,000	18,000
May	15,000	15,000
June	20,000	20,000

(4) Payment of wages

Jan. = 50% Jan. + 50% Dec
2,000 + nil = 2,000

Feb. = 50% Feb. + 50% Jan.
2,200 + 2,000 = 4,200

March = 50% March + 50% Feb.
2,300 + 2,200 = 4,500

April = 50% April + 50% March
2,300 + 2,300 = 4,600

May = 50% May + 50% April
2,000 + 2,300 = 4,300

June = 50% of June + 50% of May
2,500 + 2,000 = 4,500

Problem 8. *From the following forecasts of income and expenditure of TPK & Co. Ltd., prepare a cash budget for six months commencing from 1st June 2000 when the bank balance is estimated to be ₹ 1,10,000.*

Months	*Sales*	*Selling overheads*	*Purchases*	*Wages*	*Factory Overheads*	*Administration Overheads*	*Research Expenditure*
	₹	₹	₹	₹	₹	₹	₹
March	*82,000*	*5,000*	*40,000*	*10,000*	*8,400*	*3,400*	*2,000*
April	*88,500*	*3,250*	*37,000*	*8,000*	*5,600*	*2,500*	*2,400*
May	*84,000*	*4,100*	*40,000*	*8,400*	*5,900*	*2,760*	*2,400*
June	*93,000*	*3,710*	*39,000*	*8,800*	*5,920*	*2,480*	*2,400*
July	*72,000*	*3,210*	*39,900*	*6,000*	*5,440*	*2,600*	*2,400*
Aug.	*82,500*	*3,600*	*35,000*	*9,600*	*5,880*	*2,520*	*2,600*
Sep.	*98,600*	*3,450*	*36,400*	*8,000*	*6,000*	*2,700*	*2,600*
Oct.	*92,800*	*3,210*	*36,500*	*8,400*	*5,680*	*2,560*	*2,600*
Nov.	*1,04,400*	*3,200*	*32,000*	*7,600*	*5,360*	*2,620*	*2,400*

Lag in payment of wages : $\frac{1}{4}$ *month*

Lag in payment of factory overhead : 1 month

Lag in payment of Administration overhead : $\frac{1}{2}$ *month*

Lag in payment of Selling overhead : 1 month

Lag in payment of Research Expenditure : 1 month

Period of credit allowed by the creditors : 3 months

Period of credit allowed by the customers : 2 months

Other Information :

(i) A sales commission of 5% on sales, and due two months after sales, is payable in addition to selling overheads.

(ii) Capital expenditure planned is (a) Machinery purchased in June 2003 for ₹ 1,00,000 payable on delivery and (b) Building purchased in June 2000 for ₹ 8,00,000 payable in four half yearly instalments, the first being payable in July 2000.

(iii) Interest on Bombay Port Trust Bonds amounting to ₹ 50,000 is to be received in October 2000.

(iv) Cash sales are estimated at ₹ 2000 per month.

(v) A dividend of ₹ 10,000 is to be paid in September 2000.

(vi) Tax amounting to ₹ 30,000 is to be paid on 1st August 2000.

(vii) A call money of ₹ 2 per share on Equity share capital of ₹ 5,00,000 divided into 50,000 shares of ₹ 10 each is to be received on 1st July 2000.

Solution : **Cash Budget of TPK Ltd.**

Particulars	*June* ₹	*July* ₹	*Aug.* ₹	*Sep.* ₹	*Oct.* ₹	*Nov.* ₹
Opening balance	1,10,000	30,335	4,345	1,490	10,000	75,815
Receipts						
Interest on Bombay Trust Bonds	-	-	-	-	50,000	-
Cash Sales	2,000	2,000	2,000	2,000	2,000	2,000
Equity capital received	-	1,00,000	-	-	-	-
Amount received from credit sales	86,500	82,000	91,000	70,000	80,500	96,600
Total Receipts (A)	1,98,500	2,14,335	97,345	73,490	1,42,500	1,74,415
Payments :						
Sales Commission paid	4,425	4,200	4,650	3,600	4,125	4,930
Selling overheads	4,100	3,710	3,210	3,600	3,450	3,210
Purchase of plant & machinery	1,00,000	-	-	-	-	-
Amount Paid for the purchase of building	-	2,00,000	-	-	-	-
Dividend paid	-	-	-	10,000	-	-
Tax paid	-	-	30,000	-	-	-
Wages paid	8,700	6,700	8,700	8,400	8,900	7,800
Factory overheads	5,920	5,440	5,880	6,000	5,680	5,360
Research Expenditure	2,400	2,400	2,400	2,600	2,600	2,600
Administration						

Overheads	2,620	2,540	2,560	2,610	2,630	2,590
Amount paid to Creditors	40,000	37,000	40000	39000	39900	35000
Total payments (B)	1,68,165	2,61,990	97,400	75,810	66,685	61,490
Balance (A–B) (Surplus or deficit)	30,335	– 47,665	– 55	– 2,320	75,815	1,12,925
Overdraft (assumed)	—	+ 52,000	+ 1,545	+ 12,320	—	—
Closing Balance	30,335	4,345	1,490	10,000	75,815	1,12,925

Workings :

1. *Sales commission*

April ₹	May ₹	June ₹	July ₹	August ₹	Sep. ₹	Oct. ₹	Nov. ₹
4,425	4,200	4,650	3,600	4,125	4,930	4,640	5,220

2. *Wages*

	April ₹	May ₹	June ₹	July ₹	August ₹	Sep. ₹	Oct. ₹	Nov. ₹
$\frac{1}{4}$ of previous month	2,500	2,000	2,100	2,200	1,500	2,400	2,600	2,100
$\frac{3}{4}$ of current month	6,000	6,300	6,600	4,500	7,200	6,000	6,300	5,700
	8,500	8,300	8,700	6,700	8,700	8,400	8,900	7,800

3. *Administration overhead*

	June ₹	July ₹	August ₹	Sep. ₹	Oct. ₹	Nov. ₹
½ of previous month	1,380	1,240	1,300	1,260	1,350	1,280
½ of current month	1,240	1,300	1,260	1,350	1,280	1,310
	2,620	2,540	2,560	2,610	2,630	2,590

Credit sales

	March ₹	April ₹	May ₹	June ₹	July ₹	August ₹	Sep. ₹	Oct. ₹	Nov. ₹
Sales	82,000	88,500	84,000	93,000	72,000	82,500	98,600	92,800	1,04,400
Less : cash sales	2,000	2,000	2,000	2,000	2,000	2,000	2,000	2,000	2,000
	80,000	86,500	82,000	91,000	70,000	80,500	96,600	90,800	1,02,400

Problem 9. *From the following information and the assumptions that the balance in hand on 1.1.2002 is ₹ 75,000, prepare cash budget.*

Months	*Sales*	*Materials*	*Wages*	*Selling and Distri.cost*	*Production cost*	*Administration cost*
	₹	₹	₹	₹	₹	₹
January	*72,000*	*25,000*	*10,000*	*4,000*	*6,000*	*1,500*
February	*97,000*	*31,000*	*12,100*	*5,000*	*6,300*	*1,700*
March	*86,000*	*25,500*	*10,600*	*5,500*	*6,000*	*2,000*
April	*88,600*	*30,600*	*25,000*	*6,700*	*6,500*	*2,200*
May	*1,02,500*	*37,000*	*22,000*	*8,500*	*8,000*	*2,500*
June	*1,08,700*	*38,800*	*23,000*	*9,000*	*8,200*	*2,500*

Assume that 50% are cash sales. Assets are to be acquired in the month of February and April. Therefore, provision should be made for the payment of ₹ 8,000 and ₹ 25,000 for the same. An application has been made to the bank for the grant of a loan of ₹ 30,000 and it is hoped that it will be received in the month of May.

It is anticipated that a dividend of ₹ 35,000 will be paid in the month of June. Debtors are allowed one month's credit. Sales commission@3% on sales is to be paid.

Creditors (for goods or overheads) grant one month's credit.

Assume all expenses are paid in the following month.

Solution :

Cash Budget

Particulars	*Jan.*	*Feb.*	*March*	*Apr.*	*May*	*June*
	₹	₹	₹	₹	₹	₹
Opening balance	72,500	96,340	1,21,330	1,55,650	1,51,292	2,05,767
Receipts						
Cash Sales	36,000	48,500	43,000	44,300	51,250	54,350
Bank loan received	-	-	-	-	30,000	-
Amount received from Debtors	-	36,000	48,500	43,000	44,300	51,250
Total Receipts	1,08,500	1,80,840	2,12,830	2,42,950	2,76,842	3,11,367
Payments						
Provision of capital expenditure	-	8,000	-	25,000	-	-
Dividend paid	-	-	-	-	-	35,000
Wages	10,000	12,100	10,600	25,000	22,000	23,000
Selling and distribution cost	-	4,000	5,000	5,500	6,700	8,500
Production cost	-	6,000	6,300	6,000	6,500	8,000
Administration cost	-	1,500	1,700	2,000	2,200	2,500
Amount paid to creditors	-	25,000	31,000	25,500	30,600	37,000
Sales Commission	2,160	2,910	2,580	2,658	3,075	3,261
Total Payments	12,160	59,510	57,180	91,658	71,075	1,17,261
Closing Balance [TR – TP]	96,340	1,21,330	1,55,650	1,51,292	2,05,767	1,94,106

NOTE : Sales commission paid in the same month itself.

Working :

	Sales Commission		
Jan.	72,000 × 3/100	=	2160
Feb.	97,000 × 3/100	=	2910
March	86,000 × 3/100	=	2580
April	88,600 × 3/100	=	2658
May	10,2500 × 3/100	=	3075
June	1,08,700 × 3/100	=	3261

Problem 10. *From the following information relating to Blue Star Engineering Co. prepare a cash budget for the half year ending on 30th September 2001.*

(a) Anticipated sales, purchases and costs :

Months	*Sales* ₹	*Purchases* ₹	*Wages* ₹	*Overheads* ₹
March	*1,50,000*	*90,000*	*18,000*	*31,000*
April	*1,40,000*	*1,20,000*	*28,000*	*35,400*
May	*1,54,000*	*84,000*	*20,800*	*36,500*
June	*1,68,000*	*1,36,000*	*22,200*	*36,500*
July	*1,82,000*	*1,28,000*	*30,000*	*37,000*
August	*2,04,000*	*1,51,000*	*28,000*	*37,500*
September	*2,40,000*	*1,62,000*	*25,000*	*38,000*

(b) Other Information :

(i) Bank Balance on 1.4.2001 was ₹ 60,000.

(ii) The loan instalment of ₹ 20,000 per month was to be remitted from July to December 2001.

(iii) Sales commission@5% on Sales was to be remitted to the distributors in the month following the sales.

(iv) ₹ 65,000 was expected to be received as deposit from the distributors in the month of July.

(v) 50% of the sales are on credit, the period of credit being 1 month.

(vi) 50% of the materials purchased can be paid for after a month.

(vii) 25% of the overheads could be settled in the month following their incidence.

(viii) Wages are paid on the first working day of the following month.

Solution :

Blue Star Engineering

Cash Budget for the period of 6 months

Particulars	*April* ₹	*May* ₹	*June* ₹	*July* ₹	*Aug.* ₹	*Sept.* ₹
Opening Cash Balance	60,000	40,200	13,975	1,000	21,525	9,200
Receipts						
Cash Sales	70,000	77,000	84,000	91,000	1,02,000	1,20,000
Amount received from credit sales	75,000	70,000	77,000	84,000	91,000	1,02,000

Deposit from distributors	-	-	-	65,000	-	-
Total Receipts	2,05,000	1,87,200	1,74,975	2,41,000	2,14,525	2,31,200
Payments						
Repayment of loan	-	-	-	20,000	20,000	20,000
Sales commission paid	7,500	7,000	7,700	8,400	9,100	10,200
Amount paid to Creditors (50% cash)	60,000	42,000	68,000	64,000	75,500	81,000
Amount paid to Creditors (50% in the month following)	45,000	60,000	42,000	68,000	64,000	75,500
Wages paid	18,000	28,000	20,800	22,200	30,000	28,000
Overheads paid	34,300	36,225	36,500	36,875	37,375	37,875
Total payments	1,64,800	1,73,225	1,75,000	2,19,475	2,35,975	2,52,575
Balance	40,200	13,975	– 25	21,525	– 21,450	– 21,375
Bank OD	—	—	+ 1025	—	+ 30,650	40,000
Closing Balance	40,200	13,975	1,000	21,525	9,200	18,625

Working :

1. *Credit Sales*

	₹
March	75,000
April	70,000
May	77,000
June	84,000
July	91,000
Aug.	1,02,000
Sep.	1,20,000

2. *Sales Commission*

	₹
March	7,500
April	7,000
May	7,700
June	8,400
July	9,100
Aug.	10,200
Sep.	12,000

3. *Amount paid to creditors*

	April ₹	*May* ₹	*June* ₹	*July* ₹	*Aug.* ₹	*Sep.* ₹
50% paid in the same month	60,000	42,000	68,000	64,000	75,500	81,000
50% in the month following	45,000	60,000	42,000	68,000	64,000	75,500
	1,05,000	1,02,000	1,10,000	1,32,000	1,39,500	1,56,500

4. *Overheads*

75% current	26,550	27,375	27,375	27,750	28,125	28,500
25% of previous month	7,750	8,850	9,125	9,125	9,250	9,375
	34,300	36,225	36,500	36,875	37,375	37,875

III. Flexible Budget

Problem 1. *For production of 10,000 Electrical Automatic Irons the following are the budgeted expenses.*

Cost element	*Cost Per unit* ₹
Direct material	*60*
Direct labour	*30*
Variable overheads	*25*
Fixed overhead (₹ 1,50,000)	*15*
Variable expenses (Direct)	*5*
Selling Expenses (10%fixed)	*15*
Administration Expenses (₹ 50,000 rigid for all levels of Production)	*5*
Distribution Expenses (20% fixed)	*5*
Total cost of sale per unit	*160*

Prepare a Budget for production of 6000, 7000 and 8000 irons showing distinctly marginal cost and total cost.

[M.Com. (CA) May 2004 PU]

Solution : **Flexible Budget**

Particulars	*6,000 Units*		*7,000 Units*		*8,000 Units*		*10,000 Units*	
	CPU ₹	*TC* ₹	*CPU* ₹	*TC* ₹	*CPU* ₹	*TC* ₹	*CPU* ₹	*TC* ₹
Fixed Cost overheads	25	1,50,000	21.43	1,50,000	18.75	1,50,000	15.00	1,50,000
Administration expenses	8.33	50,000	7.14	50,000	6.25	50,000	5.00	50,000
Distribution expenses	1.67	10,000	1.43	10,000	1.25	10,000	1.00	10,000
Selling expenses	2.5	15,000	2.14	15,000	1.88	15,000	1.50	15,000
Total fixed cost	37.5	2,25,000	32.14	2,25,000	28.13	2,25,000	22.50	2,25,000
Variable Cost								
Direct material	60	3,60,000	60	4,20,000	60	4,80,000	60	6,00,000
Direct labour	30	1,80,000	30	2,10,000	30	2,40,000	30	3,00,000
Variable overhead	25	1,50,000	25	1,75,000	25	2,00,000	25	2,50,000
Variable expenses	5	30,000	5	35,000	5	40,000	5	50,000
Selling expenses	13.50	81,000	13.50	94,500	13.50	1,08,000	13.50	1,35,000
Distribution expenses	4.00	24,000	4.00	28,000	4.00	32,000	4.00	40,000
Total variable cost	137.50	8,25,000	137.50	9,62,500	137.50	11,00,000	137.50	13,75,000
Total Cost (TFC + TVC)	175	10,50,000	169.64	11,87,500	165.63	13,25,000	160	16,00,000

Working Notes :

1. Distribution expenses ₹ 5.00
   Less : fixed 1.00
   variable 4.00

   Fixed cost × budgeted production
   1 × 10000 = 10000

2. Selling expenses ₹ 15.00
   Less fixed 10% 1.50
   Variable 13.50

   Fixed cost × Budgeted production
   1.50 × 10,000 = 15,000

Problem 2. *ABC Ltd. has prepared the budget for the production of one lakh units of the only commodity manufactured by them for a costing period as under.*

Raw materials	*₹ 2.52 per unit*
Direct material	*₹ 0.75 per unit*
Direct expenses	*₹ 0.10 per unit*
Works overhead (60% fixed)	*₹ 2.50 per unit*
Administrative overhead (80% fixed)	*₹ 0.40 per unit*
Selling overhead (50%fixed)	*₹ 0.20 per unit*

The actual production during the period was only 60,000 units. Calculate the revised budgeted cost per unit. [MBA Madras]

Solution : **Flexible Budget**

Particulars	*1,00,000 units*		*60,000 units*	
	CPU ₹	*TC* ₹	*CPU* ₹	*TC* ₹
Fixed Cost				
Works overhead	1.50	1,50,000	2.50	1,50,000
Administration overhead	0.32	32,000	0.53	32,000
Selling overhead	0.10	10,000	0.17	10,000
Total Fixed cost	1.92	1,92,000	3.2	1,92,000
Variable Cost				
Raw material	2.52	2,52,000	2.52	1,51,200
Direct labour	0.75	75,000	0.75	45,000
Direct expenses	0.10	10,000	0.10	6,000
Works overhead	1.00	1,00,000	1.00	60,000
Administration overhead	0.08	8,000	0.08	4,800
selling overhead	.10	10,000	.10	6,000
Total VC	4.55	4,55,000	4.55	2,73,000
Total cost [FC + VC]	6.47	6,47,000	7.75	4,65,000

Workings : [CPU = Cost Per Unit, TC = Total Cost]

Fixed cost

1. Works overhead	2.50	(100%)
Less : fixed	1.50	(60%)
Variable	1.00	(40%)

Fixed cost 1,00,000 × budgeted production

1.50 × 10,000 = 1,50,000

2. Administration overhead	0.40	(100%)
Less : fixed 80%	0.32	(80%)
Variable	0.08	(20%)

Fixed cost × Budgeted production

.32 × 1,00,000 = 32,000

3. Selling overhead	0.20	(100%)
Less : fixed	0.10	(50%)
Variable	0.10	(50%)

Fixed cost × Budgeted production

.10 × 1,00,000 = 10,000

Problem 3. *Draw up a flexible budget for overhead expenses on the basis of the following data and determine the overhead rate at 70%, 80% and 90% of plant capacity.*

	Capacity level		
	70%	*80%*	*90%*
Variable Overheads			
Indirect labour	-	*12,000*	-
Stores including spares	-	*4,000*	-
Semi-variable Overheads	-		
Power (30%fixed, 70% variable)	-	*20,000*	-
Repairs & Maintenance (60% fixed 40 % variable)	-	*2,000*	-
Fixed Overheads			
Depreciation	-	*11,000*	-
Insurance	-	*3,000*	-
Salaries	-	*10,000*	-
Total Overheads	-	*62,000*	-
Estimated Direct Labour Hrs.	-	*1,24,000 Hrs.*	-

[B.Com. PU 2002]

Solution : **Flexible Budget**

Particulars	Capacity level 70% ₹	80% ₹	90% ₹
Fixed Cost			
Depreciation	11,000	11,000	11,000
Insurance	3,000	3,000	3,000
Salaries	10,000	10,000	10,000
Power	6,000	6,000	6,000
Repairs and maintenance	1,200	1,200	1,200
Total Fixed cost	31,200	31,200	31,200
Variable Cost			
Indirect labour	10,500	12,000	13,500
Stores including spares	3,500	4,000	4,500
Power	12,250	14,000	15,750
Repairs and maintenance	700	800	900
Total Variable cost	26,950	30,800	34,650
Total cost (FC + VC)	58,150	62,000	65,850
Estimated direct labour hours	1,08,500	1,24,000	1,39,500
Cost per hour = [Total cost/Total hours × 1 hour]	0.536	0.500	0.472

Workings :

Fixed Cost from semi variable overheads :

1. Power (100%)	₹	20,000	
Less : 30% fixed		6,000	(1) (20,000 × 30/100)
70% variable		14,000	
2. Repairs and maintenance	₹	2,000	
Less : 60% fixed		1,200	(2000 × 60/100)
40% Variable		800	

Variable Cost :

(*a*) Indirect labour	= 12,000/80 × 70	=	10,500
	12,000/80 × 90	=	13,500
(*b*) Stores including spare	= 4,000/80 × 70	=	3,500
	4,000/80 × 90	=	4,500
(*c*) Power	= 14,000/80 × 70	=	12,250
	14,000/80 × 90	=	15,750
(*d*) Repairs and maintenance	= 800/80 × 70	=	700
	800/80 × 90	=	900

Hours cost per hour :

124000/80 × 70 = 108500

124000/80 × 90 = 139500

At 70% Capacity 58150/108500 × 1 = ₹ 0.536

At 80% Capacity 62000/124000 × 1 = ₹ 0.500

At 90% Capacity 65850/139500 × 1 = ₹ 0.472

Problem 4. *Prepare a manufacturing overhead budget and ascertain the manufacturing overhead rates at 50% and 70% capacities. The following particulars are given at 60% capacity level.*

	At 60% capacity level ₹
Variable Overheads	
Indirect Materials	*6,000*
Indirect Labour	*18,000*
Semi Variable Overheads	
Electricity (40% fixed)	*30,000*
Repairs & Maintenance (80% fixed)	*3,000*
Fixed Overhead	
Depreciation	*16,500*
Insurance	*4,500*
Salaries	*15,000*
Total Overheads	*93,000*
Estimated Direct Labour Hrs.	*1,86,000 Hrs.*

[B.Com. Madurai] [M.Com. Madras]

Solution : **Flexible Budget**

Particulars	Capacity level 50% ₹	60% ₹	70% ₹
Fixed Cost :			
Doprecation	16,500	16,500	16,500
Insurance	4,500	4,500	4,500
Salaries	15,000	15,000	15,000
Electricity	12,000	12,000	12,000
Repairs & maintenance	2,400	2,400	2,400
Total fixed cost	50,400	50,400	50,400
Variable Cost :			
Indirect Labour	15,000	18,000	21,000
Indirect material	5,000	6,000	7,000
Electricity	15,000	18,000	21,000
Repairs and maintenance	500	600	700
Total Variable cost	35,500	42,600	49,700
Total Cost (FC & VC)	85,900	93,000	1,00,100
Estimated direct labour hours	1,55,000	1,86,000	2,17,000
Overhead rate [TC/T. Hrs.]	0.55	0.50	0.46

Overhead rate

Total cost/Total direct labour hrs.

85,900/1,55,000	=	0.55
93,000/1,86,000	=	0.50
1,00,100/2,17,000	=	0.46

Workings :

(*i*) Indirect material			(*ii*) Indirect labour		
600/60 × 50	=	5,000	18,000/60 × 50 = 15,000		
600/60 × 70	=	7,000	18,000/60 × 70 = 21,000		
(*iii*) Electricity	₹	30,000	(*iv*) Repairs and maintenance		3,000
Less : 40% Fixed		12,000	*Less* : Fixed 80%		2,400
Variable 60%		18,000	Variable 20%		600
18000/60 × 50	=	15,000	600/60 × 50	=	500
18000/60 × 70	=	21,000	600/60 × 70	=	700

Problem 5. *The monthly budget for the manufacturing overhead of a concern for two levels of activity were as follows.*

Capacity level	***60%***	***100%***
Budgeted production(units)	*600*	*1,000*
	₹	₹
Indirect wages	*1,200*	*2,000*
consumable stores	*900*	*1,500*
Maintenance	*1,100*	*1,500*
Power and fuel	*1,600*	*2,000*
Depreciation	*4,000*	*4,000*
Insurance	*1,000*	*1,000*

(a) Indicate which of the items are fixed, variable and semi-variable.

(b) Prepare a flexible budget for 80% of the activity.

[MCA Madras] [B.Com. Hons. - Delhi]

Solution : **Flexible Budget**

Particulars	*Capacity level*		
Capacity level	*60%*	*80%*	*100%*
Units	*600*	*800*	*1000*
Fixed Cost :	₹	₹	₹
Depreciation	4,000	4,000	4,000
Insurance	1,000	1,000	1,000
Maintenance	500	500	500
Power and fuel	1,000	1,000	1,000
Total Fixed cost	6,500	6,500	6,500

Variable Cost :			
Wages @ ₹ 2 per unit	1,200	1,600	2,000
Consumable @ ₹ 1.50 Per unit	900	1,200	1,500
Maintenance @ ₹ 1 per unit	600	800	1,000
Power and Fuel @ ₹ 1 per unit	600	800	1,000
Total variable cost	3,300	4,400	5,500
Total Cost [FC + VC]	9,800	10,900	12,000
Workings :			
Cost per unit = Total cost/output	16.33	13.62	12.00

(1) (i) *Fixed :* Depreciation and Insurance

(ii) *Variable :* Wages consumable stores

(iii) *Semi-variable :* Maintenance Power and Fuel.

(2) Budget for 80% capacity (output 800 units)

Wages @ ₹ 2 per unit	1,600
Consumable stores (1.50 × 800)	1,200
Maintenance ₹ 500 + (800 ×1)	1,300
Power and Fuel ₹ 1000 + (800 × 1)	1,800
Depreciation	4,000
Insurance	1,000
Total Cost	10,900

(3) 9,800/600 = ₹ 16.33   10,900/800 = ₹ 13.62   12,000/1000 = ₹ 12.00

(4) *Variable Cost*

(a) Wages 1,200/600 = ₹ 2 or 2,000/1,000 = ₹ 2

(b) Consumable stores = 900/600 = ₹ 1.50 or 1,500/1000 = ₹ 1.50

(c) Maintenance 1,100/600 = 1.83 1,500/1000 = ₹ 1.50

So, it is treated as semi variable

i.e., 1,500 – 1,100 / 1,000 - 600 = 400/400 = ₹ 1 is variable and ₹ 500 (*i.e.,* 1,100 - 600) is fixed

(d) *Power and Fuel :*

1,600/600 = 2.66 and 2,000/1,000 = ₹ 2

So, it is also treated as semi variable cost

i.e., 2,000-1,600/1,000-600 = 400/400 = ₹ 1 is variable and ₹ 1,000 (*i.e.,* 1,600 - 600) is fixed.

Problem 6. *The cost of an article at a capacity level of 5,000 units is given under A below. For a variation of 25% in capacity above or below this level, the individual expenses vary as indicated under B below.*

	A (₹)	B
Material cost	*25,000*	*(100% Varying)*
Labour cost	*15,000*	*(100% Varying)*

Power	*1,250*	*(80% Varying)*
Repairs and maintenance	*2,000*	*(75% Varying)*
Stores	*1,000*	*(100% Varying)*
Inspection	*500*	*(20% Varying)*
Depreciation	*10,000*	*(100% Varying)*
Administrative overheads	*5,000*	*(25% Varying)*
Selling overheads	*3,000*	*(25% Varying)*
	62,750	

Cost per unit ₹ 12.55

Find the unit cost of the product at a production level of 4000, and 6000 units.

[MCA Madras]

Solution :

Workings for flexible Budget		**Fixed Cost**
1. Material	Variable cost	Power
2. Labour	Variable cost	Repairs and maintenance
3. Power	Variable cost	Administrative overhead
4. Repair maintenance	Variable cost	Inspection
5. Stores	Variable cost	Selling overheads
6. Inspection	Variable cost	
7. Depreciation	Variable cost	
8. Administrative overheads	Variable cost	
9. Selling overhead	Variable cost	

1. Material

25,000/5000 × 4000	=	20,000
25,000/5000 × 6000	=	30,000

2. Labour

15000/15000 × 4000	=	12,000
15000/5000 = 6000	=	18,000

3. Power cost

Power cost		1,250
Less : Fixed 20%		250
Variable		1,000
1000/5000 × 4000	=	800
1000/5000 × 6000	=	1,200

4. Repairs and maintenance

Cost	₹	2,000
Less : 25% Fixed		500
Variable		1,500
1500/5000 × 4000	=	1,200
500/5000 × 6000	=	1,800

5. Stores (no fixed)		₹	1,000
1000/5000 × 4000	=		800
1000/5000 × 6000	=		1,200
6. Inspection	=	₹	500
Less : Fixed 80%			400
Variable 20%			100
100/5000 × 4000	=		80
100/5000 × 6000	=		120
7. Depreciation		₹	10,000
10000/5000 × 4000	=		8,000
10000/5000 × 6000	=		12,000
8. Ad. overhead		₹	5,000
Less : Fixed 75%			3,750
Variable 25%			1,250
1250/5000 × 4000	=		1,000
1250/5000 × 6000	=		1,500
9. Selling overhead		₹	3,000
Less : Fixed (75%)			2,250
Variable (25%)			750
750/5000 × 4000	=		600
750/5000 × 6000	=		900

Flexible Budget

Particulars	*4000 units TC (₹)*	*5000 units TC (₹)*	*6000 units TC (₹)*
Fixed Cost			
Power	250	250	250
Repairs and Maintenance	500	500	500
Ad. overhead	3,750	3,750	3,750
Selling overhead	2,250	2,250	2,250
Inspection	400	400	400
Total Fixed cost	7,150	7,150	7,150
Variable Cost			
Materials	20,000	25,000	30,000
Labour	12,000	15,000	18,000
Power	800	1,000	1,200
Repairs & Maintenance	1,200	1,500	1,800
Stores	800	1,000	1,200
Inspection	80	100	120

Depreciation	8,000	10,000	12,000
Administrative overhead	1,000	1250	1,500
Selling overhead	600	750	900
Total variable cost [VC]	44,480	55,600	66,720
Total cost (FC + VC)	51,630	62,750	73,870

$$\text{Cost per unit} = \frac{\text{TC}}{\text{No. of units}} = \frac{51,630}{4,000} = ₹\ 12.90 \quad \frac{62,750}{5,000} = ₹\ 12.55$$

$$= \frac{73,870}{6,000} = ₹\ 12.31$$

Problem 7. *The following data are available in a manufacturing company for half yearly period.*

Fixed Expenses	*₹ (in lakhs)*	*₹ (in lakhs)*
Wages and salaries	*8.4*	
Rent rates and taxes	*5.6*	
Depreciation	*7.0*	
Sundry Administration expenses	*8.9*	
		29.9
Semi-variable Expenses (at 50% capacity)		
Maintenance and Repairs	*2.5*	
Indirect Labour	*9.9*	
Sales Department salaries etc.	*2.9*	
Sundry Administration expenses	*2.6*	
		17.9
Variable expenses (at 50% capacity)		
Materials	*24.0*	
Labour	*25.6*	
Other expenses	*3.8*	
		53.4

Assume that the fixed expenses remain constant for all levels of production, semi variable expenses remain constant between 45% and 65% of capacity, increasing by 10% between 65% and 80% capacity, and by 20% between 80% and 100% capacity.

Sales at various levels are	*(₹ in Lakhs)*
60% capacity	*100.00*
75% capacity	*120.00*
90% capacity	*150.00*
100% capacity	*170.00*

Prepare a flexible budget for the half year and forecast the profit at 60%, 75%, 90%, and 100% of capacity. [MBA Anna]

Solution : **Flexible Budget**

Particualrs	*60% Capacity* ₹	*75% Capacity* ₹	*90% Capacity* ₹	*100% Capacity* ₹
Fixed Expenses				
Wages and Salaries	8,40,000	8,40,000	8,40,000	8,40,000
Rent Rates and Taxes	5,60,000	5,60,000	5,60,000	5,60,000
Depreciation	7,00,000	7,00,000	7,00,000	7,00,000
Sundry Administration Expenses	8,90,000	8,90,000	8,90,000	8,90,000
Total Fixed Cost (A)	29,90,000	29,90,000	29,90,000	29,90,000
Semi Variable Expenses				
Maintenance and Repairs	2,50,000	2,75,000	3,00,000	3,00,000
Indirect Labour	9,90,000	10,89,000	11,88,000	11,88,000
Sales Department Salaries etc.,	2,90,000	3,19,000	3,48,000	3,48,000
Sundry Administration Expenses	2,60,000	2,86,000	3,12,000	3,12,000
Total Semi Variable Cost(B)	17,90,000	19,69,000	21,48,000	21,48,000
Variable Expenses				
Material	28,80,000	36,00,000	43,20,000	48,00,000
Labour	30,72,000	38,40,000	46,08,000	51,20,000
Other Expenses	4,56,000	5,70,000	6,84,000	7,60,000
Total Variable Cost (C)	64,08,000	80,10,000	96,12,000	10,68,000
Total Cost [A+B+C]	1,11,88,000	1,29,69,000	1,47,50,000	1,58,18,000
Sales	1,00,00,000	1,20,00,000	1,50,00,000	1,70,00,000
Less : Total Cost	1,11,88,000	1,29,69,000	1,47,50,000	1,58,18,000
Profit or loss	– 11,88,000	– 9,69,000	+ 2,50,000	+ 11,82,000

Workings :

1. *Material*

   24,00,000/50 × 60 = 28,80,000
   24,00,000/50 × 75 = 36,00,000
   24,00,000/50 × 90 = 43,20,000
   24,00,000/50 × 100 = 48,00,000

2. *Labour*

   25,60,000/50 × 60 = 30,72,000
   25,60,000/50 × 75 = 38,40,000
   25,60,000/50 × 90 = 46,00,000
   25,60,000/50 × 100 = 51,20,000

3. *Other Expenses*

   3,80,000/50 × 60 = 4,56,000
   3,80,000/50 × 75 = 5,70,000
   3,80,000/50 × 90 = 6,84,000
   3,80,000/50 × 100 = 7,60,000

Problem 8. *A company, working at 50% capacity, is manufacturing 10,000 units of a product. At 50% capacity the product cost is ₹ 180 and sale price is ₹ 200. The break up of the cost is as follows.*

Particulars	*Cost per unit*	
	₹	
Materials	100	
Wages	30	
Factory Overheads	30	(40% fixed)
Administration overheads	20	(50% fixed)

At 60% working capacity, raw material cost goes up by 2% and sales price falls by 2%. At 80% working capacity the raw material cost increases by 5% and sale price decreases by same percentage i.e., 5%.

Prepare a statement to show profitability at 60%, 80% and 90% capacity.

[BBM May 2005]

Solution : **Profitability Statement**

Particulars	60% Capacity 12,000 Units		80% Capacity 16,000 Units		90% Capacity 18,000 Units	
	CPU ₹	TC ₹	CPU ₹	TC ₹	CPU ₹	TC ₹
Sales (1)	196	23,52,000	190	30,40,000	200	36,00,000
Less : Variable Cost :						
Material	102	12,24,000	105	16,80,000	100	18,00,000
Wages	30	3,60,000	30	4,80,000	30	5,40,000
Variable factory overheads	18	2,16,000	18	2,88,000	18	3,24,000
Administrative overheads	10	1,20,000	10	1,60,000	10	1,80,000
Total Variable Cost (*i*)	160	19,20,000	163	26,08,000	158	28,44,000
Contribution [S-Vc] (*i-ii*) (*iii*)	36	4,32,000	27	4,32,000	42	7,16,000
Less : Fixed Cost						
Administrative overheads	8.33	1,00,000	6.25	1,00,000	5.55	1,00,000
Factory overheads	10.00	1,20,000	7.50	1,20,000	6.66	1,20,000
Total Fixed Cost	18.33	2,20,000	13.75	2,20,000	12.21	2,20,000
Profit [Contribution – TFC]	17.67	2,12,000	13.25	2,12,000	29.79	4,96,000

[CPU = Cost Per Unit, TC : Total Cost]

Workings :

1. Number of units

   10,000/50 × 60 = 12000

   10,000/50 × 80 = 16000

   10,000/50 × 90 = 18000

2. Selling pricle at 50% ₹ 200

   At 60%

3. *Material cost at 60%*

Material cost at 50% :	₹	100
+ 2%		2
		102

Sales price	₹ 200	At 80%	
Decrease 2%	4	Raw material cost	₹ 100
	196	+ 5%	5
At 80%			105
4. Factory Overheads at 50%	₹ 30.00	5. Admt. OH at 50% cap	20.00
Less : (fixed 40%)	12.00	*Less* : Fixed 50%	10.00
Variable cost	18.00	Variable (50%)	10.00
[12 × 10,000 = 1,20,000 FC]		[10 × 10,000 = 1,00,000 FC]	

Problem 9. *The expenses for budgeted production of 10,000 units in a factory are furnished below.*

Particulars	*Cost unit* ₹
Material	*70*
Labour	*25*
Variable overheads	*20*
Fixed overheads (₹ 1,00,000)	*10*
Variable expenses (Direct)	*5*
Selling expenses 10% fixed	*13*
Distribution expenses 20% fixed	*7*
Administration expenses (₹ 50,000)	*5*
Total cost per unit	*155*

Prepare a budget for production of (a) 8000 units (b) 6000 units (c) Compute cost per unit at both the levels.

Solution : **Flexible Budget**

Particulars	*6,000 Units*		*8,000 Units*		*10,000 Units*	
	CPU ₹	*TC* ₹	*CPU* ₹	*TC* ₹	*CPU* ₹	*TC* ₹
Fixed Cost						
Fixed overheads	16.67	1,00,000	12.50	1,00,000	10.00	1,00,000
Administration expenses	8.33	50,000	6.25	50,000	5.00	50,000
Selling expenses	2.17	13,000	1.60	13,000	1.30	13,000
Distribution expenses	2.33	14,000	1.75	14,000	1.40	14,000
Total Fixed Cost (A)	29.50	1,77,000	22.10	1,77,000	17.70	1,77,000
Variable Cost						
Material	70	4,20,000	70	5,60,000	70	7,00,000
Labour	25	1,50,000	25	2,00,000	25	2,50,000
Variable overheads	20	1,20,000	20	1,60,000	20	2,00,000
Variable expenses	5	30,000	5	40,000	5	50,000

Selling expenses	11.70	70,200	11.70	93,600	11.70	1,17,000
Distribution expenses	5.60	33,600	5.60	44,800	5.60	56,000
Total Variable Cost (B)	137.3	8,23,800	137.3	10,98,400	137.3	13,73,000
Total Cost [A+B]	166.8	10,00,800	159.4	12,75,400	155	15,50,000

[CPU Cost Per Unit TC = Total Cost]

Workings :

1. Distribution Expenses ₹ 7.00
   Less : Fixed 20% 1.40
   Variable Cost 5.60

   Fixed Cost = 1.40 × Budgeted production
   = 1.40 × 10000 = **14,000**

2. Selling Expenses ₹ 13.00
   Less : Fixed 10% (13 × 10/100) 1.30
   Variable Cost 11.70

   Fixed Cost = 1.30 × 10000 units
   = **13,000**

TEST PROBLEMS

1. Quick Products Ltd. sells two products X and Y in two division North and South. The following were the budgeted and actual sales for the year 1999.

	Budget				*Actual*			
	North		*South*		*North*		*South*	
	Units	₹ *per unit*	*Units*	₹ *per unit*	*Units*	₹ *per unit*	*Units*	₹ *per unit*
Product 'X'	500	180	300	180	600	180	400	180
Product 'Y'	300	430	200	430	200	430	150	430

For the year 2000, the board of Directors has approved the proposal of sales department to increase the price of 'X' to ₹ 200 and decrease the price of 'Y' to 400. The sales estimates from the divisional managers were as follows:

North : 'X' 800 units 'Y' 500 units

South : 'X' 600 units 'Y' 300 units

An intensive advertising campaign proposed by advertising consultants is expected to result in additional sales of 20% of each product in each division over the estimated sales. Prepare the sales budget for the sales budget for the year 2000 and present it together with the budgeted and actual sales for 1999.

[**Ans.**

	Budget for 2000		1999		Actual sale for 1999	
	Qty.	*Price*	*Qty.*	*Price*	*Qty.*	*Price*
Total	2,640	7,20,000	13,000	3,59,000	1,350	3,30,500]

2. Lakshmanan Ltd. plans to sell 1,10,000 units of a certain product line in the first fiscal quarter. 1,20,000 units in the second quarter. 1,30,000 units in the third quarter. 1,50,000 units in the fourth quarter and 1,40,000 units in the fifth quarter. At the beginning of the first quarter of the current year, there are 14,000 units of product in stock. At the end of each quarter, the company plans to have an inventory equal to one-fifth of the sales for the next fiscal quarter. How many units must be manufactured in each quarter of the current year.

[Madras, B.Com.,BBA April 2007, M.Com. April 1995]

Ans.

Paticulars Units	*1st Quarter Units*	*2nd Quarter Units*	*3rd Quarter Units*	*4th Quarter Units*	*Total units*
Total units to produced	1,20,000	1,22,000	1,34,000	1,48,000	5,24,000

3. The following overhead expenses relate to a cost centre operating at 50% of normal activity. Draw up a flexible budgeted for the cost centre for operating at 75%, 100% and 125% of normal capacity.

Indicate the basis upon which you have estimated each item of expense for the different operating system.

	₹
Foreman	60
Assistant foreman	40
Inspectors	65
Shop labourers	40
Machinery repairs	100
Defective work	25
Consumable stores	20
Overtime bonus	–
Machine depreciation	110
	460

[Madras, M.C.A., April 2007; B.B.A., Nov. 2004; M.Com., Sep. 1985]

Ans.

Flexible Budget

Particulars	*50% Capacity* ₹	*75% Capacity* ₹	*100% Capacity* ₹	*125% Capacity* ₹
Total	460	580	755	990

4. Ram Engg. Co. Ltd Manufactures 2 products X and Y. An estimate of the number of units to be sold in the first 7 months of 1992 are given below:

Month	X	Y
Jan.	5,000	14,000
Feb.	6,000	14,000
Mar.	8,000	12,000
Apr.	10,000	10,000
May	12,000	8,000
June	12,000	8,000
July	10,000	9,000

It is anticipated that will be no work-in-progress at the end of any month and finished units equal to half the anticipated sales for the next month will be in stock at end of the each month (including Dec. 1991). You are required to prepare a production budget showing the number of units to be manufactured each month. *[Madras, M.Com., Oct. 1993; Sep. 1992]*

Ans.

	Jan.	Feb.	March	April	May	June
Production in units: X:	5,500	7,000	9,000	11,000	12,000	11,000
Y:	14,000	13,000	11,000	9,000	8,000	8,500

5. Alacrity co. finishes the following information. Prepare a cash budget for 6 months commencing from 1st June 1990 when the bank balance is estimated to be ₹ 1,10,000.

Month	*Sales*	*Selling Overheads*	*Purchases*	*Wages*	*Factor Overheads*	*Adminis-trative Overheads*	*Research expenditure*
	₹	₹	₹	₹	₹	₹	₹
March	82,000	5,000	40,000	10,000	8,400	3,400	2,000
April	88,000	3,250	37,000	8,000	5,680	2,500	2,400
May	84,000	4,100	40,000	8,400	5,920	2,760	2,400
June	93,000	3,710	39,060	8,800	5,440	2,480	2,400
July	72,000	3,210	39,900	6,000	5,880	2,600	2,400
August	82,500	3,600	39,400	9,600	6,000	2,520	2,600
September	88,600	3,450	36,400	8,000	5,680	2,700	2,600
October	92,800	3,210	30,574	8,400	5,360	2,560	2,600
November	1,04,000	3,200	28,000	7,600	5,850	2,620	2,400

Lag in payment of wages $^1/_4$ month.

Lag in payment of factory overhead 1 month.

Lag in payment of administration overhead $^1/_2$ month.

Lag in payment of selling overhead 1 month.

Lag in payment of research expenditure 1 month.

Period of credit allowed by creditors 3 months.

Period of credit allowed to debtors 2 months.

Other information relevant to the preparation of budget is as follows:

(*i*) A sales commission of 5% on sales and due two months after sales is payable in addition to selling overheads.

(*ii*) Capital expenditure planned is (1) plant purchased in June 1990 for ₹ 1,00,000 payable on delivery and (2) Building purchased in June 1990 for ₹ 8,00,000 payable in four half yearly instalments the first being payable in July 1990.

(*iii*) Interest on Bombay Sport Trust Bonds amounting to ₹ 50,000 is to be received in October 1990.

(*iv*) Cash sales per month–₹ 2,000.

(*v*) Dividend to be paid in september 1990 is ₹ 10,000.

(*vi*) Tax amounting to ₹ 30,000 is to be paid on 1 Aug., 1990.

(*vii*) A call of ₹2 per share on equity share capital of ₹ 5,00,000 divided into 50,000 shares of ₹10 each is to received on 1 July, 1990.

[Madras, M.com., Oct. 1993; Sep. 1992]

Ans.

	June ₹	*July* ₹	*Aug.* ₹	*Sep.* ₹	*Oct.* ₹	*Nov.* ₹
Opening balance + receipts	1,98,500	2,14,335	45,345	19,945	76,575	98,490
Total payments	1,68,165	2,61,990	97,400	75,870	66,685	65,390
Closing balance	30,335	47,655 (O.D.)	52,055 (O.D.)	55,925 (O.D.)	9,890	33,100

6. With the following data for 60% activity, prepare a budget at 80% activity.

Production at 60% capacity	-	600 units
Materials	-	₹ 100 per unit
Labour	-	₹ 40 per unit
Direct expenses	-	₹ 10 per unit
Factory expenses	-	₹ 40,000 (40% fixed)
Administration	-	₹ 30,000 (60% fixed)

[Madras, B.Com. (CS) April 2007; 1 M.Com. (ICE) Oct, 2003; B.Com. May 2001 (old); B.A. Corp Sep. 1988;]

[**Ans.** At 80% activity – Total cost : ₹ 2,20,000; Per unit : ₹ 252.5;
At 60% activity – Total cost : ₹ 1,60,000; Per unit : ₹ 266.67[

7. The expenses for the production of 5,000 units in a factory are given follows:

	Per unit ₹
Materials	50
Labour	20
Variable overhead	15
Fixed overhead (₹ 50,000)	10
Administrative expenses (5% fixed)	10
Selling expenses (20% fixed)	6

Distribution expenses (10% fixed)	5
Total cost per unit	116

You are required to prepare a budget for the production of 7,000 units.

[Madras, M.Com., (1st year) April 2003; M.Com., (1st year) (ICE) Oct. 2002; B.Com. March 1996]

[Ans. Total cost for 7,000 units : ₹ 7,69,600; Total cost for 5,000 units : ₹ 5,80,000]

8. The following details apply to an annual budget for a manufacturing company:

Quarter	1	2	3	4
Working days	65	60	55	60
Production [units per working day]	100	110	120	105
Raw material purchases				
(% by weight of annual total)	30%	50%	20%	–
Budgeted purchase price [per kg]	₹ 1	₹ 1.50	₹ 1.125	–

Quantity of raw material per unit of production : 2 kg.

Budgeted opening stock of raw material : 4,000 kg [cost ₹ 4,000]

Budgeted closing stock of raw materials : 2,000 kg

Issues are priced on FIFO basis.

Calculate the following figures:

(*i*) Quarterly and annual purchases of raw material by weight value.

(*ii*) Closing quarterly stock by weight and value.

[Madras B.A., Corp. Sep. 1997]

Ans.

	Q_1	Q_2	Q_3	Q_4	*Annual*
Production (Units)	6,500	6,600	6,600	6,300	26,000
Material consumption (kgs)	13,000	13,200	13,200	12,200	52,000
Material purchased (kgs)	15,000	25,000	10,000	–	50,000
(52,000 + 2,000 – 4,000)					
Material purchased (₹)	15,000	26,250	11,250	–	52,500
Closing stock quantity (kgs)	6,000	17,800	14,600	2,000	2,000
Closing stock value (₹)	6,000	18,690	16,080	2,250	2,250

□□□

19

Inflation Accounting

Generally, Trading account, Profit and Loss account and Balance Sheets are prepared for the purpose of presenting the financial position of the concern and displaying the operational results achieved during an accounting period. But, these financial statements are prepared on the basis of traditional concept of cost and revenue. *i.e.,* it is expressed in monetary units or rupees. The recording of business transactions under this assumption that monetary unit is constant is known as historical accounting. But, this assumption is not valid, because there have been inflationary as well as deflationary conditions. Purchasing power of rupee in India keeps changing from time to time on account of changes in the general price level.

LIMITATIONS OF HISTORICAL ACCOUNTING

The following are the important limitations of historical accounts.

(*i*) In actual practice the financial statements are prepared on the basis of the historical cost. So, the financial statements may be incorrectly interpreted unless appropriate adjustment are made on the current price level.

(*ii*) Unrealistic profit due to the depreciation calculated under the historical cost method.

(*iii*) Insufficient provisions of depreciations.

(*iv*) According to Companies Act 1956 fixed assets are shown at their historical cost and not at current cost.

(*v*) Return on capital employed is misleading, because the profits are overstated and fixed assets are understated.

(*vi*) Incorrect ascertainment of operating capacity.

(*vii*) Historical cost accounting mixes up the holding gains and its operating gains which does not help in taking effective managerial decisions.

(*viii*) Misleading inter-period and inter-firm comparison.

(*ix*) Difficulty in comparison of profitability of two plants.

To overcome the limitations of conventional accounting, accounting for price level changes is developed or advocated.

Accounting for changing prices (or inflation accounting) is a system of accounting which regularly records all items in financial statements at their current values.

APPROACHES TO THE PRICE LEVEL ACCOUNTING

Generally, there are four important approaches to the price level accounting :

(A) Current Purchasing Power Accounting [CPPA].

(B) Current Cost Accounting [CCA].

(C) Specific and General Price Level Accounting [SGPLA].

(D) Periodic revaluation of fixed assets along with the adoption of the LIFO method of inventory.

(A) Current Purchasing Power Accounting (CPPA)

According to this method any approved general price index is used to convert the values of items in the financial statement at a particular period of time. This method considers the changes in the value of item as a result of the general price level but it does not consider the changes in the value of an individual item.

Steps in Current Purchasing Power Account :

(*i*) Conversion Factor.

$$\text{Formula} = \frac{\text{Index you are converting to}}{\text{Index you are converting from}}$$

or

$$\text{Conversion Factor} = \frac{\text{Price index at the date of revaluation}}{\text{Price index at the date of existing figure}}$$

(*ii*) Mid Period Conversion.

(*iii*) Distinction between monetary accounts and non monetary accounts.

(*iv*) Determine gain or loss on monetary items.

(*v*) Cost of sales and inventories.

(*vi*) Ascertainment of profit.

(*a*) Conversion income method.

(*b*) Net change method.

(B) Current Cost Accounting (CCA)

Current purchasing power method considers only changes in the money value, but it does not take into account the changes in the value of individual item. Under this method, the value of particular item may be increased on the basis of general price index. But, the actual value of that item might have decreased. In order to overcome this limitation, the UK Government formed an Inflation Accounting Committee headed by Franis Sandilands. This committee published its report in 1975, to recommend the adoption of current cost accounting for dealing with the problem of Inflation Accounting.

In this method, historic values of items are not taken into account. Rather current values of individual items are taken on the basis of preparing profit and loss account and balance sheet. These items are not adjusted as a result of change in the general price level as they are adjusted in the current purchasing power method.

Under current cost accounting approach of inflation accounting, accounting profit is divided into three divisions.

(*i*) Unrealised holding gain.

(*ii*) Realised holding gain.

(*iii*) Current operating profit.

(*i*) Unrealised Holding Gain

Unrealised Holding Gain is the excess of the replacement cost of a non-monetary asset sold on the closing date over its historical cost.

(*ii*) Realised Holding Gain

Realised Holding Gain is the excess of the replacement cost of a non-monetary asset sold on the date of its sale over its historical cost.

(*iii*) Current Operating Profit

For the computation of current operating profit, the following adjustments are to be made in the current cost accounting method.

(*a*) Depreciation adjustment.

(*b*) Cost of sales adjustment.

(*c*) Monetary working capital adjustment.

(*d*) Gearing adjustment.

(*a*) *Depreciation Adjustment.* The current year depreciation change under current cost accounting method is obtained by apportioning the average net replacement cost over the expected remaining useful life of the fixed assets at the beginning of the period.

(*b*) *Cost of Sales Adjustment (COSA)*

Formula :

$$COSA = (C - O)\, I_a \left(\frac{C}{I_c} - \frac{O}{I_o}\right)$$

Where, O = Historical cost of opening stock.

C = Historical cost of closing stock.

I_a = Average index number of the period.

I_o = Index number appropriate to opening stock.

I_c = Index number appropriate to closing stock.

(*c*) *Monetary Working Capital Adjustment (MWCA)*

$$MWCA = C - O - I_a \left(\frac{C}{I_c} - \frac{O}{I_o}\right)$$

O = Opening monetary working capital.

C = Closing monetary working capital.

I_a = Average index number for the period.

I_o = Index number appropriate to opening MWC.

I_c = Index number appropriate to closing MWC.

(*d*) *Gearing Adjustment*

$$\text{Gearing adjustment} = \frac{L}{L+S}$$

L = Average net borrowing.

S = Average shareholders funds.

A = Total of current cost adjustments.

(C) Specific and General Price Level Accounting (SGPLA)

This approach of accounting has not been popular because it has not been proposed so far by any institutional body as other approaches have been recommended by institutional bodies.

(D) Periodic Evaluation of fixed assets along with Adoption of LIFO method of Inventory

LIFO method of inventory valuation got the world wide general acceptance and is made use of during inflation. The advantage of this method are of the view that periodic revaluation of fixed assets along with the adoption of LIFO method can reasonably reduce the effect of increasing prices.

ADVANTAGES OF INFLATION ACCOUNTING

(*i*) It helps to maintain the physical capital because of changing depreciation on their current values.

(*ii*) It facilitates comparison of profitability of the two plants set up at different dates.

(*iii*) Balance sheet exhibits a true and fair view of the financial position of a firm.

(*iv*) For supplying more meaningful information through the Ratio analysis that can be adjusted to the current values.

(*v*) To protect the employees, shareholders, and public. They are not misled, because inflation accounting shows current profit based on the current prices.

(*vi*) To help the owners, creditors and management in order to adjust the rate of return on capital employed to the current price index.

(*vii*) Profit and Loss Account will not overstate the business income.

DISADVANTAGES OF INFLATION ACCOUNTING

(*i*) So, many calculations make more complications.

(*ii*) This system is not acceptable to the income tax authorities.

(*iii*) Accounting for price level changes is not free from prejudice.

(*iv*) During the periods of deflation only lower amount of depreciation will be changed.

(*v*) Computation of profit under this system may not be a realistic profit.

TEST QUESTIONS

1. What is meant by Inflation Accounting ?
2. What are the limitations of Historical Accounting ?
3. Describe the various approaches to the Price level Accounting.
4. What is meant by Current Purchasing Price Accounting ?
5. What is meant by Current Cost Accounting ?
6. Briefly explain the advantages of Inflation Accounting.
7. What are the Limitations of Inflation Accounting ?

PROBLEMS AND SOLUTIONS

Problem 1. *Compute the net monetary result of RPMS & Co. Ltd. as on 31.12.2001. The relevant data are given below :*

	1.1.2001	*31.12.2001*
	₹	₹
Cash	*5,000*	*10,000*
Book Debts	*20,000*	*25,000*
Creditors	*15,000*	*20,000*
Loan	*20,000*	*20,000*
Retail price index numbers :		
1st January	*200*	
31st December	*300*	
Average for the year	*240*	

[B.Com. (Hons.) Delhi]

Solution :

Statement Showing the net monetary result on account of price level changes

		₹	₹
(*i*)	Monetary liabilities as on 1.1.2001 should have gone up with increase in price indices (35000 × 1.5)	52,500	
(*ii*)	Increase in monetary liabilities during 2001 which should have gone up with increase in price indices (5000 × 1.25)	6,250	
	Monetary Liabilities on 31.12.2001 should have stood at	58,750	
	However, the liabilities on 31.12.2001 stood at	40,000	
	Gain on holding of monetary Liabilities		18,750
(*iii*)	Monetary assets as on 1.1.2201 should have gone up with increase in price indices [₹ 25.000 × 1.25]	37,500	
(*iv*)	Increase in monetary assets during 2001 should have gone up with increase in price indices [₹ 10.000 × 1.25]	12,500	
	Monetary assets on 31.12.2001 should stood at	50,000	
	However, the monetary assets on 31.12.2001 stood at	35,000	
	Loss on holding monetary assets		15,000
	Net gain on monetary items		3,750

Problem 2. *Ascertain net monetary result as on 31.12.2001 from the data given below.*

	1.1.2001	*31.12.2001*
	₹	₹
Cash at bank	*15,000*	*21,000*
Debtors	*45,000*	*54,000*
Creditors	*75,000*	*50,000*
General Price Index		
	1.1.2001	*100*
	31.12.2000	*125*
	Average for 2001	*120*

[M.Com. April 2003]

Solution : Statement showing the net monetary Result

Particulars	*Historical Amount ₹*	*Adjusted Factors*	*Price Level Adjusted Amount (₹)*	*Purchasing Power Gain or Loss (₹)*
Monetary assets at the beginning of 2001				
Cash at Bank	15,000	125/100	18,750 (15,000 × 125/100)	
Accounts receivable	45,000	125/100	56,250 (45,000 × 125/100)	
Add : Increase in monetary Asset during the year				
Cash at Bank (21,000 – 15,000)	6,000	125/120	6,250 (6,000 × 125/120)	
Accounts receivable (54,000 – 45,000)	9,000	125/120	9,375 (9,000 × 125/120)	
Total	75,000		90,625	
Purchasing power loss (90,625 – 75,000)				15,625
Monetary liabilities at the beginning of 2001				
Accounts Payable	75,000	125/100	93750 (75,000 × 125/100)	
Less : Decrease in Accounts Payable	25,000	125/100	31,250 (25,000 × 125/100)	
	50,000		62,500	
Purchasing Power Gain (67,708 – 50,000)				12,500
Net Purchasing Power Gain/Less				3,125

Problem 3. *From the information given below calculate the net monetary gain or loss for the accounting year ending on 30th June 2002 :*

Net monetary assets as on 1.7.2001	₹	*1,000*
Net monetary asset as on 30.6.2002	₹	*7,000*
Transaction for the year are as follows :		
(i) Cash sales	₹	*8,000*
(ii) Credit sales	₹	*10,000*
(iii) Credit purchase of goods	₹	*7,000*
(iv) Wages incurred and paid	₹	*2,000*
(v) Other operating expenses	₹	*1,000*
(vi) Interest paid on 30.6.2002	₹	*2,000*
Index as on 1.7.2001		*100*
Index as on 30.6.2002		*150*
Average index for the year		*125*

Solution :

Particulars	*Historic Cost Accounting* ₹	*CF*	*CPP* ₹
Net monetary asset on 01.07.2001	1,000	150/100	1,500
Add : Sales	18,000	150/125	21,600
	19,000		23,100
Less : Purchases	7,000	150/125	8,400
Wages	2,000	150/125	2,400
Operating expenses	1,000	150/125	1,200
Interest	2,000	150/150	2,000
	12,000		14,000
Net monetary asset as on 30.06.2002	7,000		9,100
Less : Monetary assets on HCA basis	—		7,000
Net Monetary Loss			2,100

Problem 4. *HR & Co., has the following transaction on the given dates and price indices of the first Quarter of 2000 :*

		Price Index
Opening Balance (Jan. 1)	₹ 6,000	100
Cash Sales (Feb.)	₹ 17,500	105
Payment to creditors (Mar. 1)	₹ 12,000	108
Cash Purchase (Mar. 1)	₹ 2,000	108
Payment of expenses (Mar. 31)	₹ 2,000	110
Closing Balance (Mar. 31)	₹ 7500	110

Calculate monetary gain or loss

[B.Com. Madras]

Solution : **Conversion Table**

Particulars	*Conventional Accounting* ₹	*Conversion Factor*	*Converted Values* ₹
Receipts :			
Opening Balance	6,000	110/100	6,600
Cash sales	17,500	110/105	18,333
A	23,500		24,933
Less : Payments :			
Creditors	12,000	110/108	12,222

Purchases	2,000	110/108	2,037
Expenses	2,000	110/110	2,000
B	16,000		16,259
Closing Balance (A – B)	7,500		8,674

NOTE : If the Actual Balance is more than the Expected Balance, the difference is called monetary gain. If the Actual Balance is less than the Expected Balance, the difference is called monetary loss.

Statement of Gain or Loss

	₹
Expected Balance	8,674
Actual Balance	7,500
Monetary Loss	1,174

Problem 5. *ABC Ltd. follows LIFO system. From the following particulars given below, ascertain the cost of sales and closing inventory under CPP method.*

		General price index
Inventory 31.12.2003	₹ *5,000*	*150*
Purchase for 2002	*28,000*	*180 (Average for 2002)*
Inventory on 31.12.2004	*60,000*	*240*

Solution :

Particulars	*Historic Accounting* ₹	*Conversion Factor*	*Conversion Value*
(*i*) Cost of sales			
Opening inventory	5,000		
Add : Purchases	28,000		
Total available for sale	33,000		
Less : Closing inventory	6,000		
LIFO valuation of cost of Sales	27,000	240/180 = 1.33	36,000
(*ii*) Closing inventory			
(*a*) Current purchases	1,000	1.33	1,333
(*b*) Rest from opening stock	5,000	240/150 = 1.60	8,000
	6,000		9,333

Problem 6. *The Balance Sheet of CBC Ltd. as on 1.2.2003 and the income statement for the year ending 31.12.2003 are set out below.*

Balance Sheet as on 1.1.2003

Liabilities	₹	*Assets*	₹
Share capital	*10,000*	*New machine*	*15,000*
10% Debentures	*6,000*	*Stock*	*2,400*
Creditors	*3,600*	*Debtors*	*1,200*
		Cash	*1,000*
	19,600		*19,600*

Income Statement for the year ended on 31.12.2003

Sales		*₹ 10,000*
Cost of goods sold :		
Opening stock (FIFO)	*2,400*	
Purchases (Net)	*4,600*	
Cost of goods available for sale	*7,000*	
Less : closing stock (FIFO)	*2,000*	
		5,000
Gross profit on sales		*5,000*
Less : Operating expenses	*800*	
Depreciation	*1,500*	
Interest on debentures paid on 31.12.2003	*600*	
		2,900
Retained earnings		*2,100*

Debtors and creditors balances remained constant throughout the year. General price indices were as given below.

on 1.1.2003	*200*
Average for the year	*240*
on 31.12.2003	*300*

You are required to prepare the final accounts for the year 2003 after adjusting the price level changes under CPP method.

Solution : **(*i*) Computation of Conversion Factors**

(to represent current purchasing power of the rupee as on 31.12.2003)

$$1.1.2003 = \frac{300}{200} = 1.5 \qquad 31.12.2003 = \frac{300}{300} = 1.00$$

$$\text{Average for 2003} = \frac{300}{240} = 1.25$$

(*ii*) Income statement as per CPP method for the year ending on 31.12.2003

Particulars	*HCA* ₹	*CF* ₹	*CPP* ₹
Sales	10,000	1.25	12,500
Opening stock (FIFO)	2,400	1.50	3,600
Purchases	4,600	1.25	5,750
Cost of Goods for sale	7,000		9,350
Less : closing stock (FIFO)	2,000	1.25	2,500
Cost of goods sold	5,000		6,850
Gross profit on sales [Sales – CGS]	5,000		5,650
Operating expenses	800	1.25	1,000
Depreciation	1,500	1.50	2,250
Interest on debentures	600	1.00	600
Total expenses	2,900		3,850
Income before general price level gain or loss (GP–TE)	2,100		1,800
General price gain	—		2,550
Retained Earnings	2,100		4,350

(*iii*) Computation of monetary Gain or Loss

Particulars	*HCA (Unadjusted)*	*CF*	*CPP (Adjusted)*
Net Monetary Liabilities as on 1.1.2003	7,400	1.50	11,100
Add : Purchases	4,600	1.25	5,750
Operating expenses	800	1.25	1,000
Interest on debentures	600	1.25	600
Total	13,400		18,450
Less : Sales	10,000	1.25	12,500
Net Monetary Liabilities as on 31.12.2003	3,400		5,950
Deduct : Monetary Liabilities on HCA basis			3,400
Monetary Gain			2,550

Workings :

Cash

Opening Balance	₹	1,000
Sales Receipts		10,000
		11,000
Less : Payment on account of purchases and expenses		6,000
		5,000

(iv) Computation of Monetary Liabilities on HCA Basis

Balance Sheet

Liabilities		*Assets*	
Debentures	6000	Cash	5,000
Creditors	3600	Debtors	1,200
		Balancing figure	3,400
	9,600		9,600

Balancing figure treated as monetary liabilities = ₹ 3,400

Balance Sheet as on 31.12.2003

Liabilities	*HCA* ₹	*CF*	*CPP* ₹	*Assets*	*HCA* ₹	*CF*	*CPP* ₹
Share capital	10,000	1.5	15,000	Cash	5,000	1.0	5000
Debenture	6,000	1.0	6,000	Debtors	1,200	1.0	1200
Creditors	3,600	1.0	3,600	Stock	2,000	1.25	2500
Retained earnings	2,100	—	4,350	Machinery	15,000	1.5	22500
				Less.: Depreciation	(1,500)	1.5	(2,250)
	21,700		28,950		21,700		28,950

Problem 7. *A summary of Balance Sheet of India Ltd., is given below.*

Cash and Accounts Receivable	₹	*13,00,000*
Plant and Machinery (Net)	₹	*14,00,000*
Total Asset		*27,00,000*
Current Debts	₹	*6,00,000*
Long Term Debts	₹	*10,00,000*
Owners' Equities	₹	*11,00,000*
Total Liabilities		*27,00,000*

The Current price index is 280. The Plant and Machinery and long term debt were acquired when the price index was at 180.

You are required to revise the summary balance sheet to restate, assess equities in terms of current rupees. How will you treat the monetary gain or loss if any ? [M.Com. Delhi]

Solution : **Balance Sheet**

Liabilities	*Historical Values* ₹	*CF*	*Current Values* ₹	*Assets*	*Historical Values* ₹	*CF*	*Current Values* ₹
Current debts	6,00,000	280/280	6,00,000	Current Assets	13,00,000	280/280	13,00,000
Long term debts	10,00,000	280/280	10,00,000	Plant & Machinery	14,00,000	280/180	21,77,778
Owners' equity	11,00,000	280/180	17,11,111				
Gain balancing figure	—	—	1,66,667				
	27,00,000		34,77,778		27,00,000		34,77,778

Monetary Gain is to be added to the owners' equity

i.e., 17,11,111 + 1,66,667 = 18,77,778

Problem 8. *Markam Ltd. had the following monetary items on January 1 :*

		₹
Debtors		41,000
Bills Receivable		10,000
Cash		20,000
		71,000
Less : Bills payable	10,000	
Creditors	25,000	
		35,000
Net Monetary Assets		36,000

The transactions affecting monetary items during the year were :

(i) Sales of ₹ 1,40,000 made evenly throughout the year.

(ii) Purchases goods of ₹ 1,05,000 made evenly during the year.

(iii) Operating expenses of ₹ 35,000 were incurred evenly throughout the year.

(iv) One machine was sold for ₹ 18,000 on July 1.

(v) One machine was purchased for ₹ 25,000 in December 31.

The general price index was as follows :

On January 1	300
Average for the year	350
On July 1	360
On December 31	400

You are required to compute the general purchasing power, gain or loss for the year stated in terms of the current year-end rupee.

Solution : Statement of General Purchasing Power Gain or Loss

Particulars	*Historical Amount* ₹	*Adjusted Factors*	*Price Level Adjusted Amount* (₹)	*Purchasing Power Gain or Loss* (₹)
Conversion of monetary assets :				
Assets at the beginning of the year	36,000	400/300	48,000	
Increase in net monetary assets				
During the year : Sales	1,40,000	400/350	1,60,000	
Sale of machine	18,000	400/360	20,000	
Total	1,94,000		2,28,000	
Purchasing Power Loss (2,28,000 – 1,94,000)	—	—	—	34,000
Decrease in net monetary assets :				
Purchases	1,05,000	400/350	1,20,000	
Operating expenses	35,000	400/350	40,000	
Purchase of machine	25,000	400/400	25,000	
Total	1,65,000		1,85,000	
Purchasing Power Gain (1,85,000 – 1,65,000)	—	—	—	20,000
Net Purchase Loss				14,000

Statement of Net monetary Assets	
Price level adjusted amount of net assets (2,28,000 – 1,85,000)	43,000
Less : Purchasing Power Loss	14,000
Net monetary assets at the end of the year (1,94,000 – 1,65,000)	29,000

❑❑❑

20

Human Resources Accounting

ORIGIN OF HUMAN RESOURCE ACCOUNTING

Recognising human being as an asset is an old one. From the observation of Indian History, it is evident that Emperor Akbar gave importance to the nine jewels. Freedom fighters in India like Shri Motilal Nehru, Mahatma Gandhi, Sardar Vallabh Bhai Patel, Pandit Jawahar Lal Nehru cannot be removed from the historical pages of freedom movement of India. Inspite of the uncountable sacrifices forgone by the above individuals, no one made efforts to allocate any monetary value to such individuals in the Balance Sheet of India.

The suitable work was started to determine the cost and value of human being by behavioural scientists from 1960 onwards. The experts in this field were Shultz (1960), William Pyle (1967), Flam Holtz (1972), Morese (1973), Kenneth Sinclare (1978) and Dr Roa (1983) etc who contributed appropriate methodology and correct methods for finding out the value of the employee to the organisation.

IMPORTANCE OF HRA

In any organization, the most valuable input is the human element. The success or failure of the company depends on the quality, calibre, capability and character of the employees working in it. So, in business enterprise, a well expertised and loyal employee may be much more valuable than a stock of merchandise. It is worth recalling what Alfred Marshall said long ago that "the most valuable of all capital is that invested in human beings".

Even though this much of values is possessed by the human resources, it is unfortunate that till now there is not even a single generally accepted system to value and record the human resources as an important assets. So, the balance sheet does not exhibit the value of human resource as the most vital asset while capital invested in other assets are shown. This is one of the severe limitations of present day financial statements which prevents the user of those statements from making effective use of them.

In the face of communication and technological changes, if the management could succeed in preventing the educated, trained and efficient employees from leaving the company or increasing their professionalism, an immense benefit could be achieved by the organisation. With the help of recording and transmitting human resource capital, the management will have access to a valid and reliable measure of expenditure on equipping the personnel with requisite knowledge and operating skills.

The ultimate aim of the financial accounting is to provide detailed information about the financial aspect to the decision makers. And at the same time, the conventional system fails to generate relevant data about one important asset of the organisation *i.e.,* human asset. It is termed as intervening variables. It refers to the loyalties, attitude, motivation, high morale, performance goals, collective capacity of the effective interaction, health of the organisation and decision making. The decision makers and executors should know to what extent such assets are either appreciated or depleted during a particular period.

The outcome of this process fails to reflect the level of business performance. In the real sense, it is always a failure to measure the economic value of people by the management. For this reason, the value of human resources is not to be considered. In order to overcome this difficulty, measuring and reporting the human resources would protect the management from liquidating human resources or obtaining more profitable investment in human resources in a period of profit squeeze.

MEANING OF HUMAN RESOURCE ACCOUNTING

Human Resource Accounting is a new branch of accounting. It is an accounting for people as the organisational resources. It is the measurement of the cost and value of people to organisation.

Some important definitions of Human Resource Accounting is given below :

(*i*) *"Human resource accounting is an attempt to identify and report investments made in human resources of an organisation that are presently not accounted for in conventional accounting practice. Basically it is an information system that tells the management what changes over time are occurring to the human resources of the business".*
—Woodruff

(*ii*) *"Human resources accounting is the measurement and quantification of human organisational inputs such as recruiting, training, experience and communication".*
—Stephen Knauf

OBJECTIVES OF HUMAN RESOURCE ACCOUNTING

(*i*) To assist the management executives in monitoring effectively the use of human resources.

(*ii*) To help the management decision makers take suitable decisions regarding investment of capital resources.

(*iii*) To communicate the value and importance of human assets to the organisation and the society at large.

(*iv*) To evaluate the effectiveness and efficiency of human resources in obtaining productivity and profitability.

(*v*) To provide a determination of asset control.

METHODS OF VALUATION OF HUMAN RESOURCES

In order to measure the appropriate value of human resources, it is difficult to comply with the commonly accepted accounting principles. However, there are two important approaches for the valuation of human resources.

First one is based on the cost *i.e.,* cost incurred by the enterprise to recruit, hire, train and development of employees.

Second one is to measure the economic value of the human resource based on capitalisation of earnings.

The important methods for the valuation of human resources are given below :

(*i*) *Acquisition Cost.* Under this method, costs incurred for the purpose of recruitment, hiring and induction and training of employees are taken into account. Expenditure incurred regarding the above activities is recorded properly and a proportion of it is written off to the income of the future periods during which human resources will provide service. But, if in any situation, the human assets are liquidated prematurely, the amount which is not written off is changed to the income of the year the liquidation takes place. The historical cost of human resources is similar to the book value of other physical assets. This method is simple to understand, easy to work out and easy to implement.

(*ii*) *Replacement Cost.* In the case of acquisition cost, past costs are taken into account. But, under this approach, one takes into account how much it costs to replace a firm's existing resources and thus represents a current value approach. Under this method, historic cost is adjusted according to the current market conditions.

(*iii*) *Standard Cost.* It is the cost incurred for the purpose of recruiting, hiring, training and development of human resources in the organisation. In connection with the above activities the standard costing principles are to be applied. *i.e.,* target is set for various components of human resources which are helpful to compare the actual and find the variations from the targeted one.

(*iv*) *Opportunity Cost.* Opportunity cost is the maximum alternative earning that is earned if the productive capacity or asset is put to some alternative use. Human resource valuation under the method of opportunity cost is difficult. Because, alternative use of human resource within the organisation is restricted. And at the same time, this type of alternative use may not be identifiable in the real industrial environment.

(*v*) *Present Value of Future Earnings Method.* This model is developed by Lev and Schwartz in 1971 and is popular in India. It is otherwise called as capitalisation of salary method. According to this method, future earnings of employees are estimated upto the age of retirement and are discounted at a rate appropriate to the person or the group to obtain the present value. They have given the following formula for calculating the value of an individual.

$$Vr = \frac{I(t)}{(I+R)^{t-r}}$$

Where, Vr = The value of an individual r years old

$I(t)$ = The individual's annual earnings upto the retirement

t = retirement age

R = a discount rate

(*vi*) *Rewards Valuation Model.* It has been suggested by Flamholtz. This method identifies the important variables that determines the value of each and every individual employee in an organisation *i.e.,* his expected realisable value.

(*vii*) *Net Benefit Model.* This model was suggested by Morse (1973). According to this method, the value of human resources is equivalent to the present value of net profit earned by the enterprise from the services of the employee.

(viii) *Certainty Equivalent Net Benefit Approach.* This model has been suggested by Pekin Ogan in 1976. It is an extension of net benefit approach of Morse. Under this method, the value of human resource is determined by considering the certainty with the net profit earned by the enterprise in future.

(ix) *Aggregate Payment Approach.* This approach has been developed by Prof. S.K. Chakraborty 1976, the first Indian to develop a model on human resources of an enterprise. According to this method, the value of human resources can be calculated on a consolidated basis and not the individual basis. But, the managerial and non- managerial values are evaluated separately.

(x) *Total Cost Concept.* This approach has been developed by Prof. N. Dasgupta (1978). According to his opinion both employed and unemployed persons should be taken into account for the determination of value of human resources of the nation. In order to prepare the balance sheet of a nation, the system should be such which shows the human resources not only for a firm but also of the whole nation.

(xi) *Input Out Control Mechanism.* Dr. Rao (1983) has suggested this approach. The system of human resource accounting was developed and applied in a transport equipment manufacturing concern. The output factors of the system are described to be the indicators of human resource development and utilisation.

ADVANTAGES OF HRA

(i) It supplies quantitative information about the human capital.

(ii) It helps the management to make proper interpretation of return on capital employed.

(iii) It will help to increase the productivity of human resources through the monetary value attached to human resources.

(iv) It assists the management to evaluate management development programme.

(v) It will provide an invaluable contribution for accounting to humanity and it will lead to improved efficiency and performance of employee while preserving human dignity and honour.

(vi) When and where human element is the prime factor that places human resource accounting to a significant role.
Example : A drama company, a professional accounting firm.

(vii) The value of organisation's human resources is very much helpful for the real investors and the entrepreneurs in making long term investment decisions.

(viii) It helps the management to reorient their attitudes towards employees and improving their administrative and leadership styles.

PROBLEMS AND LIMITATIONS OF HRA

(i) There is no specific and proper guidelines for finding cost and value of resources of an enterprise.

(ii) It may lead to dehumanising and manipulation among employees.

(iii) Continuous fear of opposition from the trade unions.

(iv) The measurement of human capital bristles with many difficulties and requires huge expense.

(v) The human capital cannot be purchased or owned by the firm and it would not be recognised as asset.

(vi) Accountants express their objection because human asset cannot be objectively measured.

HUMAN RESOURCE ACCOUNTING IN INDIA

HRA can provide information for both management and outsiders. However, some models are developed for the valuation of human resources. Even though, these much of benefits are contributed by the HRA, yet its development and application in different industries has not been encouraging. Because, Indian companies Act 1956, does not provide any scope for showing any information about human resources in financial statements. Due to the development of business and industries, some of the Indian companies, both public and private, value their human resources and report this information in their annual report.

(a) Public Sector Enterprises Include

(i) Bharat Heavy Electricals Ltd. (BHEL).

(ii) Steel Authority of India Ltd. (SAIL).

(iii) Minerals and Metals Trading Corporation of India.

(iv) Cement Corporation of India.

(v) ONGC

(vi) Oil India Ltd.

(b) Private Sector Enterprises

(i) Tata Engineering and Locomotive Works.

(ii) Southern Petrochemicals Industries Corporation Ltd.

(iii) Associated Cement Company Ltd.

PROSPECTS

Until this date, Human Resource Accounting is not popular in India. So, Indian Accounting Standard and also the International Accounting Standard Committee frame the format, provisions and guidelines. Through this effort only an importance of Human Resource Accounting will be created at all levels in the industrial concerns. However, this effort will take some time to incorporate Human Resource Accounting in Indian industries.

TEST QUESTIONS

1. What is meant by Human Resources Accounting ?
2. Define Human Resources Accounting.
3. Explain the advantages of Human Resource Accounting.
4. Describe the various methods of valuation of Resources.
5. Briefly explain the objectives of Human Resource Accounting.
6. List out the various limitations of Human Resource Accounting.
7. Write Brief note about the Human Resource Accounting in India.

❑❑❑

21

Responsibility Accounting

INTRODUCTION

One of the foremost uses of management accounting is the managerial control. Among the various control techniques, 'responsibility accounting' plays a significant role.

The remaining control techniques are applicable to the organisation as a whole. But, responsibility accounting represents a method of measuring the performance of various divisions of an organisation. The main aim of this chapter is to describe the organisational structure in which the management controls processes through responsibility accounting. Responsibility accounting is similar to any other system of cost but with greater emphasis on fixing the responsibility of the person assigned and executed a specific job.

DEFINITION

Eric Kohler defines responsibility accounting as *"a method of accounting in which costs are identified with persons assumed to be capable of controlling them rather than with products or functions. It differs from activity accounting in that it does not in itself requires an organisational grouping by activities and sub activities or provide a systematic criterion of system design."*

Robert Anthony defines responsibility accounting as *"the type of management accounting that collects and reports both planned and actual accounting information in terms of responsibility centres"*.

Principles of Responsibility Accounting

(*i*) To identify the responsibility centres within an organization.
(*ii*) To define the responsibility for each responsibility centre.
(*iii*) It lays greater emphasis on human factor.
(*iv*) To specify controllable and uncontrollable activities at various levels of responsibility.
(*v*) To provide information about the performance report.

Requirements of Effective Responsibility Accounting

(*i*) The entire organisation is divided into responsibility centres *i.e.,* various responsibility centres should be created.
(*ii*) To establish a sound organisation structure.

(*iii*) To define the authority and responsibility in a clear-cut way.

(*iv*) To prepare a detailed budget with full involvement of concerned managers.

(*v*) To obtain sufficient top management support for implementing responsibility accounting.

(*vi*) The actual performance of the responsibility accounting is to be communicated to the concerned managers.

(*vii*) The performance reports for all the divisions should be prepared and if corrective measures are suggested or taken it is also communicated to the respective managers.

(*viii*) A healthy organisational environment should exist.

Advantages of Responsibility Accounting

The ultimate aim of the responsibility accounting is to help and guide the management to achieving organisational goals. The following are some important advantages of responsibility accounting.

(*i*) It provides a system of closer control.

(*ii*) It defines and communicates the corporate objectives and individual goals in an efficient manner.

(*iii*) It helps to improve the quality of decision making.

(*iv*) Each and every employee knows what is expected of him. And at the same time no one can escape from anything that goes wrong.

(*v*) It measures the performance of individual employee in an objective manner.

(*vi*) It fosters a sense of cost-consciousness among managers and their subordinates.

(*vii*) It acts as a suitable tool of cost control.

(*viii*) It is helpful in planning for future costs and revenues.

(*ix*) It guides the management to make an effective delegation of authority and responsibility.

(*x*) If necessary, corrective action can be taken and efficient control over the cost can be obtained.

RESPONSIBILITY CENTRES

A small organisation can effectively manage the business with an individual or few people of the organisation. But, in the case of large scale organisation, it is difficult to supervise by an individual or few people. In order to have an effective control of the entire activities, the large scale organisation can be divided into some small divisions or departments. Each and every unit has a separate manager and it performs its activities properly. The small units or divisions of enterprise for the purpose of effective control of its activities are called responsibility centres.

According to **Richard D. Irwin,** *"A responsibility centre is a unit of an organization under the supervision of a manager who has the responsibility for the activities of that responsibility centre."*

Responsibility centres, for the planning and control purposes, are classified into the following classes :

(i) Cost centre or Expense centre.
(ii) Revenue Centre.
(iii) Profit centre.
(iv) Investment centre.

(i) *Cost Centre.* A cost centre or expense centre is a division of an organisation in which the manager is held responsible for the costs incurred in that division. Simply, a responsibility centre is called a cost centre when the manager is solely responsible only for cost incurred in that centre.

(ii) *Revenue Centre.* A revenue centre is a unit of the organisation which is ultimately responsible for sales revenue. A manager, under this division, does not possess control over cost, but he has to control the expenses of marketing department.

(iii) *Profit Centre.* A responsibility centre is called a profit centre where the manager is held responsible for both costs and revenues. In the profit centre, input and output values are measured in monetary terms.

(iv) *Investment Centre.* A responsibility centre is called an investment centre. Its manager is responsible for costs and revenues as well as for the investment in assets used by his centre. It is defined as a responsibility centre in which inputs are measured in costs and outputs are measured in terms of revenue.

TRANSFER PRICE

A transfer price is a mechanism which is used to measure the value of goods or services furnished by a profit centre to other responsibility centres within an organisation. A correct determination of transfer price is more essential because it affects the other centres of the organisation.

Following factors taken into consideration while determining transfer price :

(i) The accurate measurement of divisional profitability.
(ii) To motivate the divisional managers.
(iii) To ensure that divisional autonomy and authority is preserved.

TEST QUESTIONS

1. Define Responsibility Accounting.
2. What is meant by Responsibility Accounting?
3. What are the principals of Responsibility Accounting?
4. Describe the requirements of effective Responsibility Accounting.
5. What are the advantages of Responsibility Accounting ?
6. Define responsibility centre.
7. What are the various classifications of responsibility centre?
8. What is cost centre ?'
9. What is revenue centre ?
10. What do you understand by profit centre ?
11. What is meant by investment centre ?
12. What is Transfer price ?

PROBLEMS AND SOLUTIONS

Problem 1. *XYZ Ltd. operates a number of divisions located in different regions. Division X incurred losses in the first half of the current year. Relevant revenue and cost data pertaining to these divisions are as follows.*

	₹
Sales revenue	*6,50,000*
Controllable variable costs	*3,50,000*
Controllable fixed costs	*2,00,000*
Attributable segment costs	*50,000*
Common firm-wide cost allocated to division X	*60,000*
Loss	*(10,000)*

You are required (i) To prepare a performance evaluation report of division X in the proper format and (ii) Advice the management whether its operation should be continued or shut down.

Solution :

(i) *Performance Evaluation Report of Division X*

Particulars	*Amount* ₹
Sales Revenue	6,50,000
Less : Controllable variable costs	3,50,000
Controllable contribution margin	3,00,000
Less : controllable fixed costs	2,00,000
Controllable segment margin	1,00,000
Less : Attributable segment costs	50,000
Segment profit contribution	50,000
Less : Common firm wide costs	60,000
	10,000

(*ii*) In the short run, division X justifies its existence as it generates a positive segment profit contribution *i.e.,* 50,000 regardless of its share of firm-wide costs. Of course, in the long run division X must collectively generate sufficient total profit contribution to allow the recovery of all firm-wide costs and the achievement of corporate profit goals.

Problem 2. *Ragal Angles Ltd. deals in three products, Ace, Nice, and Grace and these are sold directly through salesmen in three zones : Prime, Extension and Outreach. The responsibility for sales promotion rests with the headquarters and so does the overall control of distribution and sales. Cost of sales as percentage of sales are Ace 85, Nice 80, Grace 75. Details of sales, selling and distribution expenses for the year are as follows.*

Zones	*Products*	*Sales* (₹)	*Selling and distribution expenses allocated direct* (₹)
Prime Zone	*Ace*	*9,00,000*	*63,990*
	Nice	*9,00,000*	*84,465*
	Grace	*4,50,000*	*47,160*
		22,50,000	*1,95,615*
Extension Zone	*Ace*	*6,75,000*	*46,710*
	Nice	*4,50,000*	*47,700*
	Grace	*2,25,000*	*23,940*
		13,50,000	*1,18,350*
Outreach Zone	*Ace*	*2,25,000*	*18,900*
	Nice	*1,80,000*	*15,165*
	Grace	*4,95,000*	*66,375*
		9,00,000	*1,00,440*

Selling and distribution expenses at the headquarters are as follows :

	₹
Office expenses	*94,500*
Advertisement	*1,35,000*
Other expenses	*1,21,500*

Advertisement costs are allocated to zones and product on the basis of sales. Office expenses and other expenses are apportioned equally to the zones or products, while computing the profit or loss for the zones or the product as the case may be.

Prepare a comparative profit and loss statement, presenting zonal performance as distinct from product performance.

Solution : Comparative Profit and Loss Statement

[Evaluating Zonal performance.]

Particulars	*Prime* ₹	*Zones* *Extension* ₹	*Outreach* ₹	*Total* ₹
Sales revenue	22,50,000	13,50,000	9,00,000	45,00,000
Less : Cost of sales				
Ace (.85)	7,65,000	5,73,750	1,91,250	15,30,000
Nice (.80)	7,20,000	3,60,000	1,44,000	12,24,000
Grace (.75)	3,37,500	1,68,750	3,71,250	8,77,500
Total costs	18,22,500	11,02,500	7,06,500	36,31,500
Gross Profit margin (Sales – Cost of sales)	4,27,500	2,47,500	1,93,500	8,68,500

Less : Selling and distribution expenses				
Direct costs [allocated]	1,95,615	1,18,350	1,00,440	4,14,405
Advertisement Expenses [Apportioned in sales ratio 225 : 135 : 90]	67,500	40,500	27,000	1,35,000
Office expenses (apportioned equally)	31,500	31,500	31,500	94,500
other expenses (equally)	40,500	40,500	40,500	1,21,500
Total selling and distribution Costs	3,35,115	2,30,850	1,99,440	7,65,405
Net profit or loss [Gross profit-Total selling, Distribution cost]	92,385	16,650	5,940	1,03,095

Assignment Problem

Good Luck Ltd. has the following total operating results for the current year :

	₹
Sales revenue	56,00,000
Less : Variable costs	37,20,000
Contribution	18,80,000
Less : Fixed cost	10,00,000
Profit	8,80,000

The following additional information concerning the performance of each of the firm's three operating departments has been provided.

	Department		
	K	*L*	*M*
	₹	₹	₹
Sales revenue	24,00,000	20,00,000	12,00,000
Variable costs	16,80,000	12,00,000	8,40,000
Direct fixed costs	3,20,000	2,80,000	2,00,000

(*i*) Rank the three departments on the basis of their proportionate measure of relative profitability.

(*ii*) A proposal to increase advertising expenses by ₹ 1,23,200 is expected to generate 10% increase in sales in all three departments. Analyse the effect of this proposal on the firm as a whole and on each department. Assume that the cost of advertising will be allocated to divisions according to each division's percentage to sales and is to be considered as an attributable fixed cost of each department.

❑❑❑

SECTION IV : FINANCIAL MANAGEMENT

22

Financial Management

Financial Management refers to the total managerial effort for the management of sources and uses of the financial activities of the enterprises.

Financial Management is a specialised function of general management which is related to the procurement of finance and its effective utilisation for the fulfilment of common goal of the enterprises.

Some of the definitions are being reproduced below.

1. *"Financial management is the operational activity of a business that is responsible for obtaining and effectively utilising the funds necessary for efficient operations".*

—Joseph and Massie

2. *"Financial management is the application of the planning and control functions to the finance function".* **—Howard and Apon**

From the above definition it is clear that financial management is rendering a specialised service to the business in the way of obtaining and effective utilisation of the funds. Apart from this it also concentrates on financial planning, financial administration and financial control.

CHARACTERISTICS OF FINANCIAL MANAGEMENT

1. Financial management is a branch of business management.
2. It is an authentic and analytical process.
3. Centralised administration.
4. A measuring tool of performance.
5. It is essential for the management decisions.
6. Determination of Borrowing Policy.
7. Key position in the organisational structure.
8. Determination of future cash requirements.

IMPORTANCE OF FINANCIAL MANAGEMENT

Adequate finance is very much essential for the success of all the business concerns. A firm could not expand its business or at least for the survival purpose it should need sufficient amount of finance.

The following are the important areas which highlight the importance of financial management.

(*i*) It provides an easy approach to capital budgeting.
(*ii*) Promotional activities of the business organisation.
(*iii*) Financial management for optimum use of firm.
(*iv*) To obtain co-operation in business activities.
(*v*) Guidance to shareholders and investors.
(*vi*) Determinant of business success.
(*vii*) It is useful for minimising risks.
(*viii*) It has long period values and profit maximisation.
(*ix*) Helps to estimate the total requirements of funds.
(*x*) Profit Planning.
(*xi*) Controlling inventories.

OBJECTIVES AND FUNCTIONS OF FINANCIAL MANAGEMENT

Objectives of the financial management are listed below.

(*i*) Maintenance of liquid assets.
(*ii*) Maximisation of the profitability of the firm.
(*iii*) Internal resources for expansion.
(*iv*) Determining financial needs.
(*v*) Project planning evaluation.
(*vi*) Decision on capital budgeting.
(*vii*) Working capital management decisions.
(*viii*) Acquisition and mergers.
(*ix*) Ensuring fair return to the share holders.
(*x*) Establishment of reserves for growth and expansion.

FUNCTIONS

Functions of the Financial management can be classified thus.

(*a*) Executive Functions.
(*b*) Incidental Functions.

A. Executive Functions

Executive Finance Functions are those functions which require specialised administrative skill. Some of the executive functions are given below.

1. *Financial Forecasting.* This is the foremost function of financial management. It forecasts the total financial requirements of the firm during a particular period. To determine the total fund requirement, various budgets are prepared to support fund requirement decision.
2. *Financing Decision.* Supplying the required funds at an appropriate time is a primary objective of finance manager. In this regard, the financial manager should identify the sources of funds raised and the amount that can be raised from each source and the cost of funds and other aspects.

3. *Dividend Policy Decision.* Construction of the suitable dividend policy is the next important function of the financial management and managers. This decision involves the determination of the percentage of profits earned by the enterprise which is to be paid to its shareholders. In the practical sense the market price of the shares and trend of the earnings can play an important role in the construction of dividend policy of the company.
4. *Cash Flow Management.* An efficient finance manager should ensure that cash inflows and outflows must be continuous and uninterrupted. At the same time, he concentrates on the cash flow statement.
5. *Determination of Borrowing Policy.* Each and every organisation plans for the expansion and modernisation of their business. In this situation, it requires additional resources. The finance manager of a company takes correct decision about the funds received through outside sources, how long it is needed and when it is repaid.
6. *Capital Budgeting Decision.* Capital Budgeting Decisions are the most complicated one. Because, it involves long term implications. It requires huge amount of capital also. In this aspect, the financial manager is to identify the various investment proposals. The decision of the capital budgeting proposals are ranked on the basis of the urgency, liquidity, profitability and risk sensitivity.
7. *Negotiation for Various New Outside Financing.* In an organisation, finance manager must assess short term, medium term and long term financial requirements. To obtain these financial needs, he should start the negotiations at different levels for raising these funds.
8. *Checking upon Financial Performance.* For the benefit of rapid development of communication and technology, the finance manager has to employ various new software for the evaluation of financial performance of the company. An unbiased assessment of financial performance shall be of great value to the business in improving the standards, techniques and procedures of financial control.
9. *Acquisitions and Mergers.* An existing organisation may expand either by acquiring other concerns or by entering into mergers. Acquisition refers to the purchase of new firms or lease of smaller firm by a bigger firm. Merger refers to the joining of two or more firms together to form a new firm. During the periods of merger or acquisition, the major problem is the valuation of securities. In this aspect, the financial manager should follow correct valuation method, and do this process very carefully.

TEST QUESTIONS

1. What is meant by Financial Management ?
2. Define Financial Management.
3. Describe the importance of Financial Management.
4. What are the characteristics of Financial Management?
5. Critically analyze the functions of Finance manager in a Large-scale industrial establishment.
6. "Financial function is concerned with allocating funds to specific assests and obtaining the best mix of Financing in relation to overall valuation of the firm. Discuss.
7. Explain the objectives of financial management.
8. What are the functions of financial management ?

❑❑❑

23
Dividend

Dividend is the part of profits of the company which is distributed among its shareholders on the basis of their shareholding. It should be distributed according to decisions taken and resolution passed in the shareholders' meeting as well as meeting of Board of Directors.

In other words, it is the amount of profits of a company made available for the distribution among its shareholders.

It may be defined as the return that a shareholder gets from the company out of its profits on their shareholdings.

According to the Institute of Chartered Accountants of India dividend is "a distribution to shareholders out of profits or reserves available for this purpose". Normally, dividend may be paid as a fixed percentage on the share capital contributed by them or at a fixed amount per share.

Dividend should be declared only out of divisible profits. In any particular year, if there is no profit, dividend shall not be distributed in that year.

DIFFERENT TYPES OF DIVIDENDS

Dividend may be classified according to the mode of distribution as follows.

(*i*) *Cash Dividend.* Cash dividend means shareholders are paid dividend in the form of cash. If the company has sufficient cash balance, it would arrange funds for the payment of dividend.

If the company wants to have a stable dividend policy, it would prepare cash budget and meet out the regular dividend payments of the company. The cash dividend may have two classifications *i.e.,* regular dividend and interim dividend.

(*ii*) *Stock Dividend.* In any particular year, if the company does not have an adequate cash balance, it might decide to pay dividend in the form of shares. It is known as stock dividend. In this regard, the company issues its own shares to its existing shareholders in lieu of cash dividend.

(*iii*) *Scrip Dividend.* Scrip dividend means when earnings justify a dividend, but the cash position of the company is temporarily weak. During this period, shareholders are issued shares or debentures if other companies are held by the company as investment. Such payment of dividend is called scrip dividends.

(*iv*) *Bond Dividend.* If the company does not have sufficient funds to pay dividends in the form of cash, it may issue bonds to its shareholders for the purpose of dividend.

(v) *Property Dividend.* Property dividends are those dividends which are paid by the company to its shareholders in the form of property instead of payment of dividend in cash.

DIVIDEND POLICY

Dividend Policy of a company means it is the policy concerning the amount of profits to be distributed as dividend. The basic concept of the dividend policy is that the company takes future action regarding the payment of dividend with the help of the company law board.

According to Weston and Brighan, *"Dividend Policy determines the division of earnings between payments to shareholders and retained earnings".*

Factors Affecting Dividend Policy

Number of factors affect the dividend policy of a company. The major factors are :

1. *General Economic Conditions.* General Economic Conditions greatly affect the management decision to distribute its earnings as dividend. During the periods of economic depression, the firm holds large sums of money in reserve in order to meet the liquidity position of the company. But, in the case of prosperity, the company may not be liberal in dividend payments because of large profitable investment opportunity.
2. *Age of a Company.* Age of a company must decide the dividend policy. A newly established company may require huge amount of its earnings for development purpose and may formulate rigid dividend policy. But, in the case of older company it can frame a consistent policy regarding dividend.
3. *State of Capital Market.* If the capital market position of the country is more favourable to the company, the company may raise funds from different sources without any difficulty. So, the management may declare a high rate of dividend to attract the investors. But, in stock market, the shareholders are not interested in making investment so the management should follow a conservative dividend policy by maintaining the low rate of dividend.
4. *Government Policy.* Some of the policies are announced by the Government from time to time. It may affect the profit earning capacity of the organisation. Sometimes, Government restrict the distribution of dividend beyond a certain percentage in a particular industry. So, the dividend policy has to be formulated accordingly.
5. *Taxation Policy.* The tax policy announced by the Government also affect the dividends policy. High taxation reduces the earnings of the company and consequently the rate of dividend is lowered down.
6. *Past Year Dividend Rate.* At the time of formulating the dividend policy of the company, the directors must consider the dividend paid in past years. The current dividend rate should be around the average of past rates.
7. *Liquidity of Funds.* Payment of dividend represents actually a cash outflow. Availability of huge amount of cash and liquidity of the firm says it has better ability to pay dividend.

8. *Ability to Borrow*. Well established and large scale companies have better access to the capital market than the new companies. And they may borrow funds from other external sources as and when necessity arises. This type of companies may have a better dividend pay out ratio. But, smaller firms have to maintain adequate reserve and low dividend pay out ratio.
9. *Regularity and Stability in Dividend Payment*. Dividend should be paid regularly to the investors. Because, all investors expect regular payment of dividend. Through this process only, company will retain the existing shareholders on a permanent basis, and if necessary, to mobilise resources in an efficient manner.

Types of Dividend Policies

Different types of dividend policies are as follows :

(*i*) *Stable Dividend Policy*. When the company maintains more or less the stable rate of dividend, it is known as stable dividend policy. If the company has to maintain and follow stable dividend policy, the market price of its share will be of permanently higher value.

(*ii*) *Policy of Regular Stock Dividend*. It is the policy followed by the company to pay dividend in the form of shares instead of cash. Some companies follow this as a regular practice. Whenever, the stock dividends are declared by the company, it does not affect the liquidity but increases the shareholdings of the shareholder.

(*iii*) *Policy to Pay Irregular Dividend*. Generally, this policy of dividend is followed by the companies having irregular earnings or inadequate profits. Based on this policy, the company earn an higher amount of profit to pay higher dividend. If there is no profit in any particular year, the company does not declare the dividend to its shareholders.

(*iv*) *Policy of no Immediate Dividend*. It is the policy followed by the company which decides to pay no dividend even when it earns large amount of profits. Because, either it may be a new company or the firm's access to capital market is difficult.

CONFLICTING THEORIES

There are conflicting theories regarding the impact of dividend decision on the valuation of a firm.

1. Irrelevance Concept of Dividend, 2. Relevance Concept of Dividend.

1. Irrelevance Concept of Dividend

This concept was developed by Soloman, Modigliani and Miller. According to their approach, dividend policy of a firm is irrelevant as it does not affect the wealth of the shareholders. In their opinion, investors do not differentiate dividend and capital gains. There is no impact on the dividend policy or the share price of the company and further consequence.

2. Relevance Concept of Dividend

Myron Gordon, John Linter, James Walter, Richardson and others are associated with the relevance concept of dividend. According to their approach, dividend policy has a positive impact on the firm's position in the stock market. In other words there is a positive relationship between the Dividend Policy and price level of the company's shares in the stock market. Higher dividend rate increases the value of stock while low dividend decreases their value in the stock market.

WALTER'S APPROACH

He pointed out that dividend policy always affects the goodwill of the company. According to his approach, It is a relationship between the firm's return on investment or internal rate of return and cost of capital or required rate of return.

TEST QUESTIONS

1. What is meant by Dividend ?
2. Define Dividend.
3. What is cash dividend ?
4. What is meant by stock dividend ?
5. Explain the concept of script dividend.
6. What is dividend pay-out ratio ?
7. List out the two main theories of dividend.
8. What is meant by dividend policy ?
9. Describe the factors that influence the dividend policy of a firm.
10. Write note on dividend policy in practice.
11. What are the different types of dividend policies ?
12. How for do you agree that dividends are irrelevant ?
13. Explain the various factors which influence the dividend decision of a firm.
14. "A firm should follow a policy of very high dividend pay-out". Do you agree ? Why or why not ?
15. What do you understand by a stable dividend policy ? Why should it be followed ?

PROBLEMS AND SOLUTIONS

Problem 1. *Following are the details regarding three companies A Ltd., B Ltd. and C Ltd.*

A Ltd.	***B Ltd.***	***C Ltd.***
R = 15%	*R = 5%*	*R = 10%*
Ke = 10%	*Ke = 10%*	*Ke = 10%*
E = ₹ 8	*E = ₹ 8*	*E = ₹ 8*

Calculate the value of an equity share of each of these companies applying Walter's formula when dividend payment ratio (D/P ratio) is (a) 50%, (b) 75%, (c) 25%.

What conclusion do you draw ? [M.Com. Delhi-1991] [MBA Anna]

Solution :

Prof. Walter has suggested the following formula for determining the market value of a share.

$$P = \frac{D + \frac{r}{Ke}(E - D)}{Ke}$$

P = Market price of an equity share
D = Dividend per share
r = Internal rate of return
E = Earning per share
Ke = Cost of equity capital or capitalisation rate.

Value of an equity share according to Walter's Formula :

	A Ltd.	*B Ltd.*	*C Ltd.*
(*i*)	When D/P Ratio is 50% $P = \frac{D + \frac{r}{Ke}(E - D)}{Ke}$ $P = \frac{4 + \frac{.15}{.10}(8-4)}{.10}$ ₹ 100	$P = \frac{4 + \frac{.05}{.10}(8-4)}{.10}$ ₹ 60	$P = \frac{4 + \frac{.10}{.10}(8-4)}{.10}$ ₹ 80
(*ii*)	When D/P Ratio is 75% $P = \frac{6 + \frac{.15}{.10}(8-6)}{.10}$ ₹ 90	$P = \frac{6 + \frac{.05}{.10}(8-6)}{.10}$ ₹ 70	$P = \frac{6 + \frac{10}{.10}(8-6)}{.10}$ ₹ 80
(*iii*)	When D/P Ratio is 25% $P = \frac{2 + \frac{.15}{.10}(8-2)}{.10}$ ₹ 110	$P = \frac{2 + \frac{.05}{.10}(8-2)}{.10}$ ₹ 50	$P = \frac{2 + \frac{.10}{.10}(8-2)}{.10}$ ₹ 80

Conclusion :

Based upon the above calculations

(*i*) A Ltd. : This Company may be characterised as a growth firm.

(*ii*) B Ltd. : This Company may be characterised as a declining firm.

(*iii*) C Ltd. : This Company may be characterised as a normal firm.

TEST PROBLEMS

1. Anand Corporation Ltd.'s Belongs to a risk class of which the appropriate capitalization rate is 10%. It currently has 1,00,000 shares quoting ₹ 1,000 each. The company proposes to declare a dividend of ₹ 6 per share. At the end of the current fiscal year which has just be gain. Answer the following questions based on Modigliani and Miller Model and assumption of no taxes.

(*i*) What will be the price of the share at the end of the year if dividend is not declared?

(*ii*) What will be the price if dividend is declared?

(*iii*) Assuming that the company pays dividends, has a net income of ₹ 10 lakh and plans new investment of ₹ 20 lakh during the period. How many new Shares must be issued?

(*iv*) Is the MM Model realistic? What factors Might Mar its validity?

[Bharathidasan. B.Com.]

[**Ans:** (*i*) ₹ 110: (*ii*) ₹ 104; (*iii*) 15385 Shares; (*iv*) MM model is Unrealistic. Its validity is marred by unrealistic assumptions such as no taxes, no floatation's and transaction costs. No difference in the tax rates applicable to dividends and capital gains]

❑❑❑

24
Cost of Capital

INTRODUCTION

Cost of capital is one of the corner stones of the theory of financial management but it is a controversial topic in finance. And at the same time it provides suitable guidance for the formulation of capital structure of the firm. In the present financial world, it is used as a sophisticated technique of evaluating the profitability of capital investment proposals and also to examine the alternative sources of capital. In order to meet out the modern financial decision making process, in this chapter, it is proposed to discuss the concept and implications of the firm's cost of capital, procedure for the measurement of different sources of capital and also to explain its uses.

CONCEPT OF COST OF CAPITAL

The term cost of capital is the rate of return a firm must earn on its investment for the market value of the firm to remain unchanged. From the company's point of view, cost of capital is the measurement of profitability of investments and a yardstick to decide whether to make investment in particular project or not.

DEFINITIONS OF COST OF CAPITAL

(*i*) *"The cost of capital is the minimum required rate of earnings or the cut-off rate for capital expenditures".* **—G.C. Philippatos**

(*ii*) *"The cost of capital represents a cut-off rate for the allocation of capital to investment of projects. It is the rate of return on a project that will leave unchanged the market price of the stock".* **—James C. Van Horne**

(*iii*) *"In a general sense, the cost of capital is any discount rate used to value cash streams".* **—Haley and Schall.**

From the above definitions, it is clear that the cost of capital is otherwise called as cut off rate. Because, it is the suitable test of validity of committing a capital expenditure.

IMPORTANCE OF COST OF CAPITAL IN DECISION MAKING

(*i*) *Capital Budgeting Decisions.* Cost of capital may be very much used as the measuring rod for adopting an investment proposal. Generally, the company has to choose project based upon the satisfactory return on investment. It measures the financial performance and also determines acceptability of the project by discounting cash flows under present value method. Commonly, it is the technique used to accept or reject the project.

(*ii*) *Designing the Optimal Capital Structure.* The cost of capital is very much helpful in formulating firm's sound and economic capital structure. An excellent financial expert keeps an eye on the capital market fluctuations and analyses the comparative interest rate, and trend of the capital movement. Based upon the analysis, finance manager comes to correct conclusion and forms a suitable capital structure of the firm.

(*iii*) *Deciding about the Method of Financing.* An efficient financial manager has a thorough knowledge of the capital market fluctuation. The ultimate aim of the financial management is the wealth maximisation. In order to achieve these objectives, the financial manager finds the financing sources. Apart from these, comparing the specific cost of different sources of finance, the finance manager can select the most economical source of finance in a particular situation.

(*iv*) *Helpful in the Evaluation of Expansion Projects.* With the help of the cost of capital the financial manager can easily examine the financial possibilities of a given expansion project. If marginal return on investment exceeds the cost of financing, the expansion project should be accepted, otherwise it should be rejected.

(*v*) *To Evaluate the Financial Performance of Top Management.* The cost of capital can be used to evaluate the financial performance of top management people. It involves a comparison of actual profitabilities of the project undertaken with the projected overall cost of capital and an appraisal of the actual cost incurred in raising the expected funds.

(*vi*) *Other Areas.* The concept of cost of capital is also important in some other areas of decision making of the firm such as dividend decision, working capital management policies etc. The value of the firm normally depends upon its cost of capital.

DIFFERENT TYPES OF COSTS RELATED TO THE COST OF CAPITAL

The following are the various relevant costs associated with the problem of measurement of firm's cost of capital.

(*i*) *Marginal Cost of Capital.* It is the current interest on long term debt. In other words, the marginal cost of capital is the weighted average cost of new or additional funds raised by the company.

(*ii*) *Specific Cost.* Specific cost is the cost which is associated with the particular component of a capital structure.

For example : Equity shares, debentures etc. It is also known as component cost.

(*iii*) *Combined Cost.* It is the cost of capital of all the sources taken together *i.e.,* debt, equity and preference share capital. The combined cost of capital can be otherwise called as average cost or weighted cost of capital.

(*iv*) *Spot Cost.* Spot cost represents costs prevailing in the market at certain point of time.

(*v*) *Future Cost.* It is the cost which is related to the cost of funds intended to finance the expected project.

(vi) *Historical Cost.* Historical costs are the costs which are calculated on the basis of existing capital structure of the firm.

(vii) *Explicit Cost.* Explicit cost of any source of fund may be expressed as the discount rate that equates the present value of cash inflows that are incremental to the taking of the financial opportunity with the present value of its incremental cash outflows.

(viii) *Implicit Cost.* Implicit cost is the opportunity cost. It is the rate of return associated with the best investment opportunity for the firm and its shareholders that will be forgone if the project presently under consideration by the firm were accepted.

(ix) *Normalised Cost.* It is the long term cost. It indicates an estimate of cost by some averaging process from which cyclical element is removed.

DETERMINATION OF COST OF CAPITAL

Cost of capital is not only most crucial but also it is a controversial area in the financial management decisions. Under this background, determination of cost of capital is not a simple task. The finance manager has to face a lot of problems both conceptual and practical while determining the cost of capital of the company. Major problems in this regard are as follows.

(i) *Conceptual Controversy.* There is a major controversy whether or not the cost of capital is dependent upon the method and level of financing by the company. The traditional theorists pointed out a firm can change its overall cost of capital by changing its debt-equity mix. But, the modern theorists argued that the change in the debt-equity ratio does not affect the total cost of capital of the enterprise.

(ii) *Computation of Cost of Equity.* The determination of cost of equity capital is also a difficult task. In the actual theoretical point of view cost of equity capital may be defined as the minimum rate of return that a company must earn on its capital employed. So, the market price of the equity shares remain unchanged. This implies that to find out the cost of equity capital one has to require quantification of the expectations of the equity share holders. It is a very difficult task, because different authorities have tried different approaches to quantify the expectations of the equity shareholders.

(iii) *Problems in Computation of Cost of Retained Earnings and Depreciation Funds.* Cost of retained earnings and depreciation fund is determined according to the approach adopted for computing the cost of equity capital which is itself a controversial problem.

(iv) *Problems in Consideration of Historical Cost, Future Cost.* As per the decision making point of view, the historical cost is not relevant. But, future costs should be taken into account. This brings another problem whether to consider marginal cost of capital *i.e.,* cost of additional funds or whether to consider the average cost of capital *i.e.,* the cost of total funds.

(v) *Problem of Weights.* In order to ascertain the average cost of capital, the financial manager of the company has to face the problems of weights. In this aspect, computation as well as assigning of weights to each type of fund is a complicated problem. Because, there are two options in this respect, *i.e.,* book value weights and market value weights. Both of them have their own strengths and weaknesses. It is natural but results based on the two aspects differ significantly.

COMPUTATION OF COST OF CAPITAL

Computation of cost of capital involves the following :

(A) Computation of cost of each specific source of finance.

(B) Computation of weighted average cost of capital.

(A) Computation of Cost of each Specific Source of Finance

Costs of each specific source of finance are as follows :

(*i*) Debt

(*ii*) Preference shares

(*iii*) Equity capital

(*iv*) Retained earnings.

(*i*) Cost of Debt

(*a*) *Debt issued at per* : at premium or discount

$$Kd = (1 - T)\,R$$

where, Kd = Cost of debt

T = Marginal Tax Rate

R = Debenture interest rate

(*b*) *Cost of redeemable debt*

$$Kd = \frac{1 + (P - NP)/n}{(P + NP)/2}$$

where, I = Annual interest payment

P = Par value of debentures

NP = Net proceeds of debentures

n = Number of years to maturity

(*ii*) Cost of Preference Shares

(*a*) Cost of Preference Capital

$$Kp = \frac{DP}{NP}$$

where, Kp = Cost of preference share capital

DP = Fixed preference dividend

NP = Net proceeds of preference shares

(*b*) *Cost of Redeemable Preference Shares*

$$Kp = \frac{DP + (P - NP)/n}{(P + NP)/2}$$

where, Kp = Cost of preference share capital

DP = Fixed preference dividend

NP = Net proceeds of preference shares

n = Number of preference shares

(*iii*) Cost of Equity Capital

(*a*) *Dividend Price (D/P) Approach*

$$Ke = \frac{D}{NP}$$

where, Ke = Cost of equity capital

D = Dividend per Equity share

NP = Net proceeds of an equity share

(*b*) *Dividend Price Plus Growth (D/P + g) Approach*

$$Ke = \frac{D}{NP} + g$$

where, Ke = Cost of equity capital

D = Expected dividend per share

NP = Net proceeds per share

g = growth in expected dividend

(*c*) *Earning Price Approach*

$$Ke = \frac{E}{NP}$$

where, Ke = Cost of equity capital

E = Earning per share

NP = Net proceeds of an equity share.

(*d*) *Realised Yield Approach*

In order to calculate the cost of capital under this approach, it is essential to determine the internal rate of return. This internal rate of return can be calculated by the trial and error method.

(*iv*) Cost of Retained Earnings

Generally, retained earnings are undistributed profits represented by uncommitted reserves and surpluses. Computation of cost of retained earnings in the following formula.

$$Kr = Ke\,(1 - T)\,(1 - B)$$

where, Kr = Required rate of return on retained earrings.

Ke = Shareholder's required rate of return

T = Shareholders marginal tax rate

B = Brokerage cost

(B) Computation of Weighted Average Cost of Capital

Weighted average as the name implies is an average of the cost of specific source of capital employed in a business properly weighted by the proportion they hold in firm's capital structure.

Following are the Steps involved in computation of weighted average of cost of capital :

(*i*) Calculation of the cost of each specific source of finance.

(*ii*) Assigning weights to specific costs.

(*iii*) Weighted cost of all the sources of finance taken together to arrive at an overall weighted average cost of capital.

Computation of Weights

Assigning weights to specific source of finance is a difficult task. Various approaches are followed in this regard, but, two of them are commonly used (*a*) Book value approach and (*b*) Market value approach.

TEST QUESTIONS

1. What is meant by cost of capital ?
2. Define cost of capital.
3. Describe the importance of cost of capital in Decision making.
4. Explain the different types of costs related to the cost of capital.
5. Explain critically the different approaches for computing cost of equity.
6. Specific cost Vs composite cost.
7. What are the methods of computing cost of equity capital ?
8. Define the concept of cost of capital. State how you would determine the weighted average cost of capital of a firm.
9. Write a detailed note on the cost of individual components of capital.
10. What is weighted average cost of capital ? Examine the rational behind the use of weighted average cost of capital.

PROBLEMS AND SOLUTIONS

Problem 1. *From the following capital structure of a company calculate the overall cost of capital using (a) Book value weights and (b) Market value weights*

Source	*Book value (₹)*	*Market value (₹)*
Equity share capital (₹ 10 shares)	*45,000*	*90,000*
Retained earnings	*15,000*	—
Preference share capital	*10,000*	*10,000*
Debentures	*30,000*	*30,000*

The after-tax cost of different sources of finance is as follows :

Equity Share Capital : 14%, Retained Earnings : 13%, Preference Share Capital 10%, Debentures : 5%.

Solution : (*a*) Computation of Weighted Average Cost of Capital

(Book value weights)

Source (1)	*Amount (2) ₹*	*After tax cost (3)*	*Total after tax ₹ Cost (4) = (2) × (3)*
Equity share capital	45,000	14%	6,300
Retained earnings	15,000	13%	1,950
Preference share capital	10,000	10%	1,000
Debentures	30,000	5%	1,500
	1,00,000		10,750

$$\text{Weighted Average cost of capital} = \frac{10,750}{1,00,000} \times 100$$

$$= \mathbf{10.75\ \%}$$

(b) Computation of Weighted Average Cost of Capital
[Market value weights]

Source (1)	*Amount* (2) ₹	*After tax cost* (3)	*Total after tax ₹ Cost (4) = (2) × (3)*
Equity share capital	90,000	14%	12,600
Preference share capital	10,000	10%	1,000
Debentures	30,000	5%	1,500
	1,30,000		15,100

Weighted average cost of capital $= \dfrac{15{,}100}{1{,}30{,}000} \times 100$

$= \mathbf{11.61\%}$

Problem 2. *A firm has the following capital structure after tax costs for the different sources of funds used.*

Source of funds	*Amount (₹)*	*Proportion*	*After tax cost %*
Debt	*15,00,000*	*25*	*5*
Preference shares	*12,00,000*	*20*	*10*
Equity shares	*18,00,000*	*30*	*12*
Retained earnings	*15,00,000*	*25*	*11*
	60,00,000	*100*	

You are required to compute the weighted average cost of capital. [M.Sc. Dec. 2001 PU]

Solution : Computation of Weighted Average Cost of Capital

Source (1)	*Amount* (2) ₹	*After tax cost* (3)	*Total after tax ₹ Cost (4) = (2) × (3)*
Debt	15,00,000	5%	75,000
Preference shares	12,00,000	10%	1,20,000
Equity shares	18,00,000	12%	2,16,000
Retained earnings	15,00,000	11%	1,65,000
	60,00,000		5,76,000

Weighted average cost of capital $= \dfrac{5{,}76{,}000}{60{,}00{,}000} \times 100$

$= \mathbf{9.6\%}$

Problem 3. *The Servex company has the following capital structure on 30.6.2004.*

	₹
Ordinary shares (2,00,000 Shares)	*40,00,000*
6% Preference shares	*10,00,000*
8% Debentures	*30,00,000*
	80,00,000

The share of the company sells for ₹ 20. It is expected that company will pay a current dividend of ₹ 2 per share which will grow at 7% for ever. Assume the tax rate may be 50%.

(i) Compute the weighted average cost of capital based on existing capital structure.

(ii) Compute the new weighted average cost of capital if the company raises an additional ₹ 20,00,000 debt by issuing 10% debenture. This would result in increasing the expected dividend to ₹ 3 and leave the growth rate unchanged, but the price of share will fall to ₹ 15 per share.

(iii) Compute the cost of capital if in (ii) above growth rate increases to 10% .

[MBA Madras Nov. 1997]

Solution : (*i*) Statement showing Weighted Average Cost of Capital

Source (1)	*Amount* (2) ₹	*After tax cost* (3)	*Total after tax* ₹ *Cost* (4) = (2) × (3)
Equity share capital	40,00,000	17%	6,80,000
Preference share capital	10,00,000	6%	60,000
Debentures	30,00,000	4%	1,20,000
	80,00,000		8,60,000

$$\text{Weighted average cost of capital} = \frac{8,60,000}{80,00,000} \times 100$$

$$K_e = 10.75$$

NOTE : Computation cost of equity share is

$$K_e = \frac{D}{MP} + g = \frac{\text{Rs. } 2}{\text{Rs. } 20} + 0.07 = .17 \times 100$$

$$= 17\%$$

(*ii*) Statement showing Weighted Average Cost of Capital

Source (1)	*Amount* (2) ₹	*After tax cost* (3)	*Total after tax* ₹ *Cost* (4) = (2) × (3)
Equity share capital	40,00,000	27%	10,80,000
6% Preference capital	10,00,000	6%	60,000
8% Debentures	30,00,000	(8-4) 4%	1,20,000
10% Debentures	20,00,000	(10-5) 5%	1,00,000
	1,00,000,00		13,60,000

$$\text{Weighted average cost of capital } Ke = \frac{13,60,000}{1,00,00,000} \times 100$$

$$= 13.6\%$$

NOTE : Computation of cost of equity share is

$$= Ke = \frac{D}{MP} + g$$

$$= \frac{3}{15} + 0.07$$

$$= .20 + .07 = .27 \times 100$$

$$= 27\%$$

(*iii*) Statement showing Weighted Average Cost of Capital

Source (1)	*Amount* (2) ₹	*After tax cost* (3)	*Total after tax* ₹ *Cost* (4) = (2) × (3)
Equity share capital	40,00,000	30%	12,00,000
6% Preference capital	10,00,000	6%	60,000
8% Debentures	30,00,000	(8-4) 4%	1,20,000
10% Debentures	20,00,000	(10-5) 5%	1,00,000
	1,00,000,00		14,80,000

$$\text{Weighted average cost of capital } Ke = \frac{14,80,000}{1,00,00,000} \times 100$$

$$= \mathbf{14.80\%}$$

NOTE : Computation of cost of equity share is :

$$= Ke = \frac{D}{MP} + g$$

$$= \frac{3}{15} + .10$$

$$= .30 \textit{ i.e., } 30\% \ (.30 \times 100)$$

NOTE : Tax Rate *i.e.,* 50% to adjust only on Debenture after tax cost.

(*i*) Table = 10% : 50% of 10% = 5% – 5% = 5%

(*ii*) Table = 10% : 50% of 10% = 5% – 5% = 5%

(*iii*) Table = 8% : 50% of 8% = 4% – 4% = 4%

Problem 4. *Following are the details regarding the capital structure of Sridhar & Co. Ltd.*

Type of Capital	*Book value* ₹	*Market value* ₹	*Specific cost*
Debentures	*40,000*	*38,000*	*5%*
Preference capital	*10,000*	*11,000*	*8%*
Equity capital	*60,000*	*1,20,000*	*13%*
Retained earnings	*20,000*	-	*9%*
	1,30,000	*1,69,000*	

You are requested to determine the weighted average cost of capital using (i) Book value as weights (ii) Market value as weights. Do you think there can be a situation where weighted average cost of capital would be the same irrespective of the weights used.

[MBA Madras; M.Com.]

Solution : (*i*) Statement showing Weighted Average Cost of Capital

(Book value)

Sources (1)	*Amount* (2) ₹	*After tax cost* (3)	*Total after tax* ₹ *Cost* (4) = (2) × (3)
Debentures	40,000	5%	2,000
Preference capital	10,000	8%	800
Equity capital	60,000	13%	7,800
Retained earnings	20,000	9%	1,800
	1,30,000		12,400

$$\text{Weighted average cost of capital} = \frac{12,400}{1,30,000} \times 100$$
$$= 9.53\%$$

(*ii*) Statement showing the Weighted Average Cost Capital

(Market value)

Sources (1)	*Amount* (2) ₹	*After tax cost* (3)	*Total after tax* ₹ *Cost* (4) = (2) × (3)
Debentures	38,000	5%	1,900
Preference capital	11,000	8%	880
Equity capital	1,20,000	13%	15,600
	1,69,000		18,380

$$\text{Weight average cost of capital} = \frac{18,380}{1,69,000} \times 100$$
$$= 10.87\%$$

Result and Comments :

Cost of capital would be the same irrespective of the weights in case the Book value and the Market value of the securities are the same.

Problem 5. *Your company's share is quoted in the market at ₹ 20 currently. The company pays a dividend of ₹ 1 per share and the investor expects a growth rate of 5% per year. Compute :*

(*a*) *The company's cost of equity capital.*

(*b*) *If the anticipated growth rate is 6% p.a. calculate the indicated market price per share.*

(*c*) *If the company's cost of capital is 8% and the anticipated growth rate is 5% p.a., calculate the indicated market price if the dividend of Re 1 per share is to be maintained.*

Solution :

(*a*) Cost of equity capital $= \dfrac{\text{Dividend}}{\text{Price}} \times 100 + \text{Growth rate}$

$= \dfrac{1}{20} \times 100 + 5\%$

$= 5\% + 5\%$

$= 10\%$

(*b*) Market price $= \dfrac{\text{Dividend}}{\text{Cost of equity capital} - \text{Growth rate \%}}$

$= \dfrac{1}{10\% - 6\%}$

$= \dfrac{1}{4\%}$

$= .25 \times 100 = ₹\ 25$

(*c*) Market price $= \dfrac{\text{Re. 1}}{8\% - 5\%} = ₹\ 33.33$

Problem 6. *The capital structure of Reliance Ltd. is as follows :*

3000 12% Debentures of ₹ 100 each	*3,00,000*
2000 10% Preference shares of ₹ 100 each	*2,00,000*
4000 Equity shares of ₹ 100 each	*4,00,000*
Retained Earnings	*1,00,000*

The earnings per share of the company for the past years have been ₹ 15. The shares of the company are sold in the market at Book value. The company's tax rate is 50%. The shareholder's tax liability may be assumed as 25%. Find out the weighted average cost of capital.

Solution :

(*i*) Cost of Debentures

$$Kd = \frac{I}{NP}(I - T)$$

$$= \frac{36{,}000}{3{,}00{,}000} \times .50 = 6\%$$

(*ii*) Cost of preference share capital 10%

(*iii*) Cost of equity share capital 12%

(*iv*) Cost of Retained Earnings 9%

Statement showing Weighted Average Cost of Capital

Source	*Amount (₹)*	*Weights*	*Specific cost %*	*Weighted Average cost*
Debentures	3,00,000	.3	6	1.8
Preference capital	2,00,000	.2	10	2.0
Equity capital	4,00,000	.4	12	4.8
Retained earnings	1,00,000	.1	9	0.9
	10,00,000			9.5

Problem 7. *Calculate the cost of equity for a firm whose shares are quoted at ₹ 120. The dividend at the end of the year is expected to be ₹ 9.72 per share and the growth rate is 8%.*

Solution :

Cost of equity for a firm :

$$Ke = \frac{\text{DPS}}{\text{MP}} + g$$

Ke = Cost of equity capital

DPS = Dividend per Equity share

MP = Market price of an equity share

g = growth rate of dividend

$$Ke = \frac{9.72}{120} \times 100 + 8\%$$

$$= 8.1\% + 8.00\% = 16.1\%.$$

Problem 8. *The current market price of an equity share of a company is ₹ 90. The current dividend per share is ₹ 4.50. In case the dividends are expected to grow at the rate of 8%, what is the shareholders' required rate of return ?* [MBA Anna May 2003]

Solution :

Shareholders' required rate of return :

$$Ke = \frac{\text{D}}{\text{MP}} + g$$

$$Ke = \frac{4.50}{90} + 8\%$$

$$.05 + .08 = 0.13$$

i.e., $.13 \times 100 = 13\%$

Shareholders' required rate of return is 13%.

Problem 9. *(a) A company plans to issue 1,000 new shares of ₹ 100 each at par. The floatation costs are expected to be 5% of the share price. The company pays a dividend of ₹ 10 per share initially and the growth in dividends is expected to be 5%. Compute the cost of new issue of equity shares. (b) If the current market price of an equity share is ₹ 150. Calculate the cost of existing equity share capital.* [MBA Anna Dec. 2003]

Solution :

(*a*)

$$Ke = \frac{\text{D}}{\text{MP}} + g$$

$$= \frac{10}{100-5} + 5\% = 15.53\%$$

(*b*)

$$Ke = \frac{\text{D}}{\text{MP}} + \text{G}$$

$$= \frac{10}{150-5} + 5\% = \frac{10}{145} + 5\%$$

$$= 11.89\%$$

TEST PROBLEMS

1. The capital structure and after tax cost of different sources of funds are given below:

Sources of Funds	*Amount*	*Proportion to total*	*After tax cost %*
Equity share capital	7,20,000	.30	15
Retained earnings	6,00,000	.25	14
Preference share Capital	4,80,000	.20	10
Debentures	6,00,000	.25	8

You are required to compute the weighted average cost of capital. *[Bharathidasan, B.Com.]*

[**Ans:** WACC: 12% (4.5 + 3.5 + 2 + 2)]

2. You are required to determine the weighted average cost capital (Ko) of the K.C. Ltd. using (*i*) Book value weights; and (*ii*) Market value weights. The following information is available for your perusal. The K.C. Ltd.'s present book value capital structure is:

Debentures (₹ 100 per depenture)	8,00,000
Preference shares (₹ 100 per share)	2,00,000
Equity shares (₹ 10 per share)	10,00,000
Total	**20,00,000**

All these securities are traded in the capital market. Recent prices are: debentures @ ₹ 110, preference shares @ ₹ 120 and equity shares @ ₹ 22. Anticipated external financing opportunities are:

(*i*) ₹ 100 per debenture redeemable at par: 20 year maturity, 8% coupon rate, 4% floatation cost, sale price ₹ 100.

(*ii*) ₹ 100 preference share redeemable at par: 15 year maturity, 10% dividend rate, 5% flotation cost, sale price ₹ 100.

(*iii*) Equity shares: ₹ 2 per share flotation cost, sale pricve ₹ 22.

In addition, the dividend expected on the equity shares at the end of the year is ₹ 2 per share, the anticipated growth rate in dividend is 5% and the company has the practice of paying all its earnings in the form of dividend. The corporate tax rate is 50%.

[IGNOU MBA, C.S Final Dec. 1996, June 2003]

[**Ans.** WACC (Book Value): 10.23% (0.5 × 15%) + (0.10 × 10.59%) + (0.40 × 4.18%) WACC (Market Value) = 11.81% (66.26 × 15% + 7.23 × 10.59 + 26.51 × 4.18%)]

❑❑❑

25

Capital Structure

A company, in order to have successful operation, needs adequate amount of capital. The capital requirement starts right from the incorporation of the company. The foremost function of the finance manager is to make correct forecasting of financial requirements not only in present but future also. The required funds can be raised through various sources or forms.

CAPITALISATION : MEANING

The term capitalisation is the sum total of all long term securities issued by a company and the surpluses not meant for distribution.

A.S Dewing defines *"The term capitalisation is the valuation of the capital, which includes the capital stock and debt."*

According to **Gerrtenbeg**, *"For all practical purposes, capitalisation means the total accounting value of all the capital regularly employed in the business."*

CAPITAL STRUCTURE

Capital structure of a company refers to the mix of its capitalisation. A company obtains funds by issuing different types of securities *i.e.*, ordinary shares, preference shares, bonds and debentures. The combination, in which the various kinds of securities are issued is known as capital structure.

According to **Gerrtenbeg**, *"Capital structure of a company (or financial structure) refers to the make-up of its capitalisation."*

According to **Weston and Brighan**, *"Capital structure is the permanent financing of the firm, represented by long term debt, preferred stock and net worth".*

Basic Patterns of Capital Structure

(*i*) Issuing only equity shares.
(*ii*) Issuing equity shares and preference shares.
(*iii*) Issuing equity and debentures.
(*iv*) Issuing equity shares, preference shares and debentures.

Factors Affecting Capital Structure

The following factors govern the capital structure of a company.

(*i*) Trading on equity.
(*ii*) Nature of enterprises.
(*iii*) Legal restrictions.
(*iv*) Purpose of financing.
(*v*) Period of finance.
(*vi*) Market conditions.
(*vii*) Size of the company.
(*viii*) Need of investors.
(*ix*) Government policy.
(*x*) Cost of capital and availability of Funds.

(*i*) *Trading on Equity.* A company may mobilise capital either by issue of shares or by debentures. In any situation, the rate of return on total capital employed is more than the rate of interest on debentures or rate of dividend on preference shares. It is known as trading on equity. In a particular situation, a company can pay higher rate of dividend than the general rate of earnings on the total capital employed. It is the benefit of trading on equity.

(*ii*) *Nature of Enterprises.* Foremost determinant of capital structure of a company is the nature of the business enterprise. Businesses having more risks but varying income prefer equity shares. Firms, engaged in public utility services, may prefer issue of debentures and preference shares.

(*iii*) *Legal Restrictions.* Each and every company has to comply with provisions of the law regarding the issue of different kinds of securities. So, the promoter of a company has to follow the legal provisions. Specially in India, banking companies are not allowed to issue any type of securities other than equity shares.

(*iv*) *Purpose of Financing.* The purpose of financing for raising the fund must be taken into account at the time of formulating capital structure of the company. If funds are required for direct productive purpose, the company can afford to issue debentures. But, the funds are required for non-productive purposes, the company should raise funds through issue of equity shares.

(*v*) *Period of Finance.* Generally, the period of finance also determines the capital structure of companies. Short term commitment of companies are met out through borrowings. Some times, if the funds are required for 8 to 10 years, it will be met by issue of debentures. If funds are required for more than 10 years, it can be met out by issue of equity shares.

(*vi*) *Market Conditions.* Movement of the capital market also decides the capital structure of the company. During the periods of depression, the investors will look for their safety and they prefer to invest in debentures and not in equity shares. But, during the boom period any type of securities can be sold very easily in the market, hence equities also get the better market.

(*vii*) *Size of the Company.* The small scale organisations fully depend upon the owner's fund to run their business. Such companies find it difficult to obtain long term debt. But, large scale organisations are generally considered to be less risky by the investors. So, they can issue different types of securities and mobilise resources from different sources.

(*viii*) *Need of Investors.* Some of the investors prefer to invest in debentures because they provide safety of investment and stable income. Preference shares will be preferred by those who want a higher and stable income with sufficient safety of investment. Those, who want to bear higher risk, higher return and capital appreciation prefer equity shares only. So, capital structure of the company depends upon the financial status and psychological attitude of the investors.

(*ix*) *Government Policy.* Any of the monetary, fiscal, financial policies, which are time to time announced by the union government, may straight away affect the capital structure decision of the company. For example, change in the lending policy of financial institutions may mean a complete change in the financial pattern. New provisions of the SEBI also affect the capital issue policies of various companies.

(*x*) *Cost of Capital and Availability of Funds.* The appropriate term of financing is, at times, the result of the study of comparative cost of various types of financing in relation to the level of risk involved and the availability of various alternative forms of financing. But, sometimes, debentures may be issued because of their cheapness and availability, the danger of the financial position and so on.

Theories of Capital Structure

Different theories have been developed by different authors. The important theories are :

(*i*) Net income approach.
(*ii*) Net operating income approach.
(*iii*) Traditional approach.
(*iv*) Modigliani and Miller approach.

(*i*) Net Income Approach

According to NI approach, a firm can minimize the weighted average cost of capital and it can increase the value of the firm as well as market price of the equity shares by using more debt content in the company.

This approach is based upon the following assumptions :

- The cost of debt is less than the cost of equity.
- There are no corporate taxes.
- The debt content of the firm does not change the risk perception of the investors.

(*ii*) Net Operating Income Approach

This theory was suggested by Durand. It is entirely opposite to the NI approach. According to this approach, change in the capital structure of the company does not affect the market value of the firm and the overall cost of capital remains constant irrespective of the method of financing. Its implication is that the overall cost of capital remains the same whether the debt equity mix is 50 : 50, or 30 :70 or 10 : 90. Under this approach, all the structures are optimum capital structures. It is based on the following assumptions like

- The market capitalises the value of the firm as a whole.
- The business risk remains constant at each and every level of debt-equity mix.

(*iii*) Traditional Approach

This approach is also known as Ezra Solomon's approach. It is the intermediate approach between the net income approach and net operating income approach. According to this approach, the value of the firm can be increased initially. The cost of capital can be decreased by using more debt as the debt is a cheaper source of funds than equity. The optimum capital structure can be reached by an appropriate debt equity mix.

***(iv)* Modigliani and Miller Approach**

The Modigliani–Miller approach is similar to the net operating income approach. Under this approach, the value of a firm is independent of its capital structure. Simply, MM approach maintains that the average cost of capital does not change with change in the debt weighted equity mix or capital structure of the firm. The argument is based on a simple switching mechanism which is closely called arbitrage.

In the expression of Modigliani and Miller, two firms, identical in all respects except their capital structure, cannot have different market values or cost of capital because of arbitrage process. In case they have different market values or cost of capital, arbitrage will take place and the investors will engage in personal leverage as against the corporate leverage and this will again render the two companies having the same value.

Modigliani and Miller Approach is based on the following assumptions :

(i) There are no transaction costs.

(ii) All the investors are free to buy and sell securities.

(iii) There are no corporate taxes (But, this assumption has been removed later).

(iv) There are no retained earnings. However, the dividend pay out ratio is 100%

(v) Borrowings are riskless.

Balanced or Optimum Capital Structure

Optimum or balanced capital structure means an ideal combination of borrowed and owned capital that may achieve the maximisation of market value per share and decrease the cost of capital when the real cost of each source of funds is the same.

Characteristics of a Balanced Capital Structure

(i) Profitability.

(ii) Solvency.

(iii) Conservatism.

(iv) Effective Control.

(v) Economy.

(vi) Attraction to the Investors.

(vii) Ease and Simplicity.

(viii) Minimum Remuneration.

FORMULAS—FOR VALUATION OF FIRMS

1. *Valuation of Firms : NI approach*

$$V = S + B$$

Where, V = Value of the firm

S = Market value of the equity

B = Market value of the debt

Market value of Equity (S) can be ascertained as follows :

$$S = \frac{NI}{Ke}$$

S = Market value of the equity
NI = Earnings available for equity shareholders
Ke = Equity Capitalisation Rate

K = Overall cost of capital Formula for $K = \frac{EBIT}{V}$

Net Income : Amount available for Equity Shareholder

Earnings before interest and Tax	xx
Less : Interest	xx
PBT	xx
Less : Tax	xx
PAT	xx
Less : Pre-dividend (if any)	
Amount available for equity shareholders	xx

2. *Valuation of firms : NOI approach*

$$S = V - B \qquad V = \frac{EBIT}{Ke}$$

S = Value of equity
V = Value of firm
B = Value of debt
Ke = Equity Capitalisation Rate

$$Ke = \frac{EBIT - I}{V - B} \times 100$$

K = Overall cost of capital

$$K = Kd\left[\frac{B}{V}\right] = Ke\left[\frac{S}{V}\right]$$

Kd = Cost of Debt
B = Total debt
V = Total value of the firm
Ke = Cost of Equity Capital
S = Market value of Equity

3. *Valuation of firm : MM approach*

(*i*) Value of unlevered firm

$$Vu = \frac{\text{Profits available for equity shareholders}}{\text{Equity Capitalisation Rate}}$$

(or)

$$Vu = \frac{(I - t)EBT}{Ke} \qquad t = \text{tax rate}$$

(*ii*) Value of levered firm

$Vi = Vu + Bt$

$$Vi = Vu + Bt$$

Vu = Value of unlevered firm

B = Amount of debt

t = Tax rate

Vi = Value of levered firm

NOTE : The term levered firm means there is debt content in its capital structure. The term unlevered firm means there is no debt content in its capital structure.

4. *Valuation of firm : Traditional approach*

Traditional approach contains some features of NI approach and some features of NOI approach. So, there is no need for a separate formula for the valuation of firms under this approach

TEST QUESTIONS

1. Define capital structure.
2. What is meant by capital structure ?
3. List out the basic patterns of capital structure.
4. What do you understand by capital structure ? What are the major determinants of capital structure ?
5. Briefly explain the various theories of capital structure.
6. What are the characteristics of a balanced capital structure ?
7. Give a critical appraisal of the traditional approach and the Modigliani-Millers approach to the problem of capital structure.

PROBLEMS AND SOLUTIONS

Problem 1. *M/s Nagu Ltd., has a share capital of ₹ 1,00,000 divided into 10,000 equity shares of ₹ 10 each fully paid. It has a major expansion programme requiring an investment of another ₹ 50,000. The management is considering the following alternatives for raising this amount.*

(a) Issue of 5,000 Equity shares of ₹ 10 each

(b) Issue of 5,000 12% Preference shares of ₹ 10 each

(c) Issue of 10% Debentures of ₹ 50,000

The company's present earnings before interest and taxes (EBIT) are ₹ 40,000 p.a. You are required to calculate the effect of each of the above modes of financing of the EPS (Earnings Per Share) assuming (i) EBIT continues to be the same even after expansion.

(ii) EBIT increases by ₹ 10,000. Assume tax rate at 50%.

Solution :

(*i*) Computation of Earnings Per Share when EBIT is ₹ 40,000 p.a

Particulars	*Present Capital structure All Equity* ₹	*Proposed Capital structure* (*i*) *All Equity* ₹	(*ii*) *Equity + Pref* ₹	(*iii*) *Equity + Debt* ₹
EBIT	40,000	40,000	40,000	40,000
Less : Interest	—	—	—	5,000
PBT	40,000	40,000	40,000	35,000
Less : Tax	20,000	20,000	20,000	17,500
PAT	20,000	20,000	20,000	17,500
Less : Pref. Dividend	—	—	6,000	—
Profit available for Equity Share holders	20,000	20,000	14,000	17,500
Amount Available for Equity share holders	20,000	20,000	14,000	22,500
No. of Equity shares	10,000	15,000	10,000	10,000
EPS	2	1.33	1.40	1.75
Dilution against Initial EPS of ₹ 2	—	.67	.60	.25

The above solution shows that dilution of earning per share has been the least when the funds have been raised by issue of debentures.

(*ii*) Computation of Present and Projected Earnings Per Share when EBIT is ₹ 50,000 p.a. [40,000 + 10,000]

	Present Capital structure All Equity ₹	*Proposed Capital structure* (*i*) *All Equity* ₹	(*ii*) *Equity + Pref* ₹	(*iii*) *Equity + Debt* ₹
EBIT	40,000	50,000	50,000	50,000
Less : Interest	—	—	—	5,000
PBT	40,000	50,000	50,000	45,000
Less : Tax	20,000	25,000	25,000	22,500
PAT	20,000	25,000	25,000	22,500
Less : Pref. Dividend	—	—	6,000	—
Profit available for Equity Share holders	20,000	25,000	19,000	22,500
No. of Equity shares	10,000	15,000	10,000	10,000
EPS	2	1.67	1.90	2.25
Changes in EPS as against initial of ₹ 2	—	– .33	– .10	+ .25

The above table indicates that EPS has gone up by ₹ 0.25 per share as against the present EPS when the funds are raised by issue of debentures. Hence, the use of debentures is the desirable capital structure for raising funds. Because, for the other two, the EPS goes down.

Problem 2. *In considering the most desirable capital structure for a company, the following estimates of the cost of debt and equity capital (after tax) have been made at various levels of debt- equity mix.*

Debt as percentage of total capital employed	*Cost of Debt(%)*	*Cost of Equity (%)*
0	*5.0*	*12.0*
10	*5.0*	*12.0*
20	*5.0*	*12.5*
30	*5.5*	*13.0*
40	*6.0*	*14.0*
50	*6.5*	*14.6*
60	*7.0*	*20.0*

You are required to determine the optimal debt-equity mix for the company by calculating composite cost of capital. [B.Com. Adapted]

Solution :

Statement showing the Company's Composite Cost of Capital (after tax)

Debt Percentage of total capital employed	*Cost of Debt*	*Cost of Equity*	*Composite Cost of Capital*
0	5.0	12.0	5 × 0 + 12 × 1 = 12.00
10	5.0	12.0	5 × .10 + 12 × .90 = 11.30
20	5.0	12.5	5 × .20 + 12.5 × .80 = 11.00
30	5.5	13.0	5.5 × .30 + 13 × .70 = 10.75
40	6.0	14.0	6 × .40 + 14 × .60 = 10.80
50	6.5	16.0	6.5 × .50 + 16 × .50 = 11.25
60	7.0	20.0	7.0 × .60 + 20 × .40 = 12.20

Problem 3. *A new project is under consideration by Ram Ltd., which requires a capital investment of ₹ 150 Lakhs. Interest on term loan is 12% and tax rate is 50%. If the debt- equity ratio insisted by the financing agencies is 2 :1, calculate the point of indifference for the project.* [ICWA Final, Dec. 1979]

Solution :

In case of project under consideration, the debt equity ratio insisted by the financing agencies is 2 : 1.

Following are some possible alternatives :

(*i*) Raising the total capital by issue of equity shares.

(*ii*) Raising ₹ 100 lakhs by way of debt and ₹ 50 lakhs by way of issue of shares. Thus, maintaining a debt-equity ratio of 2:1.

There are two possibilities available :

(*i*) Issuing the entire capital by way of issue of equity shares.

(*ii*) Mobilising ₹ 100 lakhs by way of debt and ₹ 50 lakhs by way of issue of shares. In this situation, they can maintain a debt-equity ratio of 2:1.

In the first case, the interest amount will be zero. But, in the second case, it will be ₹ 12 lakhs.

Computation of Point Indifference

$$\frac{(x - I_1)(1 - T) - PD}{S_1} = \frac{(x - I_2)(1 - T) - PD}{S_2}$$

$$\frac{(x \times 0)(1 - .5) - 0}{15} = \frac{(x - 12) \times (1 - .5) - 0}{5}$$

$$\frac{(x \times 0.5)}{15} = \frac{(x - 12) \times .5}{5}$$

$$2.5x = 7.5x - 90$$

$$5x = 90$$

$$x = \frac{90}{5}$$

$$= ₹\ 18 \text{ lakhs}$$

NOTE : EBIT at point of indifference is therefore ₹ 18 lakhs. If EBIT is ₹ 18 lakhs, the earning on equity after tax will be 6% p.a. notwithstanding whether the capital is financed fully by equity or by any other mix of equity and debt provided. The rate of interest on debt is 12%.

Where, x = Point of Indifference or Break Even EBIT level

I_1 = Interest under plan 1

I_2 = Interest under plan 2

T = Tax Rate

PD = Preference dividend

S_1 = Number of Equity shares of plan 1

S_2 = Number of Equity shares of plan 2.

Problem 4. *(i) Murugappa & Co expects a net income of ₹ 80,000. It has 8% Debentures worth ₹ 2,00,000. The equity capitalisation rate of the company is 10%. Calculate the value of the firm and overall cost of capital rate according to the Net Income approach. (Ignoring income tax)*

(ii) If Debenture debt is increased to ₹ 3,00,000 what shall be the value of firm and the overall cost of capital ?

Solution :

(*i*) Calculate the value of the firm :

V = S + B

V = Value of the firm

S = Market value of equity

$$B = \frac{NI}{K_e} = \frac{64{,}000}{10/100} \quad \textit{i.e.,}\ 64{,}000 \times 100/10 = 6{,}40{,}000$$

Note :

(*i*) Computation of NI (Net Income)

		₹
Net Income	=	80,000
Less : Interest on 8% Debentures of ₹ 2,00,000	=	16,000
Amount available for Equity share holders	=	64,000

K_e : Equity capitalisation rate = 10%

Value the firm = ₹ 8,40,000 [6,40,000 + 2,00,000]

[Value of Debenture 2,00,000]

(*ii*) Computation of overall capitalisation Rate :

Overall cost of capital (K) = EBIT/V

EBIT = Earnings before Interest and Tax

$$V = \text{Value of the firm} = \frac{80{,}000}{8{,}40{,}000} \times 100 = 9.52\%$$

(*iii*) Computation of value of the firm when debentures raised to ₹ 3,00,000

Net income	80,000
Less : Interest on 8% Debentures of ₹ 3,00,000	24,000
	56,000

Equity Capitalisation Rate 10%

Market Value of Equity 56,000 × $\frac{100}{10}$	=	5,60,000
Market Value of Debentures	=	3,00,000
Value of the Firm		8,60,000

$$\text{Overall Cost of Capital Rate} = \frac{EBIT}{V} \times 100$$

EBIT : Earnings before interest and taxes

V : Value of the firm

i.e., EBIT : 80,000

V : 8,60,000

$$\text{Therefore, Overall Cost of Capital Rate} = \frac{80{,}000}{8{,}60{,}000} \times 100 = 9.3\%$$

Findings :

In the above computation there is increase in the debt financing and the value of the firm also increased so the overall cost of capital has decreased.

Problem 5. *(i) SLM Ltd expects a net operating income of ₹2,00,000. It has 6% Debentures worth ₹10,00,000. The overall capitalisation rate is 10%. Calculate the value of the firm and the equity capitalisation rate according to NOI approach.*

(ii) If the debenture debt is decreased to ₹7,50,000 what will be effect on the value of the firm and the equity capitalisation rate ?

Solution :

(i) Value of the firm : NOI approach

Here, S = V – B

S = Value of Equity

V = Value of the Firm

B = Value of Debt.

First Step :

$$V = \frac{EBIT}{Ke} = \frac{2,00,000}{10/100} = 2,00,000 \times \frac{100}{10} = 20,00,000$$

EBIT = Earning before interest and taxes 2,00,000

K_e = Equity capitalisation Rate 10%

B = Market value of Debenture : ₹ 10,00,000

Second Step :

S = V – B = 20,00,000 – 10,00,000 = 10,00,000

After arriving at the value of V & B, we can easily find the value of S

K_e = Equity Capitalisation Rate

$$K_e = \frac{EBIT - I}{V - B} \times 100$$

$$= \frac{2,00,000 - 60,000}{20,00,000 - 10,00,000} \times 100 = 14$$

(ii) If the debenture debt is increased to ₹ 7,50,000, the value of the firm remains unchanged at ₹ 10,00,000. The equity capitalisation rate will be as follows.

(1) Value of the firm

S = V – B

V = 20,00,000

B = 7,50,000

S = 12,50,000

(2) Equity Capitalisation Rate (K_e) $= \frac{EBIT - I}{V - B} \times 100$

$$= \frac{2,00,000 - 45,000}{20,00,000 - 7,50,000} \times 100$$

= 12.4%

Problem 6. *Two firms B and S are identical in all respects except the degree of leverage. Firm B has 6% of debt of ₹ 3.00 lakhs while firm S has no debt. Both the firms are earning an EBT of ₹ 1,20,000 each. The equity capitalisation rate is 10% and the corporate tax is 60%.*

You are required to compute the market value of the two firms.

Solution :

Value of unlevered firm : *(No debt content)*

Formula :

$$Vu = \frac{\text{Profit available for equity shareholders}}{\text{Equity Capitalisation Rate}}$$

$$= \frac{1,20,000 - 72,000}{10/100}$$

$$= 48,000 \times 100/10$$

$$Vu = ₹\ 4,80,000$$

NOTE :

Profit available for equity shareholders

Earnings before tax	1,20,000
Less : Tax Rate (1,20,000 × 60/100)	72,000
Profit available for equity shareholders	48,000

Value of levered firm

$Vi = Vu + Bt$ — $Vi = 4,80,000 + 3,00,000 \times .6$

Vi = Value of levered firm — $= 5,60,000$

Vu = Value of unlevered firm — $Vu = ₹\ 4,80,000$

B = Value of Debenture — $Vi = ₹\ 5,60,000$

t = Tax rate

TEST PROBLEMS

1. A company needs ₹ 12,00,000 for installation of a new factory which would yield an annual EBIT of ₹ 2,00,000. The company has the objective of maximizing the earnings per share. It is considering the possibility of issuing equity shares plus raising a debt of ₹ 2,00,000., ₹ 6,00,000 or ₹ 10,00,000. The current market price per share is ₹ 40 which is expected to drop to ₹ 25 per share if the market borrowing were to exceed ₹ 7,50,000.

Costs of borrowings are indicated as under:

Upto ₹ 2,50,000	10% per annum
Between ₹ 2,50,001 and ₹ 6,25,000	14% per annum
Between ₹ 6,25,001 and ₹ 10,00,000	16% per annum

Assuming the tax rate to be 50%, work out the EPS and the scheme which would meet the objective of the management.

[Bharathidasan, M.Com.; C.A. Final June 1996]

[**Ans :** EPS – I. ₹ 3.60; II. ₹ 4.20; III. ₹ 3.91]

2. A firm is considering methods to finance its investment proposal. It is estimated that initially ₹ 4,00,000 will be needed. Two alternative methods of raising funds are available to the firm; (*a*) Issue of 15% lone amounting to ₹ 2,00,000 and issue of 2,000 equity shares of ₹ 100 each and (*b*) Issue of 4,000 equity shares of ₹ 100 each. The appropriate tax rate is 50%.

(*i*) Assuming operating profit (EBIT) of: (*a*) ₹ 70,000, and (b) ₹ 80,000, which financing proposal would you recommend, and why?

(*ii*) Compute the indifference point of the financial plans.

[Delhi M.Com., 1982]

[Ans. EPS (EPIT ₹ 70,000) (*a*) ₹ 10 (20,000/2,000), (*b*) ₹ 8.75 (35,000/4,000); (EBIT ₹ 80,000) (*a*) ₹ 12.50 (25,000/2,000); (*b*) ₹ 10 (40,000/4,000); Indifference point:₹ 60,000]

3. A company is currently earning an EBIT of ₹ 12 lakh. Its present borrowings are:

11% Term loans	₹ 40 lakh
Working capital:	
Borrowing from Bank at 16%	₹ 33 lakh
Public deposits at 12%	₹ 15 lakh

The sale of the company is growing and to support this, the company purposes to obtain an additional bank borrowing of ₹ 25 lakh. The increase in EBIT is expected to be 20%.

Compute the change in interest coverage ratio after the additional borrowing.

[Madras, M.Com., Nov. 2006]

[Ans. (1) 1.05, (2) Revised interest coverage ratio = 0.93]

4. Calculate the operating leverage financial leverage and the combined leverage for the following firms and interpret results;

	P	*Q*	*R*
Output (units)	3,00,000	75,000	5,00,000
Fixed cost (₹)	3,50,000	7,00,000	75,000
Variable cost per unit (₹)	1	7,50	0.10
Interest Expenses (₹)	25,000	40,000	–
Unit selling price (₹)	3	25	0.50

[Madras, MBA. Nov. 1998]

[Ans. OP leverage: P: 2.40 times (6,00,000/2,50,000)
Q: 2.14 times (13,12,500/6,12,500)
R: 1.60 times (2,00,000/1,25,000)
Fin. leverage: P: 1.11 times (2,50,00/2,25,000)
Q: 1.07 times (6,12,500/5,72,500)
R: 1 time (1.25,500/1,25,000)
Comb. leverage: P: 2.66 times; Q: 2.29 Times: R: 1.60 times]

❑❑❑

26

Working Capital

The first and foremost objective of the financial management is to maximise the wealth of shareholders. It is possible only when the company earns sufficient profit. The profitability of the organisation fully depends upon the magnitude of sales. However, sales are not converted into cash immediately. Because there is a time gap between the sale of goods and receipt of cash. During the time gap a certain amount is required to sustain the sales volume on a regular basis. That amount is known as working capital. Suppose adequate working capital is not available, the company will not be in a position to maintain the sales volume at an expected level.

Simply, working capital means circulating capital or revolving capital. In other words, working capital means amount required for the day-to-day expenses of the business activities.

According to J.S.Mill, the sum of current assets is the working capital of a business.

"Working capital is the amount of funds necessary to cover the cost of operating the enterprise" says **Shubin.**

Gesterrberg defines, Working capital is the excess of current assets over current liabilities.

Simply, Net Working Capital = Current Assets – Current Liabilities.

CONCEPTS OF WORKING CAPITAL

(*i*) Gross Working Capital (*ii*) Net Working Capital

(*i*) Gross Working Capital

The Gross working capital refers to working capital which represents investment in current assets such as marketable securities, inventories and bills receivables.

(*ii*) Net Working Capital

Net working capital refers to working capital. It is the excess of current assets over current Liabilities. This is the most commonly accepted definition.

TYPES OF WORKING CAPITAL

Working capital can be divided into two categories on the basis of time.

(*i*) Permanent working capital or core current assets.

(*ii*) Temporary or variable working capital.

(*i*) Permanent Working Capital

Permanent working capital refers to that minimum amount of investment in all current assets which is required to carry out minimum level of business activities on a permanent basis. In other words, certain current assets which are retained by the organisation on a continuous basis is called permanent working capital or core current assets.

(*ii*) Temporary or Variable Working Capital

Temporary working capital is an investment in current assets which are fluctuating from time to time on the basis of the operations of the business. The capital, required to meet the seasonal needs of a firm, is called seasonal working capital or temporary working capital. In other words, the amount of working capital which will vary from time to time depending upon the level of business activities, is known as variable working capital.

OPERATING CYCLE

Modern business enterprises face severe competitions. They produce goods based upon the demand. In this respect, all manufactured goods are not sold immediately. And at the same time, cash for sales is also not realised immediately. From the purchase of raw material to the conversion of cash, certain time gap is taken. This time gap is technically known as operating cycle of the business.

Stages of Operating Cycle

(*i*) Conversion of cash into raw materials.
(*ii*) Conversion of raw materials into work in progress.
(*iii*) Conversion of work in progress into finished goods.
(*iv*) Conversion of finished goods into debtors.
(*v*) Conversion of debtors into cash.

Advantages or Importance of Working Capital

(*i*) Adequate working capital ensures the regular supply of raw materials and continued production.

(*ii*) Easy to get the loan from the banks and other financial institutions on easy and convenient terms.

(*iii*) It enables the firm to avail cash discount facilities on the purchases, thus it reduces the costs.

(*iv*) To follow as a prompt payment policy helps in establishment of goodwill.

(*v*) It helps the organisation to meet the financial crisis during the periods of depression or any emergencies.

(*vi*) The expansion programme of a concern is highly successful and obtains higher profitability.

(*vii*) It improves high morale among employees and executives in the organisation.

(*viii*) To encourage research programme.

(*ix*) To obtain the higher level of productivity due to effective utilisation of assets.

(*x*) Enables to pay higher return to its owner. So, automatically the firm possesses a financial soundness. In this way it helps to generate additional funds in future.

Disadvantages or Danger of Inadequate Working Capital

(*i*) A concern cannot pay its short term liabilities because of inadequate working capital. This leads to borrowing funds at higher rates of interest.

(*ii*) It may not take advantage of cash discount because the concern may find it difficult to buy its requirement in bulk quantities.

(*iii*) Low level liquidity position of the concern may lead to winding up of the firm.

(*iv*) Fixed assets could not be fully utilised on account of lack in sufficient working capital. So, the rate of return on investment falls.

(*v*) It is very difficult to obtain favourable market conditions and any of the profitable business opportunities.

(*vi*) Credit worthiness and reputation of the organisation may be damaged.

(*vii*) It leads to under-utilisation of production facilities.

Disadvantages of Excessive Working Capital

(*i*) Unnecessary purchases and accumulation of inventories lead to chances of more losses and waste.

(*ii*) Due to huge amount of idle funds the rate of return on its investment automatically goes down.

(*iii*) It leads to overtrade and chances of heavy losses.

(*iv*) Difficult to maintain the cordial relationship with the bank and other financial institutions.

(*v*) Large amount of bad debts arise.

(*vi*) It encourages mass production which may not have matching demand.

Determinants of Working Capital : (or) Factors Determining Working Capital

(*i*) Nature of Business.

(*ii*) Production Policies.

(*iii*) Length of the Manufacturing Cycle.

(iv) Terms of Purchases and Sales.
(v) Seasonal Variation.
(vi) Fluctuations in Supply.
(vii) Dividend Policy.
(viii) Requirements of Cash.
(ix) Other Factors.

(i) *Nature of Business.* Working capital of the organisation basically depends upon the nature of business. Public utility concerns like Railways, Electricity etc would need only very little amount of working capital. On the other hand, manufacturing and trading concerns need huge amount of working capital in their operations.

(ii) *Production Policies.* Production policy of the organisation is also an important factor for determining working capital. In case of labour intensive industry the quantum of working capital is required only in smaller amount. But, highly automatic plants require huge amount of working capital.

(iii) *Length of the Manufacturing Cycle.* The amount of working capital needed is highly influenced by the length of manufacturing cycle. If the manufacturing process is long, huge amount of working capital will be required and vice versa. So, utmost care should be taken to shorten the period of cycle in order to minimise the working capital requirements.

(iv) *Terms of Purchase and Sales.* If an organisation provides liberal credit facilities to its customers, large amount of working capital gets locked up in sundry debtors and bills receivable. And at the same time if continuous credit is allowed by the suppliers, it tends to cause not only postponement of payment but also payment out of sale proceeds of the goods produced. The period of credit allowed and received also determines the working capital requirements of the company.

(v) *Seasonal Variations.* Seasonal changes in the economy also affect the quantum of working capital. Huge amount of working capital is required during the periods of inflation and depression and the requirement declines during the other periods of economic cycle.

(vi) *Fluctuations in Supply.* Certain industries purchase raw material at huge level due to their irregular supply throughout the year. It is specifically applicable to the manufacturing organisation which requires an unusual type of raw material that can be purchased only with limited sources.

(vii) *Dividend Policy.* According to the new provisions of the SEBI, all the companies are compulsorily to declare the dividend to the shareholders. So, the dividend policy has a dominant influence on the working capital position of the organisation. As per the new provisions, need for the working capital is met with retained earnings. Once dividend is declared and the same has to be paid in cash requires large amounts from the pool of working capital.

(viii) *Requirements of Cash.* Need for the working capital depends upon the amount of cash required by the company for its various purposes. If greater the requirements of cash, the higher will be the working capital needs of the company and vice versa.

(ix) *Other Factors.* Apart from the above points, some other factors also affect the working capital requirements. For example, lack of transport and communication facilities, tariff policies of government etc. also influence the requirements of working capital.

SOURCES OF WORKING CAPITAL

An efficient finance manager is always interested in maintaining the correct amount of working capital at the right time, at a reasonable cost and at the best possible favourable terms. The following are the important sources of working capital.

To obtain the working capital in the following two major divisions.

(A) Long term sources.

(B) Short term sources.

(A) Long-term Sources

(*i*) Share capital.

(*ii*) Sale of debentures.

(*iii*) Ploughing back of profits.

(*iv*) Sale of fixed assets.

(*v*) Term loans.

(B) Short-term Sources

I. *Internal Sources :*

(*i*) Depreciation Funds.

(*ii*) Provision for Taxation.

(*iii*) Accrued Expenses.

II. *External Sources :*

(*i*) Trade credit.

(*ii*) Bank credit.

(*iii*) Credit papers.

(*iv*) Public deposits.

(*v*) Government's assistance.

(*vi*) Loans from directors etc.

(*vii*) Factoring.

FORECASTING TECHNIQUES OF WORKING CAPITAL

There are so many popular methods for forecasting the working capital requirements which are as follows :

(*i*) Cash Forecasting Method.

(*ii*) Balance Sheet Method.

(*iii*) Profit and Loss Adjustment Method.

(*iv*) Percentage of Sales Method.

(*v*) Operational Cycle Method.

(*vi*) Regression Analysis Method.

(*i*) *Cash Forecasting Method.* Under this method, the working capital is to be determined on the basis of the closing balance of the cash, after considering the receipts and payments made during that period.

(ii) *Balance Sheet Method.* According to this method, a forecast is made of the various assets and liabilities of the concern. The difference between two is taken which will indicate either cash surplus or cash deficiency.

(iii) *Profit and Loss Adjustment Method.* Under this method, the forecasted Profits or Losses are to be adjusted on cash basis.

(iv) *Percentage of Sales Method.* Under this method, working capital is determined as a percentage of forecasted sales. It must be decided on the basis of past observations. This method is simple and easy to understand.

(v) *Operational Cycle Method.* Under this method, working capital is determined according to the operating cycle concept. In a manufacturing organisation the working capital cycle starts from the purchase of raw material and ends with the conversion of cash. It involves purchase of raw materials, work in progress, finished goods, sales, debtors and conversion of cash. This cycle will continue again and again. Each of the cycle stage is expressed in terms of number of days of relevant activity and requires a level of investment. The amount required for these stage-wise investments will be the total amount of the working capital of the organisation.

Following formula is used to express the framework of the operating cycle :

$T = (r - c) + w + f + b$

T = Stands for the total period of operating cycle in number of days

r = Stands for the number of days of raw material and stores consumption requirements held in raw materials and stores

c = Number of days of credit allowed by creditors

W = Stands for the number of days of cost of production held in work in progress

f = Finished stock storage period

or

T = Duration of operating cycle in number of days

r = Raw materials and storage period

c = Creditors payment period

w = Work in process period

f = Finished stock storage period

b = Debtors collection period

(vi) *Regression Analysis Method.* According to this method, statistical formula is used to determine the working capital requirement. Projection of working capital is made after establishing the average relationship in the past years between sales and working capital *i.e.,* current assets.

Procedure for Computation of Working Capital

Current Assets		
Raw Material	xx	
Work in Progress	xx	
Finished Goods	xx	
Debtors	xx	
Cash	xx	
Total Current Assets		xx
Less : Current Liabilities		

Creditors	xx	
Wages	xx	
Any Other Expenses	xx	
Total Current Liabilities [TCA – TCL]		xx
Working Capital		xx
Add : Contingencies		xx
Amount of Working Capital required		xx

Workings :

(*i*) First of all uniformly we have to find out the number of units. It is the basis for computation of cost of all the elements.

(*ii*) Computation of finished goods

Raw Material Cost	xx
Labour Cost	xx
Overhead Cost	xx
Finished Goods	xx

(*iii*) Work in progress and finished goods value will be the same. But, the production occurring evenly throughout the year given in the problem means we have to find out the work-in-progress value separately.

i.e.,	Raw Material Cost	xx
	Labour Cost (It is reduced to half)	xx
	Overhead Cost	xx
	Work in Progress	xx

Value of Debtors should be calculated either including profit element or excluding profit element.

TEST QUESTIONS

1. What is the concept of working capital ?
2. Define working capital.
3. List out the various kinds of working capital.
4. What is meant by Gross working capital ?
5. What is Net working capital ?
6. What is meant by core current assets ?
7. What is meant by variable working capital ?
8. Explain the concept of operating cycle.
9. What are the stages of operating cycle ?
10. Briefly explain the various advantages of working capital.
11. Explain the various disadvantages of working capital.

12. What are the disadvantages of excessive working capital ?
13. Describe the various determinants of working capital in a business concern.
14. What are the sources of short-term working capital ?
15. Discuss the new trends in financing of working capital by banks.
16. Discuss the various techniques of forecasting working capital of a concern.
17. Explain the procedure for computation of working capital.

PROBLEMS AND SOLUTIONS

Problem 1. *From the following information, prepare a statement in column form showing the working capital requirements. (i) In total and (ii) As regards each constituent part of working capital.*

Budgeted sales (₹ 10 per unit) ₹ 2,60,000 p.a.

Analysis of Costs

	₹
Raw Materials	*3.00*
Direct Labour	*4.00*
Overheads	*2.00*
Total Cost	*9.00*
Profit	*1.00*
Sales	*10.00*

It is estimated that

(i) Raw materials are carried in stock for three weeks and finished goods for two weeks.
(ii) Factory processing will take three weeks.
(iii) Suppliers will give full five weeks credit.
(iv) Customers will require eight weeks credit.

It may be assumed that production and overheads accrue evenly throughout the year.

[M.Com. Madurai] [MCA Madras]

Solution : Statement of Working Capital Requirement

		₹
Current Assets		
Raw Materials 78,000 × 3/52	=	4,500
Work in Progress (Note)	=	9,000
Finished Goods 2,34,000 × 2/52	=	9,000
Debtors 2,60,000 × 8/52	=	40,000
		62,500
Less : Current Liabilities		
Trade Creditors (5 weeks) 5/52 × 78,000	=	7,500
Working Capital Required		55,000

Working Notes :

(*i*) Number of Units		=	26,000
(*ii*) Finished Goods			
Raw Materials	26,000 × 3	=	78,000
Direct Labour	26,000 × 4	=	1,04,000
Overheads	26,000 × 2	=	52,000
Finished Goods			2,34,000
(*iii*) Work in Progress			
Raw Material	78,000 × 3/52	=	4,500
Labour	1,04,000 × 3/52 × 1/2	=	3,000
Overhead	52,000 × 3/52 × 1/2	=	1,500
Work in Progress			9,000

NOTE : (*i*) Normally, finished goods and work in progress are taken as same value. Suppose wages and overheads accrue evenly throughout the year given in the problem, we have to find out the work in progress value separately. At that time of computing work in progress labour, overhead value is reduced to half.

(*ii*) At the time of calculating working capital, debtor value will be taken as either including profit element or excluding profit element.

Problem 2. *Prepare a working capital forecast from the following information :*

	₹
Issued share capital	*4,00,000*
12% Debentures	*1,50,000*

The fixed assets are valued at ₹ 3.00 lakhs. Production during the previous year is 1.00 lakh units. The same level of activity is intended to be maintained during the current year.

The expected ratios of cost to selling price are

Raw materials	*50%*
Direct Wages	*10%*
Overheads	*25%*

The raw materials ordinarily remain in stores for 2 months before production. Every unit of production remains in process for 2 months. Finished goods remain in the warehouse for 4 months. Credit allowed by creditors is 3 months from the date of delivery of raw materials and credit given to debtors is 3 months from the date of despatch.

Selling price is ₹ 6 per unit. Both the production and sales are in a regular cycle.

[CAIIB May 1983]

Solution : **Working Capital Statement**

	₹
Raw Materials	50,000
Work in Progress	67,500
Finished Goods	1,70,000
Debtors	1,27,500
	4,15,000
Less : Creditors	75,000
Working capital required	3,40,000

Working Notes :

Number of units = 1,00,000

Sales Value = 1,00,000 × 6 = 6,00,000

$$\text{Material} = 6{,}00{,}000 \times \frac{50}{100} = 3{,}00{,}000$$

$$\text{Labour} = 6{,}00{,}000 \times \frac{10}{100} = 60{,}000$$

$$\text{Overheads} = 6{,}00{,}000 \times \frac{25}{100} = 1{,}50{,}000$$

(*i*) Finished Goods

Raw Materials	=	3,00,000
Direct Labour	=	60,000
Overheads	=	1,50,000
		5,10,000
i.e., 5,10,000 × 4/12	=	1,70,000

(*ii*) Work in Progress

$$\text{Raw Materials} = 3{,}00{,}000 \times \frac{2}{12} = 50{,}000$$

$$\text{Direct Labour} = 60{,}000 \times \frac{2}{12} \times \frac{1}{2} = 5{,}000$$

$$\text{Overheads} = 1{,}50{,}000 \times \frac{2}{12} \times \frac{1}{2} = 12{,}500$$

67,500

(*iii*) Debtors = 5,10,000 × 3/12 = 1,27,500

(*iv*) Creditors = 3,00,000 × 3/12 = 75,000

Problem 3. *The management of G. Ltd. has called for a statement showing the working capital needed to finance a level of 3,00,000 units of output for the year. The cost structure for the company's product, for the above mentioned activity level is detailed below.*

Cost Element	*Cost per unit (₹)*
Raw Materials	*20*
Direct Labour	*5*
Overheads	*15*
Total Cost	*40*
Profit	*10*
Selling Price	*50*

Past trends indicate that raw materials are held in stock on an average for two months.
Work in progress will approximate to half a month's production.
Finished goods remain in warehouse on an average for a month.
Suppliers of materials extend a month's credit.
Two months' credit is normally allowed to debtors.
A minimum cash balance of ₹ 25,000 is expected to be maintained.

The production pattern is assumed to be even during the year. Prepare the statement of working capital determination. [MCA Madras]

Solution : **Working Capital Statement (or)**
Statement of Working Capital Requirement

Current Assets

	Raw Materials	$60,00,000 \times \frac{2}{12}$	=	10,00,000
	Work in Progress		=	3,75,000
	Finished goods	$1,20,00,000 \times \frac{1}{12}$	=	10,00,000
	Debtors	$1,50,00,000 \times \frac{2}{12}$	=	25,00,000
				48,75,000
Less :	Current Liabilities			
	Sundry Creditors	$60,00,000 \times \frac{1}{2}$	=	5,00,000
				43,75,000
Add :	Minimum Cash Balance			25,000
	Working Capital			44,00,000

Workings :

(*i*) Finished Goods

Raw Materials	$3,00,000 \times 20$	=	60,00,000
Direct Labour	$3,00,000 \times 5$	=	15,00,000
Overheads	$3,00,000 \times 15$	=	45,00,000
Finished Goods			1,20,00,000

(ii) Work in Progress

Raw Materials	$60,00,000 \times \frac{.5}{12}$	=	2,50,000
Labour	$15,00,000 \times \frac{.5}{12} \times \frac{1}{2}$	=	31,250
Overheads	$45,00,000 \times \frac{.5}{12} \times \frac{1}{2}$	=	93,750
Work in progress			3,75,000

Problem 4. *The Board of KRN Ltd. Pune wishes to know the amount of working capital which will be required to meet the programme they have planned for the year.*

You are required to prepare working capital estimate from the following information

		₹
(i) Issued Share Capital	=	*4,00,000*
5% Debentures	=	*1,00,000*
Fixed assets at cost	=	*2,50,000*
(ii) The expected ratio of cost to selling price are :		
Raw materials	=	*60%*
Labour	=	*10%*
Overheads	=	*20%*
Profit	=	*10%*

(iii) Raw materials are in stores for an average of two months. Finished goods are kept in warehouse for approximately three months.

(iv) Production during the previous year was 1,20,000 units and it is planned to maintain this level of activity in the current year also.

(v) Each unit of production is expected to be in process for one month.

(vi) Credit given by the suppliers is two months and allowed to customers is three months.

(vii) Selling price is ₹ 5 per unit.

(viii) There is a regular production and sales cycle. [M.Com. Pune 1983]

Solution : Statement of Working Capital Requirement

Current Assets

			₹
Raw Materials	$3,60,000 \times \frac{2}{12}$	=	60,000
Finished goods	$5,40,000 \times \frac{3}{12}$	=	1,35,000
Work in Progress		=	37,500
Debtors	$5,40,000 \times \frac{3}{12}$	=	1,35,000
			3,67,500

Less : Current Liabilities

Creditors	$3,60,000 \times \frac{2}{12}$	=	60,000
Working Capital Required		=	3,07,500

Working :

Number of units = 1,20,000

Sales value 1,20,000 × 5 = 6,00,000

(*i*) Finished Goods

Raw Materials	$6,00,000 \times \frac{60}{100}$	=	3,60,000
Labour	$6,00,000 \times \frac{10}{100}$	=	60,000
Overheads	$6,00,000 \times \frac{20}{100}$	=	1,20,000
Finished Goods			5,40,000

(*ii*) Work in Progress

Raw Materials	$3,60,000 \times \frac{1}{12}$	=	30,000
Labour	$60,000 \times \frac{1}{12} \times \frac{1}{2}$	=	2,500
Overheads	$1,20,000 \times \frac{1}{12} \times \frac{1}{2}$	=	5,000
Work in Progress		=	37,500

NOTE : Amount of debtors should be calculated only on cost of sales *i.e.,* excluding profit elements.

Problem 5. *Raj and Kumar who want to buy a business, seek your advice about the average working capital requirements in the first year trading. The following estimates are available and you are asked to add 10% to allow for contingencies.*

(i) Average Amount Locked up in stocks		*Per Annum ₹*
Stock of Finished Products	=	*5,000*
Stock of Stores Materials etc.	=	*8,000*
(ii) Average Credit given		
Local sales–2 weeks credit	=	*78,000*
Outside the state–6 weeks credit	=	*3,12,000*
(iii) Time available for payment		
For Purchases–4 weeks	=	*96,000*
For Wages–2 weeks	=	*2,60,000*

Calculate the average amount of working capital required. Give details of your working.

Solution : Statement of Working Capital Requirement

Current Assets			₹
Finished products and work in progress		=	5,000
Stores, Material etc.		=	8,000
			13,000
Account Receivable			
Local Sales	$78{,}000 \times \frac{2}{52}$	=	3,000
Outside the state	$3{,}12{,}000 \times \frac{6}{52} = 36{,}000$	=	36,000
Total Current Assets		=	52,000
Less : Current Liabilities			
Account Payable	$96{,}000 \times \frac{4}{52}$	=	7,385
Outstanding wages	$2{,}60{,}000 \times \frac{2}{52}$	=	10,000
Total Current Liabilities			17,385
Working Capital			34,615
Add : 10% Contingencies (34,615 x 10/100)			3,462
Working Capital required			38,077

Assignment Problem

Problem 6. *Ram Ltd decided to purchase a business and has consulted you and one point on which you are asked to advice them is the average amount of working capital which will be required in the first year workings.*

You are given the following estimates and are instructed to add 10% to your computed figure to allow for contingencies.

(i) Average amount locked up for the stocks	₹
Stock of finished products	5,000
Stock of stores materials etc.	8,000
(ii) Average credit given	
Inland sales—6 weeks credit	3,12,000
Export sales—1½ weeks credit	78,000
(iii) Lag in payment of wages and other outgoing	
Wages—1½ weeks	2,60,000
Stores, Materials etc. 1½ months	48,000
Rent Royalties etc. 6 months	10,000
Clerical Staff—½ month	62,400
Manager—½ month	4,800
Miscellaneous Expenses—½ month	48,000

(iv) Payment in advance

Sundry Expenses (Paid Quarterly in advance) 8,000

(v) Undrawn profits on the average throughout the year 11,000

Set up your calculations for the average amount of working capital required.

[M.Com. Madurai]

Answer : Working Capital ₹ 25,950, Current Assets = ₹ 53,250, Current Liabilities = ₹ 23,700.

Problem 7. *From the following estimates of Sethal Ltd. you are required to prepare a forecast of working capital requirements.*

(i) Expected level of production for the year 15,600 units.

(ii) Cost per unit : Raw Materials ₹ 90, Direct labour ₹ 40, overheads ₹ 75.

(iii) Selling Price per unit ₹ 265

(iv) Raw Materials in stock on an average for 1 month.

(v) Materials are in process on an average for 2 weeks.

(vi) Finished goods in stock on an average for 1 month.

(vii) Credit allowed by suppliers is one month.

(viii) Time lag in payment from debtors is 2 months.

(ix) Lag in payment of wages 1½ weeks.

(x) Lag in payment of overheads is one month. All sales are on credit.

(xi) Cash in hand and at Bank is expected to be ₹ 60,000.

It is assumed that production is carried on evenly throughout the year. Wages and overheads accrued evenly and a period of 4 weeks is equivalent to a month.

Solution : Statement of working capital Requirement

Current Assets			
Raw materials	1,08,000 × 1	=	1,08,000
Finished goods	2,46,000 × 1	=	2,46,000
Debtors 2 months	2,46,000 × 2	=	4,92,000
Work in progress		=	88,500
Cash in hand and at Bank		=	60,000
			9,94,500
Less : Current Liabilities			
Creditors 1,08,000 × 1		=	1,08,000
Lag in payment of wages 1½ weeks			
$48{,}000 \times \frac{3}{2} \times \frac{1}{4}$		=	18,000
Lag in payment of overheads (90,000 × 1)		=	90,000
			2,16,000
Working capital required [9,94,500 – 2,16,000]			7,78,500

Working Notes :

Estimated sales		=	15,600 units

A period of 4 weeks is taken as equivalent to one month.

Therefore, sales per month	$= 15,600 \times \frac{4}{52}$	=	1200 units
Estimated sales per month	$= 265 \times 1,200$	=	3,18,000
Raw Materials p.m.	$1,200 \times 90$	=	1,08,000
Direct Labour p.m.	$1,200 \times 40$	=	48,000
Overheads p.m.	$1,200 \times 75$	=	90,000
Cost of Sales/Finished Goods		=	2,46,000

Work in progress

Raw materials (2 weeks)	$1,08,000 \times \frac{1}{2}$	=	54,000
Labour (2 weeks)	$48,000 \times \frac{1}{2} \times \frac{1}{2}$	=	12,000
Overhead (2 weeks)	$90,000 \times \frac{1}{2} \times \frac{1}{2}$	=	22,500
			88,500

NOTE : Labour and overheads are reduced to one half as they accrue evenly during the year.

Problem 8. *Prepare an estimate of working capital and projected Balance Sheet for the year ended on 31.12.2002 from the following information.*

(i) Share capital ₹ 5,00,000, 15% Debentures of ₹ 2,00,000, Fixed assets at cost of ₹ 3,00,000.

(ii) The expected ratios of cost to selling price are Raw materials 60%, Labour 10%, Overheads 20%.

(iii) Raw materials are in stores for an average of 2 months.

(iv) Finished goods are kept in warehouse for 3 months.

(v) Expected level of production 1,20,000 units per year.

(vi) Each unit of production is expected to be in process for 1 month.

(vii) Credit given by suppliers is 2 months.

(viii) 20% of the output is sold against cash. Time lag in payment from debtors is 3 months.

(ix) Selling price is ₹ 5 per unit

(x) Labour and overheads will accrue evenly during the year.

Solution : Statement of Working Capital requirement

Current Assets

Raw Materials (2 months)	60,000
Work in progress	37,500
Stock of finished goods (3 months)	1,35,000

Debtors 3 months	1,08,000
Total Current Assets	3,40,500
Less : Current Liability	
Creditors 2 months	60,000
Working Capital required [3,40,500 – 60,000]	2,80,500

Working Notes :

Estimated production units	$\frac{1,20,000}{12}$	=	10,000 units
Sales p.m. 10,000 units × ₹ 5		=	50,000
(*i*) Finished goods :			
Raw Materials 60%	= 50,000 × 60/100	=	30,000
Direct Labour 10%	= 50,000 × 10/100	=	5,000
Overheads 20%	= 50,000 × 20/100	=	10,000
Finished goods/Cost of sales		=	45,000
(*ii*) Work in progress (1 month)			
Raw materials		=	30,000
Labour	5000 × 1/2	=	2,500
Overheads	10,000 × 1/2	=	5,000
W.I.P			37,500
(*iii*) Debtors (3months) at cost equivalent			
Cost of sales pm			45,000
Less : Cash sales 20%			9,000
Cost of sales (credit) pm			36,000
Debtors (3 months) at cost equivalent	= 36,000 × 3	=	1,08,000

Projected Balance Sheet as on 31.12.2002

Liabilities		₹	*Assets*	₹
Share Capital	2,00,000	5,00,000	Fixed Assets at cost	3,00,000
15% Debentures	30,000	2,30,000	Current Assets :	
			Raw Materials	60,000
Creditors		60,000	Work in progress	37,500
			Stock of Finished Goods	1,35,000
			Debtors	1,20,000
			Profit & Loss A/c	30,000
			Cash (BF)	1,07,500
		7,90,000		7,90,000

Problem 9. *On the basis of programme formulated to be part into operation with effect from 1.1.2003, the management of PV Ltd. desires to know the quantum of working capital required to finance the production programme.*

The following percentages which the various elements of cost bear to the selling price have been extracted from the proforma cost sheet.

Materials 50%, labour 20%, Overheads 10%.

Production in 2002 was 1,00,000 units and it is proposed to maintain the same during 2003. Following particulars are available.

(i) *Raw materials are expected to remain in the stores for an average period of one month before being issued to production.*

(ii) *Finished goods are to stay in the warehouse for 2 months on the average before being sold and send to customer.*

(iii) *Each unit of production will be in process for 1 month on an average.*

(iv) *Credit allowed by suppliers from the date of delivery of materials is 1 month.*

(v) *Debtors are allowed 2 months' credit.*

(vi) *Selling price is ₹ 9 per unit.*

(vii) *Sales and production follow a constant pattern.*

The relevant items of the Balance Sheet are	₹
Paid up share capital	*10,00,000*
6% Debentures	*1,00,000*
Fixed assets as on 1.1.2003	*7,50,000*

Prepare an estimate of Working Capital requirements as well as Forecast Profit and Loss Account and Balance Sheet of PV Ltd.

Solution :

Working Notes :

Number of units 1,00,000

Sales value 1,00,000 × 9 = 9,00,000

(i) Finished Goods

Raw materials	$9{,}00{,}000 \times \frac{50}{100}$	=	4,50,000
Labour	$9{,}00{,}000 \times \frac{20}{100}$	=	1,80,000
Overheads	$9{,}00{,}000 \times \frac{10}{100}$	=	90,000
Cost of sales/finished goods			7,20,000

(ii) Work in Progress

Raw Materials	$4{,}50{,}000 \times \frac{1}{12}$	=	37,500
Labour	$1{,}80{,}000 \times \frac{1}{12} \times \frac{1}{2}$	=	7,500
Overheads	$90{,}000 \times \frac{1}{12} \times \frac{1}{2}$	=	3,750
			48,750

Working Capital Statement

Current Assets

Raw Materials	$4,50,000 \times \frac{1}{12}$	=	37,500
Finished Goods	$7,20,000 \times \frac{2}{12}$	=	1,20,000
Work in Progress			48,750
Debtors	$7,20,000 \times \frac{2}{12}$	=	1,20,000
			3,26,250
Less : Current Liabilities			
Creditors	$4,50,000 \times \frac{1}{12}$	=	37,500
Working Capital requirement			2,88,750

Projected Trading Account

	₹		₹
To Raw materials	4,50,000	By Sales	9,00,000
To Labour	1,80,000		
To Overheads	90,000		
To Gross profit	1,80,000		
	9,00,000		9,00,000
To interest on Debenture	6,000	By Gross profit	1,80,000
To Net profit	1,74,000		
	1,80,000		1,80,000

Balance Sheet

Liabilities	₹	*Assets*	₹
Share capital	10,00,000	Fixed assets	7,50,000
6% Debentures	1,00,000	Current assets	
Interest on Debenture	6,000	Raw materials	37,500
Profit & Loss A/c (Net profit)	1,74,000	Work in progress	48,750
Creditors	37,500	Finished goods	1,20,000
		Debtors	1,20,000
		Cash (B/F)	2,41,250
	13,17,500		13,17,500

Problem 10. *Maruthi Ltd. is a newly set up enterprise. With the help of the following particulars, determine the magnitude of Working Capital.*

(i) *Various elements of cost bear the following relationship to the selling price. The cost is ₹ 200 per unit.*

Materials 40%, Labour 30%, Overheads 10%.

(ii) *Production in 1995 is estimated to be 5,000 units.*

(iii) *Materials are expected to remain in stores for an average period of 1 month.*

(iv) *Finished goods are likely to stay in warehouse for two month on average.*

(v) *Each unit of production will be in process for half a month on average.*

(vi) *50% of the sales will be on credit. Customers are allowed two months' credit.*

(vii) *Credit period allowed by the suppliers is 1 month.*

(viii) *The lag in payment to labour is one month. 50% of the overheads consists of salaries of non-production staff.*

(ix) *Allow 20% to your computed figures for contingencies.*

(x) *Assume that sales and production follow a constant pattern.* [M.Com. Bombay]

Solution :

Workings :

Number of units 5,000

Sales value 5,000 × 200 = ₹10,00,000

1. *Finished goods*

			₹
Raw materials	$10{,}00{,}000 \times \frac{40}{100}$	=	4,00,000
Labour	$10{,}00{,}000 \times \frac{30}{100}$	=	3,00,000
Overheads	$10{,}00{,}000 \times \frac{10}{100}$	=	1,00,000
Cost of sales/Finished goods			8,00,000

2. *Work in progress*

			₹
Raw materials	$4{,}00{,}000 \times \frac{.5}{12}$	=	16,667
Labour	$3{,}00{,}000 \times \frac{.5}{12} \times \frac{1}{2}$	=	6,250
Overheads	$1{,}00{,}000 \times \frac{.5}{12} \times \frac{1}{2}$	=	2,083
Work in progress			25,000

3. *Debtors*

Cost of sales = 8,00,000

Cost of credit sales = $8{,}00{,}000 \times \frac{50}{100}$ = ₹ 4,00,000

Two months' credit sales = $4{,}00{,}000 \times \frac{2}{12}$ = ₹ 66,667

Statement of Working Capital requirement

Current Assets

			₹
Raw materials	$4{,}00{,}000 \times \frac{1}{12}$	=	33,334
Finished goods	$8{,}00{,}000 \times \frac{2}{12}$	=	1,33,334

	Work in progress	=	25,000
	Debtors	=	66,667
	Total Current Assets		2,58,335
Less :	Current Liabilities		
	Creditors [4,00,000 × 1/12]		33,334
	Outstanding wages [3,00,000 × 1/12]		25,000
	Outstanding salary [1,00,000 × 50/100 × 1/12]		4,167
	Total Current Liabilities		62,501
Working capital (2,58,335 – 62,501)			1,95,834
Add :	20% for contingencies		39,166
Working capital requirement			2,35,000

Problem 11. *XYZ Cements Ltd. sells its products on a gross profit of 20% on sales. The following information is extracted from its annual accounts for the current year ended on 31st December.*

	₹
Sales at 3 months' credit	*40,00,000*
Raw material	*12,00,000*
Finished goods : 2 months credit	*32,00,000*
Wages paid—average time lags 15 days	*9,60,000*
Manufacturing expenses paid one month in arrears	*12,00,000*
Administrative expenses paid one month in arrears	*4,80,000*
Sales promotion expenses payable Half-month in advance	*2,00,000*
Cash in hand	*1,00,000*

[MCA Madras]

Solution :

Sales	₹ 40,00,000
Less : Gross Profit 20% [40,00,000 × 20/100]	8,00,000
Cost of sales	32,00,000

Statement of Working Capital requirements

Current Assets

Raw materials	12,00,000 × 1/12	=	1,00,000
Debtors	(32,00,000 × 3/12)		8,00,000

Finished goods	32,00,000 × 2/12	53,334
Prepaid expenses	[2,00,000 × .5/12]	8,334
Cash in hand		1,00,000
	Total Current Assets	10,61,668
Less : Current Liabilities :		
Creditors (12,00,000 × 1/12)		1,00,000
Manufacturing expenses (12,00,000 × 1/12)		1,00,000
Wages [9,60,000 × .5/12]		40,000
Administrative expenses (4,80,000 × 1/12)		40,000
Total current liabilities		2,80,000
Working capital [TCA – TCL]		
	[10,61,668 – 2,80,000]	7,81,668
Add : 10% Contingency	[7,81,668 × 10/100]	78,167
Working capital required		8,59,835

TEST PROBLEMS

1. A client of yours Care Ltd. is about to commence a new business and finance has been provided in respect of fixed assets. They have, however, asked you to advise the additional amount which they should make available for working capital.
They provide you with the following estimate for the first year and inform you that they have arranged an overdraft limit with they bank of ₹ 150000

	Average period of credit	*Estimate for the First year*
Purchase of raw materials	6 weeks	26,00,000
Wages	1.5 weeks	19,50,000
Overhead and Rent etc	6 months	1,00,000
Directors & Manager's Saleries	1 months	3,60,000
Travellers & office salaries	2 weeks	4,55,000
Travellers commission	3 months	2,00,000
Other overheads	2 months	6,00,000
Sales: Cash ₹ 1,40,000		
Credit ₹ 65,00,000		
(7 weeks)		

Average amount of stock and W.I.P - ₹ 3,00,000
Average amount of undrawn profit - ₹ 3,10,000

Sales were made of at an even rate for the year. You are required to prepare from the above figures and information, a table for submission to your client giving an estimate of the average amount of working capital which they provide. *[Madras, M.C.A, Nov. 1989]*

[Ans. Net working capital required = ₹ 5,71,250]

2. Kamath Ltd. is engaged in customer retailing. You are required to forecost its working capital requirements from the following information.

Projected annual sales	₹ 6,50,000
Percentage of N.P. on cost of sales	25%
Average credit allowed to debtors	10 weeks
Average credit allowed by creditors	4 weeks
Average stock carrying (in terms of sales requirements)	8 weeks
Add 20% to allow for contingencies	

[Bharathidasan M.C.A. Nov. 1997]

[Ans. Net working capital required ₹ 1,68,000]

3. Calculate estimated working capital from the following particulars:

	₹
(i) *Annual expenses:*	
Wages	52,000
Stores & materials	9,600
Office salaries	12,480
Rent	2,000
Other exp	9,600
(ii) *Average amount of stocks to be maintained:*	
Stock of finished goods	1,000
Stock of materials and stores	1,600
(iii) *Expenses paid in advance:*	
Quarterly advance	1,600 p.a —
(iv) *Annual sales:*	
Home market	62,400
Foreign market	15,600
(v) *Lag in payment of all expenses:*	
Wages	1½ weeks
Stores and materials	1½ weeks
Office salaries	½ month
Rent	6 months
Others expenses	1½ months
(vi) *Credit allowed to customers:*	
Home market	6 weeks
Foreign market	1½ weeks

[Rajasthan M.Com. 1980]

[Ans. Net Working Capital required ₹ 5,230]

❑❑❑

27

Capital Budgeting

INTRODUCTION

In the industrial and business world, all the business organisations and industries cannot have surplus money at all the times. And at the same time, they retain a certain sum of money to meet out the day to day operations. It is known as working capital. During the business period, at any time, the company has to face the problem of either replacement of fixed assets or purchase of fixed assets. In this respect, the company needs heavy capital outlay for the purpose of meeting out the capital investment in the fixed assets or development of new project. So, the capital budgeting plays a significant role in the management.

CONCEPT OF CAPITAL EXPENDITURE

Capital expenditure is one which is intended for future periods and generally includes investment in fixed assets and other developmental projects. In other words, capital expenditure is that which has to be incurred for the purpose of obtaining benefit not only for the current year but also for the specific future periods.

CAPITAL BUDGETING—MEANING

Capital budgeting refers to long term planning for the proposed capital outlay and their financing. In other words, it is the process of making investment decisions regarding the capital expenditures. Capital budgeting is also known as investment decision making, capital expenditure decision, planning capital expenditure, etc.

Charles T Horngreen has defined capital budgeting as "Capital budgeting is long term planning for making and financing proposed capital outlays".

According to Lynch "Capital budgeting consists in planning development of available capital for the purpose of maximising the long term profitability of the concern."

Need and Importance of Capital Budgeting

(*i*) Capital budgeting decision normally involves huge capital. If wrong decision is taken by the firm, it may affect the survival of the firm. So, it is very important for the firm to plan and control capital expenditure.

(*ii*) Funds involved in capital expenditure are not only huge but more or less permanently blocked in the organisation. In this respect, it involves longer time and greater risk. So, careful planning is essential.

(*iii*) Long term effect on profitability.

(*iv*) National importance—generation of employment, economic activities and economic growth.

(*v*) Complications of investment decisions.

Advantages of Capital Budgeting

(*i*) It is very useful to the concern for taking correct decision.

(*ii*) To determine the required quantum and the right source of funds for investment.

(*iii*) It influences the firm's growth in the future periods.

(*iv*) It informs about the right timings for the purchase of fixed assets.

(*v*) It guides the management for the effective utilisation of investment.

(*vi*) It minimises the risk of over-investment or under-investment of fund in fixed assets.

(*vii*) It acts as a tool for controlling capital expenditure.

(*viii*) It contributes a sound policy for depreciation and replacement of fixed assets.

Limitations of Capital Budgeting

(*i*) There may be controversial results among the application of various techniques.

(*ii*) There may be substantial loss in an investment of fund in the capital assets which are irreversible or reversible.

(*iii*) The application of capital budgeting techniques is normally a difficult task.

(*iv*) None of the various methods for evaluating profitability of the fixed assets or projects is free from drawbacks.

METHODS OF CAPITAL INVESTMENT PROPOSALS

Investment decisions of organisation may be classified in the following way :

(*i*) Independent investment proposals.

(*ii*) Mutually exclusive proposals.

(*iii*) Contingent or dependant proposals.

(*iv*) Replacement and modernization schemes.

(*v*) Cost reduction projects.

The above said investment proposals are mostly profit-oriented and therefore they may be evaluated based on their cost and benefits.

Even though the investments are made wisely, the return would be difficult to measure on the following projects.

(*i*) Educational projects.

(*ii*) Service projects.

(*iii*) Research and Development.

(*iv*) Welfare projects.

RELEVANT COST FOR CAPITAL BUDGETING DECISIONS

Normally costs and benefits, in the form of cash inflows, are associated with the capital budgeting. The following costs are generally essential for different types of investment decisions.

(*i*) Future costs.
(*ii*) Opportunity costs.
(*iii*) Interest cost.
(*iv*) Incremental or differential cost.
(*v*) Depreciation and income tax.

CAPITAL BUDGETING PROCESS

The following steps are involved in capital budgeting process.

(*i*) The capital budgeting process starts with identification of suitable investment proposals and also estimates the total cash outlay.

(*ii*) To establish capital expenditure planning committee for the purpose of screening the various proposals received from various departments.

(*iii*) Evaluation of the different investment proposals on the basis of costs and expected returns.

(*iv*) To rank the various proposals and to establish the priorities after considering their risk and profitability.

(*v*) The proposals recommended by the budget committee are sent to the top management along with a detailed report for final approval.

(*vi*) Execution of the selected proposals with sufficient allocation of funds.

(*vii*) Final stage of the capital budgeting process is an evaluation of the performance of the project after it has been fully implemented.

CAPITAL BUDGETING EVALUATION TECHNIQUES

An organisation may face a situation where various investment proposals are identified but it has to select one or some of the proposals either for shortage of funds or for some other reason. A number of project evaluation techniques are available. The most important and normally used methods are.

(*a*) *Traditional Methods :*

(*i*) Pay-back period or pay-out or pay off method.
(*ii*) Post pay back profitability methods.
(*iii*) Accounting rate of return method.

(*b*) *Time Adjusted Methods or Accounting Methods :*

(*i*) Net present value method.
(*ii*) Internal rate of return method.
(*iii*) Profitability index or cost benefit ratio method.
(*iv*) Discounted pay back method.

(*a*) Traditional Methods

(*i*) Pay-back Period Method

It is a traditional method for evaluating the profitability of investment proposals. Pay original investment of the project. Normally, shorter pay back period of the project should be recommended.

Procedure for the calculation of pay back period :

(*a*) *In the case of even cash inflows*

$$\text{Pay back period} = \frac{\text{Original Cost}}{\text{Annual Cash inflow}}$$

Annual cash inflow = Net savings or net profit + Depreciations

> **NOTE :** Suppose cash inflow is given in the problem, then there is no need to find out cash inflow. If cash inflows are not given in the problem, we have to find out cash inflow.

(*b*) *In the case of uneven cash inflows*

If cash inflows are not uniform, the calculation of pay back period takes a cumulative way *i.e.,* arriving at net cash inflow until the total is equal to original cost of the project.

(*ii*) Post Pay Back Profitability Method

Calculation :

Total cash inflow from the Proposal during its economic life	x x
Less : Original cost	x x
Post pay back profitability	x x

(*iii*) Accounting Rate of Return Method [Accounting Method]

This method is otherwise known as accounting rate return method or return on investment or average rate of return method. It can be expressed in the following ways.

(*i*) Average rate of return

$$\text{Average rate of return} = \frac{\text{Average annual profit}}{\text{Original investment}}$$

(*ii*) Return Per unit of investment method

$$\text{Return per unit of investment} = \frac{\text{Total Profit}}{\text{Net Investment}} \times 100$$

(*iii*) Rate of Return on average investment method

$$\text{Return on average investment} = \frac{\text{Profit after depreciation tax}}{\text{Average investment}}$$

$$\text{Average investment} = \frac{\text{Original Investment}}{2}$$

(*iv*) Average return on average investment method

$$\text{Average return on average investment} = \frac{\text{Average annual profit}}{\text{Average investment}} \times 100$$

(*v*) Rate of return on original investment method

$$\text{Return on original investment} = \frac{\text{Profit}}{\text{Original investment}}$$

(*b*) Time Adjusted Method or Accounting Methods

(*i*) Net Present Value Method

This method is otherwise known as excess present value or net gain method or time adjusted method

Sum of Discounted cash inflows	xx
Less : Original cost	xx
Net present value	xx

If the present value of cash inflows is more than (or equal to) the present value of cash outflows, the project would be accepted. If it is less, the project will be rejected.

(*ii*) Internal Rate of Return Method

The internal rate of return for an investment proposal is the discount rate that equates the present value of initial cost of the investment with the present value of the expected net cash flows. In other words, it is the rate which discounts the cash flows to zero. Normally, the internal rate of return is found by trial and error method. It can be stated in the following way.

$$\frac{\text{Cash inflows}}{\text{Cash outflows}} = 1$$

Procedure for Calculation

(*a*) *Where cash inflows are uniform.* In any project, the cash inflows are uniform. The IRR can be calculated by locating the factor in annuity table. The factor is calculated as follows.

$$F = \frac{I}{C}$$

Where, F = Factor to be located

I = Initial Investment

C = Cash inflow per year

The factor, thus calculated, will be located in table II on the line, representing number of years corresponding to estimated useful life of the asset.

(*b*) *Where cash inflows are not uniform.* The internal rate of return is calculated by making trial and error method.

Procedure

(*i*) *First trial rate may be calculated in the following way.*

In order to have an approximate idea about the rate, it will be better to find out the factor to be calculated in the following formula.

$$F = \frac{I}{C}$$

The above factor is treated as first trial rate.

(ii) *The second trial rate and third trial rate are determined.*

(iii) *After applying the second and third trial rates, we have to apply the following formula for the purpose of arriving at exact IRR.*

$$\text{IRR} = \text{Lower trial rate} + \frac{\text{NPV at lower rate}}{\text{NPV at lower rate} - \text{NPV at higher rate}} \times \text{Difference between higher and lower trial rate}$$

(iii) Profitability Index Method

It is a time adjusted method of evaluating profitability of the investment proposals. By calculating the profitability indices for various projects the financial manager can rank the projects according to their profitability.

$$\text{Profitability index} = \frac{\text{Present value of cash inflows}}{\text{Initial cash outlay}}$$

(Or)

$$= \frac{\text{Present value of future cash inflows}}{\text{Present value of future cash outflows}} \times 100$$

Decision Rule

Present value index of the project is equal to or more than 1 or 100% is to be selected.

(iv) Discounted Pay Back Method

Under this method, the present values of all cash inflows and outflows are calculated at an appropriate discount factor. The present values of all inflows are cumulated in order of time. The cumulative present value of cash inflows equals the present value of cash outflows. It is known as discounted pay back period.

For example,

Project cost is xxx

Year	Cash inflow	P/V	DCF
1			
2			
3			
4			
5			

Sum of discounted cash flows equals the cash outflow. It is referred as discounted pay back period. Normally, the project which gives a shorter pay back period under the discounted cash flow is accepted.

CAPITAL RATIONING

Capital rationing situation thus arises when numerous projects may compete for limited resources. It may be defined as "A situation where a constraint is placed on the total size of capital investment during a particular period".

Factors Influencing the Capital Budgeting Decisions

The following factors influence the capital budgeting decisions of the organisation.

(*i*) Amount of investment.
(*ii*) Cost of capital projects.
(*iii*) Degree of certainty.
(*iv*) Product demand.
(*v*) Future earnings.
(*vi*) Relative importance of the profit.
(*vii*) Opportunity cost.
(*viii*) Cost of production.

RISK ANALYSIS IN CAPITAL BUDGETING

Some of the important techniques of risk analysis in capital budgeting are :

(*a*) *General techniques :*

(*i*) Risk adjusted discount rate.
(*ii*) Certainty equivalent.

(*b*) *Quantitative techniques :*

(*i*) Sensitivity analysis.
(*ii*) Probability assignment.
(*iii*) Standard deviation.
(*iv*) Co-efficient of variation.
(*v*) Decision tree.

TEST QUESTIONS

1. What is meant by Capital Budgeting.
2. Explain the concept of Capital Expenditure.
3. Define Capital Budgeting.
4. Explain the need and importance of Capital Budgeting.
5. What are the advantages of Capital Budgeting ?
6. Explain the limitations of Capital Budgeting.
7. What are the principle methods employed for ascertaining the profitability of a capital expenditure project ?'
8. Give a comparative description of net present value method and internal rate of return method.
9. "Capital budgeting is long-term planning for making and financing proposed capital outlays". Explain. What are the limitation of capital budgeting ?
10. "For most investment decisions that a firm faces net present value is either a superior decision criterion or is at least as good as the competing technique". In what investment situation is the profitability index better than the net present value ?
11. Under what circumstances may NPV and IRR give conflicting recommendations ? Which criteria should be followed in such circumstances and why ?
12. Briefly explain the steps involved in the control of capital expenditure in a large scale organizations.

PROBLEMS AND SOLUTIONS

Problem 1. *Each of the following projects requires a cash outlay of ₹ 10,000. You are required to suggest which project should be accepted if the standard pay back period is 5 years.*

Year	*Project X* ₹	*Project Y* ₹	*Project Z* ₹
1	2500	4000	1000
2	2500	3000	2000
3	2500	2000	3000
4	2500	1000	4000
5	2500	—	—

Solution :

All the three projects recovered their original capital ₹ 10,000 within the period of 4 years. Here project X has constant cash inflow. Project Y initially has higher cash inflows but gradually decreased.

Project Z initially has low cash inflows but it has gradually increased.

As per the constant return point of view, project X is recommended.

Problem 2. *A Company has to choose one of the following two mutually exclusive projects. Both the projects have to be depreciated on straight line basis. The tax rate is 50%.*

Cash inflows (Profit before Depreciation and tax)

Year	*Project A* ₹	*Project B* ₹
0	15,000	15,000
1	4,200	4,200
2	4,800	4,500
3	7,000	4,000
4	8,000	5,000
5	2,000	10,000

You have to use pay-back period as the criterion. [M.Sc. ITM May 2000 PU]

Solution : **Project—A**

Year	Profit ₹	(–) Depreciation ₹	Profit After Depreciation ₹	Tax ₹	PAT ₹	Add Depreciation ₹	Cash Inflows ₹	Cumulative Cash Inflows ₹
1	4200	3000	1200	600	600	3000	3600	3600
2	4800	3000	1800	900	900	3000	3900	7500
3	7000	3000	4000	2000	2000	3000	5000	12500
4	8000	3000	4000	2000	2000	3000	5000	17500
5	2000	3000	– 1000	—	1000	3000	2000	19500

[PAT = Profit After Tax]

Pay back period = 3 years and 6 months

Working :

Investment is ₹ 15,000

Upto three years *i.e.,* first three years

Capital recovered is ₹ 12,500

Balance of ₹ 2500 recovered during the 4th year

I year	3,600
II year	3,900
III year	5,000
	12,500
Balance	2,500
	15,000

$$= \frac{12 \text{ months}}{5,000} \times 2,500 = \text{How many months ?}$$

Time taken for recovery of this amount of ₹ 2,500 = 6 months. Pay back period = 3 years 6 months.

Project—B

Year	Profit ₹	(–) Depreciation ₹	Profit After Depreciation ₹	Tax ₹	PAT ₹	Add Depreciation ₹	Cash Inflows ₹	Cumulative Cash Inflows ₹
1	4200	3000	1200	600	600	3000	3600	3600
2	4500	3000	1500	750	750	3000	3750	7350
3	4000	3000	1000	500	500	3000	3500	10850
4	5000	3000	2000	1000	1000	3000	4000	14850
5	10000	3000	7000	3500	3500	3000	6500	21350

(PAT = Profit After Tax)

> **NOTE :** If necessary only prepare cumulative cash inflows, otherwise there is no need.
> Pay back period = 4 years and 8 days

Result and decision : Project A is preferable, because it has a shorter pay back period as compared to project A.

Workings Initial investment is ₹ 15,000

Its recovered :

I year	-	3,600
II year	-	3,750
III year	-	3,500
IV year	-	4,000
		14,850
Balance		150
		15,000

Time taken for recovery of this amount ₹ 150/- = 8 days.

For recovery of ₹ 6,500 in the 5th year.

Time required = 365 days.

For recovery of ₹ 150 in the 5th year.

Time required being $\frac{365}{6{,}500} \times 150 = 8$ days

Depreciation :

Project A: $\frac{\text{Cost}}{\text{Life}} = \frac{15{,}000}{5 \text{ years}} =$ ₹ 3,000

Project B: $\frac{15{,}000}{5 \text{ years}} =$ ₹ 3,000

Problem 3. *Using the information given below, compute the pay-back period under (a) Traditional pay-back method and (b) Discounted pay-back method*

Initial outlay		*₹ 80,000*
Estimated life	*5 years*	
Profit after tax		
End of the years	*year 1*	*₹ 6,000*
	2	*₹ 14,000*
	3	*₹ 24,000*
	4	*₹ 16,000*
	5	*Nil*

Depreciation has been calculated under straight line method. The cost of capital may be taken 20% p.a. and the PV of Re. 1 at 20% p.a. is given below.

Year	*1*	*2*	*3*	*4*	*5*
P/V factor	*.83*	*.69*	*.58*	*.48*	*.40*

[MBA Nov.98 Madras] [M.Com. Calcutta]

Solution :

Year	PAT (A) ₹	Add Depreciation ₹	Profit before Depreciation but after Tax ₹	P/V factor at 20%	Present Value
1	6,000	+ 16,000	= 22,000	.83	18,260
2	14,000	+ 16,000	= 30,000	.69	20,700
3	24,000	+ 16,000	= 40,000	.58	23,200
4	6,000	+ 16,000	= 22,000	.48	15,360
5	Nil	+ 16,000	= 16,000	.40	6,400
(PAT = Profit After Tax)				Total present value	83,920
				Less : Initial investment	80,000
				Net Present Value	3,920

(*a*) *Traditional payback method*

I year ₹	22,000
II year ₹	30,000
Amount recovered for 2 years	52,000
Balance ₹	28,000
	80,000

III year profit is ₹ 40,000. But we require only ₹ 28,000 to meet the original investment of ₹ 80,000.

$$= \frac{12 \text{ months}}{40,000} \times 28,000 = \text{How many months ?}$$

i.e., 2 years 8 months

(*b*) *Discounted pay back method*

I year	18,260
II year	20,700
III year	23,200
IV year	15,360
	77,520
Balance ₹	2,480
Project cost	80,000

In the V year cash inflow is ₹ 6400. But actually we require only ₹ 2480 to meet the original investment of ₹ 80,000.

$$\therefore \quad \frac{12 \text{ months}}{6,400} \times 2,480 = \text{How many months ?}$$

i.e., 4 years 4 months

Pay back period = 4 years 4 months

NOTE : Depreciation :

$$\frac{\text{Cost}}{\text{Life}} = \frac{80,000}{5} = 16,000$$

Problem 4. *A choice is to be made between two competing proposals which require an equal investment of ₹ 50,000 and are expected to generate net cash flows as under.*

Year	*Project I* ₹	*Project II* ₹	*P/V at 10% p.a.*
1	*25,000*	*10,000*	*.909*
2	*15,000*	*12,000*	*.826*
3	*10,000*	*18,000*	*.751*
4	*Nil*	*25,000*	*.683*
5	*12,000*	*8,000*	*.621*
6	*6,000*	*4,000*	*.564*

Which project proposal should be chosen and why ? Evaluate the project proposals under discounted cash flow methods. [M.Sc. ITM May 2000 Periyar]

Solution : **Net Cash Inflows**

Year	*Project I* ₹	*Project II* ₹
1	25,000	10,000
2	15,000	12,000
3	10,000	18,000
4	Nil	25,000
5	12,000	8,000
6	6,000	4,000

Pay back period under Traditional method

Project I

I year	25,000
II year	15,000
III year	10,000
	50,000

Pay back period is 3 years.

Project II

I year	10,000	
II year	12,000	∴ 3 years 4 months
III year	18,000	
	40,000	
Balance	10,000	
	50,000	

$$\frac{2}{25,000} \times 10,000 = 4.8 \textit{ i.e., } 4$$

As per Traditional pay back period Project I is recommended, because it has shorter pay back period.

Discounted cash flow method

Project I				*Project II*			
Year	*Cash Inflows ₹*	*Discount Factor at 10% p.a.*	*Present Value ₹*	*Year*	*Cash Inflows ₹*	*Discount Factor at 10% p.a.*	*Present Value ₹*
1	25,000	.909	22,725	1	10,000	.909	9,090
2	15,000	.826	12,390	2	12,000	.826	9,912
3	10,000	.751	7,510	3	18,000	.751	13,518
4	Nil	.683	—	4	25,000	.683	17,075
5	12,000	.621	7,452	5	8,000	.621	4,968
6	6,000	.564	3,384	6	4,000	.564	2,256
	Total present value		53,461		Total present value		56,819
	Less : Original Cost		50,000		*Less* : Original Cost		50,000
	Net Present Value		3,461		Net Present Value		6,819

Criteria	Project X	Project Y
Pay back period	3 years	3 years 4 months
NPV	₹ 3,491	₹ 6,819

As per the pay back period point of view, Project X is recommended. But by NPV point of view, Project Y is recommended, because it has surplus of ₹ 6,819.

Problem 5. *A project costs ₹ 5,00,000 and yields annually a profit of ₹ 80,000 after depreciation at 12% p.a. but before tax of 50%. Calculate pay back period.*

[M.Sc. ITM May 2000 Periyar]

Solution :

$$\text{Pay back period} = \frac{\text{Original Cost}}{\text{Annual Cash Inflows}}$$

Initial investment = ₹ 5,00,000

Cash inflows = Profit after tax plus Depreciation.

	₹
Profit before Tax =	80,000
Less : Tax 50% =	40,000
Profit after Tax =	40,000
Add : Depreciation =	60,000
Annual cash inflows =	1,00,000

$$\therefore \quad \text{Pay back period} = \frac{5,00,000}{1,00,000} = 5 \text{ years}$$

NOTE : Depreciation = $5,00,000 \times \frac{12}{100} = 60,000.$

Problem 6. *ABC Ltd. is proposing to take up a project which will need an investment of ₹ 40,000. The net income before depreciation and tax is estimated as follows.*

Year	₹
1	*10,000*
2	*12,000*
3	*14,000*
4	*16,000*
5	*20,000*

Evaluate the project proposal under accounting Rate of Return Method.

Solution :

Year	*Net Income before Depreciation and Tax* ₹	*Less Depreciation* ₹	*Profit after Depreciation before Tax* ₹	*Less Tax 50%* ₹	*Profit after Tax and Depreciation* ₹
1	10,000	8,000	2,000	1,000	1,000
2	12,000	8,000	4,000	2,000	2,000
3	14,000	8,000	6,000	3,000	3,000
4	16,000	8,000	8,000	4,000	4,000
5	20,000	8,000	12,000	6,000	6,000

Accounting Rate of Return

(*i*) *Return on Average Investment Method*

$$\text{Return} = \text{Average profit}$$

$$= \textit{i.e.,} \ \frac{\text{Total Profit}}{\text{No. of Years}}$$

$$= \frac{16,000}{5} = 3,200$$

$$\text{Average investment} = \frac{\text{Original investment}}{2} = \frac{40,000}{2}$$

$$= 20,000$$

$$\text{Return on Average investment} = \frac{3,200}{20,000} \times 100$$
$$= 16\%$$

Problem 7. *Swamy Industries Ltd. purchased a machine five years ago. A proposal is under consideration to replace it by a new machine. The life of the machine is estimated to be 10 years. The existing machine can be sold at its written down value. As the cost accountant of the company you are required to submit your recommendations based on the following information.*

Particulars	*Existing Machine*		*New Machine*	
Initial cost (₹)		*25,000*		*50,000*
Machine hours p.a.	*2,000*		*2,000*	
Wages per running hour ₹		*1.25*		*1.25*
Power per hour ₹		*.50*		*2.00*
Indirect material p.a. ₹		*3,000*		*5,000*
Other expenses p.a. ₹		*12,000*		*15,000*
Cost of materials per unit		*1*		*1*
Number of units produced Per hour	*12*		*18*	
Selling price per unit		*2*		*2*

Interest to be paid at 10% on fresh capital invested.

Solution : **Statement of profit and cost**

	Existing Machine ₹	*New machine* ₹
Production p.a. (units)	24,000	36,000
Selling price per unit ₹	2.00	2.50
Sales value ₹	48,000	72,000
Expenses :		
(*i*) Materials	24,000	36,000
(*ii*) Wages	2,500	2,500
(*iii*) Power	1,000	4,000
(*iv*) Indirect material	3,000	5,000
(*v*) Other expenses p.a.	12,000	15,000
(*vi*) Depreciation	2,500	5,000
(*vii*) Interest	—	3,750
	45,000	71,250
Sales	48,000	72,000
Less : Total cost	45,000	71,250
Total profit	3,000	750
(*viii*) Cost per unit	1.87	1.98
Profit per unit	0.13	0.02

Workings :

	Existing Machine	*New Machine*
(*i*) Cost of material (24,000 × 1) (*ii*) Wages (2,000 × 1.25) (*iii*) Power (2,000 × .50)	24,000 2,500 1,000	36,000 (36,000 × 1) 2,500 (2,000 × 1.25) 4,000 (2,000 × .2)
(*iv*) Cost per unit = $\frac{\text{Total Cost}}{\text{Number of Units}}$	$\frac{45,000}{24,000} = 1.87$	$\frac{71,250}{36,000} = 1.98$
(*v*) Interest calculation	Investment in new machine *Less :* Sale value of the old machine (₹ 25,000 – Depreciation ₹ 12,500 on fixed instalment system) *i.e.,* $\left(\frac{25,000}{10} = 2,500 \times 5 = 12,500\right)$	50,000 12,500
	Fresh Investment	37,500

∴ Interest @ 10% on fresh investment is as follows.

$$37500 \times \frac{10}{100} = 3,750$$

(*vi*) Depreciation = $\frac{\text{Cost}}{\text{Life}}$ Old machine New machine

$$\frac{25,000}{10} = 2,500 \qquad \frac{50,000}{10} = 5,000$$

Problem 8. *Rank the following projects on the basis of*

(a) Pay back

(b) Accounting rate of return method

(c) Net present value

Particulars	*Year*	*Project A* ₹	*Project B* ₹	*Project C* ₹
Investment	*0*	*30,000*	*30,000*	*30,000*
Annual savings	*I*	*13,800*	*36,150*	—
	II	*13,800*	—	—
	III	*13,800*	—	*46,827*

Discount factor for the year I, II, III, are 0.909, 0.826, 0.751 respectively.

[MBA Madras]

Solution :

(a) Pay Back

Year	Project A Cash Inflows	Cumulative Cash Inflows	Project B Cash Inflows	Project C Cash Inflows
1	13,800	13,800	36,150	—
2	13,800	27,600	—	—
3	13,800	41,400	—	46,827

A. I year 13,800 + II year 13,800 = 27,600

Balance = 2,400

30,000

$$\frac{12}{13,800} \times 2,400 = 2 \text{ months } 8 \text{ days } i.e., 2 \text{ years } 2 \text{ months } 8 \text{ days.}$$

B. $$\frac{12}{36,150} \times 30,000 = 10 \text{ months}$$

C. $$\frac{12}{46,827} \times 30,000 = 7 \text{ months } 23 \text{ days}$$

(b) Accounting Rate of Return Method

$$\frac{\text{Return}}{\text{Original cost investment}} \times 100$$

$$\text{Project : A} = \frac{13,800}{30,000} \times 100 = 46\%$$

$$\text{Project : B} = \frac{12,050}{30,000} \times 100 = 40.16\%$$

$$\text{Project : C} = \frac{15,609}{30,000} \times 100 = 52.03\%$$

(c) Net Present value

If cost of capital detail is not given in the problem, we have to assume 10% as cut off rate.

Year	Project A Cash Inflows ₹	P.V. Factor at 10%	Discounted Cash Inflows ₹	Project B Cash inflows ₹	Discounted Cash Inflows ₹	Project C Cash Inflows ₹	Discounted Cash Inflows ₹
1	13,800	0.909	12,544.20	36,150	32,860	—	—
2	13,800	0.826	11,398.80	—	—	—	—
3	13,800	0.751	10,363.80	—	—	46,827	35,167
	Total present value		34,306.80		32,860		35,167
	Less : Initial cost		30,000.00		30,000		30,000
	Net Present value		4,306.80		2,860		5,167

Ranking Table

Project	*Pay back*	*Accounting Rate of Return*	*NPV.*
A	III	II	II
B	II	III	III
C	I	I	I

As per the above Ranking table project C is preferable. It gets I rank in the application of all the three techniques. So, it is recommended.

Problem 9. *Lal Ltd. is considering the purchase of a new machine which will carry out operations performed by labour. A and B are alternative models. Prepare profitability statement and work out pay back period in respect of each machine based upon the following information.*

Particulars	*Machine A*	*Machine B*
Estimated life of machine (yrs.)	*5*	*6*
Cost of machine (₹)	*1,50,000*	*2,50,000*
Cost of indirect materials (₹)	*6,000*	*8,000*
Estimated savings in scrap (₹)	*10,000*	*15,000*
Additional cost of maintenance (₹)	*19,000*	*27,000*
Estimated savings in direct wages		
Employees not required (numbers)	*150*	*200*
Wages per employee (₹)	*600*	*600*

Taxation is to be regarded as 50% of profit(ignore depreciation for calculation of tax). Which model would you recommend ? State your reasons. [M.Com. May 2000 PU]

Solution : **Profitability Statement**

		Machine A ₹	*Machine B* ₹
	Cost of the machine	1,50,000	2,50,000
Savings			
	Estimated saving in scrap	10,000	15,000
	Estimated saving in Direct wages [150 × 600]	90,000	1,20,000
	Total Savings	1,00,000	1,35,000
Expenses			
	Cost of indirect materials	6,000	8,000
	Additional cost of maintenance	19,000	27,000
	Total Expenses	25,000	35,000
	Savings [Savings – Expenses]	75,000	1,00,000
	Less : Tax 50%	37,500	50,000
	Net saving [after tax]	37,500	50,000

Pay back period

$$\frac{\text{Original Cost}}{\text{Cash Inflow}} = \frac{1,50,000}{37,500} = \frac{2,50,000}{50,000}$$

$$= 4 \text{ years} \quad = 5 \text{ years}$$

Pay back period in case of machine A is 4 years; machine B is 5 years. A has the shorter pay back period, so it should be recommended.

NOTE : Here, Depreciation is not taken into account.

Problem 10. *A Ltd. company is considering to invest in a project requiring a capital outlay of ₹ 2,00,000. Forecast for annual income after depreciation but before tax is as follows.*

Year	₹
1	*1,00,000*
2	*1,00,000*
3	*80,000*
4	*80,000*
5	*40,000*

Depreciation may be taken as 20% on original cost and taxation at 50% of net income. You are required to evaluate the project according to each of the following methods.

(a) Pay-back method

(b) Rate of return on original investment method

(c) Rate of return on average investment method

(d) Discounted cash flow method taking cost of capital as 10%

(e) Net present value index method

(f) Internal rate of return method [M.Com. Madurai] [MCA Madras]

Solution : **Profitability Statement**

Year	*Profit after Depreciation* ₹	*Less Tax* ₹	*PAT* ₹	*Add Depreciation* ₹	*Profit before Depreciation but after tax* ₹
1	1,00,000	50,000	50,000	40,000	90,000
2	1,00,000	50,000	50,000	40,000	90,000
3	80,000	40,000	40,000	40,000	80,000
4	80,000	40,000	40,000	40,000	80,000
5	40,000	20,000	20,000	40,000	60,000

(a) Pay Back Period

I year	90,000
II year	90,000
	1,80,000
Balance	20,000
	2,00,000

Balance amount recovered from IIIrd year

i.e., $\dfrac{12 \text{ months}}{80{,}000} \times 20{,}000 = 3 \text{ months}$

$\therefore$ **Pay back period = 2 years 3 months.**

(*b*) ***Rate of Return Original Investment Method***

Year	*Net Profit after Tax and depreciation* (₹)
1	50,000
2	50,000
3	40,000
4	40,000
5	20,000
Total Return	2,00,000

$$\text{Rate of Return on original investment} = \frac{\text{Return}}{\text{Original investment}}$$

Return represents the Average Return

Average Return should calculate in the following

$$= \frac{\text{Total return}}{\text{Number of years}}$$

$$= \frac{2{,}00{,}000}{5}$$

$$\text{Average Return} = ₹\ 40{,}000$$

$$\text{Rate of return on original investment} = \frac{40{,}000}{2{,}00{,}000} \times 100$$

$$= 20\%$$

(*c*) ***Rate of Return on Average investment method***

$$= \frac{\text{Return}}{\text{Average investment}} \times 100$$

$$\text{Return} = ₹\ 40{,}000$$

$$\text{Average Investment} = \frac{\text{Original investment}}{2}$$

$$= \frac{2{,}00{,}000}{2} = 1{,}00{,}000$$

$$\text{Rate of Return on Average investment} = \frac{40{,}000}{1{,}00{,}000} \times 100 = 40\%$$

(*d*) *Discounted cash flow method [Cost of capital @ 10%]*

Year	*Cash Inflows*	*Discount Factor At 10% p.a.*	*Present Value* ₹
1	90,000	0.909	81,810
2	90,000	0.826	74,340
3	80,000	0.751	60,080
4	80,000	0.683	54,670
5	60,000	0.621	37,260
		Total Present value	3,08,130
		Initial investment	2,00,000
		Net Present value	1,08,130

(*e*) *Net present value index*

$$\frac{\text{Total present value of cash inflows}}{\text{Total present value of cash outflows}} = \frac{3,08,130}{2,00,000} = 1.541$$

$$1.541 \times 100 = 154.1\%$$

(*f*) *Internal Rate of Return method.* The annual cash inflows are not uniform. We have to apply the following formula to determine the approximate rate of return.

$$F = \frac{I}{C}$$

F = Factor to be located

I = Initial investment

C = Average annual Cash inflow

$$F = \frac{2,00,000}{80,000}$$

$$= 2.5$$

Showed Table No. II at this factor rate of return in the column for 5 years is 28%.

Discounted cash flow [cost of capital @ 28%]

Year	*Cash Inflows* ₹	*Discount Factor At 28%*	*Discounted Cash Inflows* ₹
1	90,000	.781	70,290
2	90,000	.610	54,900
3	80,000	.477	38,160
4	80,000	.373	29,840
5	60,000	.291	17,460
		Total Present values	2,10,650
		Less : Initial investment	2,00,000
		Excess Present value	10,650

NOTE : The present value is higher on the level of ₹ 10,650. Now, we apply higher discount rate *i.e.,* taking 30% as cost of capital.

Discounted cash flow at cost of capital is 30%

Year	*Cash Inflows* ₹	*Discount Factor At 28%*	*Discounted Cash Inflows* ₹
1	90,000	0.769	69,210
2	90,000	0.592	53,280
3	80,000	0.455	36,400
4	80,000	0.350	28,000
5	60,000	0.269	16,140
		Total Present value	2,03,030
		Less : Initial investment	2,00,000
		Excess Present value	3,030

The excess present value at 30% is ₹ 3,030. So, the internal rate of return be slightly higher than 30%. Small amount will not affect huge level in the organisation. Hence, internal rate of return is more or less 30%.

Results and Decision :

Investigation of project with the help of all the techniques show that the new project seems to be fairly attractive.

Problem 11. *The directors of Madura limited are contemplating the purchase of new machine to replace a machine which has been in operation in the factory for the last 5 years.*

Ignoring interest but considering tax at 50% of net earnings, suggest which of the two alternatives should be preferred. The following are the details.

Particulars	*Old Machine*	*New Machine*
Purchase price (₹)	*40,000*	*60,000*
Estimated life of machine	*10 years*	*10 years*
Machine running hours p.a.	*2,000*	*2,000*
Units per hour	*24*	*36*
Wages per running hour (₹)	*3*	*5.25*
Power p.a.	*2,000*	*4,500*
Consumable stores p.a.	*6,000*	*7,500*
All other charges p.a.	*8,000*	*9,000*
Material cost per unit	*.50*	*.50*
Selling price per unit	*1.25*	*1.25*

You may assume that the above information regarding sales and cost of sales will be held throughout the economic life of each machine. Depreciation has to be charged according to straight line method. [M.Com. Madras]

Solution : **Profitability statement**

Particulars		*Old Machine*		*New Machine*
Cost of the machine (₹)		40,000		60,000
Life of the machine (yrs)		10		10
Output units.		48,000		72,000
Sales value (48,000 × 1.25)		60,000	(72,000×1.25)	90,000
Less : Expenses				
Material 48,000 × .50	24,000		(72,000 × .50) 36,000	
Wages	6,000		10,500	
Power	2,000		4,500	
Consumable stores	6,000		7,500	
Other Charges	8,000		9,000	
Depreciation	4,000	50,000	6,000	73,500
Profit before tax		10,000		16,500
Less : Tax 50%		5,000		8,250
Profit after tax		5,000		8,250

Workings :

Accounting Rate of Return **Old Machine** **New Machine**

(*i*) *Return on original investment*

$$\frac{\text{Average net earnings}}{\text{Original investment}} \quad \frac{5,000}{40,000} \times 100 = 12.3\% \quad \frac{8,250}{60,000} \times 100 = 13.75\%$$

(*ii*) *Return on Average Investment Method*

$$\frac{\text{Return}}{\text{Average investment}} \times 100 \quad \frac{5,000}{20,000} \times 100 = 25\% \quad \frac{8,250}{30,000} \times 100 = 27.5\%$$

(*iii*) *Return on incremental investment*

$$\frac{\text{Incremental earnings}}{\text{Incremental investment}} \times 100$$

$$= \frac{3,250}{20,000} \times 100 = 16.25\% \text{ or } \frac{3,250}{40,000} \times 100 = 8\%$$

NOTE :

Incremental earning = 6250 − 5000 = 1250

Incremental investment = 60,000 − 40,000 = 20,000

Result : Recommended to replace an old machinery.

Problem 12. *A project costs ₹ 1,00,000 and yields an annual cash inflow of ₹20,000 for 7 years. Calculate pay back period.*

Solution :

$$\text{Pay back period} = \frac{\text{Initial investment}}{\text{Annual cash inflow}}$$

Initial investment is = ₹ 1,00,000

Annual cash inflow ₹ = ₹ 20,000

$$\text{Pay back period} = \frac{1,00,000}{20,000}$$

= 5 years

Problem 13. *Himalaya Construction Ltd. is considering the purchase of a new machine for its immediate expansion programme. There are three possible machines suitable for the purpose. Their details are as follows :*

	Machines		
	1 ₹	*2* ₹	*3* ₹
Capital cost	*3,00,000*	*3,00,000*	*3,00,000*
Sales at standard price	*5,00,000*	*4,00,000*	*4,50,000*
Net cost of production :			
Direct material	*40,000*	*50,000*	*48,000*
Direct labour	*50,000*	*30,000*	*36,000*
Factory overheads	*60,000*	*50,000*	*58,000*
Administration costs	*20,000*	*10,000*	*15,000*
Selling and distribution costs	*10,000*	*10,000*	*10,000*

The economic life of machine No.1 is 2 years while it is 3 years for the other two. The scrap values are ₹ 40,000, ₹ 25,000 and ₹ 30,000 respectively.

Sales are expected to be at the rates shown for each year during the full economic life of expenditure resulting from each machine.

Tax to be paid is expected at 50% of the net earnings of each year. It may be assumed that all payables and receivables will be settled promptly, strictly on cash basis with no outstanding from one accounting year to another. Interest on capital has to be paid at 8% p.a.

You are requested to show which machine would be the most profitable investment on the principle of "Pay-back method". [B.Com. PU]

Solution : **Profitability Statement**

Particulars	*Machine I* ₹	*Machine II* ₹	*Machine III* ₹
Capital Cost	3,00,000	3,00,000	3,00,000
Sales (*i*)	5,00,000	4,00,000	4,50,000
Less : Expenses			
Cost of production	1,50,000	1,30,000	1,42,000
Administration cost	20,000	10,000	15,000
Selling and distribution cost	10,000	10,000	10,000
Total Cost II	1,80,000	1,50,000	1,67,000
Profit before depreciation and interest [S – TC] [*i* – *ii*] (*iii*)	3,20,000	2,50,000	2,83,000
Less : Depreciation	1,30,000	91,667	90,000
Interest on borrowings	24,000	24,000	24,000

Depreciation and interest (*iv*)	1,54,000	1,15,667	1,14,000
Profit before tax (*iii* – *iv* = *v*) *Less* : Tax 50%	1,66,000 83,000	1,34,333 67,167	1,69,000 84,500
Profit after tax *Add* : Depreciation	83,000 1,30,000	67,167 91,667	84,500 90,000
Net cash inflows	2,13,000	1,58,834	1,74,500
(*a*) Pay back period	1.41 years	1.89 years	1.72 years

Result : Machine I is preferable, because it has shorter payback period as compared to the other machine.

Working :

(*a*) *Pay back Period*

Machine I

	₹
I year	2,13,000
Balance	87,000
	3,00,000

$$= \frac{12 \text{ month}}{2,13,000} \times 87,000$$

= How many months ? = 4 months

= 1 year 4 months

Machine II

I year	1,58,834
Balance	1,41,166
	3,00,000

$$= \frac{12 \text{ month}}{1,58,834} \times 1,41,166 = 10 \text{ months}$$

Pay back period 1 year 10 months

Machine III

I year	1,74,500
Balance	1,25,500
	3,00,000

$$= \frac{12}{1,74,500} \times 1,25,500 = 8.62 \textit{ i.e., } 9 \text{ months}$$

= 1 year 9 months

	Machine I	Machine II	Machine III
Payback period	1 year 4 months	1 year 10 months	1 year 9 months

Result : As per the pay back period point of view, machine I is preferable, because it has a shorter pay back.

(*b*) *Depreciation*

	Machine I	*Machine II*	*Machine III*
$\frac{\text{Cost} - \text{Scrap}}{\text{Life}}$	$\frac{3,00,000 - 40,000}{2}$	$\frac{3,00,000 - 25,000}{3}$	$\frac{3,00,000 - 30,000}{3}$
	1,30,000	91,667	90,000

Problem 14. *The ABTS Co. Ltd. is considering the purchase of a new machine. Two alternative machines (A and B) have been suggested each having an initial cost of ₹ 4,00,000 and requiring ₹ 20,000 as additional working capital at the end of the 1st year. Earnings after taxation are expected to be as follows.*

Year	*Cash Inflows*	
	A ₹	*B* ₹
1	*40,000*	*1,20,000*
2	*1,20,000*	*1,60,000*
3	*1,60,000*	*2,00,000*
4	*2,40,000*	*1,20,000*
5	*1,60,000*	*80,000*

The company has target return on capital of 10% and on this basis, you are required to compare the profitability of the machines and state which alternatives you consider financially preferable.

Note : *The following table gives the present value of ₹ 1 due in 'n' number of years.*

Year	*1*	*2*	*3*	*4*	*5*
P/V at 10%	*.91*	*.83*	*.75*	*.68*	*.62*

[M.Com. Madras]

Solution : **Present Value Statement**

Machine A

Year	*Cash Inflows* ₹	*Discount Factor At 10%*	*Present Value* ₹
1	40,000	.91	36,400
2	1,20,000	.83	99,600
3	1,60,000	.75	1,20,000
4	2,40,000	.68	1,63,200
5	1,60,000	.62	99,200
Total Present value of cash inflows			5,18,400
Less : Total Present value of cash outflows (4,00,000 + 20,000 × .91)			4,18,200
		Net present value	1,00,200

Machine B

Year	Cash Inflows ₹	Discount Factor At 10%	Present Value ₹
1	1,20,000	.91	1,09,200
2	1,60,000	.83	1,32,800
3	2,00,000	.75	1,50,000
4	1,20,000	.68	81,600
5	80,000	.62	49,600
Total Present value of cash inflows			5,23,200
Less : Total Present value of cash outflows (4,00,000 + 20,000 × .91)			4,18,200
		Net present value	1,05,000

Result : Machine B is preferable because it has a higher net present value as compared to Machine A. So, machine B is recommended for purchase.

Problem 15. *A Company is considering two mutually exclusive projects. Both require an initial cash outlay of ₹ 10,000 each and have a life of 5 years. The company's required rate of return is 10% and pays tax at 50%. The project will be depreciated on a straight line basis. The before tax cash flows expected to be generated by the project are as follows.*

	Before Tax Cash Flows				
Year	*1*	*2*	*3*	*4*	*5*
Project A	*4,000*	*4,000*	*4,000*	*4,000*	*4,000*
Project B	*5,000*	*5,000*	*2,000*	*5,000*	*5,000*

Calculate for each project :

(i) The payback *(iii) NPV*

(ii) The accounting rate of return *(iv) PI*

Which project should be accepted and why ? [MBA Anna Dec. 2003]

Solution : **Profitability Statement**

Project A

Year	*Cash Flows* ₹	*Less Depreciation* ₹	*PBT* ₹	*Less Tax* ₹	*PAT* ₹	*Add Depreciation* ₹	*Cash Inflow (profit after tax but before depreciation)*
1	4000	2000	2000	1000	1000	+ 2000	3000
2	4000	2000	2000	1000	1000	+ 2000	3000
3	4000	2000	2000	1000	1000	+ 2000	3000
4	4000	2000	2000	1000	1000	+ 2000	3000
5	4000	2000	2000	1000	1000	+ 2000	3000

(*i*) Pay back period = 3 years 4 months

I year	3,000	
II year	3,000	
III year	3,000	
	9,000	
Balance	1,000	To recover balance amount of ₹ 1000 for how many months
	10,000	$\therefore \frac{12}{3,000} \times 1,000 = 4$

i.e., = 3 years 4 months

(*ii*) $$\text{Accounting Rate of Return} = \frac{\text{Return}}{\text{Original investment}} \times 100$$

Return = Average Profit (*i.e.,* profit after tax)

$$\text{ARR} = \text{Average profit} = \frac{\text{Total Profit}}{\text{Number of Years}} = \frac{5,000}{5} = 1,000$$

$$\text{ARR} = \frac{1,000}{10,000} \times 100 = 10\%$$

Project B

Year	*PBT* ₹	*Less Depreciation* ₹	*PBT* ₹	*Less Tax 50%* ₹	*PAT* ₹	*Add Depreciation* ₹	*Profit after tax but before depreciation (cash in hand)*
1	5000	2000	3000	1500	1500	2000	3500
2	5000	2000	3000	1500	1500	2000	3500
3	2000	2000	0	0	0	2000	2000
4	5000	2000	3000	1500	1500	2000	3500
5	5000	2000	3000	1500	1500	2000	3500

(*i*) Pay back period = 3 years 3 months

I year	3,500
II year	3,500
III year	2,000
	9,000
Balance	1,000
	10,000

To recover balance amount of ₹ 1000 in how many months

$$\frac{12}{3,500} \times 1,000 = 3 \text{ months}$$

(ii) ARP : $\frac{\text{Return}}{\text{Original cost}} \times 100$, *i.e.*, Return = Average Profit (profit after tax)

$$\text{Average profit} = \frac{\text{Total Profit}}{\text{No. of Years}} = \frac{16,000}{5} = \frac{1,200}{10,000} \times 100 = 12\%$$

Statement showing net present value

	Project I			Project II		
Year ₹	Cash Inflows ₹	*P/V fact at at 10%* ₹	*Disounted Cash Inflows* ₹	Cash Inflows ₹	*P/V Factor at 10%* ₹	*Discounted Cash Inflows* ₹
1	3,000	.090	2727	3,500	.909	3181.50
2	3,000	.826	2478	3,500	.826	2891.00
3	3,000	.751	2253	2,000	.751	1502.00
4	3,000	.683	2049	3,500	.683	2390.00
5	3,000	.621	1863	3,500	.621	2173.50
	Total Present value of cash inflows		11,370			12,138.00
	Less : Initial cost		10,000			10,000.00
	Net Present value		1,370			2,138.00

$$\text{Profitability index} = \frac{\text{Sum of discounted cash inflows}}{\text{Cash outflow}} \times 100$$

Project A

$$\text{Profitability index} = \frac{11,370}{10,000} \times 100 = 113.7\%$$

Project B

$$\text{Profitability index} = \frac{12,138}{10,000} \times 100 = 121.38\%$$

Result :

Project	Pay back	ARR	NPV	PI
A	II	II	II	II
B	I	I	I	I

Result :

Based upon the above calculation project B is preferable. Because, in all the four aspects project B would get I Rank in three techniques.

Problem 16. *Calculate the net present value for a small sized project requiring an initial investment of ₹ 20,000 and which provides a net cash inflow of ₹ 6000 each year for six years. Assume the cost of funds to be 8% p.a. and that there is no scrap value.*

[M.Com. Adapted]

Solution :

The present value of an annuity of Re. 1 for 6 years at 8% p.a., as per the annuity table is ₹ 4.623.

Hence, the present value of ₹ 6,000 is

6,000 × 4.623 =	27,738
Less : Original cost =	20,000
Net present value =	7,738

Problem 17. *The initial cost of an equipment is ₹ 3,00,000. Cash inflows for 5 years are estimated to be ₹ 2,00,000 per year. Desired rate of return is 15%. Calculate the net present value and excess present value index.* [Dec. 2004] [MBA Anna]

Solution : Present value of Re. 1 received annually for 5 years at 15% as per annuity Table = 3.352. Present value of ₹ 2,00,000 received annually for 5 years

	₹
2,00,000 × 3.352 =	6,70,400
Less : Original cost of the equipment =	3,00,000
Net present value =	3,70,400

$$\text{Excess present value index} = \frac{\text{Total present value of cash inflows}}{\text{Total present value of cash outflows}}$$

$$= \frac{6,70,000}{3,00,000} \times 100 = \mathbf{223.4}$$

Problem 18. *KVP Ltd is considering the purchase of a new machine for ₹ 1,20,000. It has a life of 4 years and an estimated scrap value of ₹ 20,000. The machine will generate an extra revenue of ₹ 4,00,000 p.a. and has an additional operating cost of ₹ 3,20,000 p.a. The company's cost of capital is 20% and tax rate 50%. Should the machine be purchased or not ?* [MBA Madras]

Solution : **Profitability Statement**

	₹
Annual revenue	4,00,000
Less : Operational costs	3,20,000
Net income before depreciation and tax	80,000
Initial investment	1,20,000
Less : Scrap	20,000
	1,00,000

Life of the machinery = 4 years

$$\text{Depreciation} = \frac{1,00,000}{4} = 25,000$$

Tax Rate = 50%

Net income before Depreciation and tax is ₹	80,000
Less : Depreciation	25,000
	55,000
Less : Tax 50%	27,500
Net income after Tax and Depreciation	27,500
Add : Depreciation	25,000
Cash inflows	52,500

Present value of Re 1 for 4 years at 20%

52,500 × 2.588 = 1,29,400

Less : initial investment

[1,00,000 + 10,000 × .482] = 1,09,640

Net present value = 19,760

Result : As per the calculation there could be a positive NPV, so the machine may be purchased.

Problem 19. *Sumanth & Co. Ltd. is considering building an assembly plant. The decision has been narrowed down to two possibilities. The company desires to choose the best plant at a level of operations of 10,000 gadgets a month. Both plants have expected life of 10 years and are expected not to have any salvage value at the time of their retirement. The cost of capital is 10%. Suggest what should be the desirable choice.*

Cost of monthly output of 10,000 units.

	Large Plant ₹	*Small Plant* ₹
Initial cost	*30,00,000*	*22,93,500*
Direct labours : First half	*15,00,000 (p.a.)*	*7,80,000 (p.a.)*
Second half	—	*9,00,000 (p.a.)*
Overheads :	*2,40,000 (p.a.)*	*2,10,000 (p.a.)*

The present value of an ordinary annuity of Re 1 for 10 years at 10% is 6.1446.

Solution : **Profitability Statement**

		₹
Direct labour for small plant for both shifts (7,80,000 + 9,00,000)		16,80,000
Direct labour for large plant		15,00,000
Savings in indirect labour (using large plant)		1,80,000
Overhead costs for small plant =	2,10,000	
Less : Overhead costs for large plant =	2,40,000	– 30,000
Net savings p.a. by using large plant		1,50,000

Present value of Re 1 saved annually for 10 years		6.1446
Present value of ₹ 1,50,000 saved annually for 10 years	= 1,50,000 × 6.1446	
	= 9,21,690	
Cost of the large plant	= 30,00,000	
Cost of the small plant	= 22,93,500	
	7,06,500	
Present value of savings from large plant		9,21,690
Less : Additional cost of large plant		7,06,500
Net present value		2,15,190

Result : In the above computation the net present value is positive. So, it is advisable to go in for the installation of large plant.

Problem 20. *PRP Ltd. is evaluating two mutually exclusive proposals for new capital investment. The following information about the proposals are available.*

Particulars	*Proposal A*	*Proposal B*
Investment cost (₹)	*80,000*	*1,00,000*
Economic life (yrs)	*4*	*5*
Earnings before depreciation and tax	*₹*	*₹*
1	*24,000*	*28,000*
2	*28,000*	*32,000*
3	*32,000*	*36,000*
4	*44,000*	*44,000*
5	—	*4,000*

The company's cost of capital is 10% and tax rate is 50%. Advise the company as to which proposal would be profitable, using NPV technique. [MCA Madras]

Solution :

Statement Showing Profitability

Proposal A

Year	*Earnings before Depreciation and Tax ₹*	*Less Depreciation ₹*	*PBT ₹*	*Less Tax 50% ₹*	*PAT ₹*	*Add Depreciation ₹*	*Cash Inflows (profit after tax but before Depreciation)*
1	24,000	20,000	4,000	2,000	2,000	20,000	22,000
2	28,000	20,000	8,000	4,000	4,000	20,000	24,000
3	32,000	20,000	12,000	6,000	6,000	20,000	26,000
4	44,000	20,000	24,000	12,000	12,000	20,000	32,000
5	—	—	—	—	—	—	—

Proposal B

Year	*Earnings before Depreciation and Tax ₹*	*Less Depreciation ₹*	*PBT ₹*	*Less Tax 50% ₹*	*PAT ₹*	*Add Depreciation ₹*	*Cash Inflows (profit after tax but before Depreciation)*
1	28,000	20,000	8,000	4,000	4,000	20,000	24,000
2	32,000	20,000	12,000	6,000	6,000	20,000	26,000
3	36,000	20,000	16,000	8,000	8,000	20,000	28,000
4	44,000	20,000	24,000	12,000	12,000	20,000	32,000
5	4,000	20,000	16,000	—	16,000	20,000	4,000

NOTE : Calculation of Depreciation

Proposal A

$$\frac{\text{Cost}}{\text{Life}} = \frac{80,000}{4} = 20,000$$

Proposal B

$$\frac{\text{Cost}}{\text{Life}} = \frac{1,00,000}{5} = 20,000$$

Statement Showing Net Present Values

Year	*Discount Factor*	*Cash Inflows ₹* (Proposal A)	*Present Value (Cash inflows × P/V factor) ₹* (Proposal A)	*Cash Inflows ₹* (Proposal B)	*Present Value (Cash inflows × P/V factor) ₹* (Proposal B)
1	.909	22,000	22,000 × .909 = 19,998	24,000	24,000 × .909 = 21,816
2	.826	24,000	24,000 × .826 = 19,824	26,000	26,000 × .826 = 21,476
3	.751	26,000	26,000 × .751 = 19,526	28,000	28,000 × .751 = 21,028
4	.683	32,000	32,000 × .683 = 21,856	32,000	32,000 × .683 = 21,856
5	.621	20,000	20,000 × .621 = 12,420	4,000	4,000 × .621 = 2,484
	Total Present Value		81,204		88,660
	Less : Initial investment		80,000		1,00,000
	Net Present value		1,2,04		– 11,340

Result : Proposal A is recommended. Because, it has the positive NPV.

Problem 21.

Initial outlay ₹ *50,000*

Life of the asset *5 years*

Estimated cash flows ₹ *12,500*

Calculate internal rate of Return.

(Cash inflows are uniform).

Solution :

$$\text{Present value factor} = \frac{\text{Initial investment}}{\text{Annual cash inflow}} = \frac{50,000}{12,500} = 4$$

To refer the Annuity Table II, the present value factor of 4 is located in the column of 5 years. The figure 3.9927 (nearer to 4) is found in the row of 8% so the internal rate of return is 8%.

Problem 22.

Initial Investment : *₹ 60,000*
Life of the asset : *4 years*

Estimated net annual Cash flows

I	*year*	*₹ 15,000*
II	*year*	*₹ 20,000*
III	*year*	*₹ 30,000*
IV	*year*	*₹ 20,000*

Calculate internal rate of return. [MBA Anna May 2005]

Solution :

Present value of Re 1 due in *'n'* number of years.

Year	*P/V factor at 10%*	*P/V factor at 12%*	*P/V factor at 14%*	*P/V factor at 15%*
1	.909	.892	.877	.869
2	.856	.797	.769	.756
3	.751	.711	.674	.657
4	.683	.635	.592	.571

Statement Showing Cash Inflows at Various Discount rates of 10%, 12%, 14%, and 15%

Year	*Annual Cash Inflows ₹*	*Discount Factor at 10%*	*Present Value ₹*	*Discount Factor at 12%*	*Present Value ₹*	*Discount Factor at 14%*	*Present Value ₹*	*Discount Factor at 15%*	*Present Value ₹*
1	15,000	.909	13,635	.892	13,380	.877	13,155	.869	13,035
2	20,000	.856	16,520	.797	15,940	.769	15,380	.756	15,120
3	30,000	.751	22,530	.711	21,330	.674	20,220	.657	19,710
4	20,000	.683	13,660	.635	12,700	.592	11,840	.571	11,420
			66,345		63,350		60,595		59,285

At the time of applying 14% of Discount rate, the present value of cash inflows is more or less equal to the outflows. So, 14% is taken as the Internal Rate of Return. If we want the exact IRR the following techniques will be applicable.

At 14% total present value = 60,595
At 15% total present value = 59,285

1,310

For the difference of 1,310, the difference in rate = 1%

For a difference of 595, what will be the difference in rate ?

$$= \frac{1}{1,310} \times 595 = .45$$

$$\therefore \quad IRR = 14\% + 0.45\% = 14.45\%$$

Problem 23. *Balimer Ltd. has a machine having an additional life of 5 years which costs ₹ 50,000 and which has a book value of ₹ 20,000. If it is sold, it will fetch ₹ 5,000. A new machine costing ₹ 1,00,000 is available. Though, its capacity is the same as that of the old machine. It will mean a saving in variable cost to the extent of ₹ 40,000 p.a. The life of machine will be 5 years at the end of which it will have a scrap value of ₹ 10,000. The rate of income tax is 50% and the company does not make an investment unless it must if it yields less than 12%. Advise the company whether the old machine should be replaced or not.*

[MBA Anna 2004]

Solution : Cash inflow if the new machine is installed

		₹
Gross savings in variable costs		40,000
Less : Depreciation (1,00,000 – 10,000) ÷ 5		18,000
Profit after depreciation		22,000
Less : tax 50%		11,000
Profit after Tax		11,000
Add : Depreciation		18,000
Total cash inflows		29,000
Present value of Re 1 receivable annually for 5 years @ 12%		3.605
Present value of cash inflow for 5 years at 12% (29,000 × 3.605)		1,04,545
Present value of scrap value of ₹ 10,000 at the end of 5th year @ 12% (10,000 × 0.567)		5,670
Cash received from sale of old plant		4,465
Discounted value (5000 × 0.893)		
Tax saving : Book value of old plant	20,000	
Sale price of old plant	5,000	
Loss	15,000	
Tax saved 50% (due to loss of ₹ 15,000) ₹ 7,500 available at the end of one year (0.893 × 7,500)		6,698
Total cash inflows		1,21,378
Cash outflows		1,00,000
Net present value		21,378

Result : The net present value is positive. So, the replacement proposal is accepted.

Problem 24. *A company is considering to expand its production. It can go either for an automatic machine costing ₹ 2,24,000 with an estimated life of 5½ years or an ordinary machine costing ₹ 60,000 having an estimated the life of 8 years. The annual sales and costs are estimated as follows.*

	Automatic Machine ₹	*Ordinary Machine* ₹
Sales	*1,50,000*	*1,50,000*
Cost :		
Material	*50,000*	*50,000*
Labour	*12,000*	*60,000*
Variable OHS	*24,000*	*20,000*

Compute the comparative profitability of the proposals under pay back period and return on investment method. Explain the difference in the results obtained under the two methods.

[B.Com. PU, M.Com. Madurai]

Solution : **Profitability Statement**

	Automatic Machine ₹	*Ordinary Machine* ₹
Cost of the machine	2,24,000	60,000
Sales	1,50,000	1,50,000
Less : Variable Cost	86,000	1,30,000
Contribution or Annual cash inflow	64,000	20,000
Pay back period = $\frac{\text{Original cost}}{\text{Cash inflow}}$	$\frac{2,24,000}{64,000}$ = 3½ years	$\frac{60,000}{20,000}$ = 3 years

Profit after the pay back period

Automatic machine = 64,000 × 2 (5½ years – 3 ½ years) = ₹ 1,28,000

Ordinary machine = 20,000 × 5 (8 years – 3 years) = ₹ 1,00,000

On the basis of the payback period only, ordinary machine should be recommended. Because it has shorter payback period. But in the case of full life of the asset, the automatic machine is preferable, because it gives a surplus amount of ₹ 1,28,000. But, ordinary machine gives only ₹ 1,00,000 for the 8 years.

Problem 25. *A project cost of ₹ 20,00,000 yielded annually a profit of ₹ 3,00,000 after depreciation @ 12½% and is subject to income tax @ 50%. Calculate pay back period.*

[MCA Dec. 2001]

Solution :

$$\text{Pay back period} = \frac{\text{Initial investment}}{\text{Annual cash inflow}}$$

Initial investment = ₹ 20,00,000

Annual cash inflows = Profit after Tax + Depreciation

Profit before Tax	3,00,000
Less : Tax 50%	1,50,000
Profit after tax	1,50,000
Add : Depreciation	
$(20{,}00{,}000 \times \frac{12.5}{100})$	2,50,000
Annual Cash inflow	4,00,000

$$\text{Pay back period} = \frac{20{,}00{,}000}{4{,}00{,}000} = \textbf{5 years}$$

Problem 26. *Rank the projects according to their desirability under the pay back method and accounting rate of returns method assuming the cost of capital is 10%.*

Project	*Initial Investment* ₹	*Annual cash flows* ₹	*Life in years*
A	*60,000*	*12,000*	*15*
B	*88,000*	*22,500*	*22*
C	*2150*	*1500*	*03*
D	*20,500.*	*4500*	*10*
E	*4,25,000*	*2,25,000*	*20*

[B.E. Anna June 2005]

Solution :

I. Ranking of the project according to pay back

Project	*Initial Investment* ₹	*Annual Cash Inflows (₹)*	*Payback Period in Years*	*Rank*
A	60,000	12,000	$\frac{60{,}000}{12{,}000} = 5$	V
B	88,000	22,500	$\frac{88{,}000}{22{,}500} = 3.91$	III
C	2150	1500	$\frac{2{,}150}{1{,}500} = 1.43$	I
D	20,500	4,500	$\frac{20{,}500}{4{,}500} = 4.55$	IV
E	4,25,000	2,25,000	$\frac{4{,}25{,}000}{2{,}25{,}000} = 1.88$	II

II. Ranking of project according to accounting rate of return method

$$\text{Formula} = \frac{\text{Return}}{\text{Original investment}} \times 100$$

Project	*Annual Cash Inflow* ₹	*Less Depreciation* ₹	*Profit* ₹	*Accounting Rate of Retrun* ₹	*Rank*
A	12,000	– 4,000	8,000	$\frac{8,000}{60,000} \times 100 = 13.33\%$	IV
B	22,500	– 4000	18,500	$\frac{18,500}{88,000} \times 100 = 21.02\%$	III
C	1,500	– 717	783	$\frac{783}{2,150} \times 100 = 36.41\%$	II
D	4,500	– 2050	2,450	$\frac{2,450}{20,500} \times 100 = 11.95\%$	V
E	2,25,000	– 21,250	2,03,750	$\frac{2,03,750}{4,25,000} \times 100 = 47.94\%$	I

Ranking of project

Project	Pay back	Accounting Rate
A	5	4
B	3	3
C	1	2
D	4	5
E	2	1

Result : As the pay back period point of view, project C has 1st Rank, so it should be recommended. But in the case of Accounting Rate of Return point of view, project E gets 1st Rank. So, it should be recommended.

Problem 27. *If expected rate of return is 30% do you recommend the following projects.*

	Project A ₹	*Project B* ₹
Capital cost	*1,00,000*	*1,50,000*
Annual Savings	*30,000*	*50,000*
Annual Savings	*30,000*	*70,000*
Annual Savings	*40,000*	*80,000*
Annual Savings	*50,000*	*50,000*

[MBA Madras Nov. 1998]

Solution :

	Project A		Project B	
Year	*Cash Inflows* ₹	*Cumulative Cash Inflows* ₹	*Cash Inflows* ₹	*Cumulative Cash Inflows* ₹
1	30,000	30,000	50,000	50,000
2	30,000	60,000	70,000	1,20,000
3	40,000	1,00,000	80,000	2,00,000
4	50,000	1,50,000	50,000	2,50,000

I. Pay back period A = 3 years

Pay back period B = 2 years 4 months

B :

I year	₹	50,000
II year	₹	70,000
		1,20,000
Balance		30,000
		1,50,000

$$\frac{12}{80,000} \times 30,000 = 4$$

i.e., 2 years 4 months

II. Return on Investment

Return = Average Return

$$i.e., = \frac{\text{Total Profit}}{\text{Number of Years}}$$

$$\text{Project A} = \frac{1,50,000}{4} = 37,500$$

Investment = Average investment

$$\text{Average investment} = \frac{\text{Original investment}}{2}$$

$$= \mathbf{50,000}$$

Project A : $= \frac{37,500}{50,000} \times 100 = \mathbf{75\%}$

Project B : $\text{Return} = \frac{2,50,000}{4} = 62,500$

$$\text{Average Investment} = \frac{1,50,000}{2} = 75,000$$

$$\therefore \quad \frac{62,500}{75,000} \times 100 = \mathbf{83.3\%}$$

The expected return is only 30%, but actual return in both the projects is more than the expected rate. So, both the projects are recommended.

TEST PROBLEMS

1. A company has to choose one of the following two mutually exclusive projects investment required for project is ₹ 1,50,000, both the projects have to be depreciated on straight line basis, The tax rate is 50%.

	Profit before Depreciation	
Year	*Project X (₹)*	*Project Y (₹)*
1	42,000	42,000
2	48,000	45,000
3	70,000	40,000
4	70,000	50,000
5	20,000	1,00,000

Calculate Pay-back Period. [**Ans.** Project X = 3 Years, 6 months
Project Y = 4 years, 9 days]

2. Determine the average rate of return from the following data of two machines A and B

	Machine A (₹)	*Machine B (₹)*
Cost	56,125	56,125
Annual estimated income after depreciation and income tax:		
First year	3,375	11,375
Second year	5,375	9,375
Third year	7,375	7,375
Fourth year	9,375	5,375
Fifth year	11,375	3,375
	36875	**36,875**
Estimated life in years	5	5
Estimated salvage value (₹)	3,000	3,000
Average income tax rate	55%	55%
Additional working capital (₹)	5,000	6,000

Depreciation has been charged on straight line basis. *[Madras, B.Com. Oct. 2002*

[**Ans.** (1) Computation of Annual Average Net Earnings, Machine A = ₹ 7,375
Machine B = ₹ 7,375 (2) Computation of Average Investment
Machine A = 21.34%. Machine B = 20.74%

❑❑❑

28

Computerised Accounting

INTRODUCTION

Computer is an Electronic Data processing machine which can do various works and at the same time quickly and accurately. Computer is a generic term. In the modern business world the role of computers and its functions are unlimited. It plays vital role not only for our day-to-day life, but also in all business activities.

EXPANSION OF COMPUTER

C – Commonly
O – Operated
M – Machine
P – Particulary
U – Used for
T – Trade
E – Education and
R – Research

ELECTRONIC COMPUTERS

Definition

The United States of American institute has defined a computer as "A device capable of solving problems, by accepting data, performing described operations on the data and supplying the result of these operations. Various types of computers are calculators, digital computers, and analog computers".

The ISO define computer as "A data processor that can perform substantial computation including numerous arithmetic and logic operations without intervention by a human operator during run".

Computer is the mechanized information converter and operators mechanically to convert information in a refined form. It analyses interprets and classify the data in the field of accounting by the employment of an electronic digital equipement. All the datas are converted into binary notion with the help of the conversion tables. Once data field into the computer in its operations is entirely self-supervised and also its operation is thousand times faster than human brain. It has a perfect meaning. Once taught to perform an operation it never forget, but a human being is not like that. All operations performed by a computer are bewildering.

COMPONENTS OF A COMPUTER

The main Components of computer are as following:

(*i*) **Input unit:** To read data fed into the storage

(*ii*) **Memory or storage units:** To retains temporarily results of sub-calculations till further processing.

(*iii*) **Arithmetic and logic units:** To perform necessary, calculations and arithmetical operations are done in this unit by taking relevant information from the memory unit.

(*iv*) **Output unit:** To obtain final information from the computer. Thus, unit transfer the final information to an outside document *i.e.*, in the printed paper.

(*v*) **Control unit:** It is otherwise called as instruction unit. Because, once data are field into the computer, each unit of the computer works under the supervision of this unit.

(*vi*) **Hardware and software:** Component parts are called hardware. Examples are hardware's are monitor, mouse, keyboard and CPU- Central Process Units.

FUNCTIONS OF COMPUTER

Generally, two categories of functions are performed by a computer, It may

(*i*) Scientific and Commercial specifically we concentrated only on commercial nature. It may be futher classified as ( ) book keeping.

(*ii*) Decision making.

(*iii*) Operational research.

CHARACTERISTICS OF COMPUTER SYSTEM

The following characteristics of computer system are as follows:

(*i*) Entire process is handled by one computer.

(*ii*) Complete list of instructions should be field into the computer it actually explain what to do.

(*iii*) It is unable to process information express in its regular manner unless otherwise an intermediary language is used.

TYPES OF COMPUTER

Computers are classified into the following two types:

(*i*) **Digital Computers:** In the present business world most of the organization employee this type of computers. Digital computer is a type of computer that which performs the work immediately after its is given a problem.

(*ii*) **Analog Computers:** It works on the basis of using a formula or a system to represent that which is being investigated. Under this computer the operation is actually based an approximate positions rather than absolute numbers.

DATA PROCESSING

The term data means a number of figures or statistics about any event. In accounting terms data are usually expreseed in monetary units and non-monitory units also.

Generally, collected data may not be used for specific purposes, because it is called Raw data processing. Data is used for specified purposes. Data processing means reassembling of facts into more meaningful terms in a professional manner and consolidation of total information in such a way so that useful inferences may be drawn upon the inferences necessary and appropriate action may be taken.

Steps involved in Data Processing

(*i*) Collection and recording of data.

(*ii*) Arranging and classifying recorded data.

(*iii*) Processing of the classified data and summarizing them into a suitable heads.

Manual and Mechanical Data Processing

Generally, collected data can be processed either manually or with help of machine. Even in the Technology development still manual method is most popular in more number of concerns in India. At present, more or less all the concerns are ready to use mechanical devices like computers with help of the manual methods of data processing.

Advantages of Mechanical Data Processing

Advantages of mechanical Data processing are as follows:

(*i*) In mechanical accounting, the accounting operations can be performed at very high speed and also provide accuracy of calculations.

(*ii*) Enable to produce quality product at the least possible cost.

(*iii*) Sound management decision can made with help of upto-date information.

(*iv*) Millions of calculations are done within few minutes with help of a computer.

Disadvantages of Mechanical Data Processing

(*i*) Huge investment requirement.

(*ii*) Manual system of data processing are slow but they are flexible as compared to the computerized accounting.

(*iii*) There may be chances for fraudulent activities.

(*iv*) Installation of a computer needs a complicated and costly task of system analysis.

(*v*) Employees are not ready to adopt the mechanical data processing.

ROLE OF COMPUTERS IN ACCOUNTING

The traditional system of accounting is the recording, classifying, summarizing the entire transaction with help of the human being. Instead of human being complete system of accounting is carried out by machine. Due to economic and industrial growth day- by-day number of transactions are increased. Impact of business growth and enormous number of business transaction various machines was developed which could store and process accounting data. Such advancement leads to number of growing successful organization. Advanced version of machine is evolved with increased speed, storage and processing capacity. A computer which can be connected and operated of these machines. So, automatically the maintenance of accounting data on a real time basis becomes almost essential. With help of the computers maintenance of accounting records become more convenient.

The computerized accounting uses the concept of data base, the purpose of database an accounting software is employed to implement a computerized accounting system. Some of the commonly used Financial Accounting software packages are Tally, Ex, Winca and Dac Easy. Its basis software which is easily access to the data contained in the data base.

COMPONENTS OF COMPUTERIZED ACCOUNTING SOFTWARE:

The following are the important components of computerized accounting software:

(*i*) Preparation of accounting documents.

(*ii*) Recording of transaction.

(*iii*) Preparation of Trial Balance and Financial statements.

TYPES OF MACHINES USED IN MECHANICAL ACCOUNTING:

(*i*) Listing, adding and calculating machines.

(*ii*) Book keeping and accounting machines.

(*iii*) Punched card processing machines.

(*iv*) Electronic computers.

Accounting Machine

Accounting machine is just like a typewriter and it does the computation of values direclty from the organisation source of a transaction to the final accounting record. As and when necessary we will get complete and accurate details of various accounts which are not possible in the manual accounting. In manual accounting there are many chances for error because recording and postings are two different functions. But, mechanized accounting original printing is correct means all other results are automatically correct. There is no chance for committing the error in mechanized accounting.

Functions of Accounting Machine

(*i*) It gives the monthly-wise results of all the accounts.

(*ii*) It gives the department-wise sales details.

(*iii*) It gives the complete details of buyers.

(*iv*) It gives the complete details of various asset and liabilities and their upto date Balances.

(*v*) It gives the details information about the incomes and expenses.

Computerized Accounting

The term Computerised Accounting means the entire stages of accounting process can be carried out *i.e.*, recording classifying and summarizing the transaction are completed with the help of computers is known as computerized accounting. Due to the industrial and economic the volume of business is increased day- by-day. In current business world computers role is more important for handling business transaction.

Transaction processing system is the starting point of computerized accounting system. The following steps could be involved while processing a transaction under transaction process system.

(1) Data Entry is the step for processing the transaction.

(2) Data validation.

(3) Processing and Revalidation.

(4) After processing and Revalidation all the valid transactions are stored in the Data Base.

(5) To produce desired information.

(6) Report preparation.

Need and Requirements of Computerized Accounting

In the present business world need for computerized accounting is increased, because manual accounting faces lot of difficulties and it can't give the accurate results.

The following are advantages supporting for the need of computerized accounting

(1) Handling large number of transaction.

(2) It provides Quick and Quality report.

(3) Reduction in paper work.

(4) Flexible reporting.

(5) It offers online facility to store and process transaction.

(6) High degree of confidence.

(7) It provides accurate reports.

(8) Scalability.

Basic Requirements of the Computerized Accounting System

Computerized accounting system needs the following basic requirements.

(1) Accounting framework.

(2) Operating procedure.

Importance of Computer System Accounting

Role and Importance of computer system in Accounting are listed below.

(1) Automatic generation of accounting documents.

(2) Information security is maintained.

(3) Quick and efficient processing of information.

(4) Decision making.

(5) Customer convenience.

(6) Efficient internal control system.

(7) To increase the efficiency of real time tranfer of funds.

APPLICATIONS OF COMPUTER

A computer can be applied more or less all types of accounting and technical matters, which are listed below

(1) Production planning and control through linear programming.

(2) Sales accounting.

(3) Purchase accounting.

(4) Payroll accounting.

(5) Inventory control.

(6) Financial statement preparation.

(7) Budget and budgetary control.

(8) Machine capacity utilisation.

(9) Profit planning.

(10) Input-output analysis.

(11) Capital Budgeting decision.

(12) Market and Marketing research.

Financial accounting software used to stored and maintain daily business transactions like purchase, sales receipts, payments, purchase returns, sales returns, deposits and withdrawals etc. various financial accounting software package are Tally. Ex, Winca and DACEASY.

Tally is the one of the important financial accounting package not only in India but also in abroad, with help of the tally package any one who may a owner, accountant, financial manager, executive, they may deal the accounting in easy manner without any difficulty. Simply says it is an tool employed by the persons who are connected with accounting for easy learning and handling.

Procedure for Operating Tally

- Starting Tally
- Creating, selecting, altering and closing a company
- Creating, display, altering, and deleting ledger accounts
- Exit from Tally.

ACCOUNTING INFORMATION

In any financial accounting, whenever the company is created, for purpose of Tally. automatically it creates two accounts *i.e.*, Cash A/c and Profit & Loss A/c other accounts are to be created as per the requirement of the user. All the accounts will not be entered in Trial Balance, Trading and Profit & Loss A/c and or Balance Sheet. In this situation, Tally should be in a position to identify which account is to be taken into which report. For example closing stock will appears in Trading A/c and Balance Sheet but not in the Trail Balance. Therefore, number of groups are given in Tally. Any account is created in Tally must belonging to any one of the groups. Generally, these account groups are based on Assets, Liabilities, Incomes and expenses. All the accounts that belongs to the group of Assets or Liabilities will taken into Balance Sheet not for the Trading & Profit and Loss A/c and the accounts that belongs to the group of Incomes and Expenses will taken into Profit and Loss Accounts not for the Balance Sheet.

ACCOUNT GROUP

According to the requirements of Indian Accounting system, Tally provides a set of 28 pre-defined groups. Among these 15 are primary groups and 13 are sub groups. The various Accounting groups are listed below:

I. Capital Account (PG)
   (1) Reserves and Surplus (SG)

II. Current Liabilities (PG)
   (1) Duties and Taxes (SG)
   (2) Provisions (SG)
   (3) Sundry Creditors (SG)

III. Loans (liabilities) (PG)
   (1) Bank OD Accounts (SG)
   (2) Secured Loans (SG)
   (3) Unsecured Loans (SG)

IV. Suspense Account (PG)

V. Current Assets (PG)
   (1) Bank Accounts (SG)
   (2) Cash in Hand (SG)
   (3) Deposits (Assets) (SG)
   (4) Loans and Advances (SG)
   (5) Stock in Hand (SG)
   (6) Sundry Debtors (SG)

VI. Fixed Assets (PG)

VII. Investments (PG)

VIII. Misc. Expenses (Assets) (PG)

IX. Sales Account (PG)

X. Purchase Account (PG)

XI. Direct Income (PG)

XII. Indirect Expenses (PG)

XIII. Indirect Income (PG)

XIV. Indirect Expenses (PG)

XV. Branch Divisions (PG)

PG: Indicates, Primary groups.
SG: Indicates, Sub-groups.

❑❑❑

QUESTION PAPERS

ANNA UNIVERSITY—COIMBATORE

M.B.A. Degree Examination—March 2010

098390005 Accounting for Management

Time : Three hours *Maximum : 100 marks*

PART A — (7 × 5 = 35 marks)

Answer ALL questions.

1. Explain any two accounting concepts.
2. What is Trial Balances?
3. Explain the meaning of Cash Flow statment.
4. Explain Debt-Equity Ratio.
5. What is Sunk Cost?
6. Explain activity based costing.
7. Explain Break-even Point.
8. What is Flexible Budget?
9. Explain the meaning of contribution.
10. What is Journals?

PART B — (5 × 12 = 60 marks)

Answer any Five questions.

11. Explain the basic concepts and conventions of accounting.
12. Explain the advantages of Budgetary control.
13. Explain the difference between Cash Flow and Fund Flow statement.
14. Prepare Profit and Loss account of M/Rajesh & Co. for the year ended 31st March, 2008

Particulars	₹	*Particulars*	₹
Opening Stock	10,0000	Sales	1,00,000
Purchases	7,000	Sales Return	5,000
Wages	5,000		
Fright inward	2,000		
Carriage inward	8,000		
Purchase return	5,000		
Advertisment	10,000		
Audit fees	5,000		
Insurance	1,000		
Salesman commission	5,000		
Rent	10,000		

Adjustments :

1. Closing Stock ₹ 50,000
2. Outstanding Rent ₹ 1,000
3. Prepaid Insurance ₹ 5,00

15. From the following details find out (*i*) Current Assets, (*ii*) Current Liabilities (*iii*) Liquid Assets, and (*iv*) Stock
Current Ratio: 2.5
Liquidity Ratio: 1.5
Working Capital ₹ 60,000

16. Draw up a flexible Budget for Overhead Expenses on the basis of the following data for 70%, 80% and 90% plan capacity:

Particulars	*Capacity Levels*		
	70% ₹	*80%* ₹	*90%* ₹
Variable Overheads:			
Indirect labour	–	12,000	–
Stores including spares	–	4,000	–
Semi–variable Overheads:			
Power (30% fixed, 70% variable)	–	20,000	–
Repairs and maintenance (60% fixed, 40% variable)	–	2,000	–
Fixed Overheads:			
Depreciation	–	11,000	–
Insurance	–	3,000	–
Salaries	–	10,000	–
Total overheads	–	62,000	–

17. Assume the cost structure and spelling prices remain the same in periods I and II, find out:

(*a*) Profit/Volume Ratio
(*b*) Break-Even Point for Sales
(*c*) Profit when sales are ₹ 1,00,000.

Periods	*Sales (₹)*	*Profit (₹)*
I	1,20,000	9,000
II	1,40,000	13,000

18. Mr. Gopal furnishes the following data retaining to manufacture of standard product during the month of April.

Pariculars	₹
Raw Material consumed	15,000
Direct labour charges	9,000
Machine-hours worked	900
Administrative overheads	20% on works cost

Selling overheads	₹ 0.50 per unit sold
Units produced	17,000
Units sold	16,000 at ₹ 4 per unit

You are required to prepare a cost sheet from the above.

PART C — (1 × 20 = 20 marks)

Compulsory Question :

19. From the following data, which product would you recommended to be manufactured in factory, time being the key factor?

	Per Unit of Product 'A'	*Per Unit of Product 'B'*
Direct material	₹ 24	₹ 14
Dierct Labour at ₹ 1 per hour	2	3
Variable overhead at ₹ 2 per hour	4	6
Selling price	100	110
Standard time to produce	2 hours	3 hours

❑❑❑

S.no. 2141 **[06 UBA 10]**

PERIYAR UNIVERSITY—SALEM

B.B.A. Degree Examination, Management Accounting

Time : Three hours *Maximum : 100 marks*

PART A — (7 × 5 = 35 marks)

Answer ALL questions.

1. Define management accounting.
2. What is cost accounting?
3. What is working capital?
4. Explain the funds form operation.
5. Define fund.
6. What is interim dividend?
7. Define ratio.
8. Explain the significance of capital gearing ratio.
9. What is budget?
10. Explain zero bare budget.

PART B — (5 × 4 = 20 marks)

Answer ALL questions.

11. (*a*) Explain the scope of management accounting.

Or

(*b*) Distinguish between management and cost accounting.

12. (*a*) Explain the uses of funds flow statement analysis.

Or

(*b*) You are given the following Balance Sheet of a company:

31st December

Liabilities	*2006* ₹	*2007* ₹	*Assets*	*2006* ₹	*2007* ₹
Accounts payable	7,000	4,500	Cash	3,000	4,700
Capital	20,000	25,000	Accounts receivable	12,000	11,500
Retained earnings	1,000	2,300	Land	5,000	6,600
			Stock	8,000	9,000
	28,000	**31,800**		**28,000**	**31,800**

Prepare a statement showing the changes in working capital.

13. (*a*) Distinguish between funds and cash flow statement.

Or

(*b*) After taking on to consideration the undermentioned items, Abi Ltd. made a net profit of ₹ 1,00,000 for the year ended 31st December, 2007.

	₹
Loss on sale of machinery	10,000
Depreciation on buildings	4,000
Depreciation on machinery	5,000
Preliminary expenses written off	5,000
Provision for taxation	10,000
Goodwill written of	5,000
Gain on sale of buildings	8,000

Find out cash from operations.

14. (*a*) What are the limitations of ratios?

Or

(*b*) The following is the Balance Sheet of a firm.

Liabilities	₹	*Assets*	₹
Share capital	30,000	Fixed assets	16,500
Creditors	8,000	Cash	1,000
Bills payable	2,000	Book debts	6,000
Provision for tax	3,000	Bill receivable	2,000
		Stock	17,500
	43,000		**43,000**

Comment upon the liquidity of the firm.

15. (*a*) What are the objectives of a budget?

Or

(*b*) From the following particulars prepare a production budget of a company for the year ended June 30, 2007.

	Sales (Units)	*Estimated Stock (Units)*	
Product		01.07.2006	30.06.2007
A	1,50,000	14,000	15,000
B	1,00,000	5,000	14,500
C	70,000	8,000	8,000

PART C — (5 × 12 = 60 marks)

Answer ALL questions.

16. (*a*) Describe the functions of management accounts.

Or

(*b*) Distinguish between financial and management accounting.

17. (*a*) From the following Balance Sheets of SK industries, prepare funds flow statement:

Liabilities	*2006* ₹	*2007* ₹	*Assets*	*2006* ₹	*2007* ₹
Share capital	60,000	65,000	Goodwill	30,000	25,000
P/L A/c	34,000	26,000	Machinery	60,000	50,000
Creditors	12,000	3,000	Cash	16,000	19,000
	1,06,000	94,000		1,06,000	94,000

Additional informations :

(*i*) Depreciation on machinery charged ₹ 20,000.

(*ii*) Dividend for ₹ 12,000 were paid during the year.

Or

(*b*) From the following prepare a statement showing sources and application of funds and schedule of charges in working capital:

Liabilities	*2004* ₹	*2005* ₹	*Assets*	*2004* ₹	*2005* ₹
Share capital	4,00,000	5,75,500	Plant	75,000	1,00,000
Creditors	1,06,000	1,00,000	Stock	1,21,000	1,36,000
P/L A/c	14,000	31,000	Debtors	1,81,000	1,70,000
			Cash	1,43,000	2,70,000
	5,20,000	6,76,000		5,20,000	6,76,000

18. (*a*) Discuss the various types of ratios.

Or

(*b*) The following is the Balance Sheet of a company as on 31st March, 2007:

Liabilities	*2004*	*Assets*	*2004*
Share capital	3,98,000	Land and Building	1,40,000
P/L A/c	30,000	Plant and Machinery	3,50,000
General Reserve	40,000	Stock	20,000
12% debentures	42,000	Debtors	1,00,000
Sundry creditors	1,00,000	B/R	10,000
Bills payable	50,000		
	6,60,000		6,60,000

Calculate :

(*i*) Current ratio (*ii*). Quick ratio (*iii*) Inventory to working capital (*iv*) Debt to equity ratio (*v*) Propriety ratio (*vi*) Capital gearing ratio

19. (*a*) Explain the objects of cash flow statement.

Or

(*b*) The comparative Balance Sheets of a company are given below:

Liabilities	*2006* ₹	*2007* ₹	*Assets*	*2006* ₹	*2007* ₹
Capital	35,000	37,000	Cash	4,500	3,900
Debentures	6,000	3,000	Book debts	7,450	8,850
Creditors	5,180	5,920	Stock	24,600	21,350
Provision for doubtful debts	350	400	Land	10,000	15,000
Profit & Loss A/c	5,020	5,280	Goodwill	5,000	2,500
	51,550	51,600		51,550	51,600

Additional Informations :

(*i*) Dividend paid amounted to ₹ 1,750

(*ii*) Land was purchased for ₹ 5,000 and amount provided for the amortization of goodwill amounted to ₹ 2,500.

(*iii*) Debentures were repaid to the extent of ₹ 3,000

You are required to prepare Cash Flow Statement

20. (*a*) With the following data for a 60% activity, prepare a budget for production at 80% and 100% capacity:

Particulars	*Units*
Production at 60% capacity	600 units
Materials	₹ 100 p/u
Labour	₹ 40 p/u
Direct expenses	₹ 10 p/u
Factory overheads	₹ 40,000 (40% Fixed)
Administrative expenses	₹ 3,000 (60% Fixed)

Or

(*b*) From the following budget date, forecast the cash position at the end of April, May and June 2007:

Month	*Sales* ₹	*Purchases* ₹	*Wages* ₹	*Miscellaneous* ₹
February	1,20,000	84,000	10,000	7,000
March	1,30,000	1,00,000	12,000	8,000
April	80,000	1,04,000	8,000	6,000
May	1,16,000	1,06,000	10,000	12,000
June	88,000	80,000	8,000	6,000

Additional Informations :

(*i*) **Sales:** 20% realized in the month of sales, discount allowed 2%, balance realized equity in two subsequent months.

(*ii*) **Purchases:** There are paid in the month following the month of supply.

(*iii*) **Wages:** 25% paid in arrears following month.

(*iv*) **Miscellaneous expenses:** Paid a month in arrears.

(*v*) **Rent:** ₹ 1,000 per month paid quarterly in advance due in April.

(*vi*) **Income tax:** First instalment of Advance tax ₹ 25,000 due on or before 15th June.

(*vii*) **Income from investment:** ₹ 5,000 received quarterly, in April and July.

(*viii*) Cash in hand ₹ 5,000 on 1st April, 2007.

❑❑❑

S.no. 3347 **[DPVL]**

PERIYAR UNIVERSITY

M.B.A. Degree Examination, March 2008

Accounting for Managerial Decisions

Time : Three hours *Maximum : 100 marks*

PART A — (7 × 5 = 35 marks)

Answer any SEVEN out of twelve questions.

1. Describe the meaning and objects of accounting principles. What are their essential features?

2. Differentiate between financial accounting and cost accounting.

3. Describe the different methods of cost and state the particular industries to which they can be applied.

4. What are the functions of a store-keeper and how should be organize the store?

5. How does management accounting help planning and control functions in an organization?

6. Explain the characteristics features of management accounting.

7. How is marginal costing useful in the decision making of a firm?

8. What is meant by cost-volume profit analysis? Describe its importance.

9. What is standard costing? State its advantages.

10. Describe the managerial uses of variance analysis.

11. What are the basis objectives for compiling a statement of sources and application of funds?

12. What are the advantages of cash flow statement?

PART B — (4 × 10 = 40 marks)

Answer any FOUR out of six questions.

13. On 1st January, 2002 a firm purchased machinery worth ₹ 50,000. On 1st July, 2004, it bought additional machinery worth ₹ 10,000 and spends ₹ 1,000 on its erection. The accounts are closed each year on 31st December. Assuming the annual depreciation is charged at 10% per annum on original cost, show necessary accounts for five years, when

(*a*) Assets accounts is maintained at written down value, and

(*b*) Assets account is maintained at cost.

14. X limited has purchased and issued the material in the following order.

	Unit	Unit costs
		₹
Jan1 Purchase	300	3
Jan 4 Purchase	600	4
Jan 6 Issue	500	–
Jan 10 Purchase	700	4
Jan 15 Issue	800	–
Jan 20 Purchase	300	5
Jan 23 Issue	100	–

Ascertain the quantity of closing stock as on 31st Jan. and state what will be its value (in each) if issues are made under the following methods:

(*a*) Average cost, (*b*) First-in-first-out, (*c*) Last-in-first-out.

15. Discuss the objectives and special features of common size statements.

16. (*a*) The sales turnover and profit during the two years were as follows:

Or

(*b*) The following is the Balance Sheet of a firm.

	Sales	Profit
	₹	₹
First year	2 Lakhs	20,000
Second year	3 Lakhs	40,000

(*a*) P/V ratio

(*b*) Fixed cost

(*c*) Break-even point.

17. The Standard estimate for materials for manufacture of 1,000 units of a commodity is 400 kgs. at 2.50 per kg. When 2,000 units of the commodity are manufactured, it is found that 820 kgs. of materials are consumed at ₹ 2.60 per kg. Calculate the material variances.

18. Explain the different types of report that are used for the internal management of an enterprise.

❑❑❑

S.no. 4138 **[PBA 07]**

PERIYAR UNIVERSITY—SALEM

M.B.A. (Pride) Degree Examination, May 2010

Financial and Management Accounting

Time : Three hours *Maximum : 100 marks*

PART A — (5 × 5 = 25 marks)

Answer ALL questions.

Each answer not to exceed 1 page :

1. (*a*) What are the accounting convertions? Explain.

Or

(*b*) What is the need for providing depreciations?

2. (*a*) What are the limitations of financial analysis?

Or

(*b*) What are the financial statement?

3. (*a*) What are the advantages of Ratio analysis?

Or

(*b*) Distinguish between Fund Flow Statement and cash flow statement.

4. (*a*) What are the essentials of effective budgetary control?

Or

(*b*) Discuss the utility of standard costing.

5. (*a*) Why cost-volume profit relationship is important in business management?

Or

(*b*) Explain 'margin of safety'. How can it be improved?

PART B — (5 × 15 = 75 marks)

Answer ALL questions.

Each question should not exceed 4 pages :

6. (*a*) The following is the Trial Balance of M/s Krishna Agencies as on 31st March, 2009. Prepare Trading and Profit and Loss account for the year ended 31-3-2009 and a Balance Sheet on the date.

Particulars	*Dr.*	*Cr.*
	₹	₹
Capital		1,00,000
Drawings	18,000	
Buildings	15,000	
Furniture and Fittings	7,500	
Motor van	25,000	
Loan from Hari @ 12% interest (1-4-2008)		15,000

Interest paid on above	900	
Sales		1,00,000
Purchases	75,000	
Opening stock	25,000	
Establishment expenses	15,000	
Wages	2,000	
Insurance	1,000	
Commission received		4,500
Sundry debtors	28,100	
Bank balance	20,000	
Sundry creditors		10,000
Interest		3,000
	2,32,500	2,32,500

Adjustments :

(*i*) The value of closing stock on 31st March, 2009 was ₹ 32,000.
(*ii*) Outstanding wages ₹ 500.
(*iii*) Prepaid insurance ₹ 300.
(*iv*) Commission received in advance ₹ 1,300.
(*v*) Allow interest on capital at 10%.
(*vi*) **Depreciate:** Building 2.5%, Furniture and Fittings 10%.
(*vii*) Charge interest on drawings ₹ 500.
(*viii*) Accured interest ₹ 500.

Or

(*b*) A company purchased a four years on lease on 1-1-2003 for ₹ 20,150. It was decided at provide for the replacement of the lease at the end of 4 years by setting up a depreciation funds. It is expected that investments will fetch interest at 4%. Sinking funds tasks show that to provide to requisite sun at 4% at the end of 4 years an investment of ₹ 4,74,502 is required. Investments are made to the nearest rupee. On 31-12-2006 the investment were sold for ₹ 14,830 on 1-1-2007 the same lease was renewed for a further period of 4 years by payment of ₹ 22,000.

Given the important ledger accounts to record the above.

7. (*a*) From the following Profit and Loss accounts of Suresh Ltd for the year ended 31st March, 2007 and 2008. You are required to prepare comparative income statement.

Particulars	*2007* ₹	*2008* ₹	*Particulars*	*2007* ₹	*2008* ₹
To cost of goods	60,000	75,000	By Net Sales	80,000	1,00,000
To operating expenses					
Administrative exp	2,000	2,000			
Selling expenses	3,000	4,000			
To net profit	15,000	19,000			
	80,000	1,00,000		80,000	1,00,000

Or

(*b*) Explain the usefulness of trend percentages in the interpretation of financial statements.

8. (*a*) Following are the ratios of the trading activities at National Traders Ltd.

Debtors velocity	=	3 Months
Stock velocity	=	8 Months
Creditors velocity	=	2 Months
Gross profit ratio	=	25%

Gross profit for the year ended 31-3-2008 amounts to ₹ 4,00,000. Closing stock of the year is ₹ 10,000 above the opening stock. Bills Receivable amounts to ₹ 25,000 and Bills Payable to ₹ 10,000

Find out

(*i*) Sales. (*ii*) Sundry debtors. (*iii*) Closing stock. (*iv*) Sundry creditors.

Or

(*b*) Vijaya Kumar Ltd. present the following financial statements for 2008 and 2009. Prepare a sources and applications of funds and evaluate your findings.

Liabilities	*2007* ₹	*2008* ₹	*Assets*	*2007* ₹	*2008* ₹
Sundry creditors	8,26,000	12,54,000	Cash	1,06,000	62,000
Bills payable	4,52,000	6,28,000	Investment	1,74,000	-
Loan from bank	2,00,000	4,70,000	Sundry debtors	6,92,000	10,56,000
Reserve and surplus	13,84,000	4,70,000	Stock in trade	8,64,000	13,66,000
Share capital	12,00,000	12,00,00	Net fixed assets	22,26,000	27,96,000
	40,62,000	52,80,000		40,62,000	52,80,000

Depreciation of ₹ 3,78,000 was written of on fixed assets.

9. (*a*) From the following information regarding a standard product, compare

(*i*) Price

(*ii*) Usage and

(*iii*) Mix variance

Mutual	*Standard*			*Actual*		
	Quantity kilos	*Unit price*	*Total*	*Quantity kilos*	*Unit price*	*Total*
A	4	1.00	4.00	2	3.50	7.00
B	2	2.00	4.00	1	2.00	2.00
C	2	4.00	8.00	3	3.00	9.00
Total	8	2.00	16.00	6	3.00	18.00

Or

(*b*) Prepare a cash budget for the months of May, June and July 2009 on the basis of the following information.

Months	Credit Sales	Credit Purchases	Wages	Manufacturing Expenses	Office Expenses	Selling Expenses
March	60,000	36,000	9,000	4,000	2,000	4,000
April	62,000	38,000	8,000	3,000	1,500	5,000
May	64,000	33,000	10,000	4,500	2,500	4,500
June	58,000	35,000	8,500	3,500	2,000	3,500
July	56,000	39,000	9,500	4,000	1,000	4,500
Aug	60,000	34,000	8,000	3,000	1,500	4,500

(*i*) Cash balance on 1st May 2009 ₹ 8,000.

(*ii*) Plant costing ₹ 16,000 is due for delivery in July, payable 10% on delivery and the balance after 3 months.

(*iii*) Advance Tax ₹ 8,000 each is payable in March and June.

(*iv*) Period of credit allowed by suppliers two months and to customers one month.

(*v*) Lag in payament of manufacturing expanse ½ month.

(*vi*) Lag in payament of office and selling expanse one months.

10. (*a*) The sales turnover and profit during two periods were as follows:

Period	*Sales ₹*	*Profit ₹*
I	20,00,000	2,00,000
II	30,00,000	4,00,000

Calculate :

(*i*) P/V ratio

(*ii*) BEP

(*iii*) Margin of Safety

(*iv*) The sales required to earn a profit of ₹ 5 lakhs and

(*v*) The profit when sales are ₹ 10 lakhs

Or

(*b*) Arul Karthick sales a popular brand of Men's Sports shirts at an average price of ₹ 28 each. He purchases the shirts from a supplier at a unit cost of ₹ 18. The costs of operating his shop are all fixed costs and amount to ₹ 54,000 a year. He pays a commission to his salesman at the rate of ₹ 1 for every shirts sold through the particulars salesman required.

(*i*) How many shirts must be sold in a year to break-even ?

(*ii*) Compute the sales revenue at the break-even point.

(*iii*) Compute the monthly sales revenue required to earn a net profit before tax of ₹ 45,000 in a year.

❑❑❑

ANNA UNIVERSITY—COIMBATORE

X1006

M.B.A. Degree Examination—March 2008

First Trimester

MBA 016 — Financial and Management Accounting

Time : Three hours *Maximum : 100 marks*

PART A — (20 × 1 = 20 marks)

Answer ALL questions.

Choose the correct answer :

1. Financial accounting deals with
(*a*) Finding out cost (*b*) Finding out profit
(*c*) Finding out prices (*d*) None of the above.

2. Accounting concepts are based on
(*a*) Certain assumptions (*b*) Certain facts and figures
(*c*) Certain records (*d*) Certain assets.

3. Business entity concepts are based on
(*a*) Business and Business (*b*) Individual and individual
(*c*) Individual and business (*d*) None of the above.

4. Current Assets includes
(*a*) Land (*b*) Furniture
(*c*) Machinery (*d*) Stock.

5. Non-current liability includes
(*a*) Cash (*b*) Outstanding salary
(*c*) Prepaid rent (*d*) Mortgage loan.

6. Balance Sheet indicates
(*a*) Trading results (*b*) Results of profit
(*c*) Cash in hand (*d*) Assets and liabilities.

7. Cash flow statement is also called as
(*a*) Sources and application (*b*) Sources and uses
(*c*) Balance sheet (*d*) Trial balance.

8. Break-even point is a point
(*a*) Where there is profit (*b*) Where there is loss
(*c*) Where there is no profit no loss (*d*) None of the above.

9. Financial accounts records
(*a*) Actual figures (*b*) Budgeted figures
(*c*) Standard figures (*d*) None of the above.

10. Going concern concept assures
(*a*) Business as dissolving concern (*b*) As a realising values
(*c*) As a continuing concern (*d*) None of the above.

True or False :

11. Depreciation of machinery is application of funds.
12. Cash flow consists of cash in hand and cash at bank.
13. Cost sheet profit differs from financial profit.
14. Direct materials is an example for controllable cost.
15. An opportunity cost is the cost for the advantage foregone.

Fill in the blanks :

16. Outstanding wages appears in the .... side of the Balance Sheet.
17. Current Ratio deals with Current Assets and ....
18. Current Assets minus Current Liability is called as .... capital.
19. Liquidity ratio is also known as .... ratio.
20. 1 : 1 is the standard .... ratio.

PART B — (10 × 2 = 20 marks)

Answer any TEN questions.

21. What is a Trial Balance ?
22. Mention different types of Budgets.
23. What is a Cost Center ?
24. Mention two differences between Trial balance and Balance Sheet.
25. Mention the three different formulas for the Debit and Credit.
26. What do you mean by cash flow ?
27. Fixed expenses ₹ 2,40,000, Selling price per unit ₹ 30, Variable cost per unit ₹ 15. Find out the Break-even sales in Units.
28. What do you mean by budgetary control ?
29. What is the standard costing ?
30. What do you mean by Accounting Ratios ?
31. What is a flexible budget ?
32. What is fund flow ?

PART C — (5 × 10 = 50 marks)

Answer any FIVE questions.

33. Give the format of a COST SHEET.
34. Explain the different accounting concept.
35. From the following Profit and Loss Account. Find out (*a*) Gross Profit Ratio (*b*) Net Profit Ratio (*c*) Operating Ratio (*d*) Operating Profit Ratio.

	₹		₹
To Opening stock	26,000	By sales	1,60,000
To Purchase	80,000	By Closing stock	38,000
To Wages	40,000		
To Gross profit c/d	52,000		
	1,98,000		1,98,000

	₹		₹
To Selling expenses	4,000	By Gross profit b/d	52,000
To Administration expenses	24,000	By Compensation for	
To Value of furniture cost in fire	800	acquired land	4,800
To Net profit c/d	28,000		
	56,800		56,800

36. The stand cost of a chemical mixture is as follows :
8 tons of material A at ₹ 40 per ton
12 tons of material B at ₹ 60 per ton
Standard yield is 90% of input actual cost for a period is
10 tons of material A at ₹ 30 per ton
20 tons of material B at ₹ 68 per ton
Actual yield is 26.5 tons
Compute all material variances.

37. Following are the budget expenses for the production of 10,000 units. Prepare a Flexible Budget for 6000 and 8000 units.

	Per unit
Direct material	60
Direct labour	30
Direct expenses	25
Flexible expenses (1,50,000)	15
Variable expenses (direct)	5
Selling expenses 10% fixed	15
Administration expenses (50,000)	5
Distribution expenses (20% fixed)	5
Total cost	160

38. What basis would you follow for distribution of the following overhead expenses ?
(*a*) Factory Rent
(*b*) ESI
(*c*) Insurance on Building
(*d*) Welfare Department Expenses
(*e*) Electric Light.

39. From the following Balance Sheet prepare the FLOW CHART.

Balance Sheet

	Last Year ₹	*This Year* ₹		*Last Year* ₹	*This Year* ₹
Share Capital	5,00,000	7,00,000	Machinery	80,000	1,20,000
Profit and Loss a/c	1,00,000	1,60,000	Building	5,00,000	8,00,000
General Balance	50,000	70,000	Stock	1,00,000	75,000
Sundry Creditors	2,00,000	2,45,000	Debtors	1,50,000	1,60,000
			Cash	20,000	20,000
	8,50,000	11,75,000		8,50,000	11,75,000

Additional information :

(*a*) ₹ 50,000 has been charged for depreciation on Machinery.

(*b*) ₹ 20,000 dividend paid.

40. From the following particular calculate :

(*a*) Contribution

(*b*) P/V ratio

(*c*) Break even points in units and also in rupees

(*d*) Selling price per unit if the break even point is brought down to 25000 units.

Fixed expenses	₹ 1,50,000
Selling price per unit	₹ 15
Variable cost per unit	₹ 10.

PART D — (1 × 10 = 10 marks)

Compulsory Question

41. From the following TRIAL BALANCE prepare the Final. Accounts and BALANCE SHEET as on 31st March 2007.

Trial Balance

	Debit ₹	*Credit* ₹
Capital Account		90,000
Machinery	80,000	
Sales		4,07,000
Purchase	2,60,000	
Returns	6,000	5,750
Opening Stock	30,000	
Discount	350	800
Bank Charges	75	
Debtors	45,000	
Creditors		25,000
Salaries	26,800	
Wages	40,000	
Carriage Inwards	750	
Carriage Outwards	1,200	
Bad Debts Provision		525
Rent and Taxes	10,000	
Advertisement	2,000	
Cash	6,900	
Furniture	20,000	
Total	5,29,075	5,29,075

Adjustments :

(*a*) Closing Stock ₹ 35,000

(*b*) Provide 10% depreciation on Machinery

(*c*) Provide 2% reserve for Bad Debts

(*d*) Outstanding Wages ₹ 9,000.

ANNA UNIVERSITY—COIMBATORE

X1006

M.B.A. Degree Examination—November/December 2007

First Trimester

MBA 016 — Financial and Management Accounting

Time : Three hours *Maximum : 100 marks*

PART A — (20 × 1 = 20 marks)

Answer ALL questions.

State Whether The Following Are 'True' or 'False'.

1. The figures given in the Balance Sheet are the future estimated values of assets and liabilities.
2. Drawings will appear in the asset side of the balance sheet.
3. "Business is different from business man" and the above concept is called as dual aspect concept.
4. Stock is a part of liquid asset.
5. Rule of thumb for acid test ratio is 1 : 1.
6. A ratio is an arithmetical relationship of one number to another number.
7. Goodwill is a current asset.
8. Cash flow statement is a substitute of cash account.
9. Decrease in creditors is Inflow of cash.
10. Sources and uses statement is also called as Fund Flow Statement.

Choose the correct answer :

11. Rent received in advance will appear in the
    (*a*) Balance sheet asset side (*b*) Balance sheet liability side
    (*c*) Trading account (*d*) None of the above.
12. The net worth of a limited company is equal to
    (*a*) Current assets minus current liabilities
    (*b*) Fixed assets minus long-term liabilities
    (*c*) Fixed assets minus current liabilities
    (*d*) The total of share holders funds/proprietors funds.
13. Standard current ratio is
    (*a*) 2 (*b*) 1
    (*c*) 3 (*d*) 4.
14. The difference between actual sales—break even sales is called as
    (*a*) Break even point (*b*) Standard cost
    (*c*) Marginal cost (*d*) Margin of safety.
15. Liquid ratio is also known as
    (*a*) Quick ratio (*b*) Current ratio
    (*c*) Operating ratio (*d*) Operating profit ratio.

Fill up the blanks :

16. Current asset-current liabilities is ....

17. Debt equity ratio is ....

18. For every debit there is a corresponding credit and this is called as .... aspect.

19. Total cost is equal to total sales and this is called as ....

20. Operating profit ratio is 100 .... ratio.

PART B — (10 × 2 = 20 marks)

Answer any TEN questions.

21. Give four examples for current assets.

22. Current ratio 2.5
Liquid ratio 1.5
Working capital ₹ 60,000
Calculate
(*a*) Current assets
(*b*) Current liabilities
(*c*) Liquid assets
(*d*) Stock.

23. What do you mean by Fund flow ?

24. What is a Trial Balance and how does it differ from a Balance Sheet ?

25. From the following find out the raw materials to be purchased for product A.
Estimated consumption (UNITS) 1,20,000
Estimated opening stock (UNITS) 16,000
Estimated closing stock (UNITS) 20,000

26. What do you mean by Master Budget ?

27. Mention the formula for material price variance.

28. What is P/V ratio ?

29. Define marginal cost.

30. What is flexible budget ?

31. Current ratio : 2.6 : 1
Liquid assets : 1.5 : 1
Current liabilities ₹ 40,000
Find out (*a*) Current asset (*b*) Current liability.

32. Sales ₹ 2,00,000, G.P. ratio is 20% find out the cost of goods sold.

PART C — (5 × 10 = 50 marks)

Answer any FIVE questions.

33. What is meant by ratio analysis ? Discuss its objects and limitations.

34. Briefly explain the accounting concepts and conventions.

35. Describe the essential steps of a budgetary control system.

36. Following is the Balance Sheet of A Ltd., as on 31st December 2006.

Liabilities	₹	*Assets*	₹
Equity Share Capital	5,00,000	Building	3,50,000
Debentures	2,00,000	Machinery	2,50,000
Bank Loan	1,50,000	Cash at Bank	80,000
Sundry Creditors	75,000	Debtors	85,000
Bills Payable	50,000	Bills Receivable	1,05,000
Outstanding Expenses	5,000	Stock	1,00,000
		Prepaid Expenses	10,000
	9,80,000		9,80,000

Calculate :

(*a*) (*i*) Current Ratio

(*ii*) Acid Test Ratio

(*iii*) Absolute Liquid Ratio

(*b*) Comment on the short-term financial position.

37. The following information relates to a flexible budget at 60% capacity. Prepare a flexible budget for 50% and 70% capacity and also determine the overhead rates.

Expenses at 60% capacity

	₹
Variable overheads :	
Indirect labour	10,500
Indirect materials	8,400
Semi-variable Expenses :	
Repairs and maintenance (70% fixed)	7,000
Electricity (50% Fixed)	25,200
Fixed Expenses :	
Salaries	70,000
Insurance	4,000
Depreciation	20,000

Estimated direct labour hours 1,20,000 (Hours)

38. From the following balance sheets of a company as on 31st December 2006 prepare a CASH FLOW STATEMENT.

Liabilities	*Year 2005*	*Year 2006*	*Assets*	*Year 2005*	*Year 2006*
Share capital	1,00,000	1,25,000	Building	1,00,000	95,000
General Reserve	25,000	30,000	Machinery	75,000	85,500
Profit and loss A/c	15,250	15,300	Stock	50,000	37,000
Bank loan (Long-term)	35,000	–	Debtors	40,000	32,100
Creditors	75,000	67,600	Cash	250	5,800
Provision for taxation	15,000	17,500			
	2,65,250	2,55,400		2,65,250	2,55,400

Additional Information :

(*a*) Dividend paid ₹ 11,500

(*b*) Dividend received ₹ 5,000

(*c*) Depreciation on Building ₹ 5,000

(*d*) Further Machinery purchased ₹ 19,000

(*e*) Depreciation written off on Machinery ₹ 6,000.

39. From the following calculate :

(*a*) Material cost variance

(*b*) Material price variance

(*c*) Material usage variance

Products	*Standard Quantity (Units)*	*Standard Price* ₹	*Actual Quantity (Units)*	*Actual Price* ₹
A	1050	2.00	1100	2.25
B	1500	3.25	1400	3.50
C	2100	3.50	2000	3.75

40. The sales turnover and profit during two years were as follows :

Year	*Sales* ₹	*Profit* ₹
2005	1,50,000	20,000
2006	1,70,000	25,000

Find out :

(*a*) PV ratio and fixed cost

(*b*) Break even point

(*c*) Sales required to earn a profit of ₹ 40,000

(*d*) Profit made when sales are ₹ 2,50,000

PART D — (1 × 10 = 10 marks)

Compulsory Part

41. Problem :

From the following trial balance prepare the Trading, Profit and Loss Account and the Balance Sheet as on 31.12.2005

Particulars	*Debit* (₹)	*Credit* (₹)
Capital		60,000
Drawings	7,200	
Opening Stock	20,500	
Purchases	68,000	
Carriage Inwards	1,500	
Sales		1,40,500
Sundry Debtors	23,500	
Sundry Creditors		14,300
Cash-in-Hand	500	

Cash at Bank	2,200	
Carriage Outwards	1,700	
Salaries	20,000	
Bills Receivable	5,300	
Bills Payable		4,200
Insurance	1,200	
Furniture	10,000	
Machinery	28,000	
Rent	2,000	
Wages	21,500	
Provision for Doubtful Debts		1,000
General Expenses	6,900	
	2,20,000	2,20,000

Adjustments :

(*a*) Closing stock is ₹ 27,000

(*b*) Provide for Doubtful debts at 5% on sundry debtors

(*c*) Unexpired Insurance ₹ 300

(*d*) Outstanding wages ₹ 3,500

(*e*) Depreciate machinery by 10%

ANNA UNIVERSITY—CHENNAI

G4506

M.B.A. Degree Examination, May/June 2007
First Semester
BA 1606 — Accounting for Management
(Regulation 2005)

Time : Three hours *Maximum : 100 marks*

PART A — (10 × 2 = 20 marks)

Answer ALL questions.

1. What is the relationship between Management, Cost and Financial accounting ?

2. Who are the users of Balance Sheet and Profit and Loss Account ?

3. What are the Basic records used before preparing Trading, Profit and Loss A/c and Balance Sheet ?

4. State any four methods of Depreciation.

5. From the following details of a concern, calculate Liquidity Ratios.

Current Assets ₹ 1,90,000

Quick Assets ₹ 1,50,000

Current Liabilities ₹ 75,000.

6. Draw a specimen form of Funds Flow Statement.

7. Distinguish between Variable, Fixed and Semivariable Costs.

8. What is Break-even Point ?

9. Write a short note on make or buy Decision.

10. What is Cash Budget ?

PART B — (5 × 16 = 80 marks)

11. (*a*) The Income Statement of CRM Ltd., are given for the years 2004 and 2005. Convert them into common-size income statement and interpret the changes. (16)

Income Statements for the year ending 2004 and 2005

	2004 ₹	*2005* ₹		*2004* ₹	*2005* ₹
To Cost of Sales	5,95,000	6,15,000	By Gross Sales	7,25,000	8,15,000
To Gross Profit	1,05,000	1,85,000	*Less* : Returns	25,000	15,000
	7,00,000	8,00,000	Net Sales	7,00,000	8,00,000
To Operating Expenses :			By Gross Profit b/d	1,05,000	1,85,000
To Selling and distribution expenses	23,000	24,000	By Other Income	1,200	8,050
To Administrative expenses	12,700	12,500			

To Non-operating expenses	17,500	19,400			
To Net profit during the year	53,000	1,37,150			
	1,06,200	1,93,050		1,06,200	1,93,050

Or

(*b*) Discuss the concept of Human Resource Accounting. Explain its importance in the present context. (16)

12. (*a*) Write short notes on : (16)

(*i*) Business entity concept

(*ii*) Going concern concept and cost concept

(*iii*) Money measurement concept

(*iv*) Double entry concept.

Or

(*b*) From the following Trial Balance, prepare (*i*) Trading and Profit and Loss a/c and (*ii*) Balance Sheet.

Trial Balance as on 31.12.2005

Debit Balances	₹	*Credit Balances*	₹
Cash in Hand	2,000	Capital	2,00,000
Machinery	60,000	Sales	2,54,800
Stock	50,000	Sundry Creditors	40,000
Bills Receivables	1,600	Bank Overdraft	22,000
Sundry Debtors	50,000	Return Outwards	3,000
Wages	70,000	Discount Received	1,800
Land	40,000	Bills Payable	1,800
Carriage Inwards	2,400		
Purchases	1,80,000		
Salaries	24,000		
Rent	4,000		
Postage	1,000		
Return Inwards	3,200		
Drawings	10,000		
Furniture	18,000		
Interest	600		
Cash at Bank	6,600		
Total	5,23,400		5,23,400

Adjustments:

(*i*) Stock as on 31.12.2005 was ₹ 25,000.

(*ii*) Outstanding Rent ₹ 4,000

(*iii*) Provision for Bad Debts is to be 10%. (16)

13. (*a*) (*i*) State the uses and significance of cash flow statement. (8)

(*ii*) What are the limitations of Ratio Analysis ? (8)

Or

(*b*) From the following details, make out a Balance Sheet with as many details as possible.

(*i*) Stock velocity = 6

(*ii*) Capital turnover ratio = 2

(*iii*) Fixed assets turnover = 4

(*iv*) Gross profit ratio = 20%

(*v*) Debtors velocity = 2 months

(*vi*) Creditors velocity = 73 days.

The Gross profit was ₹ 60,000. Reserves and surplus amounts to ₹ 20,000. Closing Stock was ₹ 5,000 in excess on Opening Stock. The cost of goods sold is ₹ 2,40,000. (16)

14. (*a*) Discuss various basis of classification of cost and various types of costs. (16)

Or

(*b*) From the following data, you are required to calculate (*i*) P/V ratio (*ii*) Break-even sales (*iii*) Sales required to earn a profit of ₹ 4,50,000 (*iv*) Contribution per unit.

Fixed expenses = ₹ 90,000

Variable cost per unit :

Direct Material = ₹ 5

Direct Labour = ₹ 2

Direct Overheads = 100% of direct labour

Selling price per unit = ₹ 12. (4 × 4 = 16)

15. (*a*) Explain different types of Budgets and its uses. (16)

Or

(*b*) (*i*) What is Responsibility Accounting ? (8)

(*ii*) The components of an item are manufactured by another unit under the same management. The unit at present manufactures 1,00,000 units (the present requirements of the main factory) at the following costs :

	₹
Materials	5,00,000
Labour	2,50,000
Overheads	2,00,000
	9,50,000

Labour is paid at ₹ 2 per unit, the fixed D.A. and other allowances monthly. The components required by the main factory are to be increased by 20%. The components factory can increase production upto 25% without any additional labour force, overheads are variable to the extent of 25% of the present amount.

The additional requirement may be purchased from the market at ₹ 8.50 per unit. Suggest which will be better ? (8)

ANNA UNIVERSITY—CHENNAI

E4044

M.B.A. Degree Examination, May/June 2007
First Semester
BA 105 — Accounting for Management
(Regulation 2002)

Time : Three hours *Maximum : 100 marks*

PART A — (10 × 2 = 20 marks)

Answer ALL questions.

1. State different classifications of Accounts. Also state the rules of Accounting.
2. Differentiate between a Trial Balance and a Balance Sheet.
3. Define Depreciation. What are its cause ?
4. State the components of Shareholders' equity.
5. State the need for Financial Statement Analysis.
6. Explain the merits and demerits of Ratio Analysis.
7. Define Marginal Costing.
8. State the significance of Break-even Analysis.
9. Differentiate between Fixed and Flexible Budgets.
10. What are the advantages of Standard Costing ?

PART B — (5 × 16 = 80 marks)

11. (*a*) Discuss in detail the various Accounting Concepts and Conventions.

Or

(*b*) Explain in detail the accounting for merchandising Transaction.

12. (*a*) M/s Ritesh Ltd., purchased a second hand machine on 1st January 2001 for ₹ 3,70,000 and immediately spent ₹ 20,000 on its repairs and ₹ 10,000 for installation. On 1st July 2002, it purchased another machine for ₹ 1,00,000. On 1st July 2003, it sold off another machine for ₹ 2,50,000 and bought another for ₹ 3,00,000. Depreciation was provided on the machine @ 10% on original cost annually on 31 December. With effect from 1st January 2004, the company changed the method of providing depreciation and adopted the Written Down Value method and the rate of depreciation @ 15% per annum. Show machinery account for four years.

Or

(*b*) Bring out the differences between Funds Flow Analysis and Cash Flow Analysis.

13. (*a*) Following are the summarized Balance Sheets of Dinesh Ltd., as on 31st December 2003 and 2004 :

Liabilities	*2003*	*2004*	*Assets*	*2003*	*2004*
	₹	₹		₹	₹
Share Capital	2,00,000	2,50,000	Land and Buildings	2,00,000	1,90,000
General Reserve	50,000	60,000	Plant and Machinery	1,50,000	1,69,000

Profit and Loss A/c	30,500	30,600	Stock	1,00,000	74,000
Bank Loan	70,000	–	Sundry debtors	80,000	64,200
Sundry Creditors	1,50,000	1,35,200	Cash	500	600
Pro. for Taxation	30,000	35,000	Bank	–	8,000
			Goodwill	–	5,000
	5,30,500	5,10,800		5,30,500	5,10,800

Additional information supplied :

During the year ended 31st December, 2004 :

(*i*) Dividend of ₹ 23,000 was paid;

(*ii*) Assets of another company were purchased for a consideration of ₹ 50,000 payable in shares. The following assets were purchased Stock. ₹ 20,000 Machinery ₹ 25,000.

(*iii*) Machinery was purchased for ₹ 8,000.

(*iv*) Depreciation written off : Buildings ₹ 10,000; Machinery ₹ 14,000

(*v*) Income tax paid during the year ₹ 28,000 Provision of ₹ 33,000 was charged to Profit and Loss Account.

(*b*) What do you understand by Zero Base Budgeting ? How is it different from Traditional Budgeting ?

14. (*a*) A company budgets for a production of 1,50,000 units. The variable cost per unit is ₹ 14 and fixed cost is ₹ 2 per unit. The company fixes its selling price to fetch a profit of 15% on cost.

(*i*) What is the BEP ?

(*ii*) What is the P/V Ratio ?

(*iii*) If it reduces selling price by 5%, how the revised selling price affect the BEP and P/V Ratio ?

(*iv*) If a profit increase of 10% is desired more that the budget, what should be the sales at the reduced prices ?

Or

(*b*) State the different methods of Costing. Explain each one of them in detail.

15. (*a*) "Variance Analysis is an integral part of Standard Cost Accounting". Explain this statement.

Or

(*b*) The following details relating to the product 'X' during the month of June 2005 are available. You are required to compute the material and labour cost variance and also to reconcile the standard and the actual cost with the help of such variance :

Standard cost per unit :

Material 50 kg	@ ₹ 40 per kg
Labour 400 hours	@ ₹ 1 per hour

Actual cost for the month :

Material 4900 kgs.	@ ₹ 42 per kg
Labour 39600 hours	@ ₹ 1.10 per hour

Actual production = 100 units.

ANNA UNIVERSITY—CHENNAI

Z4506

M.B.A. Degree Examination, January 2007

First Semester

BA 1606 — Accounting for Management

(Regulation 2005)

Time : Three hours — *Maximum : 100 marks*

PART A — (10 × 2 = 20 marks)

Answer ALL questions :

1. Define Financial Accounting.
2. What do you mean by Inflation Accounting ?
3. Define Inventory Turnover Ratio.
4. Define Process Costing.
5. What do you mean by Margin and Safety ?
6. What do you mean by Cash from Operation ?
7. Define Target Costing.
8. What do you mean by Material Mix Variance ?
9. Define Incremental Analysis.
10. What do you mean by Responsibility Accounting ?

PART B — (5 × 16 = 80 marks)

11. (*a*) Define Human Resources Accounting. Explain their uses and abuses ?

Or

(*b*) Prepare Trading and Profit and Loss Account for the year ended 31st March, 1990 and Balance Sheet as at the date from the following Trail Balance of K. Rama Rao

Dr. Balances	₹	*Cr. Balances*	₹
Drawings	45,000	Capital	1,60,000
Goodwill	80,000	Bills Payable	33,800
Land and Buildings	60,000	Creditors	70,000
Plant and Machinery	40,000	Purchases Returns	2,650
Loose Tools	3,000	Sales	4,18,000
Bills Receivable	3,000		
Stock, 1st April, 1989	40,000		
Purchases	2,51,000		
Wages	20,000		
Carriage Outwards	500		
Carriage Inwards	1,000		
Coal	5,800		
Salaries	35,000		

Rent, Rates and Taxes	2,800
Discount	1,500
Cash at Bank	25,000
Cash in Hand	400
Sundry Debtors	45,000
Repairs	1,800
Printing and Stationery	500
Bad Debts	1,200
Advertisements	3,500
Sales Returns	2,000
Furniture	11,200
General Expenses	5,250

Adjustments :

(*i*) Closing Stock on 31st March, 1990 was ₹ 35,000.

(*ii*) Depreciate Plant and Machinery, Tools and Furniture by 10% and Land and Building by 5%.

(*iii*) Provide ₹ 1,500 for wages.

(*iv*) Advertisements prepaid are ₹ 500.

(*v*) Provide 5% on Debtors against bad debts and 2% against discount.

12. (*a*) Explain various methods of pricing the Inventory ?

Or

(*b*) A company purchased a four years 'lease on April 1, 1987 for ₹ 10,00,000. It is decided to provide for the replacement of the lease at the end of four years by setting up a depreciation fund. It is expected that investments will fetch interest at 12%. Sinking fund tables show that ₹ 0.209234 invested each year will produce ₹ 1 at the end of four years at 12% per annum. Investments were made in 12% Bonds of ₹ 100 each available at a face value. Interest was receivable yearly on 31st March.

On March 31st, 1991, the investments were sold for ₹ 6,98, 940. On 1st April, 1991 the same lease was renewed for a further period of 4 years by payment of ₹ 12,00,000.

Show journal entries and give the important ledger accounts to record the above.

13. (*a*) Define Ratio Analysis. Indicate uses and abuses ?

Or

(*b*) The following are the summarized Balance Sheets of Good Luck Ltd., as on 31st December, 1999 and 31st December, 2000.

Liabilities	*31st Dec. '99* ₹	*31st Dec. '00* ₹	*Assets*	*31st Dec. '99* ₹	*31st Dec. '00* ₹
Equity Share Capital	2,00,000	2,40,000	Land and Buildings	1,05,000	1,50,000
8% Debentures	50,000	—	Plant and Machinery (at cost)	2,90,000	3,20,000
Share Premium	—	10,000			
General Reserve	30,000	50,000	Furniture (at cost)	9,000	10,000
Profit and Loss Account	48,000	68,000	Inventories	1,30,000	1,05,000
Sundry Creditors	1,30,000	1,50,000	Sundry Debtors	75,000	85,000
Proposed Dividend	20,000	24,000	Cash	15,000	26,000

Provision for Depreciation :				
Plant and Machinery	1,40,000	1,50,000		
Furniture	6,000	4,000		
Total :	6,24,000	6,96,000	6,24,000	6,96,000

Additional information is as follows :

(*i*) Furniture which cost ₹ 5,000, written down value ₹ 1,000 was sold during the year 2000 for ₹ 2,000.

(*ii*) Plant and Machinery which cost ₹ 20,000 and in respect of which ₹ 13,000 had been written off as depreciation was sold during the year 2000 for ₹ 3,000.

(*iii*) The dividend of 1999 was paid during 2000.

You are required to prepare :

(1) A statement of changes in working capital during 2000

(2) Funds flow statement for the year 2000.

14. (*a*) Explain the Uses and Abuses of Marginal Costing and Cost Volume Profit Analysis ?

Or

(*b*) The following figures of sales and profits for two periods are available in respect of concern :

	Sales ₹	*Profit* ₹
Period I	1,00,000	15,000
Period II	1,20,000	23,000

You are required to find out :

(*i*) P/V ratio

(*ii*) Fixed cost

(*iii*) Break-even point

(*iv*) Profit at an estimated sale of ₹ 1,25,000

(*v*) Sales required to earn a profit of ₹ 20,000

15. (*a*) Define Budget. Indicate the procedure for introduction of Budgetary Control in an Organization.

Or

(*b*) A factory is producing three joint products A, B and C. The actual joint expenses of manufacture for a period were ₹ 19,600. The other details are as follows :

	Subsequent Expenses		
	A ₹	*B* ₹	*C* ₹
Material	1,500	1,300	1,000
Labour	200	150	100
Overheads	800	550	400
	2,500	2,000	1,500
Selling Price	30,000	24,000	20,000
Estimate Profits on Selling Prices	30%	25%	20%

Show how you would propose to apportion the joint costs of manufacture.

ANNA UNIVERSITY—CHENNAI

Q6506

M.B.A. Degree Examination, May/June 2006

First Semester

BA 1606 — Accounting for Management

Time : Three hours *Maximum : 100 marks*

PART A — (10 × 2 = 20 marks)

Answer ALL questions.

1. Define Management Accounting.
2. What is the Convention of Consistency ?
3. What is Revenue Expenditure ?
4. Give four examples of intangible asset.
5. What is the formula for calculating Average Collection period ?
6. How cash flow statement is different from fund flow statement ?
7. Define Activity based costing.
8. What is Target Costing ?
9. What is a Production Budget ?
10. Give four uses of marginal costing.

PART B — (5 × 16 = 80 marks)

11. SV Limited budgeted the manufacture of 30,000 units of its only product A for the next quarter. The capacity of the factory has not been fully utilized.

The variable costs per unit of product A are as under :

	₹
Direct material	48.00
Direct wages (₹ 4 per hour)	36.80
Factory variable overheads	27.60
Selling overheads-variable	18.00

Product A is sold at ₹ 200 per unit. Fixed overheads for the quarter are ₹ 15,00,000. At present the company manufacturers component P, one unit of which is used in each unit of product A. The cost of this component is already included in the cost structure of product A as aforesaid. Anyhow, the cost per batch of 1,000 units of the component P is separately supplied as under :

	₹
Direct material	6,000
Direct wages	4,800
Factory variable overheads	3,600
Fixed overhead apportioned to the component	3,600
Total Cost	18,000

It is proposed to utilize the spare capacity by manufacture of 1,500 units of product B for export. The details are as under :

	₹
Export selling price	228 per unit
Direct material costs	80 per unit
Direct labour	16 hours per unit
Variable selling expense applicable to this product	20 per unit

Factory variable overheads have to be charged, calculated on the basis of direct labour hour rate applicable to product A.

It has to be noted that component P is not used in the manufacture of Product B.

(*i*) Present a statement showing the profit as originally envisaged in the budget.

(*ii*) State whether component P should be manufactured or bought from the market if this can be procured at a price of ₹ 16 per unit.

(*iii*) Calculate the contribution on account of accepting the export order of Product B. (5 + 5 + 6)

12. (*a*) (*i*) Explain any four concepts used in accounting.

(*ii*) How financial accounting and cost accounting are related ? (8 + 8)

Or

(*b*) The following is the Trial Balance of B Govil on 31st March 2000.

	Dr.	*Cr.*
Cash in hand	540	
Cash at bank	12,630	
Purchases account	1,40,675	
Sales account		2,58,780
Returns inwards account	2,680	
Returns outwards account		1,500
Wages account	20,480	
Fuel and power account	4,730	
Carriage on sales account	3,200	
Carriage on purchases account	2,040	
Stock account (1st April, 1999)	25,760	
Buildings account	30,000	
Freehold land account	20,000	
Machinery account	20,000	
Patents account	7,500	
Salaries account	15,000	
General expenses account	13,000	
Insurance account	600	
Drawings account	15,245	
Capital account		82,000
Sundry debtors	14,500	6,300
	3,48,580	3,48,580

Taking into account into the following adjustments, prepare Trading and Profit and Loss account and Balance Sheet :

(*i*) Stock on hand on 31st March, 2000 is ₹ 26,800.

(*ii*) Machinery is to be depreciated at the rate of 10% and patents at the rate of 20%.

(*iii*) Salaries for the month of March 2000 amounting to ₹ 1,500 were unpaid.

(*iv*) Insurance includes a premium of ₹ 170 on a policy, expiring on 31st September 2000.

(*v*) Wages include a sum of ₹ 2,000 spent on the erection of a cycle shed for employees and customers.

(*vi*) A provision for bad and doubtful debts to be created to the extent of 5 per cent on sundry debtors.

13. (*a*) On 1st July, 1997 a company purchased a machine for ₹ 3,90,000 and spent ₹ 10,000 on its installation. It decided to provide depreciation at 15% per annum, using written down value method. On 30th November, 2000 the machine was dismantled at a cost of ₹ 5,000 and then sold for ₹ 1,00,000. On 30th November, 2000 the machine was dismantled at a cost of ₹ 5,000 and then sold for ₹ 1,00,000. On 1st December, 2000 the company acquired and put into operation a new machine at a total cost of ₹ 7,60,000. Depreciation was provided on the new machine on the same basis as had been used in the case of the earlier machine. The company closes its books of account every year on 31st March. Prepare Machinery Account for four accounting year ending 31.03.2001.

Or

(*b*) (*i*) Calculate the value of stock under.

(1) LIFO

(2) FIFO

Opening stock 1000 units - ₹ 10,000.

Receipts	
01.03.2006	500 units @ ₹ 12
05.03.2006	1000 units @ ₹ 15
10.03.2006	750 units @ ₹ 20
15.03.2006	500 units @ ₹ 25
Issues	
02.03.2006	750 units
07.03.2006	900 units
13.03.2006	500 units

(*ii*) What are the different methods of valuing goodwill ? (10 + 6)

14. (*a*) From the Balance Sheets of A Limited, make out :

(*i*) Statement of changes in the working capital

(*ii*) Funds flow statement.

Balance Sheets

Following is the additional information available :

Liabilities	*2004*	*2005*	*Assets*	*2004*	*2005*
	₹	₹		₹	₹
Equity Share Capital	3,00,000	4,00,000	Goodwill	1,15,000	90,000
12 % Redeemable preference Share Captial	1,50,000	1,00,000	Land and Building	2,00,000	1,70,000
General Reserve	40,000	70,000	Plant	80,000	2,00,000
Profit and Loss A/c	30,000	48,000	Debtors	1,60,000	2,00,000
Proposed Dividends	42,000	50,000	Stock	77,000	1,09,000
Creditors	55,000	83,000	Bills Receivable	20,000	30,000
Bills Payable	20,000	16,000	Cash in Hand	15,000	10,000
Provision for Taxation	40,000	50,000	Cash at Bank	10,000	8,000
Total	6,77,000	8,17,000		6,77,000	8,17,000

(1) Depreciation of ₹ 10,000 and ₹ 20,000 have been charged on Plant and Land and Buildings respectively in 2005.

(2) An interim dividend of ₹ 20,000 has been paid in 2005.

(3) Income tax of ₹ 35,000 has been paid in 2005.

Or

(*b*) With the following ratios and further information given below, prepare a Trading Account, Profit and Loss Account and a Balance Sheet of Shri Narain :

(*i*) Gross profit ratio 25%

(*ii*) Net profit/sales 20%

(*iii*) Stock-turnover ratio 10%

(*iv*) Net profit/capital 1/5

(*v*) Capital to Total Liabilities ½

(*vi*) Fixed assets/capital 5/4

(*vii*) Fixed assets/total current assets 5/7

(*viii*) Fixed assets ₹ 10,00,000

(*ix*) Closing stock ₹ 1,00,000

15. (*a*) The company manufacturers a particular product the standard direct materials cost of which is ₹ 10 per unit. The following information is obtained from the costing records :

(*i*) Standard Mix :

Material	*Quantity Units*	*Rate* ₹	*Amount* ₹
A	70	10	700
B	30	5	150
	100		850
Less (15%)	15		–
	85		850

(*ii*) Actual results for June 1998 :

Material	*Quantity* Units	*Rate* ₹	*Amount* ₹
A	400	11	4,400
B	200	6	1,200
	600		5,600
Less (10%)	60		–
	540		5,600

Compute :

(1) Material price variance;

(2) Material mix variance;

(3) Material yield variance;

(4) Material usage variance; and

(5) Total material cost variance.

Or

(*b*) A small tool company uses job costing. The following cost data is obtained from the books of the previous year ended December 31.

Particulars	*Amount* ₹
Direct materials	90,000
Direct wages	75,000
Profit	60,900
Selling and distribution overheads	52,500
Administration overheads	42,000
Factory overheads	45,000

Required

(*i*) Prepare a job cost sheet indicating the prime cost, work cost, production cost, cost of sales, and sales.

(*ii*) In the current year, the company has received orders for a number of jobs. It is estimated that direct materials required will be ₹ 1,20,000 and direct labour cost ₹ 75,000. What should be the price for these jobs if the factory intends to earn the same rate of profit on sales, assuming that the selling and distribution overheads have gone up by 15%. The factory recovers factory overheads as a percentage of direct wages and administration and selling and distribution overhead as a percentage of works cost based on cost rates prevailing in the previous year. (8 + 8)

ANNA UNIVERSITY—CHENNAI

G8156

M.B.A. Degree Examination, January 2006.

First Semester

BA 1606 — Accounting for Management

(Regulation 2005)

Time : Three hours *Maximum : 100 marks*

PART A — (10 × 2 = 20 marks)

Answer ALL questions.

1. Define Financial Accounting.
2. What are GAAP ?
3. What is depreciation ?
4. What are intangible assets ?
5. What are ratios ?
6. Define the term 'fund'.
7. What is CVP Analysis ?
8. What is Process costing ?
9. What are incremental costs ?
10. What is master budget ?

PART B — (5 × 16 = 80 marks)

11. (*i*) The Managing Director of A Pvt. Ltd., asks for your assistance in arriving at a decision as to continue manufacture a component X; or to buy it from an outside supplier. The component X is used in the finished products of the company. The following data are supplied.

The annual requirement of component X is 10000 units. The lowest quotation from an outside supplier is ₹ 8.00 per unit.

The component X is manufactured in the machine shop. If the component X is bought out, certain machinery will be sold at its book value and the residual capacity of the machine shop will remain idle.

The total expenses of the Machine Shop for the year ending 31.3.2004 are as follows. During that year the Shop manufactured 10,000 units of X :

	₹
Material	1,35,000
Direct Labour	1,00,000
Indirect Labour	40,000
Power and Fuel	6,000
Repairs and Maintenance	11,000
Rates, Taxes and Insurance	16,000
Depreciation	20,000
Other Overhead Expenses	29,600

The following expenses of the machine shop apply to manufacturing of component X :

	₹
Materials	35,000
Direct Labour	56,000
Indirect Labour	12,000
Power and Fuel	600
Repairs and Maintenance	1,000

The sale of machinery used for the manufacture of component X would reduce Depreciation by ₹ 4,000 and insurance by ₹ 2,000.

If the component X is bought out, the following additional expenses would be incurred :

Freight ₹ 1.00 per unit

Inspection ₹ 10,000 per annum

You are required to prepare a report to the Managing Director showing the comparison of expenses of Machine Shop (1) When the component X is made and (2) when bought out. (10)

(*ii*) From the following average figures of previous quarters, prepare a manufacturing overhead budget for the quarter ending March 2005. The budgeted output during this quarter is 4,000 units.

Fixed overheads ₹ 20,000

Variable overheads ₹ 10,000 (Varying @ ₹ 5 per unit)

Semi Variable overheads ₹ 10,000 (40% fixed and 60% varying @ ₹ 3 per unit) (6)

12. (*a*) Explain the various accounting concepts and conventions which are used in the preparation of accounts.

Or

(*b*) The following is the Trial Balance of Miss Biba Ganguly on 31st December 2004.

	Debit ₹	*Credit* ₹
Capital		20,000
Plant and Machinery	25,000	
Office Furniture and Fittings	1,300	
Stock on 1-1-2004	24,000	
Motor Vehicle	6,000	
Sundry Debtors	22,850	
Cash in Hand	200	
Cash at Bank	3,250	
Wages	75,000	
Salaries	7,000	
Purchases	1,06,750	
Sales		2,40,000
Bills Receivable	3,600	

Bills Payable		2,800
Sundry Creditors		26,000
Returns Inwards	4,650	
Provision for Doubtful Debts		1,250
Drawings	3,500	
Returns Outwards		2,750
Rent	3,000	
Factory lighting	400	
Insurance	3,150	
General Expenses	500	
Bad debts	1,250	
Discount	3,250	1,850
	2,94,650	2,94,650

The following adjustments are to be effected :

(*i*) Stock on 31st December 2004 ₹ 26,000.

(*ii*) Furniture to be depreciated by 5%.

(*iii*) Factory lighting is due for 3 months, but not paid ₹ 150.

(*iv*) Write off further bad debts ₹ 350.

(*v*) The provision for doubtful debts to be increased to ₹ 1,500 and provision for discount on debts at 2% to be made.

(*vi*) During the year, machinery was purchased for ₹ 10,000 but it was debited to purchases account.

You are required to prepare the Trading and Profit and Loss Account and the Balance Sheet as on 31st December 2004.

13. (*a*) What is Inventory ? Describe the various methods of pricing issue of materials.

Or

(*b*) Vijay and Co. purchased a machine on 1st January 2000 for ₹ 9,250 and immediately spent ₹ 750 on its erection. On 1st July 2001, it purchased another machine for ₹ 2,500 and on 1st July 2002, it sold off the first machine purchased in 2000 for ₹ 7,000 and on the same date it purchased another machine for ₹ 6,250. On 1st July, 1998, the second machine purchased for ₹ 2,500 was also sold off for ₹ 500. Depreciation was provided on the machinery on written down value basis at 10%. Give machinery account for four years commencing from January 1,2000.

14. (*a*) What are Accounting Ratios ? Explain its uses and limitations.

Or

(*b*) From the following Balance Sheets of X Ltd., as on 31st December 2000 and 2001, you are required to prepare

(*i*) Schedule of changes in working capital and

(*ii*) Funds Flow Statement.

Liabilities	*2000* ₹	*2001* ₹	*Assets*	*2000* ₹	*2001* ₹
Share Capital	1,00,000	1,00,000	Goodwill	12,000	12,000
General Reserve	14,000	18,000	Building	40,000	36,000
P&L A/c	16,000	13,000	Plant	37,000	36,000
Sundry Creditors	8,000	5,400	Investments	10,000	11,000
Bills Payable	1,200	800	Stock	30,000	23,400
Prov. for Tax	16,000	18,000	Bills Receivable	2,000	3,200
Prov. for Doubtful Debts	400	600	Debtors	18,000	19,000
			Cash at Bank	6,600	15,200
	1,55,600	1,55,800		1,55,600	1,55,800

Additional informations :

(1) Depreciation charged on plant was ₹ 4,000 and on building ₹ 4,000.

(2) Provision for taxation of ₹ 19,000 was made during the year 2001

(3) Interim Dividend of ₹ 8,000 was paid during the year 2001.

15. (*a*) "A firm can avoid standard costing but, of course, at its own peril". Elucidate it and explain the advantages and limitations of standard costing.

Or

(*b*) The sales turnover and profit during two periods were as follows :

Period 1	Sales ₹ 20 lakhs	Profit ₹ 2 lakhs
Period 2	Sales ₹ 30 lakhs	Profit ₹ 4 lakhs

Calculate :

(*i*) P/V ratio

(*ii*) Sales required to earn a profit of ₹ 5 lakhs and

(*iii*) Profit when sales are ₹ 10 lakhs.

ANNA UNIVERSITY—CHENNAI

Y4044

M.B.A. Degree Examination, November/December 2006

First Semester

BA 105 — Accounting for Management

(Regulation 2002)

Time : Three hours *Maximum : 100 marks*

PART A — (10 × 2 = 20 marks)

Answer ALL questions.

1. What are the functions performed by the accounting system ?
2. What are the components of current assets ?
3. Define the nature of cash.
4. What do you understand by accounts receivable ?
5. What are the methods of financial statement analysis ?
6. What is a cash flow statement ?
7. What is meant by cost-volume-profit analysis ?
8. What do you understand by job order cost accounting ?
9. What are the essentials of a sound system of budgeting ?
10. Describe the managerial use of variance analysis.

PART B — (5 × 16 = 80 marks)

11. (*a*) Define and explain briefly the following :

(*i*) Flexible budget.

(*ii*) Sales budget.

(*iii*) Labour budget.

(*iv*) Overhead budget.

Or

(*b*) (*i*) Discuss the relevance of zero base budgeting for the present situation. (10)

(*ii*) What are the advantages of profit budgeting ? (6)

12. (*a*) The current credit terms of Kailash Ltd., are "net 30". It is considering to change them to "3/15, net 45" credit terms in order to increase its sales.

The proposed change is expected to have the following implications :

Current sales	₹ 50,00,000
Estimated increase in sales	10%
Estimated total sales that will avail discount offer	₹ 15,00,000
Estimated increased investment in receivables	4,00,000
Estimated increased costs :	
Bad debt losses	1% of increased sales

Production administrative and selling costs	74% of increased sales
Required return on investment	10%
Cash Discount	3% of sales

You are required to state whether it is desirable to introduce the changes in credit terms or not. Why ?

Or

(*b*) "Efficient cash management will aim at maximizing the availability of cash inflows by decentralizing collections and decelerating cash outflows by centralizing disbursements". Discuss.

13. (*a*) Explain the different techniques of analysis and interpretation of financial statements.

Or

(*b*) From the following balances, you are required to calculate cash from operations :

	31st December 1999 ₹	31st December 2000 ₹
Debtors	50,000	47,000
Bills Receivable	10,000	12,500
Creditors	20,000	25,000
Bills Payable	8,000	6,000
Expenses O/S	1,000	1,200
Expenses prepaid	800	700
Accrued Income	600	750
Income Received in Advance	300	250
Net Profit made	–	1,30,000

14. (*a*) You are given the following data for the year 2004 of the company :

Variable Cost	₹ 6,00,000
Fixed Cost	₹ 3,00,000
Net Profit	₹ 1,00,000
Sales	₹ 10,00,000

Find (*i*) P/V ratio (*ii*) B.E.P. (*iii*) Profit when sales amounted to ₹ 12,00,000 (*iv*) Sales required to earn a profit of ₹ 2,00,000.

Or

(*b*) The product of a manufacturing concern passes through two processes A and B and then to finished stock. It is ascertained that in each process normally 5% of the total weight is lost and 10% is scrap which from processes A and B realizes ₹ 80 per tonne and ₹ 200 per tonne respectively.

The following are the figures relating to both the processes :

	Process A	*Process B*
Materials in tonnes	1,000	70
Cost of material in rupees per tonne	125	200
Wages in rupees	28,000	10,000

Manufacturing expenses in rupees	8,000	5,250
Output in tonnes	830	780

Prepare Process Cost Accounts showing cost per tonne of each process. There was no stock or work-in-progress in any process.

15. (*a*) A department of company X attains sales of ₹ 6,00,000 at 80% of its normal capacity and its expenses are given below :

Administration Costs :	
Office Salaries	₹ 90,000
General Expenses	2% of sales
Depreciation	₹ 7,500
Rates and taxes	₹ 8,750
Selling Costs :	
Salaries	8% of sales
Travelling Expenses	2% of sales
Sales office	1% of sales
General Expenses	1% of sales
Distribution Costs :	
Wages	₹ 15,000
Rent	1% of sales
Other Expenses	4% of sales

Draw up flexible administration, selling and distribution cost budget, operating at 90%, 100% and 110% of normal capacity.

Or

(*b*) Is it necessary to separate variable-overhead and fixed-overhead variances ? What is the fundamental difference between these two kinds of variances ?

ANNA UNIVERSITY—CHENNAI

E8044

M.B.A. Degree Examination, November/December 2005

First Semester

BA 105 — Accounting for Management

Time : Three hours *Maximum : 100 marks*

PART A — (10 × 2 = 20 marks)

Answer ALL questions.

1. What are the functions of accounting ?
2. What do you mean by accounting cycle ?
3. What is meant by ratio analysis ?
4. What you mean by depreciation ?
5. How will you calculate cash from operation ?
6. Why do firms control Inventories ?
7. Differentiate between standard cost and estimated cost.
8. Explain the managerial use of variance analysis.
9. What do you mean by process costing ?
10. Explain the relationship of budgetary control and budgeting.

PART B — (5 × 16 = 80 marks)

11. (*i*) Explain the methods of financial statement analysis. (8)

(*ii*) The summary of Balance Sheet in respect of A Ltd., and B Ltd., is as under :

	A Ltd.	*B Ltd.*
	₹	₹
Buildings	1,00,000	4,50,000
Machinery	3,00,000	7,50,000
Share Capital	4,50,000	14,50,000
Retained Earnings	50,000	33,000
Debtors	1,15,000	1,60,000
Stocks	60,000	2,17,000
Cash	10,000	5,000
Prepaid Expenses	5,000	3,000
Creditors	91,000	1,00,000
Liability for Expenses	9,000	17,000
Preliminary expenses	10,000	15,000

Prepare common-size Balance Sheets. (8)

12. (*a*) (*i*) Discuss the objectives and advantages of cash flow statement. (8)

(*ii*) From the following Balance Sheets as on 31st December, you are required to prepare a cash flow statement : (8)

	2003 ₹	2004 ₹		2003 ₹	2004 ₹
Share Capital	1,00,000	1,50,000	Fixed Assets	1,00,000	1,50,000
Profit and Loss a/c	50,000	80,000	Goodwill	50,000	40,000
General Reserve	30,000	40,000	Inventories	50,000	80,000
16% Bonds	50,000	60,000	Debtors	50,000	80,000
Sundry Creditors	30,000	40,000	Bills Receivable	10,000	20,000
Expenses o/s	10,000	15,000	Bank	10,000	15,000
	2,70,000	3,85,000		2,70,000	3,85,000

(*b*) (*i*) Explain the main components of current assets in a manufacturing concern. (8)

(*ii*) Kailash Ltd., gives the following Balance Sheet. You are required to compute the following ratios :

(1) Liquid ratio

(2) Debt-equity ratio

(3) Solvency ratio

(4) Stock-working capital ratio. (8)

Balance Sheet as on 31st Dec.

	₹		₹
Equity Share Capital	15,00,000	Fixed Assets	14,00,000
Reserves and Surplus	1,00,000	Stock	5,00,000
6% Debentures	3,00,000	Debtors	2,00,000
Overdraft	1,00,000	Cash	1,00,000
Creditors	2,00,000		
	22,00,000		22,00,000

13. (*a*) (*i*) Discuss the importance of the following in relation to marginal costing :

(1) Break-even Points

(2) Margin of Safety

(3) Contribution

(4) P/V Ratio. (8)

(*ii*) The particulars of two plants producing an identical product with the same selling price are as under :

	Plant A	*Plant B*
Capacity utilization	70%	60%
	(₹ in Lakhs)	*(₹ in Lakhs)*
Sales	150	90
Variable cost	105	75
Fixed cost	30	20

It has been decided to merge plant B with plant A. The additional fixed expenses involved in the merger amount to ₹ 2 lakhs.

(1) Find the break-even point of plant A and plant B before merger and the break-even point of the merged plant.

(2) Find the capacity utilization of the integrated plant required to earn a profit of ₹ 18 lakhs. (8)

Or

(*b*) (*i*) What do you mean by the term Batch Costing ? How is Economic Batch quantity determined ? (8)

(*ii*) Compute the economic batch quantity for a company using batch costing with the following information :

Annual demand for the parts	4,000 units
Setting up cost	₹ 100
Cost of manufacture : one unit	₹ 200
Rate of interest per annum	10%

(8)

14. (*a*) (*i*) Explain the difference between a forecast and a budget. (8)

(*ii*) Prepare a flexible budget for overheads on the basis of the following data. Ascertained the overhead rates at 50%, 60% and 70% capacity :

	At 60% capacity (₹)
Variable Overheads:	
Indirect material	6,000
Indirect labour	18,000
Semi-variable overheads :	
Electricity (40% fixed 60% variable)	30,000
Repairs (80% fixed 20% variable)	3,000
Fixed overheads :	
Depreciation	16,500
Insurance	4,500
Salaries	15,000
Total overheads	93,000
Estimated direct labour hours	1,86,000

(8)

Or

(*b*) (*i*) What do you understand by zero base budgeting ? How is it different from traditional budgeting ?

(*ii*) From the following particulars, prepare a production budget of a company for the year ended June 30, 2004 : (8)

Product	*Sales (units)*	*Estimated stock (units)*	
	(as per sales budgets)	*1st July 2003*	*30th June 2004*
A	1,50,000	14,000	15,000
B	1,00,000	5,000	14,500
C	70,000	8,000	8,000

15. (*a*) (*i*) Explain the importance and advantage of direct costing. (8)

(*ii*) Calculate the material mix variance from the following : (8)

Material	*Standard*	*Actual*
A	90 units at ₹ 12 each	100 units at ₹ 12 each
B	60 units at ₹ 15 each	50 units at ₹ 16 each

Or

(*b*) (*i*) Discuss the importance of combination costing system : (8)

(*ii*) The labour budget of a company for a week is as follows :

20 skilled men @ 50 paise per hour for 40 hours	= 400
40 unskilled men @ 30 paise per hour for 40 hours	= 480
	880

The actual labour force was used as follows :

30 skilled labour men @ 50 paise per hour for 40 hours	= 600
30 unskilled men @ 35 paise per hour for 40 hours	= 420
	1,020

Analyse labour variance. (8)

ANNA UNIVERSITY—CHENNAI

Z3505

M.C.A. Degree Examination, January 2007

First Semester

MC 1605 — Accounting and Financial Management

(Regulation 2005)

Time : Three hours *Maximum : 100 marks*

PART A — (10 × 2 = 20 marks)

Answer ALL questions.

1. Define Accounting.
2. What is funds flow statement ?
3. What are the elements of cost ?
4. What is breakeven point ?
5. Define zero base budgeting.
6. What is master budget ?
7. What are the goals of financial management ?
8. What is weighted average cost of capital.
9. What is optimum capital structure ?
10. What are the two concepts of working capital ?

PART B — (5 × 16 = 80 marks)

11. (*a*) What are accounting ratios ? Explain its uses and limitations.

Or

(*b*) The following is the Trial Balance of Shree Ganesh on 30th June 2006.

Name of Account	*Debit (₹)*	*Credit (₹)*
Capital		1,86,000
Drawings	15,735	
Stock (1.7.2005)	17,280	
Sundry Creditors		18,900
Sundry Debtors	43,500	
Machinery	60,000	
Patents	22,500	
Freehold Land	30,000	
Buildings	96,000	
Sales		2,96,340
Purchases	1,22,025	
Sales Returns	2,040	
Purchases Returns		1,500
Cash at Bank	7,890	

Cash in Hand	1,620	
Insurance	1,800	
General Expenses	9,000	
Salaries	45,000	
Wages	25,440	
Factory Fuel and Power	14,190	
Carriage on Purchases	6,120	
Carriage on Sales	9,600	
Rent		27,000
	5,29,740	5,29,740

The following adjustments are to be effected :

(*i*) Stock on 30th June 2006 ₹ 20,400.

(*ii*) 5% on Sundry Debtors is to be written off as bad.

(*iii*) Salaries for the month of June 2006 amounting to ₹ 4,500 were unpaid.

(*iv*) Insurance include a premium of ₹ 510 on a policy expiring on December 31st 2006.

(*v*) Rent ₹ 3,000 is accrued but not received.

(*vi*) Depreciate Machinery @ 10% and Patents @ 20%.

You are required to prepare Trading and Profit and Loss Account and the Balance Sheet as on 30th June 2006.

12. (*a*) "A firm can avoid standard costing but, of course, at its own peril". Elucidate it and explain the advantages and limitations of standard costing.

Or

(*b*) The sales turnover and profit during two periods were as follows :

Period 1	Sales ₹ 20 lakhs	Profit ₹ 2 lakhs
Period 2	Sales ₹ 30 lakhs	Profit ₹ 4 lakhs

Calculate :

(*i*) P/V Ratio

(*ii*) Sales required to earn a profit of ₹ 5 lakhs; and

(*iii*) Profit when sales are ₹ 10 lakhs. Also show the verification for your answer.

13. (*a*) Define Budgetary Control. Explain its uses and limitations.

Or

(*b*) The expenses for budgeted production of 10,000 units in a factory are furnished below :

	Per Unit (₹)
Materials	70
Labour	25
Variable Overhead	20
Fixed Overhead (₹ 1,00,000)	10
Variable Expenses (Direct)	5
Selling Expenses (10% Fixed)	13

Distribution Expenses (20% Fixed)	7
Administration Expenses (₹ 50,000)	5
Total cost per unit (to make and sell)	155

Prepare a budget for production of

(*i*) 8,000 units

(*ii*) 6,000 units and

(*iii*) Indicate cost per unit at both the levels.

Assume that administration expenses are fixed for all levels of production.

14. (*a*) What are the basic financial decisions ? How do they involve risk-return trade off ?

Or

(*b*) A limited company is considering investing in a project requiring a capital outlay of ₹ 2,00,000. Forecast for annual income after depreciation but before tax is as follows :

Year	₹
1	1,00,000
2	1,00,000
3	80,000
4	80,000
5	40,000

Depreciation may be taken as 20% on original cost and taxation at 50% of net income.

You are required to evaluate the project according to each of the following methods :

(*i*) Payback method

(*ii*) Rate of return on original investment method

(*iii*) NPV method taking cost of capital as 10%

(*iv*) NPV index method.

Year :	1	2	3	4	5
PV factor @ 10%	.909	.826	.751	.683	.621

15. (*a*) Explain the various factors which affect the capital structure of a firm.

Or

(*b*) Explain the various factors influencing the working capital requirements of a firm.

ANNA UNIVERSITY—CHENNAI

K3505

M.C.A. Degree Examination, January 2008

First Semester

MC 1605 — Accounting and Financial Management

(Regulation 2005)

Time : Three hours *Maximum : 100 marks*

PART A — (10 × 2 = 20 marks)

Answer ALL questions.

1. Define "Going concern convention" in accounting.

2. Define the term "Funds".

3. What is meant by "Margin of Safety" ?

4. Calculate Break-even point from the following particulars :

Fixed expenses	₹ 1,50,000
Variable cost per unit	₹ 10
Selling price per unit	₹ 15

5. What is a budget manual ?

6. Define "Zero Base Budget".

7. What is meant by "Risk" ?

8. What do you mean by Financial Leverage ?

9. How net working capital is different from working capital ?

10. What is the need for a dividend ?

PART B — (5 × 16 = 80 marks)

11. (*a*) From the following information, prepare a Balance Sheet. Show the workings.

(*i*) Working capital	₹ 75,000
(*ii*) Reserves and surplus	₹ 1,00,000
(*iii*) Bank overdraft	₹ 60,000
(*iv*) Current ratio	1.75
(*v*) Liquid ratio	1.15
(*vi*) Fixed assets to proprietor's fund	0.75
(*vii*) Long-term liabilities	Nil

Or

(*b*) What is Ratio Analysis ? List the major categories of ratio analysis and discuss any four ratios with an illustration. (2 + 4 + 10)

12. (*a*) "Marginal costing is a valuable aid for managerial decisions" - Discuss.

Or

(*b*)

Material	*Standard*			*Actual*		
	Qty kg.	*Price* ₹	*Total* ₹	*Qty* kg.	*Price* ₹	*Total* ₹
A	500	6.00	3,000	400	6.00	2,400
B	400	3.75	1.500	500	3.60	1,800
C	300	3.00	900	400	2.80	1,120
	1,200			1,300		
Less 10% Normal loss	120			220		
	1,080		5,400	1,080		5,320

Calculate material variances.

13. (*a*) Briefly discuss the steps in the installation of a system of budgetary control and explain the main functions of a budget controller ?

Or

(*b*) Draw out cash budget for Jan. to Mar. from the following information :

(*i*) Cash and Bank balances on 1.1.1997 ₹ 2,00,000

(*ii*) Actual and budgeted sales

Months	₹	
Sep.	6,00,000	(Actual)
Oct.	6,50,000	"
Nov.	7,00,000	"
Dec.	7,50,000	"
Jan.	8,00,000	(Budgeted)
Feb.	8,20,000	"
Mar.	8,90,000	"

(*iii*) Purchases—Actual and budgeted figures are :

	₹	
Sep.	3,60,000	(Actual)
Oct.	4,00,000	"
Nov.	4,80,000	"
Dec.	4,50,000	"
Jan.	4,80,000	(Budgeted)
Feb.	4,00,000	"
Mar.	5,00,000	"

(*iv*) Wages and expenses—Actual and budgeted

Months	*Wages* ₹	*Expenses* ₹
Nov. (Actual)	1,50,000	50,000
Dec. (Actual)	1,50,000	60,000
Jan. (Budgeted)	1,80,000	60,000
Feb. (Budgeted)	1,80,000	80,000
Mar. (Budgeted)	2,00,000	80,000

(*v*) Special items

(1) Advance payment of income tax in March 1997 ₹ 50,000

(2) Plant acquired and price paid in Jan. 1997 ₹ 1,00,000

(*vi*) 10% purchases and sales are on cash basis

(*vii*) Time

Credit sales	2 months
Credit purchase	1 month
Wages	½ month
Expenses	¼ month

14. (*a*) Explain the various techniques that are adopted to infuse the element of risk in capital budgeting.

Or

(*b*) M/S XYZ Ltd., decided to install a machine with a life of 5 years and no salvage value. The capital outlay of the firm was expected to be ₹ 3,10,500. Earnings before depreciation but after tax were expected to be :

1st year ₹ 70,000, 2nd year ₹ 1,00,000

3rd year ₹ 1,30,000 4th year ₹ 90,000 and

5th year ₹ 60,000.

You are required to work out Internal rate of return of the project (IRR).

15. (*a*) Discuss the importance (advantages) of working capital for a manufacturing concern.

Or

(*b*) Draw out and explain the various criterias for determining "pattern of capital structure" and also explain the factors influencing the pattern of capital structure.

ANNA UNIVERSITY—CHENNAI

Q5505

M.C.A. Degree Examination, May/June 2006

First Semester

MC 1605 — Accounting and Financial Management

(Regulation 2005)

Time : Three hours *Maximum : 100 marks*

PART A — (10 × 2 = 20 marks)

Answer ALL questions.

1. Define Accounting.
2. Mention the various accounting concepts and conventions.
3. What are the various elements of cost ?
4. Explain — (*a*) Contribution and (*b*) P/V ratio.
5. Define Standard costing.
6. What is ZBB ?
7. What is time value of money ?
8. Explain :

   (*a*) Specific cost of capital and

   (*b*) Weighted average cost of capital.
9. Define capital structure.
10. What are the various types of dividend policies ?

PART B — (5 × 16 = 80 marks)

11. The following Trial Balance is extracted from the books of Mr. Pillai on 31.03.2002 :

Particulars	*Debit* ₹	*Credit* ₹
Furniture and Fittings	640	—
Motor Vehicles	6,250	—
Buildings	7,500	—
Capital	—	12,500
Bad Debts	125	—
Provision for Doubtful Debts	—	200
Sundry Debtors and Creditors	3,800	2,500
Stock as on 1.4.2002	3,460	—
Purchases and Sales	5,475	15,450
Bank Overdraft	—	2,850
Sales and Purchase Returns	200	125
Advertising	450	—
Interest on Bank Overdraft	118	—

Commission	—	375
Cash	650	—
Taxes and Insurance Preminum	782	—
General Expenses	1,250	—
Salaries	3,300	—
Total	34,000	34,000

Adjustments :

(*i*) Stock on hand on 31.3.2002 ₹ 3,250.

(*ii*) Depreciate Buildings @ 5% p.a. Furniture @ 10% p.a. Motor Vehicles @ 20% p.a.

(*iii*) ₹ 85 is due for interest on bank overdraft.

(*iv*) Salaries ₹ 300 and taxes ₹ 200 are outstanding.

(*v*) Insurance premium amounting to ₹ 100 is prepaid.

(*vi*) One-third of the commission received is in respect of work to be done next year.

(*vii*) Write off a further sum of ₹ 100 as bad debts from debtors and create provision for doubtful debts @ 5% on debtors.

Prepare a trading and profit and loss account and balance sheet of the company.

12. (*a*) Explain the concept of CVP analysis. Discuss its managerial applications.

Or

(*b*) What is standard costing ? How does it differ from budgetary control ?

13. (*a*) Explain the concept of budgeting and budgetary control. What are the essentials of an effective budgetary control system ?

Or

(*b*) Prepare a cash budget for the first four months from the following estimated revenues and expenses.

Month	*Sales* ₹	*Purchases* ₹	*Labour (Wages)* ₹	*Overheads-Administrative* ₹	*Overheads-Distribution* ₹
April	60,000	60,000	12,000	2,000	1,200
May	66,000	42,000	14,000	2,200	1,400
June	72,000	40,000	16,000	2,200	1,400
July	78,000	36,000	18,000	2,400	1,600
August	84,000	34,000	20,000	2,600	1,600

Additional Informations :

(*i*) Cash balance on 1st April was ₹ 35,000.

(*ii*) 50% of sales are on credit basis which are realized in the subsequent month.

(*iii*) Suppliers are paid in the month following the month of supply.

(*iv*) Delay in payment of wages and overheads is 30 days.

(iii) Suppliers are paid in the month following the month of supply.
(iv) Delay in payment of wages and overheads is 30 days.
(v) Dividends on investments amounting ₹ 10,000 may be received in April and July.
(vi) The company plans to purchase a machine for ₹ 60,000 for which it has to pay the consideration in three equal instalments in the month of April, June and July.

14. (a) ABC Co., is considering two machines, only one of which can be purchased. The available data on the two machines is given below :

	Machine A	*Machine B*
Cost (₹)	48,000	85,000
Life of the Machine	5 years	7 years

Annual savings (after taxation)

Years	*Machine A (₹)*	*Machine B (₹)*
1	8,000	18,000
2	10,000	25,000
3	15,000	30,000
4	22,000	40,000
5	30,000	20,000

Neither machine will have any salvage value. The cost of capital is 10%. Compute the profitability index for each machine. Based on the profitability index, which machine should be purchased ?

Or

(b) A firm's after tax cost of capital of specific sources and its capital structure are as follows :

Sources of capital	*After tax cost of capital*	*Book value (₹)*
Debt capital	8%	3,00,000
Equity capital	17%	5,00,000
Preference capital	14%	2,00,000
Total		10,00,000

Calculate the weighted average cost of capital of the firm using book value weights.

15. (a) Define capital structure. What are the elements of a capital structure ? What do you mean by optimum capital structure ? What are the features of an appropriate capital structure ?

Or

(b) Explain the concepts of working capital. What are the determinants of working capital needs of a firm ?

BHARATHIAR UNIVERSITY—COIMBATORE

[05 MCA 15]

(For the candidates admitted from 2005 onwards)

M.C.A. Degree Examination, November 2006

First Semester

Accounting and Financial Management

Time : Three hours *Maximum : 100 marks*

SECTION A — (10 × 1 = 10 marks)

Answer ALL questions.

Choose the correct answer :

1. Cash drawn from bank for personal purpose is debited to
   (*a*) Cash A/c (*b*) Drawings A/c
   (*c*) Office Expenses A/c (*d*) None
2. Salary A/c in Trial Balance is to be debited to
   (*a*) Trading A/c (*b*) Profit and Loss A/c
   (*c*) Salary A/c (*d*) None
3. Quick assets exclude
   (*a*) Cash and Bank (*b*) Inventory
   (*c*) Debtors (*d*) Bills Receivable
4. Return on Investment Ratio is a
   (*a*) Current ratio (*b*) Profitability ratio
   (*b*) Activity ratio (*d*) None
5. The term 'fund' as used in Funds Flow Statement is
   (*a*) Cash (*b*) Current assets
   (*c*) Current liabilities (*d*) Current assets-current liabilities
6. Which is the following an application of fund ?
   (*a*) Purchase of asset (*b*) Sale of asset
   (*c*) Funds from operation (*d*) Dividends received
7. The first step in preparing a budget is
   (*a*) Cost forecast (*b*) Production forecast
   (*c*) Sales forecast (*d*) Working capital forecast
8. The difference between fixed expenses and variable expenses assumed significance i
   (*a*) Cash budget (*b*) Sales budget
   (*c*) Flexible budget (*d*) Production budget
9. Total of all indirect expenses
   (*a*) Total cost (*b*) Prime cost
   (*c*) Overheads (*d*) Cost of production
10. At BEP
   (*a*) Sales = Total cost (*b*) Sales > Total cost
   (*c*) Sales < Total cost (*d*) None

SECTION B — (5 × 3 = 15 marks)

Answer ALL questions.

11. (*a*) Bring out the rules for Double Entry Book Keeping.

Or

(*b*) Rahim A/c was settled by issuing a cheque for ₹ 12,950 (Total amount due ₹ 13,200). Pass journal entry.

12. (*a*) What is current ratio ? How it is calculated ?

Or

(*b*) Calculate inventory turnover ratio :

Opening stock	₹ 20,000
Closing stock	₹ 30,000
Purchases	₹1,60,000

13. (*a*) How funds from operations is calculated ?

Or

(*b*) Opening balance of machine ₹ 1,90,000

Depreciation provided	₹ 25,000
Closing balance	₹ 2,00,000

Find the machinery purchase.

14. (*a*) Define Budgetary Control.

Or

(*b*) Prepare production budget for June, 2006.

Estimated sales 10,000 units

Desired closing stock 1,500 units

Opening stock 500 units.

15. (*a*) Give the elements of cost with examples.

Or

(*b*) Selling price ₹ 10/unit

Variable cost ₹ 5/unit

Fixed expenses ₹ 25,000

Find out B.E.P.

SECTION C — (5 × 10 = 50 marks)

Answer ALL questions.

16. (*a*) Define accounting. Discuss the advantages of accounting.

Or

(*b*) From the following Trial Balance of Mr. Balu prepare the final accounts for the year ended 31st December, 2005.

	₹		₹
Opening Stock	22,500	Capital	42,650
Purchases	1,12,500	Sales	2,10,000
Machinery	37,500	Creditors	7,500
Trade Expenses	5,000	Bills Payable	1,100

Carriage Inwards	1,250	
Factory Rent	1,500	
Debtors	30,000	
Office Rent	1,500	
Printing and Stationery	300	
General Expenses	1,400	
Advertising	7,500	
Bill Receivable	1,500	
Drawings	3,000	
Salary	9,000	
Manufacturing expenses	10,500	
Furniture	3,750	
Cash in Hand	6,000	
Cash at Bank	6,250	
Insurance	300	
	2,61,250	2,61,250

Adjustments :

(*i*) Closing Stock ₹ 17,000

(*ii*) Provide depreciation : Machinery and Furniture @ 10%

(*iii*) Insurance pre-paid ₹ 100.

17. (*a*) Give the advantages and limitations of ratios as a tool of Financial Statement Analysis.

Or

(*b*) Calculate Debtors and Closing Stock from the following data :

Debtors velocity	3 months
Stock velocity	1.5 times
Gross profit ratio	25%
Gross profit	₹ 2,00,000
Bills receivable	₹ 10,000

Closing stock is 20% more than the opening stock.

18. (*a*) Explain the concept of funds flow and funds from operations.

Or

(*b*) From the following Balance Sheet of X Ltd.

Prepare fund flow statement :

	2004 ₹	*2005* ₹		*2004* ₹	*2005* ₹
Share Capital	50,000	80,000	Fixed Assets	40,000	43,000
Reserves	20,000	25,000	Stock	25,000	45,000
P and L A/c	10,000	15,000	Debtors	10,000	20,000
Creditors	5,000	8,000	Cash and Bank	10,000	20,000
	85,000	1,28,000		85,000	1,28,000

(*i*) Depreciation on fixed assets ₹ 15,000

(*ii*) Dividend paid ₹ 5,000

Or

19. (*a*) Discuss the objects of budgetary control.

(*b*) Draw a flexible budget for overhead expenses on the basis of the following data for 80, 90 and 100% capacities :

Expenses	*at 80%* ₹
Variable :	
Indirect labour	1,20,000
Stores and spaces	40,000
Semi-variable :	
Power (30% fixed)	2,00,000
Repairs and maintenance (60% fixed)	20,000
Fixed :	
Depreciation	1,10,000
Insurance	30,000
Salaries	1,00,000
Total	6,20,000

20. (*a*) Explain the classification of costs.

Or

(*b*) From the following data calculate

(*i*) P/V ratio

(*ii*) Profit when sales are ₹ 2,40,000.

(*iii*) New B.E.P. if selling price is reduced by 20%.

Fixed expenses ₹ 80,000.

Break even sales ₹ 2,00,000.

❑❑❑

APPENDIX

Appendix 1

TABLE I

Present Value cf ₹ 1

Years	*5%*	*6%*	*8%*	*10%*	*12%*	*14%*	*15%*	*16%*	*18%*	*20%*	*22%*	*24%*	*25%*	*28%*	*30%*
1	0.952	0.943	0.926	0.909	0.893	0.877	0.870	0.862	0.847	0.833	0.820	0.806	0.800	0.781	0.769
2	0.907	0.890	0.857	0.826	0.797	0.769	0.756	0.743	0.718	0.694	0.672	0.650	0.640	0.610	0.592
3	0.864	0.840	0.794	0.751	0.712	0.675	0.658	0.641	0.609	0.579	0.551	0.524	0.512	0.477	0.455
4	0.823	0.792	0.735	0.683	0.636	0.592	0.572	0.552	0.516	0.482	0.451	0.423	0.410	0.373	0.350
5	0.784	0.747	0.681	0.621	0.567	0.519	0.497	0.476	0.437	0.402	0.370	0.341	0.328	0.291	0.269
6	0.746	0.705	0.630	0.564	0.507	0.456	0.432	0.410	0.370	0.335	0.303	0.275	0.262	0.227	0.207
7	0.711	0.665	0.583	0.513	0.452	0.400	0.376	0.354	0.314	0.279	0.249	0.222	0.210	0.178	0.159
8	0.647	0.627	0.570	0.467	0.404	0.351	0.327	0.305	0.266	0.233	0.204	0.179	0.168	0.139	0.123
9	0.645	0.592	0.500	0.424	0.361	0.308	0.284	0.263	0.225	0.193	0.167	0.144	0.134	0.108	0.094
10	0.614	0.558	0.463	0.386	0.322	0.270	0.247	0.227	0.191	0.162	0.137	0.116	0.107	0.085	0.073
11	0.585	0.527	0.429	0.350	0.287	0.237	0.215	0.195	0.162	0.135	0.112	0.094	0.087	0.066	0.056
12	0.557	0.497	0.397	0.319	0.257	0.208	0.187	0.168	0.137	0.112	0.092	0.076	0.069	0.052	0.043
13	0.530	0.469	0.368	0.290	0.229	0.182	0.163	0.145	0.116	0.093	0.075	0.061	0.055	0.040	0.033
14	0.505	0.442	0.340	0.263	0.205	0.160	0.141	0.125	0.099	0.078	0.062	0.049	0.044	0.032	0.025
15	0.481	0.417	0.315	0.239	0.183	0.140	0.123	0.108	0.084	0.065	0.051	0.040	0.035	0.025	0.020
16	0.458	0.394	0.292	0.218	0.163	0.123	0.107	0.093	0.071	0.054	0.042	0.032	0.028	0.019	0.015
17	0.436	0.371	0.270	0.198	0.147	0.108	0.093	0.080	0.060	0.045	0.034	0.026	0.023	0.015	0.012
18	0.416	0.350	0.250	0.180	0.130	0.095	0.081	0.069	0.051	0.038	0.028	0.021	0.018	0.012	0.009
19	0.396	0.331	0.232	0.164	0.116	0.083	0.070	0.060	0.043	0.031	0.023	0.017	0.014	0.009	0.007
20	0.377	0.312	0.215	0.149	0.104	0.073	0.061	0.051	0.037	0.026	0.019	0.014	0.012	0.007	0.005

Appendix 2

TABLE II

Present Value of ₹ 1 Received Annually for N Years

Years	*5%*	*6%*	*8%*	*10%*	*12%*	*14%*	*15%*	*16%*	*18%*	*20%*	*22%*	*24%*	*25%*	*28%*	*30%*
1	0.952	0.943	0.926	0.909	0.893	0.877	0.870	0.862	0.847	0.833	0.820	0.806	0.800	0.781	0.769
2	1.859	1.883	1.783	1.736	1.690	1.647	1.626	1.605	1.566	1.528	1.492	1.457	1.440	1.392	1.361
3	2.773	2.676	2.577	2.847	2.402	2.322	2.283	2.246	2.174	2.016	2.042	1.981	1.952	1.868	1.816
4	3.546	3.465	3.312	3.170	3.037	2.914	2.855	2.798	2.690	2.589	2.494	2.404	2.362	2.241	2.166
5	4.330	4.212	3.993	3.791	3.605	3.433	3.352	3.274	3.127	2.991	2.864	2.745	2.689	2.532	2.346
6	5.076	4.917	4.623	4.335	4.111	3.889	3.784	3.685	3.498	3.326	3.167	3.020	2.951	2.759	2.643
7	5.786	5.582	5.206	4.868	4.564	4.288	4.160	4.039	3.812	3.605	3.416	3.242	3.161	2.937	2.802
8	6.463	6.210	5.747	5.335	4.968	4.639	4.487	4.344	4.078	3.837	3.619	3.421	3.329	3.076	2.925
9	7.109	6.802	6.247	5.759	5.328	4.946	4.772	4.607	4.303	4.031	3.786	3.566	3.463	3.184	3.019
10	7.722	7.360	6.710	6.145	5.650	5.216	5.019	4.833	4.494	4.192	3.923	3.682	3.571	3.269	3.092
11	8.306	7.787	7.139	6.495	5.937	5.453	5.234	5.029	4.656	4.327	4.035	3.776	3.656	3.335	3.147
12	8.863	8.384	7.536	6.814	6.194	5.660	5.421	5.197	4.793	4.439	4.127	3.851	3.725	3.387	3.190
13	9.394	8.853	7.904	7.103	6.424	5.842	5.583	4.342	4.910	4.533	4.203	3.912	3.780	3.427	3.223
14	9.899	9.295	8.244	7.367	6.628	6.002	5.724	5.468	5.008	4.611	4.265	3.926	3.824	3.459	3.249
15	10.380	9.712	8.559	7.606	6.811	6.142	5.847	5.575	5.092	4.675	4.315	4.001	3.859	3.483	3.268
16	10.383	10.106	8.851	7.824	6.974	6.265	5.954	5.669	5.162	4.730	4.357	4.033	3.887	3.503	3.283
17	11.274	10.477	9.122	8.022	7.120	6.373	6.047	5.749	5.222	4.775	4.391	4.059	3.910	3.518	3.295
18	11.690	10.828	9.372	8.201	7.250	6.467	6.128	5.818	5.273	4.812	4.419	4.080	3.928	3.529	3.304
19	12.082	11.158	9.614	8.365	7.366	6.550	6.188	5.877	5.316	4.844	4.442	4.097	3.942	3.539	3.311
20	12.462	11.470	9.818	8.514	7.469	6.623	6.259	5.929	5.355	4.870	4.460	4.110	3.954	3.546	3.316

Appendix 3

TABLE III : Compound value of ₹ 1

Period	1%	2%	3%	4%	5%	6%	7%	8%	9%	10%	12%	14%	15%
1	1.010	1.020	1.030	1.040	1.050	1.060	1.070	1.080	1.090	1.100	1.120	1.140	1.150
2	1.020	1.040	1.062	1.082	1.102	1.124	1.145	1.166	1.188	1.210	1.254	1.300	1.322
3	1.030	1.061	1.093	1.125	1.158	1.121	1.225	1.263	1.295	1.331	1.404	1.482	1.521
4	1.041	1.082	1.126	1.170	1.216	1.262	1.311	1.360	1.412	1.464	1.574	1.689	1.749
5	1.051	1.104	1.159	1.217	1.276	1.338	1.403	1.469	1.539	1.611	1.762	1.925	2.011
6	1.062	1.126	1.194	1.265	1.340	1.419	1.501	1.587	1.677	1.772	1.974	2.195	2.313
7	1.072	1.149	1.230	1.316	1.407	1.504	1.606	1.714	1.828	1.949	2.211	2.502	2.660
8	1.183	1.172	1.267	1.369	1.477	1.594	1.718	1.851	1.993	2.144	2.476	2.853	3.518
9	1.094	1.125	1.305	1.423	1.551	1.689	1.838	1.999	2.172	2.358	2.773	3.252	3.518
10	1.105	1.219	1.334	1.480	1.629	1.791	1.967	2.159	2.367	2.594	3.106	3.707	4.046
11	1.116	1.243	1.384	1.539	1.710	1.898	2.105	2.332	2.580	2.853	3.479	4.226	4.652
12	1.127	1.268	1.426	1.601	1.796	2.012	2.252	2.518	2.813	3.138	3.896	4.818	5.350
13	1.138	1.294	1.469	1.665	1.886	2.133	2.410	2.720	3.066	3.452	4.363	5.492	6.153
14	1.149	1.319	1.513	1.732	1.980	2.261	2.579	2.937	3.342	3.797	4.887	6.261	7.076
15	1.161	1.346	1.558	1.801	2.079	2.397	2.759	3.172	3.642	4.177	5.474	7.138	8.137
16	1.173	1.373	1.605	1.873	2.183	2.540	2.952	3.426	3.970	4.595	6.130	8.137	9.358
17	1.184	1.400	1.653	1.948	2.292	2.693	3.159	3.700	4.328	5.054	6.866	9.276	10.761
18	1.196	1.428	1.702	2.026	2.407	2.854	3.380	3.896	4.717	5.560	7.690	10.575	12.375
19	1.208	1.457	1.754	2.107	2.527	3.026	3.617	4.316	5.142	6.116	6.613	12.056	14.232
20	1.220	1.486	1.806	2.191	2.653	3.207	3.870	4.661	5.604	6.728	9.646	13.743	16.637
25	1.282	1.641	2.094	2.666	3.386	4.292	5.247	6.848	8.623	10.835	17.000	26.426	32.919
30	1.348	1.811	2.427	3.243	4.322	5.743	7.612	10.063	13.268	17.449	29.960	50.950	66.212

Appendix 4

TABLE IV : The Compound value of an Annuity of ₹ 1

Period	*1%*	*2%*	*3%*	*4%*	*5%*	*6%*	*7%*	*8%*	*9%*	*10%*
1	1.000	1.000	1.000	1.000	1.000	1.000	1.000	1.000	1.000	1.000
2	2.010	2.020	2.030	2.040	2.050	2.060	2.070	2.080	2.090	2.100
3	3.030	3.060	3.091	3.122	3.152	3.184	3.215	3.246	3.278	3.310
4	4.060	4.122	4.184	4.246	4.310	4.375	4.440	4.506	4.573	4.641
5	5.101	5.204	5.309	5.416	5.526	5.637	5.751	5.867	5.985	6.105
6	6.152	6.308	6.468	6.633	6.802	6.975	7.153	7.336	7.523	7.716
7	7.214	7.434	7.662	7.898	8.142	8.394	8.654	8.923	9.200	9.487
8	8.286	8.583	8.892	9.214	9.549	9.897	10.260	10.637	11.028	11.436
9	9.368	9.755	10.159	10.583	11.027	11.491	11.978	12.488	13.021	13.579
10	10.462	10.950	11.464	12.006	12.578	13.181	13.816	14.487	15.193	15.937
11	11.567	12.169	12.808	13.486	14.207	14.972	15.784	16.645	17.560	18.531
12	12.682	13.412	14.192	15.026	15.917	16.870	17.888	18.977	20.141	21.384
13	13.809	14.680	15.618	16.627	17.713	18.882	20.141	21.495	22.953	24.523
14	14.947	15.974	17.086	18.292	19.598	21.015	22.550	24.215	26.019	27.975
15	16.097	17.293	18.599	20.023	21.578	23.276	25.129	27.152	29.361	31.772
16	17.258	18.639	20.157	21.824	23.657	25.672	27.888	30.324	33.003	35.949
17	18.430	20.012	21.761	23.697	25.840	28.213	30.840	33.750	36.973	40.544
18	19.614	21.412	23.414	25.645	28.132	30.905	33.999	37.540	41.301	45.599
19	20.811	22.840	25.117	27.671	30.539	33.760	37.379	41.446	46.018	51.158
20	22.019	24.267	26.870	29.778	33.066	36.785	40.995	45.762	51.169	57.274
21	23.239	25.783	28.676	31.969	35.719	39.992	44.865	50.422	56.764	64.002
22	24.471	27.299	30.536	34.248	38.505	43.392	49.005	55.456	62.872	71.402
23	25.716	28.845	32.452	36.618	41.430	46.995	53.435	60.893	69.531	79.542
24	26.973	30.421	34.426	39.082	44.501	50.815	58.176	66.764	76.789	88.496
25	28.243	32.030	36.459	41.645	47.726	54.864	63.248	73.105	84.699	98.346
30	34.784	40.567	47.575	56.084	66.438	79.057	94.459	113.282	136.305	164.491

Index

❑❑❑